To/

Ken

Happy 50th Birthday

From Richard & Janet

(tight lines ?)

THE BROCKHAMPTON PRESS

Complete Book of
FISHING

BROCKHAMPTON PRESS
LONDON

This edition published 1995 by Brockhampton Press,
a member of Hodder Headline PLC Group,
20 Bloomsbury Street, London, WC1B 3QA

This arrangement © 1988 Marshall Cavendish Ltd

Prepared by Marshall Cavendish Books Ltd
58 Old Compton Street, London W1V 5PA

Printed in EC
ISBN 1-86019-101-0

CONTRIBUTORS

John Bailey: Rudd. **Des Brennan**: Mullet, Tope, Ling. **Geoffrey Bucknall**: Fly Casting. **Dietrich Burkel**: Wels, Sharks. **George Burrows**: Lough Erne System, Eire, the Coast. **Len Cacutt (Editor)**: General Introduction, Coarse, Sea and Game Introductions. **Kevin Clifford**: Wild carp. **Richard Dawes**: Potato. **Ron Edwards**: Dogfish, Flounder, Plaice, Whiting, Sole. **Neville Fickling**: Zander. **Tony Fordham**: Float Rods, Spinning Rods. **Frank Guttfield**: Chub, Barbel, Tench, Wels, Bait Additives, Sweetcorn, Laybys and Eddies, Hot Spots. **Ian Heaps**: Underarm Casting, Float Fishing, Swingtips and Quivertips. **John Holden**: Bass, Skate, Rays. **Trevor Housby**: Off-shore Fishing. **Bill Howes**: Groundbaiting, Worms, Maggots, Casters, Groundbait. **Charles Landells**: Slugs, Weighing-in Scales. **Billy Makin**: Plugs. **Mike Millman**: West Country, Pollack, Wreck Fishing, Sea Leads, Rubby-Dubby, **Leslie Moncrieff**: Turbot. **Arthur Oglesby**: River Trout. **Alan Pearson**: Natural Flies, Wet Fly Lines, Wet Fly Fishing. **Barry Potterton**: River Trout. **Mike Prichard** : Chub, Pike, Wrasse. **Barrie Rickards**: Perch, Pike, Zander, Spinning, Spinners. **Reg Quest**: Conger. **Gerry Savage**: Carp. **Peter Stone:** Playing and Landing, Bread, Freshwater Hooks, Swimfeeders, Centrepins and Multipliers. **Deryck Swift**: Plugs, Spinning Flights, Catapults and Bait Throwers. **Fred J Taylor**: Chub, Tench, Gravel Pits, Lake Margins. **Harvey Torbett**: Bream, Barbel, Dace, Chub, Eel, Float-ledgering, Cheese, Fixed-spool Reel, Knots, Landing Nets, Keepnets. **Kenneth Torbett:** Nylon Line. **Paul Vincent:** Paste and Crust. **Richard Walker**: Grayling, Fly Lines. **Alywne Wheeler**: Perch, Crucian Carp, Fish Senses, Black Bream. **Ken Whitehead**: Deadbaits, Rod Rests, Forceps and Disgorgers, Freshwater Traces, Keepnets, Swivels. **John Wilson**: Roach, Norfolk, Summer Lakes. **Norman Worth**: Seedbaits.

CONTENTS

INTRODUCTION

FISHING IS A SPORT and pastime for all seasons, all people, young, old and every age in between, and most important of all it is the world's greatest tension remover. To go fishing is to be a part of nature's peace and relaxation takes the place of that tension that so often seems to be part of our everyday existence. It can be practised wherever there is water holding fish, but on the other hand I've known anglers who seem to be able to catch fish where there just should not be any! They have through years of hard-won experience acquired the knack of 'reading the water', a phrase which sums up their expertise and enables them to know, really know, that this or that area on what might seem to the onlooker to be a place apparently identical to all others close by will be just the spot to fish.

In its most simplest form fishing is putting a bait in the water to attract a fish, which will take the bait (and the hidden hook) or swim away. That, in the tiniest of tiny nutshells, is fishing. But this is a simplistic description that conceals a vast complex of skills, knowhow, techniques, a myriad baits and lures, many different models of rods, reels and accessories, most of which are designed to help the angler to catch fish. However there are not a few on the market with the sole objective of luring an inexperienced angler close enough to be tempted to spend money unwisely.

At this point some words must be addressed to the newcomer to the sport. When the fishing bug bites, an early symptom is an almost irresistible urge to draw out the life savings and head towards the nearest fishing tackle shop – and it would be very easy to spend a small fortune in these days of carbon and boron rods and reels, expensive accessories and clothing and a huge range of literature which is also becoming dearer and dearer. To resist such an impulse to engage upon a spending spree is difficult, but resisted it must be. For a start, the newcomer will not know good tackle from bad, and this applies to rods, reels, hooks, line, and especially those intriguing accessories festooning the walls and crowding the cases in tackle shops. There is so much gear on offer, stand after stand of rods, rows and rows of reels; colourful and attractive (mostly to the angler) spinners and plugs of every colour, size and shape. It is essential that a fishing friend goes with the novice, someone with a good deal of experience in old Izaak Walton's art who will assist him to obtain the few necessary, basic items suitable for the first fishing outings at local waters.

The first decision to make is: where shall we go fishing? If the beginner lives at or near the coast the sea may well be irresistible. Then comes the next decision: will it be off the beach, pier, rocks or out in a boat? Each of these kinds of sea fishing needs a different set of tackle, with matching reels, line and accessories. A beachcasting rod, for example, is virtually useless out in a boat, where the terminal tackle is usually dropped over the side. Here, the length of a beachcaster is nothing more than a hindrance in these conditions. On the other hand, a boat rod has not the beachcasting rod's length, which provides the leverage for throwing the terminal tackle out to where it will be most effective, sometimes 100 yards or more. Pier fishing can demand something in between, depending upon the state of the tide and many other factors.

The angler's home base might of course be inland, and here the choice of fishing is just as varied as that found by the coast. It can be a slow-moving river, a fast, bubbling stream, a near-stagnant canal, a farm-pond (but don't knock these delightful and attractive places, some hold excellent heads of fish, especially rudd), a natural lake or a vast man-made reservoir.

Every kind of fishing has its great attractions and those who fish any one of them will tell you that their favourite water is the best! Never take their word – try them out (by borrowing a pal's fishing tackle, if you know him well enough) and find out for yourself which kind of fishing you prefer and which gives you the most pleasure.

All branches of sport have a competitive element that seems so necessary for many of us before the powerful internal drive to succeed is raised to the level where we can use our skills to the best advantage. Of course, some sports are wholly competitve – boxing, wrestling, darts and so on to name but a few are only possible when one has an opponent. Angling is different and here probably is where it can be described as more of a pastime than a sport. The solo angler's competition is the fish and he is applying his skill to 'convince' the fish that the hooked offering or lure is worthy of close attention and edible.

Like other sports, too, the search for more effective equipment, tactics and applications has led to a steady advance in the fishing gear available to all anglers. In coarse matchfishing the necessity to catch large numbers of small fish has become the priority of some extremely skilful matchmen, anglers who often find themselves allotted a peg on a stretch of river or canal, perhaps quite featureless, and with similarly expert matchmen on either side. Here their skills are tested to the full and they must rely upon previously acquired knowledge of similar situations, using 'secret' groundbaits and hookbaits and adopting ultra-fine methods to attract the fish and thus overcome the oppostion.

Sea fishing matches on the beach or out in boats give the ordinary angler much more of a chance against the experts because the fish shoals over which they might hope to be anchored, or the stretch of beach where they are fishing might not have the fairly predictable shoals that work along freshwater rivers and canals. The proximity of the anglers there also demands much finer and cautious fishing than at sea where the boat might be in 25 fathoms or more and the fish of mixed species, some large and powerful.

For some anglers, the author including himself among them, the sea holds a fascination impossible to ignore. To be with a couple of reliable fishing friends out in a well-equipped and intelligently skippered charterboat can provide a truly exciting and rewarding fishing session. It is the uncertainty and unpredictability of what is happening deep down on the seabed far below that creates the huge feeling of anticipation as your baited hook and weight sinks down and down into the darkness, the line pulling off the reel under the control of your thumb resting on the spool of the multiplier. There may be a shark, a conger as strong as a pony, a skate the size of a grand piano, any of these might be lurking right where your bait is headed. Feeding casually, one of them may sense your bait, home in and suddenly the rod in your hand is pulled viciously down to the gunnel: your heart misses a beat, thumping away as you contact the fish and begin to assess the situation. The experienced sea angler can often tell during those first few hectic moments what species of fish he has hooked and will adjust his tactics accordingly. There is one thing the beginner will learn early on in his sea fishing career the first time he hooks a 'big'un': there are fish down there which are stronger than him, which can either break his line or rod, ruin the reel – even pull him overboard if the tackle is ultra-strong and he is not settled safely into a fighting chair.

The sea, however, is not alone in producing fish with strength. On a smaller scale, there are freshwater fish capable of breaking an angler's tackle. On one occasion while fishing the Thames with lightish tackle, and seeking roach, my bait was taken by something that just kept on swimming away upstream. There was nothing my fine line could do, the fish simply kept on swimming deep and strongly upstream and its motion suggested to me that I had hooked one of the powerful Thames barbel.

The flyfisherman's graceful skills must not be ignored. This angler's pleasure is two-fold: he enjoys the action of his beloved fly rod as it flexes and works in his hand to cast the nigh-on weightless artificial fly or lure to a distance of 30 yards (and more in the expert hand). This would of course not be possible were it not for the flexibility of the whippy fly rod and the weight of the fly line, both acting in concert. Weight is supplied by the line and that and the spring inherent in the rod combines to throw the line first back and then forward to unfurl in a beautiful curve eventually to float the artificial down to the water's surface, gently enough to give the impression of a spent fly. To watch an accomplished fly fisherman casting for chalkstream trout is to witness artistry of a high order. Mind you, be careful not to make your presence too obvious, for once your silhouette intrudes into the trout's circular horizon the chances of it being tempted by a fly however well presented are slender.

There has been an extraordinary increase in the numbers of anglers taking to reservoir trout fishing in recent years. This branch of game fishing has the advantage of providing excellent fly fishing at reasonable cost and is available to many anglers unable to afford or even gain access to the select chalkstreams where the dry fly is paramount. On reservoirs the wet fly is necessary, lures fished deep and imitating small fish and aquatic insect life. Though the wet fly is cast by fly line its method of presentation to the trout has been described as little different from ledgering or spinning, especially when the wet fly is allowed to sink to the bottom. Anglers who use predominantly coarse fishing methods quickly adapt to reservoir flyfishing and it allows them to fish when the close season for roach, carp, chub and so on is in force.

Unlike the powerful wild brown trout of the great game fishing rivers which feed on fish and a varied diet of insect and crustacean life, most of the stewpond-bred trout destined for reservoirs, some browns but mostly rainbows, which do not breed readily in British rivers, are fed on protein-rich pellets which while providing all the elements necessary for growing do not give the flesh that distinctive taste formed by natural, living food. Reservoir trout can be bred to huge size, up to 20lb, and while the rod-caught record from wild brown trout is 19lb 9oz 4dr, that for the rainbow is just 1oz 4dr lighter.

Every angler must be aware of the law as it affects his sport. There is very little free fishing in freshwater and Water Authority rod licences are obligatory as well tickets to fish. Both are usually available on day, weekly, monthly and season bases. There are also close seasons for coarse and game fish, during which fishing is illegal. While the sea has no such restrictions, the fish themselves create seasons by migrating to faraway areas in order to spawn. But no matter what kind of fishing the angler practises he must retain the highest respect for his fishy quarry and for all other users of the water.

Remember, too, that tomorrow's angling depends upon today's care and conservation both of the fish, all the associated wildlife and also of the surroundings in which he fishes. It is his skills and wits against some of the world's most ultra-cautious and cunning creatures.

COARSE FISHING

TODAY'S COARSE fisherman employs methods, tactics and tackle that are highly sophisticated – they need to be, for the numbers of anglers to be seen in action throughout Britain where this very popular branch of fishing is carried out, are as high as they have ever been. In well-fished waters where large bags of fish could once have been taken with comparative ease and modest skills the fish have now become conditioned to almost continual angling pressure and in consequence will be extremely wary of anything that does not act in a perfectly natural way.

The result of what can only be described as the 'fishing explosion' that began some 25 years ago has, then, led to the modern angler of necessity being more skilful, especially the matchfisherman who has to compete not only against the ultra-cautious fish but against similarly expert anglers lining the waterside on either side of him. Even the lone pleasure angler has had to acquire a high degree of skill to get the best from the advanced tackle the manufacturers produce. Perhaps this increase in general, all-round skill is reflected in the steady advance seen in the record weights of some species. The pike record of 51lb 8oz, a superb Redmire fish caught by that totally dedicated specimen hunter Chris Yates, brings that elusive 55lb carp nearer and surely we will see the magic figure of 15lb alongside a tench record in the not too distant future. Yates' carp beat at long, long last the late Richard Walker's famous 44lb 'Clarissa' taken from the same water in 1952.

In this section of the book we take a long look at Britain's fine coarse fish species and the best tried and tested methods for catching them. The knowledgeable reader will note that the gudgeon, bleak, charr and a few small, exotic species that figure in the records lists do not appear here. There is a valid reason for this in that no single volume can cover all species, styles, baits, and tackle of the three disciplines of angling – coarse, sea and game. But every major angling species is here and given its due space, is properly described and with the traditional methods of capturing it explained.

Following the opening sections devoted to the fish themselves there is a very informative article on the fish and how they react to the world around them. All thinking anglers need to know more about their quarry than that it lives in water!

The angler should know how to treat fish with consideration and to do this he must know something about their various lifestyles without delving into the realms of fish biology. Simply knowing how to handle a fish by the use of a wet cloth instead of the bare hands, or why the fingers or any foreign object should never come into contact with the sensitive gills – these are but two examples indicating the things a considerate angler ought to be aware of.

The skills a successful angler employs are developed over the time he spends at the waterside. Usually they are his own special adaptations of fishing methods that have been with us for centuries. These basic skills are the magic float and ledger combination, float fishing followed by its straightforward underarm casting technique, and spinning, a subject about which volumes could and have be written.

If there is one single topic guaranteed to excite the angler's imagination and to start his pulses throbbing it is baits. That old, classic storybook tale of the worm and the bent pin was no figment of the author's imagination – that familiar worm is probably the most effective and natural bait of all, for most freshwater fish will encounter the wriggling, tasty worm in their natural element, either from being washed into the water by rain, being dropped by a passing bird or finding its way there by just falling in. But a lifetime's fishing using only one bait, the worm, as well as being not particularly innovative, ignores many other natural offerings which will catch fish. The inventive angler experiments with all kinds of things from the domestic larder – and do not be put off by thinking that fish will not take something they will never encounter in their own element. Take bread: how many fish will ever see a nice, new, large white loaf? But the familiar loaf proves a really effective bait, as well as being the main constituent of many sorts of groundbait. In the bait section you will find bread in its various forms and a whole range of other proven items that will catch fish. The possible list is as long as your arm: if it can be manipulated to sit on the hook, try it. The subject is very important and every angler must think hard about it, for when his favourite bait fails him he must use another. No angler should ever go fishing without at least two alternative baits in his tackle bag.

Every angler has his or her favourite fishing places and these are usually waters where their first good catches were made. One of the most important elements for a successful life is confidence and if one has confidence in particular waters the chances of taking fish there are greater than swims where effort has been unrewarded. This is not to imply that the latter waters do not hold good fish, for it is very much a state of mind. It must not prohibit you from visiting other places, certainly those that have a reputation for good fishing.

Fishing tackle – now here is a single angling subject that could easily fill three books this size. One's impressions on entering a large, well-stocked fishing tackle shop for the first time are of amazement that the sport should be so complicated. Another feeling the angler experiences is that he wonders how on earth he managed to fish before and not having all those intriguing gadgets without which the respectable angler could just not be seen on the waterside. This book has already described those main elements of rod, reel, line, hook, bait – five items. So what about that angler staggering along the waterside festooned with holdalls, rod bags, landing nets, keepnets, groundbait cannisters and bait tins? Does he really need all that paraphernalia? Yes and no! Yes if he is a better angler with it; no if he just feels that he just might want this or that item because it looked so terrific in the tackle shop.

There are a good many accessories which are of great help to the angler, among them those obvious rod rests, landing nets, keepnets and forceps. The last item, one should note, has taken the place of that old-fashioned instrument of fish torture known as the disgorger. Even the way it was used was clumsy, being poked into the fish's mouth to release the hook. Used carefully and with consideration for the fish it was perhaps acceptable, but more often than not the lining of the fish's mouth was torn and in extreme cases, such as when a small perch took the bait right down, to use the disgorger was to kill the fish. It is still on sale but for all anglers who have a concern for the fish the best thing is a pair of good forceps, which grip the shank of the hook firmly and allow it to be gently withdrawn. Used correctly, it does far less injury to the fish, a point of great importance when one is to return that fish to the water.

The angling press loves success stories and those photographs of matchmen hauling huge keepnets bulging with large numbers of small fish to the scales have led to much of the adverse and well-founded criticism about keepnets. One way to avoid this is to have your camera with you. When you do land that beauty of a tench or roach, unhook it carefully while holding it in a wet towel, photograph it, then return it.

It will have been noted when looking down the list of coarse fishing articles that there is no mention of lead shot or weights. The omission was very deliberate for a very good reason. Lead is virtually banned for use by anglers in freshwater. In 1986 the Royal Society for the Protection of Birds asserted that each year between 3,370 and 4,190 mute swans die from lead poisoning in English waters and the biggest single killer was alleged to be the lead shot lost or discarded by anglers. The swans, it was claimed, take the lead in while feeding. Naturally, angling organisations were adamant that there must be some other explanation for the deaths since, after all, lead shot has been used for very many years by anglers so why, suddenly, should these unfortunate swans now begin to die? And what about all that lead in the form of shot used by 12-bore shot guns?

The protestations were of no avail, though, and the Government took action with Statutory Instrument 1886, No. 1992, which came into operation in January 1987. Under the Control of Pollution (Angler's Lead Weights) Regulations 1986 the importation and sale of lead weights below 1oz for angling was banned. The National Federation of Anglers also played its part by banning the use of weights between 0.13gr and ½oz in its National Championships and the finals of other NFA events. Most angling organisations strongly urged the abolition of the 'problem sizes' of lead. All clubs and anglers have voluntarily stopped using lead. Now, lead shots are practically non-existent. There are even centres where clubs and angling organisations can take their no-longer legal lead shot and for which they receive the going price for scrap lead. Full information can be obtained from the Lead Development Association, 34 Berkeley Square, London W1X 6AJ.

What, then, is replacing lead? Early attempts to manufacture alternative substances were not satisfactory, but today there are a number of quite acceptable lead-substitutes and the reader is recommended to write to the National Anglers' Council for a very useful booklet entitled ANGLERS' CHOICE, A Guide to Alternatives to Lead Weights. It was produced by the Royal Society for the Protection of Birds in conjunction with the National Federation of Anglers and not only describes the substitutes but offers some excellent material as how they can best be used in various angling situations. This booklet is available from the National Anglers' Council, 11 Cowgate, Peterborough, PE1 1LZ. Any references in the part of

Still with the Law in mind, anglers must always be aware of the fact that all rivers and enclosed waters are property and that either the owners themselves or those who have leased the water have the right to give permission to fish or to charge for the privilege. At the same time there are Water Authorities who have a number of interests to consider which in some instances conflict with fishing. These pursuits include sailing,

Lastly, of great importance is the way that anglers act when they go fishing, both while they are in action and when they have finished. The waterside must be left clean and tidy and no oddments of tackle, food or bait left about. Line especially is a killer, for birds can get their claws and legs enmeshed in it and die a slow death.

Common bream

Colouring water or the stirring of reeds may mean that a shoal of bream are grazing at your feet. But do you know enough about the species to capitalize on those first tentative signs?

The freshwater bream, *Abramis brama*, has a dark green or brown back, but in older fish it may take on a slate grey hue. The flanks of the bream are olive-bronze and their white or creamy underside is often marked with scarlet streaks. The body is heavily covered with a thick layer of slime, which sometimes gives the fish a blue appearance. The bream is deep-bellied and full-backed. The tail is asymmetrical, the lower lobe being longer than the upper lobe. A long anal fin extends almost from the middle of the belly to the tail.

Habitat

The body shape of the bream gives some clue to its habits. Not only is the shape suited to bottom living, but also enables the fish to swim easily through the closely-spaced stems of reeds and sedges common in sluggish and stillwaters. This increases the potential feeding grounds for the fish as well as providing ready shelter from predators.

Normally bream are bottom feeders, and as shoals may contain as many as 50 fish they must cruise continuously to find food. They feed extensively on algae, plankton, insect larvae, crustaceans and molluscs, also grubbing among the bottom debris for the many micro-organisms which live there.

Once feeding, the shoals move slowly along the bottom rather like a flock of sheep working its way across the meadow when grazing. The comparison is apt because the fish soon denude the bottom of food,

like sheep cropping grass. Fortunately, when the bream have passed, other small bottom-living creatures soon take up residence.

When feeding in earnest a large shoal will stir up a great deal of mud. Gases are released which carry the colour of the mud quickly to the surface, even in quite deep waters. Anglers seeking bream should be aware of this, and keep an eye open for both the bubbles and the muddy colouring. In stillwaters this is in-

Graham Marsden returns a 9lb 3oz bream to a Cheshire Mere where it lives among the reed stems along the lakebed.

valuable in locating feeding fish. In rivers some judgement is required to decide how far the current has washed the colour from the feeding place, and whether or not to fish up or downstream. Fortunately bream also like to roll about, playing on or near the surface prior to feeding.

Twilight and dusk are good times to seek bream, which take advantage of the failing light to enter the shallower marginal waters in search of food. Sometimes they give themselves away by gently moving the marginal reeds, and a bait presented on the edge of the margins will often take fish.

Spawning occurs in May or June. After a severe winter anglers will sometimes take bream spawning as late as the end of June and even after the season has opened. The males can be recognized by the tubercles on the head and shoulders, typical of cyprinoids during spawning. The fish usually seek wide reedy bays and margins, and sometimes enter the tangles of waterside tree roots which extend below undercut banks. Once spawned they move into deeper water, remaining there throughout the summer, cruising when feeding, or lying motionless.

When frost sets in they seek out the deeper gullies and holes in the bottom, moving out at intervals to feed, and remaining quite active, especially at night when the water is warmer than the air, or by day during bright sunny spells. In still-waters, bream tend to become comatose during winter, moving only when tempted out of their sleepiness by warmer weather.

Bream growth

The freshwater bream generally attains a length of 3-4in during the first year. During the second year it will probably double its length, and weigh up to 2oz. This is the angler's typical 'tinplate bream'. In the third year the body fills out and the fish attains 9in, and by the time it is four to five years old it is 12in long. A specimen of 7lb is probably 10 years old, and fish in the record class of approximately 12lb may be between 12 and 15 years old. In Britain this is probably close to the maximum life span of the bream.

The search for big bream has continued for many years. Before the war the British Record Fish lists noted many fish over 12lb, and during the war a 13lb 8oz record was set by Mr E. Costin fishing at Chiddington Castle lake.

Some of the best fishing is found in Ireland. This angler is about to net a bream from Grove Lake, Tulla, in County Clare.

ASK THE EXPERT

Do bream always feed on the bottom?
Generally, yes. But when large shoals are about some fish often lie above the main shoal and float fishing tackles 1ft off the bottom may well take fish 'on the drop' or when 'swimming the stream'. Sometimes you can take fish like this when shoals are moving from one river feeding area to another.

I've been told, 'You know when it's a bream on the hook'. Are the bites really so recognizable?
Bream bites on float tackles are distinctive; the float first trembles, then tilts, before moving sideways across the surface and submerging. Sometimes, if your shots are close to the bait, the float simply falls flat before sliding slowly away. (Arrange the lower shots 12-15in from the hook.) Sometimes, the float trembles, moves a little, then remains quite still for a moment before the pronounced movement.

When should I strike?
Usually it's wise to await that lateral and continuous movement of the float. But unfortunately on some days it's necessary to hit the first float movement. You simply have to vary your technique from swim to swim and day to day.

When are ledgers or paternosters more suitable for bream than float tackle?
When the water is too deep for float tackle or when fishing at distances where floats are unmanageable. Awkward bank angles, too, can provide bites you cannot connect with. Then a very light ledger tackle enables bites to develop fully before a fish becomes suspicious. Here, too, a sensitive swingtip may be effective.

These older records were abandoned when the new British Record (rod-caught) Committee was set up. The current record is a 16lb 6oz bream caught by A. Bromley while fishing a private water in Staffs on 8 August 1986. Ten-pounder bream are listed from both the River Thames and the River Lea.

The freshwater bream is common in most parts of England except the western extremities. It is also plentiful in Ireland, where the average run of fish is larger than elsewhere. It is less common in southern Scotland, and absent north of Loch Lomond; it is found throughout Europe north of the Alps and the Pyrenees, except in the west and north of Scandinavia, and in the south and west of the Balkans. Anglers on holiday in Europe have a chance of good bream fishing.

Throughout their range, bream are as much at home in lakes as in

rivers. They prefer sluggish waters and in swift large rivers tend to be found in the slower reaches. They attain the best sizes in stillwaters, but fight better when taken in such faster waters as the Thames, Trent, or Great Ouse, where they turn their broad flanks to the current when hooked. Some of the best bream waters are in the Norfolk Broads waterways, and in the Lincolnshire and Fenland drain systems. Traditionally, too, the Arun, Nene, Welland and Witham are noted for bream. Some of the best specimens in the last few decades, however, have been taken from the reservoirs of Walthamstow, Tring, Staines and Marsworth, close to Tring.

Confusion with rudd

Bream are not easily confused with roach, but may be mistaken for large rudd. The short anal fin of the rudd should separate them. Unfortunately, bream spawn in similar places to those sought by roach and rudd, and the species occasionally interbreed accidentally when fish on the edge of shoals intermingle. Eggs from one shoal are sometimes fertilized by milt from the other, and the resulting hybrids are fairly common.

In England the common roach/bream hybrid was once believed to be a separate species, and called 'Pomeranian bream'. It even warranted its own specific title, *Abramis buggenhagii*, which is still found in older text books on fish. Now it is known to be a hybrid which is nevertheless popular with anglers. Sharing the characteristics of its parents it sometimes attains good weights. When it exceeds three or four pounds there is a danger of wishful thinking, and the fish is put up as a record roach, or at least as a specimen. No angler should make such a mistake because the anal fin of each fish is distinctive, bearing a specific number of branched rays. True roach have 9-12, true bream 23-29, and the hybrid 15-19. This is a very simple count to make and if the branched rays are counted at the outside edge of the fin they cannot easily be confused with the unbranched rays at the fore-edge.

The rudd/bream hybrid is not often found in England, but is common in Ireland, where, to complicate matters further, the native true rudd has traditionally been called 'roach'. Such hybrids are fortunately easy to recognize if the anal fin

Eric Baines with a respectable net of bream from the River Shannon. The bream in this river run larger on average than their counterparts in English rivers.

Inset: *Unhook a bream over a keepnet. This is necessary if a fine specimen is not to jump free and squirm back into the water.*

Methods	Rod	Reel	Reel Line	Terminal Tackle	Hooks	Leads/ Weights	Bait	Groundbait/ Attractor	Time of Season	Habitat	Distribution
Float—Slider	13ft match rod	Fixed-spool	3lb	Single hook	18-14	Split shot bunched 15in from hook	Maggot, casters	Loose hookbait samples	Summer, autumn	Lake, mere, reservoir, slow river	Widely distributed except for parts of the North-West and Northern Scotland
Float—Fixed peacock quill (slow-sinking 'on-the-drop')	12-13ft match rod	Fixed-spool	3lb	Single hook	12-8 / 18-14	Split-shot bunched under float	Bread or worm / Maggot, caster	Loose hook-bait samples/ cloudbait	Summer, autumn	Lake, mere, reservoir, canal	
Float—Avon	13ft match rod	Fixed-spool, centrepin	4lb	Single hook	16-10	Split shot in two bunches: one in mid-water, one 9in from hook	Bread, worm, maggot	Hookbait and fairly stiff groundbait	Summer, autumn	River with fairly strong current	
Ledger— Paternoster	11ft rod with 1¼lb test curve	Fixed-spool	4lb	Single or double hook	18-8	¼-1oz bomb	Maggot, caster, bread, worm	Breadcrumb, bran, stale bread	Summer, autumn, winter	Lake, mere, reservoir	
Ledger—Link	11ft rod with 1¼lb test curve	Fixed-spool	4lb	Single hook	18-8	¼-1oz bomb	Maggot, caster, bread, worm	Breadcrumb, bran, stale bread	Summer, autumn, winter	Lake, mere, reservoir	
Ledger— Rolling bullet	11ft rod with 1¼lb test curve	Fixed-spool	4lb	Single hook	18-8	¼-1oz bullet	Maggot, caster, bread, worm	Loose hook-bait samples plus bread groundbait	Summer, autumn	River	
Ledger— Swimfeeder	11ft rod with 1¼lb test curve	Fixed-spool	4lb	Single hook	18-12	Included in swimfeeder	Maggot, caster, sweetcorn	Fill feeders with hookbait	Summer, autumn, winter	Lake, mere, reservoir, river, canal	
Spinning	9-10ft spinning rod	Fixed-spool	4lb	Small, silver Mepps spinner	Spinner	None	Spinner	None	Very early season	Lake, mere, reservoir, river	
Fly fishing	9-10ft reservoir rod	Fly	No 7-9 (sinking)	4lb leader	Wet	None	Polystickle	None	Summer	Lake, mere, reservoir	

Bite indicators for the four ledgering techniques.
Paternoster-ledger: swingtip or quivertip
Link-ledger: various butt indicators

Ledgered rolling bullet: rod top, quivertip or touch (holding the line between your fingers—always the most sensitive indication)
Ledgered swimfeeder: swingtip, quivertip or butt indicator.

ray count is carried out. True rudd have 10-13 branched rays and the hybrid has 15-18. If your specimen has more than 13 branched rays in its anal fin it cannot be a rudd. If more than 12, it cannot be a roach.

Almost all roach baits will take bream, but usually bream like a good mouthful. The bait must therefore be bigger and presented on hooks up to size No 8 or No 6. Good baits are bread derivatives, sweet-corn, worms, swan mussels and gentles. A bunch of gentles will often work, and a large lobworm will often take the better fish. When fish are coy a maggot or a brandling may tempt them to bite.

White bream
The white or silver bream, *Blicca bjoerkna*, is only found in a few slow flowing rivers and stillwaters in the east of England. It is similar in shape and colour to the common freshwater bream but the pale flanks have a silvery sheen. Other distinguishing features are the two rows of pharyngeal teeth and a 'V'-shaped pattern under the ab-domen where the scales lie back to back along the ridge.

White bream are similar to the common bream in habitat and diet, but tend to be more selective in their feeding and are less confirmed bottom-feeders. Bream caught in midwater are always worthy of a close scrutiny. White bream are small, reaching a maximum length of about 15in and the current British Record (rod-caught) is open at 1lb, and will perhaps be surpassed by the first angler who can correctly recognize the species.

Chub

On warm evening in late summer, you may see chub move on the surface in search of food. But by nature specimen chub are shy, solitary fish, well known for their cunning and their bold bite

Predominantly a river fish, the chub *(Leuciscus cephalus)* is found where currents flow fast over gravel or stony beds. It is a fish of clean, unpolluted waters where both oxygen and food exist in plenty. The species provides fishing of quality for the angler prepared to stalk this cautious and stealthy prey with great care and skill. A specimen chub is shy in habit—a thick-bodied ghost that fades into the depths at sight or sound of man or beast. Yet the chub is renowned for the dogged resistance it displays to the efforts of angler and rod.

Location

Though thought of as a pure river fish, the chub has been successfully introduced to stillwaters where it thrives and can grow larger than its river counterpart. Where rivers are diverted, notably by the construction of motorways, stillwaters are formed which are populated by chub, barbel and dace. The Muskham Fishery (close to the River Trent below Newark) which was created in 1979, has several stillwaters containing chub. These fish, introduced along with carp, tench and bream, are succeeding within their man-made habitat reaching weights of 5lb. It appears that the fish become more free-taking in the open lake environment, no doubt conditioned by their lack of the territorial behaviour which they exhibit in river habitats.

Unlike the tench and carp, which can be regarded as fish of the warmer months, the chub remains a year round angling species when seeded into suitable stillwaters. It remains to be seen whether the food availability of this highly fertile fishery will produce fish approaching the chub caught from the River Annan.

Left: *During daylight, chub roam in shoals near the surface of strong, fast flowing currents. The merest disturbance is enough to send them back into the depths.*

Chub are even found in stretches of river set aside for trout fishing. Anglers are sometimes encouraged to fish for them during the trout close season and to remove their catch to conserve the game fish.

While the chub is found throughout most of England, it is absent from west Wales and from Scotland above the Forth-Clyde valley. Until recently the species was not thought to exist in Ireland, but reports indicate the possibility that the fish has been introduced into the Blackwater river system, as livebait by pike fishermen.

Identification

The chub belongs to the carp family, though it does not resemble the carp in appearance. The mature fish is solidly built, with a blunt head, large mouth and thick, pale lips. The back is greenish brown, the flanks silvery, and the belly a yellowy white. The fins, which are well defined and powerful, can range from colourless to a rich red. It is easy to identify by its large scales, which have a slight black edging, and can only be confused with other fish when young, when it is often mistaken for a dace. The distinction between the two should be clear, however, for the chub has large fins with rounded, convex rear edges, especially noticable on the anal fin, and 44–46 scales along the lateral line, while the dace's fins have concave rear edges and its lateral line averages 47–54 scales.

Spawning

Like other coarse fish, the chub spawns in the spring. Different water and weather conditions affect breeding times but this usually occurs between April and early June.

This tiny pool on the River Itchen, Ovington, Hampshire, has all the signs of chub territory. Here chub will feed on berries, insects and food particles dropped from the overhanging willow tree, and nymphs, larvae, shrimps and snails from the reed margins. Although basically a river fish, the chub will thrive in suitable stillwaters.

ASK THE EXPERT

Will chub take surface-presented bait?
Yes, at certain times of the year the fish will take a free-lined, surface fished bait such as a natural insect which the fish expects to find falling from the overhanging vegetation. Beetles, moths, grubs, seeds and small fruits are also taken by chub.

Where is the best place to ledger for chub?
This species likes to lie in secure places, so try rolling a ledgered bait under the banks downstream of your fishing position. When ledgering for the larger specimens 4-6lb nylon is advisable to get the fish moving toward the rod soon after hooking. Big fish need to be kept fighting, not diving for their lie.

What breaking strain should be used when chub fishing?
Choice depends on the style of angling and the environment. Float fishing, on a deep slow-running river, would call for lines of 1-4lb, the stronger breaking strain for situations of long trotting over distances of 25-40 yards. Much of a chub's fight comes from the power of the current that it lives in. They are crafty fish that use the river flow, obstructions on the river bed and prolonged sulking to strain the line to its utmost.

Does the chub hybridize with other fish?
Yes, though not as often as other cyprinids. It is possible that there are chub/dace, chub/roach hybrids, but identifying them with any certainty is extremely difficult.

The female releases between 100,000-200,000 eggs—about 0.7 mm diameter—which stick to plants and river debris. After 8-10 days hatching takes place in the shallow water of the gravelly runs favoured by the species. After cleaning itself in the fast waters of the shallows, the fish will slowly head for deeper waters, where it has both security and space.

The rate of growth of the chub is slow. In its first year it may attain a length of between 5-8cm, growing to around 22cm at full maturity. The male matures between 3-4 years, while the female only reaches maturity between 4-5 years.

While the chub is one of Britain's bigger coarse fish, it rarely exceeds 6lb, though weight tends to vary in different parts of the country. A good Hampshire Avon chub, for example, may weigh some 7lb, while a weight of 3lb would be considered good in Norfolk. The present record fish weighed 7lb 6oz and fell to Bill Warren at the Royalty in 1957.

Specimen chub are more solitary than other river species and tends to establish a definite territory. Old fish, particularly, will seek out a hole and lie up for long periods. All rivers have known chub holes, which the seasoned angler can point out to the newcomer, but it is unlikely that more than one or two chub can be caught from the swim. Younger chub do shoal and form mixed shoals with dace and roach in areas that can provide the necessary abundance of food.

Hybridization occurs as a result of this mixed shoaling and cross-breeding between the chub and the bream, roach, rudd or dace is quite common. This can lead to identifica-

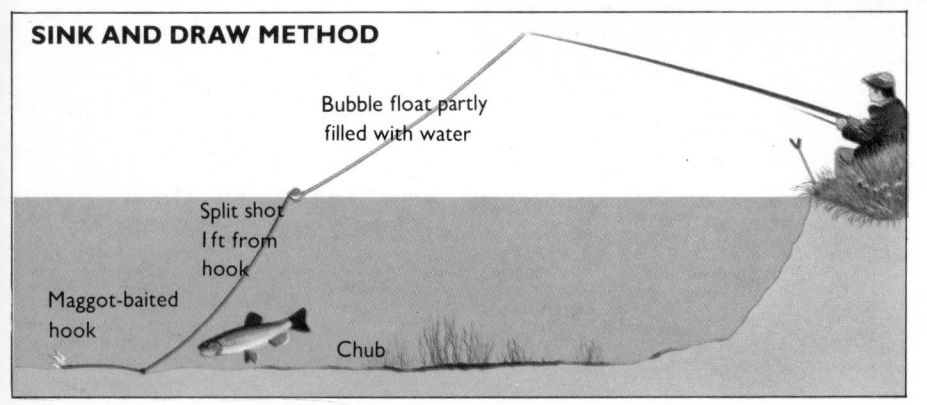

SINK AND DRAW METHOD

Bubble float partly filled with water

Split shot 1ft from hook

Maggot-baited hook

Chub

Left: *This method involves using a bubble float, stopped about a foot from the hook with a split shot and partly filled with water to add casting weight. When the tackle lands in the water the bait's weight pulls the line through the eye of the bubble float and allows the bait to fall naturally to the bottom. The bait needs to be fairly substantial —large bunches of maggots or knobs of cheese. The effect can be dramatic, with chub charging at the bait and even attacking the bubble float. On windy days, when it might be difficult to see the float, try freelining with knobs of cheesepaste big enough to cover the hook.*

16

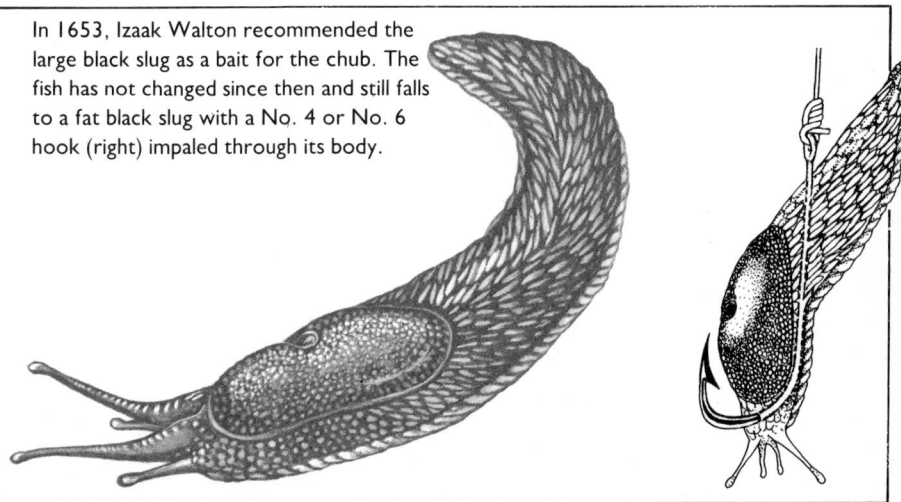

In 1653, Izaak Walton recommended the large black slug as a bait for the chub. The fish has not changed since then and still falls to a fat black slug with a No. 4 or No. 6 hook (right) impaled through its body.

tion problems, especially for the claimant to a record for a species.

Natural feeding patterns

The chub rises, trout-like, from deep water to take a small fish, fly or anything edible that disturbs the surface. A rapid rise in air or water temperature will encourage the fish to lie, head to current, just beneath the surface, watching for anything the current brings along above it.

Remember that fruits fall constantly into rivers and that the chub expects to feed on them. Baits such as elderberries may not be an obvious choice, but they produce results, especially after high winds or other disturbances have swept a

Left: *This 5lb-plus summer chub was caught on the River Wensum using sweetcorn bait.*
Below: *Chub often lie in slack water just downstream of submerged roots. In order to coax a stubborn fish out, it is best to use a powerful rod such as a 10ft Avon with 6lb line. A chub which reaches the safety of a snaggy hole may be impossible to extract on lighter tackle.*

lot of fruit or berries into the water. The young chub feeds on flying insects, water insects, worms, molluscs, fish eggs, seeds and sometimes plants.

Baits

Chub are famed for their wide-ranging appetites and can be taken on a variety of baits. Try float-fishing with cheese, ripe-fruits, especially berries, worms, silkweed, dried blood, slugs or maggots. Natural and artificial flies can also be used, as can other insects and grubs. The smaller members of a shoal will feed on aquatic insects and bottom-dwelling invertebrates, while the older fish will add a substantial amount of vegetable matter to their diet and will chase and eat the fry of many species, including their own.

Other baits at the water's edge include crayfish, which can be gathered by scraping the undercut banks below the water level, and swan mussels.

The chub's taste for many types of bait and the fact that it can be caught at any time of year, if the right technique is used, make it something of an all-rounder for the angler. It can be relied on to give good sport and to repay the concentration and patience with which it must be hunted. The chub can also provide a fine bonus to a day spent fishing for other species for it sometimes quite unexpectedly and impulsively takes a bait such as a lobworm float-fished along the far bank, which it may have been ignoring for hours.

SLACK WATER CHUB

Slack water

Current is diverted away from bank out into mid-stream by tree roots or bushes, etc.

← Flow

Chub lying in slack water here

Summer stalking

In summer it is possible to stalk fish, to select and to catch the biggest of the bunch. Stealth and a quiet approach will catch summer specimens, and provided the bait is acceptable and presented correctly, the tackle strength can be substantial. I have never found chub to be tackle shy. They are shy of anglers and of baits on which they have been hooked before; but there is no point in presenting a big bait on a big hook to a chub lying in a bulrush pocket if your line is not strong enough to pull it out, but there are times when it is necessary. If you enjoy a long, traditional fight with a fish in open water your chances of specimen chub are greatly reduced.

Many summer baits will succeed, when applied with common sense. Luncheon meat, sweetcorn, casters and tares have suddenly found favour, and are used so regularly by so many anglers that the need is for something subtler.

Subtlety lies in knowing where the chub are likely to be. If you know a big chub's lie, you do not need to use great handfuls of maggots or dollops of groundbait. The fish will probably eat that and ignore your hookbait. Throw in enough to whet his appetite. You can often dispense with groundbait altogether. Put a good bait to a good chub without scaring it, and there is a fair chance that it will be yours.

Simple and natural

Having dismissed luncheon meat and so forth as run-of-the-mill, it may seem strange to recommend lobworms and crayfish as good early season baits. They too are in common use, but they are natural. Chub get used to them; on heavily fished waters they even become scared stiff of them. But only the simplest of

An experienced chub fisherman trots his float down hard under the far bank of a broad, quick-moving river.

tackle is needed when using these baits to extract big chub from an undercut bank, a hole in the lily pads, underwater roots, the branches of an overhanging willow, or a gravel bar. A hook tied directly to the reel line is usually sufficient.

If the chub can be seen, the bait should be dropped not in front, but behind it. That is the way to fool the biggest in the bunch. Try to hit its tail with a big crayfish mounted on a No 2 hook. All too often, one of the smaller chub will spot the bait and snatch it as it slowly sinks, but just once in a while the really big specimen chub swirls and takes it without any preliminary inspection.

Monster frogs

When frogs were thick on the ground it was generally accepted that small frogs were good chub baits. But they are good only for small chub! For specimens you need monster ones mounted on No 6 hooks. The biggest chub I ever hooked took an enormous dead frog which I dropped in front of it and began to twitch back slowly. But there was too much bait and not enough hook and I lost the fish. Using the natural baits, keep out of sight and allow the bait to drift down naturally with the current or sink slowly in pockets of stillness, thereby not arousing suspicion.

Chub will often chase a worm or crayfish as it is being retrieved upstream. Nothing could look less natural than, say, two lobworms creeping upriver off the bottom, but sometimes it does the trick. And when a chub hits a bait moving in this way it usually hooks itself and there is little chance of escape. Use a No 4 or 6 hook with worms, unless you wish to add an extra worm for weight in which case you can go a size bigger.

I have spent quite a lot of time playing around with artificial baits. If the right one is used where big chub are known to lie, chances are good. Chub are not as predatory as pike, and small plugs intended for chub often end up half swallowed by jacks. But many really big chub are almost as predatory, and I have hooked two on sprats meant for pike. I am sure there is a case for

20

Above: *Swingtipping and ledgering out to the shadow of the bush on the opposite bank.*

Below: *Chub favour clean, running water and adopt sharply defined territories.*

Why is it that the smaller rivers seem to hold the bigger chub?
Big chub are often taken from large rivers, too. But generally speaking the fish density is less in smaller waters, thus allowing the chub there are to reach bigger average proportions. (Obviously this is an over-simplification of a complicated phenomenon.)

Why is it that although my local water holds many 2-3lb chub, I cannot break the 3lb barrier?
You are probably concentrating on the swims that hold several 'school' fish. Try the pegs with more character, and look for that elusive solitary creature aloof from the rest.

Are minnows good chub baits?
Excellent. So, too, are gudgeon, bleak—even small chub. Many good sized chub have fallen to a freelined, lip-hooked minnow on a size 8 hook.

Why is there no talk of high protein baits or amino acids in chub fishing?
Carping is a waiting game centred on stillwaters, where scent is of prime importance. Specimen chub are more sensitive to the vibrations or the sight of a morsel of food, and would not necessarily home in on an artificially created scent.

Swimfeeders are popular with matchmen who win on a catch of chub. Are they useful for specimen chub hunting?
Not very often. The contents of a swimfeeder attract smaller fish and, besides, specimen chub which have survived long enough to grow big through a degree of wariness, are suspicious of anything unnatural in their habitat. The bait that takes them will be that which appears natural.

ledgering with deadbaits in winter, when highly coloured water prevents the pursuit of fish that you can actually see. I keep deadbaits moving in the current so as to resemble live fish.

Winter specimens from small rivers
Summer offers the best chance of seeing, hooking and hauling out a big chub, but winter fish are stronger and in better condition. They also move around less in extreme cold. (It may be worthwhile to carry a thermometer and check the water temperature.) In winter, the best chances of specimen chub are in small rivers of character. These waters, with shallows and deeps, bends and scours, undercuts, gravels and glides call for simple ledger tackle.

There is more water in the river,

the rushes and reeds have died down, the lily pads are gone. The river has changed character and yet many of the summer haunts remain popular with the chub.

Waters and backwaters, overgrown for most of the summer, have been scoured almost clean. Rafts of debris gather against overhangs; fast runs develop under high opposite banks; little turbulent eddies widen into pools; the silkweed from the shallows disappears and the deep run below it is clear. There is a gap between the over-hanging willow branches and the bank where the current is now pushing through a little faster. The sharp bend has widened into a clear defined run; the current from the ditch opposite now hits the bank below the angler's feet and sets off diagonally at a lively rate. These are all chub lies.

Methods	Rod	Reel	Reel Line	Terminal tackle	Hooks	Leads/Weights	Bait	Groundbait/Attractor	Time of Season	Habitat	Distribution
Float: Avon	12ft hollow-glass, soft tip	Centrepin or fixed-spool	3-4lb	2-3lb hook length	18-12	2 BB to 3 AAA	All baits	Groundbait, hookbait	All season	Fast-flowing rivers, weir-pools	Throughout England, southern Scotland, east Wales
Float: slider	13ft hollow-glass or carbon	Fixed-spool	3lb	2-3lb hook length	18-12	2-3 swan bulk shot	All baits	Stiff groundbait, hookbait	All season	Deep slow water	
Float: waggler (straw, peacock)	13ft hollow-glass or carbon	Fixed-spool	2-3lb	1-2lb hook length	20-16	Light terminal shot	Maggots or casters	Loose-fed casters or maggots	Mainly summer	Far bank of rivers and canals	
Float-stick	12ft hollow-glass or carbon	Centrepin or fixed-spool	2lb	1-2lb hook length	20-16	Strung out shot	Maggots or casters	Loose hemp, casters and maggots	All season	Rivers with steady flow	
Ledger: paternoster	10ft 6in hollow-glass, 1½lb test	Fixed-spool	3-5lb	2-4lb	18-6	Arlesey bomb or swan shot	All baits	Groundbait and hookbait	Mainly winter	Deep holes under river banks	
Ledger: bullet, roller	10ft 6in hollow-glass or split cane, 1½lb test	Fixed-spool	3-5lb	2-4lb hook length	10-4	Bullet lead	Crust, cheese, worm	Loose particles	All season	Fast-flowing rivers, weir-pools	
Blockend or open-end feeder	10ft hollow-glass, quivertip	Fixed-spool	4-8lb	3-6lb hook length	16-12	Swimfeeder	Maggots, casters, red worm	Samples in feeder	All season	Larger rivers	
Spinning	10ft 6in hollow-glass, 1½lb test	Fixed-spool	5lb	5lb	Small Mepps	Swan shot	None	None	Summer	Rivers, weir-pools, lakes, pits	
Plugging	10ft 6in hollow-glass, 1½lb test	Fixed-spool or multiplier	5lb	5lb	Small plug	Often none	None	None	Summer	Rivers, lakes, pits	
Fly	9ft hollow-glass, AFTM 6	Fly	DT6F	6lb nylon tapered cast	10-8	None	Large wet or dry fly	None	Summer	Rivers, small streams, weir-pools	
Freeline	10ft 6in hollow-glass, 1½lb test	Fixed-spool	4lb	4lb	12-6	None	Bread, lobworm, cheese, crayfish, slugs	None	All season	Rivers, small streams	

From the above table, it becomes apparent that the chub falls to a limitless variety of different baits and fishing methods. He is a bold feeder with a big mouth, and when feeling secure in his environment devours almost anything that is edible, big or small.

Noticeably smaller hooks and finer lines are used for the stick float and waggler techniques, primarily because these tend to be associated with match fishing. On such occasions, the presence of anglers at regular intervals along the river bank reduces even the greedy, voracious chub to a cautious and worthy adversary.

Wild Carp

Although it does not grow to the same enormous size as its domesticated cousins, the cunning wild carp is popular with many anglers who like a long and furious fight

The wild carp is among the most majestic and beautiful of our freshwater fish — and the most difficult to catch. To Izaak Walton it was 'the queen of rivers'. With an ample supply of food it can grow to a large size to become an extremely strong and tenacious fighter and a fish with a cunning second to none.

Unfortunately, the wild carp is slowly becoming less widespread, not only in Britain, but throughout the world. One reason suggested for this is that the introduction of the 'King' carp strain into many habitats has caused interbreeding, thus losing forever the purity of the wild carp stock. However, there is evidence to suggest that with adequate spawning facilities, the true wild carp and the selectively bred 'King' carp will not spawn together.

Probably, the most significant reasons for the drop in numbers have been, with the enormous increase in popularity of carp fishing since the 1950s, the detrimental changes which have taken place in their particular habitats, and because the species has been overshadowed to some extent by the faster-growing 'King' carp.

Identifying the wild carp

The wild carp has a much more slender body, similar in some respects to that of the chub, than the cultivated species, which is often hump-backed and much deeper. In Britain the wild carp seldom exceeds 10lb in weight, although a few over 15lb have been captured, and the maximum, under favourable conditions, is probably about 25lb.

Coloration is variable, depending mainly on the environment. Usually, the top of the head and body are dark brownish-blue, the sides bright golden, and the underside off-white near the head, changing to a yellowish near the tail. The dorsal fin has the same colour as the top of the body, as does the upper portion of the tail, while the lower part of the tail often has a reddish-orange tinge. The pectoral, ventral and anal fins vary between slate grey and pale reddish-

The carp is one of the most important and popular species of freshwater fish.

orange. Variations in colour in individual fish can take place throughout the year, and are especially noticeable during spawning.

Maturity is usually reached between 2−4 years, with the male often maturing earlier than the female. The time taken appears to depend to a large extent upon temperature, for under artificially controlled conditions carp have reached maturity after only 4-8 months.

The wild carp is an adaptable fish, which is capable of living in a wide variety of habitats in Britain. Generally, however, it favours shallow lakes and ponds, rich in aquatic vegetation, and still, sluggish, or slow-moving rivers and canals. Since Britain is at the northernmost limit of the area in which carp reproduce, it follows that, in general, the distribution and occurrence of the species are greater in the south of these islands than in the north. The most northerly wild carp fisheries in the British Isles are Brayton Pond, near Aspatria in Cumbria, and Danskine Loch, in Scotland.

Adult wild carp typically inhabit warmer environments, such as shallow areas of ponds and lakes, or slack eddies in rivers, usually where there is aquatic vegetation. On rare occasions, they have been noted in swift mountain trout streams, and netted to depths of nearly 100ft.

Spawning

Spawning generally takes place be-

Below: *When light enters water at an angle of more than 10°, it is refracted (bent) downwards. This enables a fish to see an object (such as an angler) standing on the bank close to the water, so keep low or well back if you don't want to be seen, and approach with great care.*

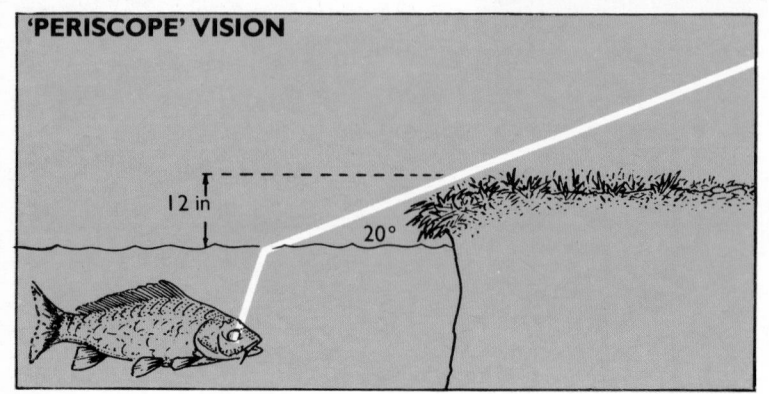

'PERISCOPE' VISION

12 in

20°

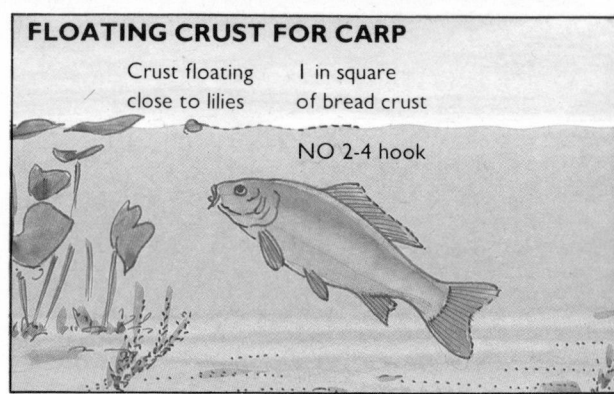

FLOATING CRUST FOR CARP

Crust floating close to lilies

1 in square of bread crust

NO 2-4 hook

tween early May and late July, and is primarily dependent upon water temperature. Usually, this needs to be in excess of 17°C (62.6°F) to stimulate the wild carp into spawning. There is strong evidence to suggest that spawning is often prolonged over a period of several days, or even weeks, although whether different fish are involved, or the same fish makes repeated efforts, is not clear.

The eggs are usually shed in shallow water, on soft aquatic vegetation. In deep ponds and lakes, with no shallows, the carp has been known to come close to the margins to spawn on overhanging vegetation, and even on fibrous roots and branches. The female is generally accompanied by two or more males, and the actual spawning is carried out very energetically so that the splashing of the fish may be audible over considerable distances.

The small, translucent-grey eggs, 1mm in diameter, swell and are sticky on contact with water, becoming attached singly to whatever medium the carp are spawning over. The amount of eggs carried by the female is directly related to her size, but may also vary according to environmental factors. The proportion by weight of eggs in a female wild carp, just prior to spawning, is less than in the cultivated 'King' carp variety, amounting to approximately 10—20% of body weight, while the roe of a female 'King' carp can represent up to one third.

The eggs hatch in 4—8 days, depending on the temperature, the newly hatched larvae having a yolk-sac on which to feed initially. The larvae are able to attach themselves to plants, or will lie on the bottom, before floating to the surface after two or three days to fill their swimbladders with air. They then become free swimming, and feed on microscopic algae, rotifers and water fleas. Growth is variable and depends mainly on the amount of food available and water temperature, but other factors, such as the oxygen content, also have an effect.

Basic carping

Next to presenting bread crusts on a greased line, perhaps the most effective of all carping methods — and

Above: *In situations where bankside disturbance might drive fish away, the best method of catching carp is to fish long-range with a standard fixed-spool reel.*

Left: *The typical habitat of the carp: shallow lakes or slow rivers, with plenty of weed and cover. Although naturally a herbivore, the carp can be caught on worm and maggot, as well as bread, meat, potato and cereal baits. Other effective baits include cat-food and sweetcorn.*

Below: *One of the most basic methods for catching carp is floating crust. Terminal tackle is the simplest available — a hook, a greased line, and a 1 in-square piece of bread crust.*

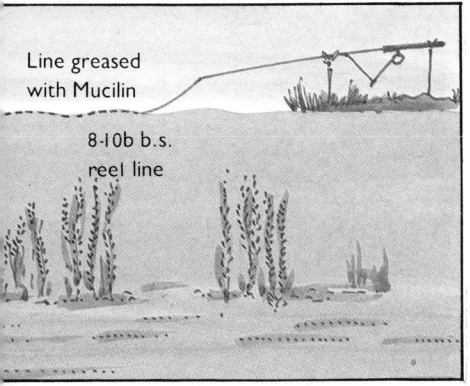

Line greased with Mucilin

8-10b b.s. reel line

Why is it often easier to catch carp at night than during the day?
Carp are easily scared away by any kind of movement or disturbance on the bankside. At night, when things have quietened down, there's less chance of them being spooked.

Why do anglers sometimes sponge their spools with washing up liquid before freelining for carp?
One of the secrets of successful freelining is getting the line to sink quickly and lie flat along the bottom. The washing up liquid overcomes the surface tension of the water, enabling the line to sink immediately and rapidly.

Why are carp found mostly in shallow waters?
This is mainly because water temperature has a marked effect on their rate of breeding. Carp do not breed at all in the deepest, coldest lakes and gravel pits, but in shallow waters such as farm ponds which warm up quickly and maintain their temperature, they breed very successfully indeed. This has caused a great deal of trouble in Australia, where carp that were introduced into the Murray River system found conditions so much to their liking that they multiplied with great rapidity. These large numbers of carp began to affect the existence of the local species, and today they are considered vermin.

Why are mirror and leather carp sometimes referred to as 'naked' fish?
Because the leather carp is almost bare of scales: it has just a few near the fins. The mirror carp, too, is only partly covered, with a few large scales near the head and tail or along the lateral line.

there are many — is to 'freeline'. The secret behind this most sensitive presentation is to choose a bait large and heavy enough to be cast accurately without the addition of shots or float, and simply to offer it on the bottom on a completely 'freeline'.

Good freelining swims are close to beds of surface weed such as broad leaf potamogeton or lilies, alongside fallen trees or where brambles trail into the water, on the top of a shallow, gravel bar, or wherever carp have been seen moving even very close in alongside marginal rushes or sedges. In short, almost any area within 20 to 30 yards of the bank. Beyond that distance freelining techniques can cause problems to the inexperienced.

Care must be taken to ensure that most of the line lies perfectly flat along the bottom, or 'line bites', where a fish swims into a 'hanging'

line, might occur.

Good, heavy, baits are lobworms (try two on the hook), breadflake, luncheon meat, small whole freshwater mussels straight out of the shell, and various pastes such as tinned cat food, or sausage meat stiffened with wholemeal flour. Use hook sizes 2 to 6 depending on baits, and tie direct to 8-10 lb b.s. line. Where there are no weeds or snags or where the carp average on the small side, line strength can be reduced to 6-7lbs. In each case use an 'all through action' rod.

Bites are usually bold when freelining because the carp simply feels minimum resistance as it sucks in and makes off with the bait, so allow some 'slack' or a 'bow' in the line to hang down from the rod tip and watch it carefully where it enters the water. Alternatively, and especially

in windy conditions, use a foil indicator between reel and butt ring. After a preliminary 'twitch' or sometimes without any prior warning the line will suddenly and confidently rise up through the water. Wait for it to fully tighten before striking hard and far back. This is most important when using big hooks which do *not* penetrate the carp's rubbery mouth easily. To help penetration, crunch down the barb flat with a pair of forceps and really sharpen the outside edge between point and barb with a carbrundum stone. It is worth the extra few minutes, because a carp is often lost within seconds.

Learn to walk slowly, quietly, and not to make any sudden arm movements around a carp water, and you will even hook fish which confidently swim into within mere feet of where you sit.

FISHING FOR CARP

Method	Rod	Reel	Line	Terminal tackle	Hooks	Lead Weights	Bait	Groundbait Attractor	Habitat	Time of season	Distribution
Antenna float or betalight float	Fibreglass or carbonfibre, 11ft 6in, 1¼lb test	Fixed-spool	5-8lb	Single hook below antenna/ betalight float	4-10	Balanced split shot	Naturals, particles, some pastes, specials	Usually same as hookbait	Usually stillwaters, occasionally moving water	All times, especially winter	Widely distributed in southern England and the Midlands, becoming scarce further north
Slider float	Fibreglass or carbonfibre, 12-13ft, 1¼lb test	Fixed-spool	5-7lb	Single hook below slider float	4-10	Balanced split shot	Naturals, particles, pastes, specials	Usually same as hookbait	Usually stillwaters	All times, especially winter	
Link ledger	Fibreglass or carbonfibre, 11ft, 1¼-1½lb test	Fixed-spool	6-12lb	Swan shot or bomb link with single hook	2-8	¼-2oz bomb or variable swan shot	Naturals, particles, pastes, specials	Usually same as hookbait	Moving and stillwaters	All times	
Paternoster	Fibreglass or carbonfibre, 11ft, 1¼-1½lb test	Fixed-spool	6-12lb	Arlesey bomb, single hook	2-8	¼-2oz bomb or variable swan shot	All types	Usually same as hookbait	Moving and stillwaters	All times	
Swimfeeder	Fibreglass or carbonfibre, 11ft 6in, 1½lb test	Fixed-spool	6-10lb	Swimfeeder, single hook	4-8	Swimfeeder	Natural particles, usually maggots	Usually same as hookbait	Moving and stillwaters	All times	
Freelining	Fibreglass or carbonfibre, 11ft, 1¼-1½lb test	Fixed-spool	6-12lb	Single hook only	2-8	No weight	Usually paste specials, some naturals	Usually same as hookbait	Stillwaters	Usually summer and autumn	
Freelined floating bait	Fibreglass or carbonfibre, 11ft 6in, 1¼-1½lb test	Fixed-spool	6-12lb	Single hook only	2-6	No weight	Crust, air-injected worm, some specials	Few samples, same as hookbait	Stillwaters	Usually summer	
Ledgered floating bait	Fibreglass or carbonfibre, 11ft 6in, 1¼-1½lb test	Fixed-spool	5-8lb	Arlesey bomb or link with single hook	2-8	¼-2oz bomb	Crust, air-injected worm, some specials	None	Usually stillwaters, occasionally moving water	Usually summer and autumn	
Margin fishing	Fibreglass or carbonfibre, 10-11ft, 1½lb test	Fixed-spool	8-12lb	Single hook only	2-8	No weight	All types	Usually same as hookbait	Stillwaters	Mostly summer	

FISHING TECHNIQUE

Beware of faddists and wonder baits, says Gerry Savage. In carp fishing there is no substitute for a flexible and intelligent approach, a lively respect for the species, and a first-class angling technique

Above: *Charlie Clay took this 17½lb leather at night when the fish venture into the margins to feed in seeming safety.*

In 1952 Richard Walker broke the British carp record with his famous 44lb common carp from Redmire Pool. At that time the norm in carp tackle was a cane rod of about 10ft and a centrepin reel or, if you were fortunate, one of the claw-type fixed-spool reels.

The record still stands in the British record committee's official list but there is no doubt that it was broken by Chris Yates in 1980 when he caught and photographed a carp weighing 51lb 8oz, again from the now legendary Redmire Pool. The late Richard Walker's fish is still in the record book because Yates did not submit the body of the fish for inspection at the time of its capture.

Nowadays, tackle and tactics are far more sophisticated. Cane has vir-

tually disappeared from the tackle shops, although the discerning angler who can afford it may choose to build his own cane carp rod. For many carp enthusiasts, cane has magical memories but today's angler prefers glass or carbon rods.

Davenport and Fordham were one of the first firms to offer glass carp rods back in the early 1960s. The 'D & F' rod was a standard 10ft version, but now length varies from this to as much as 13ft, with the general preference being for fast-taper versions of about 11ft. These thin-walled, purpose-built rods can cast a bait over 70 yards, while 80-90 yards

is claimed for stiffer models.

These rods are suited to the experienced carp angler, but the beginner should start with one of 10 or 11ft with a fast taper. I use a ledger rig—which as well as being a useful bottom fishing aid, is a must for presenting a floating bait at long range. The weight of the ledger depends on the distance at which you want to fish. If the carp are on the surface, say some 50 or 60 yards out, you will require a ¾oz or 1oz ledger. I use the well-known Arlesey bomb with a swivel, as this makes for free running and minimal resistance. I tie about 2-3in of line to the bomb and then attach the free end to a split ring.

Maximum casting distance

Some carp anglers prefer to use a small swivel and a ledger stop but I prefer the split ring ledger without the stop. My floating crust bait hides a No 2 or No 4 hook, though sometimes when the bait is smaller I use a No 6, allowing the running weight to rest against the hook-bait. This gives maximum casting distance, while this split-ring method also guarantees that the crust will rise very quickly to the surface, even in weedy areas, where a swivel link can become clogged.

You will need a ledger-stop to fish a small bait on the bottom at long range, but there will also be days when the carp are right under the rod tip, and this is when the art of freelining in the margins comes into its own. In 1976 I caught a 22¾lb mirror carp in 3ft of coloured water lapping a bankside clump of reeds. I had previously flicked a few small pellets of paste into the swim as an attractor and then patiently waited a couple of hours until the big carp came along and took the bait. When using two rods, I often elect to fish one at long range and the other close in. I have taken more fish at long range, but the better-quality fish often inhabit the margins, so it is well to be flexible in your approach.

As for waters, in my home county, Kent, there are several day ticket venues that boast a good head of carp. At Dartford, just off the A2, there is the famous Brooklands Lake. Here you have an excellent chance of a 20lb carp, and double-figure specimens are regularly taken by anglers who purchase their tickets at the waterside. On the A225, which links Dartford and Farningham, is the pretty village of Sutton-on-Hone and just south of Sutton lies the productive Horton Kirby complex, where the carp fishing is superb and day permits are available on the bank.

Other Kent carp waters
Day permits are also available at Dennis Johnson's lakes at New Hythe, near Maidstone, where carp to 30lb have been taken. At Faversham, carp anglers can fish the Faversham Angling Club's School Pool and the best carp to date is a 34¾lb specimen—just one pound short of the current county record. Nationally, the Leisure Sport Angling Club offers fishing for carp on a smaller scale, and other companies offer similar facilities.

Whatever you choose to fish, there are important steps to follow if you want to catch carp. For example, if no information is forthcoming regarding the depth of the water, you will have to plumb the lake. Look for islands, as these denote the shallows which carp are known to frequent. If you discover weed beds, shallows and gravel runs, so much the better.

Reeds, lily pads and sandbanks are also popular carp haunts, and it is a good idea to watch what other carp anglers are doing. If the water is virtually free of bankside noise and heavy pedestrian traffic, the margins are a good bet. But quiet waters today are the exception, and in the main I choose to fish at long range during daylight hours and under the rod tip at night.

Now to the complex question of baits. Unfortunately, great emphasis is laid on what is used at the business end of the line, and although this is important, watercraft and technique count for a lot too. A 'killer' bait is of no use at all if it is not cast to where the fish are, and, equally, if your presentation is at fault, you will not tempt carp, the most wily of all the coarse species.

When asked what my favourite carp bait is, I reply: 'Whatever the carp are taking on the day'. I say

28

Top: *Floating crust accounted for these four double-figure carp taken by Peter Ward.*
Above: *Winter fishing for carp can be slow and conditions muddy, but on the right water, very productive indeed.*

Right: *This tricky carp swim is full of snags and has few unobstructed footings at the waterside from which to wield a landing net.*
Below: *No such problems for the captor of this 8½lb mirror carp.*

How can I thwart the bait-robbing little fish that spoil my carp fishing when I'm using sweetcorn?
The only solution seems to be to use bigger baits than corn—try a par-boiled potato or a large paste concoction.

Must I really perfect casts of 60 yards and more before I catch carp?
Only if the carp have been driven out to the middle of a lake by bankside disturbance do you need long-distance casting. If it is relatively quiet, or if you are night fishing, there's no reason why you shouldn't catch them a few yards from the bank.

How can I tell if a water holds specimen carp?
Try to visit the water on a very hot day with a pair of polarized sun-glasses. You will soon see carp if they are there, their big black shadows moving along the surface with their dorsal fins just creating a wake in the surface film.

Just how big could this country's carp grow?
The 50lb mark has recently been passed here. Fish well in excess of 60lb have been taken on the Continent, so there's no reason why the same is not possible here.

Do I choose strength of line according to the size of carp I am after?
Only partly: the main deciding factor is the nature of the water to be fished. A snag-free venue does not call for the same beefy tackle as a lake rife with sunken trees or emergent plant life.

that because today the choice of baits is so varied: one day the carp will devour floating crust as if their very survival depended on it, the next it will be high protein *à la carte* that takes fish.

To start with, there are the old-established favourites: potato, worms, bread, cheese, maggots, honeyed paste and, as already mentioned, floating crust, all of which catch carp. Particle baits—sweet-corn, beans, peas, and the like—have all become popular during the last few years. Then there are the topical high-protein baits.

Fred Wilton started anglers on the high protein gambit back in the late 1960s, since when high protein has accounted for hundreds of carp. HP, as it is known, is expensive, although there are several ready-made mixes that contain a high protein percentage available at most tackle shops.

The more successful protein baits contain casein (milk protein) and the vitamin B complex found in yeast, which is soluble in water. Protein is a top scorer in waters where carp seldom reach 20lb because of competition with other stock for natural

Above: *Beside this handsome catch are potato baits of the same size as the one which caught it.*
Below: *One bait suggestion and a recommended rig.*

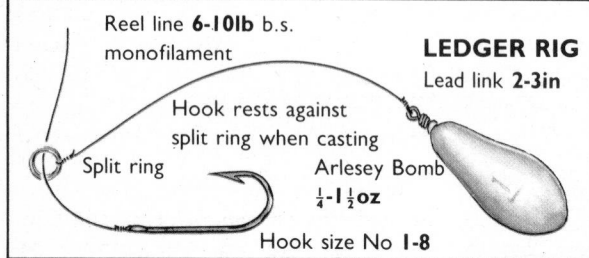

Reel line **6-10lb** b.s. monofilament

LEDGER RIG

Lead link **2-3in**

Hook rests against split ring when casting

Split ring

Arlesey Bomb $\frac{1}{4}$-1$\frac{1}{2}$oz

Hook size No 1-8

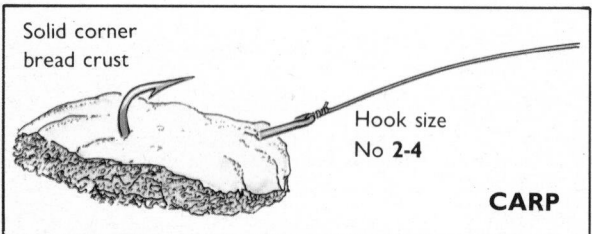

Solid corner bread crust

Hook size No 2-4

CARP

Above: *A specimen mirror carp is brought to the net from the bank of a small water happily underrated and overgrown.*

food, where demand exceeds supply. HP will also catch carp on food-rich waters, but often will *not* score while mini-baits, sweetcorn and beans, for example, are taking fish.

When preparing high protein baits, some anglers mix with eggs instead of water. Six eggs are usually sufficient to mix 10oz of protein powder. The most widely used constituents are wheatgerm, soya, flour, casein, yeast mixture and, in some cases, gluten (as already stated there are available at least four ready-made protein mixes, each of which, when the price of each individual ingredient is taken into consideration, represents good value for money). After mixing the eggs and protein powder to a firm paste, roll into balls and boil for about a minute. The result is a bait with a 'skin' that defeats the attentions of

any unwanted 'nuisance' fish.

Protein baits are so widely used nowadays that groundbaiting is really unnecessary. Indeed, the trick is to add one or two smells of your own. I have taken to flavouring the bait with a gravy mix or soup stock. This has paid off handsomely, for I have been fortunate enough to land six carp over 20lb, with the best tipping the scales at 29lb 14oz in one season. But remember, there is not, and never will be, an ultimate bait.

Finally, a couple of bait preparation tips. If I want to fish a soft bait at long range I begin by rolling the mix into a dozen or so balls, each weighing about an ounce. Afterwards I put them into the freezer and leave them there until I go fishing, when I take them to the lake in a vacuum flask to preserve their hardness. They are hooked by

threading the line through the hard bait with a baiting needle. The hook is then tied on and drawn back into the bait. No other weight is required and the bait—remember it weighs about 1oz—is easily cast the required distance. Now, here is the bonus: just a few minutes after coming to rest on the bottom, the frozen bait becomes soft again and even at long range the hook is set quite easily on the strike.

Alternatively, soft baits can be mixed at the lakeside. This is done by using the lake water to mix the paste—a growing habit with the carp angler—and by using a small piece of ballpoint pen tube to prevent the line splitting the bait.

Barbel

On fast streamy waters between June and October, you might, if you know where to look, encounter the elusive barbel, perhaps the toughest of the river species

Once the angler hooks his first barbel he will find himself equally hooked on barbel fishing. The sheer power and strength of this stubborn fighter has to be experienced to be believed. Salmon anglers who have inadvertently taken barbel all agree that, weight for weight, there is little to choose between the two species for endurance and power.

The barbel, *Barbus barbus*, is predominantly a bottom-feeding species, as a quick examination of its large underslung, crescent-shaped mouth will show. Four large barbules hang from the leathery lips, one from each corner of the mouth, and two from just under the snout. These barbules are equipped with taste and touch cells and are admirably suited to their task. Like external tongues they enable the fish to feel and taste food without having to open its mouth. The rounded snout is used to root about on the bottom, rather like a pig snuffling for truffles. It is hardly surprising that these features, together with the disproportionately small eyes, have earned the barbel the nickname of 'pigfish'.

The body is well adapted to its way of life. The broad forehead tapers sharply in a curve to the rounded snout. This gives the head a wedge shape which is quite obvious when you look down on a fish in the water. The barbel offers this wedge-like profile towards the flow of the stream and the current holds the fish firmly on the bottom.

Colouring

On its dark brown or green-brown back the pointed dorsal fin echoes the shape of the upper tail lobe. On its cream or buff underside the small scales give it a pearly appearance, and the rounded edges of the lower tail lobe and the anal fin are not, as you might expect, due to wear and tear on the bottom, but by Nature's design, finishing the near-perfect adaptation of the barbel to its bottom-living life.

Curiously, you will not usually catch a young fish, except when fishing near the surface where the barbel has adventurously joined the dace swims, stealing the single maggot intended for dace. The year-old

During the summer months, early mornings and late evenings are the most productive times for catching barbel, especially in hot weather.

31

fish, only 5-6in long, has a lightly speckled body, and is therefore similar in marking and body shape to the gudgeon. The two, however, are not easily mistaken. Gudgeon have two large barbules, the barbel four, and in young barbel these are small and undeveloped.

By the end of the second year the young barbel will have doubled in length, and by the end of the third attained 15in or more. A five-year-old fish will be between 18in and 21in long. By the time it reaches 7lb or 8lb it is 24-25in long and 7-8 years old. At 10lb it will be as many years old and the elusive 14-pounder will probably have reached the age of 13-15 years.

Size

Throughout the age range, size for size, barbel are lighter than most species. A typical 14in barbel weighs a pound, but a roach of this size tips the scale at about 1lb 12oz, a carp 1lb 14oz, and a chub 1lb 8oz. An 18in barbel weighs only 1½-2lb while at this length carp, roach, chub and perch would all be over the 3lb mark.

Like trout, barbel prefer swift, well-oxygenated water, although they can survive in water with low temperatures and oxygen levels where trout would perish. They settle just below the trout zones,

Left: *Landing a barbel requires a wide, deep net—a double figure barbel may be over 3ft long and very powerful.* **Below:** *A cross-section of a typical barbel swim. Barbel may hide in undercut banks when not feeding.*

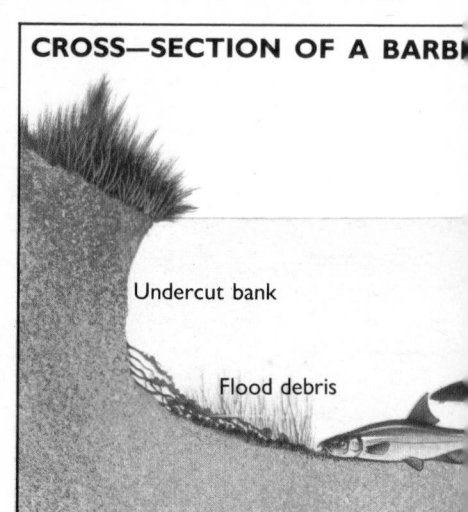

CROSS—SECTION OF A BARBE

Undercut bank

Flood debris

Above: *When actively feeding, barbel venture away from the cover of streamer weeds to grub in adjacent stretches of open river.*
Top right: *Playing a barbel on the Upper Severn. For this, strong tackle is essential.*

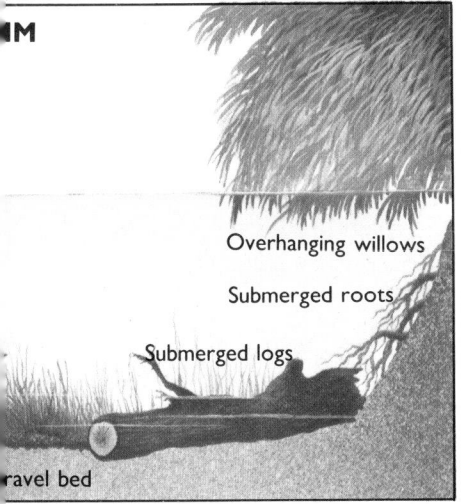

Overhanging willows

Submerged roots

Submerged logs

ravel bed

seeking out the clean water and hard bottoms with layers of silt and mud where their food requirements are met in the profuse weed growth or reed margins. They often live in the thick of the weed, especially where the current has isolated pockets of weed and islands of reed in the middle of the stream.

Barbel spawn early in summer. They move into the clear gravelly shallows, scoop out a small depression with the tail, deposit their eggs, and sometimes cover them. They then move into their weir pools and swift runs to clean themselves. They can often be seen right under the lip of the weir at this time, later working back into the pool itself. By midsummer they are back in their usual feeding haunts, where they often share the swims with dace. Towards the onset of autumn they move back into deeper water and by winter have become semi-hibernatory, feeding only when tempted out of their sleepiness by warm, sunny spells.

Barbel have considerable appetites and, when conditions suit them, will often feed continuously throughout the day. Some days, however, they will feed for only a brief spell, and other days intermittently. They are omnivorous, indiscriminately feeding on plants and animals. Much of their food is

harvested from the minute organisms in the bottom silt layers, and when feeding the barbel cleans the bottom like a vacuum cleaner. They also display a marked fancy for minnows, frogs, crayfish, and fish fry. Their pharyngeal teeth are large and strong, being hooked and pointed enough to deal with the shells of crayfish or snails, which they eject after chewing. Anglers know them to be fond of meat, and use sausages, liver, slugs and petfood as well as the natural baits to catch them. Good fish are often taken after judicious groundbaiting.

Bait and tackle

Barbel will also take such traditional baits as wheat, hemp, barley, maggots, silkweed, and all manner of 'secret' pastes concocted by the angler. When they are fastidious it is essential to use comparative tackle, hooks and light baits to tempt them. This spells out the paradox of barbel fishing. The

angler has not only to locate his fish, but also to seek them with hooks and lines that are not so heavy as to scare them away, but strong enough to subdue and land a powerful fish.

Barbel are indigenous to the swift flowing waters that run to the East Coast of England. They are common in the Thames, Yorkshire Ouse, and Derwent, as well as in the Kennet, Swale, Nidd, and Wharfe. They do not naturally occur in the slow flowing lowland rivers of East Anglia and are not found in any rivers that flow to the south or west.

Restocking

Pollution has probably reduced barbel populations over the past 50 years, as well as reducing the number of rivers that once had natural barbel stocks. These trends have been reversed recently, and are compensated by restocking in many waters where barbel have become rare or non-existent. Many waters without barbel have been success-

fully stocked with them, bringing barbel fishing to many areas where before it did not exist.

The most obvious and notable examples are the Hampshire Avon and Dorset Stour which were stocked by Mr Gomm in 1896. A hundred Thames fish were released in the Stour near Iford Bridge, which is not very far from the confluence of the Stour with its neighbour the Hampshire Avon. Some of these introduced fish dropped down to Wick Ferry, where these two rivers share the same short estuary, and spread into the Avon itself. Since then not only have barbel thrived in these waters, but the Avon has eclipsed all other British rivers in the quality and quantity of these fish. More recently stocks have been transferred to the Severn, Medway, Welland, Great Ouse, Nene, and other rivers. In most situations reports indicate that the barbel has successfully acclimatized itself in suitable reaches.

FISHING TECHNIQUE

Hot or cold, day or night, says Frank Guttfield, the barbel are there for the catching. But it is not that easy, you have to know how and where to look, how and with what to bait up and when to strike—and that's just the beginning

Barbel can be caught by a variety of methods, on many baits, and at all hours. In pages 31–34 the habitat and biology of the barbel were discussed, with the generally accepted baits, such as meats, and traditional angling methods—notably ledgering. This section of the article will concentrate on how and when to tempt the formidable barbel.

First, when are the chances greatest? The barbel once had the reputation of being solely a summer- and autumn-only species. Of course summer and autumn are regularly productive, but late autumn and early winter can be equally rewarding for the keen angler. In fact, several of the most successful Thames and Kennet barbel experts consider October right through to early December as *the* time for the really exceptional specimens. Whatever the time of year, the key factors that control the barbel's feeding pattern are air and water temperature, coupled with flow and water level.

To some degree, the hotter it is the more a barbel feeds. In the sizzling summer of 1976, when the Thames and Kennet were as low as ever and water temperatures soared well into the eighties, the barbel fed with predictable and clockwork regularity. There is very little evidence to suggest that there is an upper water-temperature limit. As with most other species, settled conditions are important—any wild fluctuation in temperature, wind, flow or level is not conducive to good fishing.

In winter, the water temperature does become more critical. There has now been sufficient evidence gathered by observant anglers to establish the minimum feeding temperature. This critical level is thought to be about 5·6° (42°F) or under, but at 7·1°C (45°F) and above the chances are excellent. So the reason why November, and even December, can be so productive is that there are far more days and nights when the water temperature is within feeding range.

Left: *Mick Mulhearn with a barbel caught from the Ouse in Yorkshire. Steadily flowing water over a gravel or clay (not mud) river bed offers the best chances.*

When to fish for barbel

From January to mid-February, when winter usually begins to bite, there will be few, if any, opportunities when conditions are right. Then, from mid-February until the end of the season, the chances are on the increase, particularly for the angler who lives close to the river (or knows someone who does) and can therefore take advantage of opportunities at short notice.

Having established that the barbel is a fish of all seasons, what time of day is best? Again, it is difficult to generalize for barbel have been caught in the darkest of nights and during the brightest summer day. The general concensus of opinion among successful anglers is that barbel fishing is most consistently productive during the hour or so before, and subsequent two hours after dark.

In summer, barbel will sometimes feed on and off throughout the night, but often there will be a dead spot of, perhaps, two hours from 2300 hours to about 0100, while in the winter an evening session will invariably end before midnight. But do not fall into the trap of thinking that the feeding habits of the barbel are strictly nocturnal. The middle part of the day in summer and autumn often produces a short spell of frenzied feeding activity, but catching them then is difficult. The night-time approach is relatively simple, for the barbel at this time tends to be less cautious than in daytime. Tactics, baits and methods tend therefore to be finer and more sophisticated during the day.

Locating barbel swims comes slowly with hard-won experience. Reading a stretch of river is an art that cannot be acquired overnight.

Weirpool barbel

In summer and autumn, when rivers are low and sluggish, barbel tend to prefer the faster and well-oxygenated places such as weir pools. These places have often been favoured by traditionalist barbel anglers, but the fish are difficult to locate in them.

But barbel are not always found in the fastest, most turbulent water. In summer they do prefer water with a

bit of 'push', but there must be a steady flow without turbulence and back-eddies. During summer, the barbel tend to steer clear of the more open stretches in daytime. In the Kennet, for instance, they are found holed up among the dense beds of streamer weed, while in the Thames they will be down among the underwater 'cabbages'. As darkness falls, the barbel will venture out into the open stretches in search of food.

Baits for daytime barbel

To catch these holed-up, daytime fish is not easy; stealth and delicate bait-presentation are needed. Small baits, such as maggots, are often best, and to present them effectively fine tackle and small hooks are needed—but a 3lb b.s. line and No 16 hook are of little use to heaving a 9lb barbel from dense weed. So the angler new to barbel fishing should

Above: *Barbel fishing on the Throop in Dorset where barbel hide among the streamer weed.*
Below: *Feeling for bites—the most sensitive bite indication of all.*

make a start in the late evening and night, in the more open swims.

Having established the importance of a nice, steady flow, what other basic factors should the would-be barbel catcher look for? undoubtedly these fish prefer swims with a hard bottom, not necessarily gravel, and undercut clay banks are a regular haunt.

Relatively deep swims with a steady flow are usually a good bet, particularly under the near bank. Further experience will reveal that each swim has a particular hotspot.

Barbel hotspots

Like carp, barbel have the fascinating habit of rolling (and occasionally leaping), but a rolling barbel may not be a feeding barbel. However, when consistent rolling is seen it is often indication of a hotspot and sooner or later it will produce fish.

To recap: in summer, be on the look-out for swims with above-average current and, after heavy rains, the barbel will often feed well when the level is on the way up. In winter almost the reverse situation applies: the slower-than-average stretches need to be noted. A fast-rising, coloured river is not good, but when it is fining down, and during a mild spell, conditions will be more or less ideal.

Wind, or rather the lack of it, is another factor to watch. Blustery conditions are to be avoided, while still, muggy days or nights are often mostly productive.

Ledgering by day or night is by far the most effective method, and the beginner will be well advised to start this way. Essential tackle is an 11ft hollow-glass rod with a test-curve of 1½lb, combined with a reliable fixed-spool reel holding line

How can I sort out quality barbel?
Smaller 'school' barbel tend to live, throughout the summer and autumn, on the same pegs or within a small area. Avoid these noted hotspots and look for pegs with character where there is more chance of solitary quality barbel.

Do barbel feed well in winter?
They can be caught in small numbers throughout the winter, providing the water temperature is high enough. Long mild spells in November and December usually result in barbel catches. On artificially heated rivers like the Trent, they are caught even in the coldest conditions, their feeding stimulated by large discharges of hot water from power stations.

How should I set about night fishing?
Make sure that you know exactly where you want to fish before the light fades. Note the direction of swims to which you will cast and look out for potential snags. Tackle will not differ greatly, but decide whether you are going to doze or sit up alert, and choose a visual or audible bite indicator accordingly.

What bait would you recommend to combat dense streamer weed?
Any bait which completely covers the hook—such as a soft cheese paste or luncheon meat—should prevent frequent snagging.

Does a swimfeeder work in barbel fishing?
It works incredibly well for the smaller, shoal barbel. In fact, in the last few years, match fishermen competing along the Severn have scorned any other method.

between 6 and 9lb b.s., depending on conditions. A lead attached to a 6in link and a small swivel is preferable to a lead running direct on the reel line. The distance the link ledger is stopped from the hook depends on the current, the type of bait, and the amount of weed in the swim. Usually this distance will vary between 12 and 18in, but when fishing the gaps in streamer weed you may find that it needs to be doubled.

The beginner should concentrate on well-proven meaty baits such as sausage or luncheon meat. Use hook sizes between 10 and 4, depending on the size of bait. Avoid meat baits with a high fat or gristle content; the lumps can prevent the hook penetrating. The most effective method of detecting barbel bites is to hold the rod and feel for them with line held between thumb and forefinger. At the same time, watch the rod top for movements. At night a beam from a torch on to the rod tip is a major asset and it does not ap-

pear to scare fish. But it must not be flashed on and off into the water.

For the novice perhaps the most important matter is the identification of barbel bites on the ledger, for they can vary enormously. Most barbel bites are quite characteristic and fall into four predominant types:

1. The 'rod-wrencher'. Without warning, this pulls the rod top right round almost wrenching the rod from your hands. The fish invariably hooks itself, yet occasionally it is missed, leaving the angler dazed.

2. The slow 'steady pull' that moves the tip round a few inches, sometimes preceded by a characteristic gentle 'tap-tap'. These are bites from confidently feeding barbel.

3. The sudden 'lunge'. This is a very strong, but all-too-short pull that needs lightning reflexes from the angler. A frustrating bite, nearly always missed and probably the result of the barbel feeling something suspicious. The sudden

'lunge' bite often arises from the barbel being scared by the terminal tackle. It can be caused by the use of too light a lead. Many times, the angler has been told to use 'just enough lead to hold bottom'. But in a strong flow the lead and terminal tackle will bounce along the bottom as soon as a barbel mouths the bait. So use a lead that really holds, it is less likely to scare the fish.

4. The 'vibrator'—a series of tiny tweaks and trembles on the line or rod tip when small baits are being used. Occasionally a fish will be hooked when a 'vibrator' is struck at, but the experienced angler will sometimes wait for a more positive pull to develop, for vibrating can be the prelude to a positive take and can last several minutes.

Below: *Fishing into a swim overshadowed by bushes on the River Ure. The bait is sausage meat (inset). Providing the water is deep, and pushing on vigorously, there is more chance here than in the centre of the river.*

Perch

Strikingly beautiful, the perch is one of the most popular of freshwater fishes among anglers. Though lacking the bold aggressiveness of pike, the perch is a worthy adversary

Though known to be a wanderer and a voracious eater, perch roam in shoals in search of food along well defined routes.

The perch is perhaps one of the most popular freshwater species in the British Isles, especially with the young angler. The reason for this is that perch are voracious eaters and will willingly take bait, especially worms, placed quietly under their noses. For the young angler the capture of two or three perch, even if they are only 6in long, can enliven an otherwise fishless day. Though perch of this size are rarely of interest to the experienced angler, to the novice they offer good sport and the opportunity to develop a wide range of angling skills.

The boldness of the perch, *Perca fluviatilis*, is matched by its bold appearance. No other species of British freshwater fish has such characteristic colouring—dark greenish brown above, olive green below, and a series of vertical dark bars down the sides. The pelvic, anal and lower tail fins are orange red, the two dorsals and the upper part of the tail fin are a darker greenish brown, except for the spiny dorsal fin, which has a black blotch near its rear end. The basic coloration is, however, very variable—some perch are almost blue on the back and sides, others may be light brown.

Colour changes

Undoubtedly, this colouring varies with the habitat, but it also changes with the responses of the fish—an aggressive perch, faced with another of the same size, will become darker, the bars turning almost black, and the dorsal fin spot showing jet black and conspicuous on the elevated fin. This fin spot probably acts as a false eye so that, seen from the side, it may suggest to a competitor, or predator, that the fish in front is much larger than in reality. The function of the spot, however, seems never to have attracted the attention of students of fish behaviour.

The other major feature of the perch is its spines. The first dorsal fin has 13-16 strong spines, the second dorsal, the anal, and the pelvic fins, one or two each. A flattened, but stout spine on each gill cover supplements these spines, and even the scales have numerous short spikes on their free edges, giving the perch its characteristic rough feel. It is worth pointing out the falsity of the belief, held even by experienced anglers, that perch spines are venomous. Certainly, their spiny fins can give a nasty jab if handled carelessly, but it is a clean wound. Any subsequent infection is probably caused more by a soiled handkerchief wrapped round the hand than by the fish.

The ruffe

The ruffe, *Gymnocephalus cernuus*, also known as one time as the pope, is less distinctive, but nevertheless easy enough to identify in British waters. It too has a high and spiny first dorsal fin, but this is joined to the second dorsal, not separate as in the perch. Again, the pelvic and anal fins have spines, as have the gill covers, but the spines tend to be more slender than in the perch. A very distinctive feature of the ruffe is the large cavities underlying the skin on the lower side of the head. These are specially developed sensory canals, forming part of the lateral line system. The coloration of the ruffe is much less striking than that of the perch, being basically olive above, yellowish on the sides and fins, with liberally scattered dark spots and blotches.

While the perch is widely distributed throughout the whole of the British Isles—although less widespread in Scotland—its presence in the North and West is in large part due to its being introduced there for purposes of angling or food, or out of sheer curiosity. The ruffe, on the other hand, has not attracted such interest.

Its spread throughout the country is thought to be due to accidental or natural restocking processes, involving transfer with other species during restocking, or the carrying of eggs by waterfowl. Both fish are members of the family Percidae, to which the zander also belongs.

Perch form shoals of variable size throughout their lives. From the middle of their larval development, when about 10-20mm long, they form small shoals and swim actively, if slowly, both horizontally and vertically, in pursuit of rotifers and copepod crustaceans. The shoal keeps together by visual contact, and so at night it breaks up and the larvae sink singly to the bottom. At a length of 20-30mm they are found in depths of about 5ft.

The perch's diet
For the perch of up to 5cm, small planktonic animals, chiefly crustaceans and midge larvae, are the main food, and continue to be, with the addition of fresh-water shrimps, un-

Top left: *When handling perch, keep your fingers away from the sharp spines.*
Above: *Prime perch caught in southern England despite the widespread disease which almost destroyed stocks.*

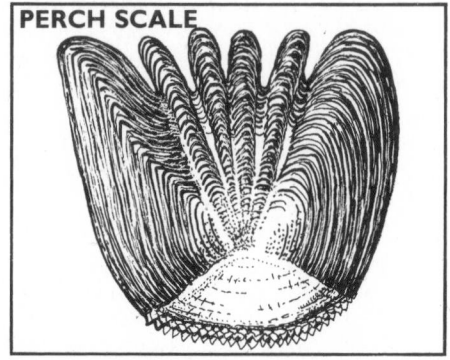

PERCH SCALE

Above: *A perch scale's distinctive shape.*
Right: *The perch's natural habitat contains a wide variety of food, including most of the smaller cyprinids and sticklebacks. Mature perch also feed on young perch.*

WATER BEETLE

STICKLEBACK

WEEDY SHALLOWS

CRAYFISH

til the fish reaches a length of 10cm. At about this length, fish become increasingly important as food, most of the actively swimming carp-like fishes, and ruffe and younger perch, figuring in the diet. However, this dietary graduation from invertebrates to fish varies greatly from one water to another and may depend very considerably on the fauna there. Research on the perch population of a Norwegian lake showed that they were still eating bottom-living invertebrates at a length of 30cm, but that there were relatively few prey fish, other than perch, available for consumption.

Competition with the zander

The tendency to cannibalism in perch over 15cm is very marked, and must have considerable bearing on the age structure of lake populations. Interestingly, zander are also highly cannibalistic in years when there are many young zander around, and studies of the biology of the two species in the Netherlands have shown that in their first year both prey on the same food. Competition for food does not seriously affect their growth in the large waters studied, but in more restricted areas it may be severe. It is certainly a factor to bear in mind in England, following the ill-judged

TREE ROOTS

ROACH

STONY BOTTOM

introduction of the zander.

Both the perch and the zander, even in the earliest stages, feed by selecting by eye each item of food before snapping it up. Ruffe, in contrast, tend to live near the bottom, favouring murky or clouded water, and rely very little on sight to find their food. The elaboration of the lateral line canals on the underside of the head must be seen as a result of evolutionary processes in this kind of environment. The ruffe's diet consists of small animals, chiefly crustaceans, bloodworms, worms, and amphipods (fresh-water shrimps), most of which are bottom-living organisms detected by vibrations through the sensory canals. The diet remains virtually unchanged for life, the ruffe never becoming a fish-eater. The ruffe is also sensitive to noise and other vibrations, and young fish have proved very difficult to keep in captivity.

Spawning in perch takes place from April to May in Britain, but the farther north the later it occurs. The extremes for the species throughout its geographical range are February and July. Although it may seem that temperature is the factor that triggers off the process, the local time of spawning must be a result of natural selection to ensure that breeding produces post-larvae and fry at a time when food for them is in good supply.

The species' spawning habits

Generally, spawning takes place in warm shallows with dense vegetation, or among underwater tree roots or the twigs and branches of fallen trees. The perch is not fussy about the place in which it spawns, and in the absence of such plants or twigs, may shed its eggs on rough rocky or stony shores in, for example, upland lakes. Usually, each female is accompanied by several males, which shed milt close to her vent as the egg strand is extruded. Spawning is a slow process, the female winding her way between the plants, roots, or twigs, and leaving on them a lacy, intertwined mass of eggs. In captivity, the female has been seen to defend the egg mass, but such behaviour has not been observed in the wild.

Why do a fish's colours fade when the fish is dead?
Much of a fish's colouring is under nervous control, its eye and brain in turn triggering a response to the tone and colour of surroundings. The mechanism for colour change is in the skin of a fish, in colour cells—red, yellow and black—which overlie the fish's silvery white background colour. These expand or contract according to signals from the fish's brain. Once the fish is dead, these colour cells contract so that the fish becomes paler.

Can stunted perch grow again if overcrowded stocks are thinned out?
Fish are the only vertebrates to keep growing throughout their lives, and the survivors of a thinned population will continue to grow, though further growth is small if the fish are old. Young stunted fish grow better, given a second chance, but will never make specimen status.

Why don't ruffe and perch form hybrids?
Their general life-style and their spawning behaviour in particular mean that the two species don't mingle while they are spawning. The perch's habit of one female pairing off with two or three males to spawn would mean, too, that a male ruffe joining in would quickly be chased off.

Do perch or ruffe swim great distances?
These species adopt a home range and stay within it. Perch transported 30 kilometres ($18\frac{1}{2}$ miles) will find their way home if at all possible—so they *can* swim considerable distances: it seems they prefer not to.

Above: *Unhooking a small perch. Disengaging the hook is not always an easy job as perch are notorious for gorging a bait.*

The number of eggs produced, all shed at a single spawning, varies strikingly between localities, and to some extent with the size of the female fish, the extremes being 950 and 210,000. The eggs hatch in 2-3 weeks, depending on temperature, and the success rate is usually high.

Growth depends very largely on the food available, which is mainly a function of the richness of the habitat. In lakes where food is plentiful the average length has been recorded at 8-10cm at one year, 16-19cm at two years, 20-24cm at three years, 22-26cm at four years, 27-29cm at five years and about 31cm at six years. Poor growth lakes, such as Dubh Lochan in Scotland, gave mean total lengths for the first five years of 5, 8, 9, 11 and 12cm.

Sexual maturity

In fast growth lakes, some of the male fish are sexually mature at the end of their first year and take part in spawning. The majority of males are sexually mature at two years —at a length of around 15cm —while most females mature at three years and a mean length of 20cm. Males live for 6-7 years, but females survive, continuing to grow slowly, for up to 10 years. It is virtually certain that large specimens will be females from productive waters with fast growth rates.

The perch is well-known for its tendency to overrun a lake with fish all about the same size. This phenomenon has been studied intensively in Lake Windermere, for which records go back to 1941. Many lakes contain stunted populations of perch of similar size and age. The generally accepted explanation for this is that the weather, especially in spring and summer, affects the survival of the post-larvae and fry. Years with particularly high survival rates are warm and sunny. In the case of Windermere, this has been expressed numerically as the total number of degrees that the daily surface water temperature exceeds 14°C (57.2°F) so that, for example, 10 days at 19°C (66.2°F) gives a total of 50 day degrees. When the index is above 400, a good survival rate will be ensured; if it is below 150, survival is poor.

Dominant survivors

The factors causing these differences are indirect, but are certainly connected with the availability of the right type of food as the young perch develop. Good years result in an abundance of young perch. In the absence of a large stock of bigger perch, they will continue to thrive, but by the time the next year's young are active they will have reached a size to turn cannibal and many, if not most, of these young will be eaten. The survivors of a good year class, therefore, tend to dominate the fish—especially perch —population of a water until their numbers decline and they cease to be significant predators. The stage is then set for another year class to dominate the water.

It should be added, however, that reports of this year class dominance have been most notable in lakes in the North and West of the British Isles, where the species is not indigenous. In rich lowland habitats the difference between one year class and another is not so marked, the population being kept in check by predators, chiefly perch and pike, and possibly by disease. The catastrophic perch disease which swept through the country a few years ago resulted in the virtual extermination of the species in many waters. The disease is still active in a few waters, but now we are seeing a revival of the species in fisheries that were thought to be barren because of the disease.

Ruffe—perch's poor relation

In comparison with the very extensive research that has been conducted on the perch, little is known of the ruffe. Variations in growth rates in different habitats have been observed, but the causes are not properly understood. The maximum

Below: *Perch thrive in slow or moderately flowing rivers where eddies such as that on the River Kennet seem always to have a resident 'stripey'.*

recorded lengths in the first four years are 8, 15, 18 and 19cm, but more usual figures are around 6, 9, 11 and 12cm. Most ruffe are sexually mature at the end of their first year, and all are by the end of their second. Spawning takes place on the lake or river bed on exposed hard surfaces such as gravel, sand or clay in a series lasting from April to June. It is doubtful that ruffe live for longer than six years, or attain more than 25cm, specimens of this length having been recorded only on the Continent. The ruffe is very much the poor relation of the perch —timorous and retiring, fussy about its spawning places, only locally distributed, relatively colourless, and small—and few anglers know much about it, and still fewer care.

FISHING FOR PERCH

Methods	Rod	Reel	Reel Line	Terminal Tackle	Hooks	Leads/Weights	Bait	Groundbait/Attractor	Habitat	Time of Season	Distribution
Float: peacock quill	11ft glass, 1lb test, progressive Avon-type	Fixed-spool	4lb	Single hook tied direct	14-6 depends on size of bait	1 swan shot	Brandling, lobworm, marshworm	Light cloud of hook samples	November	Lake, pit, reservoir	Widespread throughout British Isles
Float: trotter	12ft glass match	Fixed-spool	4lb	Single hook to fine nylon link	14-8	Stabilizer shot, bulk shot, small bottom shot	Maggot, brandling, lobtail	Medium feed including hook samples	All Season, subject to conditions	Rivers and streams	
Ledger: long-range swivelled	10ft glass carp or Avon-action	Fixed-spool	6lb	Single hook tied direct	6-4	1oz bomb	Large lobworm	—	December onwards	Deep pits and reservoirs	
Ledger: short-range link	11ft glass, 1lb test	Fixed-spool	3-5lb	Single hook tied direct	—	Nylon swan-shot link	Small redworm	—	November onwards	Slow-moving rivers and streams	
Ledger: fixed single shot	12ft soft-action glass	Fixed-spool	2-4lb	Single hook separate link	12-10	1 swan shot	Maggots, small worm or worm portion	Light cloud of maggot samples	June to September	Slow rivers, canals and drains	
Paternoster: short range fixed	12ft glass match	Any	4lb	Two single hooks	12-6	Pear lead	Worm and minnow	—	June to September	Near banks of small and large rivers	
Paternoster: sliding long-range	10ft glass carp or Avon	Fixed-spool	6lb	Single hook tied direct	6-4	Bomb on long link	Large worm	—	November onwards	Deep stillwaters	
Freeline	12ft soft-action glass	Fixed-spool	4-6lb	Single hook tied direct	10-6	—	Worm, deadbait or crayfish	—	All Season	All slow or stillwaters	
Spinning artificials	6-9ft hollow-glass, fast taper	Fixed-spool	3-5lb	Two very small swivels	—	Small anti-kink	Mepps (0) Ondex (0)	—	All Season	Any weed-free water	
Spinning deadbaits	10ft soft-action glass	Fixed-spool	3-5lb	Two very small swivels	Small treble (14)	Small anti-kink	Dead minnow, loach, bleak, gudgeon	—	All Season	Any weed-free water	
Plug fishing	10ft fast-taper glass	Fixed-spool	3-5lb	Small snap-swivel	Plug	—	Small shallow or deep-diving plug	—	All Season	Any weed-free water	
Fly fishing	9ft distance fly rod (glass or carbon-fibre)	Single-action fly reel	Floating or sinking flyline	Streamer, bucktail, flasher flies	10-4	—	—	—	June-November	Any weed-free water	
Deadbaiting	10ft carp or Avon glass	Fixed-spool	4-6lb	Flight of two tiny trebles	16-14	Small barleycorn	Dead minnow, bleak, gudgeon or perch	—	All season	Any weed-free stillwater	
Jigging	10ft Avon glass, sometimes 12ft for lowering and jigging near bank	Fixed-spool or centrepin	5lb	Hair or feather jig	Off-set weighted	(See Hooks)	—	—	All Season	All waters. Good for weed holes and snaggy areas near bank	

FISHING TECHNIQUE

Fierce, greedy and impetuous, perch combine the qualities that make fishing rewarding and fun. Their boldness is startling; their good looks enough to thrill the most blasé angler

Above: The small eddies around wooden pilings and the supports of bridges and landing stages seem to attract perch, perhaps due to the shelter they provide for small food fishes. This landing stage on a picturesque stretch of the Thames at Laleham is a typically attractive example.

Few fish catch the imagination quite so much as the colourful perch, which is interesting because it is not one of our bigger species, growing to 4lb-plus but rarely. It is a relatively small and crafty predator, unlike all others such as the pike, zander, chub and trout.

With no other species is the difference between young and old fish so marked. Baby perch are gullible to an astonishing degree, engulfing with enthusiasm lobworms as big as themselves and seemingly ignoring or unaware of bankside disturbance. On the other hand, large perch may well be about the most difficult fish in freshwater to catch, certainly with any degree of predictability or regularity.

The perch does not grow into a heavyweight so rods present no problems. For short-range fishing a 10-11ft Avon rod, carrying a line of 3-5lb line is about right, while in some circumstances it is good, but not essential, to use a long, hollow-

glass matchman's rod for swinging out a lobworm on float tackle into water lilies, for example. For long-range ledgering a Mark IV carp rod is about right while a fly rod, too, can be most useful. Choice of reel is easy; any good quality fixed-spool reel, or centrepin for short-range fishing or trotting.

The traditional way

A worm suspended under a float is one of the traditional ways of catching perch and it is as good today as ever it was. Usually the float was a porcupine or crow quill and the angler searched likely perch lies against camp sheeting—not so common now. Man-made features, though, such as jetties, the stonework of bridges, parts of weirs or culverts seem to attract perch shoals.

These fish also congregate near natural features such as sidestream junctions, sharp changes in slope on gravel pits, sunken trees and logs –

—anywhere other than stretches of flat, uniform water.

The roving perch angler

One of the great pleasures of perch fishing is to take a bag of worms and the bare essentials of tackle, and walk from spot to spot dropping the worm into each likely hole. If the water is relatively shallow, up to 5ft deep, it is wise to have either a self-cocking float or at least the shot well above the hook so that the worm sinks slowly. When it has reached the bottom, or the end of its travel if you are fishing off the bottom, wait a few minutes and then give it a twitch of a few inches. The worm rises enticingly and then slowly sinks again. You can use exactly the same method in deep water, although here one should use a sliding float, for contact and feeling with the bait is dulled. The results can be the same, however, if you are sensitive to the delicate signals that your tackle gives.

Above: *Perch from a Yorkshire lake.*
Right: *A lovely specimen is carefully consigned to the keepnet.*

But which of the many different worms should you use? The lob-worm beats all other baits, but at times a small red worm or, alternatively, a brandling, will work quite well. With a big lob you need a larger hook, anything from a No 12 to 4, but with tiny red worms, or even bloodworms, go as small as 16 or 18 as necessary. Sometimes perch will take a very small offering on a very small hook, and then perhaps you should be thinking about staying at the swim and working it up with maggots. Unless a longish cast is required the worm should be hooked once, so that you get a lively wriggle rather than a bunched-up offering. It is difficult to advise about striking. Usually the float makes a preliminary sudden dive. Wait for it to come up and then slide away. If it doesn't come up, strike! If you miss the fish it may be a very small one but in any event give the next bite a little longer before striking. If you continue to miss bites use a piece of lobworm or a small hook and small species of worm.

The author has taken large bags of perch by wandering from hole to hole but it sometimes pays not to move on too quickly. One can often find a big shoal of perch and the larger specimens may only come after a lot of fishing. 'Small ones first, larger ones later', is often the rule after a quiet spell.

Sometimes it is necessary to get the bait right among the rush and reed stems. A self-cocking float is ideal, very smoothly rubbered at both ends, or attached at one end only. A bait sinking very close to the stems may be taken, while one only a foot away is ignored, probably because the perch are lurking in the weeds. On some small rivers, a long rod is an advantage for dropping baits into these positions, as it is for stret-pegging, which is also effective at times. Strangely, perch sometimes prefer dead worms. The author has experienced this more than once, but it is probably more common than generally supposed.

Now for other livebaits—small fish. Maggots will not be introduced here for the methods are the same as for any other species. One thing to remember is that when using a single maggot the arrival of perch in the swim is often signalled by a lightning dip of the float, which you promptly miss. But of small live baits, the soft-bodied fishes (minnow, gudgeon, and loach) are far better than harder or spiny baits (sticklebacks, perch, roach, rudd and so on). A big minnow or small gudgeon is ideal—one can even use roach or rudd. In fact, perch weighing anything above 3oz take small gudgeon and minnows.

Small trebles, no wire

A wire trace is not needed and for hooks you want a large single or very small trebles. Baits and tackle will on occasion be lost to pike but not to perch. It is a mistake to think

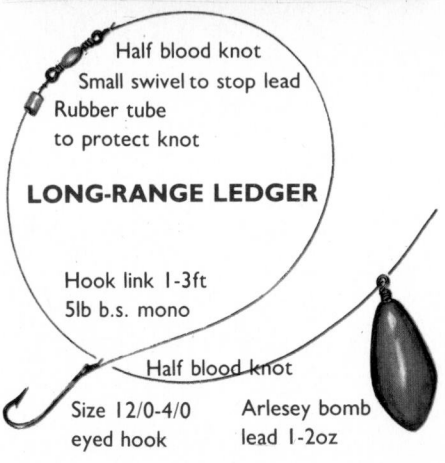

LONG-RANGE LEDGER

Half blood knot
Small swivel to stop lead
Rubber tube
to protect knot

Hook link 1-3ft
5lb b.s. mono

Half blood knot

Size 12/0-4/0 eyed hook

Arlesey bomb lead 1-2oz

Top: *The attractive body stripes show up clearly here. A good sized fish is always a colourful sight.*
Above: *The rig for which Richard Walker invented the now famous Arlesey bomb. The best bait for this kind of ledgering is a large lobworm.*
Right: *A rig for the roving angler or for use in a swim which has been 'worked up' with loose-fed maggots.*
Top, far right: *A buoyant, mid-water bait which does not involve the gathering of livebait is a large lobworm injected with air. Single-hooked, its length will lend it a little lifelike 'waggle'.*
Top centre: *This confluence on the Kennet promises excellent fishing for perch which are tolerant of still and fast-moving water.*

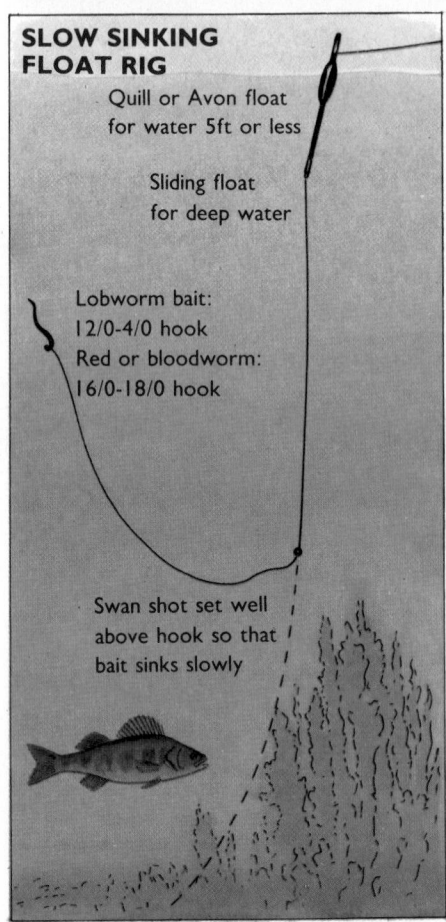

SLOW SINKING FLOAT RIG

Quill or Avon float for water 5ft or less

Sliding float for deep water

Lobworm bait: 12/0-4/0 hook
Red or bloodworm: 16/0-18/0 hook

Swan shot set well above hook so that bait sinks slowly

that small perch will avoid live fish. They do not. When float fishing for perch you need a slightly larger cork-bodied float than for worming, but not above ½inch in diameter for a circular body. For paternostering with or without the float, use the tiniest of lead weights (perhaps a swan shot) rather than the ½oz Arlesey bombs that you would use for piking. The reel line need only be

around 5lb b.s. and the paternoster link (which is tied to a swivel about 1ft above the bait) should be about 3lb b.s. and 3ft in length.

Spinning

Spinning for perch is an effective method. A wire trace is not needed. Sometimes one may need a celluloid or plastic anti-kink vane fixed on the line about 12-18in above the lure.

PATERNOSTER LIVEBAIT RIG

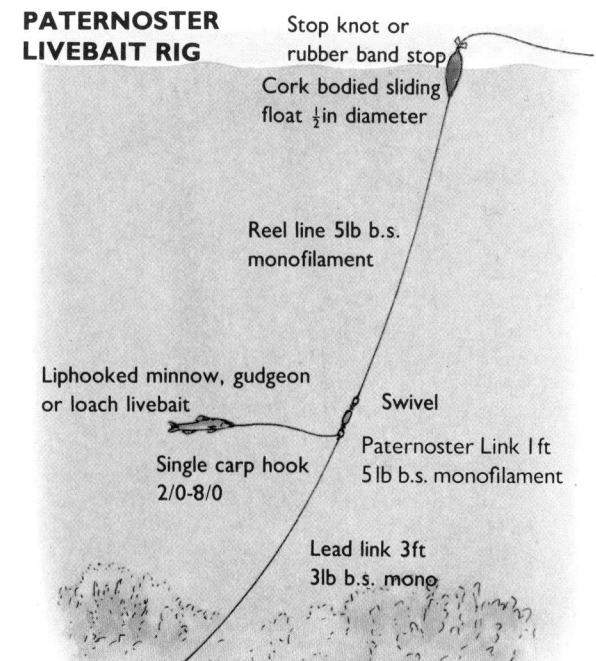

Stop knot or rubber band stop

Cork bodied sliding float ½in diameter

Reel line 5lb b.s. monofilament

Liphooked minnow, gudgeon or loach livebait

Swivel

Single carp hook 2/0-8/0

Paternoster Link 1ft 5 lb b.s. monofilament

Lead link 3ft 3lb b.s. mono

Below: *Coaxing a beautiful perch out of the shallows of a gravel pit. Pit perch are caught from around underwater obstacles like sunken trees.*

Is it true that perch eat their own fry?

Oh yes. Many a specimen has been landed using a small perch as livebait but this may be distasteful to you, either in view of the move away from livebaiting or because the species has suffered enough over the last decade thanks to perch disease.

Why are perch so often found close to underwater obstacles.

A perch shoal stays close to its food supply. These obstacles provide a rich larder for the fry which, in turn, are eaten.

Using lobworm as my bait, I find that I'm missing more than half my bites.

You are probably striking too soon. When a perch first takes your bait, allow 2-3 seconds to ensure that the part of the worm containing the hook is inside the fish's mouth.

How can I fish lobworms at long range?

Although the traditional porcupine quill float is still best for close range, zoomer and antenna floats are more effective over long distances. As for casting weights, Richard Walker developed his Arlesey bomb specially for making long casts to specimen perch in Arlesey lake, though its uses are now many and varied.

Is there a cheap, effective spinner on the market specifically for perch?

The tiny, twinkling fly spoon has been a favourite with perch anglers for generations, and it is still as cheap and efficient as ever.

Crucian carp

Smaller than its close relatives, the common and king carp, the crucian is nevertheless a hardier fish which will often survive in conditions where other species would die

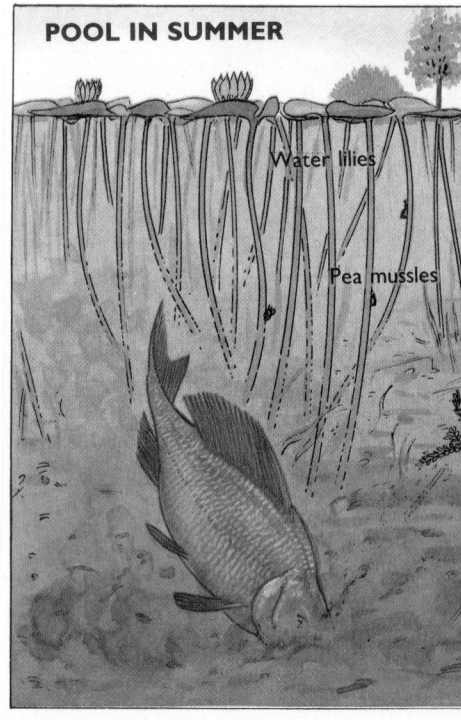

POOL IN SUMMER

Water lilies

Pea mussles

Among the freshwater fish of the British Isles there are many fine sporting species with devotees dedicated to their capture and study. There are also many small species, like minnows, which the angler regards only as prey for bigger fish or as bait. Between the two extremes lie a number of species with some appeal to the angler but which few attempt to catch. Probably the most common of these is the crucian carp, *Carassius carassius*.

The crucian carp is not a well-known species to the angler, perhaps because of its poor distribution. Originally thought to be a native of the east of England, roughly the region covered by Yorkshire rivers, the Trent, the Great Ouse, and the Thames systems, today, by the intervention of man, it is found well outside these river systems. There is even some doubt as to whether it is native to the Thames basin at all, its distribution being very patchy in that area. Whether this is due to sporadic introduction by man or the destruction of so many suitable natural habitats in this area is uncertain. Whatever the truth of this, the crucian is not found in many parts of the British Isles. It is absent from Scotland and Ireland, and Wales has only isolated populations as do the extreme southwest and the north of England.

Freshwater migration
The reason for this sparse distribution owes nothing to the crucian's need for special habitat (for it will survive where most other species would die) but in the prehistory of these islands. Following the last Ice Age, obliterating all the native freshwater fish in Britain, a land connection between England and the Continent persisted for two to three thousand years in the area now covered by the North Sea. Through the lakes and streams which dotted this area, native freshwater fishes migrated to recolonize our rivers. This is why, even today, the eastern rivers of England contain more species than many of the western rivers. While fish like the dace and the roach colonized new waters, others, like the crucian and the silver bream, did not, staying roughly in the area they inhabited

Below: *This crucian was taken from the River Thames; you will find them more often in swampy or heavily overgrown stillwaters.*

Above: *A pond in summer provides abundant food for the crucian carp, which will forage on the surface and below.*

48

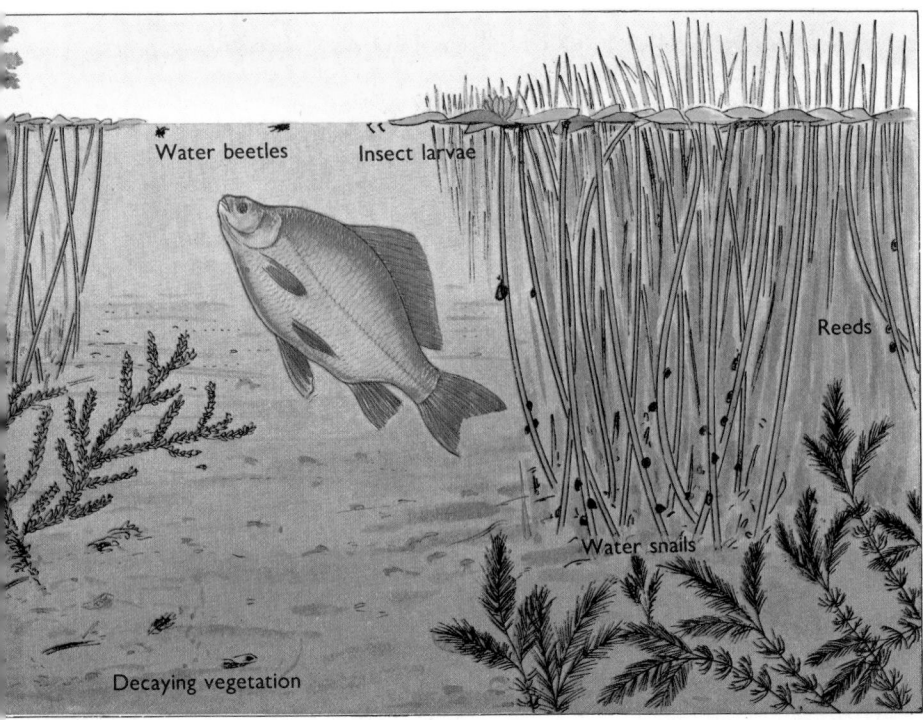

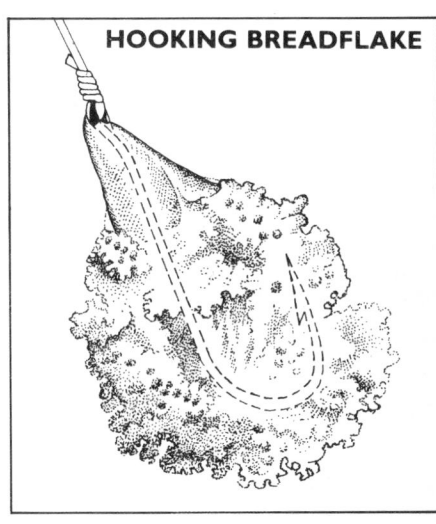

Above: *Bread that flakes easily in the water is a good crucian bait.* **Left:** *Trevor Housby fishing for crucian in a small lake.*

when the North Sea was finally formed.

Adaptation to change

The crucian carp thrives in the kind of swampy region that best resembles the prehistoric North Sea landbridge. It is found in overgrown, weedy pools and lakes choked with vegetation, both growing and decaying on the bottom. An extremely hardy fish, it is able to tolerate a wide range of temperature and oxygen variations. So tolerant is it, in fact, that it can survive where few other fish will. Very low levels of dissolved oxygen such as often exist in densely weeded pools, especially at night when the plants are producing deadly carbon dioxide rather than oxygen, or in winter when the vegetation has died down and is rotting to the detriment of dissolved oxygen, fail to kill the crucian carp. Able to face long frozen periods, low oxygen levels beneath the ice and near zero temperatures, high summer temperatures only make the crucian more active.

Given such adaptability, the crucian is often put into waters in which it will survive and breed—but never grow to any great size. Its natural habitat, the lowland pools and marshes in flood plains of rivers, where plant growth is rich and suitable food abundant, no longer exists in England today. As a result, places where the crucian now lives are fre-

49

quently less than ideal and are often man-made lakes and pools. Small woodland pools, the result of some long-forgotten landscape gardener's work, with a thick residue of rotting leaves from nearby trees and too few plants, and old claypits made in the days when clay was dug by hand, are frequently its habitat.

Two types of crucian

There are two types of crucian carp: one big-headed and flat-bellied, the other solid, dumpy with a small head. The slender-bodied, big-headed mini-crucians of so many of these pools are the result of their food-deprived environment. In Europe these fish are often referred to as the *humilis* form of the crucian (a name proposed in 1840 by a scientist who thought the variation from the normal crucian shape so extreme that it must be another species). In fact, they are simply half-starved crucians. From aquarium experiments it seems that given abundant food they will grow to resemble the full-bodied fish, if they were not too old when captured.

The plump, full-bodied crucian found in the larger, richer lakes is richly coloured, with the back a deep bronze-green, the sides bronze or yellow, the ventral fins tinged with red and the tail and dorsal fin dark. Its small head, humped back, and solid body show a fish that has never been short of food. They feed when young on the minute crustaceans, including water fleas and copepods, abundant in rich, still freshwaters, graduating to insect larvae (especially bloodworms and mosquito larvae), larger crustaceans, and even small water snails as they grow. When well-grown there are few invertebrates that the crucian carp will not tackle. Remains of plants, especially the finer leaves of the pondweeds, are often found in crucians' stomachs, although it is possible that the plant is eaten for the sake of some animal, such as snails, or perhaps their eggs, living on it.

Given abundant food the growth rate can be quite rapid. In central European lakes one research worker found growth as follows:

Age	1	2	3	4	5
Males	2in	3¼in	4½in	5¾in	6½in
Females	2in	3¼in	4½in	6in	7¼in

These figures, for a wild population, show two features of interest. First, the lakes from which the samples were taken were large and the growth-rate good (many small-lake crucians that have been examined are less than 5in in length at six or seven years). Second, the figures suggest that females grow faster and larger than males. The largest crucians examined have always proved to be female (they live up to 12 years in England). Females take four or five years to mature, while males generally mature at three years.

Growth rates of this order are fair approximations to those found in the more favoured English habitats for the species.

Controlled breeding

In East Germany and Poland some fish farmers grow crucian carp for the food market, mainly because the

Above: *A New Forest pool, typical of the crowded waters where crucians are found.* **Below left:** *In winter crucians slow down and lie in the mud.* **Below:** *Stocking with crucian in the Tri-Lakes Fishery, Sandhurst.*

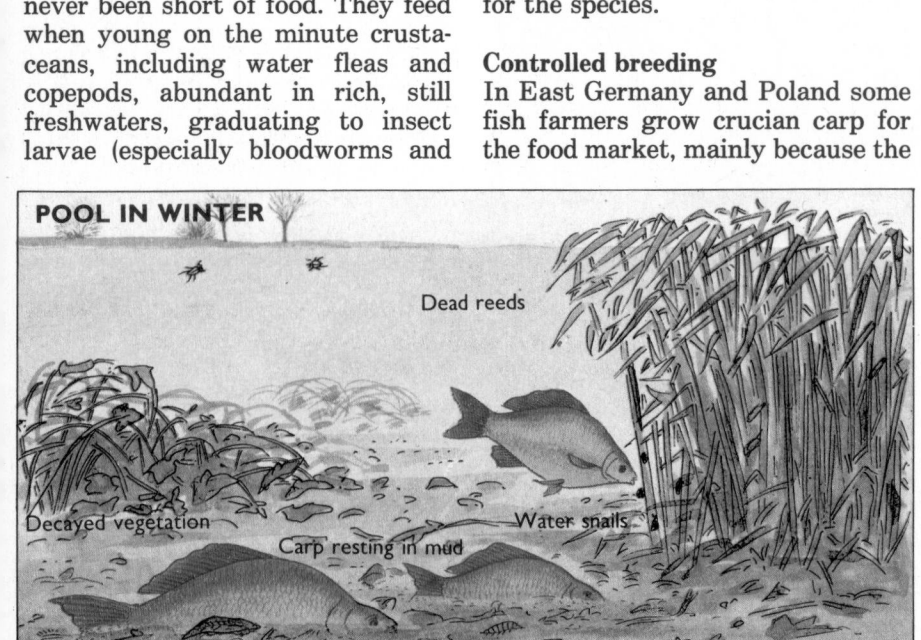

POOL IN WINTER

Dead reeds

Decayed vegetation

Carp resting in mud

Water snails

common carp, *Cyprinus carpio*, proves to be rather delicate and slow-growing in their cold continental climate. Here, by selective breeding and of course, food feeding, they have produced deep-bodied farm fish known as Spechthausen which mature at two years when they reach a length of 5-6in. Clearly, such selection could be practised on a small scale by fish farmers in this country to produce fast growing, large fish for the angling market. In the course of a generation or two, however, such fish may revert to the normal-growing, often stunted population of so many lakes, due to spawning.

Spawning

Spawning takes place from May to June—sometimes in cool summers, as late as July. The eggs are golden to pale red in colour and stick to the leaves of plants. They hatch in five to seven days depending on the temperature, and even as long as 10 days in cool weather although this results in high mortality. The fry

hatch out at about 4.5mm in length and hang on the leaf by a special sucker on the head for a further two days while they absorb the last of the egg's yolk which at first forms a bulge on the belly. After this their survival and growth depend on the amount of food available. The female crucian carp lays between 150,000 and 300,000 eggs in several spawning sessions. This number is not particularly large—only one-quarter to one-third the number produced by a 10lb common carp—and the abundance of crucians cannot be due to high egg production. Where the crucian has the advantage over such fish as the common carp, with which it is frequently found, is in its adaptability and toughness, and the much higher rate of survival of the newly hatched young. While this, no doubt, has advantages for the survival of the species, it often tends to be a disadvantage to the individual population. All too often one finds large numbers of small crucians in a lake stunted in their growth simply

Pondweed on the surface, reeds lining the edges—ideal crucian territory.

because there are too many mouths for the available food.

Annual netting to remove some of the excess population is possibly the best solution to this problem. If this proves impractical, a club rule that all crucians caught have to be killed is the solution. It sounds unkind, but in the interest of future angling it is often necessary.

Crucian carp and the common carp are often spoken of as if they are close relatives. In fact, the relationship is not especially close. The crucian is more closely related to the goldfish, *Carassius auratus,* and when young it is sometimes difficult to tell the two apart. This, however, is not likely to cause many anglers problems, although it can be a problem for fish breeders as the two will readily breed together to produce a crucian/goldfish hybrid. The problem for the angler is more likely to be difficulty in distinguishing the crucian carp from the crucian/common carp hybrid. This is not always very difficult, although sometimes the odd hybrid can give the angler identification problems.

Aids to identification
First, remember that crucians have no barbules round the mouth and the shape of the dorsal fin is smoothly curved outwards (convex). Second, the common carp has a barbule at each corner of the mouth and its dorsal fin is curved inwards (concave). Hybrids usually have one barbule, either on the left or the right side. Sometimes they have two tiny barbules, not much more than pimples, on each side. Very rarely it may be that they have no barbules. The dorsal fin shape is literally in-between the parent species, usually high in front, but with only a shallow dip in the outline, but often straight edged. Other features, such as the number of pharyngeal teeth, tend to be intermediate between the parent species but in the really difficult cases examination of the pharyngeal teeth is necessary.

FISHING FOR CRUCIAN CARP

Methods	Rod	Reel	Line	Terminal tackle	Hooks	Lead Weights	Bait	Groundbait/ Attractor	Time of Season	Habitat	Distribution
Freeline	11ft hollow-glass 1-1½lb test	Fixed-spool	5lb		8-4	None	Luncheon meat, cat-food, paste/ flake, worm	Hookbait samples	Summer and autumn	Lake, pit, pond	South and South-East England
Ledger	11ft hollow-glass 1-1½lb test	Fixed-spool	5lb	Link-ledger	12-4	Pear lead on a nylon link	As above, plus maggots, sweetcorn, casters	Hookbait plus maggots, sweetcorn, casters	Summer and autumn	Lake, pit, pond	
Paternoster	11ft hollow-glass 1-1½lb test	Fixed-spool	5lb	Paternoster-link	12-4	Pear lead on a nylon link	As above, plus maggots, sweetcorn, casters	Hookbait plus maggots, sweetcorn, casters	Summer and autumn	Lake, pit, pond	
Swimfeeder ledger	11ft hollow-glass 1-1½lb test	Fixed-spool	5lb	Swimfeeder	16-4	Swimfeeder	As above, plus maggots, sweetcorn, casters	Hookbait plus maggots, sweetcorn, casters	Summer and autumn	Lake, pit, pond	
Float	13ft hollow-glass match	Fixed-spool or closed-face	2-4lb	Antenna or waggler; antenna-slider	18-12	Split-shot	Mainly maggots, and casters	Hookbait plus maggots, sweetcorn, casters	Summer and autumn	Lake, pit, pond	

Crucians are fish of season. In winter, midday—when the water has warmed up—is the best time for them. In summer, they feed most actively early in the morning and in the late evening, although they can be kept feeding by the judicious addition of groundbait. Sheltered swims, away from the prevailing wind, and holes between weedbeds are the most likely hotspots.

FISHING TECHNIQUE

For once, the specimen hunter need not suffer freezing winds, snow and other hardships to catch his fish. Some of the biggest and best crucian carp fishing is done on small ornamental lakes in summer, says Jim Gibbinson

Many prizes are won each year with crucian carp that are not true crucians—not fraudulently, but simply through mistaken identity. In some waters, crucian carp hybridize with common carp. The offspring closely resemble true crucians, often satisfying all the external identification tests. They have barbuleless lips, and scale and fin-ray counts often betray no difference. The only positive means of identification in difficult cases is by dissecting out the pharyngeal teeth.

Identification difficulties
I have seen a 9lb fish which defied the efforts of experts at the Natural History Museum to make a categorical identification without internal examination. Only its phenomenal weight encouraged the captor to persist until proof was given that it was not a true crucian but a crucian × common carp hybrid. Unfortunately, many large fish are not so thoroughly investigated and are accepted as crucian. Sometimes, identification is even based on photographic evidence alone.

A rarer cause of confusion is the goldfish—the ordinary swim-round-and-round-in-a-glass-bowl-on-the-sideboard goldfish. These golden

carp *(Carassius auratus)* live wild in a few waters and, over a few generations, revert to natural carp-type coloration. I used to catch them from a small park lake where they averaged 3–4lb (the occasional six-

Below: *No great depth of water is needed to support a population of big crucians. They live among the water lilies of this lake.*

pounder was taken). We assumed that they were small carp until it was noticed that they had no barbules. Subsequent research revealed their true identity.

'Bomb crater' fishing

Crucians are frequently found in small waters. I used to catch them in Essex ponds no larger than the average living room, but these 'bomb crater' waters are found all over the southern counties. Even in tiny waters of that sort, crucians tend to proliferate. Hordes of tiny, stunted fish result, and in such waters a half-pounder would be a monster. Big crucians are generally found in food-rich waters where circumstances combine to prevent over-breeding, and enough pike and perch exist to crop the young fish and reduce the survival rate. On these waters, a 2lb crucian is a big fish. Most anglers have never seen a crucian of that size, far less caught one. Persistent fishing in a quality water may eventually produce a few specimens of $2\frac{1}{2}$lb.

If you want to catch three-pounders, you will have to put in long, persistent effort in an above-average water, or find a truly exceptional water. While seeking some big mirror carp, I discovered a very fertile lake and caught some colossal crucians of up to $3\frac{1}{4}$lb. But I believe it to have held fish of 6lb-plus.

There is a tendency among specimen hunters to over-complicate fishing with extravagant, sophisticated extras. In crucian carp fishing, this takes the form of ultra-sensitive tackle. Float rigs are used that are capable of registering lifts and dips of less than a millimetre! In my experience crucians do not warrant such refinements. They sink the float out of sight, while, in ledgering, they pull an indicator right up to the rod. In freelining with the bale-arm open, the crucians trundle off with the bait in runs worthy of any carp. By all means ruin your eyesight watching for millimetric movements of a float; but by simply freelining you will be giving the fish enough rope to hang themselves.

For freelining, use heavy baits such as paste, on a fine-wire size 8 hook with a barb and small eye.

Best times for big fish

I have caught crucians during every hour of the day and night, but the best times for big fish are from dawn to mid-morning and through the night. Quite obviously, there are variations from water to water and from one week to another on the same water. Technique makes a difference too. Crucians sometimes respond to floating baits in the middle of a blazing afternoon.

For specimens the best time of year is from the start of the season until late July. August is sometimes good, but generally unreliable. September can be excellent. By the end of September, crucians become scarce. I have caught them in January by accident, while winter carp fishing. But generally winter is good only for stunted pond fish which feed avidly throughout.

Catching big crucians while fishing for specimen carp, I have concluded that scaled-down carp tactics are the best for catching specimen crucians.

Rods need not be heavy. A 3lb crucian is a huge fish, so the sort of rod used for tench, bream or roach is ideal. I have a pair of thin-walled, fast-taper 11ft blanks, with a test-curve of about 1lb. (The term 'test-curve' is not really appropriate when applied to fast-taper rods.) The rings are of the best quality hard-chrome, except for the tip, which is lined with friction-free magnesium oxide and is kind to fine lines. My handles are not covered with corks; simply a short length of plastic shrink-tube with a whipped-on, lightweight, snap-lock, Fuji reel fitting.

These rods are a pleasure to use. They make an ideal marriage with 5lb lines, but, owing to the tolerance of fast-taper glass, will handle a range from 3 to 8lb. I mostly use a 5lb line, which may seem too heavy, but then I do not see the point of fishing light for the sake of it—only if it is the one way to get bites.

Crucians are found in shallow water. The north-east corner of a lake gets the benefit of prevailing warm south-westerlies and is often well-endowed with food forms such as insect larvae. The westerlies prevalent in autumn blow leaves and floating weed to this area over the years, so the bottom is rich with humus in which water plants can grow. The northern side of the lake gets most of the sunshine too, especially if the lake is surrounded by trees. A mellow south-westerly blowing into the north-east corner of the lake on the day of the fishing trip is most propitious.

In very difficult waters, as many as three rods may be used, but two are usually sufficient. Do check the terms of your rod licence, however, for the number of rods permissible.

Rods are set up horizontally 2ft above the ground, unless strong winds prove troublesome, in which case the tips are submerged. A wind often drops away after dark, however. A bobbin indicator is hung between the first and second ring. For daytime fishing this can be anything from a pea-sized piece of

When is the best time of day to fish for specimen crucians?
Like the tench, crucians are at their most active during the early morning and evening, though night fishing often produces the best fishing of all.

How can I avoid tench when I'm after crucians?
This is an unfailing problem as the feeding times and preference for baits are so similar. You must either find a fishery holding carp exclusively, or put up with catching a tench or two.

I only seem to catch crucians during warm weather. Should I change my tactics in the autumn?
You are probably doing nothing wrong. It is just that crucian fishing drops off steeply as soon as the first frosts arrive.

Why is cat-food paste so effective?
The meaty ingredients of cat food releases an attractive scent into the water drawing fish to a swim from many yards away.

Why do I fail to hook any fish when using floating crust?
You are obviously striking much too soon. Wait until your line starts to run rather than striking on impulse.

I like to use three rods, but how can I avoid tangling when I get a bite on one of them?
Fan out the baits so that they are well separated. If a hooked fish swims towards your other lines, drop the tip of the spare rod in the water and keep your line well free of the water so as to bring the fish to the surface. Please note that many ticket waters do not allow the use of more than two rods.

LUMINOUS BOBBIN RING

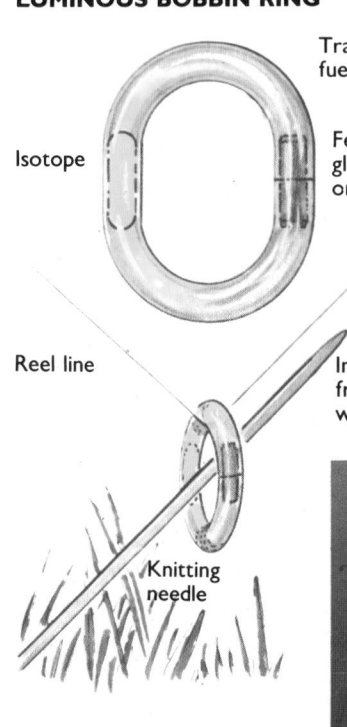

Transparent fuel pipe

Isotope

Ferrule glued in one end

Reel line

Indicator is free to slide off when bite occurs

Knitting needle

SECURE CASTING TIP

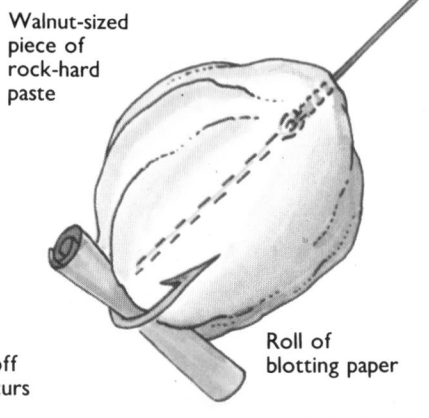

Walnut-sized piece of rock-hard paste

Roll of blotting paper

Left: *John Watson with five fine crucians caught on bread flake.*
Right: *An ambitious rig, each rod fitted with an audible bite detector. But could their tones be distinguished?*

Dace

A dace's delicate lips are more seductive to an angler than its vital statistics, for although it is smaller than roach or chub, its shy reserve and nervous nibbles are an endearing challenge

The dace (*Leuciscus leuciscus*) is common throughout England and Wales, except in the extreme West. It is rarely found in Scotland, and until recently was not recorded in Ireland. It is essentially a river fish, flourishing in the swifter, well-oxygenated reaches along the barbel zone, extending upstream into the trout zone, and downstream into the roach and bream zones. It is unusual to find it in lakes, and when found there its presence is often due to pike anglers having released unwanted livebaits at the end of the day; or because the fish have been cut off from a river by the formation of an ox-bow or horseshoe-shaped bend formed from a meander.

In Lancashire the dace is generally called the graining, and, as such, was once believed to be a different species. Modern authorities on fish do not distinguish it from the dace. In the West of England it is known as the dare or dart—a name probably derived from the manner in which dace forge their way upstream against very swift currents by a series of darting movements.

It is a slender, graceful fish, generally brown or green coloured on the back, with dorsal and tail fins to match. The flanks are of a striking silver, and the underside is white. The lower fins are white or grey, sometimes with pink or yellow tints. The head and mouth are small and the eye has a distinctly yellow iris—never the roach red.

Confusion with roach or chub

The dace is sometimes confused with young roach or chub, but usually the sparkling metallic silver of the flanks distinguishes it from both species. Roach and chub are coloured either like pewter or bronze, but dace have the white lustre of freshly polished silver. Older chub are sometimes mistaken for dace, usually due to wishful thinking on the angler's part.

Dace are a small species, the average run of fish being less than 8oz—a fish of 12oz is a good one, a pounder a very much-sought-after specimen. Chub of this size are common and the angler can be forgiven for hoping when his mixed bag of small dace and roach contains a chub of 1½lb.

However, such confusion should not last, for chub bear distinctly convex-edged dorsal and anal fins, while dace have fins with concave edges. Chub also have a large head and mouth, which contrasts with the small, oblique mouth of the dace.

Dace are at their best in small streams, or in the swift upper reaches of the river where the water is shallow and clear. Here can sometimes be seen large shoals darting from cover into the streamy runs for a morsel, or moving swiftly downstream when scared by an anglers' shadow on the water. In waters such as these one occasionally spots a grandfather dace, attended by one or two similar-sized companions. To have attained a weight of nearly 1lb such dace must have long outlived the rest of the shoal with which they grew up, and have developed in isolation.

Best dace are in trout zones

Any angler anxious to catch these fish must fish fine and far off, and yet be swift in his reflexes when a fish takes. The best dace specimens of all are often found among trout zones, where their superb quality often goes unnoticed by the fly fisherman seeking trout, and it is such waters that the specimen-dace hunter would love to be allowed to test his skill.

Dace are also common in large,

broad, slower-flowing waters, where they often appear in roach swims. They usually feed higher in the water than the roach shoals, and tend to predominate in the centre runs, where the stream is swiftest. Although they are generally considered to be surface and middle-water feeders, in fact they do continually change depth, feeding alternatively at the top and on the bottom, as well as in-between.

Good-quality dace are taken on most of the major river systems —the Thames, Trent, Ribble, Severn, Hampshire Avon, Dorset Stour, Kent Stour, Waveney, Kennet, Windrush and many others. They are loved by anglers because, size for size, they fight far better

Above: *Feeding dace dimple the surface in their own distinctive way.*
Right: *Trotting for dace. A trotting reel has no handle and is spun by the angler's fingers batting the rim.*
Below: *Specimen dace from one of Norfolk's broadland waters.*

than roach or chub, and perhaps above all because they take the bait so swiftly that the angler can pride himself on being able to hit every second bite.

The seasonal movements of dace shoals are similar to those of roach. With the opening of the season they are found on the gravelly shallows, where swift, streamy runs predominate, or scouring in weirpools and shallow, fast-moving stretches. Within a few weeks, usually earlier than roach, they move into the main river, seeking out the swifter reaches, and patrol continuously in search of food. Like roach, they lie under the cover of overhanging weed tendrils and fringes, usually close to the surface, where they intercept food items passing down and then flash back to cover again. As autumn approaches, they work into deeper waters, except during the flood or spate, when they seek refuge from the main torrent in ox-bows, lay-bys and back eddies, or in holes under the banks. They still forage into the turbulent waters, but the shoals divide into smaller groups to move around. With winter, when the floods have gone, they work into deeper waters and re-form shoals.

The dace usually spawns between March and May, although it may be earlier or later depending on the season. The species breed communally, moving to spawning beds in feeder streams over sandy or stony bottoms. At this time the males develop spawning tubercles all over their bodies. The females each lay, on the river bed, between 3,000 and 27,000 eggs of 1½-2mm in diameter. In temperatures of about 13°C (55°F) these hatch after some 25 days.

The young grow to about 6cm in a year, reaching maturity—with a length of 10-20cm, and rarely exceeding 25cm—after two to three years. The current British record fish weighed 1lb 4oz 4dm when caught in 1960, although specimens of over 1lb are rare.

The feeding patterns of dace are also similar to those of the roach, but have a different emphasis. Like roach, they live on insects, plants, crustaceans, and molluscs, but the proportions differ. Roach take about half their food from plants, but dace only a quarter. Their main diet—about a third of their total intake—consists of insects.

The rest is composed of crustaceans and molluscs. Like roach, they are able to live for lengthy periods with little or no food, subsisting on body reserves during the leaner winter months if they have too.

Baits for dace

Dace will take most baits offered to roach at one time or another, according to prevailing circumstances. Bread baits, including paste, crust, crumb and flake, are popular, and cereals such as wheat, hemp, or tares also account for large bags, especially in winter, when insect life is less easily found by the fish. Many anglers like to groundbait the swim with hemp, while using elderberry on the hook. This is worthwhile, as the fish hang on to the bait a little longer, giving the angler fractionally more time to synchronize his strike with the disappearance of the float.

In summer, maggots, caddis grubs, woodlice, earwigs, or freshwater shrimps and worms are all good dace baits, and the angler must experiment to see which best suits existing conditions and the whims of the fish on a particular day.

Almost any float or ledgering method can be employed, according to preferences and the water fished, but the sparing use of groundbait is always useful for attracting shoals to the vicinity.

The style for large rivers

On large rivers such as the Thames, Severn, or Trent, where the stream is both broad and deep, float fishing fine and far off is an excellent style, well-suited for taking good bags. Tackle must be carefully selected: the float should be as light as possible to suit the weight of the current and the distances to be cast. It must also be heavy enough to be controllable at a distance and at the same time provide good visibility when it suddenly dips out of sight.

In such situations most experienced anglers prefer to use a centrepin rather than a fixed-spool reel. This is because it maintains closer contact with the float, permitting a more immediate reaction and a swifter strike. A 4in diameter reel drum is suitable, and this must be smooth and free-running to allow the line to

trickle freely off as the pull of the stream dictates. Once contact is made with the shoal, the angler can usually take several fish before the bites cease. He must then adjust his float to locate the depth at which the shoal has settled, and be prepared to repeat this throughout the day as these fickle fish alter their level in the water.

In a shallow river, especially

Right: *Wading, with reeds behind him to break up his outline, the angler trots for dace.*
Below: *The trotting rig has an artificial caddis as bait. Two nymphs are also shown. The ledger rig is braided with maggot.*
Bottom: *The dace zone is broadly between the slow bream stretch and the faster barbel reach. But dace will also move upstream, and rarely drop downriver to where the temperature of the water may well reach over 20°C (68°F).*

where the water is clear, the angler must take good care not be seen. A favourite strategy is to locate feeding shoals by eye and then select a suitable pitch well upstream, preferably with a good weedbed between the angler and the fish. A few maggots are tossed in as groundbait and the angler then wades out a little, pegs down his keepnet in the margins and starts to fish. If he can

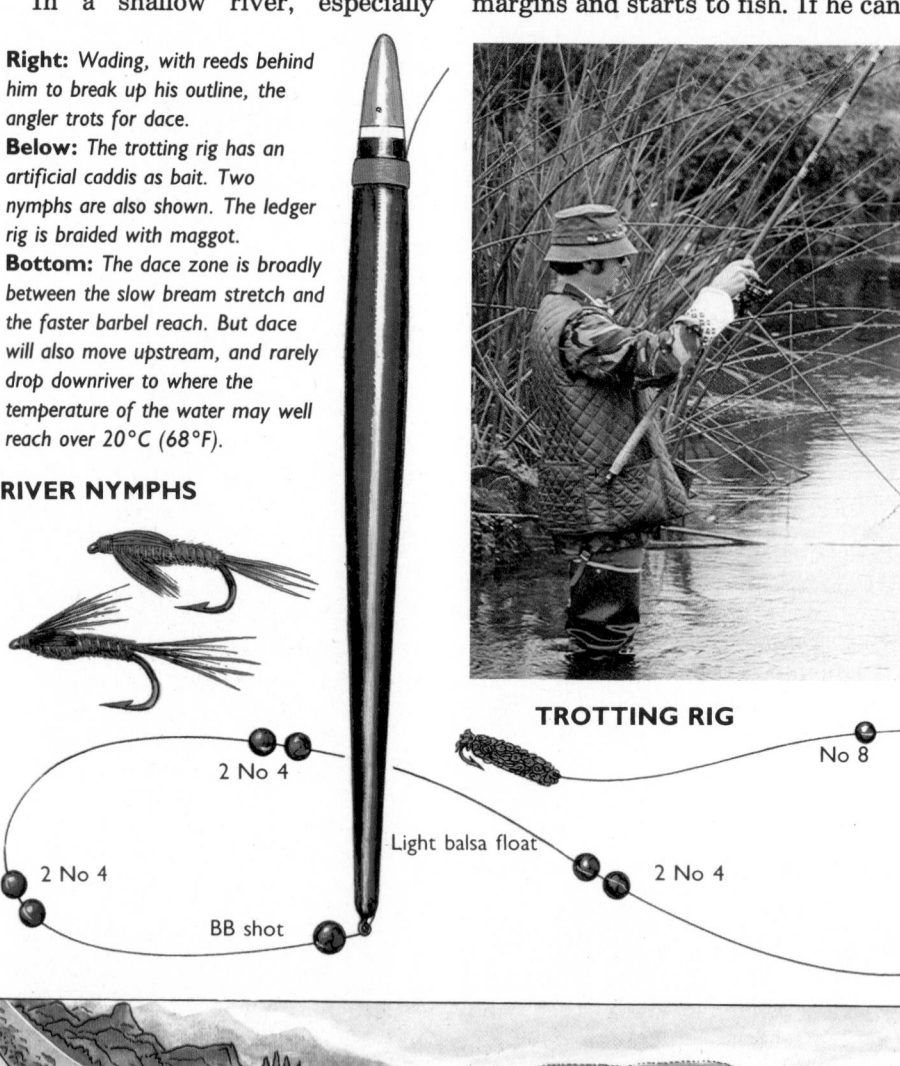

RIVER NYMPHS

TROTTING RIG

2 No 4

2 No 4

BB shot

Light balsa float

2 No 4

No 8

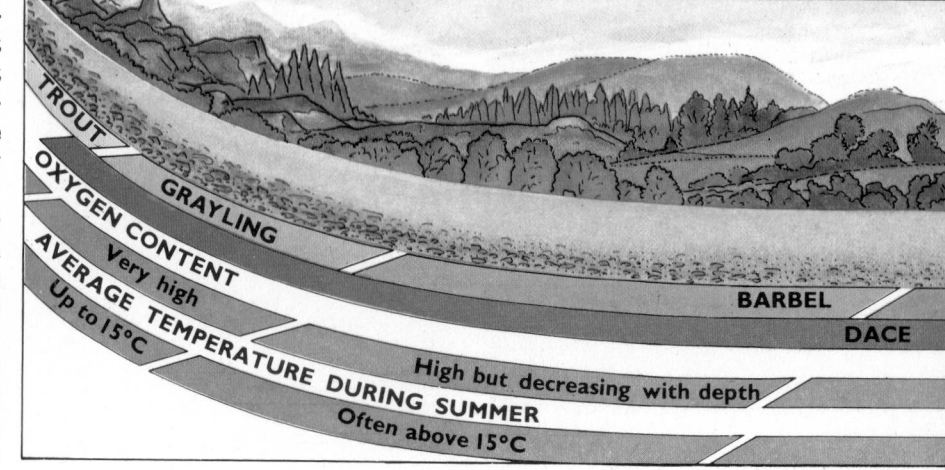

TROUT

GRAYLING

OXYGEN CONTENT
Very high

AVERAGE TEMPERATURE DURING SUMMER
Up to 15°C

High but decreasing with depth

Often above 15°C

BARBEL

DACE

wade as far as midstream he does so, stirring up the bottom gently to get a little colour into the water downstream. The maggots are held in a cloth bag with small holes in each end, which the angler ties to his waist to provide a regular trickle of maggots into the stream.

Cast lightly downstream
The angler then casts lightly downstream a few yards to enable adjustment of his tackle for depth. Once the tackle is properly set, he casts downstream, trotting the bait down to the fish. As it approaches weedbeds he checks the line momentarily to swing the bait up over the weed, then resumes the trot down to the waiting shoals. Bites are fast and furious so long as the fish do not suspect his presence. He makes sure of this by retrieving line swiftly with taps on the drum, rather than by winding the handle, in order to remove hooked fish from the shoal with as little disturbance as possible to the other dace.

A further alternative, both in deep, heavy water or in shallow streams, is to use ledger tackle. A light swivelled pear-lead, stopped by shot 18in from the hook and used in conjunction with a fixed-spool reel, enables accurate casting to the fish. In shallow waters the angler casts above the shoals, raising the rod tip so that the ledger weight rolls down toward them, although groundbaiting will bring the fish up towards the bait if necessary. The rod tip is kept in direct contact with the light line, and, fishing by touch, the angler prepares to meet the swift bites with an equally speedy strike.

Where are the best areas of rivers to find dace?
Always look for the fast streamy runs and, as the water temperature drops, a nice steady, roachy glide should prove productive.

How strong does my tackle need to be?
It is highly unlikely that you will hook any fish of over 12oz, so a small hook and a 1-2lb line can be used. This is one of the pleasures of dace fishing. Coupled with a light match rod, light-line fishing can be great fun.

Can a dace put up any sort of fight?
Despite its size, the dace pound for pound is a spirited little scapper on correctly balanced tackle and can present all kinds of problems in awkward swims.

Is elderberry a good bait?
Yes, but only at the right time of year. Try trotting a single fruit under an overhanging bush on which there are ripe berries. Later in the year, a maggot or caster is more likely to be effective.

Do dace live in canals?
Only if the water is sufficiently pure. The Oxford Canal between Banbury and Oxford is teeming with dace, but they rarely grow to above 4oz.

How do you distinguish dace from chub?
Look at their mouths: a chub's is very large and almost square, whereas a dace has a small, pert mouth. A further help is the anal fin which is convex on the chub but concave on the dace.

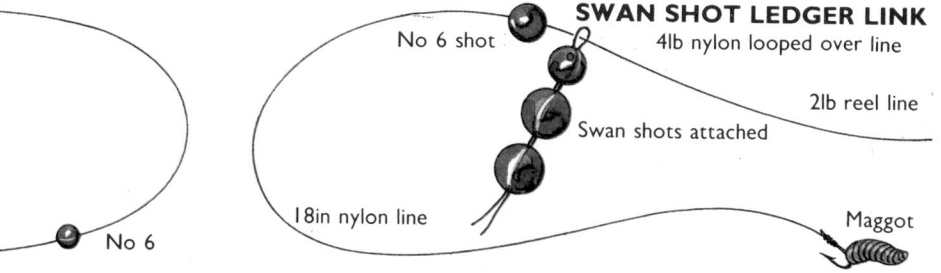

SWAN SHOT LEDGER LINK

No 6 shot

4lb nylon looped over line

2lb reel line

Swan shots attached

18in nylon line

No 6

Maggot

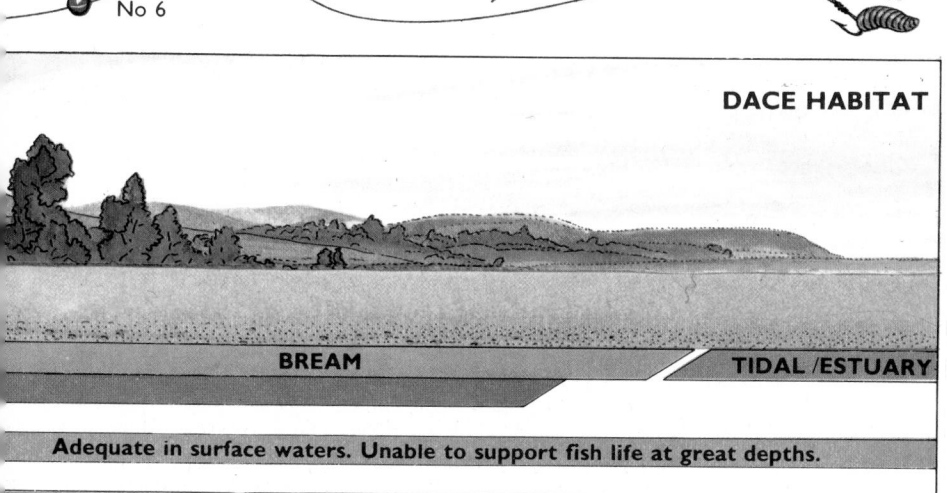

DACE HABITAT

BREAM

TIDAL /ESTUARY

Adequate in surface waters. Unable to support fish life at great depths.

Often up to 20°C and higher

Often above 20°C

Grayling

Bridging the gulf between coarse and game angling, the grayling—the 'lady of the stream'—has come to be appreciated only since pollution has made it a rarity in most waters

The grayling *(Thymallus thymallus)*, a member of the salmon family, is widely distributed throughout the British Isles, except in Ireland. Its enormous dorsal fin, with the tiny adipose fin characteristic of members of the Salmonidae, enables it to be readily distinguished from any other species.

Arguably, the grayling when alive is the most beautiful of all British fishes. The metallic scales show tinges of gold, green, pink and magenta, while the fins show bars, spots and lines of brown, crimson and purple. Sadly all these glorious colours fade within a few minutes of the death of the fish, and the angler returns home with a rather plain silvery-grey fish.

The grayling spawns between late March and early May, the eggs being shed in a hollow scooped in gravel by the female fish, after which they are covered in the same way as are the ova of salmon, sea trout and brown trout. When in breeding condition, the male fish are much darker in colour than the females, and are usually larger. The eggs are much smaller than those of trout, and the female grayling produces twice to three times as many eggs per pound of body weight than the female trout does.

Left: *Arthur Oglesby nets a grayling from the River Nidd, Yorkshire.*
Below: *Bob float and redworm—traditional grayling tackle.*
Right: *A 2lb fish from West Beck, Driffield.*
Below right: *Grayling need fast-flowing clean water over a stone and gravel bed.*

That all important food supply

As with every other species, growth rates depend very much upon the food supply. In the Hampshire chalkstreams, a grayling may reach a weight of 2lb in six or seven years. The largest grayling ever taken on rod and line was one of 4½lb caught by Dr T Sanctuary from the River Wylye at Brimerton in 1885. One of 4¾lb was netted from the Hampshire Avon in the same year; but nowadays it is far from common to catch a grayling as large as 2lb from these chalkstreams.

Proprietors of Wiltshire, Hampshire and Dorset fisheries continue to wage unrelenting war upon the grayling on the grounds that it competes with trout for food. As all these waters are now artificially stocked with trout raised in stewponds to takeable size or bigger; as most of these trout are rainbows, and as most of them are caught before they have been more

than two or three months in the river, it is hard to see how grayling can affect their size or numbers.

It is true that grayling eat much the same food as trout, namely insects, molluscs and crustacea, but they usually occupy different areas of river and it is doubtful if they offer very severe competition. Unlike trout, they form shoals and where the angler finds one, he will usually find several.

The grayling is intolerant of pollution, and will disappear from a water in which the degree of pollution is not such as to destroy trout or even seriously to inhibit their growth. If grayling find water to their liking, they will proliferate amazingly, but there are numerous instances of their introduction having failed. For example, they were introduced into the rivers Ivel and Ousel, in Bedfordshire, and the Beane in Hertfordshire. The two latter rivers supported a breeding population of trout, but the grayling failed to breed, though the original stock survived and put on weight, until they died of old age or capture.

The grayling is the subject of some very curious notions; one is that it smells of thyme, though some describe its smell as resembling cucumber. It certainly has a characteristic smell.

It has also been alleged that, by raising its large dorsal fin, it can instantly inflate its swimbladder and thus raise rapidly to the surface. In fact, nothing of the sort happens, though a grayling can and often does shoot up to the surface from a

ASK THE EXPERT

What are the best natural baits for grayling fishing?
Juicy wrigglers such as redworms, brandlings and bronze maggots are highly recommended. Wasp grub, too, is popular and successful.

Are there more specimen grayling in the South or the North of England?
Catches indicate that the average weight of southern grayling is higher than that of fish caught in the north. Such figures may say more about the distribution of wild and gentle waters throughout England than the size of grayling.

Can grayling be caught in really shallow waters?
Many specimen grayling are taken from water less than 12in deep.

Is it true that they have soft mouths?
No, on the contrary, their mouths are particularly hard. Many fish are lost because the hook fails to penetrate properly—not because it has torn free. Because of this toughness in the lip, many experts favour barbless hooks which make a surer entry though they call for additional skill.

Can I catch a grayling using an artificial other than a fly?
Yes, in northern Europe it is possible to catch grayling on tiny spinners—a technique which makes for delightful sport.

How can I best prepare grayling for the table?
They may be smoked, in the same way as trout. Impregnated with the savour of hot woodsmoke, they make first-class eating. But a fresh grayling, simply grilled in butter, is delicious.

Freshwater shrimps

Mayfly

Clear water

Water moss

Stony bottom

Caddis larva

...siderable depth. Then, so too can numerous other species.

The grayling's big dorsal fin

The big dorsal fin does, however, enable a hooked grayling to resist the angler's efforts to bring the fish to the landing net. In a brisk current, playing a big grayling is reminiscent of flying an underwater kite. In clear water, the fish can be seen with its dorsal fin fully erect, moving at an angle to the current, and, unless the angle of pull is changed, the fish may take a long time to subdue.

Yet another fallacy about grayling is that they cannot be caught when there is mist on the river. I have caught far too many in mist and fog to believe this; but they do not like its equivalent in the water, namely, a muddy flow, and seldom bite when a river is coloured with suspended particles after rain.

Primarily fish of running water, grayling thrive in clean lakes, though they seldom if ever breed in such waters. The reason for this is probably due to lack of suitable spawning areas, as with trout.

One of the points in favour of grayling is that, unlike most other fish, they will continue to feed freely when water temperature has fallen below that critical figure of 4°C (39.2°F), the temperature at which water is at its heaviest and below which no other British freshwater species will feed very actively. The grayling is the exception, and good catches can be made when the river is fringed with ice and the line is freezing to the rod-rings.

To many modern anglers, the other great attraction which the grayling provides is that it is coming into its best condition just when the trout season is ending. As it can be caught readily by fly-fishing, it thus extends the period during which this method can be used right through the winter, until the middle of March. Most anglers, however, prefer to stop fishing for grayling a month earlier. The fish becomes gravid—pregnant—in February.

Grayling tend to wander, and what proves a good spot one day will not necessarily be so on other occasions. I have spotted a shoal of good-

sized fish in a particular area, and arriving the next day full of hope, have found the fish gone. I also remember sitting watching a vacant gravel-bottomed run, which had remained devoid of grayling for a week, when suddenly seven good fish came dropping back from somewhere farther upstream, and took possession. Not for long; within half an hour six—all between 1¼ and 1½lb were in my bag; the survivor took fright and left.

Very large catches of grayling are sometimes possible. A few years ago I secured 50 fish weighing 56lb in one day. On the other hand, there have been days on excellent grayling waters when, try as I would, I could not catch a single fish, usually when rain had muddied the water.

The grayling, treated properly, is an excellent fish to eat, but a grayling that spends the day dead in a bag and the night in a larder, especially if in a plastic bag, will be tasteless or worse, however cooked.

Where the angler is catching several grayling from one spot, the

fish can be kept alive in a keepnet until it is time to stop fishing. If they are then killed and put directly into an insulated box with some ice-packs, and on arrival home placed in a refrigerator or a deep-freeze, the flavour when they are cooked will be found excellent. Scales are easily removed before cooking, and the bones after.

Where fishing is conditional upon all grayling being killed, as is regrettably the case on some fisheries, it is worth remembering that a grayling makes an excellent deadbait for pike, whether fished static or on wobbler tackle. It is a very firm fish, and will cast long distances. It is also much more resistant to attack by eels, so if you are a pike fisher, deep freeze any grayling you don't eat.

Below: *A matching pair, fly fished from a prime game river. A catch, when it does come, often heralds further successes.*
Right: *The stupendous colours, which contribute so much to the thrill of catching a grayling, quickly fade on its death.*

FISHING FOR GRAYLING

Methods	Rod	Reel	Reel Line	Terminal Tackle	Hooks	Leads/ Weights	Bait	Groundbait/ Attractor	Time of Season	Habitat	Distribution
Float	Glassfibre or carbonfibre 11ft 6in trotter	Fixed-spool or centre-pin	3lb	Single hook	Short shank, bronze or gold, 10-16	Split shot	Redworm, brandling, lob tail, maggots, bread	None	October to March	Streams, rivers, lakes	Widely distributed in British Isles but not in Ireland.
Cork on quill	Glassfibre or carbonfibre 11ft 6in trotter	Fixed-spool or centre-pin	3lb	Single hook	Short shank, bronze or gold, 10-16	Split shot	Redworm, brandling lob tail, maggots, bread	None	October to March	Streams, rivers, lakes	(Several lakes now fully stocked, eg Broadlands Lake, Romsey, Hants)
Stick float	Glassfibre or carbonfibre 11ft 6in trotter	Fixed-spool or centre-pin	3lb	Single hook	Short shank, bronze or gold, 10-16	Split shot	Redworm, brandling, lob tail, maggots, bread	None	October to March	Streams, rivers, lakes	
Quill	Glassfibre or carbonfibre 11ft 6in trotter	Fixed-spool or centre-pin	3lb	Single hook	Short shank, bronze or gold, 10-16	Split shot	Redworm, brandling, lob tail, maggots, bread	None	October to March	Streams, rivers, lakes	
Ledger (rarely used)	Glassfibre or carbonfibre 11ft 6in trotter	Fixed-spool	3lb	Single hook swan shot ledger	Short shank, bronze or gold, 10-16	Swan shot	Worm	None	October to March	Streams, rivers, lakes	
Fly fishing	9-7ft glassfibre, split cane, carbonfibre	Fly reel	5-6-7 fly line floating	7ft leader	Artificial flies	None	Coch-y-Bondhu, Red Tag, Soldier Palmer, Killer Bug, Welham Nymph	None	Throughout the season	Streams, rivers, lakes	

Grayling are members of the salmon family. When alive they are well-coloured fish; the tinges of gold, green, pink and magenta and lines of brown, purple and crimson on their scales fade soon after their death, and you will take home a plain silver-grey fish. Spawning takes place between late March and early May. Grayling feed on a wide variety of insects, molluscs and crustaceans.

Tench

Though normally associated with stillwaters, tench may be found in slow-flowing rivers. Among freshwater fishermen the tench has a reputation as a hardy fish and a powerful, determined fighter

The tench, *Tinca tinca*, is a powerful fighting fish, much valued by the freshwater specimen hunter. The species belongs to the carp family and has a short, thick-set body, oval in cross-section. A copious layer of slime almost hides the diminutive scales—smaller than the pupil of the eye—that are deeply embedded in the skin. The scale count along the lateral line varies between about 90 and 120.

The back rises gradually from the head to the dorsal fin, while the belly line is almost horizontal. Tench have a head with a slightly protruding

The tench used to be called the 'doctor fish' because it was believed that if a sick fish rubbed itself against the slimy body of the tench it received a 'miracle' cure.

mouth and a short pair of barbules on the upper lip. The dorsal fin is high and arched, and has three or four hard and eight or nine soft rays, and the caudal fin is wide and squarish, rather like a rudder. Pectoral and pelvic fins are thick, and the latter, in the mature male, have a sturdy ray on the outer edge.

The tench is a very hardy fish, able to live in poorly oxygenated

waters and often the only species to survive pollution and oxygen starvation. It can survive out of water longer than any other freshwater fish, with the possible exception of the eel and carp, staying alive for up to two or three hours in a damp sack. This makes it an easy fish to transfer from water to water.

Mature tench vary in length from about 12 to 30in, a fish of 12in weighing about 1½lb and one of 24in around 4lb. The current British rod-caught tench record stands at 14lb 3oz, caught on 28 June 1987, but this fish, like many others in excess of 6lb, contained a lot of spawn. Just how big a 'clean' tench grows is debatable. One hears stories of anglers seeing fish well into the 'teens', but these are usually found to be spawning. For a 'clean' tench, an eight-pounder seems to be near the upper limit.

Tench at the other end of the scale are not often taken. The few waters where tench of less than a pound are caught regularly also yield other fish of only two or three ounces.

Distribution

The species is well distributed throughout England, Ireland, and Wales, but is not so common in Scotland. While the dark olive, occasionally almost black, thickset fish is the more widely distributed, there also exists, in southern England, another variety of tench. This is the much lighter coloured 'golden' fish, which is more slender and streamlined. The governing factor appears to be the pH value (indicating the acidity or alkalinity) of the water. These 'golden' tench are quite common in the alkaline chalk pits, while the dark variety is native to more acid lakes and pits.

Where to find tench

Tench prefer stillwaters of all kinds, down to the tiniest village pond, but are by no means restricted to them. Several slow-moving rivers such as the Thames and Great Ouse also hold good tench, but they are not evenly distributed; an intimate knowledge of these rivers is needed to track them down. The famous Hampshire Avon at Christchurch has another good tench swim.

The tench spends much of its time on or near the bottom, often close to dense weedbeds during the daytime. At night, it frequently ventures into open water and the margins to feed.

To learn about the habits of the tench, it pays to study the fish in its natural environment without the aid of rod and reel. The results of studies over the years suggest that the tench congregate in different kinds and sizes of shoal. The size of this will vary according to the size of the individual fish and also with the characteristics and geography of the water. Generally, the smaller fish form larger groups. With tench of under 4lb the shoal may hold several hundred fish, while with specimens of 4–5lb, there will probably be between 40 and 50 fish. The really large tench of 6lb and 7lb or more tend to move about in much smaller groups of four or five fish, and in some cases they will even swim in pairs. This tendency is a common occurrence in the smaller broken-up gravel pits where there are numerous small pools, nooks and crannies and interconnecting channels. These features seem to produce small groups or lone fish.

Spawning can take place any time between May and August depending primarily on water temperature. The ideal temperature is 18°C (64°F), and it is unfortunate that this is rarely reached during the coarse fish close season (15 March—15 June, inclusive). It is most common for tench to spawn in late June, July, or even August, although lots of spawnbound females are caught in the first weeks of the fishing season. A female tench with a normal weight of 5lb is quite capable of weighing well over 7lb with spawn.

Frenzied spawning

Spawning and its prelude can be a spectacular sight, with shoals of fish literally heaping themselves up and thrashing about in the shallow weedy margins. This activity can be so frenzied that fish have been known to get stranded high and dry on the banks. Tench prefer to spawn in well lit and warm, gravelly shallows no more than 2ft deep. Often the spawning territory is adja-

cent to beds of reed mace or bullrushes, which the female rubs against to clean itself after spawning. It lays 100–200,000 eggs of which perhaps half a percent survive. They are greenish, with a sticky protective covering, and are about 1.5mm in diameter. They are shed over weed, submerged twigs or branches, or the fine roots of willow trees where they adjoin the spawning ground. The eggs develop in 4–8 days, and after 12 days the embryo measures about 12mm. In one year it will have reached some 30mm, in two years 60mm, and 95mm after

Top: *With the rod well up, the angler here is putting pressure on a 4lb tench hooked in the reeds of Ireland's river Shannon.*
Above: *The tench usually feeds on or near the bottom on crustaceans and molluscs. When feeding on muddy or silty bottoms, tench often betray their presence by sending up patches of bubbles to the surface. These are easy to distinguish from marsh gas as the patches are small and frothy and occur in vast quantities.*

three. Males reach maturity, with a length of about 125mm, at three years and the females at four.

The angler's knowledge of the diet

ASK THE EXPERT

What purpose does the body slime serve?

It's a lubricant. As the fish flexes its body in swimming, the scales overlap and slide partly over one another. The largest scales are at the front of the body, which flexes least; the smallest are at the tail. The mucus, or slime, is secreted by cells in the *epidermis* or transparent outer layer of skin which protects the scales from invading fungus and parasites.

Do tench feed in the middle of the night?

On busy fishing waters especially, tench are put down by noisy anglers during the day and only venture to the food-rich margins during the night, mopping up residual groundbait. In June, July and August there is a dead interval of two hours between midnight and 2am when the angler does best to catch a nap. For the rest of the time he may well encounter tench feeding close in. And they are less tackle-shy after dark.

Some tench seem bloated without being full of spawn: are they diseased?

Many large tench are 'dropsical' — suffering from dropsy, in which water gathers in the peritoneum and causes bloating and finally death.

Is the meat of tench edible?

If you look hard enough, you can find it for sale in this country, but on the Continent and throughout China, tench is a popular delicacy. If you cook your own catch, a muddy taint can be avoided by keeping the fish alive in fresh water for some time after it's caught. Better still, return it alive. Few anglers will thank you for taking a large tench from their favourite water.

of the tench is lacking. To learn what food fish eat, you must either watch them feeding in their natural environment or kill them and examine the contents of their stomachs.

Feeding habits

Most of the feeding is done on the bottom, the tench rooting among the mud, silt or gravel for food. Young, developing tench take in much plankton-type food as they swim in mid-water; they also eat considerable quantities of algae. Examples of food found on the bottom are insect larvae such as dragon flies, damsel flies and midges. The mature tench also eats crustaceans, such as water slaters, and molluscs, of which the pond snail is the most common example. The younger fish also like water fleas, water mites, and chironomid larvae. Contrary to popular belief, tench do not eat weed, although small quantities are accidentally eaten when the tench 'vacuum cleans' the insect life from the weeds.

But knowing what kind of natural food makes the tench grow big does

Freshwater mussels make excellent bait for tench. Pass the barb of the hook through the fleshy part of the mussel. Mussels can be grubbed by hand from lakes, reservoirs and ponds.

not really help the angler with his choice of bait. As most of the food that the tench eats is minute, presenting a similar sized bait is not practical on conventional tackle. Microscopic hooks and ultra-fine lines would be needed, yet these would hardly be suitable for hauling out 6lb of muscular tench from a heavily weeded swim. Generally, the angler is restricted to common baits such as worms, maggots, or bread in its various forms, although these can hardly be considered to be 'natural' baits.

The swan mussel

One of the few exceptions is the swan mussel. Many waters holding good tench also hold vasts beds of mussels, and in fact, the noted big-tench waters are rarely without them. Also, it is very rare to find a water containing mussels which has no tench, so there may be a link, although it is not absolutely proved. Whether the tench is capable of crunching up a whole mussel in its natural state is a point for debate, but it certainly enjoys the juicy 'insides'. Mussels are therefore good bait, and fishing with this bait is one of the most exciting ways of tempting bigger-than-average specimens.

Tench fishing methods are

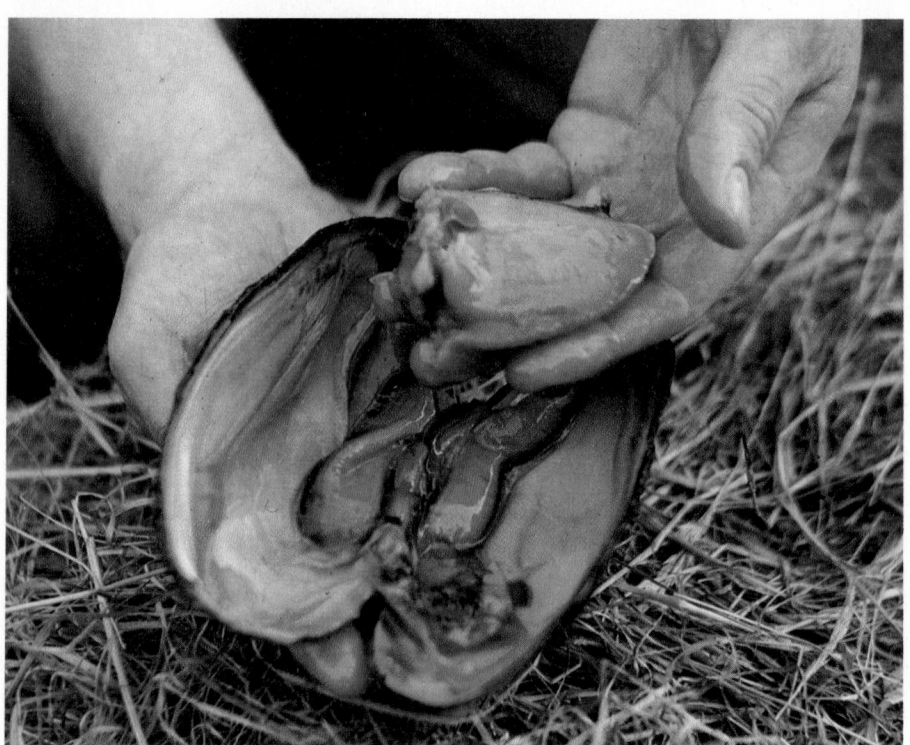

A lobworm kept in moss becomes well scoured, and it will be able to withstand long range casting.

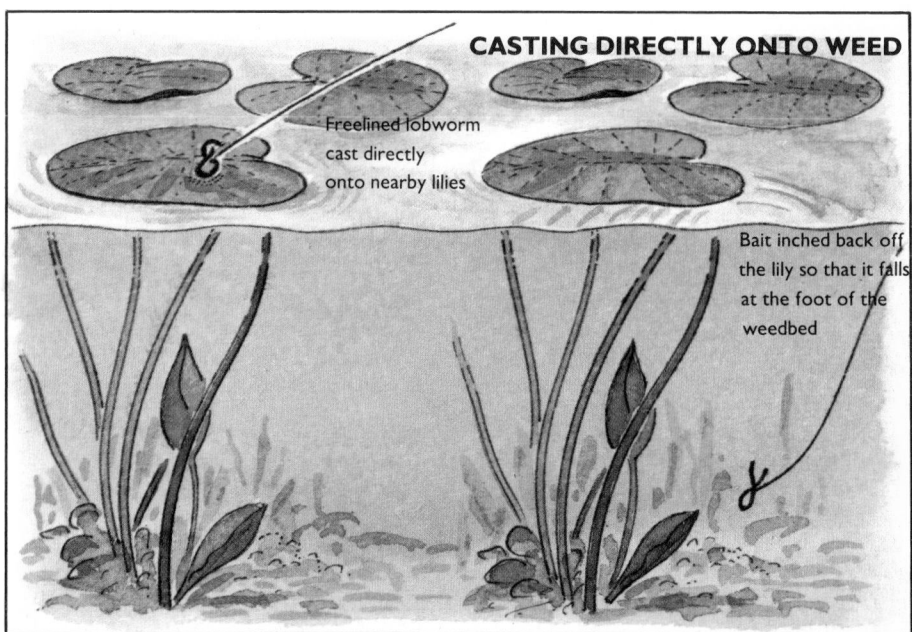

CASTING DIRECTLY ONTO WEED

Freelined lobworm cast directly onto nearby lilies

Bait inched back off the lily so that it falls at the foot of the weedbed

Above: *Cast your bait onto a lily near the edge of the bed to avoid difficulties in landing your catch.*

Below: *The 'lift' bite technique is one of the most successful methods of catching tench.*

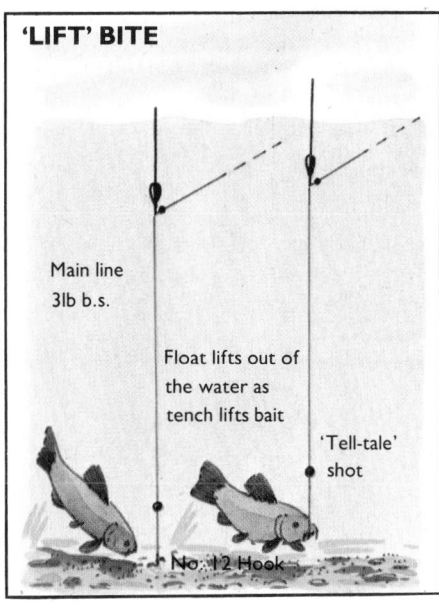

'LIFT' BITE

Main line 3lb b.s.

Float lifts out of the water as tench lifts bait

'Tell-tale' shot

No. 12 Hook

numerous and varied. Four widely used and effective techniques form the basis of serious tench fishing: conventional float fishing or 'laying-on'; ledgering; float fishing using the very sensitive 'lift' method with the bait presented just touching the bottom; freelining—with the bait on the bottom, and a line without floats, leads or shot.

All these methods hinge on a bottom-fished bait as this is where the tench does much of its serious feeding. Some feeding is done just off bottom however, or even in mid-water, and often the tench will be receptive to a slowly sinking bait; but in these conditions, specialized skills and knowledge are required.

For the newcomer, the best method is probably freelining. It is the simplest and involves only absolute essentials—rod, reel, line, and baited hook. For the angler to use float tackle with maximum efficiency, a thorough knowledge of contours and depths is essential, particularly when the delicacy of the balanced 'lift' method is used. With freeline tactics the bait will invariably end up in the right place—on the bottom, and when a tench takes there will be only minimal resistance. There will be no dragging of a float and no friction on the line due to the ledger weight.

Once the bait has settled on the bottom, the rod is simply placed on two rests and an 'external' indicator, such as a dough bobbin, is attached to the line between the reel and the butt ring.

The only limitation of the freeline method is its range, but you will be amazed how far you can gently lob a large piece of breadflake or a large worm—15 yards is no problem. In any event, you rarely need to fish

farther than that. All too often you will find your tench within 15ft of the bank, provided you use stealth and caution. If you need additional weight, increase the size of your bait or add another worm; alternatively, use a single swan shot a foot or two from the hook.

When the tench bites, you will probably get a couple of preliminary knocks followed by a steady lift or 'run'. Whenever there is a steady positive draw on the line, however slow, this is the time to strike your tench, and then the fun begins.

Tackle selection
Choice of tackle depends on local conditions and the ability of the angler. For freelining and ledgering a fairly powerful hollow-glass rod of 10½–11ft with a test curve of about 1½lb is suggested. For float fishing, a similar rod with an extra few inches may well be desirable. Most tench waters have a fair share of weed for at least part of the summer, which, particularly if there are other submerged snags like trees, means that you cannot afford to fish too fine. In snaggy conditions you will need line of at least 5lb b.s., or even 7 or 8lb in really difficult spots. If you are fortunate enough to locate your tench in snag and weed-free reservoir-type waters, you can drop to 3lb providing you have experience of handling bigger fish. For hooks, the choice is wide, depending on the rest of your tackle and bait.

FISHING TECHNIQUE

There may be a 2lb difference between what constitutes a specimen tench in one water and in another, say Fred J Taylor and Frank Guttfield. A hunter's achievement is measured by the difficulties he has had to overcome

AT-A-GLANCE

Specimen sizes
5lb to 7lb, depending on the average weight for the individual waters. In some areas 3lb may be very good; in others the heavier weight applies.

Tackle, bait, techniques
Rod
9ft to 13ft

Reel
Fixed-spool

Line b.s.
2lb b.s. to 8lb b.s.

Hooks
No 16 to No 2

Bait
Bread, brandlings, freshwater mussel, sweetcorn, maggot and many others

Groundbait
Worms, trout pellets, soaked maize, bread and all hookbaits

Techniques
Ledgering, freelining, float fishing

If a specimen is regarded as a fish worthy of mounting in a glass case or one weighing half as much as the existing record, then the specimen hunter's first task is to locate a water holding such fish. But if, as I believe, a specimen is a fish that is above average for the water concerned, then any tench angler can consider himself a specimen hunter.

Where the pleasure lies
I have had access to waters holding 4, 5, 6, and 7 pounders and can claim to have seen (and tried desperately hard to catch) double-figure tench. But I do not regard taking a 5-pounder from such waters as a greater achievement than catching a 3-pounder from a modest pond that normally yields fish of half that size. The pleasure comes from trying to catch a good tench from any water, and from the variety tench fishing offers from season to season.

Persistence pays
There is, generally, little hope of sorting out big tench from small. So if you use the traditional methods recommended by tench fishers you will, despite the many disadvantages, catch tench. And if you persist for hours, season after season, the chances are that a specimen will eventually come your way in time.

The situation can be expressed in percentages. I once calculated over a five-year period, that on a certain water I had to catch ten 4lb tench before I caught a five-pounder. Had I been catching *all* four-pounders, my ratio of specimens would have been 1 to 10, but there were many more fish under 4lb so the actual percentage was probably less than half that. Those figures would not apply to every water but they could be of interest to the angler who seeks something a little better than average and could indicate the chances involved.

The key to specimen tench
It pays to take a fresh look at the way you catch tench, however. If you accept as gospel that tench are bottom feeders and that you need to present a big bait hard on the bottom to catch them, you will end up with fewer tench and hence fewer specimens than if you experiment with different rigs, tackles, baits and presentations. Experimentation is nearly always the key to successful tench specimen hunting.

In traditional, shallow, soft-bottomed lakes tench tend to be reasonably active for much of the summer. They forage a lot, moving around in search of food, and can be attracted and held in raked and baited swims. If they are prepared

Below: *Ledgering for specimen tench in a Wraysbury gravel pit. When the fish are there, but not biting, rig for lift-bites on really fine tackle.*

to accept a bottom-fished lobworm and bites are coming frequently, there is no need to change your approach, but if bites are few and far between, and there is obvious activity in the swim, finer tackle and more subtle tactics may be necessary.

The lift style

It was this situation that led to the development of the well-known lift style, which has probably accounted for more specimen tench than any other method during the past 25 years. It does not work everywhere, but, like the recent patterns of long antenna floats, should always be given a chance. The principle is simple and based on the fact that tench tend to suck in and blow out small baits. The lift rig is shotted so that any such behaviour by the tench causes the single bottom shot to move, and the movement of that shot causes the float to lift in the water and lie on the surface. The rod has to be placed in a rest, and the tackle, which is set deeper than the water, is drawn taut until the float, attached at the bottom end only, cocks. The float is over-loaded by the single shot which means that it sinks completely if both bait and shot are not on the bottom.

The disadvantages of this are that the buoyant peacock quill float always strives to rise to the surface and lift bites are usually fast. This means that the strike has to be made very quickly and, as the rod cannot be hand-held for fear of upsetting the delicate balance of the rig, intense concentration and sharp reflexes are essential. They, however, come with practice and it is an exciting and challenging way of dealing with specimen tench.

Big windbeater or driftbeater floats on the market today work on the same principle, but because they are shotted differently and are exceptionally stable, the whole bite sequence is, or appears to be, slowed down. This means that the angler can relax more, his bites appear more positive, his strikes may be more leisurely and his control over a hooked fish will be immediate but not frantic.

Large floats with buoyant sight bulbs are ideal for fishing at night in the light of a torch beam. The tench is not necessarily nocturnal, but I have taken more five-pounders after dark than in daylight, many on illuminated float tackle and windbeater floats. Specimen tench feed more confidently after dark on many waters, and where boating, swimming, sailing and other activities

Above: *Tench fishing is traditionally the first expedition of a coarseman's season.*

disturb the bigger fish by day, the night offers the best chance of specimens. If the beam of the torch is shone *across* the water and not directly into it, tench do not seem in any way disturbed by it; they are not attracted to lights as has been suggested. Powerful torch beams can, however, irritate other anglers, so illuminated float fishing should be practised discreetly.

Deepwater tenching

For extremely deep water (which is not common in traditional tench lakes) the slider attachment is useful, and particularly effective for illuminated float fishing at night, even in comparatively shallow water. It bulks all the weight at the bottom end of the tackle and allows an accurate, underhand cast to be made *along* the torch beam which should always remain static once it has been set.

During the day when delicate bites, calling for tiny baits, are experienced, a thin antenna-type float shotted so the bait barely touches the bottom will give exceptionally good bite registration.

It was once believed that the thin

antenna floats were ideal for windy conditions. The whole of the antenna was left out of the water and remained reasonably still on a wave-tossed lake, but it was not an easy style. Today's very fine antenna floats work better in calm conditions. Suitable for medium-range work, they should be shotted down so that an inch or slightly more of the antenna shows above the water. Again, this type of float, allied to sensitive shotting, shows delicate bites well, and tends to slow down those that would appear as lightning dips on a flat-topped float.

In almost all stillwater tench fishing the float is fixed at the bottom end only, and there are many methods of attachment. Occasionally, however, when tench will accept a bait moving slowly along the bottom, the float is best fixed both top and bottom.

Drifting the bait
During the day, float tackle, set so that a moderate breeze causes it to drift along the surface and drag the bait with it, often accounts for good tench. For obvious reasons it should be capable of dragging the bait (*and* a bottom shot to slow the movement down) without being drawn under. Some top buoyancy is necessary in these circumstances and a little shoulder should be left out of the water to ensure support.

Dense rushbeds, where many really big tench often hole up during the day, call for a rather special kind of approach. The bait should be placed either directly into, or very close to the edge of the rushbed. Sometimes this can be achieved from the bank by lowering the tackle in on the end of a long rod; at other times it may be necessary to approach the margin by boat and cast towards it.

Either way, it is dangerous fishing and expensive floats are better left in their boxes. Instead, use simple float tackle, which because of its method of attachment is almost snag-proof. It can be made up by threading the reel line completely through a length of peacock quill, and a single large shot pinched on to the line immediately below it will make sure it does not slip, and ensure that the bait sinks slowly under

its own weight. Most baits are taken while they are sinking, and this could be similar to the natural situation where the tench sheltering in the rush beds dislodge food from the stems and take it as it sinks.

Make float changing simple
Several situations call for float fishing and it is not always possible to select the ideal rig immediately. Quick changes are necessary from time to time, so a separate float attachment kept permanently on the line is often advisable. This makes float changing simple with shotting adjusted without dismantling the whole tackle.

Rigs and tackle are not alone in accounting for success. As already said, locating the fish is all-important. Many really big tench are found in weedy shallows and, during the day, their paths can be plotted by the string of bubbles they send up to the surface.

Despite the weed, however, many stay put, feeding mainly at night. In theory they should not like areas of thick weed at night because of the lack of oxygen, but small, cleared patches have produced amazingly large specimens during the first few hours of darkness. Big baits have been taken freely and boldly, the line running off the reel spool in the manner associated with carp. So, tench, which need the utmost coaxing at dawn and during the day, are often very easy to hook in these circumstances. This could be because of that brief period they are foraging and (unlike other tench fishing situations) there appears to be little need for groundbait.

Boat tenching
There are several other styles of fishing, but because many tench lakes are heavily weeded, long-range ledgering is mainly unsuitable. In these waters boats can play an important part in the locating and catching of big tench, and there are situations where boat fishing offers the only chance of a specimen. Where banks are heavily trodden and fished, many of the worthwhile specimens often spend most of their time out of casting range, but can be tracked down in hot weather and

Above: *Pete Tilotson returns a 7lb 11oz gravel pit tench.*
Below: *On heavily fished waters, a boat may be the only way to reach the specimens.*

70

Why do some waters hold very big tench and others only average-size fish?
Fish tend to grow according to the quantities of food available. A lush Southern gravel pit, with adequate weed growth and a nice balance between the species, should produce quality fish.

How can I tell if a water holds specimen tench?
The only sure way is to make enquiries into the catch-record of the water. A rough and ready rule is that big waters hold big fish—but don't count on it.

Why should raking out a swim improve the fishing?
In the first place, the colour stirred up is an attraction. Once in the swim, the tench can happily feed on all the bottom-dwellers disturbed from their homes. The gentlest raking dislodges thousands of tiny creatures.

Can I use any of the water creatures disturbed by raking as hook-baits?
Unfortunately most of them are too small, with the possible exception of the swan mussel. It's better to introduce loose samples of your bait into the swim immediately after raking it. The best results can then be expected a couple of hours later.

Specimen fish are reputed to be solitary creatures. Does this apply to tench?
Tench tend to be little more gregarious in later life than other species but it is true to say that the specimen-sized fish are usually found in smaller shoals than their smaller relations.

clear water conditions by a boat search. Stealth and quietness are essential, and the boat should only cause minimal water disturbance.

Once the tench are located, you should not try to fish for them immediately. It is reasonable to expect them to be around that area some time later, and the groundbaiting overnight will usually attract and hold the shoal. If there is a choice, prebait the area holding the smaller shoal, for it will contain the bigger specimens. In very big gravel pits, where there are great depth variations, this is a particularly effective method of contacting specimens.

Spotting the fish
There is no better means of selection than actually spotting the fish, as trout and carp anglers know well. It is not always possible with tench,

but if you are prepared to put in time watching, big tench frequently show themselves over shallow bars in gravel pits. You cannot expect to catch them at once, but they do follow a routine. They may pass over the bar several times in an hour, or only twice in a day, and because they are nomadic they can be waylaid. If you wait your chance, you can hope to pick up a fish each time the shoal moves through. Heavy groundbaiting is not helpful, however, because these fish do not usually stay. In many situations it will merely attract small, unwanted roach or rudd, or, if bream and tench are present, the bream will dispose of the groundbait before the tench arrive. In these circumstances, leave a few samples of hookbait on the bar and place a similar hookbait among them. Floats, leads or shots are

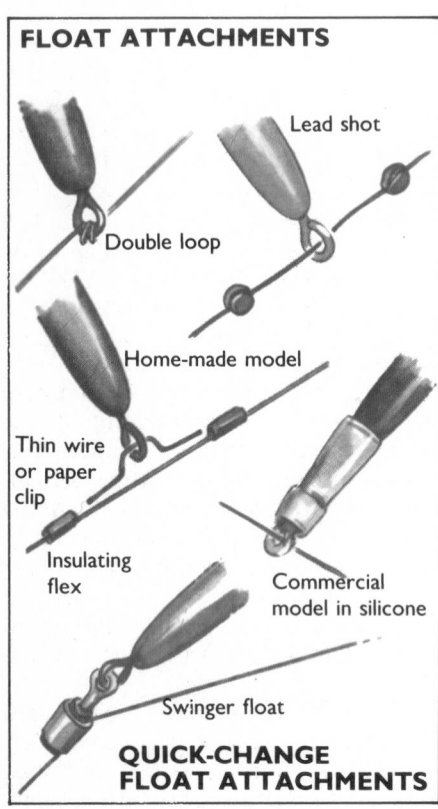

Lead shot

Double loop

Home-made model

Thin wire
or paper
clip

Insulating
flex

Commercial
model in silicone

Swinger float

**QUICK-CHANGE
FLOAT ATTACHMENTS**

TENCH LAKE SPOTLIGHT

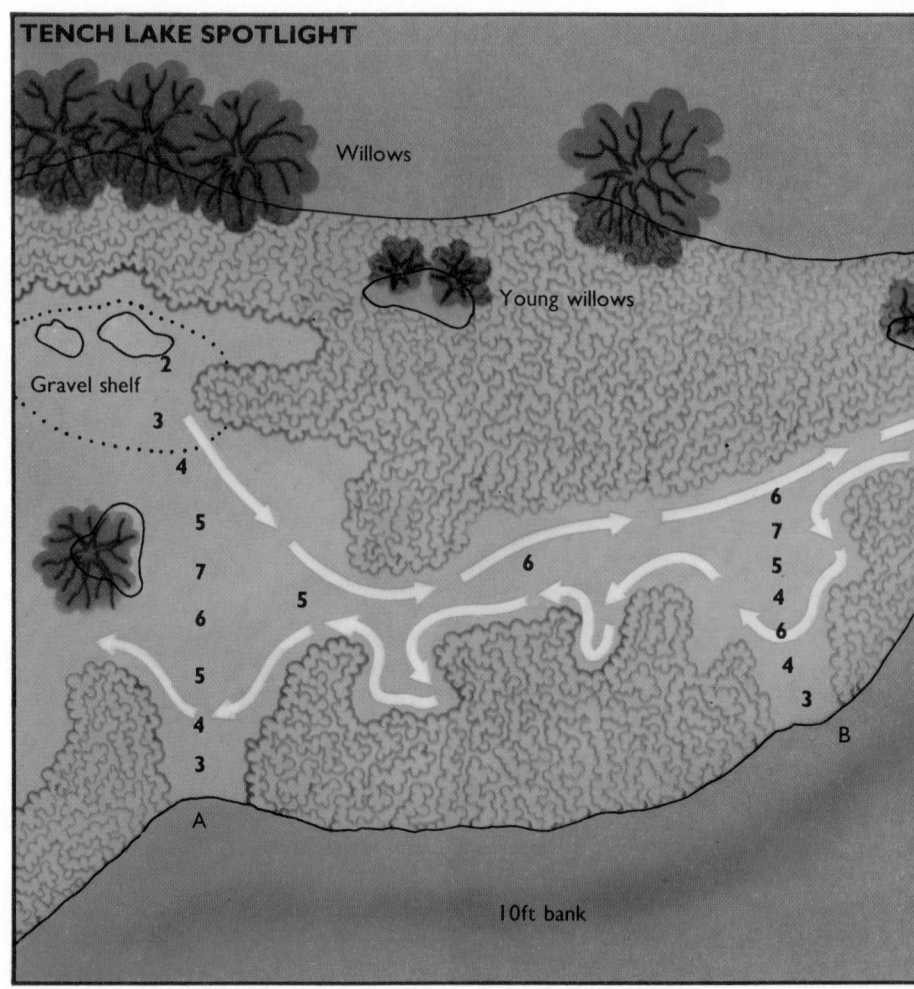

Willows

Young willows

Gravel shelf

2
3
4
5
7
6
5
4
3
A
5
6
7
5
4
3
B
10ft bank

Right and far right: *Plan and cross-sections of a typical gravel pit tench swim.*
Below: *Graham Frith proudly displays the tench bag of a lifetime—two beautiful fish weighing 6lb 4oz and 6lb 11oz.*

seldom necessary. If tench feed on the way through you will not mistake the run-off bites they give, but do not act impatiently and try to move the bait into their immediate vision. Leave it lying there, and be prepared to see the fish pass over it without showing any interest. You can never be sure when they will begin feeding, but the chances are that they will eventually. It is also possible that they will do this when you are not there, but that is part of the game. Hunting specimen tench is exciting but frustrating.

Rod length, hook size and line strength are really a matter for individual choice and should be selected with the size of fish expected and the nature of the water in mind. There is little point in going to great lengths to hook a specimen tench if the tackle is not capable of holding it. No one would expect to drive home a No 4 hook with a line of 2lb b.s., and delicate float tackles will not work with heavy lines. The

thin antenna floats described earlier fish better with a 3lb line than with one twice as strong. In fact, 4lb b.s. is about the heaviest you should use.

Big windbeater floats accommodate lines up to 6lb b.s., while simple lift floats made of peacock quill and attached by a silicone or plastic band can confidently be fished on 5lb line. Where big fish are expected, tie the hook directly to the reel line and do not use finer hook links or bottoms. Every join or knot is a weakness, and tying an eyed or fine-wire spade end to the reel line eliminates them all. Simple precautions, such as testing the line in advance, making sure that hooks are sharp and that there are no rust spots, should also be carried out.

Other essentials are an umbrella, a large landing net, a reliable torch for night fishing, and an eye shade or polarized sunglasses (or both) for use in bright sunshine. Accessories such as bite alarms, bite indicators, swingtips, Betalights, and rod rests

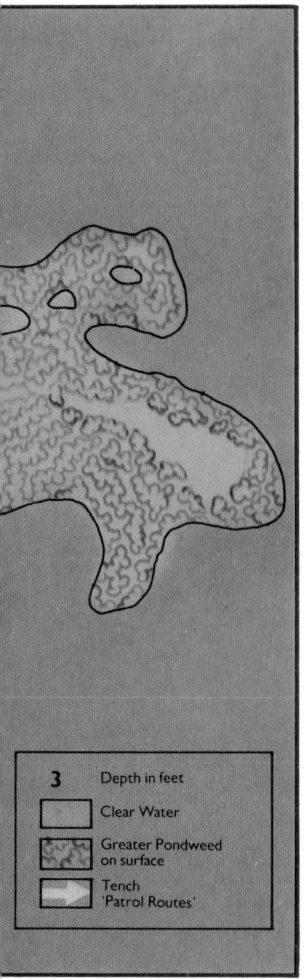

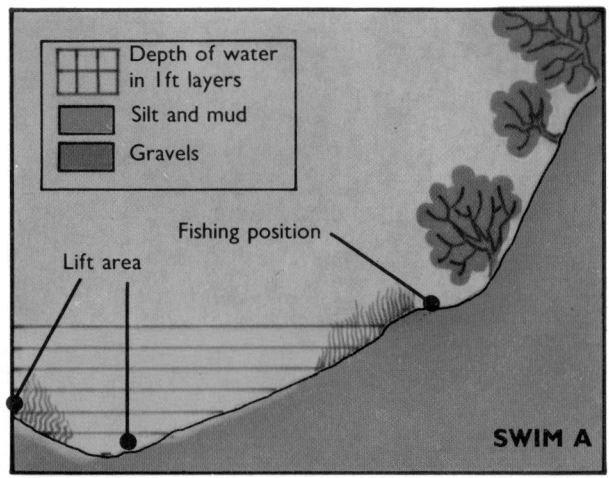

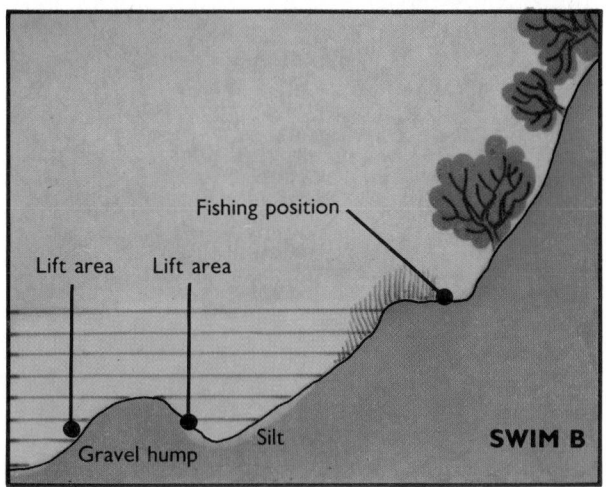

SWIM A diagram labels: Depth of water in 1ft layers; Silt and mud; Gravels; Fishing position; Lift area

SWIM B diagram labels: Fishing position; Lift area; Lift area; Gravel hump; Silt

Legend (left map): 3 — Depth in feet; Clear Water; Greater Pondweed on surface; Tench 'Patrol Routes'

attract tench into a given area. The maize itself is not the best of hookbaits, however, because it never really softens, and hooked fish tend to come adrift. Instead, it is better to fish a sweetcorn hookbait. Soft paste made from maize meal and allowed to 'go off' is also very effective when used with soaked maize.

Canned sweetcorn is particularly good for tench and carp. Maggots and casters, redworms, black slugs, snails, caddis, grubs, freshwater mussels—and innumerable other baits, natural and manufactured—are also good. Although all will take fish many of them are of little value except, perhaps, as talking points amongst anglers. With few exceptions most 'odd-ball' baits are less likely to produce specimen tench than the tried and tested alternatives.

From time to time there are reports of big tench taken on unusual baits not intended for them, but there are seldom subsequent catches on the same bait. I once hooked an enormous tench on a piece of dead fish intended for an eel, but as I had eel-fished that spot for many years previously with chunks of dead fish as hookbaits, I knew I had not discovered anything revolutionary! This fish had learnt to avoid the usual baits and, having changed its diet completely, had grown enormous. It is perhaps this change of diet that produces the odd specimen in a water where they are thought not to live.

Frank Guttfield's Spotlight

The disused gravel workings of the southern counties possess all the ingredients that allow fish to grow big quickly. Carp, bream, roach, rudd, pike and tench thrive, and tench reach specimen proportions—5lb and above—more frequently than some of the other species.

The topography can vary enormously. Some pits are bleak, vast expanses of 60-100 acres, while others are lush, island-studded waters of three or four acres. The biggest pits probably yield the largest tench but smaller waters are more interesting to fish. Such waters have taught me a great deal about watercraft.

should be chosen by the individual.

My own rods range from 9ft to 13ft. Each has its own application, although there is no need for an armoury of rods at the outset. I prefer soft-actioned rods to rigid pokers, but friends prefer the opposite. My soft-actioned wand that weighs but a few ounces is ideal for tench fishing from a boat, while for bank fishing I would choose something much longer, especially for use with a float. Whatever the length or action of the rod, it should be applied to a suitable line. My soft rods are not likely to break a fine 2lb b.s. line; my heavier rods would be too hard on lines under 6lb b.s.

Reliable baits

In these days of fashionable baits—high protein, magic, seed, particle, secret, cereal and others—it seems odd to suggest that a loaf of bread and a tin of worms are still an effective bait for most tench fishing. But they are, because tench become wary of certain baits as the season progresses, and it often pays to change. In the early days of the season, sensible-sized hookbaits are just as likely to be taken as single maggots or casters. I have caught more big tench on small crust cubes (which, at ⅜in square, are huge compared with a single maggot) than any other bait. Brandlings are also excellent, especially when used in advance as groundbait.

On certain waters, freshwater mussels used whole (without shells, of course) or as snippets, have probably accounted for as many big day-time tench as any other bait, while trout pellets as groundbait, and hookbaits made up of soaked brown bread and softened pellets, have proved an excellent combination in recent years.

Soaked maize

Soaked maize, left until it has fermented and developed an unbearable smell, will undoubtedly

Wels

For 100 years introductions have been attempted of Europe's largest freshwater fish. Even now anyone who has caught a Wels here can regard himself as a pioneer

The Danubian Catfish (*Silurus glanis*) is a member of a large group of fishes found in the freshwaters of Europe and Asia. The species is also known in this country by its German name Wels, a name which is probably better than the former, for the species is not confined to the River Danube and its tributaries, but occurs over the whole of central and eastern Europe and farther east into western Asia.

It is not native to Britain, where its introduction has been completely artificial, for it is one of the many species which did not reach these islands from continental Europe following the withdrawal of the ice sheets after the last major ice age.

Successful introduction

Many attempts at introduction have been made throughout Britain, but few have been successful. Specimens from these successful waters have been used to start new populations, which have maintained themselves. The best known of these introductions was that at Woburn Abbey in the 1880s, providing specimens for other parts of the country.

The Wels, like all members of the *Siluridae* group, is characterized by a long, sinuous body which is laterally compressed. The head is relatively short, and is slightly compressed on top and below. Also characteristic of the family is the very small dorsal fin, which is situated well forward and has a maximum of only four individual rays.

The anal fin is extremely long, running down more than two-thirds of the body, and is supported by about 90 individual branched rays. There is little space between the anal fin and the relatively small, oval-shaped tail fin. The pelvic fins, also small, are set immediately in front of the anal fin. The pectoral fins are nearly three times as large as the pelvic fins and are set about halfway between the latter and the front of the head.

Common feature

Common to all catfish, and probably the feature from which they derive their English name, are the barbules found around the mouth, both on the upper and lower jaw. Individual species or groups of species have their own number of barbules. The species of the Wels group, for example, have two very long barbules on the upper lip that extend from near the corners of the mouth. The Wels itself has four extra, much shorter barbules on the underside of the lower jaw, these being evenly spaced in an arc which follows the outline of the jaw. Only two of these short lower barbules are found in the Aristotle Catfish, which is otherwise identical to the Wels.

Feelers

The long upper barbules are extremely mobile and may be directed forward as well as up, down or sideways. They are used by the Wels as a means of searching for food and to avoid obstacles while swimming, so that they should be considered as feelers rather than barbules. This substitute for sight is clearly necessary, for the species has extremely small, inconspicuous eyes, which are only apparent because of the narrow, bright yellow or golden ring which surrounds the pupil. The fish appears to have a well developed sense of smell, for it displays relatively large nostrils at the base of the long upper barbules or feelers.

Taking into account that all these features are found on all other types of catfishes, it is not surprising that there are many mis-identifications.

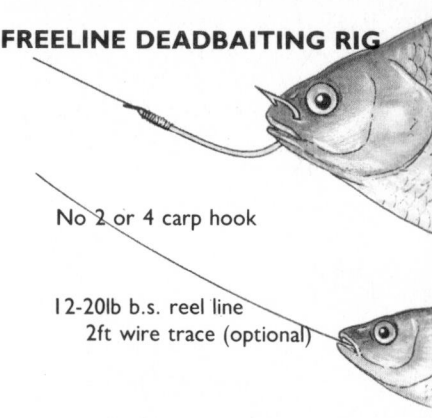

FREELINE DEADBAITING RIG

No 2 or 4 carp hook

12-20lb b.s. reel line
2ft wire trace (optional)

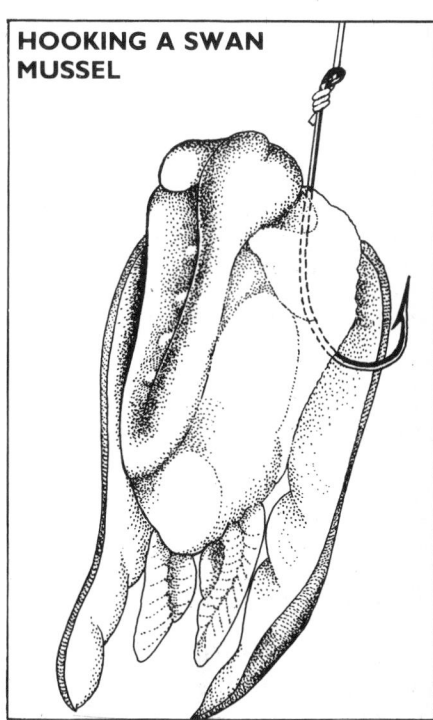

Above: *The ideal static offering for a Wels. But don't lose the barb in the bait.*

Above and right: *The shovel-mouth of the Wels. Though the teeth are small, and grind rather than tear food, the gape is wide enough to ingest prey in proportion to the size of fish.* **Left:** *A lip-hooked deadbait (fresh or putrid) on a trace strong enough to withstand the grinding action of a Wels' teeth.*

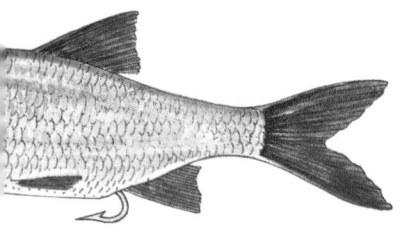

It is sometimes difficult to distinguish between the different types of catfishes found in this country. These cases involve an entirely separate species which originated in North America and which in most cases finds its way into our waters from aquaria which it has outgrown. This species is a member of the *Ictalurus* group of catfishes which, in their country of origin, go under various names, including Bullheads, Horned Pout, and Catfish.

The only similarity between this species, or members of the group as a whole, and the *Silurid* catfishes, is the presence of the barbules or feelers around the mouth. The *Ictalurid* catfishes are much shorter than the Wels types, have much larger dorsal fins, much smaller anal fins, and usually two additional short barbules between the long ones on the upper jaw. Even if none of these features can confirm that it is not the Wels the presence of an adipose fin, that is, a fleshy fin without rays, situated between the dorsal and the tail fins, should make it very obvious that the specimen requires more description than the term Catfish, which anglers in this country tend to apply only to Wels.

Like the North American species,

75

the Wels has no scales on any part of its body. Its colouring can vary greatly. The back always has dark blue-black, olive-green or brown tones. These lighten somewhat down the side of the body to give way to white on the belly, although the darker tone of the sides continues over the anal and pelvic fins. The flanks, and often the fins have a marbled appearance produced by irregular patches of colour. Partially or even completely albino specimens are not too uncommon.

The mouth of the Wels is extremely large and is situated across the end of the head. The lower lip protrudes slightly beyond the upper, giving the mouth a shovel-like appearance. It is not equipped with the large teeth associated with predatory fish, having instead a band of small teeth in each jaw.

Spawning

The number of eggs laid by the species is very high, indicating that the survival rate of the young larvae must be relatively low. Examination of specimens on the Continent, where, in some areas, it is a fairly important food fish, has shown that the female produces about 15,000 eggs per pound of body weight. This occurs on its reaching maturity, at the end of the third or fourth year, when it has attained a length of 23½-27½in and a weight of 2-4lb. The male, which has a slightly faster growth rate, is already mature by the end of the second or third year.

Spawning takes place at the end of spring or in early summer, but only if the water temperature exceeds 18°C. If not, it may occur as late as July or August in northern waters such as Britain's, where such temperatures may not be reached before mid or late summer, if at all. The development of the eggs requires 140-210 day-degrees, that is, 14-21 days at a temperature of 10°C, or 7-11½ days at twice the temperature. The high temperature required for spawning, together with the length of development of the eggs in late summer or early autumn, may result in several years passing during which the Wels does not successfully reproduce, so that introductions will perhaps not con-

tinue to flourish. Furthermore, even if the eggs do hatch, the larvae may die off because of the lack of food at that time of year.

The yellow, sticky eggs, about 3mm in diameter, are deposited in a 'nest' prepared by the parent fish in the shallow, reedy margins of lakes and rivers, or even on flooded marginal meadows. This site, a small area cleared of vegetation, is watched over by the parents for a time with the male often guarding the eggs until they hatch. The newly hatched tadpole-like larvae are about 7mm long and for the first few

Top: *Frank Guttfield strikes into a big Wels.*
Above: *Ledgering at Woburn Abbey where some of the earliest and most advertized introductions of Danubian Catfish were made.*
Right: *Tiddenfoot Pit near Leighton Buzzard—known to hold some large specimens.*

days of life cling to the vegetation surrounding the nest by means of an adhesive gland. They remain there while they absorb their relatively large yolk-sac, but as soon as this is done they become active swimmers and begin to feed on planktonic animals. Growth can be extremely rapid if the water is a rich one with an abundant supply of this type of food, so that they may reach a length of 1-1½in at the end of four weeks. This growth rate continues, and at the end of the first year they may reach a weight of 1lb.

Largest freshwater fish

As they grow, the size of their prey increases to take in, besides fish, small aquatic creatures such as amphibians and small mammals like voles, and even small water birds.

The Wels must be considered as one of the largest freshwater fish in the world and is certainly the largest freshwater species in Europe. Records of weights indicate that it reaches a length of 7-8ft and a weight of 500lb. Even now, specimens of 200lb are still relatively common and every year sees the capture of several fish of over 100lb by Continental anglers.

The species is relatively shy, frequenting the deeper parts of slow-flowing rivers or stretches of rivers and lakes where vegetation, debris

How big do Wels grow?
Nothing over 50lb has been caught in this country, but specimens ten times bigger than that have been caught on the Continent.

My local lake holds Catfish, but night fishing is banned. Is it worthwhile fishing during the day?
If you choose a warm, overcast day, preferably after two or three warm days and nights, you may strike lucky.

Is there an effective groundbait for Wels?
Chopped fish or any meaty waste matter will bring hungry Catfish around. Add a few drops of pilchard oil and dried blood to the mixture.

What rod is best for Catfish?
No specialist rod exists because the species is still so rare, but a good carp or pike rod will do the job.

Are Catfish likely to colonize a local lake if a few stock fish are introduced?
If your lake is in the South, you have more of a chance than Northern areas. But it is very hit and miss. Ensure that the local water authority approves before making any transfer of fish.

Do Catfish feed all year round?
No—at least it is unlikely that you will see any evidence of the species once the first frosts arrive.

Since a Wels is predatory, will it chase a spinner?
Spinners have never proved effective, probably because the Catfish is more of a scavenger than a hunter. But livebaits, usually intended for pike, have accounted for some catches.

from trees, or even overhanging rock ledges, can provide cover in which they can hide during the daylight hours. Generally, it will only leave its hiding place in search of food at night or during thundery weather on hot summer days, when it moves about close to the bottom. Night fishing, which, unfortunately, is not allowed at most British fishing venues must therefore be considered the most productive approach for the angler.

Much has been written for and against the introduction of this alien species to new waters in this country. While any introduction of alien species, whether fish or mammal, can have disastrous results, as has been shown on numerous occasions, a survey of those waters where the Wels exists indicates that other indigenous species manage to survive extremely well in its presence, as anyone who has fished the Woburn Lakes can verify. There is little chance of Wels taking over a water because our climatic conditions make its reproduction rather unreliable. On the other hand, its potential size and great fighting qualities make it a fine addition to the list of British freshwater species.

Frank Guttfield writes:
There is little doubt that the Wels Catfish is the largest inhabitant of British freshwaters: the 43½lb record breaker from Wilstone reservoir is a tiddler compared to some fish that have been seen or hooked and lost.

The Cat is sluggish in shape and sluggish by nature; it is in no way built for speed. Largely dependent on the senses of taste, feel and smell, the Catfish is predominantly a scavenger feeding on virtually anything dead, rotting or very slow moving. Dead fish constitute a significant part of the Cat's diet and so do large freshwater (swan) mussels. The gaping maw of even a smallish Cat is powerful enough to crush a mussel with ease.

The Wels in England is essentially a summer fish and has rarely been caught in water temperatures of less than 65°F. It thrives in hot conditions and appears to be most active in water temperatures between 75 and 85°F. Although Cats will feed at any time of day or night (they are the most unpredictable of fish) dark, muggy nights with plenty of cloud cover seem the most productive.

In many ways the tactics and tackle for this freshwater leviathan closely resemble those of the big eel specialist. The angler cannot afford to use fine or sophisticated tackle for these giants; brute force and simplicity are essential. The rod needs to be a powerful weapon with a test curve between 2-4lb, and it is most important that the reel fittings are reliable. A quality fixed-spool reel loaded with at least 100 yards (preferably 200) of line between 12 and 20lb is also essential.

Roach or gudgeon dead bait
Freelining with a dead fish bait is by far the most productive way to tempt a Wels. The preferred fish bait is a smallish roach or gudgeon of 4-5in long, either lip-hooked or with line threaded through the mouth. The hook size is generally a No 2 or 4 and it is important to use a really strong, reliable, sharp hook. Some specialists prefer a bait that is a few days old and 'off', while others have done equally well with freshly killed baits. Other than fish baits the freshwater mussel must rate as a very close second. Find the largest mussel possible and lightly hook it on the 'foot' together with the loose entrails. The use of a wire trace is a matter of personal preference. There have been cases where it was felt that the teeth had ground down a nylon line and eventually caused a break, but generally a line of 12lb b.s. and upwards in good condition should suffice. The landing net needs to be big—at least 3ft in diameter and 4-5ft deep. Pre-baiting with offal, chopped fish or mussels can help.

FISHING FOR WELS

Method	Rod	Reel	Line	Terminal Tackle	Hooks	Lead Weights	Bait	Groundbait/ Attractor	Time of Season	Habitat	Distribution
Freeline ledgering (for 30-60lb) specimens	10½-11½ft hollow glass 2¼-3¼lb test. Screw reel-fitting desirable	Fixed-spool e.g. Mitchell 300 or heavy-duty	14-25lb	Freelined ledger or stone attached with PVC soluble tape	2 or 4 strong-eyed e.g. B James carp hook	None	Small deadbait —gudgeon, bleak, roach— swan mussel, liver and other meats	Samples of hookbait	Summer, early autumn. Very warm, sultry weather is preferable	Snaggy areas in lakes, pools and pits	Exceptional waters, all in South Central England e.g. Woburn, Tiddenfoot Pit, Claydon Lakes
Freeline ledgering for fish up to 30lb	10½-11½ft as above, but 1¾-2½lb	As above	9-15lb	As above	As above	None	As above	As above	As above	In more open waters of the kind above	

Wels do not yet run to the giant proportions recorded in their native Danube, and distribution here is still limited. However, the record has reached 43lb 8oz. A Wels can be distinguished from the American Catfish by having six barbules rather than eight. Its huge, shovel-like mouth, displaying an expanse of gums and small teeth, is capable of seizing ducklings and voles.

Rudd

More, perhaps, than any species, rudd reward clever management of a coarse water. A controlled population may produce handsome fish—but so too may clever fishing

Of all the coarse fishes there is perhaps none more handsome than the fully mature rudd, especially during the early season when the sunshine brings out all the subtleties of colour. Very few anglers can resist pausing momentarily to admire it before slipping it into the keepnet.

It is no mean fighter either. Size for size, the rudd fights better than the roach, which is hardly surprising because size for size it runs heavier. The rudd is a lake and pond fish, which thrives especially well in a stillwater habitat. However, it is also found in limited numbers in slow and sluggish rivers, or in the almost still reaches of older canals. In such waters it prefers these slow reaches and pools and rarely mixes with roach populations found in the faster reaches, except when it moves in shoals between one fairly still water region and another.

Overgrown chalk pits also produce shoals of rudd and where such populations are well balanced with good pike, perch or even wild bird predators, the resident rudd do well. In other waters they are prone to become too profuse and as a result become small and stunted. Ruthless netting will often alleviate this problem and when transferred to waters where food is plentiful the fish often increase their growth rates.

Useful predators
Introducing pike and perch into such waters will also improve rudd growth rates, as well as producing good quality perch and pike. A permanent balance is difficult to achieve, however, and problem waters often pass through long cycles when different species gain a passing prominence and produce stunted perch and rudd at intervals between excellent ones.

Growth rates are therefore highly variable from one water to another. In fertile waters rudd will reach a length of 2in during their first year and 4in in the second.

Since the rudd is largely a surface

Norfolk angler John Nunn with a rudd caught on ledgered bait close to the lake bed.

What tackle is best for rudd fishing?

Any light rod and float tackle will do when fish are feeding close to the bank. But a rod of 12-14ft, able to cast 40 yards, with all-through action capable of throwing three swan shot, and an antenna float, will bring best results. A fixed-spool reel is essential; hooks may vary from 14 to 18, according to bait. Lines of 2-3lb are probably the most suitable.

What is the current record rudd?

The 4lb 8oz fish taken by Rev C Alston in 1933 from Ringmere near Thetford was beaten by a fish of 4lb 10oz from Pitsford Reservoir, Northants, in 1986, thus cancelling a long-standing record. A few others have been claimed but not authenticated and may have been hybrids. Any rudd over 2lb merits specimen status: fewer than 30 fish over 3lb have been recorded.

Which British waters might produce specimen fish?

The lakes of Norfolk and Lincolnshire are proven, and Slapton Lea is renowned. The most unremarkable waters can produce specimens: gravel, chalk and sand pits, even ornamental lakes. Avoid waters with large rudd populations; look for a lake known for pike, with some carp and only the occasional rudd. The water should be clear, weedy, and of varying depth.

Is it worth bottom fishing for rudd?

As a rule you will catch *more* near the surface. But better quality fish often lie deeper and feed on the bottom. The specimen hunter will fish deep and forego frequent catches. Fish the top first, then use tackle which quickly passes down through the shoals.

and middle water feeder its diet consists mostly of insects and plants with a sprinkling of crustaceans and molluscs. It also shows a marked fondness for fish fry (often its own kind) during the early season, and it is less likely to feed on the bottom for chironomids and many mud-dwelling life forms.

The rudd's feeding habits are suggested by the strongly upturned mouth and in summer it takes a large part of its food from surface flies, pupae, nymphs and beetles. The rudd is therefore more easily seen when feeding, and this tendency for surface activity is always useful to the angler. Perhaps this is why the rudd is considered to be easier to catch than the roach, which does not give its position away.

Rudd shoals often consist of fish of varying sizes, the large ones tending to lie somewhat below the main shoal. Rudd like to feed in or over weed beds and will often move close to the shore, and even among the

Below: *A specimen is boated on Lough Annaghmore. Ireland is renowned for big catches: in 1957 a 5lb 2oz (unverified) rudd was taken from the River Shannon. While many large rudd inhabit the water, there are a number of hybrids which can be confusing.*

weedy margins—their thin-sectioned bodies are well adapted for swimming between the reed stems, where they forage.

Rudd spawn in May or June, and are often taken still unspawned in mid-June, when even the slightest handling causes the spawn to be shed. Throughout summer the rudd feeds heavily, becoming somewhat less active in autumn, and in winter being almost in a state of coma. However, a bright sunny day may bring it to the slightly warmer surface layers in bays and backwaters.

The species is widely scattered throughout England, particularly in the South East. It becomes less common in the North and West, and in the extreme West and North it is uncommon or even rare. The rudd does not occur in Scotland or west Wales but is common in Ireland, where it is known as roach.

Some variety of colour is evident, some waters producing highly attractive rudd with yellow fins. An albino form, known as golden rudd, with colouring similar to goldfish, is also found in some waters.

At one time the so-called 'blue roach' received considerable attention both from anglers and fish specialists. Over the years these specimens have proved, upon expert examination, to be true rudd. It is possible that the 'blue' colour variation is more apparent than real. Any fish copiously covered in slime often appears bluish when viewed in strong sunlight—this is often noticeable in bream. Perhaps the reason for this blue colour is that the rudd taken shortly after spawning still bears a heavier slime layer than when fully scoured, and exhibits this same blue cast.

Whatever the cause, nobody can be blamed for occasionally mistaking a large roach for a rudd, or vice versa, especially on a cursory examination. A closer look usually reveals that the dorsal fin in the roach is set with its origin roughly level with that of the pelvic fin roots, but in the rudd the dorsal fin is decidedly further back from the pelvic fin root level. Large fish of both species are full-bodied, and may even be similar in colour, the brassy-tinted variety of roach being

Left: *Landing a two-pounder caught by swingtipping.* **Above:** *A catch of 20 rudd, ranging from 1lb 9oz to 2lb 5oz.*

similar to the normally golden colouring of the rudd. Such problem fish are not necessarily important unless their weight is sufficient to warrant consideration as a specimen or record fish. This is indeed one of many reasons why the Record Fish Committee insists on examining the fish claimed as a record. The pharyngeal teeth provide proof of identity. Roach pharyngeals—teeth set in the throat behind the gills—consist of a single row of only five teeth. Rudd pharyngeals bear two rows with five teeth in the outer row and three in the inner row. Furthermore, rudd pharyngeals are more strongly hooked than those of roach and are distinctly pectinated.

A further complication in such cases is that rudd do occasionally mate both with roach and bream, producing a hybrid. Anal fin ray counts, however, will always separate the rudd from the bream, and the hybrid from both. Rudd have 10-13 branched rays, bream 23-29, and the hybrid 15-18. Any angler can carry out such a check.

Rudd/roach hybrids

Rudd/roach hybrids are far more difficult to identify and the anal fin ray count is of no value in determining species or hybridization. Fortunately such hybrids are unusual, and in

any case rarely deserve closer examination, since their size is unlikely to warrant record claims. Nevertheless, only dissection can prove such a case beyond dispute.

Rudd frequently provide a fair bag and the early season lake angler can look forward to a peaceful day when the rudd are obliging.

Surface and middle-water fishing methods are clearly indicated, and if shoals of rudd are seen well off-shore the angler must shot-up a fairly heavy tackle to provide long casting. Rudd feeding well off the shoreline are not unduly shy, but most anglers prefer to take no chances.

Fishing for rudd

A useful strategy is to cast well beyond the shoal, where the splash of tackle hitting the surface will not be noticed. The tackle is then drawn slowly towards the angler and into position over the shoal. Runs are often signified by a determined lateral and oblique movement of the float as fish take the bait along with them, rather than diving with it. In these situations a bubble-float partially filled with water often provides casting weight, permitting light shotting. Alternatively, a controller lying flat on the surface rather than being cocked like a float, allows swift bite detection on finer

tackle than might otherwise be required. Whichever method is adopted, good eye-sight and swift reflexes are necessary.

When shoals of rudd do venture close inshore, great care is necessary to avoid alarming them. Fish hooked must be drawn aside from the shoal without allowing them to splash on the surface. This means employing side strain with the rod tip low until the fish can be landed.

Weed-filled haunts

In many gravel pits the depth of water may well be more than 30ft. Weed beds, invisible from the shore, are often deep rooted, but extend upwards to within 12ft or so of the surface. These are often likely rudd haunts, and the regular visitor will get to know their positions. Shoals may be feeding 10ft or more from the surface, foraging among the top of the weed, constantly changing depth and coming to the surface.

Whatever the feeding locations, the angler should use tackles as light as conditions will allow. When long casting he must make certain that his shotting is disposed along the cast to prevent the hook flying back and tangling over the float or upper shots during flight. Usually it is expedient to ensure that the lowest shot is more than halfway down the cast from the float. This also enables slowly sinking baits to be presented as required.

Rudd frequently rise to a well-cast fly. The fly should be small, and almost any good imitative pattern will take fish. Nymphs should also be tried. Many anglers like to attach a maggot or a piece of white leather to the tail of the fly as an additional inducement. In conditions where rudd are rising freely this is a most enjoyable and effective way of taking fish regularly without alarming the rest of the shoal.

The fly may be fished dry, although timing the strike is sometimes a problem, or it may be fished wet, a foot or so below the surface. Wet flies should be drawn very slowly as rudd are not inclined to chase a moving bait. During the early season when fish fry are frequently eaten by rudd, a small flasher-type fly, fished in short irregular jerks, is sometimes very effective. This may also account for better quality fish than ordinary bait methods, because larger, more mature fish are more prone to take fish fry at this time of year.

Free-feeding rudd

When rudd are feeding freely their presence and activity is so obvious that groundbaiting is quite unnecessary. When there are no feeding signs on the water it is advantageous to tempt them into a feeding mood, or draw feeding fish within casting distance by the careful use of groundbait. Since the rudd is predominantly a surface feeder, there is little point in using heavy groundbaits intended to lie on the bottom, and cloudbaits—used little and often—are useful.

When boat fishing on the larger waters of the Norfolk Broads, local anglers often fasten a piece of bread to a length of line attached to a stone. This is then anchored in the vicinity of reeds or weed beds, and the boat is then moved quietly away to a suitable fishing position. An alternative is to float small pieces of bread downwind at intervals, either from the boat or the shore. If there are gulls or ducks in the vicinity, this can do more harm than good —cloudbait is then the only answer.

Some of the best rudd fishing is to be found in many of the waters of the Norfolk Broads, which are also noted for the excellence of their pike fishing. Fishing from the bank is possible in few of these waters and the best rudd areas are the shallower reed-fringed portions where cruising boats do not venture, as the depth varies from one or two to four or five feet. Excellent rudd are also found in the little known ponds and meres of Shropshire and the Fens of East Anglia, and perhaps the best known water is Slapton Lea, also known for large pike. Many waters contain rudd over 2lb, but their presence is never suspected until the pond is drained, or electrically fished, when fine rudd are found in the nets with hundreds of smaller fish.

FISHING FOR RUDD

Methods	Rod	Reel	Reel Line	Terminal Tackle	Hooks	Leads/ Weights	Bait	Groundbait/ Attractor	Time of Season	Habitat	Distribution
Long-distance ledgering	13ft, 1lb test	Fixed-spool	2lb	Running link	10-14	$\frac{1}{4}$-$\frac{1}{2}$oz bomb	Bread maggot, worm	Golden crumbs and hookbait	Late summer/ winter	Stillwater	Ireland, South-West Southern, and South-East England
Short-distance ledgering	10ft/soft action	Fixed-spool	3lb	Freeline	10	None	Bread, worm	Mashed bread	Early summer	Stillwater	Ireland, South-West, Southern, and South-East England
Surface-crust fishing	12ft	Fixed-spool	3lb	Freeline	8-10	None	Crust	Samples of hookbait	All seasons at night	Stillwater	Ireland, South-West, Southern, and South-East England
Bubble-float fishing	13ft	Fixed-spool	2lb	Single hook	8-10	2 No 6s	Flake	Samples of hookbait	Summer	Stillwater	Ireland, South-West, Southern, and South-East England
Short-distance float fishing with a small sinking bait— small quill or pole float	12ft	Fixed-spool	2lb	Single hook	16-20	2 dust shot	Maggot, caster, sweetcorn	Hookbait	Summer	Stillwater	Ireland, South-West, Southern, and South-East England
Fly fishing	Trout fly	Fly	Floating line	2lb trace	10 and 12		Small wet or dry flies and nymphs	None	Summer	Stillwater	Ireland, South-West, Southern, and South-East England

Rudd like small, heavily weeded ponds or gravel pits and still, quiet rivers throughout Ireland (where they are called 'roach'), SW, S and SE England, particularly East Anglia—the Norfolk Broads and the Wensum valley. The record is 4lb 10oz (Pitsford Reservoir, Northants, 1986) but that size is rare – any rudd taken over 3lb would be a notable specimen.

FISHING TECHNIQUE

The waters with a reputation for large bags of mixed species are not the ones for a specimen hunter of rudd. Vulnerable to competition and shy of anglers, big rudd hate crowds

Rudd are shy, sensitive fish that must never be underestimated. To catch good, specimen rudd, the experienced and successful angler has familiarized himself with the precarious life cycle of the species, its movements, habitat, and feeding patterns from hour to hour.

Good rudd waters are often found near the coast. Slapton Ley and the marshes of Lincolnshire and East Anglia, for example, are fine rudd waters. Fittingly, a lot of my fishing for this handsome species is done on beautiful estate lakes in Norfolk.

Rudd in stately home waters
These lie next to stately homes, nestled in large parks. Norfolk is still an agricultural county and has many estate lakes, some private, but the majority fishable. They all have certain features in common: for example, they are manmade, generally in a valley, so that they utilize an existing water-course; all of them have dam walls, few are deep and most of them are at least a century old. Shallowness and age have led to silting and reed encroachment in all of them. Bit by bit the picture of an ideal rudd habitat begins to emerge.

Lately, most of my rudding is done in sand or gravel pits. With 1500-2000 acres of new water every year, this is the fastest-growing aspect of coarse fishing. Not all pits suit rudd: many are too deep, some have little weed or marginal vegetation. Shallow, weeded rudd pits exist all over Southern England. Many are controlled by large groups like Leisure Sport or the London Anglers' Association and others are controlled by individuals or by private companies like Norfolk's Swanton Morley Fisheries. Successful rudd pits have a similar geography—bays, ridges, extensive shallows, islands and weed growth.

Rudd and their neighbours
The most important thing in determining the potential of a rudd water is not the food supplies nor the weed growth. It is the fish population of the water. Rudd are hypersensitive, so that other species have a real influence on them. Let us look at two identical pits that I know. Both are of three or four acres, and are exceptionally rich in underwater life and weed. Both have shallows and reed margins and the same pH values.

The effects of other fish species
Yet one pit—call it A—holds rudd of over 3lb, while, in B, a 4oz fish is a specimen. This situation exists purely because of the stocks of other fish.

The rudd in Pit A are big because they compete for food with just a few roach and a handful of carp. Their numbers are culled at every stage in their development—as spawn and fry they are food for eels, as 2oz fish they are kept down by the plentiful perch, when bigger they are thinned by the stock of good pike. At no stage does the rudd stock outgrow its available food supply. Perhaps only a few dozen fish mature, but their size is guaranteed.

Pit B is in a sorry state, because a misguided club official put bream, tench and crucian carp in with the rudd. Food is so scarce that all the species are thin and stunted. As a further consequence, big bags of hungry fish are assured and so the pit is heavily fished. Local boys remove large quantities of eels,

which means that the spawn of other species is not cropped. In the winter they catch pike and, being inexperienced anglers, allow large numbers to die, so that more small fish escape their natural fate as pike prey.

This is an extreme example, but the message is clearly there: if you want good rudd there should not be many in the water. If you go on a summer evening and see fish rising everywhere, you can forget the specimens. If you get an immediate bite on a new water, ignore that too. But if you are fishless on your first outing, keep trying.

Even after ten years of carp fishing, I still rate big rudd as the shyest freshwater fish. This must be remembered when locating swims. Nearly all my rudding has to be at distances of over 20 yards, often beyond 40 yards. But there are exceptions to this rule, for every big fish finds a place where it feels completely secure. This is invariably an area that is little fished, perhaps because of distance from the banks or because of snags. Some of my rudd safe areas are tucked behind islands or in an arm solid with lilies. One shoal has its hideout under a sunken alder tree, another beneath the remains of a boat-house.

Safe areas are not difficult to discover, but do require a certain amount of ingenuity to fish. You might need polarized sunglasses to watch the fish take the bait, sometimes thigh boots to get you through swamps, and, frequently, heavy tackle to bully fish into the open so, for this sort of fishing, I use a 13-footer. It has a test curve of $1\frac{1}{4}$lb and I team it with 4lb b.s. line and hooks to match—a No 10 with flake, a 12 with maggots.

I usually wait for the rudd to move into open water and begin to feed properly. As the light fades, and then right through until dawn, the shoals leave their refuges and patrol the lake. They can be meticulous in their timekeeping. A famous shoal on Hickling Broad passed through a bay every night between twelve and one, and that was the only time a bite would come.

Rudd will follow contours on the bottom; gravel bars, for example. They are like wolf packs that keep to the heights to see food better at a distance. Bigger fish often move close to the bank facing the wind, favouring bay mouths where there are concentrations of daphnia and nymphs. They will follow routes through weedbeds, or patrol the channels between islands. Despite this, the swims I fish are the most open and exposed in a lake, for enclosed swims seem to make the bigger rudd nervous, in much the same way as big bream react, according to the experts. I also favour the water that the wind hits hardest, especially if the depth is between 3 and 9ft. Perhaps broken water stimulates rudd to feed by introducing oxygen, or by concentrating food, or just masking the sound of

Below: *Float fishing for rudd on the calm waters of a canal. Perfect peace and quiet is needed to catch these sensitive fish.*

ASK THE EXPERT

Should I use a float or a ledger for big rudd?
Where the fish move within easy float casting range use a float if conditions are right. Often though, the big fish are found at ranges greater than 25 to 30 yards and ledgering is a must.

If rudd are primarily surface feeders how can ledgering work?
Smaller rudd up to a pound or so certainly swim high in the water during the summer months, but the bigger than average fish appear to fall for a bait fished on or near to the bottom.

Does floating crust work for big rudd?
It can but it is more likely to attract the smaller fish who will rapidly whittle it down to nothing. A 'balanced' crust is much better. This is a combination of flake and crust that barely sinks so that fish can be taken on the drop or once it has settled on to the bottom.

Would you groundbait when using a 'balanced' crust?
Yes, with very fine golden breadcrumbs. If they are mixed up soft enough to break up on impact with the water, a fine cloud will slowly descend. Rudd will invariably come to investigate and might well see your slowly sinking balanced crust as an easy meal.

Would you fish casters in the same way?
Mix a few casters in with the breadcrumbs so that the surface feeders are attracted. These will soon follow the rest of the casters down. Use two or three floating casters on the hook: they will sink slowly and produce many more bites than sinking casters.

tackle and groundbait hitting water.

Sighting big rudd is an important part of location. In the day, you might see the occasional red fin, but movement is greatest as dusk falls. A rudd roll is a very distinctive action. It is not quite like a bream's, nor is it the smooth, dolphin arc of a tench, but a splashy half-jump. Often, there are several rolls as a shoal prepares to feed.

I do not mean to suggest that rudd are solely nocturnal feeders. Between June and September, any day that is overcast and windy will produce fish. In autumn and winter the daylight hours are again often the most productive if there is a breeze and air temperatures are not below 9°C. I do not like an easterly winter wind, but all the rest are fine and I can fish in a Force 8 if need be.

Left: *Jim Tyree tenderly places a 2lb 3oz rudd into his keepnet, but for as short a time as possible.* **Below:** *Lough Annaghmore—famous for its rudd.*

I fish with the least confidence when there is a flat calm, especially when the sun or moon is bright.

Fish are very much more sensitive than humans to climatic conditions. I have noticed winter roach begin to feed if the water temperature rises half a degree. Summer tench come on to feed if the light value drops by one F-stop on the camera exposure-meter. The biggest silver eel runs occur in Norfolk rivers when there is a storm out on the North Sea. Likewise, the threat of rain or wind spurs rudd to feed.

Most big rudd are taken by fishing on the bottom. Small fish up to 1lb can be caught in mid-water or on the surface, but mature rudd feed deeper. Accordingly, I usually ledger. The method has its advantages, for it needs quite a lot of expertise to present a bait well enough on float tackle to fool a big rudd. Furthermore, most anglers find it difficult to floatfish efficiently at more than 25 yards and the big fish can be feeding over 50 yards out.

Butt-bobbins

Once a rudd takes the bait, the bite is bold. My indicator is the butt-bobbin, the shop-bought isotope kind, and because bites are so strong it does not matter if you use a fixed paternoster or a running link ledger. But I prefer the latter. I stop the ledger link 2-4ft from the hook with a plastic ledger stop, never a split shot. I make the running ledger from the green collar of a ledger stop, a length of nylon and an Arlesey bomb. One end of the line is tied to the ring of the bomb, the other is threaded through the ledger stop, brought back and tied on the bomb ring next to the first end. The length of the link depends on the depth of silt or weed and the plastic ledger stop keeps the reel line away from obstructions.

The size of the bomb depends on the length of the cast to be made, but always choose a weight heavy enough to get there easily. A strained cast is an inaccurate one and can wrench the hook out of a soft bait.

I have some 30 rods in my tackle room, yet I nearly always use the same one for rudd fishing. It is 12ft long with an all-through action. It is not too 'tippy' like an all-through-action match rod, yet it is not at all sloppy. Lines of 3lb b.s. work well with it and for rudd I use them almost exclusively, unless the water is gin-clear, when I go lighter, or snag ridden, when I go heavier.

The tackle for rudd is straight-forward, and the art lies in the choice of bait and skilful ground-baiting. Big rudd are uncannily quick to learn from experience and not many fish need to be caught on a particular bait or from a particular swim before they vanish. To catch good rudd consistently, I always need to be a step ahead of them and so I never fish the same lake quite the same way three times in succession. The swim, the bait or the

groundbait must be varied. The angler fishing in a stereotyped manner will never catch, or even suspect the presence of big rudd, while the innovator will score.

The bait I use at the beginning of the season is bread flake. A piece about the size of a thumbnail, on a size 10 hook, is about right. When that 'goes off', try crust of the same size, on the same-sized hook. A few fish later, maggots may become necessary. Use three on a size 12. Then, casters take their place. Sweetcorn can be tried next—two grains on a 12, or one on a size 14 or 16. Wheat can then be tried, but after that the rudd will want worms again. Half a lobworm on a size 8 or a brandling on a size 14 are both effective. It might take a whole season to cover this cycle, but you can always start again the following year with flake.

Groundbaiting cycle

Broadly speaking, my groundbaiting has three stages. First, the rudd accept soaked bread stiffened slightly with white crumb. Then groundbait has to become more sophisticated and so I mix some golden crumb with enough water to make the mix sloppy. Into this I mix two good handfuls of casters, then squeeze them hard so that some burst. I then add a few 1p-sized pieces of crust and mix in just enough white crumb to stiffen it for catapulting. This groundbait will break up as it hits the water and go down slowly. Burst casters will rise and sink and rise again, but the pieces of crust work themselves loose and drift into mid-water.

All groundbait must be delivered by catapult—not thrown out. A catapult with good, strong elastic gives you much greater accuracy and distance. It keeps balls of groundbait intact until they hit the water. After a while, the rudd become suspicious of any cereal groundbait and you are left with three alternatives. You can catapult-out loose offerings of groundbait, but if the distance is too great, it may be possible to deposit the feed from a boat. If not, it can be cast out in a swimfeeder. Try to get enough offerings out before the rudd appear,

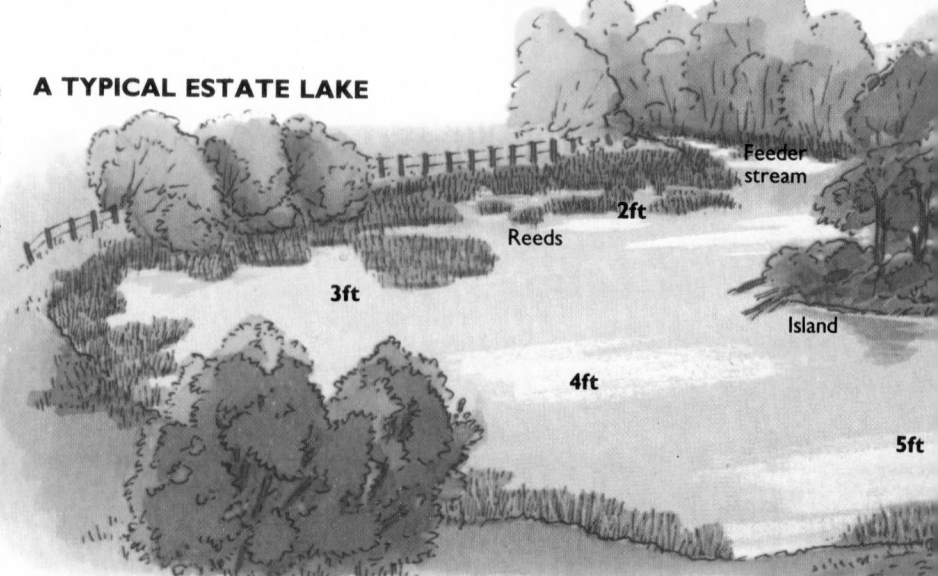

A TYPICAL ESTATE LAKE

Feeder stream

2ft

Reeds

3ft

Island

4ft

5ft

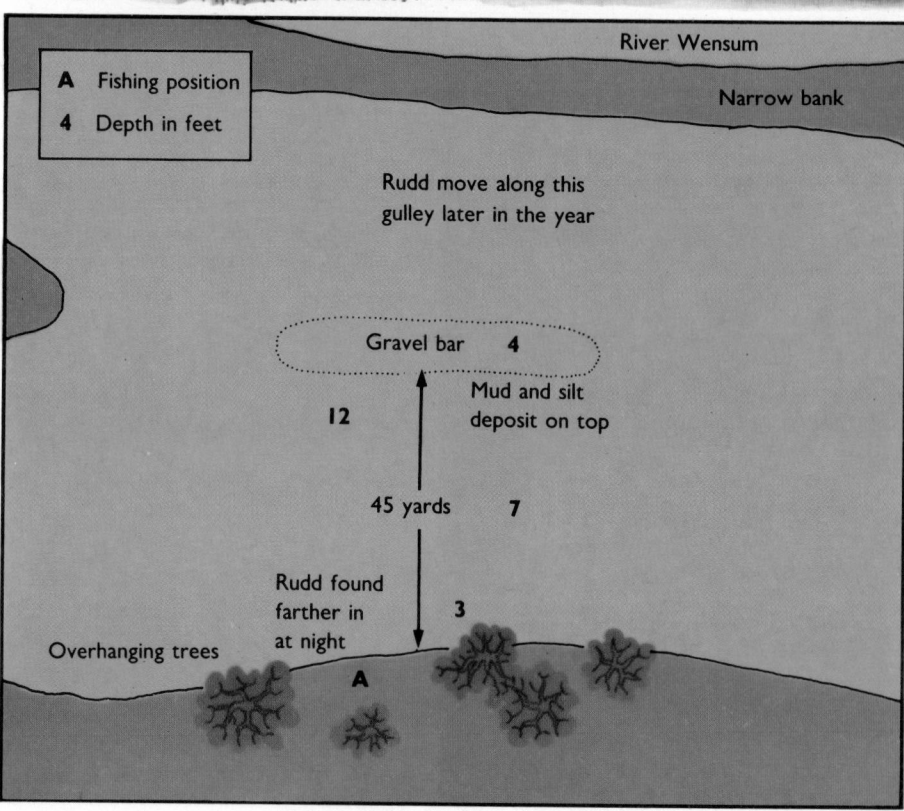

A — Fishing position
4 — Depth in feet

River Wensum

Narrow bank

Rudd move along this gulley later in the year

Gravel bar   4

12

Mud and silt deposit on top

45 yards   7

Rudd found farther in at night

3

Overhanging trees

A

because the splash of a feeder is likely to disturb them. Choose a big open-ended feeder and pack it with casters or maggots. Block the ends with as little groundbait as possible. Ten to 20 casts with the swimfeeder should put down enough feed to hold a good shoal a while.

Carp baits have received a lot of attention recently, and I believe a lot of the new thinking could be adapted to rudd fishing. I am not sure about the advances in the use of high protein and am more interested in the new particle baits and amino

acid additives. As examples of the former, I have found rice and hemp to make very effective groundbait for big rudd. On the hook I have had promising results with sultanas. Alternatively, go to a large seed merchant and look around. You will be amazed by the variety of potential baits. Certainly, many remain untried for rudd, yet they could prove to be a dramatic success.

The most notorious carp-fishing development is the introduction of amino acids into baits. There is a lot of secrecy about them, perhaps

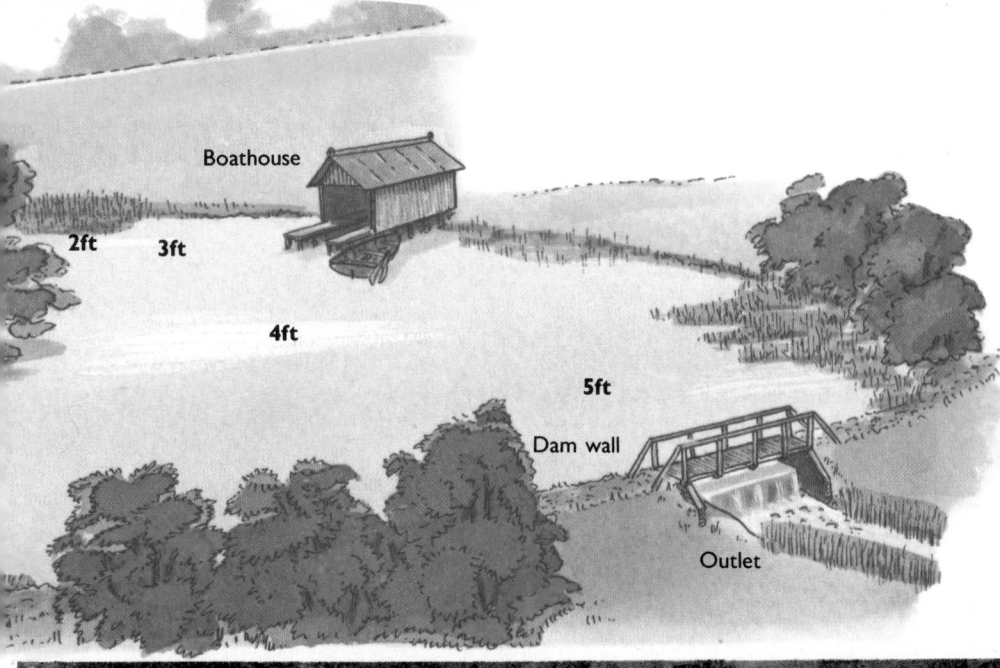

Boathouse
2ft
3ft
4ft
5ft
Dam wall
Outlet

Left: *The extensive shallows—the water's maximum depth is only 5ft—and the abundant weed growth of this typical estate lake often characterizes good rudd waters. The rich weed growth, favoured by rudd, does present problems for the angler, however.* **Below left:** *Plan of the Wensum Valley gravel pit, Norfolk—a mature rudd water. Though not abundant, rudd of over 3lb can be found here. During the day rudd patrol the gravel bar 45 yards out, moving in at night.* **Below:** *Early evening and, regular as clockwork, rudd begin to feed. Note the very large keepnet—essential if rudd are to be returned to the water unharmed.*

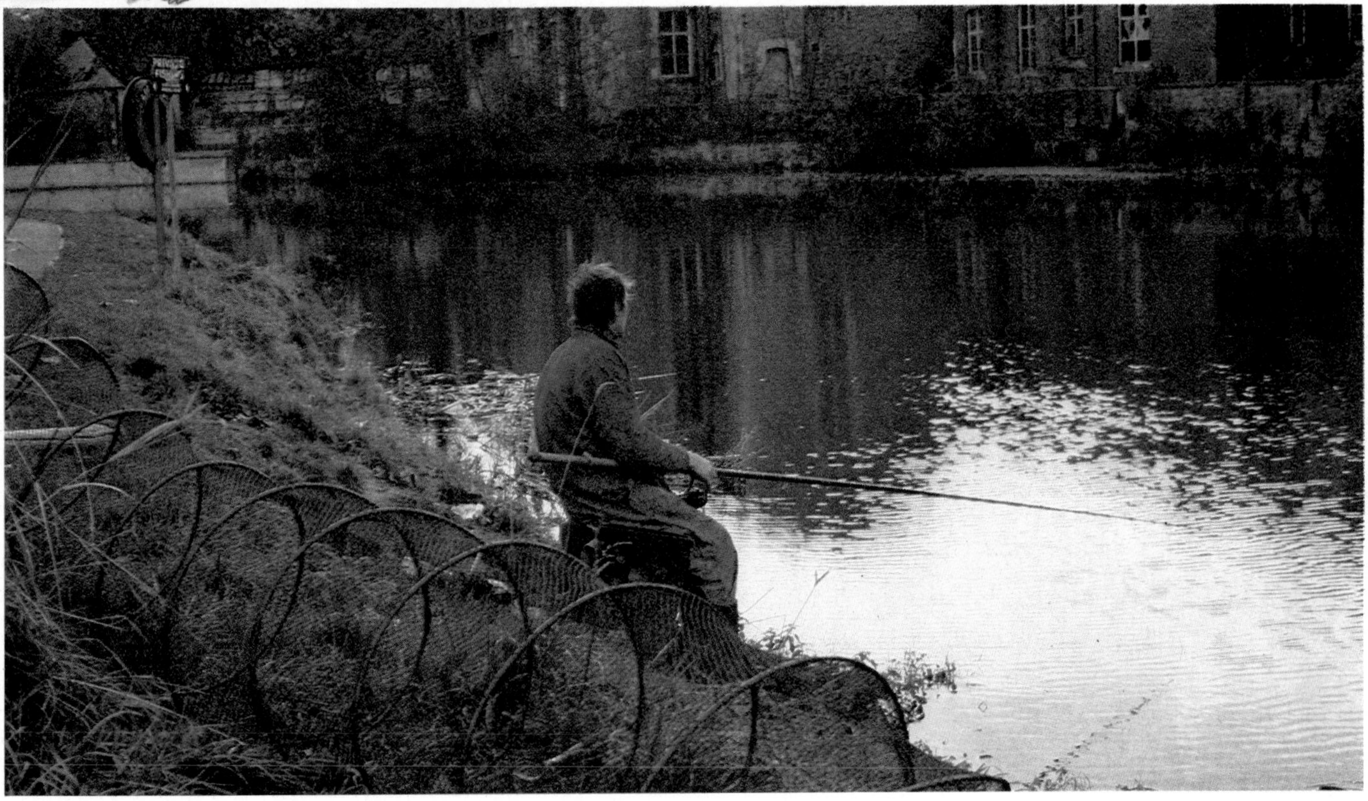

because they do work well. They are costly, although I have bought them to mix with bread flake. Results certainly do improve but no more than by using the shop-bought additive, Black Magic.

These ideas are not way-out and I am sure they are going to revolutionize fishing. Nobody now would dream of using plain bread flake for carp, yet we still do for rudd. It is high time for a change of attitude.

Because rudd are highly strung, they fare badly in keepnets, especially over prolonged periods. If you watch them, they continually prod the mesh with their noses in an effort to escape. This can cause cuts which let in fungus and disease. I once kept nine 2lb rudd in a keepnet for five hours to photograph later. Five died immediately they were returned to the water. I took them out and examined them—there was nothing visibly wrong and I believe they died of nervous strain. Now, the only time I keep a rudd is when it is a single specimen and I am waiting for better light for a photograph. I look after it in the net, which is 15ft long, putting weed over the net to block out the light and make the fish lie quieter. I go to this trouble not just on humanitarian grounds, but because I know many of the best rudd waters have limited populations of big fish. In small lakes the stock may be only one or two shoals of 20 fish each, and so to kill just one fish would be to destroy a significant percentage.

Hybrids vary from the obvious to the virtually undetectable. My advice is not to worry about it unless you are going to be claiming a record.

Pike

The pike, an exciting adversary for the freshwater angler, is a voracious predator which feeds on a wide range of prey—its diet can include small water birds and even other pike

Ask any freshwater angler which fish he fears most and with certainty he will say, 'the pike'. Why the pike (*Esox lucius*) should be feared is debatable. The fish is by no means the only freshwater predator—the perch and the brown trout also eat other species. Indeed, the trout kills more immature shoal fish than either the pike or the perch.

The solitary pike

Streamlined, powerful but graceful, the pike is the supreme predator in our rivers and streams because of the enormous size it can grow to. It leads a solitary life, lying in ambush to dart out and feed on smaller shoal fish—species such as roach, rudd and bream. The pike is built for speed, but only over short distances.

It prefers to wait until an unwary fish comes within striking distance, then, in a burst of energy launches its body forward to grasp its prey.

As the pike gets older and slower it becomes a scavenger, seeking out ailing fish and searching the bottom of the lake or river for dead fish. In this way the pike contributes to the balance of Nature, regulating the numbers of fish that any water is able to support. At the same time, by removing sickly or stunted fish, the feeding habits of the pike ensure the long-term health of the other coarse fish species.

The pike is widely distributed throughout the British Isles. It is found in both flowing and stillwaters. Lakes, especially those containing vast shoals of fodder fish, will hold the larger pike. Loch Lomond and similar large expanses of water have an enormous food potential. Pike there feed on salmon smolts, trout and coarse fish in large numbers. River pike, on the other hand, have to keep up a never ending battle against running water in order to breathe and maintain control over their territory before they even attempt to make a kill.

Maturity and spawning

The female pike will always grow larger than the male, which rarely exceeds 10lb in body weight. During spawning, which can occur at various times, depending on the geographical location and the temperature, a number of male fish will accompany each egg-laden female. Often these male fish are only a pound or so in weight. They become sexually mature after the third year of life, whereas female fish mature slightly later—between the third and fifth year. Spawning begins in March but may extend to June in northerly areas. Pike seek out shallow parts of a lake or stream and have a liking for flooded grassland around the perimeters of stillwater, and for the water meadows that border some of our rivers. The slightly sticky eggs are released haphazardly to adhere to grass stems and waterweed.

If the temperature is right—about 11°C—the eggs will hatch in 10-15 days. The tiny pike will remain at-

Can pike be gaffed without harm?
Expert pike anglers will play out their fish before inserting the gaff into the V of the underjaw. But it's so easy to get carried away with the imminent capture of a fish that a large landing net is a more sure way of landing a pike without harming it.

Do I have to use a wire trace for piking?
The wire trace is only necessary when spinning or trolling an artificial lure. A spoon or plug invites a savage attack from a pike which often closes its jaws across the trace: only pliable wire can withstand that.

Does the pike hybridize with perch to produce the pike-perch?
No. The so-called pike-perch is an entirely different species, *Stizostedion lucioperca,* more correctly called zander.

Can I fish for pike on the opening day of the coarse season?
It depends where you live. Some Water Authorities do not allow pike fishing before September, whereas in Scotland and Ireland there is no closed season. There's certainly a moral question as to whether we *should,* in pursuit of record catches, fish for female pike heavy with eggs.

Are pike edible?
Yes, indeed there are a number of ways of cooking pike, though they are all rather rich and expensive. A pike stuffed with thyme, marjoram, oysters, anchovies and butter then roasted in claret, was a great favourite with Izaak Walton. No less exotic is pike stuffed with veal then baked on a bed of mushrooms, garlic and red wine for 45 minutes.

tached to the plant stems for a few days until they absorb the yolk sac. An adhesive pad on the head prevents their being swept away by currents. When the sac has been absorbed and the mouth fully formed, the larvae become free-swimming, moving to the surface to feed on minute water life. If the water is warm enough, the larvae grow fast over the first few months, attaining 3-7in in a year, but many of them will be eaten by other predatory fish. Over a period of two or three weeks a female pike of 14lb probably spawns around 100,000 eggs, of which only a few will make a year's growth, with even fewer growing to the size of the female parent.

Record pike

The present record pike weighed 44lb 14oz when caught from Ardleigh Reservoir, Essex, by Mike Linton on 4 January 1987, but numerous specimens of over 40lb, and one of 53lb have been taken from Irish and Scottish water. A 43lb pike was caught in this country in 1974 but following a spurious claim the fish was never credited to its true captor whose name did not enter the record fish lists. There is some evidence for the existence of pike of up to 70lb in British waters. Certainly, if you wish to join the record-breakers, it is advisable to fish in the early part of the season when many of the female fish are heavy with spawn. But conservation-minded anglers may object to this.

Learning to 'read' the water is something all anglers should do. It involves studying the area and

Above: *After attacking and grasping its prey (in this case another pike), the pike moves away a few yards before swallowing it head first.*

Right: *The mottled green and brown flanks of the pike, speckled with lighter spots, enable the fish to blend into the bed of similarly coloured reeds.*

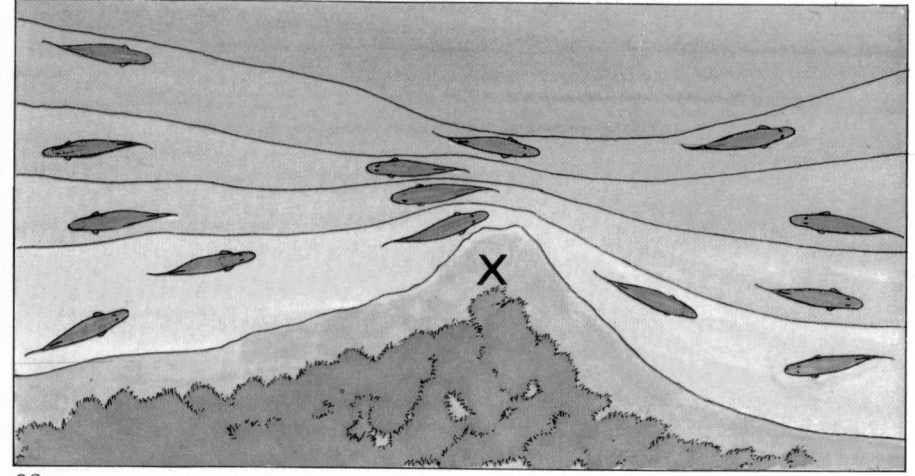

Left: *Pike tend to keep to constant depths when they are patrolling for food. They also hang around protruding ledges such as that marked 'X' in the diagram, which would be a good place from which to fish for them.*

Right: *The colouring of a pike alters as it reaches maturity. A fish of less than 2lb will have light-coloured bars on its flanks; older fish have only spots.*

deciding where fish are likely to be found. And to do this an understanding of the pike's habits and needs is invaluable. Pike often lie in holes in the undercut banks of rivers and streams. Where a tree has fallen into the water it diverts the flow and sets up an eddy, which produces a drastic slowdown in the current. This creates a natural lie for a predator. On stillwaters the pike will pounce from the edge of beds of reedmace, water lilies and rushes, coming out from gaps between the stalks, where it has cover.

Large lakes, reservoirs and other stillwaters lack the identifying features which aid the angler's search. Underwater contours assume importance in this situation. Natural fall-offs in the slope of the lake bed, ledges and underwater obstructions are the places to find pike. But as these places are invisible to the angler he must locate them by plumbing.

Pike can be made to come to the angler in just the same way as smaller fish are lured. Groundbait, though not of the cereal type, can attract pike. They are able to detect blood in the water over long distances. Finely ground fish offal mixed with pilchard oil is therefore an effective groundbait.

Pike can be caught by a variety of methods. Because of the fish's voracious appetite, it will attack both live and deadbaits. Fish, for example, can be presented either live, swimming in mid-water, or as deadbait, lying on the bottom. Practically any species can be used as a livebait—even small pike are an attractive lure for the larger ones. The most important thing is to use a lively bait that will work well, swimming strongly in order to arouse the attention of a pike. However, many anglers consider the use of one fish to catch another as cruel.

Artificial lures play an important part in pike fishing. Spinning is both a pleasurable and successful method. Almost any material can be employed in the manufacture of lures but metal is most often used. Essentially, this is because metal can be worked and bent to the required shape to provide the spinner or spoon with an attractive action when pulled through the water. Obviously metal has its own weight so there is little need to add lead to the end tackle in order to cast it. There is much controversy about the type of action that a spinner should have to make it attractive to the pike and other fish. Trout and perch will dash after a minute blade spinner that

MONA'S LENGTH WEIGHT PIKE SCALE			
in	lb	in	lb
20	2·500	41	21·537
21	2·894	42	23·152
22	2·327	43	24·845
23	3·802	44	26·602
24	4·300	45	28·476
25	4·882	46	30·457
26	5·492	47	32·444
27	6·150	48	34·585
28	6·860	49	36·774
29	7·621	50	39·062
30	8·437	51	41·453
31	9·309	52	43·940
32	10·240	53	46·524
33	11·230	54	49·207
34	12·282	55	51·992
35	13·398	56	54·880
36	14·580	57	57·872
37	15·829	58	60·972
38	17·147	59	64·180
39	18·537	60	67·500
40	20·000		

represents a small, lively fish. On the other hand, pike, especially the big ones, are only prepared to surge after a lure over short distances. Often if you cast out a ledgered deadbait, then spin a small artificial lure over the top of the resting place of the ledger bait, pike can be drawn into the swim by the lure, but fall casually to the natural bait because it is easier for them to take.

The spoon should be larger for pike and incorporate good-quality treble hooks. Bright colours seem to attract pike. A copper spoon with one side painted red will give alternating flashes that simulate the appearance of an escaping rudd, while a silver spoon with red stripes resembles a roach. The colour combinations are never-ending and should be experimented with. Quite often a black-painted spinner is the only type that induces pike to attack. It could be that the pike sees the lure as a moving silhouette, which annoys it. An attack (that cannot be called a 'feeding response') is often made on an artifical lure. Is the pike responding to an invasion of its territory when it strikes to kill or drive away? There is still a great deal to be learned about fish behaviour of this kind.

Plugs came to us from America, where they are used successfully to catch a wide variety of species. Made of wood or plastic, they do not really resemble anything found in Nature. Anglers rely on the action built into the plug to attract fish. The shape of the plug, position of the diving-vane and treble hooks all serve to give the plug a motion that urges pike to attack.

Above: *Another Norfolk pike—a 16½lb specimen taken by Dave Plummer on the River Waveney.*

Below: *Herring is a very effective deadbait for pike. The technique shown here is used by John Wilson when boat fishing for pike on the Norfolk Broads, the smell of the bait luring the pike out of the weedbeds.*

BINOCULAR VISION

Right field of vision

Hunter's binocular vision

Blind field

Left field of vision

Right field of vision

Prey's binocular vision

Blind field

Left field of vision

Above: *As it is a predatory fish, the pike needs a good field of binocular vision to help it judge angles and distances between itself and its prey. Non-predatory fish need less binocular vision, but they have wider overall vision to help them evade capture.*

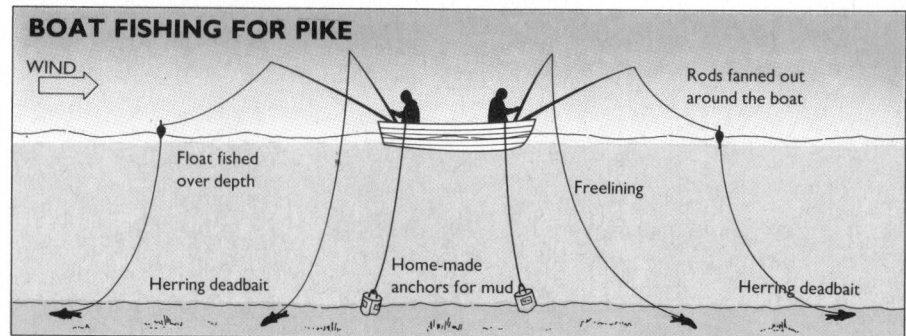

BOAT FISHING FOR PIKE

WIND

Rods fanned out around the boat

Float fished over depth

Freelining

Herring deadbait

Home-made anchors for mud

Herring deadbait

FISHING TECHNIQUE

Like a pride of lions, young pike inhabit a home base from which to strike at passing prey, sometimes acting in concert to make the best of a shoal of food fish, says Barrie Rickards. Like lions, too, in old age pike lead a lonely, scavenging life, feeding often on putrid flesh

More folklore and complex thinking surrounds the subject of how to fish for pike than any other species. Not all of it is traditional, for a great deal of modern muddled thinking exists. In fact, fishing for pike is a relatively simple matter once you have faced up to a few home truths, unpalatable though these may be.

The prime fallacy is that the pike is a solitary beast—the lone wolf of the fishy world. It is not. Most of the time, the pike the angler fishes for—say over 5lb—is in the company, often close, of other pike. In this way, considerable areas of water may contain nothing but jack, or young, pike. Rather than the lone wolf idea, we should think of the comparison with a pride of lions. We should not compare them with a wolf pack either, for pike rarely hunt as a pack except when they corner unusually large shoals of bait fish.

Lions live as a pride with a home base. Any game which wanders through that area is safe if the lions are not hungry, but meets instant death if they are. Occasionally lions go on the rampage, hunting far and wide, and not necessarily as a pack, or even as a loose group. The pike's behaviour is very similar. Days when big pike seem to be mad to feed throughout a water, are those when their hunting urge has spread them far and wide. Most of the time they frequent a relatively small area, which elsewhere I have referred to as a hotspot.

Feeding patterns

Within a hotspot pike have feeding patterns. Considerable numbers may come on the feed at roughly the same time each day and feed for a very short period. When conditions are adverse—due, for example, to dropping temperature and barometer—only a few pike may respond to the careful angler, but again, it will be at the same time of day.

Generally speaking, these feeding periods last about an hour. In the autumn they tend to be not long after first light with a second (often shorter) period towards dark, often

Left: *Jim Tyree with a 12½lb Waveney pike. Sometimes a strong young pike can put up a better fight than a weary old specimen.*

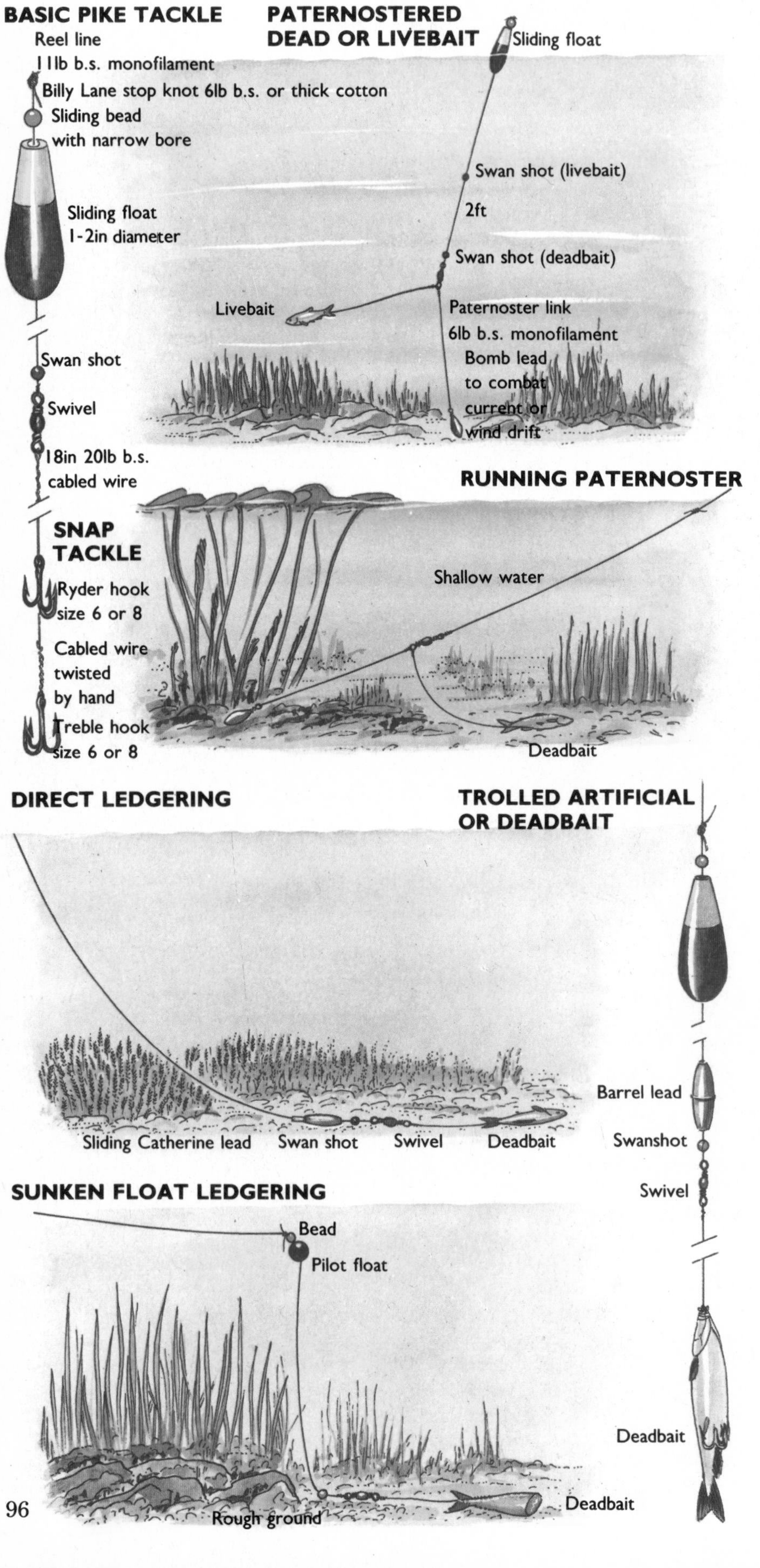

BASIC PIKE TACKLE

Reel line
11lb b.s. monofilament
Billy Lane stop knot 6lb b.s. or thick cotton
Sliding bead
with narrow bore

Sliding float
1-2in diameter

Swan shot

Swivel

18in 20lb b.s.
cabled wire

SNAP TACKLE

Ryder hook
size 6 or 8

Cabled wire
twisted
by hand

Treble hook
size 6 or 8

PATERNOSTERED DEAD OR LIVEBAIT

Sliding float

Swan shot (livebait)
2ft
Swan shot (deadbait)

Livebait

Paternoster link
6lb b.s. monofilament
Bomb lead
to combat
current or
wind drift

RUNNING PATERNOSTER

Shallow water

Deadbait

DIRECT LEDGERING

Sliding Catherine lead   Swan shot   Swivel   Deadbait

SUNKEN FLOAT LEDGERING

Bead
Pilot float

Rough ground   Deadbait

TROLLED ARTIFICIAL OR DEADBAIT

Barrel lead

Swanshot

Swivel

Deadbait

Deadbait

about 1½ hours before nightfall. In the winter the feeding period may be later in the day, often about midday, but generally the extent of feeding is less spectacular, even under good conditions, because water temperatures are lower and metabolic requirements are less.

The fact is, unpalatable though it may be, that you have to get up in the morning and fish hard and long for a day or two until you have the feeding pattern—always assuming that you have found the hotspots in the first place. It should be emphasized strongly that there is nothing quite like sitting in a place you know to be a hotspot, waiting for the feed—you *know* it will happen and that the prize can be yours.

All other problems of rods and tackle pale into insignificance beside those just dealt with. While not implying that there are not several good rods, reels and techniques, let me describe the extremely simple approach that has produced for me more than 600 pike over 10lb in the last 15 years.

96

ASK THE EXPERT

Is it necessary to use a wire trace for deadbaiting?
Absolutely crucial—and make sure that any trace is at least 12in long. A big pike can easily engulf a smallish deadbait and take it well down the throat before you are aware of it.

Do I need heavyweight line to fish canals or small drains?
Double-figure pike are common, even on small waters. In fact, fish of 30lb have been taken from waters you could almost jump across. Any line of less than 10lb breaking strain would be fool-hardy.

What are sink-and-draw tactics?
A deadbait is cast well out into the swim, allowed to sink and then drawn up to the surface. This process is repeated until the deadbait is near to the side, when it is recast and brought in at a slightly different angle, so that all the water can be covered.

Is it true that many waters ban the use of livebaiting?
Before you even consider using a livebait, check your licence or ask the owner of the water. Often, too, you may meet with considerable opposition to livebaiting from fellow anglers.

What is gorge tackle?
It is an illegal form of pike fishing where the fish is allowed to turn and swallow the bait before the strike is made. You must always strike when the first run is made to avoid deep hooking, especially when you intend to return the pike alive.

The pike rod

First, the rod. A model like the Mark IV carp rod is too soft, not for playing pike, but for casting the baits so commonly used in piking. However, a stepped-up carp rod is ideal. Several of these are available, in hollow glassfibre, but the best type are those with progressive action as opposed to the tip action associated with fast taper blanks.

Fast taper blanks with a test curve in the range of 2¼-2½lb have their place in piking, for example in firing 2oz leads and small baits a long distance (up to 70 yards). A slow action rod, however, will not only cast heavy deadbaits a long way (4-5oz up to 80 yards in average weather conditions) but can be used for shorter range float paternoster rigs for live and deadbaiting.

Personally, I find a 10ft slow action rod ideal for most of my piking, which includes use of artificial baits much of the time. When spinning I would probably use lighter bait casting rods as well, but my concern here is to outline an outfit that can

Above: *A pike of over 20lb fetches an admiring crowd of young pike anglers.*
Far left: *Six rigs for taking pike. Large, heavy baits call for powerful tackle, but to maintain an element of sport and subtlety your line should not be too heavy.*

be used with great success and versatility for almost all styles of pike fishing you are likely to encounter.

When considering reels a ruthless approach cuts out thoughts of multipliers and centrepins, and homes in on the versatility of a good quality fixed-spool reel. I use those with roller pick-ups and able to carry 200 yards of 15lb b.s. lines. The b.s. of monofilament line that I normally use is 11-12lb, even for very big pike. Only in heavily weeded or snag-ridden waters would I go up to 14-15lb b.s., although I use 20lb line when trolling. Breaking strains under 11lb considerably increase the risk of snapping the cast when hurling out 4oz of mackerel for 70 yards, while lines of 14-15lb b.s. drastically reduce distance.

Using this rod, reel and line com-

Above: *Some waters hold so many small pike that none have the chance to grow big. The whole population remains stunted.*

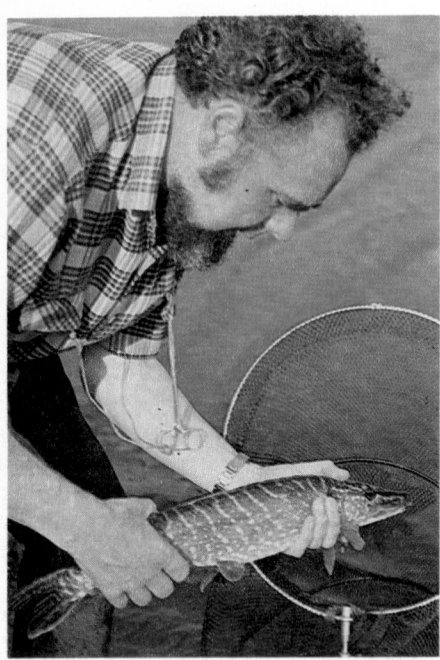

bination, the most common method I employ uses a 12in diameter spherical sliding float with a home-made snap tackle on the business end. The float has a hole of a sixth of an inch through the middle so that it slides very freely on the reel line. Above it is a bead with a small hole through which the line comfortably passes, and above this and set at the required depth, is a stop knot of 6lb b.s. monofilament or of thick cotton, which has less of a tendency to cut into the reel line.

The snap tackle consists of, at one end, a swivel, and at the extreme of the other end a No 6 or 8 treble hook. Between them is a sliding Ryder hook of the same size. These two items are fixed by passing 2in of the cabled wire trace through the eyes, laying them back and twisting them together firmly with the fingers. The application of some Araldite adhesive can be made, though this is not really necessary.

Dead or live bait

This basic tackle can be used for laying on with deadbait, for suspending deadbait, or for using a freeswimming livebait. Paternostered dead- or livebait is fished by tying a length of 6lb b.s. monofilament to the swivel

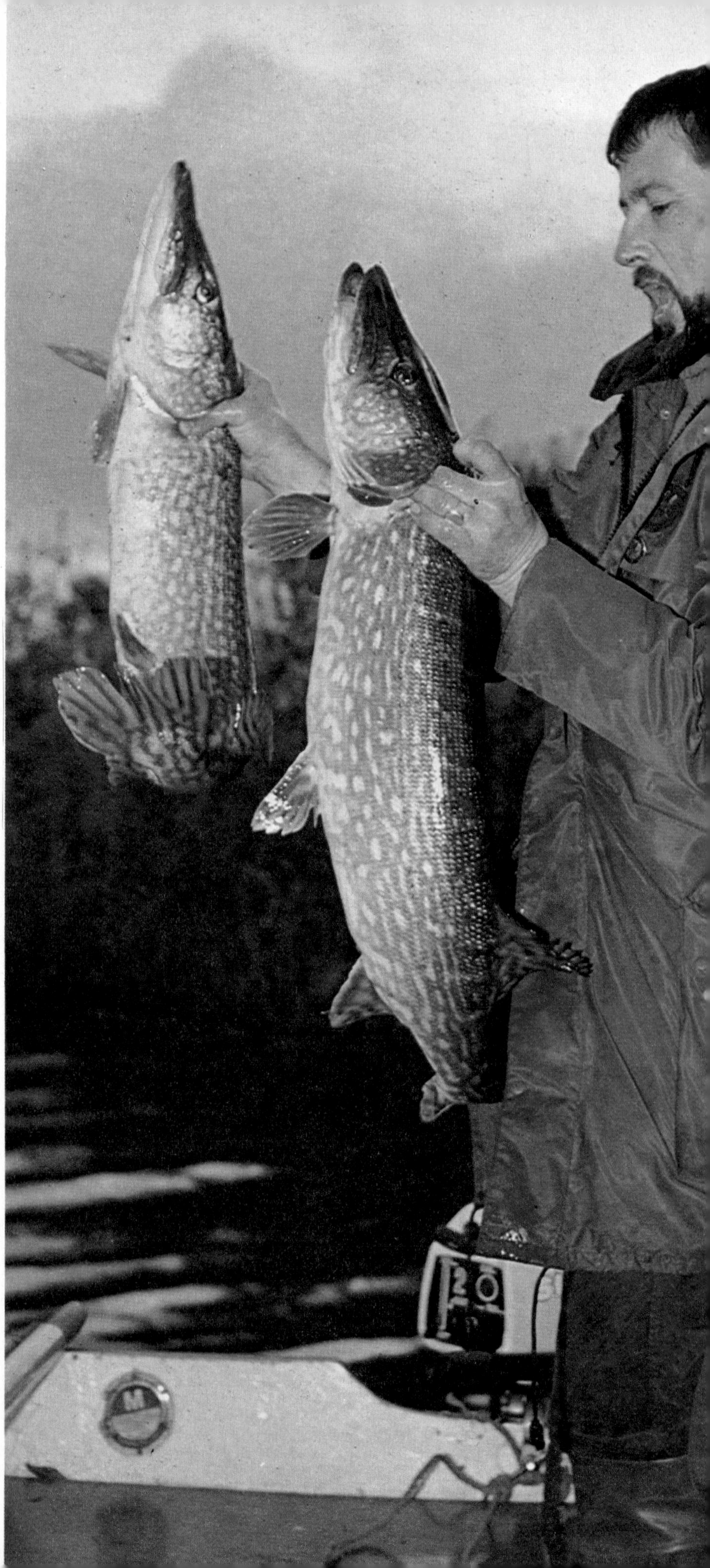

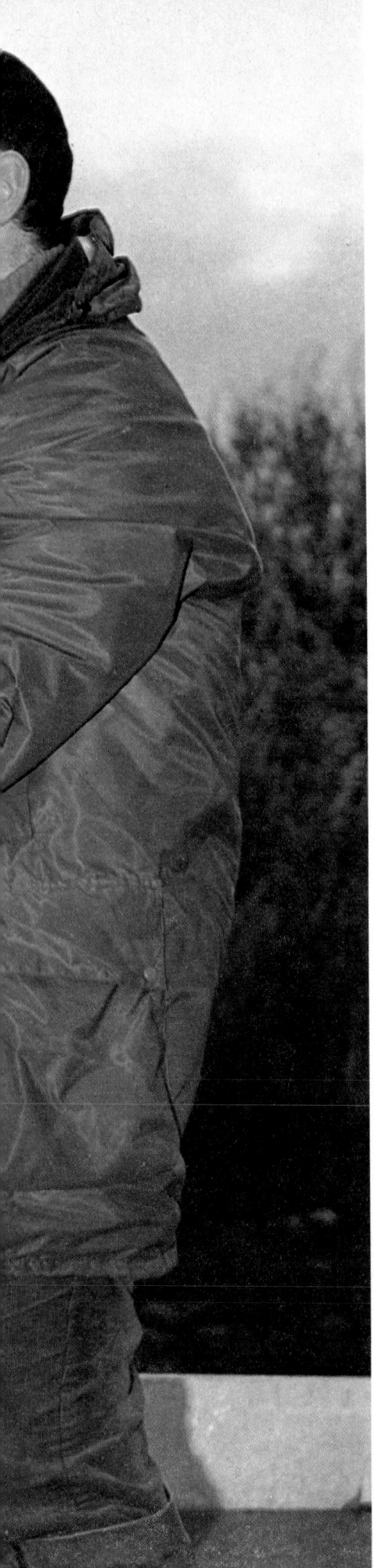

at the top of the trace, and to the bottom of the paternoster link is added a lead suitable to combat the current or wind drift. The depth is set so that the bait is the desired distance off the bottom. In order to prevent the sliding float from dropping over the trace a swan shot should be placed either just above the swivel for deadbait fishing, or about 2ft above it if you are going to be livebait fishing.

So arranged, the tackle is suitable for much of the pike fishing that the average angler is likely to practice. However, to achieve greater distance, or to avoid scaring pike in shallow water, the float can be dispensed with and a simple paternoster arrangement reverted to. Similarly, direct ledgering can be carried out by breaking off the paternoster line and adding the appropriate sliding lead to the reel line. Alternatively, the tackle can be fished completely freeline, one of the deadliest piking techniques for close range fishing. Whichever variation you decide to use, the same hooks, line, reel and rod are employed.

Only if I used a very large dead- or livebait would I change to a multi-hook system—probably just two

snap tackles—but I have not done this for several years. For spinning I remove the float and snap tackle and add the appropriate trace and lure. The bead and stop knot can be left on the reel line in case a rapid change is again made. Trolled artificials or deadbaits, used in conjunction with float tackle, can be fished on the same gear, but a barrel lead of appropriate weight is added to the reel line just above the swan.

It should be clear now that such an outfit enables you to fish livebaits and suspended deadbaits at close to medium range, and to use all these methods from boat or bank. The same rod can be used for floatless trolling of lures in conjunction with heavy lines. This is the first change of tackle we have made which takes more than a few moments. Fishing in heavy weed would require the same change of reel spool, hardly a long job.

Left: *Two nice River Waveney pike for John Wilson. Floatless trolling evidently brings about dramatic results.*
Below: *A pike is brought to the net from the River Bure. With fish of this size it is vital to get the landing net deep and bring it up directly under the struggling pike.*

Zander

Zander—like the Vikings—came to Britain amidst rumours of ruthless slaughter. It has taken them a century to live down these accusations and become an accepted sporting fish

The zander or pike-perch (*Stizostedion lucioperca*) is the largest member of the widespread perch family *(Percidae)* of fish. It is not, as some believe, a pike/perch hybrid, but is a separate species.

The zander is a native of Eastern Europe, but spread to the countries bordering the English Channel before finally arriving in England during the 19th century. In Europe it is a popular sport-fish and is appreciated as excellent eating as well as for its fighting qualities, but it has yet to be caught, or even seen, by most British anglers.

Many of the features of our native perch and ruffe are visible in the zander. Though having something of the elongated body of the pike, there is little mistaking the characteristics that indicate the zander's close relationship to the perch in particular. There are two dorsal fins, the first spiny, with about 14 hard rays, the second soft. These spines, and others on the gill cover and anal fin, mean that the fish must be handled very carefully.

The body is long, the head small and narrow. The mouth is large compared with the perch and ruffe, but small relative to the cavernous jaws of the pike. What the zander's jaws lack in size however, they make up for in the size of the teeth they contain. On both, the front of the lower and upper jaws are found pairs of large fang-like teeth. These fit into hollows in the opposite side of the jaws and are used to stab the prey, inflicting a fatal wound, and then to hold it.

The eyes are large and have a peculiar glassy look. This is because they incorporate a reflective plate or tapetum, which increases their sensitivity at night and in poor light.

Zander are not particularly vivid in colour, neither is there much variation from habitat to habitat as there is with other fish. The back is usually grey or brown in colour, with black dappling occurring in vague stripes. These are much less well defined than in the perch though they are clearer in the young fish,

Left: *The author with an 8lb 15oz zander.*
Below: *Section through a bony fish eye explaining the acuity and night vision of zander, carp, crucians, goldfish and ruffe.*

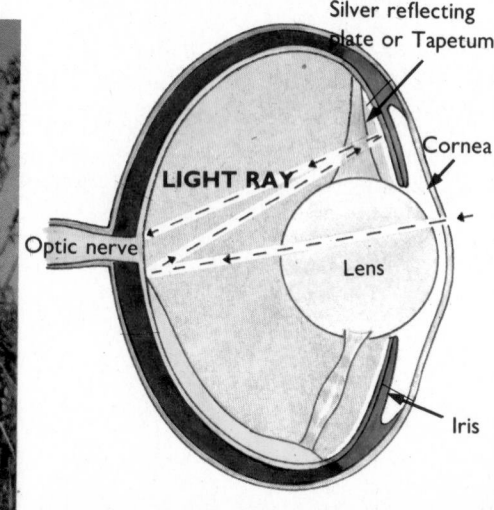

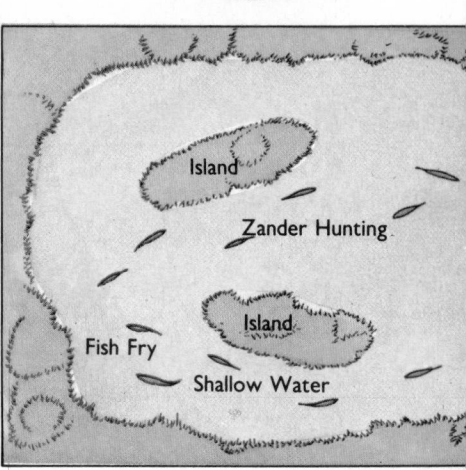

while often disappearing completely with maturity. The flanks of the young zander are silver, while those of the older fish have a greenish-gold hue. The underside and lower fins are white, although a hint of blue is sometimes noticeable. The dorsal fins, especially the spiny one, carry black spots over a grey and yellow background. The tail is speckled grey with white lower lobe.

Preferred habitat

Although a comparative newcomer to this country, the zander has spread quickly from its original home at Woburn Abbey. It prefers larger, open waters, rather than smaller, weed-filled ones. As they do not tolerate poorly oxygenated waters, zander do not thrive in smaller, stagnant waters. Unlike pike, they actually prefer to live in murky and coloured conditions. This undoubtedly has something to do with their excellent eyesight, which enables them to find the small fish on which they prey before their

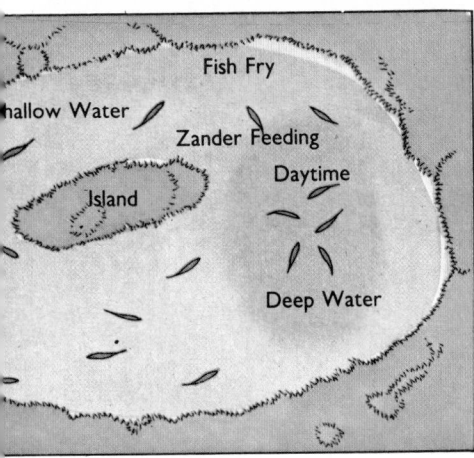

victims spot the looming predator.

The distribution of the zander in Britain is fairly concentrated, the main area being, apart from a few lakes in Bedfordshire, the vast network of rivers and drains of the East Anglian Fens. The Bedfordshire lakes include the first British waters to be stocked with zander—Woburn Abbey lakes and Claydon Lake.

Location of zander

In the Fens, a pit near Mepal, Cambridgeshire, received zander and, shortly afterwards, they were introduced into the Great Ouse Relief Channel near King's Lynn, Norfolk. It was these fish that spread throughout the Ouse system and even to the River Stour in Essex. The main zander waters in Fenland include the Relief and Cut-Off Channels, the Ouse and the Delph, Old Bedford Drain, Sixteen Foot, Middle Level and Roswell Pits, near Ely. A few other waters around the country are known to hold zander, some of which have been transferred illegally from the Fens, including lakes in Yorkshire, Leicestershire, Greater London, Warwickshire and Surrey. Zander are likely to spread and become established in many of our river systems.

Like the perch, zander shoal, often in large numbers. Usually, those in a shoal are of similar size and, probably, age. The larger the fish, the smaller the shoal and it is likely that big zander lead a solitary existence for part of the time. However, when there are large shoals of fry in a restricted area of water, zander of all sizes, and even pike and perch, will sometimes gather to take advantage of the food supply.

The zander is like a freshwater wolf, hunting in packs over large distances. They are very discriminating about feeding times, spending long periods hanging in mid-water or just off the bottom. When dusk or dawn arrives, however, they will move off to hunt, sometimes moving into shallow water, for this is where much of their food is found.

Above left: Former record holder Bill Chillingworth fishing for zander on the Great Ouse Relief Channel at dawn.
Left: Typical enclosed zander water.

Are zander as ravenous as some anglers suggest?
Zander do eat a lot of small fish and it is perhaps because of this that they have gained a rather bad reputation. But in fact they eat no more than other predators—about $2\frac{1}{2}$ to 4 times their own bodyweight in a year.

When do zander feed most avidly?
Unfortunately, zander are at their hungriest in May and June before the season opens, though they do feed well right through the summer and autumn. Only in winter does feeding decrease and angling become chancy.

Are livebaits more certain of success than deadbaits?
Zander eat both live and dead fish, so either may work. Most zander can be caught quite effectively on dead roach, bream and bleak. Salt-sea fish baits, are generally a waste of time.

What's the best way of cooking zander?
The flesh of a zander weighing 6lb or less is the finest and may be eaten with a cheese sauce which complements flavour of the fine flesh. Zander can also be smoked with excellent results.

Where will the next record zander be taken?
Zander are now widespread, so predicting which water has record potential becomes increasingly hazardous. However, if the Fenlands recover from their present problems, the Relief Channels will probably come to the fore again. In the next few years Old Bury Hill Lake near Dorking and Coombe Abbey Lake near Coventry will be worth watching.

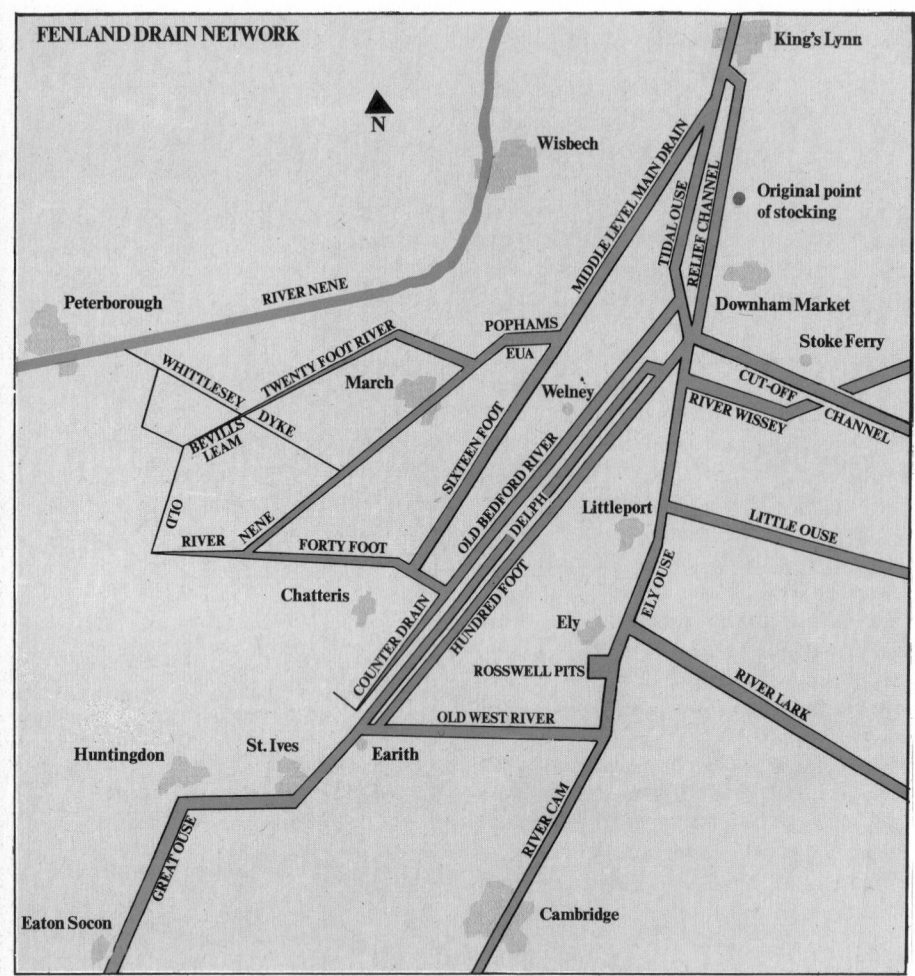

FENLAND DRAIN NETWORK

King's Lynn

Wisbech

Original point
of stocking

Peterborough

RIVER NENE

Downham Market

Stoke Ferry

POPHAMS
EUA

WHITTLESEY
TWENTY FOOT RIVER

March

Welney

CUT-OFF
CHANNEL

RIVER WISSEY

BEVILLS
LEAM
DYKE

SIXTEEN FOOT

OLD BEDFORD RIVER

Littleport

LITTLE OUSE

OLD
RIVER NENE

FORTY FOOT

DELPH

Chatteris

HUNDRED FOOT

COUNTER DRAIN

Ely

ELY OUSE

ROSSWELL PITS

RIVER LARK

OLD WEST RIVER

Huntingdon

St. Ives

Earith

RIVER CAM

GREAT OUSE

Eaton Socon

Cambridge

MIDDLE LEVEL MAIN DRAIN

TIDAL OUSE

RELIEF CHANNEL

Above: *Head-on confrontation with a
specimen zander showing its array of
stabbing fangs as well as many smaller teeth.*
Left: *From its first point of introduction in
the Fens on the Tidal Ouse Relief Channel,
the zander has found its way into all the
Drains. But steps have been taken to prevent
it entering the River Nene.*

Sometimes, feeding continues into
the night, especially on cold, starlit
nights. During the day they feed
sporadically but sometimes, when
the water becomes coloured due to
flooding or strong winds, they feed
all through the day.

Eating habits
The diet of the zander depends largely on the food available. Any species
of fish is fair game for the zander's
toothy jaws, even its own kind. They
are particularly fond of the smaller
fish species, especially the bottom
feeders such as gudgeon and their
own relation, the ruffe. They prefer
smaller fish than pike do, and they
chase and grasp their prey by the
tail or any part of the body they can
get hold of. They then swallow the
fish tail or head first, not turning it
in the way pike do. Any fish they
cannot swallow is ejected and then
probably picked up dead from the
bottom. Zander readily take dead
fish and have been known to join

together with their shoal mates to
dismember the corpse. Apart from
fish, zander also eat freshwater
shrimps and water slaters.

An Old Wives Tale, popular with
some anglers, has it that the zander
kills for the sake of killing. It is far
more likely that because the species'
feeding methods are more 'hit and
miss' than those of other predators,
a prey sometimes escapes, to die of
its wounds, suggesting that the
zander has killed senselessly.

Another misconception that dies
hard is that the zander will eat all
the other fish in any water into
which it is introduced. Every fish
has to eat to live, of course, and any
fish that ate every other would soon
die of hunger. Nature does not allow
this to happen and the zander
flourishes without annihilating
other species.

In March or April, when the water
temperature reaches between 12°
and 14°C, male and female fish pair
off in preparation for spawning. The

female matures at three years and
the male a year earlier. The eggs
number between 100,000–300,000
depending in the size of the fish.
These are small—about $\frac{1}{16}$in diameter
—and are laid on sand, weed or
sticks. In Europe zander are encouraged to lay their eggs on
bundles of sticks. It is then possible
to transfer the sticks to a pond for
hatching. The male is unusual in
that it guards the eggs while they
are hatching. However, this is as far
as parental responsibility goes.
When hatched after 10—15 days,
the tiny zander may be merely additional food for the adults.

Immature zander
The young zander is initially a
plankton feeder, taking daphnia and
cyclops, gradually progressing to
larger invertebrates and eventually
to small fish. Even when only 3in
long, however, the zander is already
a predator and will attack insects
and immature fish.

FISHING TECHNIQUE

Your motives for catching a big zander will decide the way you fish for it: invite it to fight on light tackle, or subdue and land the makings of a fine meal, using pike techniques

AT-A-GLANCE

Specimen sizes
Few waters which have held zander for any length of time will be unable to give zander of 10lb. Fish of over this figure can be considered to have attained a specimen size.

Tackle, baits, techniques
Rod
10-12ft (test curve of $1\frac{1}{4}$-$2\frac{1}{4}$lb)

Reel
Fixed-spool

Line
7-12lb b.s.

Hooks
Size 8-12 trebles
Size 2-2/0 singles

Baits
Live/dead fish to 8oz. Small spoons, spinners, running plugs, flies

Techniques
Ledgered and freelined live/deadbaits, float-fished livebaits—free-swimming or on a paternoster; wobbled deadbaits, spinning, plugging.

What is a specimen zander? Life is too short to live in terms of record fish, so any fish over 10lb can probably be considered a specimen. Probably no other fish gives the angler such a good chance of getting close to the British Record of $17\frac{1}{4}$lb. Until July 1978, 59 over 12lb had been recorded, and the record was broken—although not always officially—10 times between 1968 and 1978. That is an average of once a year—although Bill Chillingworth's record of 15lb 5oz stood from 1971 until 1977.

Falling records
Some earlier records have, of course, been beaten several times. I broke the British record twice myself, the second time with a fish of 12lb 5oz, but my best fish is now 13¼lb. I have had five myself, and my friends Neville Fickling and Bill Chillingworth have had, respectively, 8 and 18 over 10lb. It takes a lot of fishing to consistently catch ten-pounders, but even the less-devoted specimen hunter might expect fish over 5lb fairly regularly.

In 1978, the Anglian Water Authority changed its byelaws. Zander fishing now opens on June 16 and closes on March 14, the same as for all other coarse fish. Most of my successful zandering is done after October 1.

Whatever the time of year, there is little doubt that the best times for zander are dusk and dawn. Zander can see better in twilight and in the dark than in daylight, and low light is necessary before they feed. On all the waters I have fished, dawn —from about an hour before first light to about an hour after—is best. Most consistently, you get runs when it is not quite light enough to see what you are doing.

Silent nights
Next to dawn and dusk, night is the best time. Summer nights produce few runs, but runs come in short bursts every few hours in winter. Nevertheless, you still have to be patient through the inevitable long periods of inactivity.

During the day, the chances of fish are even less, particularly if it is calm, bright and sunny. Factors, such as strong colour, which decrease visibility, increase the chances of runs, and for this reason drains or rivers are always more likely to produce fish during the day than are rarely coloured stillwaters. Handling tackle may be difficult when drains and rivers are in flood or lightly coloured, but at these times there is not only more chance of zander, but of big zander too.

My own experience bears this out. My 13¼lb fish came from coloured water not long after dawn; my 12lb 5oz fish came during the day from brown floodwater; a 10lb 6oz fish fell at dusk on a dull day with a strong wind and big waves; and all the other good ones came around dawn or from coloured water during the day. I admit that there are exceptions, but the specimen hunter needs optimum conditions, tackle and locality for a good chance of big fish.

Night-feeding zander
I have one theory as to why zander are not taken more frequently at night. They move about more in the dark, so that ledgering dead-baits at night is not very productive. For example, when I fished Landbeach Lakes at night, I found that the fish came up off the bottom and searched for fry near the surface and in the margins. Then, the only way to get results was to floatfish a livebait or worm at a depth of about 2ft on the drift.

Zander hunters fall into two

Above: *Heavy duty tackle and a 6oz roach—a bait calculated to attract only the very largest zander in the locality. Coarse fish are a better zander bait than sea fish.*

Supertwin, and Ryobi, this last being extremely smooth—but any good model is suitable. I can see no point in considering closed-face reels, centrepins or multipliers.

The two brands of nylon monofilament that I regularly use are Intrepid Superline dyed with hot-water Dylon, and 11lb sorrel-coloured Sylcast, which I prefer. It is hard and dull, but becomes reasonably supple after an hour or so of use. I avoid soft lines (which have poor knot strength) and pre-stretched lines. The latter are thinner but have no stretch to cushion the strike, which I need with my striking technique.

At the business-end, I use home-made snap tackle with size 8-10 treble hooks. Some people fish without wire traces, but I can see no sense in it; not only because zander have sharp teeth, but because results prove conclusively that wire traces are not detrimental to success. The wire I use is Tidemaster or Alasticum, or a similar dark, fine, cabled wire.

The trace is around 1ft and is attached by an ordinary standard swivel. At the end of the trace I use a Mustad treble and above this a sliding Ryder treble. Both the bottom treble and swivel are attached by simply passing 1in or so of the wire through the swivel or hook eye

schools—those who scale-down their tackle to 7-9lb b.s. lines specifically for zander, and those who still use sophisticated pike tackle (the Fens are full of pike), including 11-12lb lines and size 6 or 8 treble hooks. I come into the lattter category, although I have caught many zander on scaled-down tackle. Results are not adversely affected by the use of pike tackle, except in one aspect—the fight of the fish is reduced. But, like most zander men, I go for the fish because it is plump, good looking, clean to the touch, and cooks well; not because of its ability to put up a good fight.

Float-paternostered livebait

My basic tackle is a float-paternostered livebait, exactly the same rig as I use for pike. The rod can be a Mk IV Carp rod, an Avon, or one of the hollow-glass equivalents. I also use a 10ft Farstrike made by Davenport and Fordham and, at the heavier end of the scale, a Piker 10 made by the East Anglian Rod Co and a 10ft stepped-up carp rod by Olivers of Knebworth. The only special feature of these rods is that all have hard chrome rings. I alternate choosing between Fuji handle fittings and ordinary sliding winch fittings.

I use fixed-spool reels—Mitchell 300 and 410, Intrepid Elite and

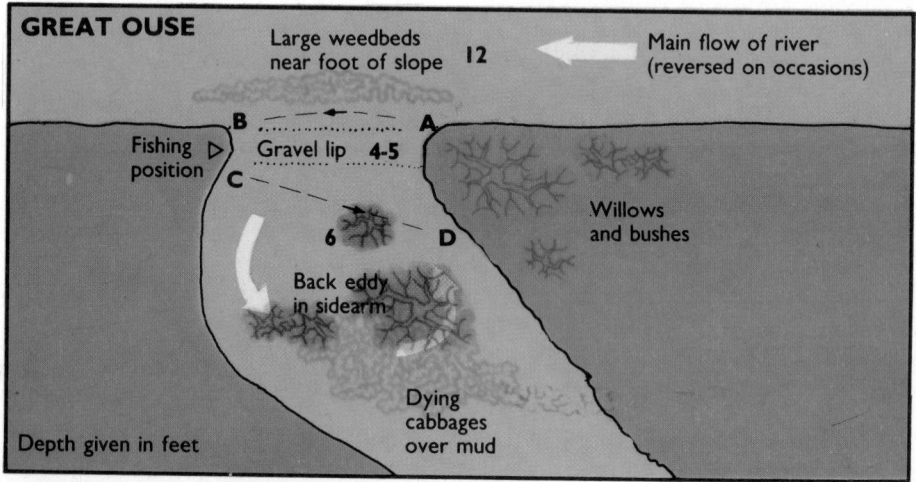

GREAT OUSE

Large weedbeds near foot of slope 12

Main flow of river (reversed on occasions)

B ← A
Gravel lip 4-5
Fishing position ▷
C

6
Back eddy in sidearm

D

Willows and bushes

Dying cabbages over mud

Depth given in feet

FLOODWATER ZANDER

Worn away side bay

Small fry shoal in back eddy out of main stream

9ft deep

Zander are attracted by small fry

and then twisting the wire together. The twist can be Araldited or Superglued but slip never occurs even without glue.

Cut down on weight

A three-way swivel can be used to attach the paternoster line, but again I hardly feel this is necessary. Use just enough weight to hold bottom in the current or drift. As well as the main lead, I also use a swan shot clipped on about 2ft above the trace swivel.

I use what used to be called pilot floats, of $\frac{1}{2}$-$1\frac{1}{4}$in diameter. These are simply a sphere with a hole through the middle. I often make my own in a few minutes from balsa dowel rod, although I make them cigar-shaped and fish them fat-end downwards —so that they give less resistance on the take.

The float is stopped with a Billy Lane knot tied on the line at the appropriate depth. Tie the knot with cotton or with 6lb b.s. monofilament. Cotton does not cut into the line, as nylon sometimes does, but stays firm for a shorter period; a nylon stop knot often stays on my line for weeks.

Between the stop knot and the pilot float, attach a small lead or bead with a hole just large enough to take the reel line comfortably. This bead stops the float slipping over the knot. The beads sold in tackle shops always have large holes and so are unsuitable. I buy a cheap 'pearl' necklace, with dozens of suitable beads on it. One is used to stop the hole in the float. All you then have to do at the bankside is to tie the stop knot. I prefer it to any of the free-swimming float rigs that you see people using, except when the fish are feeding in the shallows and there is a surface drift.

If you wish to fish a very shallow bait, it can still be used; simply lengthen the paternoster link. It makes casting a bit difficult, unless you loop up the link and tie it with PVA strip, but I have cast paternoster links up to 10ft long with little or no trouble.

Another modification is to remove the float to make a simple paternoster rig, which can be teamed with heavy leads for long-range or floodwater fishing. In such cases, set up the tackle taut, with the rod pointing at about 45° to the sky, and fish the paternoster either fixed or sliding. In the second case, attaching the paternoster by a swivel above the trace swivel is better.

Although I usually use treble hooks, a lot of anglers prefer one large single, especially when deadbaiting. A large single is particularly useful when using a leaded or leadless ledgering rig. Use a size 2/0 on a 1ft trace. In the past, this rig accounted for zander up to 9lb on Woburn and Claydon Lakes. It is in favour again for specimen hunting with small deadbaits such as rudd, gudgeon and eel portion.

Fish strips

Roach and bream are just as good as deadbaits, but small strips are perhaps better than whole fish. Although zander occasionally fall to sea fish like herrings, sardines and sprats, they do not like them as much as they do coarse deadbaits.

As with most species, zander takes vary a lot. One of my big zander merely held the float 2in below the surface and continued to do so until I hit it hard. Others twitch away for minutes on end, but a strike produces nothing. A third kind of bite results in a searing run

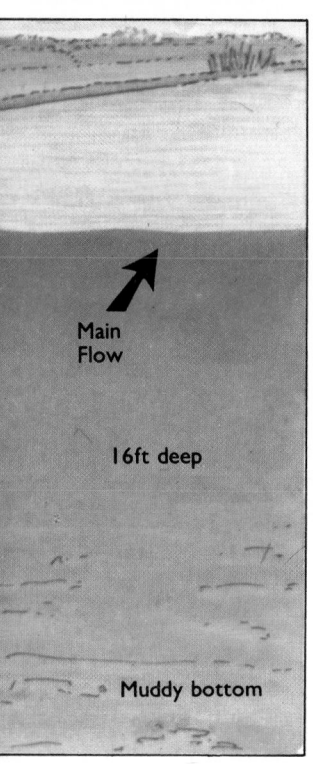

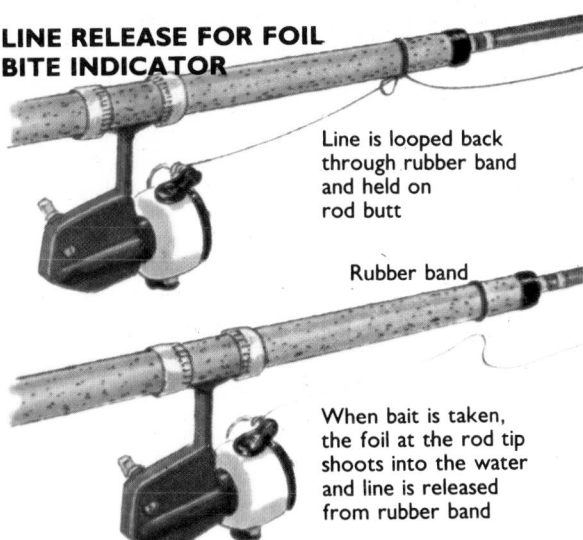

LINE RELEASE FOR FOIL BITE INDICATOR

Line is looped back through rubber band and held on rod butt

Rubber band

When bait is taken, the foil at the rod tip shoots into the water and line is released from rubber band

Main Flow

16ft deep

Muddy bottom

Above left: *Barrie Rickard's spotlighted swim on the Great Ouse. Confluences are always rich in potential.*
Above: *Where there is flow or drag, bites are best shown by a piece of tin foil on the line near the rod tip.*
Left: *Shallow laybys are frequent haunts of zander in times of flood when fry shoal there out of the main flow.*

that bounces the rod in the rest. It is impossible to generalize about strike timing, but strike technique is another matter. I always put on the pick-up, wind up until I feel the fish, and then strike as quickly as I can. The fight is not worth mentioning, and unhooking is exactly the same as for pike, except the zander's jaws are much stronger.

Barry Rickards' Spotlight

Because of modern drainage practice, most zander swims—in both drains and rivers—tend to look much the same. They are all more or less straight and featureless, although some are deeper than others. In most cases it is like fishing a long bath!

But one exception is a favourite swim of mine on the Great Ouse. Here I fish from a spot which projects against the usual flow of the river, with a shallow sidearm going across in front of me and to my right and with the main river passing to my left. The divergence of the two streams creates an eddy in the sidearm whose strength depends on the speed and direction of flow of the main river.

Occasionally the flow of the Great Ouse is reversed so that it flows in a normally upstream direction. On these occasions, I am able to cast my float paternoster rig to B and allow it to work to A. But normally I cast to A and work very slowly back to B, taking perhaps $\frac{1}{2}$ hour over a 25-yard cast. All the time the bait is held near a gravel lip in front of my fishing position, the lead being on the main-river side of this lip.

Takes usually run out into the main river and across the dense weedbeds at the foot of the lip. The zander come out of the weeds up to the lip, then turn away across the river. The lead itself may catch the

weedbed during the run, so that a ledger link as weak as 3lb b.s. may be advisable. Often the lead is lost, so I use a small nut rather than a proper lead.

When the river is in flood, zander move into the sidearm and hide in the cabbages. So, I shallow the tackle a little, use a long paternoster link, and let the rig search slowly around the area C on the sidearm edge of the lip. The main river can be quite unfishable during floods, but takes in the sidearm are often good. The fish rarely run into the main river but go up the sidearm, towards the spot marked D. Usually I strike long before they get there, but if I get an odd jerky run, caused by a zander around 1lb, I leave it to develop awhile. These small fish either stop at D and drop the bait, or turn at high speed and make a strikeable run to the right.

Whether zander are hooked in the sidearm or in the main river, they rarely go for the weed or cabbage clumps, but always fight in open water. Fortunately, they prefer open water by day—perhaps because of their poor daytime vision. If they did go for the many snags, the angler would have great difficulty in stopping them, particularly if they used the currents. Once hooked,

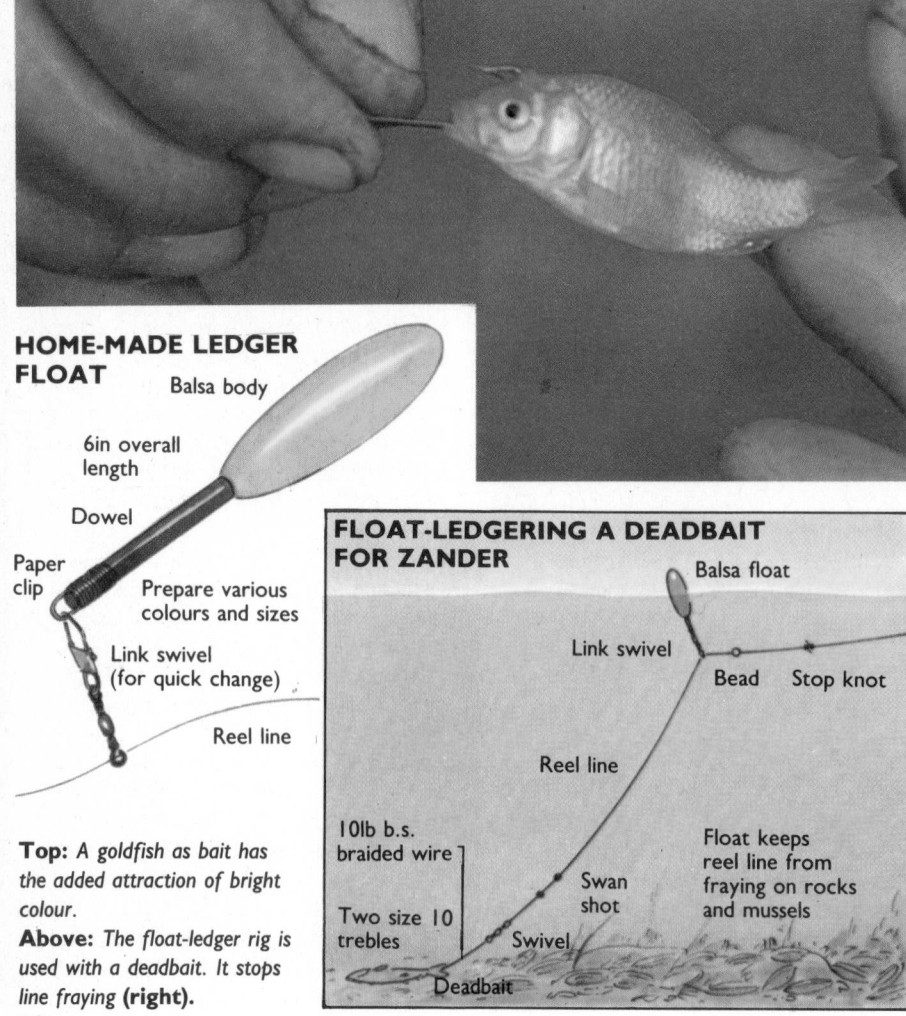

HOME-MADE LEDGER FLOAT

Balsa body

6in overall length

Dowel

Paper clip

Prepare various colours and sizes

Link swivel (for quick change)

Reel line

Top: *A goldfish as bait has the added attraction of bright colour.*

Above: *The float-ledger rig is used with a deadbait. It stops line fraying (right).*

FLOAT-LEDGERING A DEADBAIT FOR ZANDER

Balsa float

Link swivel

Bead   Stop knot

Reel line

10lb b.s. braided wire

Two size 10 trebles

Float keeps reel line from fraying on rocks and mussels

Swan shot

Swivel

Deadbait

Above: *The former holder of the zander record, Bill Chillingworth, fishing on the Great Ouse Relief Channel in the Fen Country, a long established zander water.*

they are usually netted. Because the water pushes towards the angler, they can be backed over a waiting net without seeing it.

Neville Fickling Writes
Though the zander is spreading farther and farther afield every year, the number of waters which have a stock of specimens are few. It takes eight or nine years for a zander to reach 10lb, so one's choice of water is limited to those which have had zander for at least that period. In time, more and more waters will support specimens. A few unsung rivers may have one or two very big fish—the early colonists from adjoining water—but the chances of contacting these fish are remote.

The zander specimen hunter chooses a water with a long history of zander, such as the Great Ouse Relief Channel or the adjoining Cut-Off Channel. Other Fenland waters worthy of attention include the Great Ouse, the Delph, the Sixteen Foot and Middle Level, the Wissey, the Old and New Bedford Drains and Roswell Pits, near Ely. Outside this area, a number of pits in Bedfordshire may have specimen zander, while the lakes at Woburn and Claydon are certainly worth a visit. A few waters in Yorkshire and

Warwickshire also hold zander. Nearer London, Old Bury Hill Lake, near Dorking, contains zander and these may reach specimen weights in the near future.

Elusive species
Zander very seldom show themselves. They do not frequent shallow water or feed near the surface, except at night or during floods. The angler has to get to grips with his quarry by indirect means. On a featureless piece of water such as a Fen Drain it pays to select a stretch —between two bridges, say—and get to know that piece of water. Fish it systematically, noting any variations in depth. On calm, sunny, summer evenings a walk along the bank will show where the zander's small food fish are most numerous. These areas should be tried, along with any where drains enter the main channel.

While fishing, the angler may encounter beds of zebra mussels anywhere from the marginal shelf to the middle. These may attract zander but the heavy tackle losses caused by the sharp shells may

ASK THE EXPERT

When are the best times to fish for specimen zander?
The hour before first light and the hour after sunset are usually the most productive, but zander will feed all through the night, putting in an appearance from time to time in short bursts of frenzied activity.

Why do I miss so many takes when I use deadbaits on a single hook?
There are two simple answers to this problem. Either delay your strike so that the fish has completely gorged the bait, or use two sets of treble hooks, mounted as 'snap tackle'.

Does the zander put up a fight?
Strangely enough, a zander is one of the poorest, pound for pound, of all our freshwater fish when it comes to fighting an angler.

Wouldn't it be more sportsmanlike to fish fine?
It would if it were not for the likelihood of hooking a large pike in your efforts to catch a zander. No sportsman could be in favour of a pike breaking free and swimming off with a mouthful of hook and fine line.

Is it true that I can catch zander while a river is in flood?
This is one of the best times to seek out quality zander. They are unlike other species in that the dirty water stimulates them to hunt, and if you can find a secluded backwater you are almost certain to strike lucky.

Where, in a gravel pit, should I begin to look for zander?
If there are islands dotted around, the channels between them will produce a catch or two. Channels linking one pit to another are also reliable hotspots.

107

prove prohibitive. Zander will probably be encountered all along a stretch of drain. On some waters there is no easily discernible consistency, but on others a pattern emerges, showing that the larger-than-average zander frequent a certain area. Once a good area has been found, it pays to stay with it, for packs of zander will constantly be moving in and out. The angler should not chase about from one spot to another.

Holed-up by day
Large stillwaters, such as Roswell Pits, where bank fishing is very limited, call for a boat. Zander are likely to hole up in areas of deep water during the day. But the bank angler can still catch specimens, provided he fishes at a point on the zanders' regular patrol route. Good swims are found where two pieces of water are connected by a narrow channel, and between islands, but the water in the gap must be deep.

It is possible to catch big zander at any time of the year, but once the water temperature drops below 5°C, the chances are remote.

June and July provide first-class zander sport on many waters. The small food fish will be scarce after the winter and will not reach an edible size. The zander may then become preoccupied during high summer with the multitudes of fry. This can make August, especially, a slow month. Traditional zander months are September and October, when many big fish are caught. The shortening days also make it possible to fish throughout daylight hours without undue strain.

Feeding periods, noted on the Relief Channel during the summer of 1978, differed from those of the year before. It is essential therefore to consider each new season with an open mind. If unable to glean more detailed knowledge from repeated trips, fish at dawn, dusk and night.

Large zander, in particular, are greatly influenced by the weather, by the interaction of light, wind and temperature. Their effects differ, according to whether the fish are actively hunting for food, or simply resident in one area nibbling at anything that strays into sight.

The very worst weather, with

strong winds whipping the water to a foam and colouring it cocoa-brown, brings out the best zander. Brisk winds and clear sky, with lots of sunshine, encourage zander packs to move about the water, giving the angler a chance of contacting all sizes. Luck plays a very big part in these conditions, as the angler can do nothing to select a big fish out of a pack hunting through his swim.

Zander packs, however, usually comprise similar-sized fish, the biggest packs frequently being made up of 3-4lb fish. The largest often tag on behind, but mingle with the pack when large numbers converge on big fry shoals.

There is no reason to feel deterred even on a hot, sunny day with no wind. Somewhere, a semi-static pack of zander will be willing to feed. Once located, the swim may produce large numbers of bites as long as the angler is prepared to work hard and try a number of swims. The popular technique of 'leapfrogging' rods

Left: *John Watson with a 13lb zander he took from the Great Ouse using a ledgered deadbait.*

along the bank can pay off under these conditions.

One of the most frustrating problems facing the zander specimen hunter is how to sort the big zander from the small ones. The basic rigs described in part 52 will catch zander of all sizes. How can the specimen hunter improve his chances of a big one?

By increasing the size of the live or deadbait to as much as $\frac{1}{2}$lb it is certainly possible to eliminate many of the smaller fish. But the attendant problems are many. Small zander make abortive runs on large bait. Fewer runs are experienced. Finally, when a big zander does take, it is less easily hooked and more easily lost on a larger bait.

Blanket coverage

Most serious specimen hunters have opted for small or medium-sized baits, on the principle that bigger fish will come every so often if methods are geared towards catching as many zander as possible.

Any type of coarse fish can be used for live or deadbait, whole or halved. Larger fish baits can be cut up into strips or chunks. The most commonly used are roach, rudd, dace, bream and eel portions. Few small zander seem willing to tackle a 4-6oz live perch; larger zander are not worried by the spines.

Sustaining interest

Seafish such as herrings, sprats and mackerel make poor baits, although they have taken a few specimens, so it is always worth experimenting. At the end of a successful day it is a good idea to chop up the remaining deadbaits and catapult them out into the swim. It may help to keep the zander interested—useful if you plan to return the next day.

Freshly killed deadbaits are not always easily come by. Though somewhat soft on thawing, frozen freshwater baits catch plenty of zander. With soft baits it pays to thread them on to a large single hook with a baiting needle or, when using trebles, to tie the hooks to the bait in the region of the tail. Long casts are then possible without losing the bait, which will often be recovered on landing the zander.

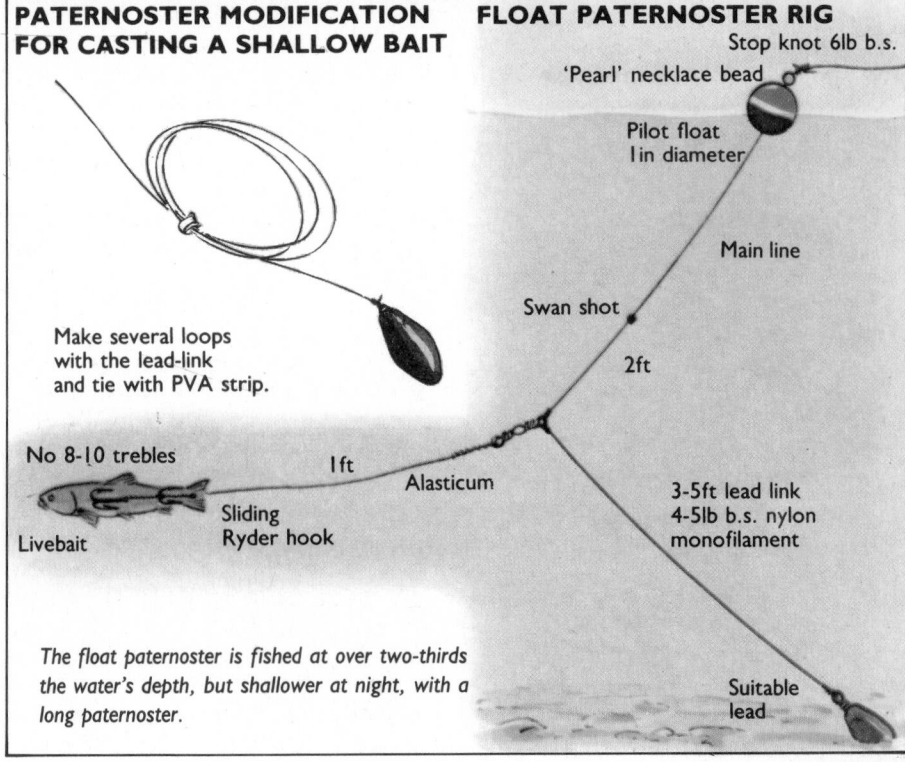

PATERNOSTER MODIFICATION FOR CASTING A SHALLOW BAIT

Make several loops with the lead-link and tie with PVA strip.

No 8-10 trebles

Livebait

1ft

Sliding Ryder hook

Alasticum

FLOAT PATERNOSTER RIG

Stop knot 6lb b.s.

'Pearl' necklace bead

Pilot float 1in diameter

Main line

Swan shot

2ft

3-5ft lead link 4-5lb b.s. nylon monofilament

Suitable lead

The float paternoster is fished at over two-thirds the water's depth, but shallower at night, with a long paternoster.

Above: *Fenland drains such as this can hold an excellent head of zander. The angler here is spinning. Although this is a perfectly valid technique, it does not account for as many specimen fish as ledgering does.*

Left: *Gordon Burton in the very act of subduing a 9lb 12oz zander on the Fenland Delph.*

There are times when zander give long, fast runs, swallowing the bait quickly. On these days, resistance from floats and leads is largely ignored. At other times they tend to be very finicky and only the most sensitive methods will produce fish. Leads and floats should be as small as possible.

Where no flow or drag occurs, small dolly-type indicators can be fixed to the line between the open reel spool and butt ring. These drop off, quickly offering the minimum resistance. Where there *is* flow or drag, a small square of kitchen foil can be attached to the line in front of the rod tip. The reel line is then tucked lightly under an elastic band on the butt. A run is indicated by the foil shooting off into the water. In extreme conditions of flow there may be no alternative but to slacken the clutch on the fixed-spool reel and watch the rod tip for the initial taps which signal a zander run.

If a lot of runs are being missed even with the most sensitive set-up, the culprits are probably small zander. The best solution is to move to another swim, for a shoal of tiny zander will soon strip hooks without getting caught.

With small treble hooks on a small bait, most zander will be hooked if struck instantly. When using a single hook it pays to wait a while to let the zander swallow the bait. A barbless hook helps, for a lot of fish are deep hooked on single hooks.

Sometimes the rivers and drains become so swollen with rain that they take on a dirty brown colour. Old trees, dead weed and all the refuse associated with farming are pushed down. This should not deter the zander specimen hunter, provided the weather is mild and the water is not the product of melting snow.

Strong flows and suspended rubbish cause problems of presentation. Tackle is quickly dragged from posi-tion, so it is necessary to fish more crudely than one would normally do. Floats need to be larger and leads may weigh anything up to 2oz. But during floods big zander do not seem put out by heavy tackle, and a large lively livebait can pay off. The vibra-tion and flash of a living fish attract the zander much quicker than a ledgered deadbait.

It has become the fashion for several years to kill big zander. The reasons vary from plain ignorance to a hatred of the species. Specimens can fight very strongly, but, unfor-tunately, this tends to weaken them, so their return to the water must be as quick as possible. Hold the fish upright facing any current until it recovers and swims off.

Zander do not like keepnets and it is inadvisable to confine numbers together. They should be released a few yards from where you are fishing. Keep a big fish only long enough to photograph.

Eel

The eel was once thought to spawn 'in the entrails of the earth'. That myth has been disproved, but mystery still surrounds the eel's life-cycle

The eel (*Anguilla anguilla*) has a long thin body which is particularly slimy, giving rise to the saying 'as slippery as an eel'. The protruding lower jaw is noticeably longer than the upper, the pectoral fins are small and rounded, and the dorsal, anal and tail fins are joined together. It has no ventral fin, and the body is covered with minute scales, unlike the conger, which is scaleless. It grows to a maximum length of 54in (137cm) and it can be as heavy as 20lb (9kg).

Bone and muscle structure
It was once believed that there were at least four different species of European eel—long-nosed and short-nosed eels, the frog-mouthed eel and the bull-headed eel. Leading authorities categorized them according to distinct physical differences. In 1896, however, it was shown that the bone and muscle structures were similar in each type and that physical differences were due only to age, sex, and stage of development. Now, all European eels are regarded as belonging to a single species.

An air of mystery has always surrounded the eel. This is because its origins and mating habits were, for a long time, not understood. As early as 350BC, Aristotle noted with surprise its apparent lack of seminal fluid or eggs. Seemingly devoid of a reproductive system, the eel was thought to come directly from 'the entrails of the earth'.

Knowledge of the eel was gradually built up until in the late 19th century the larva *Leptocephalus brevirostris* was identified as that of the eel. Previously, this had been

thought to be a separate species, while the origins of the eel itself had been unknown.

The little leptocephalid, a leaf-shaped creature only 3in long, was, after much research, found to originate in the Sargasso Sea, off Bermuda, from where all eels inhabiting European waters travel.

The life-cycle of the eel is complicated. Hatched at about 1,600ft (500m) below the surface in the Sargasso Sea, the leptocephalid rises to the surface, where it is carried in vast numbers by oceanic currents towards the European Continental Shelf. During the three-year journey it develops and attains a size of about 3in by the time it reaches the European coasts. Here it finally assumes the shape of the elver or young eel we know. It then enters rivers and streams from the Baltic and Scandinavian coasts to the Mediterranean coasts and as far south as Madeira and the coasts of North Africa.

'Eel-fare'
The elver 'run' or 'eel-fare' takes place at different times in different countries, according to the distances travelled by the larvae. In the Baltic and the North Sea it is between March and April; in the Mediterranean it is between October and December.

Eels work their way far inland from the sea, even travelling overland on damp, moonless nights. This 4lb adult eel was taken from a Lancashire brick pit.

Having entered the estuary, the elvers run up river. Many thousands leave the water and travel overland from ditch to ditch, entering lakes, ponds and watercourses totally unconnected with the sea. The elvers travel by night, either in the darker, deeper waters or overland on moonless damp nights during heavy rains, when a heavy dew enables them to remain moist enough to survive. They also take advantage of autumn floods.

The elvers have now become yellow eels, and spend between eight and 18 years in freshwater, feeding on crustaceans, insects, molluscs and fish. They are slow growers, and it is estimated that an eel of 12-15in (30-40cm) is roughly seven to eight years old. Growth rates vary enormously from place to place, the females growing more swiftly than the males and reaching greater ages.

Maturity

When the eels are sexually mature they take on a silver hue in preparation for their return to the sea. The silver eels begin to move seaward in the autumn, travelling overland as the need arises, and moving mostly at night. Finally, they enter the sea for the final journey across several thousands of miles of the Atlantic Ocean. Their bodies then adapt for the oceanic voyage. The eye enlarges, the gut atrophies, the jaws weaken, and the gonads greatly increase in size.

Previously, it took the eels three years to arrive as leptocephalids, carried largely by currents. Now they must combat the same currents. It is not known how long the journey takes, or indeed whether these eels ever succeeded in spawning. Some authorities consider that the migrating European eels never reach their spawning grounds. They hold the view that the progeny of American mature eels, spawned in the same place, are carried by the currents to renew the contingents of European eels. Other authorities believe that sufficient numbers of the European returners succeed in spawning and so maintain the species. There is still no definite answer to this question.

LEDGER RIG FOR EEL FISHING

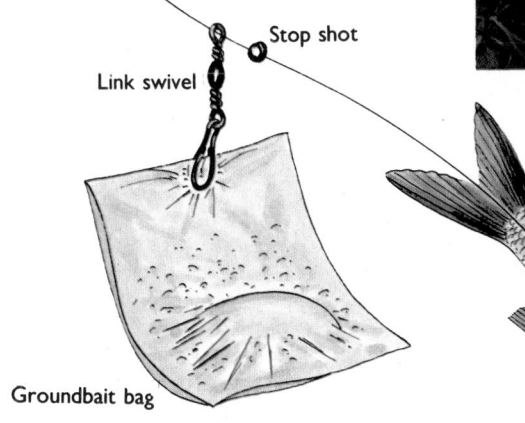

Stop shot

Link swivel

Groundbait bag

Barleycorn lead inside fish

No 4 carp hook

Top right: *Basic tackle for eel fishing: a wire trace, ledger weight and lobworms.*
Above: *Variation on a theme: ledgered deadbait. The paper falls apart quickly in the water to release the contents.*

ASK THE EXPERT

Should a landing net be used for eels?
Unless your lines are very fine and the eel very big, it's better to swing the eel straight on to the bank. This prevents it coiling itself round the line or tangling in the net. Drop it on to newspaper which, for some reason, usually quietens it for long enough to cut the line above the hook.

Ought small eels to be returned alive?
If they are lightly lip-hooked and you don't want to eat them, yes. But the hook is usually well down the throat and is virtually impossible to remove without damaging the gills. The fish is unlikely to survive and it is better to kill it quickly and humanely. Cut the backbone behind the head or close to the tail.

Must eels be skinned before cooking them?
All the best cookery books recommend it, but if you buy live eels from the fish shop they aren't skinned and few housewives bother. Eel scales are minute and embedded: you won't be aware of them when eating it.

Is eel blood poisonous?
It can cause inflammation if it gets into cuts or abrasions when fresh. Cover any cuts before you start fishing and wash after handling an eel. The blood isn't poisonous when cooked.

Why are eels sometimes seen as vermin?
In trout and salmon waters they eat fish spawn and can affect stocks. Waters like this are often electrically fished or netted. On match sites eels are usually welcome as they count towards winning catches.

Capacity to survive

Perhaps the most surprising characteristic of eels is their capacity to survive out of water for long periods. Anglers know that carp and tench can survive for an hour or two when kept in damp grass, but the eel surpasses them. This is largely due to the structure of the gills. Most fish gills collapse when out of water, but those of the eel are rigid enough for the gill plates or laminae to remain largely separated when out of water, and this enables direct gas exchange to take place. Provided the eel is cool and damp, it can survive for up to 10 hours out of water. This characteristic has always been of commercial importance, since it enables eels to be transported alive and fresh.

Any angler grasping his catch is soon aware of the copious layer of slime which covers the eel. It is of vital importance, providing a barrier which helps make the eel watertight. It may seem strange that a creature spending its life in water should need to be watertight, but fish like lampreys, salmon, and eels, which migrate from sea water to fresh,

or vice versa, depend on such mechanisms to survive.

When eels are in the sea, water losses due to osmosis occur through the gills and to a lesser extent through the skin. To replace these losses, sea fishes drink considerable amounts of water and this further raises the salt content of the blood and lymphatic systems. Excess salt is therefore removed through the gills, maintaining the osmotic pressure at a balance consistent with the sea water in which they are living.

This balance is upset when the elvers enter the estuary, for they are in a condition in which their body fluids are saltier than the

freshwater. The osmotic process is then reversed and water enters through the gills and skin. To counter the excess amount of water in the body, and to maintain a balance, the kidneys have to expel large amounts of diluted urine.

Later, when the eel leaves the freshwater system on its return journey, a reverse process again occurs. In fact, estuarine eels need to be more slimy than river eels, so that the slime acts as a barrier to losses through the skin.

The specimen hunter hopes for large female eels, which grow to far greater sizes than the males. The current record (rod-caught) is a fish of 11lb 2oz. The record is low considering the sizes eels are known to attain. Tate Regan mentions an eel of 10lb, and one of 20lb was reported taken near Norwich in 1893. According to the reporter of this catch, the biggest eels are to be taken in lakes and dykes of the Norfolk Broads, and in the extensive Lincolnshire dykes and drains.

Anglers generally agree that still and sluggish waters, preferably predominantly muddy and highly

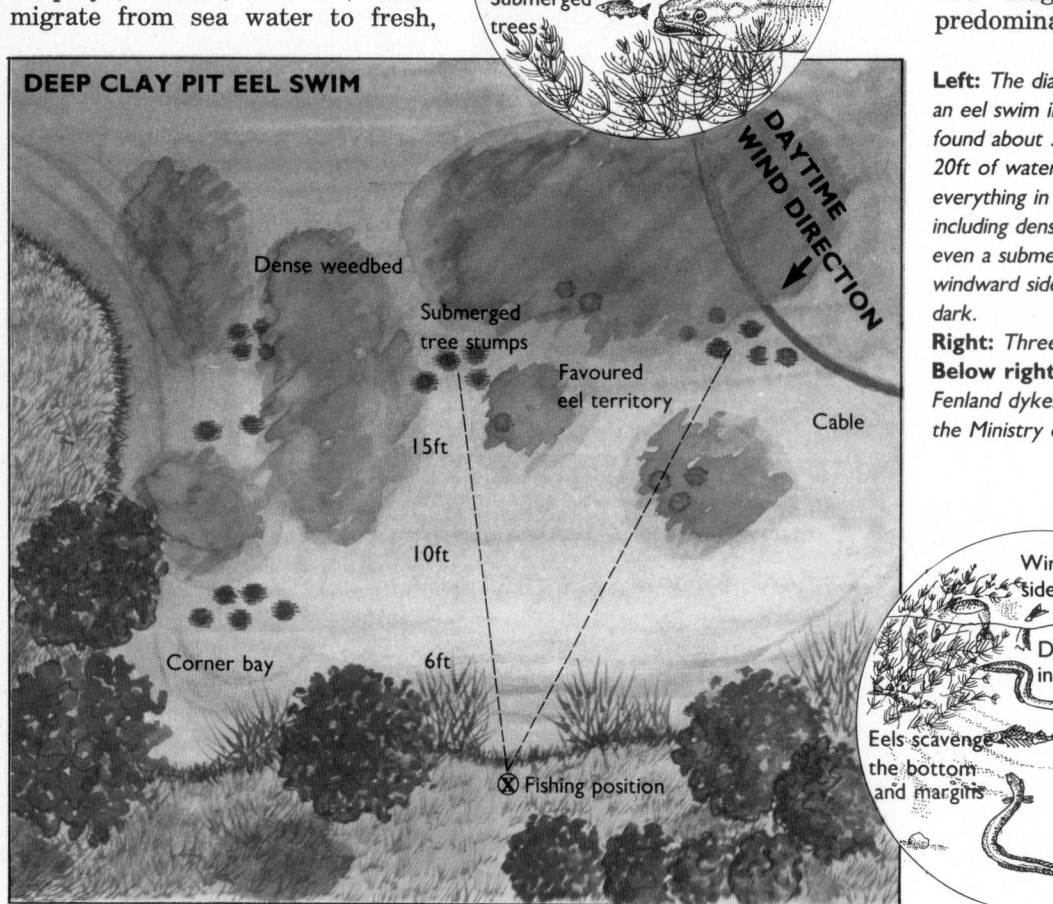

DEEP CLAY PIT EEL SWIM

Dense weedbed

Submerged tree stumps

Favoured eel territory

Cable

15ft

10ft

6ft

Corner bay

Ⓧ Fishing position

DAYTIME WIND DIRECTION

Dense weedbed

Submerged trees

Windward side of lake

Dead fish drift into margins

Eels scavenge the bottom and margins

Discarded ground bait

Left: *The diagram shows a typical example of an eel swim in a deep clay pit. Eels will be found about 30 yards from the bank in about 20ft of water. The swim has almost everything in terms of cover or refuge, including dense weedbeds, sunken trees and even a submerged cable. The margins on the windward side will be profitable for eels after dark.*
Right: *Three mature eels.*
Below right: *Eel netting is widespread in all Fenland dykes and drains with the support of the Ministry of Agriculture.*

coloured, produce the best eels. Muddy estuaries are good places for large catches, and the best time for fishing is after dark when the eels are on the move, which is when they are feeding in earnest.

Traditionally, eels have a reputation for damaging game fishing by eating vast amounts of game fish spawn. Water Authority officials spend a great deal of time electrically catching eels on the trout fisheries for it is certain that the eel competes with salmon and trout for food. Whether it damages future stocks is open to conjecture.

Fishing for eels

Certainly, the eel specialist knows that eels will eat almost anything of animal origin, live or dead. A favourite bait for the rod is a dead fish. The countryman seeking eels will often leave a sack of rabbit guts overnight in the river and find eels in the morning.

Tackle needs to be tough—lines of up to 15lb b.s. are not too heavy if the bait and place are right. The rod should be powerful enough to hold a strong fish hard, because once given its head, the eel will invariably seek refuge in submerged roots, which defeat the best lines. A dead dace or roach is used for bait, but a mackerel slice would do as well, depending on the area fished. Long shanked hooks are preferable because premature striking loses fish and the eel gets the bait well into its throat with a longer hook.

Killing an eel

Once the eel is landed, the best expedient is to cut the line and start again with a fresh hook. The catch is kept in a large damp sack. To kill the eel it is necessary to cut through the vertebral column, usually near the tail, or to cut its head off. Nevertheless, the sack is still needed since the nervous system operates for some time after death, and many an angler will tell of an eel which slithered back into the water minus its head.

Commercial eel fisheries are big business, especially in Holland. In Britain fixed traps are set up every year with the support of the Ministry of Agriculture.

FISHING TECHNIQUE

When it's light enough to spot big eels, it's too light for eels to be about. But if you solve the problem of finding a specimen water, there are a variety of ways of catching its occupants

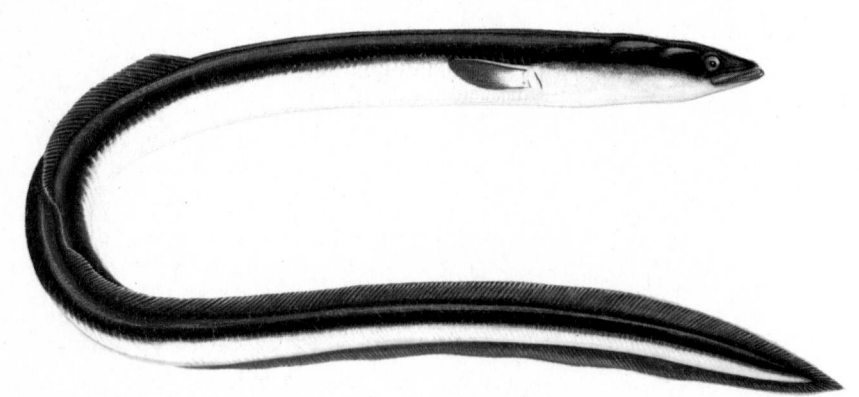

For many years knowing anglers have suggested that the long-standing 8lb 10oz record held by Alan Dust was not really representative of the growth potential of the eel. This belief was substantiated in 1978 by the 'surprise' new record eel of 11lb 2oz caught by Stephen Terry from Kingfisher Lake in Hampshire.

This will be an exceedingly difficult record to beat, even though there is little doubt that bigger eels exist: a 20-pounder is certainly within the realms of possibility.

It is much more difficult to single out waters that do *not* hold eels than it is to find water that do. Nearly every stretch of river, canals, lake, gravel-pit, and even the tiniest village pond will have, with certainty, an eel population.

The ideal training ground

If you are happy to catch quantities of medium-sized eels, say from 1lb to 3½lb, your best bet will be to concentrate on slow rivers, drains and canals. Slow rivers such as the Great Ouse and the Fen Drains have a big eel population, and such waters provide an ideal training-ground for the angler who eventually intends to hunt the really big ones. When I was in my teens I certainly spent quite a number of exciting and invaluable nights catching eels on the river Ouse at places like St Neot's, Offord and Little Paxton.

The search for big-eel waters

Finding a big-eel water where there is a chance of fish of 4lb upwards is more difficult, and searching out a water with record-breaking potential is a virtual impossibility—unless of course you *know* they are in there. The reason is that they hardly ever show themselves, for eels are very sensitive to light. They are also extremely sensitive to vibrations from the bankside and there is no doubt that they can detect these from a great distance. If you have serious intentions of catching a big eel you must have a contant awareness of these two factors.

In all the hundreds—if not thousands—of hours I have spent fish-watching, there are only a few occasions when I have been able to watch eels in their natural habitat. So going eel-spotting in the late close season as the carp or tench angler does is just not on: you will not see any!

The secret of success

I cannot over-emphasize the importance that leg-work and research play in the eventual downfall of a big fish. The only sure way of locating a big-eel water is to find one that has produced good fish consistently for a few years. By consistently I mean half a dozen fish of 5lb-plus in a season, but even two or three such fish should be a good indicator of

excellent prospects.

Nevertheless, catching several medium-sized eels does not guarantee a specimen. The greatest difficulty in pinning-down a big-eel water is that a high percentage of really big specimens are taken completely out of the blue from waters without a big-eel history. The new record eel comes into this category. Why are big eels caught so rarely? First, big eels feed infrequently and you need a great deal of time. Second, they are extremely powerful and ruthless fish when hooked, so when he finds himself struggling with one by accident the inexperienced angler does not stand a chance. There is little doubt that rivers carry the largest head of eels.

Roach

Seasonal changes in the roach's food, habitat and inclination to feed thwart the unimaginative angler whose tackle, station and techniques remain unaltered all season long

Roach are very often the first species encountered by the young fisherman, but the fun of catching them grows over the years as he progresses from boggle-eyed, stunted tiddlers packed into farm ponds to those deep-sided 2lb roach with scarlet fins and silvery blue flanks —the roach fisher's ultimate goal.

Such fish, however, are usually found only in rich waters, their size determined by the environment. 'Reading a water' is therefore the key to successful roaching, whether you desire quantity or quality.

One of the most important factors is water temperature. During the summer, roach move through upper water layers and take food from the surface—they may even be caught on a dry fly. But during the winter they are loath to move more than a few inches from the bottom to intercept a bait.

Below: *A self-confident roach fisherman brings a nice specimen to net without so much as standing up.*

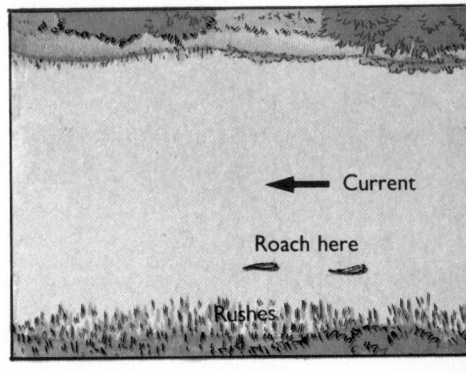

Below: *Where the current is moderately fast, the link swivel ledger will get your bait to the fish when float-fishing fails.*

Current

Roach here

Rushes

LINK SWIVEL LEDGER

Link swiv

Loop in end
of hook trace

Also important is water colour. In bright conditions and with clear water, even the finest tackle is quite visible. You must then be ultra-cautious, be as quiet as possible, and use bankside shrubbery to cam-ouflage your silhouette. Being a shoaling fish, the roach is highly sensitive to alien vibrations, surface shadows, or anything suspicious. One frightened fish can easily lead the shoal out of the swim or make them disinclined to feed. Therefore the best roaching, particularly for larger, wiser specimens, is done in coloured water, at dusk and dawn.

Tackle for roach fishing

Despite the wide variety of condi-tions and waters in which roach are found, two rods suffice: a 12-13ft match rod and a 9ft ledger rod with a threaded tip ring for a swingtip or quivertip. The reel can be either a fixed-spool with a sensitive clutch for light lines, or a free-running cen-trepin. The former is probably better because long and accurate casting is sometimes called for. Two spools are needed, one with 2lb b.s. line for float fishing, the other with 3-4lb line for ledgering.

Alternatively, of course, you may decide to do away with a rod altogether and use a roach pole. In recent years their standing has

Above: *Roach fishing on light float tackle.*
Below: *A river angler prepares to ledger a swimfeeder under the far bank. See rig above.*

Above far right: *A 74½lb mixed bag made up mostly of roach from Colebrook River, County Fermanagh.*

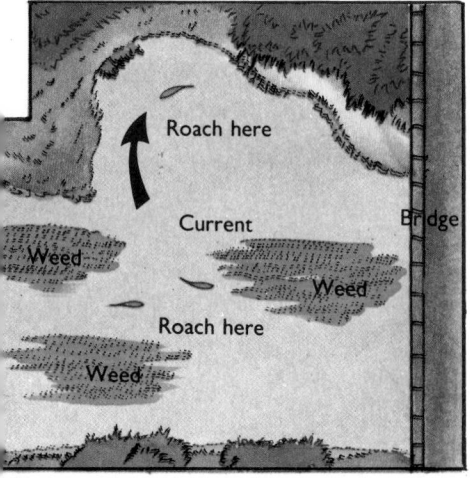

Roach here

Current

Bridge

Weed

Weed

Roach here

Weed

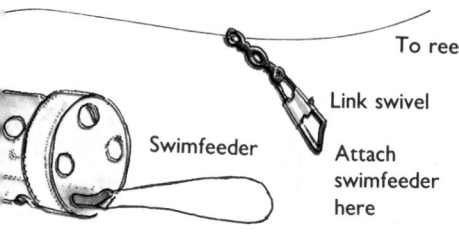

To reel

Link swivel

Swimfeeder

Attach
swimfeeder
here

grown steadily, for they present a bait very precisely. They are highly effective but nevertheless most roach anglers still prefer rod and line.

A sensible range of floats
Do not collect hundreds of beautiful, different patterned floats, because you will not know whether your float is wrong or your method of fishing, although nearly always it will be the latter. A sensible range would be a set of four stick floats, carrying shot from 1BB to 5BB, for trotting in slow to medium-fast swims; a set of Avons, also for trotting, but taking shots ranging from 4BB to three swan and used to combat much faster, even turbulent water; a set of zoomers or antenna floats, with shotting ranging from 2BB to 4AA for sensitive presentation in still-waters; and a few Canal Greys for ultra-sensitive work.

As far as hooks are concerned, round-bends take a lot of beating. For large baits, such as worms and breadflake, use eyed hooks from No 10 to No 6, and tie them directly on to the line. For small baits, where neatness of presentation is essential, spade ends are better. These can be tied either direct or to a hook length of 1-1½lb b.s. line when, for example, clear or very cold water deters

the roach from paying attention to hooks tied to thicker line because the bait behaves unnaturally.

A good selection of split shot is also required, plus an assortment of small swivels, Arlesey bombs, and open-ended and block-ended swimfeeders for fishing far out or in fast water. The easiest spots to catch roach are stillwater lakes, pits or farm ponds. On such waters, many different techniques can be tried until you have success.

The basic technique
On a small, well-coloured water in summer, for example, start off float fishing with a 2BB quill float, with ⅛in of the tip showing and a size 14 hook holding two maggots. Begin by fixing both shots 6in from the hook and set the float overdepth to lay the bait on the bottom. Then scatter a few maggots around the float every so often and you will soon have the roach feeding.

But if bites are not forthcoming, or they suddenly stop, the loose maggots may have been taken on the way down. So push the float down the line a little and slide one of the two shot up just beneath it. Fix the other shot about 2ft from the hook. Then cast out and watch carefully as the float cocks. If the bait is taken 'on the drop', the float

Left: *Hot weather, and the roach are feeding high in the water. There's a need for more caution in the angler's approach to the water, but the shoals may well be visible, and receptive even to such baits as dry fly.*
Above: *As a day's fishing progresses, roach shoals often move farther and farther out, so that by midday long-distance casting is called for.*
Right: *Forceps being used to remove the hook from a fine roach in the prime of condition. Specimens are rarely caught other than early or late and from murky, coloured water.*

will take longer to settle than it should. Alternatively, bites may come a few seconds later, and the float will slide under positively. In either case, strike at once.

In windy weather, or when fishing over some distance in large lakes or pits, an antenna float rather than a Canal Grey should be used. It may be fixed either by the bottom end only, or as a slider, which is really necessary when you are fishing in very deep swims.

To reduce wind disturbance, ensure the line is well sunk by over-casting and then winding the tackle back to the desired spot with the rod tip held beneath the surface. When this is done, you can then fish in the same way as for close-range fishing —although presenting loose feed or small balls of groundbait far out calls for both a catapult and skill.

Feeding the swim
Provided water temperatures are high, roach can be expected to feed at almost any depth. So if the swim goes dead, try varying the depth until bites materialize. Alternative-ly, try another bait—for example, sweetcorn, a couple of brandlings or breadflake. But always use feed sparingly and step up the rate only if bites are regular.

Overfeeding a roach shoal is probably the most common reason why bites stop. A deepish hole in a small, clear-water river may contain just a dozen or so roach. Although such fish may well be large, they will not consume vast quantities of food, so building up the swim for a lengthy session with lots of loose feed is not worthwhile.

Mobility and sensitive tackle
It is far better on small waters to be mobile and to use the sensitive freelining method. Use polarized sunglass to spot a shoal, then creep quietly upstream and, with just a No 8 hook holding a large piece of breadflake on the line, allow the current to trundle the bait down to the shoal. Watch the line where it enters the water if the water is not clear enough for you to actually see a fish suck the bait in. Sometimes the line will tighten quickly, the rod tip will even be pulled round, sometimes

there is just a mere slow 'pluck', and sometimes the line may even fall slack momentarily as a roach swims upstream with the bait. Whatever happens, strike quickly at any unnatural movement.

You will have trouble holding bottom in fast, deep holes, so for these pinch a swan shot 12in from the hook. Or in even fiercer conditions, such as when fishing weirpools, rig up a two or three swan shot link ledger or a running Arlesey bomb ledger and watch the rod top or quiver tip for bites.

In small rivers expect to take just one, or perhaps two, roach from a swim and then to move on to another—a delightful and very interesting method of roaching.

Conditions are different on medium-sized rivers, however, and these are best fished with a float. As you cannot see your quarry, you must use a plummet to obtain a fair idea of both the depth and the nature of the bottom. Search for any even-paced stretch with a clean gravel or silty bottom and consistent depth. Then set up a stick float carrying sufficient shot to allow the bait a natural passage.

Tiny hooks in cold water
In very cold water, put a tiny dust shot 12in from the hook and use smaller hook sizes, even as small as No 22, holding a single maggot or caster. You can expect only tiny bites, so shot the float well down and hit anything suspicious.

In the summer, however, bites are more positive, and larger baits can be used, particularly at dawn and dusk. Early in the morning, roach lie on the bottom, so the best method is to fish well overdepth and lay on with a large piece of breadflake, a crust cube, sweetcorn, or perhaps two grains of stewed wheat. As the day progresses, the fish tend to rise, so trotting with smaller baits becomes the preferred method. Maggots, casters, wheat, sweetcorn, and bait such as hempseed (or other seedbaits) and elderberry, can all be deadly. But bites can often be very quick, so slow them down by feeding sparingly, putting a large grain or an elderberry on the hook. Casters are particularly good, and often sort

out the better fish, but check after each cast that the inside has not been sucked out by an unseen bite.

Adjusting trotting tackle
Plan on the roach accepting the bait when it is just tripping bottom, and allow for the current when catapulting loose feed upstream. Fix the float top and bottom—then if you get no bites as the tackle trots through the swim unchecked, hold it back a little, allowing the bait to swing enticingly upwards. If roach only accept the bait when holding the float back, experiment with the shotting. Start off with two groups—one at mid-depth and a small shot 10in from the hook—and then space the lead out more evenly between float and hook.

On large, wide or fast rivers, you should change your tactics yet again. Ledgering is often the most productive method here. You can either watch the rod tip for bites or screw in a swingtip (or a quivertip in fast-flowing rivers).

Loose feed must be concentrated
Concentrate your loose feed by using a blockend feeder for strong currents or an open-ended feeder on medium to slow waters. These can be stopped 12in from the hook by a split shot, fished on a separate link via a pair of swivels, or even fixed paternoster-fashion. Try to place the tackle consistently into the same area so that a concentration of bait builds up.

Exciting ledgering
Ledgering is also useful on slow or stillwaters, particularly for larger fish which prefer the bottom. Baits can be large, such as a bunch of maggots or breadflake, and tackle should be kept to a minimum. Use just enough lead to reach the swim or to hold bottom, set the rod low to the water in two rests, pointing at the bait, and use a ledger bobbin clipped on the line between the butt and second rod ring to indicate bites. By using a luminous bobbin, you can fish that last hour of daylight and even later into darkness, when the biggest roach show up. A more exciting way of taking a specimen roach does not exist.

Fish senses

Without a complex system of sense organs fish would not be able to survive the rigours of their environment. But exactly how sophisticated this system is has only recently been revealed

Any animal that is not well adapted to its environment will not survive long either as an individual or as a species. The fish is finely tuned to its environment, but because its environment is one in which we can see little, hear poorly and smell not at all, it has taken a long time for us to begin to understand how well equipped a fish is.

How well can fish see? The fish eye is basically similar to that of man and other vertebrates. Beneath the outer surface (the cornea) which is often partly covered by a clear fatty eyelid to assist streamlining, the central part of the eye is occupied by a hard, clear, spherical lens. This lens is virtually optically perfect and transmits light without distortion on to the sensitive cells of the retina which lines the back of the eye.

In some fish, notably those which depend on sight for finding their food, such as the trout, the lens is not perfectly spherical but slightly oval. The lens can be moved backwards or forwards by special muscles, and its shape means that it has two focal lengths. The ability to move the lens rearwards means that it moves closer to the retina at the back of the eye, and this gives the fish its forward vision. A trout can,

therefore, focus at the same time on a distant object and one close by—seeing clearly the angler's waders and at the same time the fly in front of its nose.

Rods and cones

The retina contains light-sensitive cells of two types—rods and cones. The rods are more sensitive and respond to poor light, while the cones respond to bright illumination and are responsible for colour vision. Fishes active in daylight have retinae with more cones than rods, while those which live in the deep sea or are active at night have fewer cones. Pike, trout and the carp family are daylight feeders and have numerous cones in the retina. These enable them to see in colour and in conditions of full daylight. Eels and burbot, however, which are mainly dusk or night time feeders, are equipped with many rods in the retina. Trout, however, can see in the twilight, for their vision switches from cones to rods as the light fades. In poor light, young salmon have been observed to sink into deeper water, so that food is thrown into contrast against the brighter surface of the water, and then to watch and take items as small as

Left: *The lateral line conceals a tube that conveys a vast range of information to the brain.* **Inset above:** *Wrasse are thought to communicate by grinding their teeth.*

water fleas (Daphnia) with ease.

Because fish do not have visible ears, it was long assumed that they could not hear. In fact, their ears are sensitive enough for them to hear well, although different groups can perform better than others. In the carp family, which includes most of our freshwater fishes—roach, dace, chub, barbel and carp—we have one

Above: *Does muscle rustling account for the uniform behaviour of fish in a shoal?*
Inset above: *The gurnard—the tips of its pectoral fins are as sensitive as fingers.*

of the most sensitive groups of fishes. In this family the inner ear itself is elaborated in various ways. The sounds are transmitted to the inner ear by a chain of small bones called Weberian ossicles.

This capacity to hear sounds so well (the North American catfishes, *Ictaluridae*, can detect a range of vibrations up to 13,000 cycles per se-

cond) has been a major factor in the success of the large group of fishes, which includes the carp family, the characins, and the catfishes, which have colonized freshwaters. No doubt the turbid nature of most freshwaters, which are darkly coloured by plant plankton, silt or rotting vegetation, has meant that such fishes find it necessary to take advantage of their hearing ability.

Fish noises
Even without the swimbladder connection, which is a feature of the

carp family, other fishes can hear well. Many fish make noises by releasing small bubbles of gas, originating in the swimbladder, and schools of pilchard and herring can be detected in calm weather by the altered water surface where the bubbles burst. Others, such as wrasses, grind their teeth—and cod, haddock and gurnards use their swimbladders to amplify the noises that they make.

One can only assume that these noises are made to be heard by others of the same species. Even swimming produces noises of a characteristic type, and it is likely that schooling fish are assisted in keeping together as a shoal by the continual rustle produced by the muscles of the other fish. It has also been established that some sharks can detect these swimming noises. Tape recordings of a struggling fish speared by a diver have been played with success to attract sharks towards the sound source.

All fishes have a good sense of smell, but those with eyes developed for poor light tend to have more elaborate and sensitive nasal organs. Most fish have two nostrils, the front one being raised on a short tube, while the posterior one opens flat on the surface of the head in front of the eye. The front nostril leads into a nasal pit which has a rosette of deeply folded skin heavily laden with sense cells. The flow of water in the rosette carries odour particles over these cells, and out through the hind nostril.

The freshwater eel has particularly well-developed nasal organs with a long rosette, and experiments have proved that it is very sensitive to smells. At a dilution of only one part in ten thousand million million of water, pure organic substances can be detected when only two or three molecules of the substance are in the olfactory organs.

Other fishes, such as the carp, are possibly less sensitive, although not much so. There is little doubt that they can detect and avoid injurious or unpleasant substances such as those that cause pollution. Much of a salmon's movement, returning to its native stream to spawn, is believed to depend on its ability to detect

Fish senses

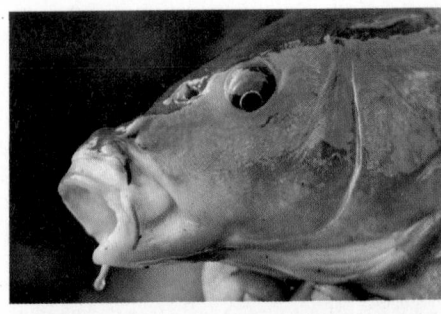

Below: Some of the main components of the nervous system of a barbel. The olfactory and optic lobes are parts of the brain which deal with smell and sight. The otolith and semicircular canals are parts of the internal ear.

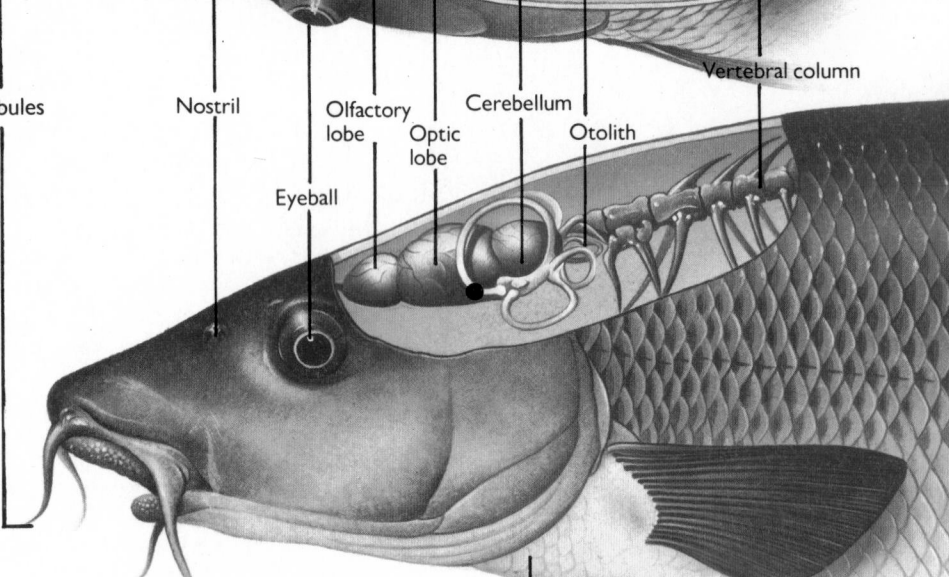

Semicircular canal ●

Barbules

Nostril

Olfactory lobe

Optic lobe

Eyeball

Cerebellum

Otolith

Vertebral column

Lateral line

Gills

NASAL SENSITIVITY

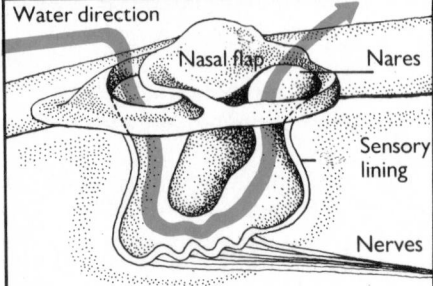

Water direction

Nasal flap

Nares

Sensory lining

Nerves

Key to lateral line canal diagrams

1 canal passage through scale
2 front end of scale
3 epidermis
4 lateral line canal
5 lateral line nerves
6 external opening of lateral line canal
7 rear end of scale
8 sense organ

SIDE VIEW OF SCALES AND LATERAL LINE CANAL

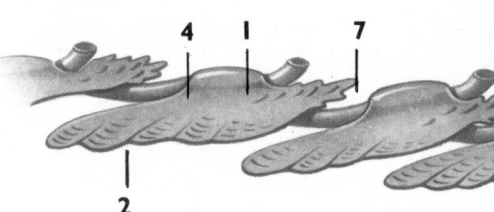

4   1   7

2

Left and above left: The barbules on the mouths of many fish serve a dual function as organs of taste and of touch. Those of the barbel are much more developed than those of the carp.
Above: The eyes of the grayling have distinctively elongated pupils.
Right: The eel has a very sensitive sense of smell, being able to detect substances in minute concentrations.

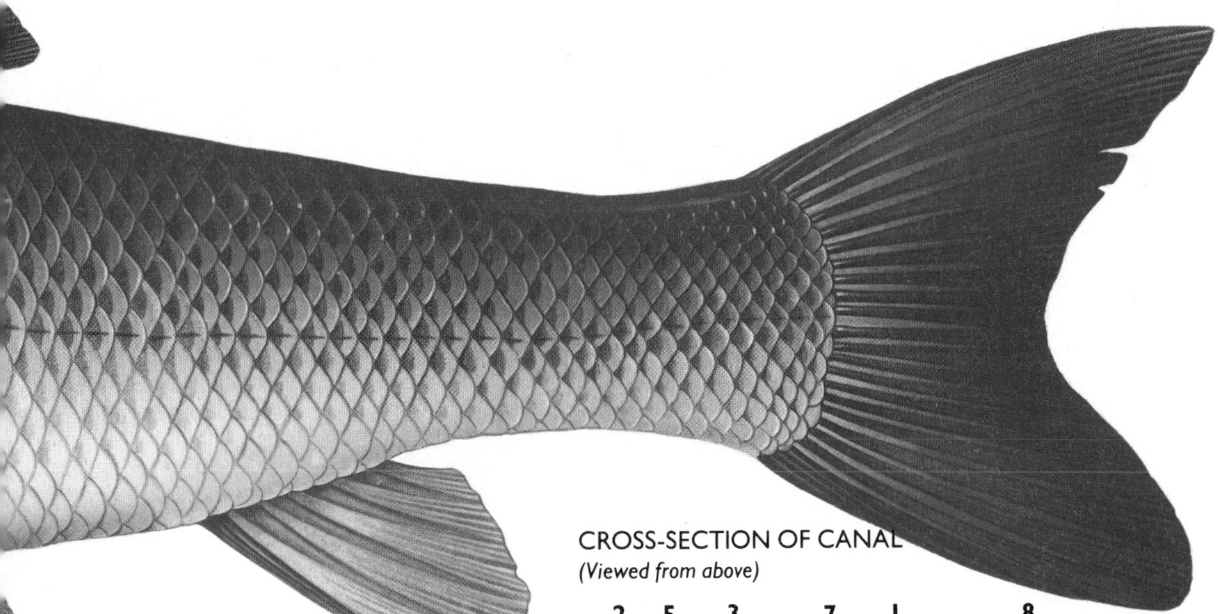

CROSS-SECTION OF CANAL
(Viewed from above)

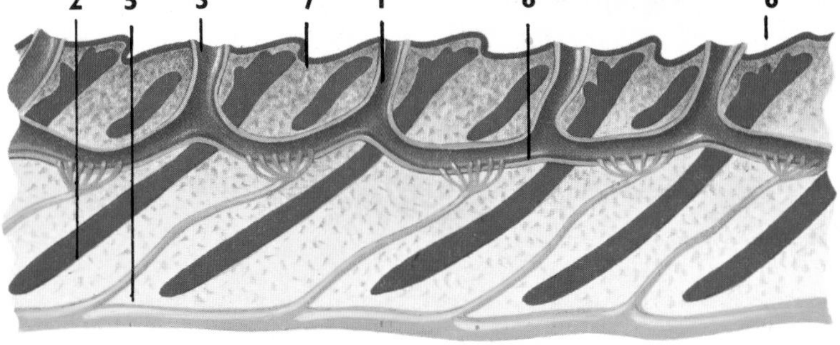

2 5 3 7 1 8 6

6

TYPICAL LATERAL LINE CANAL AND SCALES ARRANGEMENT
These two diagrams show how the lateral line canal of a fish opens on to its body surface, and contains sense organs which are connected to its central nervous system.

the characteristic odour of the spawning stream.

This again implies an ability to detect only a few molecules of scent passing through the nostrils—and it means that the fish reacts positively to increasing amounts of odour as it gets closer to 'home'.

Taste in man is a sense confined to the region of the mouth. But in fishes it is spread farther. The mouth of a fish contains large numbers of cells, known as taste buds, on the lips, the underside of the snout and around the mouth, especially on any barbules.

Pouting and cod, when feeding, swim around with their chin barbules extended forwards, sampling the sea bed for edible items as they move—and no doubt gudgeon and barbel also can taste an offered bait without taking it into their mouths. Gurnards have taste cells on the long pectoral rays which they use for searching out molluscs, crustaceans and worms.

It is known that carp have a sense of taste, and can distinguish saltiness, sweetness, bitterness and acidity. There is also no reason to think that they do this less efficiently than man. Gurnards and other fishes detect the extract of the worms or clams on which they normally feed, but seem indifferent to sensations of sweetness or saltiness. Not surprisingly, some research at marine fishery laboratories has explored taste sensitivity of fish in search of an artificial substitute which tastes like the natural food but stays fixed to the hook better!

Lateral line

The lateral line is a conspicuous sense organ in most of our fishes. It varies a little from species to species, but basically is noticeable as a series of scales along the side of the body bearing a tube on part of their length. It then continues as a sunken tube and has openings over the head, around the eyes, on the cheeks and on the lower jaw.

The sensitive part of the lateral line is a small cell, the neuromast. When pressure within the canal changes due to outside influences, these neuromasts detect the alteration and a message travels through the dense nerve network of the canal to the brain. Experiments with captive fishes show that the lateral line system can detect a variety of vibrations. The North American catfish or bullhead can detect vibrations of between 20 and 100 cycles per second by means of these organs, and it seems that at the upper range where this system fades out the animal's sense of hearing takes over.

It can be concluded that by means of its lateral line system, a fish can detect localized disturbances caused either by currents or by an approaching predator. This also acts as a distant touch sense. Change of water pressure from objects or prey can allow the fish to detect their presence without actually coming into contact.

A further aptitude found in fishes, and which is unique to them, is that some are capable of producing electrical discharges. It is most extreme in the electric ray or torpedo. Some tropical fish, such as the electric eel and the electric catfish, also produce a strong stunning current. Less noticeable is the low capacity electrical ability of the rays and skates. They have weakly developed electricity-producing organs in the tail muscles, although they are rather reluctant to discharge their current, which is delivered at a voltage of about four volts. In the skates and rays this function is not fully understood, but possibly the electric field produced can serve as an early warning system to alert the fish of approaching potential predators. More probably, it serves as a species-recognition system keeping a school of rays together at mating time and ensuring that the same species mate.

Fish are well adapted for the conditions in which they live. With such a battery of acute senses on the side of the fish it is no wonder that the successful capture of specimen fish is a feat of skill and endurance.

Below: *The amazing feats undertaken by a salmon to return to its spawning redds may be in response to a familiar odour which the fish can recognize and 'track'.*

Groundbaiting

Groundbaiting as a method of attracting fish can be very effective, but a little dropped in the right place works a lot better than random scattering over a wide area

Groundbaiting is carried out to attract fish into a swim and set them feeding. There are various methods of groundbaiting, depending mainly upon the type of water, the rate of flow, and the species of fish sought.

Groundbaiting in fresh water
Groundbaiting with a heavy mixture which drops to the bottom fast is needed at times, but once there it should break up quickly. In fast flowing water, when barbel or bream are the quarry, a ball of groundbait which sinks quickly is thrown in slightly upstream so that when it hits the bottom and breaks up, the particles drift along the bottom and

through the swim. Bream usually swim in large shoals, feeding on the bottom, and large amounts of groundbait are often needed to concentrate the shoal in the swim. A large bucketful of groundbait is generally the minimum required for a day's fishing.

Baiting up a swim several days in advance can pay dividends, particularly when bream, tench or carp are sought. This can draw a big shoal of bream into the swim and hold them there until fishing starts, even though their usual tendency is to be on the move.

A ball of groundbait can be used to land a quantity of loose maggots on the bed of a deep swim. In strong flowing water, such as a weir stream, bank clay can be worked into the mixture for this purpose. It is then moulded in the shape of a cup, the cavity filled with maggots, worms or another bait, and the top closed over. A strong flow, coupled with the action of the wriggling bait, will soon break up the balls, sending the hookbait samples trickling along the bottom to bring fish close.

Groundbaiting from a boat
When fishing from a boat, groundbait can be dropped over the side or lowered to the bottom in a meshed bag weighted with stones. An occasional tug on a cord attached to the bag will release and circulate particles of the groundbait through the mesh and into the swim.

When ledgering, it is essential to get the groundbait in the right place, and then to fish the baited hook in the middle of it or as close as possible—on the downstream side.

Groundbaiting is frequently done with the use of mechanical devices, such as bait-droppers, swimfeeders and catapults. One sure way of landing loose maggots, or other hookbait samples, on the bottom, is to put them there by means of a bait-

Fishing for tope from a boat. Balls of groundbait made from mackerel or oily pilchards or herrings, pounded to a pulp with a blunt instrument, and then mixed with bran—with blood added to thicken the mixture—can be a deadly bait. Known as rubby dubby in Cornwall, the pieces of fish sink, while the oil floats on the surface to form a trail leading tope to the baited hook.

LEDGERING TECHNIQUES

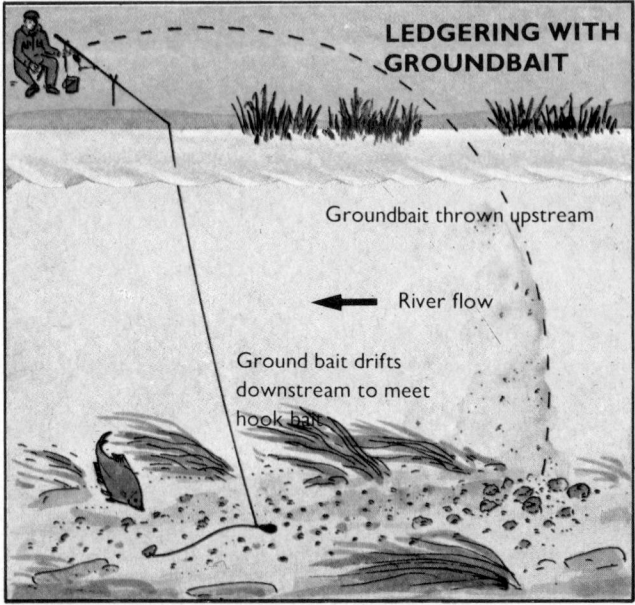

LEDGERING WITH GROUNDBAIT

Groundbait thrown upstream

River flow

Ground bait drifts downstream to meet hook bait

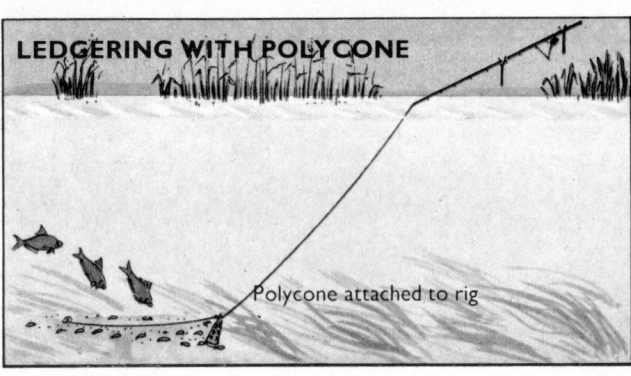

LEDGERING WITH POLYCONE

Polycone attached to rig

FLOAT FISHING FROM A BOAT

Anchored boat

Mesh bucket containing groundbait

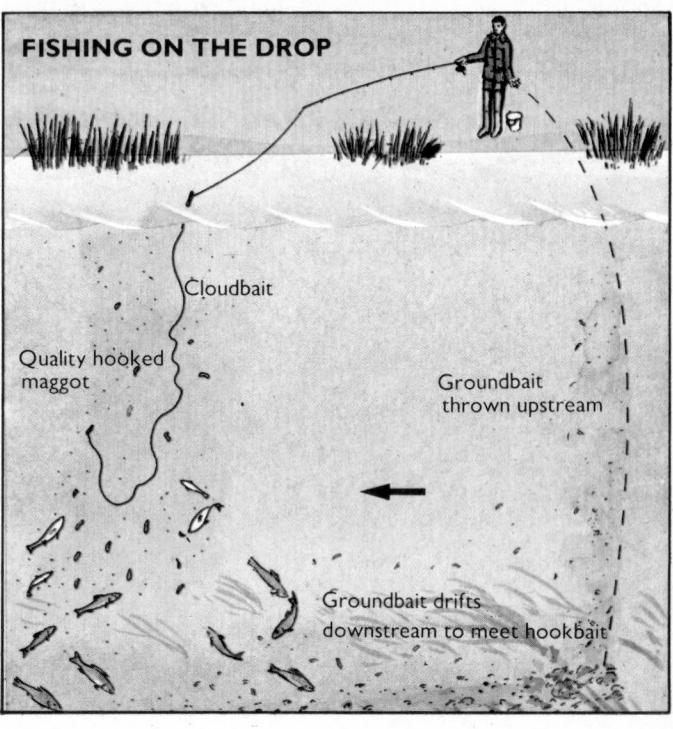

FISHING ON THE DROP

Cloudbait

Quality hooked maggot

Groundbait thrown upstream

Groundbait drifts downstream to meet hookbait

dropper, of which there are various kinds on the market. The loaded bait-dropper is lowered to the bottom of the swim, when a trip wire opens the lid and releases the contents. The match angler usually starts by putting down several droppers full of hookbait samples. Once the fish move into the swim, the bait-dropper should be used with caution, for it may scare the fish.

Scattering by hand
Bait-droppers are obviously not so useful when fishing on the drop, or if taking fish from under the surface when small fish are relied on to make up the match weight. Scattering bait loosely by hand or by catapult is more effective in that case.

Good catches of fish are often made by using choice maggots as hookbait and groundbaiting with inferior maggots, or feeders as they are known. Feeders are generally used in conjunction with a cloudbait. As one becomes expert in casting with one hand and tossing the feed or attractor in with the other, both hookbait and groundbait will enter the water together. The choice maggots on the hook will sink slowly and enticingly amidst the dissolving cloudbait and the feeders.

Use of the swimfeeder
When ledgering the midstream an effective way of getting maggots down to the bed of the river is to use a gadget known as a swimfeeder. These come in various designs and sizes, but the basic model is a celluloid tube that is attached to the ledger tackle. The open-ended type is packed with maggots, with breadcrumbs as plugs at both ends.

With groundbait plugs the feeder can also be used to concentrate hempseed or casters in the vicinity of the baited hook. The closed or blockend type of feeder is filled with maggots only.

After the tackle is cast out it reaches the bottom and the flow of water swings the baited hook to a position downstream of the swimfeeder. From this the maggots will wriggle out through the holes and into the right place—around the baited hook.

A swimfeeder deposits groundbait exactly where it is needed—but it does not always put enough there.

Ledgering with groundbait: Balls of groundbait are cast upstream to break up and settle near the hook bait.

Ledgering with a Polycone: The Polycone swimfeeder used as a weight in ledgering.

Float fishing from a boat: Feeding a swim from a boat by the use of a mesh bag or bucket. It can be placed directly upstream to drift downstream to meet the hook bait.

Fishing on the drop: The use of cloud and groundbait.

Below: Near to the bank, particles can be thrown by hand; for swims farther off you need a boat or catapult.

LAYING PARTICLE GROUND BAIT

A catapult is used if a boat is not available.

Below: *The Polycone swimfeeder filled with maggots. With a swimfeeder you can cast your groundbait accurately. The maggots wriggle out around the baited hook.*

Below centre: *Balls of groundbait can be liberally laced with maggots.*

Below right: *If you don't have a catapult, try adding a stone to your groundbait—it aids casting accuracy and distance.*

This is why, when ledgering, groundbaiting the swim manually is sometimes employed at the same time as offering the hookbait samples in the swimfeeder.

Care must always be exercised when groundbaiting a swim where specimen fish are the quarry. On a river, the introduction of a large quantity of groundbait will invariably attract shoals of small fish, and these can prove a nuisance.

Cloudbaiting

A form of groundbaiting which is effective in many types of waters, particularly for surface and mid-water species, is cloudbaiting. This means clouding the water by introducing minute particles which the fish will search through, looking for more substantial food.

After taking note of the rate of flow of the water, the angler regularly throws small balls of cloudbait into the swim. This is done upstream, so that the cloud drifts down and through the area being fished. The float tackle is cast out immediately after, following the groundbait closely through the swim.

Drip-feeding

For roach, dace and chub fishing on a small, secluded river, regular swim-baiting can be made by the use of a 'drip-feed'—a tin with a few holes punched in the bottom, which is filled with maggots and hung from a bridge or overhanging branch. The steady trickle of maggots over a long period will entice fish from some distance away into the swim.

As match fishermen know, regular groundbaiting of the swim is very important no matter what hookbait is used. Without it, the angler is fishing on a hit-and-miss basis.

ASK THE EXPERT

What is the best catapult to buy?
Buy big rather than too small, with a wide U-shape and forks turning out slightly at the top. The cup should be rigid, not flexible, and the elastic square in cross-section with a soft spring to it, fastened through holes in the fork ends. A reliable catapult costs about £3.50.

When do I use a catapult and when a bait-thrower?
Both are for delivering groundbait or feedbait to distant swims. The catapult is suitable when the groundbait can't be pressed into a heavy ball—bread or biscuit, for instance, while the bait thrower can cope with greater weights. The longer the stick, the farther you can throw a heavy (eg. clay-mixed) ball.

I've seen boat anglers throwing paper-bagfuls of bait into rivers: are they litter louts or is this a valid method?
There are various ways of groundbaiting flowing water from a boat. One is to fill small paper bags with groundbait plus a few stones, tear off the two bottom corners of each bag, and twist the top closed. As it enters the river, the stones help the bag to sink. Then water enters the holes and forces open the bag.

Isn't there a traditional method of groundbaiting for rudd?
Tethered crust has long been used for rudd, particularly on stillwaters. Crusts of bread are anchored close to reedbeds by a length of string tied to a stone, from a boat. Alternatively, slices are thrown loose, to drift downwind while the boat follows quietly behind. Splashes and a nudging of the bread show that rudd have started feeding. Floating or slow-sinking flake is then cast as hookbait close by.

Float ledgering

Float ledgering in its various forms is almost unlimited in its effectiveness; but the delicate balance of forces between the tackle and the current or wind demands careful adjustment

As its name suggests, float ledgering combines many of the advantages of ledgering with those of normal float fishing. The simplest and best known method of float ledgering is widely known as 'laying-on'. Anglers often resort to laying-on when fish are responding to float tackle either in midwater or near the bottom. By changing style, they are able to fish the bottom itself to seek the more wily and larger specimens.

When laying-on, the float is raised to a position on the line about a foot or so greater than the water depth (measured with a plummet). When the tackle is cast into position the float fails to cock because the weights or shotting, lying in a heap on the bottom, exert no pull on the line. The line is then tightened with a turn or so of the reel, drawing the float towards the bank and at the same time taking up the slack between the float and the shotting. The shotting straightened out, the shots exert a downward pull on the float, which cocks somewhat obliquely.

This is a far finer presentation of the original tackle than simply float fishing with the bait on the bottom, because the float is now set well away from the bait. The line runs obliquely and is less likely to cause shy fish to become suspicious of the bait when it is well presented.

Modifying the tackle
Although a simple change to laying-on from normal float tackle can be very effective, you can improve your tackle with several modifications. The shotting can be rearranged to provide a more immediate reaction to bites or the float can be changed to suit the slightly different balances of forces now operating between float, shots, and current or wind. The combination of float and shotting should be varied to suit the widely varying water conditions met by the angler. Laying-on is just as effective with a light porcupine quill and a single shot in stillwaters as with a heavy cork or balsa-bodied antenna float with several shots in a light stream.

In the proper hands, laying-on

The usual principle applies when you are laying-on: keep well clear of the bank.

tackle can be extremely sensitive and very effective. Bites are normally signified by a light trembling of the float, which eventually slides under, giving the angler ample time to tighten on a good fish. Good bream, roach and other species often succumb to laying-on techniques, and the method is particularly suited to fishing in slow and sluggish waters or in the stillwaters of lakes and ponds.

Laying-on also enables the angler to carry out a number of useful manoeuvres. In stillwater he can raise the rod sufficiently to draw the float a foot or so closer. This moves the bait nearer to him and he then fishes the water where it has settled. Repeating this tactic at intervals enables him to fish thoroughly the water between himself and the bait's original position. Often the bait is taken shortly after such a move, especially if a marauding perch is attracted by the sporadic movements of a worm or maggot.

Laying-on in slow waters

The same strategy can be used in slow or sluggish waters. Lifting the rod tip allows the current to lift the shot and bait before dropping them downstream a little, when the float again sits obliquely. As before, this tactic can be repeated, the bottom tackle being drawn downstream and towards the bank to search a swim thoroughly. Again, a bite often follows shortly after a movement.

Laying-on tackle can be made more sensitive by replacing the bottom shotting with a single drilled bullet or a pear lead and swivel. To retain the sensitivity of the float, it is now necessary to counterbalance it with shotting set directly underneath it or by twisting lead wire about its base. Alternatively, subsitute a self-cocking float. Either way, a fish taking the bait pulls line through the eye of the swivel without experiencing any resistance from the weights or even from the float's buoyancy.

In fast waters such a rig may be ineffective. Often, the pull of the current simply causes the float to sink out of sight, making it difficult to keep it in position for more than a few minutes. Some anglers take

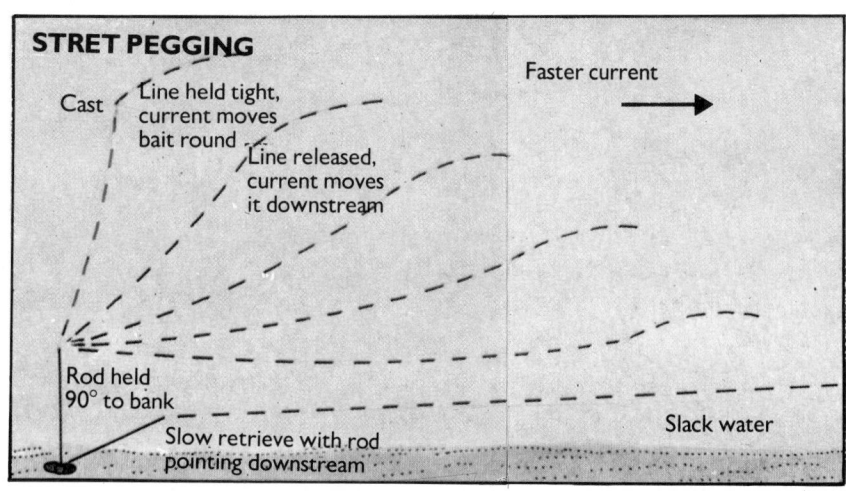

STRET PEGGING

Cast — Line held tight, current moves bait round ...

Line released, current moves it downstream

Faster current

Rod held 90° to bank

Slow retrieve with rod pointing downstream

Slack water

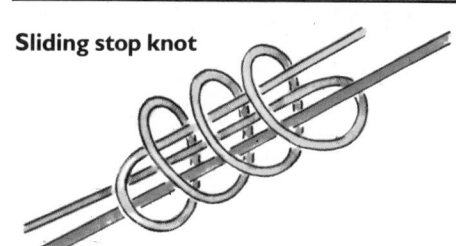

Sliding stop knot

Above: *Stret-pegging requires the rod to be held at all times.* **Right:** *A slider float, free to run along the line, can be held by a stop-knot (left).* **Below:** *A simple float ledger rig, which combines the qualities of float fishing with the subtleties of traditional ledgering.*

FLOAT LEDGER RIG

advantage of this situation, however. Allowing the shots to work downstream, they can fish into holes and over weedbeds. By holding the float back momentarily, the shots are pulled off the bottom by the current and waver over the weed or in midwater until the rod tip is lowered again. Then the bottom tackle sinks down and for a few moments the float rides ready to signal an instant bite. This method is generally known as 'stret-pegging' and can be as easily done with a light pear lead

and swivel as with a more orthodox float and heavy shotting. Both methods are very sensitive, but if sliding weights are used the float must be counterweighted or a self-cocking float used. It is necessary to hold the rod throughout.

Laying-on tackles are probably best used in still waters where the depth does not exceed the length of the rod. A 13ft rod, for example, with a float set at 12ft and the fishing depth at, say, 10ft, allows the angler to cast well out into

ASK THE EXPERT

What species am I likely to catch by float ledgering?
Virtually all species—with the possible exception of surface feeders such as bleak or rudd.

Can I use any sort of rod?
Because of the need to fish over-depth a long float rod of about 13ft is needed. Shorter rods are best kept for straightforward ledgering.

Can I use a pole?
Certainly. When a river is in flood, a float ledgering rig attached to a pole is an ideal way of presenting a still bait while avoiding all the rubbish that usually accumulates on the line.

A bait doesn't have to be static, does it? Twitched baits seem to do well.
A float-ledgering rig is one of the best set-ups for twitching. A moving bait catches the fish's eye as, with each movement of the ledger, a little cloud of mud is disturbed. To ground-bait for a twitched bait, introduce feed in a 10ft line then twitch the bait along the line. Few methods are deadlier.

I've heard that its a solution to very weedy bottoms. Is this true?
Float ledgering will certainly prevent a bait drifting and, if the ledger is attached to a short link, there will be no friction problems, even if it sinks into the weed.

Line-bites are a problem when I ledger for bream. Would float ledgering help?
Match anglers often employ the technique for this very reason. A line lying along the bottom from ledger to rod tip invites line-bites along its entire length. A line from float to rod overcomes the problem.

swims where ordinary float tackle will often not hold bottom because surface drift or wind on the line create forces which combine to sink the float. If surface winds are strong, it is useful to place a single dust shot on the line just above the float so it will ride correctly.

Submerge your rod tip
If the rod tip is submerged slightly, all the line between float and rod tip will also sink. This means that no surface wind or wave action can interfere with the line, allowing the tackle to be particularly effective. In a heavy popple, when waves are formed by the wind, it may be necessary to use an antenna float for good visibility. Once again, this tackle can be retrieved a few inches at intervals to search the bottom, covering all the ground between each cast and ensuring that the angler thoroughly covers those sections of the water where his ground-bait has been deposited.

All laying-on tackles can be used with swimfeeders instead of weights in slow and sluggish waters, or with bait droppers in stillwater. They all ensure that the angler, casting accurately, is actually fishing where his groundbait is placed.

In very deep stillwaters, where the

Laying on with small baits was reponsible for these two beautiful roach.

depth is greater than the length of the rod in use, float ledgering with a slider float can be used to good advantage. A slider float must be free to run on the line and can often be attached by two wire loops, one at the base of the float and one two-thirds up. The float is then stopped at the required depth by means of a simple bloodknot tied with a separate few inches of nylon on the line. The loose ends of the knot should be slightly greater than the diameter of the lower float loop. When the tackle is cast, the line is then left loose long enough for the float to rise to the knot, where it is held and sits in view.

Minor depth adjustments can be made by sliding the knot itself along the line and then re-tightening it. The angler can also make minor adjustments by sinking the rod tip and line and drawing in or letting out a little line to make the float ride properly. Slider floats used in this way also need to be counterbalanced so that they become self-cocking. This can be done by twisting lead wire around the base, or, with some designs by taking the cap off the float and placing a few shots inside.

Playing and landing

When you have learned to read the water and present your bait properly there are further skills to acquire. Playing and landing a hooked fish are vital elements in successful angling

Despite thousands of words of sound advice from fishing writers on the subject of playing and landing, many fish are neverthless lost by anglers who lack this basic skill. The most common weak spots are: little or no understanding of the slipping clutch on the frequently used fixed-spool reel, and not knowing how to coax out a fish that has run into weed (which can happen to the most experienced angler). First, then, the slipping clutch.

Before making the first cast, hold the rod in one hand and place one finger lightly on the edge of the spool. With the other hand take hold of the end of the line and pull as hard as possible. The clutch should not slip. If it does so before reaching maximum pressure the clutch is set too loose, while if the line breaks the clutch is too tight. With the spool set correctly it is impossible for a running fish to break the line, providing, that is, that everything else

is done properly. When a fish is hooked, immediately apply one finger of the rod hand to the rim of the spool. In this way, when the rod is held at an angle of between 15 and 30° to the vertical, maximum pressure is brought to bear on the running fish. The line will be almost at breaking point but, if the slipping clutch is correctly set, will not actually break.

Pumping and netting
When the fish stops its run, line is recovered by the pocess known as 'pumping'. For this, assuming the fish is stationary or nearly so, turn the reel handle, at the same time lowering the rod until the tip is at waist level. Then increase finger pressure on the spool rim and bring up the rod to its former position. Repeat the process until the fish runs again or is ready for the net.

Good angling technique. Eddie Harris puts side-strain on a fighting barbel hooked in the fast water of a Kennet weirpool.

It is now—at the point of net-ting—that most mistakes occur. When the fish is played out, the net is placed in the water, ready for use. With the fish wallowing or lying on the surface, bring the rod tip down to waist level once more, and, with the other hand holding the net, draw the rod back over the shoulder, maintaining strong pressure on the spool all the time. Steady the net about 12in below the surface and draw the fish towards and over it. Do not lift until it is over the net.

Two rules of netting

Sometimes, as the fish is drawn to the net, it will suddenly find new strength and either swim off or change direction. Let it do so for it is unlikely to take line. Keep the finger on the spool and allow the rod to take the strain. Two important points must be remembered: first, as the fish comes over the net make sure that the rod is no farther back than 30° to the vertical. If it is, you will not have complete control over the fish. Secondly, never move the net towards the fish but keep it still and pull the fish over it.

The problem of the fish that runs into weed is one that requires swift action. Some fish, especially roach and chub, however quick one's reflexes are, will manage to transfer the hook to the weed and escape. Other species, barbel and tench in particular, are not so clever and must be extracted from the weed by 'pumping'. As soon as the fish reaches the weed, use the technique described earlier, repeating the pro-cess without stopping and keeping the finger down hard on the spool. Once the fish starts to move, keep control of the situation with con-tinual pumping, as this will, in the majority of cases, get the fish out of the weed. This technique relies on knowing how much pressure your line will take—something that only comes with experience, and not nor-mally before the loss of a fish.

Coaxing a fish through weed

When a fish runs into streamer weed *(Ranunculus)*, you must get downstream of it in order to extract it. Trying to coax a fish through this weed from upstream only worsens

134

LANDING A CHUB

A chub is hooked in a pool heavily overhung with trees and bushes. Immediately there is a problem, the fish must be controlled and played carefully to the landing net.

Much of the fight has left the fish now. But this is the time when great care must be taken, and the angler must be alert to any sudden flurry of movement if the fish plunges towards the branches dipping into the water or banks of rushes and weed growth.

There is a technique in netting a fish properly. When the fish is beaten and close in, never plunge the net into the water and try to scoop the fish into it. You must lower the net below the surface and hold it still while the fish is drawn over the rim.

Here the net is a little high in the water, but the chub has been played out sufficiently for it to make no sudden attempt to break away. The net must now be lifted to take the weight of the fish and brought back from the water's edge. Keep the line from the fish's mouth loose by following the path of the net with the rod top.

John Wilson lifts the net carefully from the water. The net is capacious and capable of holding large fish in absolute safety. Never try to net a fish whose length is more than the diameter of the net, especially if there is still fight left in it.

Holding the chub carefully in order to avoid harm (a wet rag is useful here), John removes the hook. The fish has given sport and pleasure to the angler, and should now be returned to the water — none the worse for its experience.

ASK THE EXPERT

What happens if the rod drops too low while pumping?
A sudden dive by the fish can result in an instant breakage as the 'give' in the rod no longer comes into play.

How long should a landing net handle be?
About 6ft long. A longer one is all right, but you may have trouble lifting it enough to get the fish inside. Whatever you do, don't use a handle of less than 4ft when fishing from a high bank you can't reach; worse still, there is a danger of falling in. And you lose all control when the rod has to be brought way back over the shoulder to get the fish near enough to the net.

When pumping a fish from a weedbed, how soon will the fish begin to move?
This depends on how far the fish has gone in and the density of weed. But, providing you keep pumping, it should start moving within 20 seconds and be completely free in half a minute.

Can glass fibre handles break when lifting heavy fish?
Never try to lift a fish of more than 2lb with a glass fibre pole. Slide both net and fish to the bank. At the water's edge, drop the handle and catch hold of the arms of the frame. Off high banks a net should be lifted vertically.

Which type of net is best – micromesh or a larger mesh?
For matchfishing, micromesh is best because the very small shots matchmen use cannot get tangled in the mesh. With bigger fish, though, needing a bigger net, waterlogged micromesh can become extremely heavy and difficult to lift out.

the situation. Although fish of all sorts can be forced out of 'cabbages' (underwater lilies) or various types of weedy growth, it is extremely difficult to move a fish from a lily patch by 'pumping' and many battles have been lost here.

Playing a fish on a centrepin reel is much easier than on a fixed-spool. Immediately the fish is hooked, turn the handle slowly, keeping the line tight. If the fish runs let it take line, but rest the palm of the hand lightly against the rim of the reel, facing upwards. In this way, by applying a light but insistent pressure, the fish has to fight for every inch of line but will not break it.

To sum up, when playing a big fish the important thing is not to allow the fish to take control. If this happens then it is likely to be lost. Do not hurry the playing—a sure way of losing the fish—yet do not drag it out longer than necessary, for the object, it must be remembered, is to get the catch on the bank. Maintain a steady pressure and give line only when you have to.

Normally, one holds the rod pointing upwards, as described, but remember that fish do turn sideways and, when they do, sideways pressure must be applied. Bring the rod down to the horizontal position and keep it there while playing the fish running to the side.

Above right: *A good-sized Kennet dace being played by Peter Ward. See how the angler is keeping the rod at just the right angle to allow the flexible top to do the work.*
Below: *A grayling comes to the waiting net quietly and without fuss.*

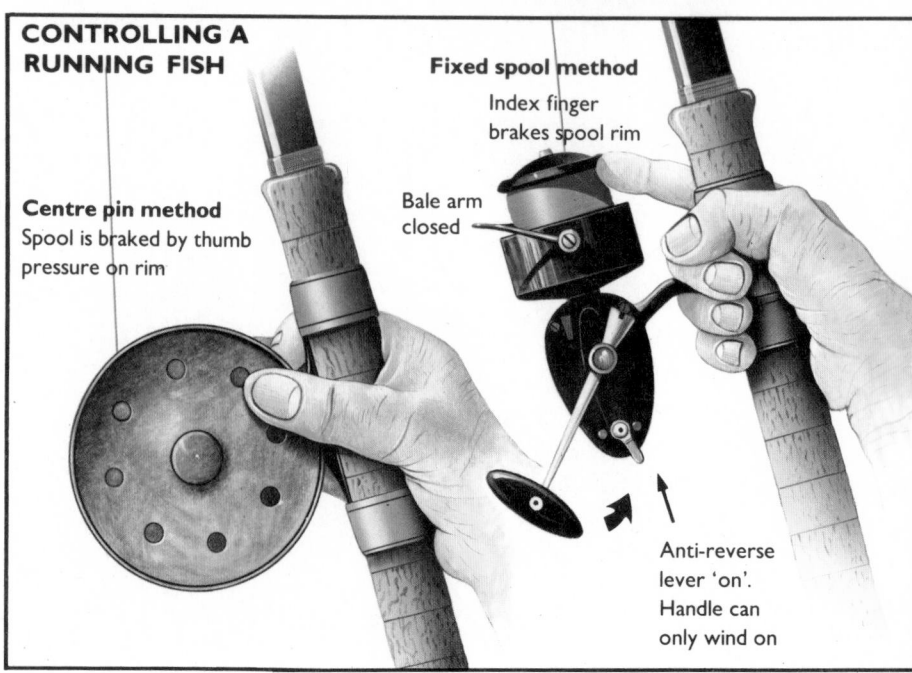

CONTROLLING A RUNNING FISH

Centre pin method
Spool is braked by thumb pressure on rim

Fixed spool method
Index finger brakes spool rim

Bale arm closed

Anti-reverse lever 'on'. Handle can only wind on

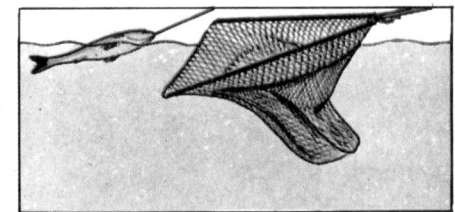

Good netting technique. The fish is being drawn steadily towards and over the edge of the straight-mouthed landing net.

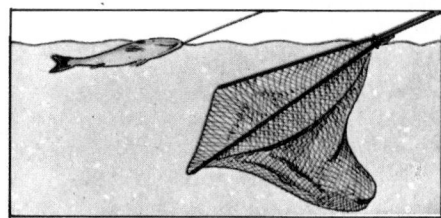

The mouth of the net here is too deep. When it is lifted, the resulting displacement of the water can cause the fish to panic.

A good tench, its head covered with weed, is brought quietly to the waiting net. Any jerky movement at this stage may cause the fish to thrash dangerously about.

'PUMPING' A FISH

To 'pump' a fish, lower the rod to horizontal while reeling in. Stop the spool with finger pressure and raise rod to 60°. Repeat till the fish is ready to net

The fish is brought nearer with each successive 'pump'

USING SIDESTRAIN

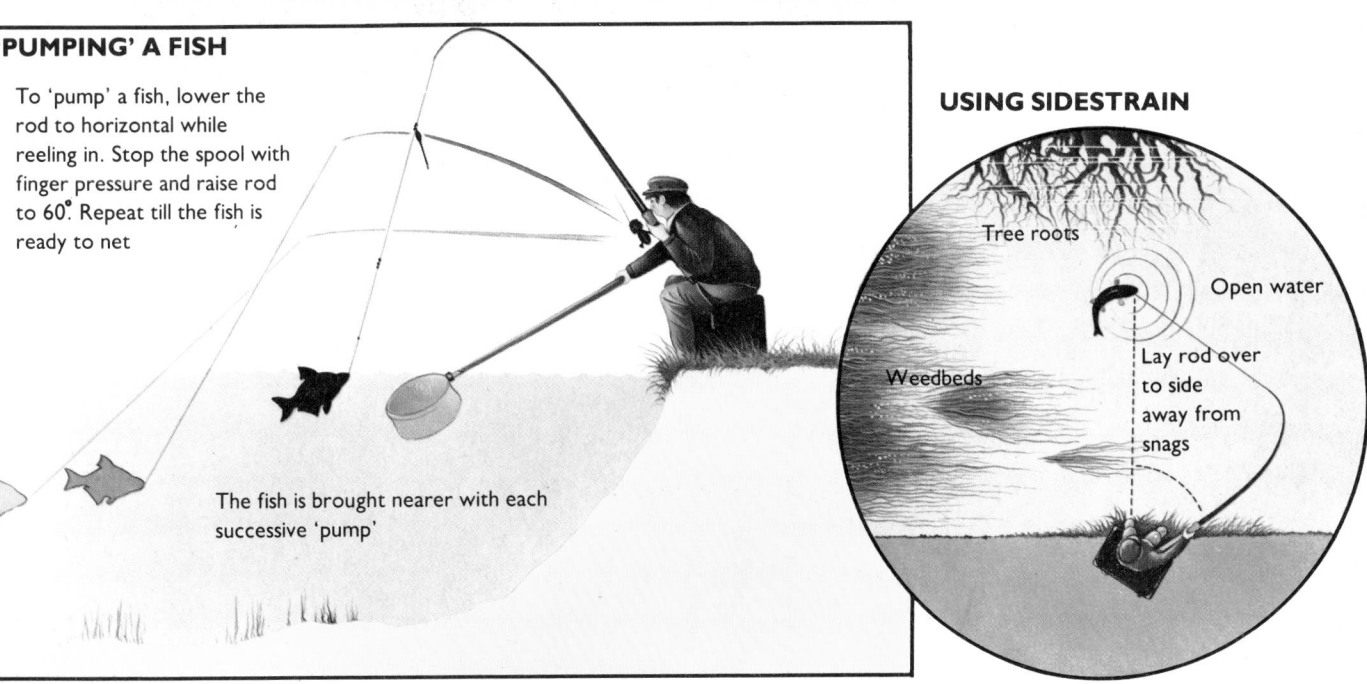

Tree roots

Open water

Weedbeds

Lay rod over to side away from snags

Spinning

Spinning is one of the most effective ways of catching predatory fish. But success depends upon presenting a spinning bait at the right depth, spot and time

Spinning is the art of casting and retrieving a lure designed to look or act like a small fish, frog or mouse. Spinning is often a deadly method and most sea, game or coarse anglers find it necessary to spin at times. Using a variety of spinner-spoons and plugs, anglers use it for a number of different species on waters throughout the country.

Spinning is also one of the best methods of fishing for young anglers to use. Armed with one or two plugs, a closed-face fixed-spool reel and a decent spinning rod, the novice will learn both to cast and to catch a sizeable fish.

Species caught with spinners
Most game fish take a spinner readily. Many sea fish, even flounders, fall to them, and in coarse fishing, pike, perch and chub take these lures often, while other fish in the carp family (bream, carp, tench, and others), and zander will also take them occasionally.

Generally speaking, spinning is a good method for the open river where there are deep pools, or for large stillwaters, gravel pits and reservoirs. One should not spin, if unskilled, in confined spaces, as retrieval will be difficult. If the river is overhung with much vegetation though it may hold good fish, bad casting will result in lost lures.

Choice of rod depends on the water more than anything else. On big rivers, gravel pits or reservoirs you may need a powerful, two-handed, stepped-up carp rod to throw biggish spoons, spinners or plugs a long way. In contrast, on small rivers, canals or ponds, short casts with a 7-8ft spinning rod of hollow glass for use with lines of 5-8lb b.s. may be adequate.

A certain amount of common sense is needed in choice of rod: big

pike or salmon on a small river, for example, would need a powerful line, from 10lb to 20lb b.s.

The choice of reels is legion. It is possible, though, for the experienced angler to spin directly from a top-class centrepin. With plugs you can pull off loops of line from the rod rings, while for sizeable plugs and heavy spinners you may use a multiplying reel. Multipliers are accurate on short to moderate casts, but difficult to use for light baits.

Other than for light spinning,

closed-face reels are rarely used. For playing heavy fish they prove to be ineffective since the line within the housing goes through too many angles, creating considerable friction. Many open-faced fixed-spool reels are, however, superb. One with a roller pick-up and a reliable, easily reached anti-reverse switch is especially useful.

The species of fish also governs the choice of rod, reel and line. In weedy water, like the Fenland drains, you need heavy line and a powerful rod to hold the fish. The same applies to heavy fish in small waters. On the other hand, when perch or chub fishing, a MK IV carp rod, or its lighter version, the Avon, in glass or split cane, are excellent.

Ultra light spinning is proving to be increasingly popular. For this, a sawn-off length of fly rod, 5-6ft, with a line of 4lb b.s. is recommended. A tiny fixed-spool reel of high quality,

like one of the small Shakespeares, Daiwas, or Ryobis, and small lures, almost down to big flies in size, but with diving vanes or propellors, are also necessary. You can, in fact, make your own lures on big single hooks, and catch more carp species with this than you would on conventional spinning gear.

The wide range of rods and reels provides great versatility of spinning techniques. Lines are also varied, but a good standard line is a simple monofil, usually dyed dark in colour, and supple. Some anglers use plaited nylon, particularly on multiplying reels, but monofil generally has more stretch. Other spinning, such as trolling from a boat, may require special lead-cored lines, and some sea spinning is done with wire lines. Different strengths of nylon monofil together with appropriate weights to get the spinner down, usually prove adequate.

Wire traces

If a fish has sharp teeth you may need a wire trace on the line. This applies particularly to pike and zander and many sea fish, but not when spinning for game fish, or coarse fish such as perch or chub.

Cabled, supple, dark coloured wire is better than made up, plastic coated, shiny traces. Add a swivel to one end and a safety-pin link swivel to the other by passing 2in of cable wire through the swivel eye. Laying it back parallel, twist the two parts together by hand. Crimp-on sleeves can be used to secure the join, or strong glue, but in fact these are not usually needed.

Minimum of equipment

At the waterside, remember that you are always on the move, so a minimum of equipment is advisable. A small rucksack on your back is best, to hold food and waterproof clothing, and an angler's waistcoat with numerous pockets for spinners, spoons and miscellaneous items of tackle such as a spring balance, forceps for removing lures from fishes' jaws, a sharpening stone for blunted hooks, scissors and other small items, will prove useful. For landing salmon a small, collapsible net, gaff or tailer is necessary.

Always take enough clothes to keep warm. If possible wear plimsols or walking boots rather than wellingtons or waders, although weight and heat saving on footwear is not always a good thing. Clothes should be drab, and the approach to the waterside quiet. It is a good plan to fish through the spot you intend standing at, particularly on a coarse fish water where another angler's groundbait may have attracted shoal fish and predators close in to the bank.

Where to cast

Where to cast? First, with a sinking spinner, find out the depth of water working on the principle of retrieving slow and deep. Cast out and

A pike of nearly 20lb—the fish of a lifetime for most anglers—falls to a well used spoon. As this catch clearly demonstrates, it is not always necessary to offer a new, shiny lure in order to take a fine specimen fish.

ASK THE EXPERT

How do I strike?
You rarely have to. Occasionally you will get a slack-line take as the hooked fish swims towards you: then wind up as fast as humanly possible and hit it hard.

Should I point the rod at the lure?
No. The best angle is usually 30-40 degrees to the side: just enough to avoid breakage on a savage take and not too much to result in a soft strike.

An angler who is spinning is constantly making sudden movements. Why doesn't he frighten fish away?
He may. You must be extra careful, when fishing through the bankside swim in front of the spot you intend to occupy *before* standing there. Big lures will frighten fish on small waters and in small, weedy holes: try a tiny lure first. Always wear drab clothing and don't be too proud to kneel down.

My line has become crinkled after an hour's spinning. Why?
The lure is rotating in a way that twists the line. You need an anti-kink vane or a lure with reversible vanes.

Is wading an advantage?
When working in shallows, along gravel bars of gravel pits, for example, wading may be an advantage. But wearing waders in summer can be uncomfortably warm.

Will the same rod serve for sea and freshwater spinning?
In many instances, yes. For heavy work in freshwater, a sea rod, line and so forth are fine. Equally, light spinning tackle normally used off rocks may be used in freshwater.

allow the spinner or spoon to sink with the pick-up off, and judge the time it takes the spinner to strike the bottom. As the spinner nears the bank, raise the rod top to avoid the lure running into the slope. Casting in a fan-wise fashion, each cast being some five degrees to the side of the previous cast, is also used, but this can make for boring fishing, except from an anchored boat. It is probably better to cast where you think the predator will be.

Having explored the most likely places—ledges, sunken branches, and holes behind boulders—move on and try another spot.

Some anglers have difficulty estimating how far out the lure is. To remedy this, tie a nylon stop knot, such as a Billy Lane stop knot, to the line at a fixed length above the lure, perhaps 15ft. As the knot clicks through the top ring you will know where the spinner is. This is particularly useful for night spinning—one of the most exciting forms of fishing there is.

For night spinning you also need a shot clipped on the line just above the trace swivel, or if not using a trace, some 2ft up the line. This prevents the trace swivel being reeled into the end ring of the rod, or the spinner itself being retrieved too close to the rod tip. It should usually hang a couple of feet from the rod tip prior to a cast. Another important consideration when spinning at night is to know how far you have cast. Fortunately this is fairly easy. In daylight measure out a suitable-length cast by pulling line off the reel, then secure a rubber band round the spool before reeling the line back on to the reel. This avoids overcasting.

Colours and sizes

Spinners, spoons and plugs come in all colours and sizes. Simple spoons are egg-shaped and can be made from dessert spoons. Despite their simplicity they will take almost anything that swims. Drill a hole out at each end and by using a split ring, add a treble hook at one end and a swivel at the other. Elongated, concave-convex spoons, with or without fins, are also useful.

Bar spoons are attached at one end to a bar forming an axis around which the blade spins. The tiny sizes will take trout, sea trout and perch,

Below: *A typical stretch of river showing the most likely spots where fish will congregate (A to I). X marks each successive casting spot and the dotted lines the direction the spinning lure will take.*

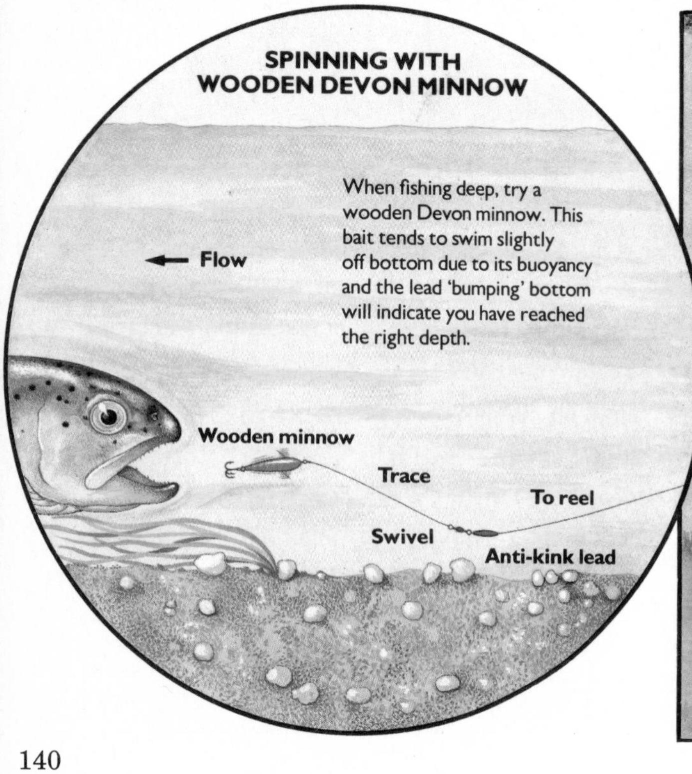

Right: *A selection of spinners and spoons.*
Below right: *The single-handed overhead cast can begin with the rod tip at eye level. The rod is raised to almost vertical and brought smartly forward.*
Below: *A spinning rig incorporating a Wye lead to prevent the line from kinking.*

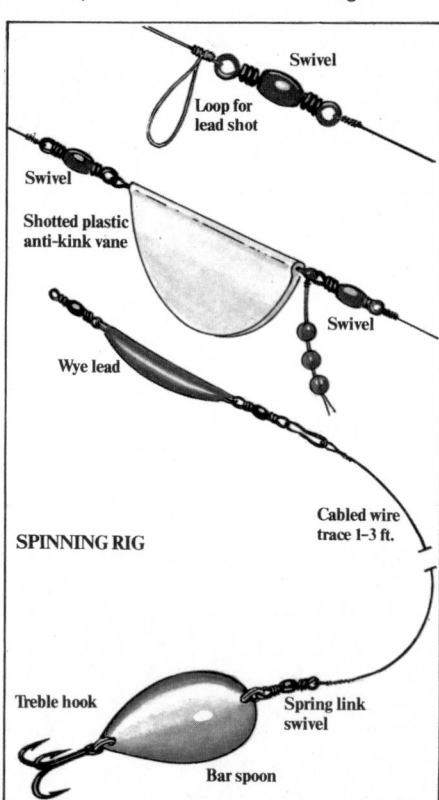

Swivel
Loop for lead shot
Swivel
Shotted plastic anti-kink vane
Swivel
Wye lead
Cabled wire trace 1–3 ft.
SPINNING RIG
Treble hook
Spring link swivel
Bar spoon

SPINNING WITH WOODEN DEVON MINNOW

When fishing deep, try a wooden Devon minnow. This bait tends to swim slightly off bottom due to its buoyancy and the lead 'bumping' bottom will indicate you have reached the right depth.

← Flow

Wooden minnow
Trace
To reel
Swivel
Anti-kink lead

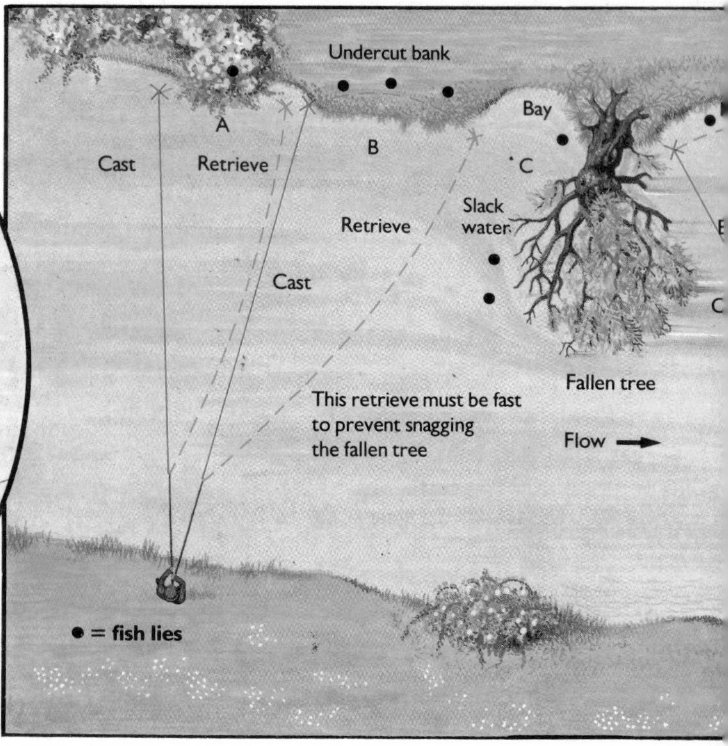

Undercut bank
Bay
A
Cast   Retrieve   B   C
Retrieve   Slack water
Cast
Fallen tree
This retrieve must be fast to prevent snagging the fallen tree
Flow →

● = fish lies

and the large sizes pike and salmon. They retrieve with greater vibration, but, unlike many spoons, retrieve in a more or less straight line unless the angler alters the position of the rod end. Fly spoons are a kind of small bar spoon, while many other spinners, like some minnows, and mackerel spinners, have a hole through them and rotate about their whole length.

Plugs can be floaters (poppers or crawlers), floaters which dive to various depths, or sinking plugs. These are available in one piece, or with two or more pieces. Some plugs dive shallow, some deep. Perhaps the most versatile, all-purpose plug is the smallest. Around an inch in length, with wood, fur and feather attached, it is almost as good as the fly-type lures. This type of plug can be fished on fly rods or with ultra-light gear.

The action of the spinner in the water is essential to a successful catch. For most species this should be slow and steady; for trout, fast and steady. Occasionally aim to retrieve in short bursts, swinging the rod from side to side. This will vary the direction and add a lifelike flutter to your spinner. When retrieving try not to be too quick, as the lure will rise high in the water; on the other hand, one should not retrieve too cautiously for fear of snagging your lure.

Plugs and spinners can easily be made at home, adding in many ways to one of the most enjoyable aspects of fishing.

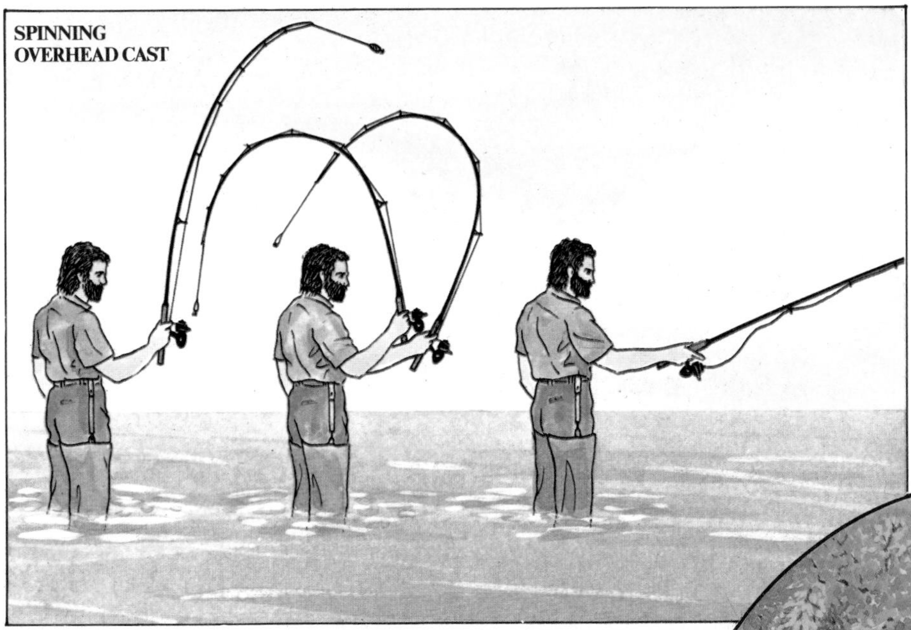

SPINNING OVERHEAD CAST

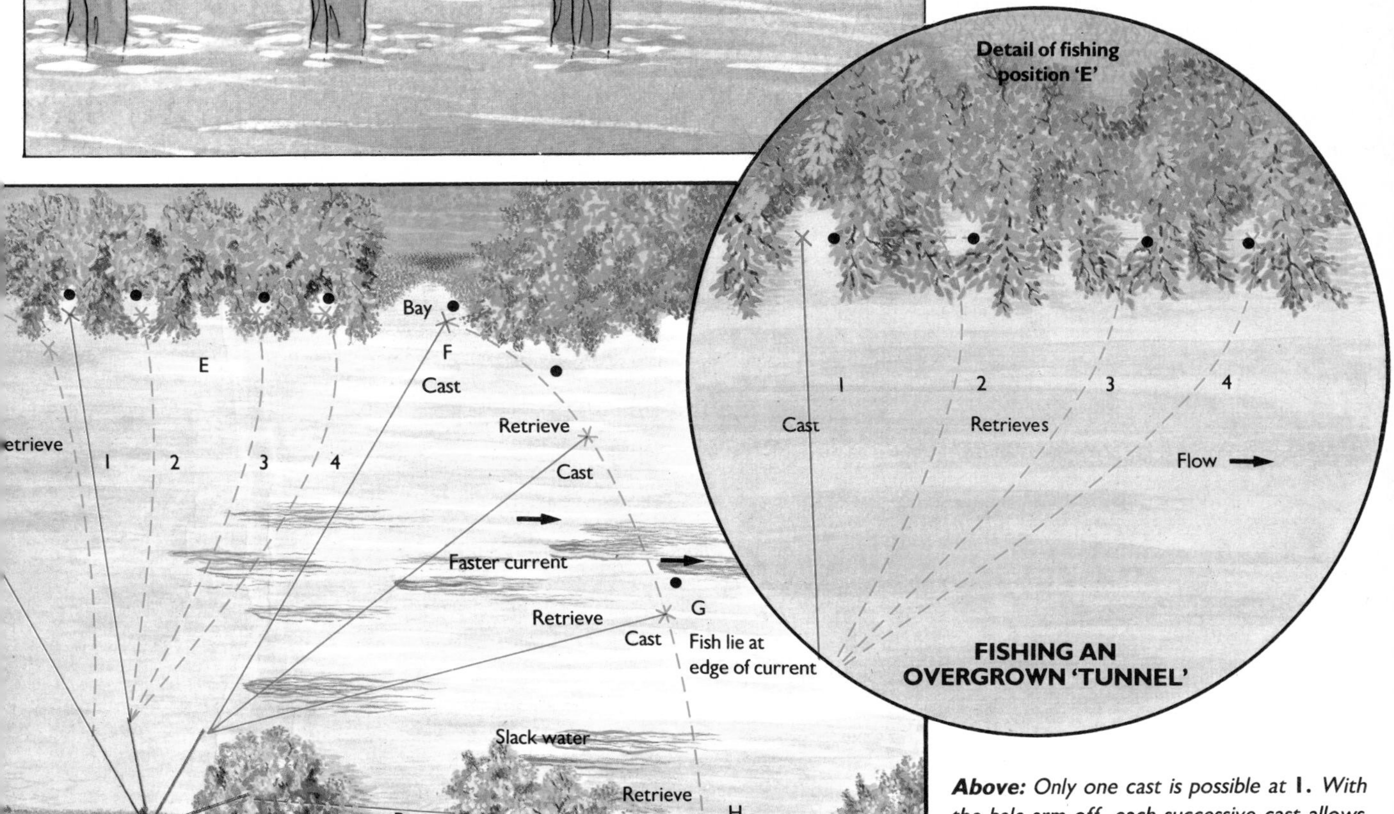

Detail of fishing position 'E'

Cast
1 2 3 4
Retrieves

Flow →

FISHING AN OVERGROWN 'TUNNEL'

retrieve
1 2 3 4

E

Bay
F
Cast

Retrieve

Cast

Faster current

Retrieve   G
Cast Fish lie at
edge of current

Slack water

Retrieve

Bay
1
Bring rod over towards bank
to retrieve lure beneath trees

Bay
H
Bay

Above: Only one cast is possible at 1. With the bale arm off, each successive cast allows the lure to drop further downstream before retrieving. **4** *is reached without snagging bottom by careful weight adjustment.*

141

Underarm casting

There are two reasons for perfecting this gentle casting skill: to deliver unwieldy end tackle and complex shotting patterns without mishap and to reach those inaccessible, overhung swims

UNDERARM CAST

One of the most neglected skills of many anglers is casting. It should be a smooth operation designed to use the action of the rod to place the tackle in the required spot. It is easy to find anglers who have not even mastered that basic skill, so it is little wonder that they have not explored the various alternative casting techniques.

One particularly useful skill is the underarm cast. This technique once turned an apparently hopeless peg in a national match on the Severn into a productive spot. It is also useful in casting delicate baits, such as wasp grub, which would be ripped off the hook by the force of an overarm cast. The peg on the Severn had a 6ft gap between the water and some overhanging willow branches. Quite a lot of competitors in that match would surely have given up, but the author was able to underarm cast a loaded slider float 15-20 yards into the main flow and catch fish.

Perhaps the actual term, underarm cast, while commonly used, is something of a misnomer. The correct description should be the 'backhand cast', for in many instances the cast is more of a side sweep delivered from the back of the hand. It is similar to the action of a spin bowler in cricket involving a nice steady arm movement across the body, with a smooth sharp delivery imparted by the wrist.

The starting position for underarm casting is with the rod positioned across the body and the point down. The bait is held in the free hand. So, if you are right-handed, the rod is in that hand and the bait in the left, the line being tight to the rod top—not too tight, though, as

you can easily hook yourself. The rod tip should be positioned on your left side—vice versa if you are left-handed—with the point near to the surface of the water.

The 'follow-through'

A smooth, sweeping action then sends the tackle on its way. The next second is vital to the action, for the rod must 'follow through', with the tip raised high and pointing directly at the spot aimed for. As the end tackle starts to fall the rod tip is used to straighten or mend the line—either by moving it upstream or, on a stillwater, against the wind—while the line is 'feathered' off the reel with the forefinger to retard the float and allow the length between float and hook to straighten out and so enter the water smoothly.

The rod tip is now dropped and should finish up just above the surface of the water again, if the line is to be sunk.

It all sounds easy, and it is, with practice. Most probably, the first few attempts will be disastrous, but practice will make perfect and a skill that leads to improved catches will have been acquired.

Points to watch are the follow-through—vital for direction; dropping the rod point, and 'feathering' the line off the reel to eliminate tangles and give clean entry. Do not expect to cast as far with the underarm method as with an overhead throw if using similar tackle. You need plenty of weight in the float, but, properly placed, it will not affect bait presentation. Loaded floats, such as the author's own sliders, and stick floats, which carry weight in their base, are the right

choice for this job.

Shotting is important. With a 'waggler' or loaded slider, normal shotting is right—the bulk shot should be about 5ft from the hook with the tell-tale shot around 18in from the hook. The stop-shot—to stop the float running down and fouling the bulk shot—should be 10ft 6in from the hook. When fishing shallower water, the shot should be positioned in proportion.

Correct shotting

If you are using a stick float, then the shotting should be 'poker-line', that is, the shot strung out at regular intervals between float and hook. If the shot is not correctly placed, too much fishing time will be spent unravelling tangles at the business end.

Slightly modifying this method by putting a little more 'bite' into the delivery and keeping the rod tip low, will produce a flat cast which is very useful in windy conditions. Keeping the end rig low and fast minimizes the effect of the wind, helps accuracy, and leads to far less of a 'bow' in the line, thus giving quicker control of the float. This method is practised extensively on the Staffordshire canals, where it has been

Top left and **top**: *Peter Ward begins and follows though on the underarm cast.*
Above: *To trot the far bank, the angler had to slot his end tackle in under its overhang.*

Can an underarm cast be useful for fishing at long range?
Only rarely: long range casting calls for the beefier action and the higher trajectory of an overhead cast.

Why do I end up in a tangle every time I try the underarm cast?
The reason lies either in your shotting patterns or your failure to follow through smoothly. Persevere, though, adjusting these elements. Once mastered, the technique can make many pegs productive which were previously unfishable.

How should I cast when using a centrepin?
An underarm cast is the way to use a centrepin reel. The line is pulled into a loop from between the rod rings with the left hand, then the float is smoothly cast out with a slight flick of the wrist, at the same time releasing the line.

Could the cast be applied to ledgering?
Yes, but only at very close range. Any distance beyond 20 yards will demand a more orthodox cast to ensure the necessary distance and accuracy.

Why is this style of casting associated with light tackle and line?
If you are casting to the opposite bank, your line is going to come to rest across the entire territory of the fishes below. It must touch down lightly (which is a matter of technique) but it must not be too thick or obtrusive.

developed into a fine art.

It seems appropriate to emphasize one or two general points about casting, for these apply to the underarm technique as well. First, see that the reel spool is correctly loaded. The line must be just fractionally below the lip of the spool. Do not fill it level otherwise there is a danger of line spillage and 'bird's nests'. If the line does not fill the spool to within, say, $\frac{1}{16}$in, then energy is wasted in lifting it over the lip, causing a potential loss of casting distance.

As in all casting the most important aspect is accuracy, particularly at long range. To improve this, try casting with the rod point positioned above the opposite shoulder to your rod hand. As with underarm casting, the rod is across the body, but with the point up in the air. A smooth sweep with the rod tip moving in the direction of the required point will give you accuracy and, with practice, distance.

Though rarely used in the North of England, Midlanders have developed it to a fine art, the advantages being most aparent in canal and drain fishing. Where it is necessary to land the bait close to the far bank, particularly under overhanging trees and bramble bushes, an overarm cast just will not do the job because of its high angle of trajectory. An underarm cast, however, can skim the float across the canal a few inches above the water with the bonus that the float preceeds the bait. Where the far bank is lined with foliage, often dipping into the water, it is important to allow the unchecked entry of the float to prevent the bait from looping over, with the inevitable snagging that follows.

Because of the extremely fine tolerances required in fishing the far bank of a canal or drain, it is a pointless exercise if wind or surface drift is allowed to pull the float away from the cover so much sought by fish. The answer lies in careful treatment of the line, by squirting a little washing-up liquid on to the spool, to ensure rapid sinking.

Float fishing

To many the epitome of angling happiness is watching any old float bobbing up and down in the water. There is, however, a lot more to modern float fishing than this

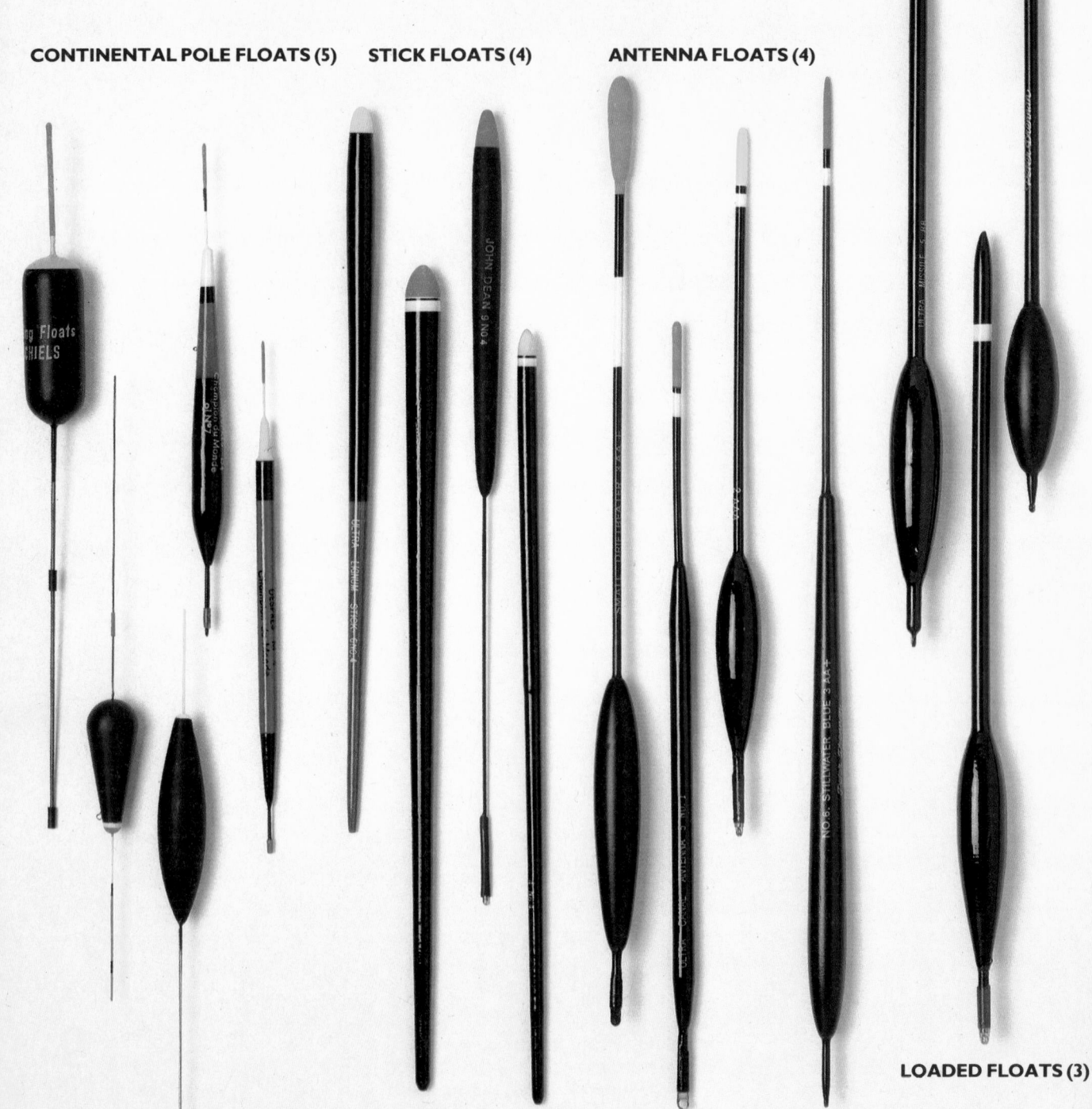

CONTINENTAL POLE FLOATS (5) **STICK FLOATS (4)** **ANTENNA FLOATS (4)**

LOADED FLOATS (3)

WAGGLERS (7)

TROTTING FLOATS (3)

QUILL FLOATS (3)

SLIDERS (2)

145

Float fishing is probably the most popular form of coarse fishing. There are a great number of different types of float and different methods of float fishing, but too many anglers, having found that one tactic and one float work reasonably well, stick to this without considering other methods. Rather than just settling for the most convenient method, the angler should try to achieve the best possible presentation of the bait in each situation. He should go for the most effective method. This might not be the easiest, but it is the angler with the techniques and ability to do this who will more often than not catch the most fish.

The waggler

The large antenna float—the waggler—seems to be the float most abused by lazy anglers. Certainly, in the past few years, it has been reponsible for winning a lot of matches. Yet is this because this is the most effective float, or because it is being used when it shouldn't be?

This is not as contradictory as it sounds. People are winning matches with the waggler, but it is possible that with other floats, such as a stick, they would have won with even more fish. And while a waggler is comparatively easy to fish, it will not allow the angler to get the best out of every swim.

The reason for this is simple. The waggler does not allow the same degree of control over the presentation of the bait as a double-rubbered float. When the waggler is being properly used it is fished attached by its bottom end only and has a lot of tip showing above the water. This is because it is fished with a shot dragging the bottom and the float must not be sensitive enough to be dragged under.

Even so, despite its size, try to hold it back against the water flow, so that the bait is presented in a slow, attractive manner, and what happens? It merely goes under because of the drag of the line between rod tip and float—unless you have achieved a degree of expertise and control of the float possessed by very few anglers. In contrast, a stick or balsa, fished double-rubber, can

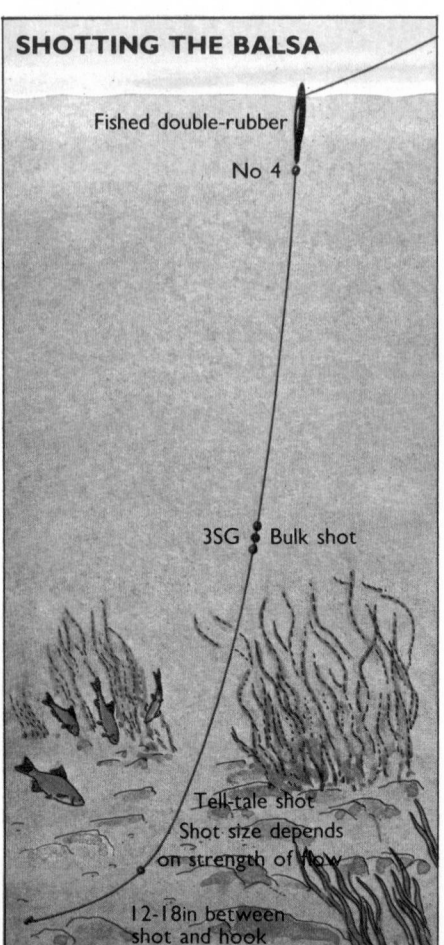

SHOTTING THE BALSA

Fished double-rubber

No 4

3SG • Bulk shot

Tell-tale shot
Shot size depends
on strength of flow

12-18in between
shot and hook

Left: *Shotting the balsa is relatively simple, with bulk shot roughly halfway between float and hook and the tell-tale weighted according to current.* **Above:** *A good grayling taken on a trotted bait is netted.* **Below:** *Float-fished bread is a dependable method of catching roach.*

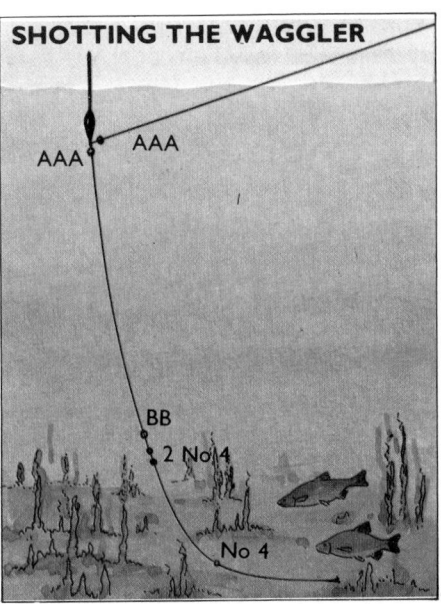

SHOTTING THE WAGGLER

AAA   AAA

BB
2 No 4

No 4

Above: *Shot pattern for the waggler.* **Left:** *Using an extending landing net to bring in a fish caught on the waggler.*

be held in the stream so that the bait just trickles along.

This is not to say that the waggler cannot be a very useful float in certain circumstances. In difficult conditions, rough water and fierce downstream wind, for example, or when the fish are biting freely three or four rod-lengths out—when it has the edge in speed—it can be ideal. In other circumstances, on rivers such as the Ribble, which has an uneven flow, other floats, such as the Avon balsa, are more successful.

The Avon balsa
The size of the balsa is important. It must be big enough to carry sufficient weight to allow you to pull back on the rod without it dragging into the bank too quickly. A float which can carry about two or three swan shot serves the purpose. Shotting is simple: all you need is a small shot, say a No 4 (directly under the float to stop it sliding down the line under the pressure of striking), the bulk shot roughly halfway between the float and the hook, and the tell-tale which goes 1ft to 18in from the hook. The purpose of the tell-tale shot is to regulate the presentation of the bait. The tell-tale's size will depend on the strength of the flow.

The method with this rig is to cast out to the area you wish to

fish—with this rig the under-arm cast is a must if tangles are to be avoided—and then to mend the line—that is to lift the line and swing it upstream if it threatens to put drag on the float and bait—until the float settles. Then lift the rod tip high in the air so that the line goes directly to the float tip without touching the water.

If you choose a float with plenty of bulk and weight-carrying capacity, it will strip line from the reel at the pace you dictate and carry on the current far more smoothly than a waggler. Furthermore, if you check the line on the rim of the spool with your fingertip, you can slow the float right down or even momentarily stop it—something you can't do with a waggler.

There's no doubt that this pays off. If you have studied the swim, you should know what part of it may produce a fish; you can then slow up the float when it is approaching the area, relaxing again when it has passed downstream.

Big stick floats
Big stick floats are another useful tool ignored by many anglers nowadays. When the wind is blowing upstream and out from the bank, the big stick is probably easier to handle than a waggler. This is

Why do floats come in such a variety of colour combinations?
Floats are coloured so that they can be seen at a distance against various backgrounds. Choose a black tip when fishing in open water, an orange or yellow tip against a dark background. Although there is no conclusive proof that fish are affected by the colour of a float, a blue or grey finish, when seen from below, seems more likely to blend with the sky.

Where can I buy float making materials?
Float-making kits can be ordered from John Towle of 31 Charles Avenue, Spondon, Derbyshire. Most tackle dealers sell peacock quills and corks while balsa is available from model shops. Few floats are more sensitive than the crowquills you find lying around everywhere in the countryside.

If I buy my son half a dozen floats to start him off, what lengths, colours and shapes should I go for?
Porcupine floats come in various lengths and colours and are really robust. Two each of 4in, 6in and 8in would do for a start, a couple black tipped for bright backgrounds, a couple in orange or yellow for dark or broken backgrounds.

Can you recommend an up-to-date book on float patterns and how they are used?
The late Billy Lane wrote an excellent book on floats and their uses: a revised edition — *The New Encyclopedia of Float Fishing* — by Billy Lane and Colin Graham, Pelham Books, price £9.95. It is doubtful if there is a more comprehensive book, either for novice or expert.

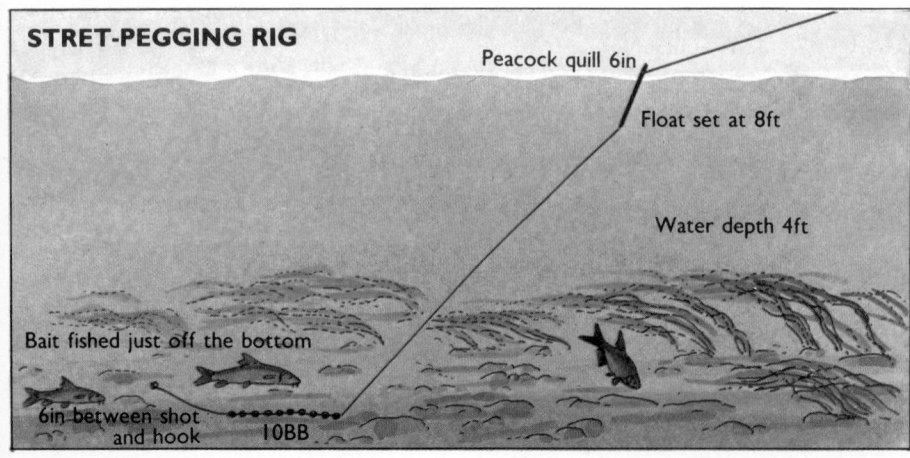

STRET-PEGGING RIG

Peacock quill 6in

Float set at 8ft

Water depth 4ft

Bait fished just off the bottom

6in between shot and hook

10BB

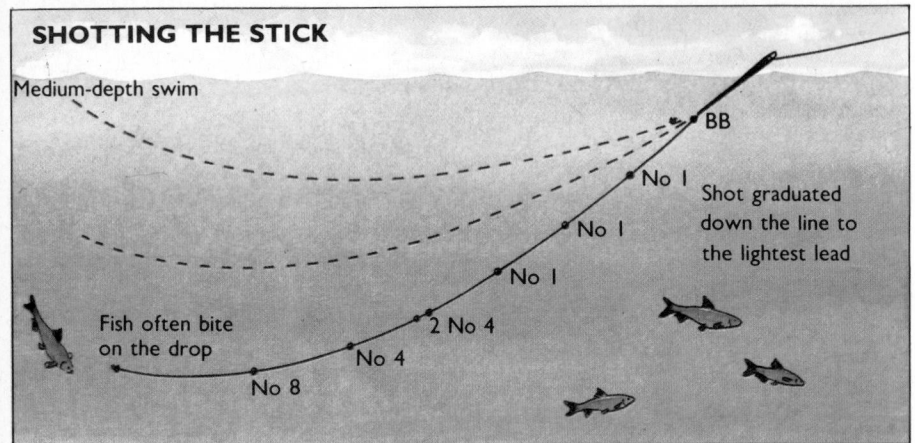

SHOTTING THE STICK

Medium-depth swim

BB

No 1

No 1

Shot graduated down the line to the lightest lead

No 1

No 1

2 No 4

No 4

Fish often bite on the drop

No 8

Above left: *Stret-pegging is sometimes the only way to fish fast-flowing rivers with success.* **Left:** *The shotting pattern for big stick floats is a steady graduation from the top down, with No 8 shot as the heaviest.* **Above:** *A 2lb roach taken from the River Tud on float-fished bread.*

because the effect of the wind on the line when the float is being fished double-rubber slows down the bait without any effort from the angler. Again, underarm casting is essential.

Another 'old-fashioned' method of fishing which receives too little attention nowadays is stret-pegging. It has largely been abandoned in favour of swing tip rods and there is little doubt that when bait is wanted hard on the bottom in the middle of the river the swingtip is by far the best solution. Nevertheless, if the fish are closer in, then stret-pegging is deadly, particularly if the river is carrying a lot of water.

When stret-pegging, the float—a peacock is ideal—is fished double-rubber, over-depth and over-shotted. Basically, this means that line between float and hook should be about twice as long as the water is deep and should carry roughly double the amount of shot the float can support. For example, if you have a 6in length of peacock quill capable of carrying half a dozen BB shot, load

it up with 12 BB, concentrated around 6in from the hook and if the water is 4ft deep, set the float at 8ft. The bait then bobs around in the current just off the bottom, while the line stretches at an angle of 45 from the float to the weight.

The technique is basically simple. Just cast out and allow the tip to pull round. But although this sounds simple, it is not that easy. The line must be held tight between float and rod tip and the float literally held up—otherwise, being heavily over-shotted, it just dives to the bottom. However, if used properly, you'll be surprised at just how positive the bites are.

If the fish are not biting, try varying the presentation of the bait by slightly lifting the rod and 'inching' the business end of the rig across the bottom.

A stillwater alternative to ledgering is the lift method of float fishing for which, conveniently, you can use the same piece of peacock as for stret-pegging. But instead of a bunch of small shot, use one big one,

say a swan, although once again the rig is fished over-shotted, and over depth as with stret-pegging. The difference is that the float is fished peg-leg—that is attached by its bottom end only. Furthermore, unlike stret-pegging, the hook should be very near to the shot, say, only two or three inches away.

With the lift method, cast out to your swim, and allow the shot to hit bottom. The float will, of course, lie flat. Then gently tighten up the line until the float cocks and is dotted down—that is, it only has the smallest amount possible showing. When a fish picks the bait off the bottom—this method is particularly effective for tench—the result is the most dramatic bite in fishing. To swallow the bait, the fish must also pick up the shot and the float pops up like a Jack-in-the-box!

Curiously enough, the big shot does not seem to put off the fish—although obviously the method can be scaled down using, say, a reversed crowquill or an even more sensitive pheasant-tail quill.

Worms

Cheap, versatile and plentiful, earthworms are one of the most effective baits available to the coarse fisherman. But for best results you need to know how to look after them properly

Most garden lawns contain a plentiful supply of earthworms. The best time for the collection of earthworms is after dark, especially following a shower of rain.

Earthworms have been used as a bait for fish for a thousand years and more, and today they are just as effective. All species of freshwater fish can be caught on worms, and indeed several record fish have fallen to this bait. Even the salmon or trout may be taken in this way, sometimes deliberately, sometimes by chance.

Collecting worms
There are some 25 kinds of earthworm found in Britain, but only three species are of real interest to the coarse fisherman—the lobworm, the redworm and the brandling. The lobworm, sometimes called the dewworm, is the largest, the most used as bait and probably the easiest to find. It can be fished whole for the bigger species, but just the head or tail, commonly offered to roach and dace, will often take larger fish too.

Lobworms may be gathered from a lawn, but if the grass is long it may be difficult. Cricket pitches and close-cut sports fields will also yield lobworms in plenty if access, at the right time, is available to the angler. The best periods are after dark and following a heavy dew or shower or, when conditions are dry, after a lawn has been watered. Early morning can also prove fruitful for worm collecting. It is important to move stealthily, for worms are very sensitive to vibrations and will soon dig themselves in if disturbed. At night it is necessary to use a dim torch or a beachcaster's lamp that straps on to the head and leaves both hands free.

A worm must be seized quickly and firmly when it has come partly out of its hole on to the wet grass.

Carry a tin of fine sand in which to dip your fingers to give them a grip on the slippery creature. The lobworm has tiny clusters of erectile bristles at intervals along its length, and these enable it to grip the sides of its burrow. So having got hold of the worm, maintain a steady pressure until it relaxes and comes out smoothly with its fish-attracting tail intact.

The redworm
The redworm is a smaller species, not usually over 4in long, and is a useful roach, dace, bream and perch bait, although any species of worm may appeal to all freshwater fish. This worm is found in compost heaps, and under large stones or rotting logs; any sizeable object in the garden could conceal enough worms for a good day's fishing.

The brandling is of similar size to the redworm but is distinguishable by a series of yellowish rings around its red, often shiny, body. It can be collected from manure piles or compost heaps. The presence of a compost heap will, of course, mean a regular supply of worms. If the wormery is tended by adding potato peelings, tea leaves and vegetable waste, the worms will grow much bigger and probably breed there, thus supplying a constant store of bait. Where grassy conditions are suitable, worms can be dug at the river bank. Be careful to fill all the holes in and not leave places which other anglers can stumble over.

Cleaning and toughening
Although very effective on the hook, most worms become soft and lifeless very quickly in water and often drop off the hook during casting out. Their quality can be improved to overcome this by allowing the worms to work through a good soil for a few days prior to use. Sink a box in the earth, providing small holes in the bottom for drainage. Place the worms on a bed of soil (a dark, loamy kind is best) and cover with sacking. In wriggling through the soil they will scour themselves to emerge brighter and so more attractive to the fish. They will also be tougher, and will stay on the hook

ASK THE EXPERT

How do I keep tight hold of a worm for long enough to hook it?
Dip your finger tips in sand before picking up each of your bait worms, in the same way as you did in order to pull them out of the ground.

Is it possible to use worm as a pike bait?
Though not normally regarded as a bait for pike, a bunch of lobworms, fished in 'sink and draw', has caught pike when other traditional baits have failed.

Can worm pieces be used in combination with other things to make cocktails?
Yes, bread paste or flake with the hook point 'tipped' with a small piece of worm tail is particularly killing. Try a cocktail of maggot and worm tail, too.

How successful is worm as a deadbait?
A dead worm is useless and should be discarded well away from your stock of bait as it will quickly cause wholesale deaths among the rest.

Are the tiny red bloodworms that live in the water butt any use as a worm bait?
Certainly: the bloodworm, which is the larval form of the midge family, is used a lot by match fishermen to take small fish. But it is also successful with large – even specimen – fish such as carp and tench, when fished in bunches on a fine wire hook.

COMMON BAIT WORMS

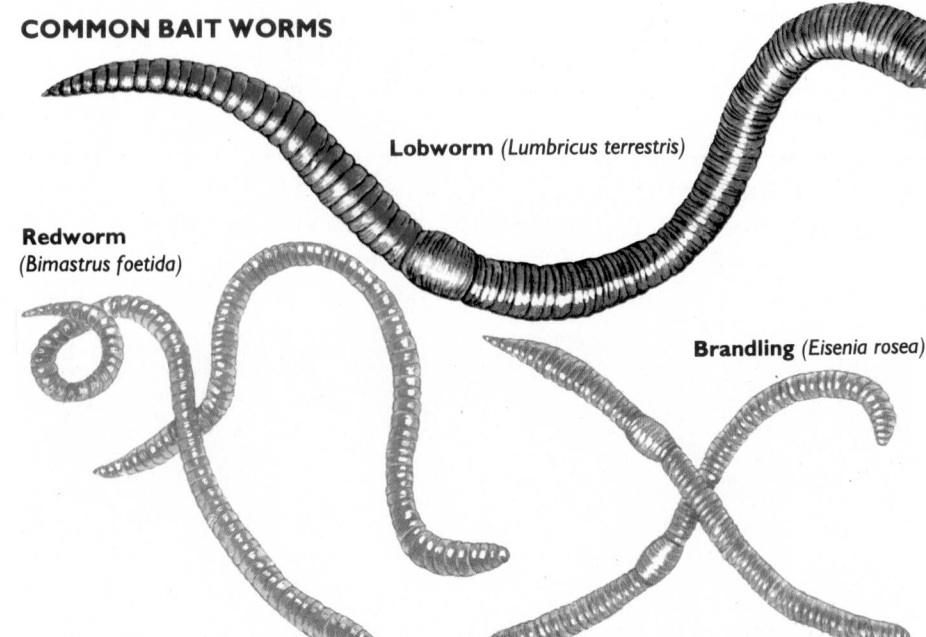

Lobworm (*Lumbricus terrestris*)

Redworm (*Bimastrus foetida*)

Brandling (*Eisenia rosea*)

All freshwater fish are attracted by earthworms but roach, dace, bream and perch are particularly susceptible to the smaller, brighter coloured redworms.

longer and wriggle more enticingly. 'Faddist' used to recommend that worms be kept in fine red sand or brickdust, suggesting that this gave them an added colouring as well as making the texture of their skins much tougher.

Alternatively, a bucket containing sphagnum moss (obtainable cheaply from a florist) provides a medium for cleaning and toughening your worm bait. They will burrow through the moss, which should be damp but not wet. To keep worms fresh immediately before and during use, put them in clean moss and place in a linen bag. Tins and jars should be avoided, for they do not allow the worms to breathe properly. Remember also to weed out dead and dying worms, for one dead worm in a bait tin tends to trigger off an extremely fast mass mortality among the rest.

Hooking the worm
It is important to hook a worm correctly, for this ensures that it stays on the hook and that it will wriggle naturally to attract the fish. A whole worm can be hooked anywhere along its length. If necessary, pierce a long worm several times and feed it along the hook. Tails or pieces of worms should present no problem and stay on the hook. In general do not try to cover the hook, for a worm is a very tempting bait and, if lively, will probably wriggle enough to expose part of the hook anyway.

Apart from using a single hook, there is the two-hook rig known as pennell tackle, and the two- or three-hook Stewart Tackle. These multiple-hook rigs are best when the whole of a big lobworm is used.

Look after worms, they are an all-purpose, all-weather angling bait.

HOOKING A WORM
If using a single hook (left) make sure that it pierces the body of the worm twice, or alternatively, you can use two hooks (right).

Natural flies

What sweeter revenge on the flies and insects that have stung, bitten, buzzed and bothered you at the water's edge than to hook up on a juicy natural bait and catch a specimen fish with it!

Collecting insects in a butterfly net from the long grasses alongside the River Otter, near Honiton, in Devon.

Many anglers today seem to think that it is impossible to catch coarse fish unless they have ample supplies of maggots and casters. In the match fishing world, this does, indeed, seem to be true. For the pleasure angler, or specimen hunter, however, the maggot has a distinct disadvantage: it is a bait which lends itself too readily to the capture of small fish. There are very many other baits freely available to the angler prepared to seek them out. They cost nothing but a little time devoted to their collection, and provide excellent sport with a variety of coarse fish. One of the most interesting is natural flies.

For a great many years, it has been standard angling practice to fish a natural fly 'on the dap'. This is particularly true when fishing for trout in large stillwaters such as the Scottish lochs, or Irish loughs, where at times there can be very heavy hatches of large flies such as the mayfly. The tackle used is very simple: a long rod, a 12 or 13ft glassfibre match rod, combining lightness with strength would be ideal; a centrepin reel loaded with a blow line of undressed floss silk, usually coloured light green, and a short leader of nylon monofilament of about 5lb b.s. with a fine wire eyed hook tied on.

Technique, too, is simple. First, collect a number of suitable flies from around the shoreline of the lake. Store these in a dry bottle, so that just one or two can be shaken out as required. Angling usually takes place from a boat moored in a suitable position or allowed to drift very slowly with the wind. There has to be a wind for the light line to be carried out, allowing the fly impaled on the hook to dibble on the water's surface in a realistic way.

Flies for surface feeders

The mayfly, or some of the other flies that regularly appear on trout lakes, are rarely seen on coarse fisheries. This is not important, however, because the technique is the same. Insects such as the daddy long legs are very suitable bait for the surface-feeding varieties of coarse fish—particularly the rudd, a shoal fish which spend much of its time at the surface. Grasshoppers are also used, as are any insects that might be blown on to the water and which can be easily collected.

Having collected a good supply of bait, set off in the boat, keeping a sharp look-out for a shoal of rudd. When you have found it, moor well upwind. Select a hook to suit the size of bait. A size 12, for example, will be about right for a daddy long legs, while you will need a size 10 for a grasshopper, a drone fly or a small bumble bee. Pass the hook through the body of the bait, then allow the wind to blow the line away from you towards the rudd shoal, keeping the rod vertical. Keep on paying out line until you are covering the shoal. Drop the rod tip slightly, allowing the fly to fall to the surface. It does not matter if it lifts off every now and again—this is a realistic imitation of the struggles of an insect trying to escape from the water.

Coarse fish on fly

Coarse fish usually take a natural insect from the surface very confidently. There may be a big splashy rise, or just a tiny dimple, but either way the fly will vanish from sight and the leader will move and tighten as the fish turns away from the surface. Now is the time to strike. The strike must be firm because there is usually a big bow in the line which has to be taken up before striking.

Maggots

When all you've caught after a long day's fishing is a cold, then its time to review your choice of bait. Maggots are good bait for many kinds of fish, and breeding them yourself is easy

The maggot is the most popular coarse fishing bait used in Britain. Almost all our freshwater species may be taken on it, major competitions have been won on it, and it has also accounted for some record fish.

Maggots are small, easy to buy, transport and use. Not so long ago they were cheap, but prices have risen steeply. Maggots now cost about £1 a pint. They are sold this way because pint beer glasses were once used to scoop them up for sale.

The maggot is the larva, or grub, of the fly. The maggots of the bluebottle, greenbottle, and common housefly are the ones which are used by the angler.

There are four stages in the life-cycle of a fly: egg — grub — pupa — fly. The female of the common housefly lays between 120 and 150 eggs at a time and deposits several batches during its lifetime.

Maggot breeding

Breeding maggots is big business. Millions are sold every week by tackle dealers all over the country. Professional breeders use bluebottles for mass production of the ordinary maggot. The common housefly's maggots are known as 'squatts', and being smaller than the bluebottle larvae they are used as 'feeders' thrown in to attract fish. Maggots

from the greenbottle are called 'pinkies'. These are also small and used as 'feeders', but may be used on the hook when circumstances require very fine tackle.

Commercial fly houses holding the breeding stocks are maintained at constant temperatures of 21.1°C-23.9°C (70-75°F). This enables maggot production to meet the year-round demand.

Maggot breeding starts when meat or fish is placed in the fly house so that the breeder flies can lay their eggs. When this is done the meat is said to be 'blown'. The meat is then removed from the fly house and placed on trays in long sheds. When the maggots hatch they begin to feed and grow. On reaching bait size they are transferred to another tray filled with bran or sawdust. As they wriggle through this they are cleaned and then ready for despatch, usually in large biscuit tins, to tackle shops. There they are kept in fridges to prevent them reaching the pupa (or chrysalis) stage too soon.

Maggots are usually sold in saw-

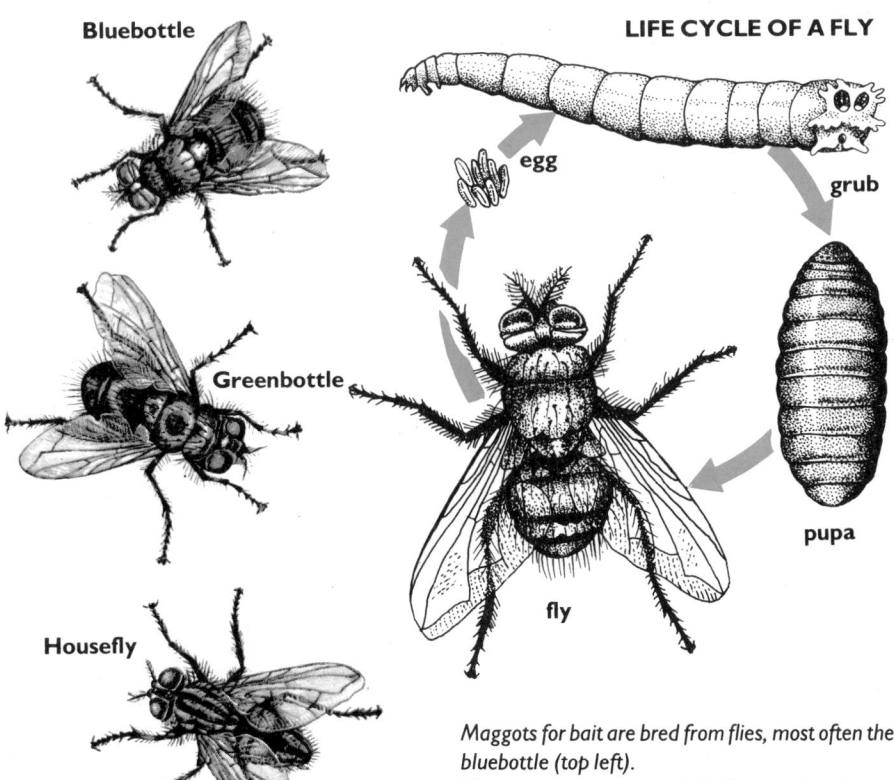

Bluebottle

Greenbottle

Housefly

LIFE CYCLE OF A FLY

egg

grub

pupa

fly

Maggots for bait are bred from flies, most often the bluebottle (top left).
The maggots known as 'pinkies' come from the greenbottle (centre left), and the housefly (bottom) produces 'squatts'.

dust or bran. To improve their taste remove them from the sawdust or bran and transfer them to a clean bait box containing custard or blancmange powder, flour, or a similar substance. As they crawl through this they become well-coated and tiny specks flake off in the water to add an extra attraction for the fish.

Breeding your own maggots
Many anglers are now breeding their own maggots, and producing very high quality hookbait. This must be done in garden sheds or somewhere away from the house. (Even professional breeders are often asked by local authorities to move on because of the smell associated with their business.) Quality maggots may be obtained from chicken carcasses. Put these in a container — a large biscuit tin is ideal — and make sure the lid fits perfectly. Make a 2-3in diameter hole in the top and leave the tin outdoors. After a couple of days the chicken flesh will be blown, with clusters of eggs visible.

Wrap the blown chicken carcass in old newspaper and replace it in the tin. The eggs will hatch a few days later

How long will maggots keep?
This depends on how warm they are kept. In summer they will not last more than three or four days before turning into the brittle chrysalis.

Can you stop maggots turning into chrysalids?
Only for a short time. Put them in a plastic box, with very small pinholes, and place it in the fridge — getting permission first! No harm will come to food there so long as the maggots remain in the box. They will become limp and white, and keep for several weeks. When returned to a warm atmosphere they soom come back to life.

Why do fish like maggots?
This must be due to a combination of their wriggling sending 'fishy' vibrations through the water, their movement and shape which make them look like small fish or tadpoles, and the 'smell' or taste given off by any additive on them.

Are maggots harmful to the angler?
Not in the normal way of picking them up and putting them on the hook. But it has been estimated that one maggot might carry as many as 350,000 bacteria, so keep them off your sandwiches!

Why are maggots so popular?
Because they stay on the hook well, can be cast well out, and because they attract all the coarse species. Even pike and trout have been taken on maggots. But always have another bait with you and be prepared to change if fish stop taking maggots.

BREEDING MAGGOTS

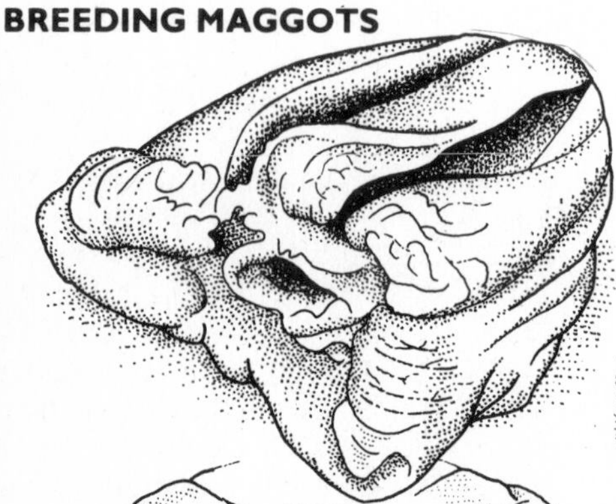

A pig or sheep heart, drained and cut open, is best for breeding gozzers.

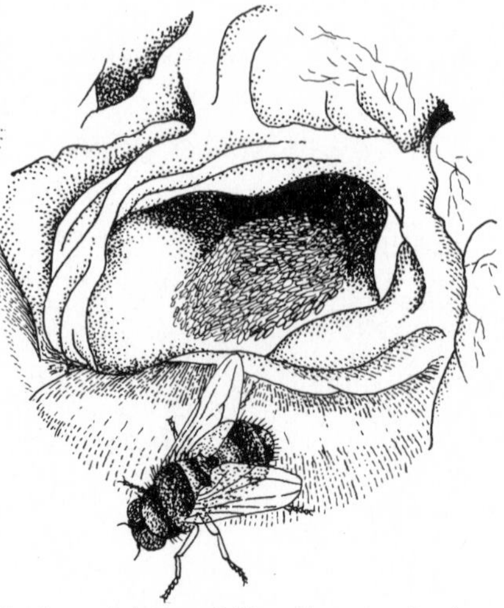

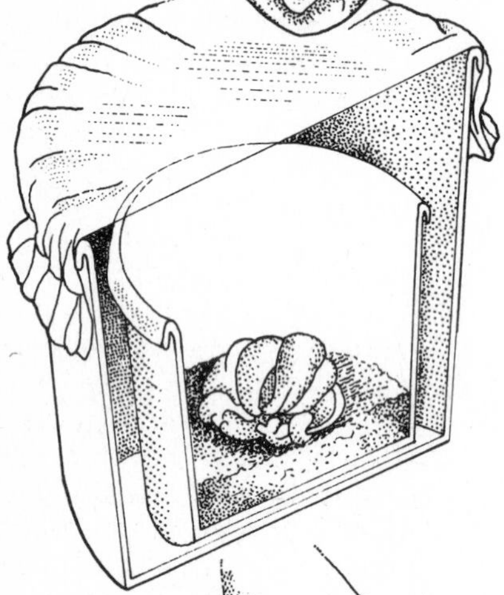

The heart is laid on 2-3in of bran in a bucket, which is covered to prevent unwanted additional 'blows' and kept in a cool, dark place.

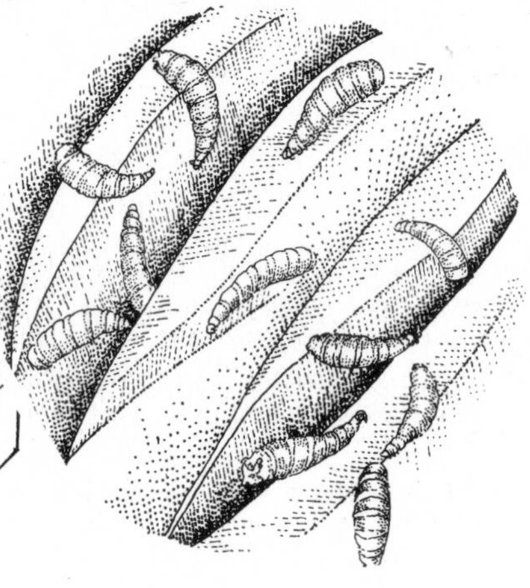

When grown, the maggots are riddled and put into clean bran.

Below: *Hook the maggot through the vent at the blunt end. This will allow it to wiggle attractively to tempt the fish.*

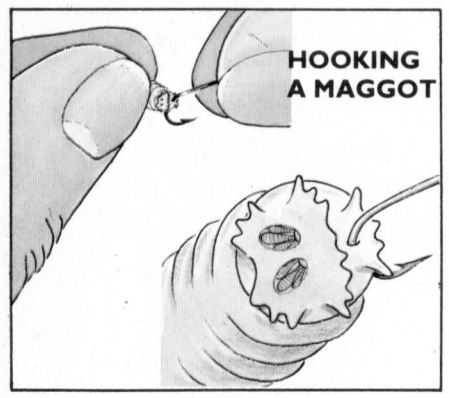

HOOKING A MAGGOT

and the grubs will begin to feed on the nutritious meat. To help the maggots grow fat, add soft brown sugar or even the cream off the top of the milk.

Keep the chicken wrapped in the paper, watching at intervals to see how the maggots are growing. When they stop feeding, place the maggots in bran for 24 hours. Next, tip onto a sieve and allow the bran and maggots to separate. Now add clean bran, plus more sugar, which will ensure that they remain soft until needed.

The 'gozzer' is a very soft, white maggot, the larval form of a type of bluebottle, reared mainly on pigeon carcass, pig's or sheep's heart. After

five or six days of feeding, these should be given a final bran 'bath' and left until required.

A very succulent maggot, the 'gozzer's' powers of attraction are highly valued.

Coloured maggots

Some years ago it was the practice to use maggots coloured pink, yellow, orange, red and bronze. It defied explanation, but at times fish seemed to prefer a certain colour to all others and this gave the matchman an advantage if he had the taking coloured maggots. Light and water colour conditions were probably the reasons.

However, it gradually became feared that the dyes, Chrysiodine R for orange and bronze, Auramine O for yellow and Rhodamine B for red, were agents capable of causing cancer in humans. Anglers would obviously have freely handled the dyed maggots and in the process transfer the dye to the skin of their hands.

The seriousness of the matter is illustrated by the fact that ICI issued a statement insisting that even the dyes containing food-colouring substances should not be used for dyeing maggots. Today, tackle shops that once sold various coloured maggots now offer only white, natural maggots.

The 'annatto' is a special colour-fed maggot whose yellow colour comes from the dye used to colour butter. Gozzers and other extra soft maggots produce the best results with this dye. Annatto is bought in roll form and must be cut into slices and mixed into a thin paste with water before use.

To prevent your maggots from turning into chrysalids, or casters, before you want them to, when the weather is warm, place them securely in a plastic box with extra bran and store them in your fridge where they will become cold and still. Make sure the lid of the box is securely closed, but remember that maggots need air, so ensure your bait boxes are ventilated with pinholes.

Lastly, if buying maggots from a shop, be sure they are fresh and do not include remnants of last week's stock.

Casters

Hailed by many as the new 'wonder' bait of recent years, casters need to be firm and dark red to ensure success. For this reason many anglers have turned to producing them at home

The chrysalis, or pupa, of the fly is known to anglers as a caster. At this point in its life-cycle (from egg to grub, or maggot, to pupa, to fly) it is an excellent bait. First made popular by match anglers in roach waters, some experts consider casters to be the most important new bait adopted in recent years. Although the maggot remains the most popular general bait, the time may be near when the caster will have replaced it. As well as roach, chub and dace are partial to it and it has accounted for bream, gudgeon and tench. When first introduced to a stretch of water the fish may be uninterested but, once sampled, every caster is likely to be taken. The fish probably gets its food more easily from the insect at this stage of its lifecycle than it did when it was a mere maggot.

Casters can be purchased from a tackle shop or bait dealer and kept in

Above: *Casters and maggots laid out at the swim.* **Right:** *To hook a caster hold it gently between thumb and forefinger, pierce the head with the point of the hook and sink the bend and most of the shank into the bait.*

a refrigerator for about a week. Home production can work out to be more expensive than buying them ready-bred, but the angler needs chrysalids (or casters) as sinkers: too fast a metamorphosis and the caster becomes a floater, of no practical use except as a means to check on the presence of fish in unknown water. The keen angler who needs a constant supply, therefore, will want to produce his own, in order to control the speed of change. After a little trial and error the angler can have casters in perfect condition and colour in the quantities he needs as and when he wants them.

Whether you buy casters from the dealer or raise maggots yourself,

you will need about five pints of maggots to produce three pints of good quality casters—enough for a match or a day's fishing.

For large casters, choose large maggots. To test for freshness if you are buying the maggots, look for the food pouch—the small black speck under the skin. This pouch carries all the food the insect needs to complete the stages of its development to a fly, and should still be visible.

It takes a fresh maggot, one that has just been taken from its feed medium, five to six days to turn into a chrysalis with the temperature at between 65° and 70°F (18° to 21°C). To slow development, put the maggots, in a plastic box, into the refrigerator for three days—more in very hot weather, less in cold.

Tip the maggots on to a sieve to be riddled and cleaned, then into tins of dry sawdust, so that maggots and sawdust cover the bottoms of the tins to a depth of not more than a couple of inches. The maggots should now be kept in a cool place: a garage or cool outhouse is ideal.

After about 24 hours the first of the casters will be seen. Once this stage is reached put the contents of the tins on to a riddle over a larger container and the maggots will wriggle through, leaving the already-turned casters on the mesh. Any dead maggots that you find amongst them should be thrown away.

HOOKING A CASTER

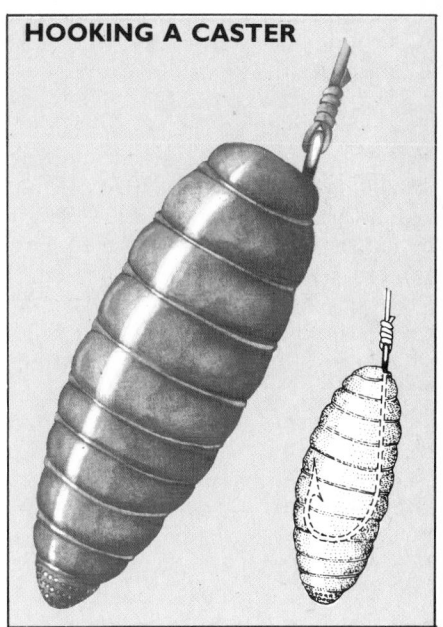

FROM MAGGOTS TO CASTERS

Top: Five pints of maggots give a day's supply of casters.
Above: In five or six days most of the maggots turn to casters. Remove all dead maggots (right).

Return the live maggots to their tins. Repeat this inspection and selection process every 7 or 8 hours. Each batch of casters can be rinsed in water to remove bits of sawdust, drained on the riddle, sealed in plastic bags and placed in the refrigerator, at not less than 34°F.

Removing floaters

By rinsing the casters, any floaters can be removed at this stage. Damp casters can sour in the refrigerator and some anglers prefer to omit rinsing at this stage as a final check should may be made before setting off, or at the waterside.

If you do not want to use the refrigerator for collecting the bags of casters, you can put them direct from the riddling into a bucket, just covering them with water and adding to their number as they develop. Floaters can thus be eliminated as they appear and the bucket kept in the same cool outhouse as the tins of maggots.

Whichever method you use, you will find that the casters vary in col-

our. Casters of a uniform dark red colour—the favourite—can be achieved quite simply. On the evening before use, wrap all the casters in a wet towel and leave in a bucket overnight. Next morning all the casters will be the same colour.

The choice of hook size will be governed by the size of the caster. The biggest you can use will probably be a 14, but generally a 16 or 18

will be necessary. The hook must be buried in the caster. Hold the caster between thumb and forefinger and, with the hook in the other hand, pierce the head of the caster with the point. Turn the hook very gently into the caster and, with some of the shank still showing, lightly tap the top of the shank until the hook sinks into the caster.

Casters may be fished singly, or in

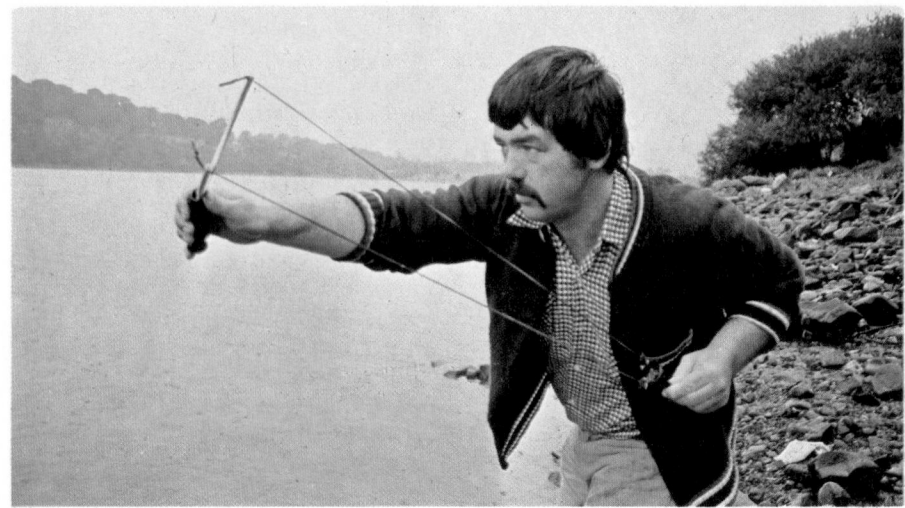

156

twos, threes and fours. In deepish, fast flowing water, casters are best introduced as groundbait. Where there are plenty of fish and they start to take, you can put as many as two dozen casters in every cast. Casters can also be used in combination with other small bait, such as worm tail, hempseed or tares. When groundbaiting the swim with a mixture of hemp, it is essential to make sure the casters are fast sinkers. Floaters drift with the flow and could attract fish out of the swim.

Big fish bait

Casters are not just small fish bait—fairly good bream, chub and barbel have been caught on casters. But big fish require larger hooks with more than one caster placed on the hook. As a rough guide, a 10lb barbel might take a bunch of five casters on a size 12 hook. But an 11lb 8oz barbel has been known to take a small bunch of maggots with a single caster on the tip of the hook.

When fishing deep water at long range, a quantity of casters can be mixed with a cereal groundbait to resemble a 'plum duff' with crunchy casters worked into the groundbait ball. Thrown into the top of a swim by hand, the ball will drop quickly to the bottom before breaking up—an ideal groundbaiting method when ledgering casters. Little and often is always a good maxim when groundbaiting with casters because it is easy to over-feed the swim.

When fished singly, casters need fine and delicate tackle. An easy casting rod is advisable when fished far off—too vigorous a cast will flick the bait off the hook. Quality casters are thought to be a good roach bait on any canal or river. With the approach of autumn they can be unbeatable on some waters.

Casters work best on clear waters, so when a river is coloured it may pay to revert to the maggot.

What makes a good caster?
A correctly bred quality maggot makes a fine chrysalis. This means a large, plump and well coloured caster which will sink quickly.

How best can I identify and separate floaters?
On the morning you go fishing, tip all the casters into a bucket of water. The floaters will remain on the surface, of course, and can be skimmed off easily.

Which fish can I catch with floaters?
Floaters can be a deadly bait for rudd, small roach, dace and bleak—fish which feed close to the surface. They are also useful when you are being bothered by a shoal of small fish. Simply throw in floaters at intervals and as the casters wash downstream they will take with them the unwanted fish—out of your swim.

Why are fine wire hooks recommended for casters?
The casters will burst as you attempt to bait-up, unless fine wire is used.

Can casters be mixed with other baits?
There are various combinations that prove effective. Try feeding a swim with hempseed but using caster on the hook, for instance. The advantage is that casters on the hook fetch more positive bites than hemp.

Can left-over casters from one day's fishing be used on another?
Yes, but only within a few days. Keep the casters in water or in a fridge (not a deep freeze). Even so, they will only last for two or three days. After that they will go sour and should be thrown away.

Left: *When using a catapult to hurl casters into a distant swim, make sure the pouch is cup-shaped to avoid crushing them.*

Above: *A particularly deadly bait for catching bream is to use a 'cocktail' mixture of worm with a single caster on the tip.*

157

Slugs

Slimy and grotesque-looking, despised by the gardener—that's the much-maligned slug. But freelined it's a killing bait for the most wary chub and free for the collecting besides

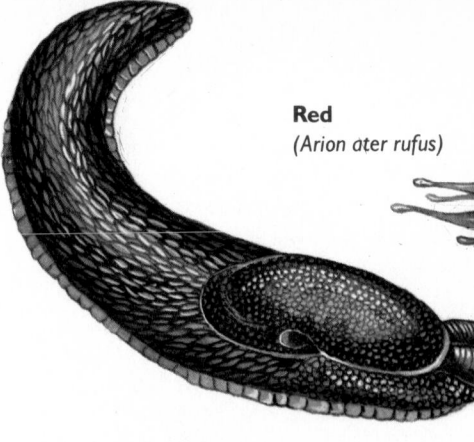

Red
(Arion ater rufus)

Left: *A freelined slug bait will prove irresistible to big chub like this one.*
Above: *Three of the many species of slug found in Britain.* **Below:** *Casting a slug baited hook into a likely chub lie. The offering will soon be accepted.*

Most people think of the slug as a slimy and unpleasant creature which must be treated with distaste. To the hard-working gardener it is a major pest, eating young green shoots. But for the big-fish angler the slug is almost a thing of beauty and a bait that will attract even the most wary chub.

There are over 20 species of slug to be found in Britain. They can be considered as snails that have lost their shells, for the internal anatomy of a slug is very similar.

The best slugs
For the angler, the best slugs are undoubtedly the black, *Arion ater,* the great grey, *Limax maximus,* and the red, *Arion ater rufus.* Most of the other British slugs are too small to use as a big-fish bait.

As slugs tend to lie-up when frosts appear in late October or November, one must construct either a holding area or a place where they can be allowed to breed. By far the best way to keep them is in an aquarium. This will enable you to see what is going on inside without having to disturb the inmates.

An ideal size is an aquarium measuring 48in×8in×15in. It should have as a cover a well-fitting lid of ¼in plate glass.

Place about 6in of garden soil in the bottom and make sure that you have a few good-sized lobworms in it as well. On top of the soil place some small pieces of plywood, about 6in×6in. The food for the slugs is placed on these slabs.

As slugs like to hide during the day you must prepare somewhere for them to go, so put a couple of inverted flower-pots on top of the soil.

Keep moisture down
The atmosphere in the tank is kept moist by the tight-fitting lid. This creates rather too much moisture, so if the aquarium is kept propped up at one end the moisture will filter down and form a pool which should be siphoned out from time to time.

It is important to keep the pool of condensed water low since for some reason the slugs tend to crawl into it and drown. Therefore it is best if the 'sluggery' is kept in a garden shed or garage, for the smell of decomposing slug is very potent.

On a rainy day, place them on the lawn for a 'run'. But keep an eye on them for they can move surprisingly fast and disappear into the grass.

Food for the slugs can be all kinds of household waste, greengrocery and garden cuttings. Add potato-peelings and greens such as cabbage.

Great grey
(Limax maximus)

Black
(Arion ater)

Below: *Your slug will be attacked by chub without any preliminaries, resulting, more often than not, in a neat lip-hooking.*

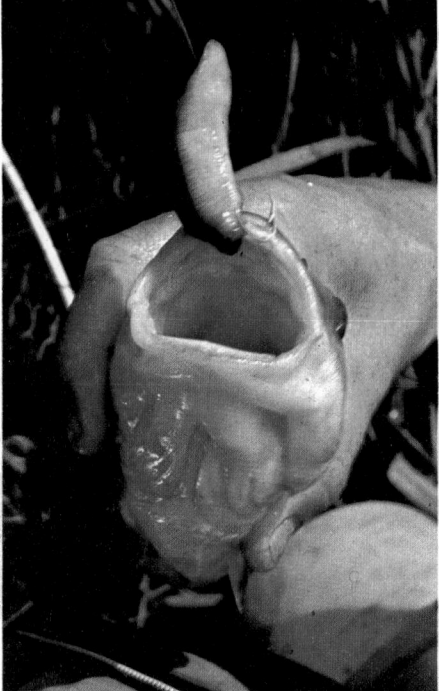

ASK THE EXPERT

Where can I look for slugs 'in the wild'?
A compost heap is a favourite place, especially after dark. But on any moist, mild night, pathways are strewn with slow-moving slugs.

Can I breed slugs in a compost heap?
It would be more difficult to **stop** slugs breeding in a heap. No matter how many you collect there will always be plenty more.

Can slugs get out of a lidless container?
Certainly. A gardener's ploy for trapping unwelcome slugs is to invert flowerpots over garden canes. The slugs *climb the canes* but are defeated somehow by the downward journey. If you don't seal a breeding container with a ventilated lid, your bait will disappear overnight.

Do fish ever show a preference for the different breeds of slugs?
Occasionally a switch from a red slug to a black one will produce an immediate response. Coincidence? Top matchmen always take two or three different colours of maggots to the waterside, so clearly there is something in the principle of colour-change.

Why is a big hook necessary?
A slug is a big bait and a chub has a big mouth. Besides, long experience has shown a good ratio of bites to fish taken when big hooks are used.

What species might I catch with this bait other than chub?
In rivers the odd barbel will add variety to your catch. And tench occasionally fall to a slug in stillwaters.

Check the tank regularly and remove any dead slugs. When the tank is established and the slugs are feeding well, they will probably breed. So in late October or November place some sheets of newspaper on the soil. The slugs will lay their clusters of small white eggs on the paper, and some on the insides of the inverted flower-pots on top of the soil.

After the eggs have been laid, remove the slugs. They will soon die as they only live about a year. Any rotting food must also be taken out. Now cover the sides and top of the aquarium with polystyrene sheeting to keep in the warmth.

When spring arrives, very small slugs will be seen. Often, the tight lid and condensation attract tiny flies and mites. The young slugs will feed on these, but get them 'weaned' on to potato-peelings and green-stuffs as soon as possible.

A few fresh slugs from the garden ought to be put in, but it seems that some species cannot get on together. The large black slugs do not live with the red. So keep to one sort which you can find locally. The slugs should be about 3in long by May and in June they can be fattened up for the summer's fishing.

Fattening them up
Three days before you go out on a fishing trip, get a whole melon and cut a small hole in the tough skin. If you place this in the sluggery they will crawl in and gorge themselves, often leaving nothing but the melon's tough skin. The largest slug I have bred using this method is one that measured an incredible 7½in long. This may be a record!

Bread

If you want a cheap, plentiful, easy to use and highly effective coarse fishing bait, try bread. Most species can be taken on it, and it's especially good for caching carp and tench

Above: *One of the standard bread baits used by carp fishermen is the floating crust.*

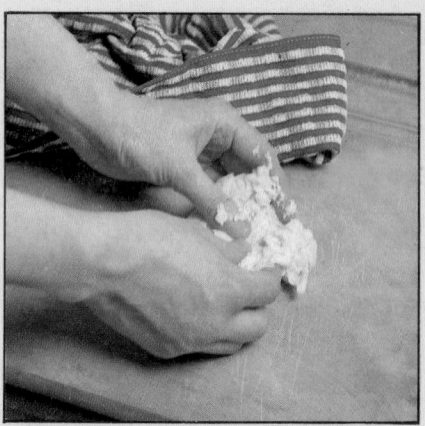
Bread is not only an old-fashioned bait but also a very successful one. In recent years, and on many waters, it has been neglected, perhaps because its uses are not fully understood. Four different baits can be made from a white loaf —flake, crust, balanced crust and paste. The first two of these come from a new loaf, the fourth from an old loaf, the third from both.

Flake

Flake is the name given to the crumb of new bread. The crumb of a two-day-old loaf is difficult, if not impossible, to place on the hook. When removing the crumb from the loaf a light touch is essential. Take hold of the crumb and lightly pull it from the loaf: it should be like a sponge with one edge sealed between thumb and forefinger. With the other hand take the hook, push the shank into the 'sponge' and gently pinch the crumb over it. Both the bend—or part of it—and the point of the hook will be exposed. The two sides of the crumb must be joined together with the minimum of pressure. If the sponge falls apart the bread is too old: one light edge-pinch should be sufficient to keep it together. If the flake is pinched too tightly the bait will be hard and unattractive.

The size of flake, and therefore the size of hook, depends upon the fish you expect to catch, the water you are fishing and the time of year. Chub, barbel, carp and tench during the early part of the season, and big roach in waters not too heavily fished, can all be taken on a No 6 hook. For bream, chub in winter, roach in some waters, tench, grayling and crucian carp, use a No 10. For dace in heavily fished waters, or in winter, use a No 12; in exceptional circumstances, when for example, the fish are shy or in very cold water, use a No 14.

Many anglers dislike flake because it is difficult to cast. The cast must always be a soft one, smooth and unhurried. Generally a sideways cast is best, or when fishing close in, an underhand one. When proficient, overhead casts can be made without bait and hook parting company in mid-air.

An advantage of flake is that, whether trotted or ledgered, small particles constantly break off, thus attracting fish from downstream into one's swim.

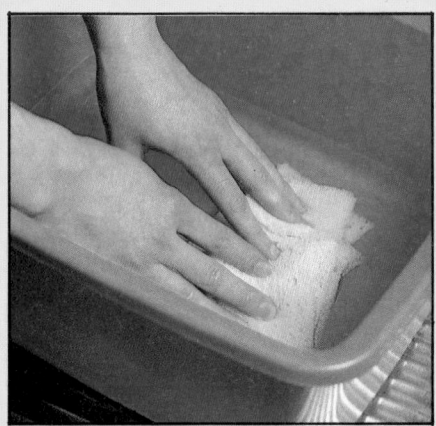

Soak the trimmed slices in a bowl of cold water, making them soggy but not so wet that they disintegrate.

Wrap the soaked slices in a clean cloth (such as a tea towel) and squeeze them firmly to remove all excess water.

The finished paste. Some anglers mix additives such as aniseed, brown sugar or custard powder into their paste.

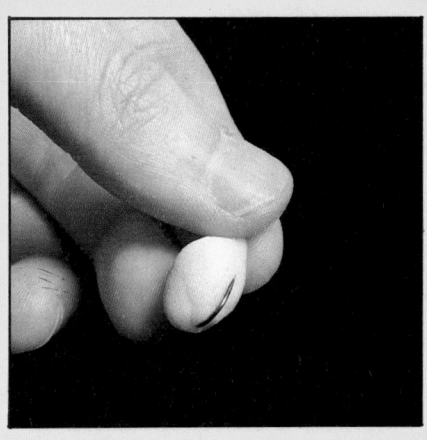

Bread paste should be moulded around the shank and bend of the hook, leaving the point exposed.

Can you think why I might be missing so many strikes using flake?

It depends on which fish you are trying for, of course, but you may be pinching the flake too tightly around the hook. Though it is much less attractive like this, some fish will still rise to it. But the hook then fails to penetrate because the flake's still partially attached.

For how long should a piece of crust be dunked?

Two seconds—no more. By then it will be sufficiently weighty to cast, without being so waterlogged that it drops off.

Has bread anything to offer the roving angler?

Take half a loaf in search of 'little river' roach and you'll find out. In mild weather, and with low water levels, freelined or laid-on breadflake will interest fish of specimen proportions.

I have caught rudd on breadflake, but they become suspicious of it so quickly that it is soon useless. What then?

Progress from flake to crust then, a few fish later, use a bunch of maggots. Before the day is out, you may also need sweetcorn, wheat and lobworm. It is the species to blame, not your technique.

Is it true that the colder the water, the less effective bread is as bait?

No, but in cold water fish become lethargic, use less energy, and therefore require less food. A big piece of crust may well be ignored or just pecked at. But a small piece—mounted on a 14 hook, say—could be devastating.

Crust

Crust must come from a newish loaf, not more than two or three days old. The loaf should be kept in the shade, because once hardened the crust is useless. Depending upon the species being sought, sliced and unsliced loaves can be used. For roach, dace and grayling, a cut loaf is best: where larger pieces are required for such species as chub and carp, an uncut loaf is necessary, especially when using floating crust.

The best way to cut the crust from an unsliced loaf is to insert the point of a sharp knife into the side of the crust. Cut through the crust in the shape of a square. When you pull the square of crust away from the loaf, a chunk of the soft flake beneath it will also come away.

Floating crust is very popular among carp and chub fishermen. The crust must be soft, so the baking of the loaf and its freshness are very important. Hard, brittle crust is useless. Some fastidious anglers order specially-baked loaves, but this should not be necessary if you choose a loaf which has been baked to a light brown colour.

Crumbly or too-hard crust from stale loaves is also useless, breaking up as the hook is pushed through it. A fairly large piece of crust, say 1½in square, is often used with a cast of 20 yards or more. For distance-casting the corners and

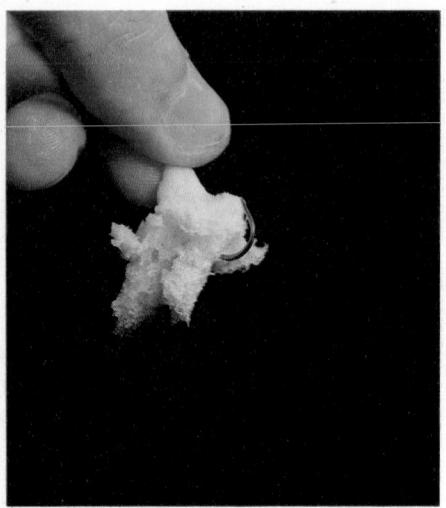

Above: *When using flake, it should be moulded firmly around the shank of the hook, leaving the bend and point exposed.*

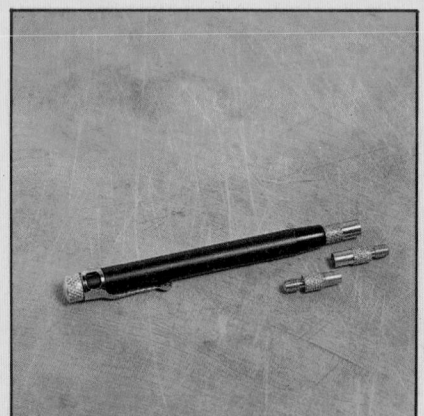

The bread punch, with a selection of chuck sizes, is used for making small pellets of bread flake.

A piece of fresh sliced white bread is placed on a hard surface, and the bread punch is pushed into it.

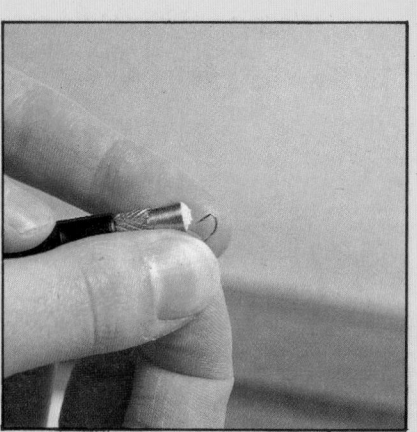

The hook is pushed into the slug of compressed bread inside the chuck of the bread punch.

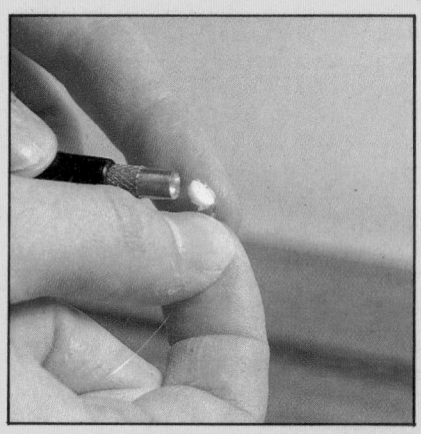

With a gentle twisting action the hook, with the pellet of flake impaled on it, is withdrawn from the punch.

edges of the loaf are, for a given size, heavier than the flat areas and therefore cast better. When no floats or weights are used, however, some weight must be given to the bait, so just before casting the crust is dipped into the water for a moment. This is called 'dunking'.

Hooking the crust

Opinions differ as to which side up the crust should lie. To make the bait hang crust side down take the crust and the hook, push the hook into the crumb side, out of the crust, then back through the crumb until both bend and part of the shank of the hook protrude. The opposite actions will make the bait hang with the crust up. About half the shank with the point and barb should always protrude from the crust. A hook slightly larger than the thickness of the crust must be used. If the hook is completely buried, the wet crust is liable to fall or cast off.

Crust will catch fish in all seasons but it is especially useful in winter, fished stationary close to the bottom. The distance it is presented off the bottom is determined by how far the weight is stopped from it: 6in from the crust and the crust will be fishing about 6in off the bottom.

In June and July crust is especially good for tench, fished either under a float, 'lift' style, or simply ledgered. It can be fished in rivers, trotted and ledgered, and floatless

on a weightless line. In stillwaters, ledgered and floating crust has probably accounted for more carp than any other bait.

Ledgering

Ledgered bread crust is one of the deadliest of baits for chub, while smaller pieces of crust will take tench, roach and even dace.

Crusts tend to be buoyant, so for ledgering the weight should be stopped very close to the hook to hold the bait near the riverbed: an Arlesey bomb is ideal and should be stopped an inch away from the hook.

The size of the ledger depends on the size of the bait and the flow of the river. Ideally, the weight should

be such that the crust should just stay held in position in the current.

Don't be afraid of using really big chunks of crust for chub fishing, especially in summer. A chub will soon make short work of a wad of crust the size of a matchbox. Chub will often feed from the surface in rivers and when you can see fish cruising like this, a wad of crust floated down to them seldom fails. A large piece of crust will sink quicker if you dunk it in the water before casting. Avoid soaking too much, however, or it will soften and fly off your cast.

Although a soft bait, crust will withstand quite a hard, forceful cast—an overhead cast is best.

Bait additives

No bait manufacturer can package and put a price tag on success, much as he would like you to think so. Additives need intelligent handling before they begin to improve your fishing

Above: *Fishing for bream and carp using Roubaisen, a light, fine textured additive said to consist of 20 ingredients.*

Since the days of Walton the topic of 'secret deadly baits' has captured the imagination of anglers. The whole question of wonder additives and closely guarded recipes is emotive to say the least. It can confuse, frustrate and disillusion the novice. However, additives continue to be in vogue and are obviously here to stay. In fact there are thousands of possible additives belonging to eight common groups: oils, essences, colouring, meat extract, blood, sweeteners, pulverized seeds and natural juices. In recent years a great deal of effort has been expended (mainly by the carp fishing fraternity) in developing special meat and 'high protein' baits. The way to success with any bait or mixture is to experiment for yourself. The kitchen larder is full of surprises.

'Deadly' aniseed?

Aniseed is probably the best known and most controversial 'deadly' additive of them all, yet there are thousands who have been taken in by its mythical reputation. The author rates the results he has achieved with it as being quite inconclusive. There are a number of expensive 'revolutionary' fish attractors on the market, most of which are based on aniseed—try not to get caught! Aniseed is also supposed to be a deadly attractor of cats and dogs, but when the author tried it on several cats they at best ignored it—at worst they positively turned up their noses!

The traditional way to use oils like aniseed is to incorporate them in a breadpaste, while a few optimists immerse their hookbait in a concentrated 'dip'. Some additives, notably aniseed, are even supplied in aerosol cans so that you can give your baits a spray at the water's edge.

Oil of geranium

Another additive, reputed to go down well with roach, is oil of geranium. It is not very pleasant to us humans, but apparently it has worked for some anglers. Some years ago, the chemists in Hertfordshire sold out when the rumour leaked out that local experts were using it to make exceptional catches.

If you can tolerate the mess and obnoxious smell, pilchard oil is certainly an additive that can be used to advantage in pike fishing. A variety of methods can be used to introduce this into your swim; the most effective is probably to mix the oil with groundbait and scatter it around. This will attract the small fish which in turn will draw the pike. This attractor in many ways resembles the 'rubby dubby' well proven by sea anglers.

Household essences

There are several common essences used by the housewife that have been borrowed, with moderate success, by carp and tench anglers. These include vanilla, almond and banana essence. All are blended into conventional breadpastes and, unlike many renowned additives, their smells are not obnoxious. All three of the above additives have been proved to some degree by anglers of repute who have carried out carefully planned 'control' experiments with identical tackle and plain bait set-up in the same swim as a rig using an essence additive. The most notable devotee was probably Bob Reynolds who, in the late 1950s, made some formidable carp captures at Billing using banana essence to flavour his baits.

There are many colourings available, the most widely used being the maggot dyes, and these can also be used to colour pastes and groundbait. The whole question of whether

fish hunt by scent or colour-sensitive vision, or a combination of both, is most complex. Nevertheless, a change in colour *can* make all the difference in certain conditions. Frequently the angler does not know why, but reasons seem unimportant while his success lasts! The author had a very successful tench season some years ago when, for some reason, the tench showed a quite definite, temporary preference for yellow breadpaste.

Sausage meat and gravy

A variety of meat extracts are widely used by carp and barbel anglers. They are simply commercial culinary products such as gravy browning, Bovril, Marmite and Oxo and are not to be confused with the much more sophisticated recipes for high protein baits. But they do have a place among the other purpose-mixed preparaions.

Continental additives

In recent years Continental bait additives and groundbaits have been imported in ever increasing quantities. Much of their popularity stems from the match performances of foreign teams, particularly the French, when competing in international events.

Although dozens of products are now appearing on the market, three of them are proven fish attractors. Probably the most popular is a pro-duct called 'Roubaisen'. This is an extremely light and fine mixture of fish attractors containing 20 different ingredients. Bream of all sizes are attracted by its smell and as the product contains little, if any, cereal, the fish do not feed on it. The effect is to excite them into a feeding frenzy and if your hookbait is correctly presented, the bites that result are positively amazing.

'Magic', like Roubaisen, is a combination of many ingredients, reportedly 14, the base of which is a strong chocolate smelling substance. As in most Continental feed baits, ground hempseed is added for its oily content. This groundbait is again particularly effective for bream but also seems capable of attracting the majority of British fish.

An ideal additive to traditional cereal groundbait is Sensas 2000. This product is extremely effective in rivers owing to its bulky nature when mixed, yet is capable of breaking up on the river bed, giving off a scent which attracts fish from downstream swims.

To get these additives into perspective, it must be remembered that they are not an easy way of catching fish; they are merely attractors and stimulators. The most important factor is the correct use of the correct bait in the right place.

Below: *A treacle dip, or a drop or two of flavour concentrate, really spices up a bait.*

ASK THE EXPERT

Do bait additives really work?
The short answer is yes, but don't forget that they only represent a small proportion of what fishermen term as skill. Experience and dedication count far more.

Do different additives attract different species?
Undoubtedly so. Predators are invariably attracted by oil or blood-based additives, while bream, roach and most other coarse fish seem to approve of sweeter ingredients such as vanilla or banana essence.

Is it true that curry powder added to baits fished on canals works well?
Like Continental groundbaits, curry powder is a mixture of many different ingredients whose fish-attracting qualities are somewhat dubious. However, coriander, which forms the basis of most curry powders, does seem to work for canal fish for whatever reason.

Why, if aniseed works, is it not used more often?
Probably because it has attracted more anglers than it has fish. Few successful anglers are at all convinced of its supposed effectiveness.

When should I use meat extracts with my groundbait?
These are most commonly used by carp and barbel anglers when using a meaty bait such as sausage or luncheon meat. These are perhaps the most successful additives yet discovered.

Are Continental additives only used for match fishing?
As a general rule yes, but if they work for matchmen there's no reason why they shouldn't work for all anglers.

Paste and crust

One loaf represents a versatile range of killing baits—but only to the angler versed in preparing, balancing and offering something different from the pulpy, year-round glut of bread

Left: *Trotting a bread bait for dace brings a bite on the river bend.*
Right: *Roach like this will fall to a similar bait and technique.*

Breadpaste is one of the oldest and probably most successful baits. Correctly mixed—and surprisingly few anglers can do it properly—it is a very effective offering, capable of catching most species at all times of the season. Many of the past Thames anglers used little else, while as a roach and bream bait, even today, it has few equals.

Paste must be made from an old loaf, four days old at least. The loaf is prepared by removing the crusts then cutting it into slices an inch thick. Take one slice and dip it into a bowl of water, removing it almost immediately. Placing it into the palm of one hand, knead it into a paste with the other hand. Keep kneading until all the lumps have disappeared and it is soft. Now repeat the procedure with each slice in turn until you have sufficient for your fishing needs.

Put all the balls of paste together and knead the mixture, making sure that the texture is right by adding water if necessary. The texture is most important. The paste should be soft but not tacky. Should any

stick to your fingers, mix another slice to a slightly drier consistency and work in. The final kneading should be made immediately prior to fishing. Place a piece on the hook, cast and retrieve. If it remains on the hook during the retrieve it is too hard; if it flies off during casting it is too soft. Adjust it accordingly.

Mixing the paste
Mixing paste should be done over a clean bowl, for if the bread is right it will crumble. (If it doesn't it is not old enough.) Pick up the fallen pieces and mix them in with the paste. New—even fairly new bread—will not make good paste; the results are glutinous, slightly grey in colour and contain lumps. Stale bread does not go lumpy, the texture is constant and it retains its whiteness. And whiteness is part of the bait's attraction because it can be seen clearly by the fish.

When mixed, the paste should be kept in a clean plastic box, wrapped in a clean cloth. At all times it must be shielded from the sun; if not, a thin crust will form, rendering the

outside useless for fishing.

At one time it was recommended that oils and aniseed should be added to the paste to make it even more attractive to the fish. In my experience, however, this is not necessary. Nevertheless, there is one additive that has been found to be very successful—custard powder. Sprinkle some custard powder in a bowl, place the paste on to it and mix thoroughly until the paste is bright yellow in colour. Both the smell and colour attract fish, especially roach, bream and dace.

A favourite trick of Northern canal anglers is to add a few crystals of red maggot dye to the bait as they press the mix together. Red vegetable dye works equally well, but remember to aim for a pink shade, not a deep red, so be sparing and add only a little dye at a time. Halve the paste and add a little more dye to one half so that a colour change of bait is available.

The angler is now equipped with paste that is white, custard yellow and two shades of pink. It is quite extraordinary how the fish react to

these variations of colour in different weather and water conditions.

Some anglers mould their paste on to the hook in a pear shape. While this does not prevent fish eating it, the author prefers to use it rough, simply pinching it on to the hook lightly with the minimum fuss. The less paste is handled, the better.

Hook sizes suitable for breadpaste range from 4 to 20 depending on the fish sought. For roach, bream, dace and grayling, 14 to 20 are right; chub, bream, tench and sometimes large roach need size 10; 8 for chub and barbel; 4 or 6 for carp.

Groundbait appetizers

Neither paste nor bread is a natural bait, but it is nevertheless unlikely that big fish will not have come into contact with it in some form, at some time or other. Feeding the ducks, throwing left-over sandwiches out of a boat, abandoning groundbaits after a day's fishing: all these help educate fish to a diet of bread and groundbait mixture, so groundbaiting in its usual sense is unnecessary. It is better to cast the paste to the likeliest spot and simply scatter around it half a dozen tiny balls of the same bait. Each moulded ball becomes soft in the water and presents an appetizer which is not substantial enough to overfeed.

Match fishermen prefer to use finely sieved cereal groundbait. Mixed lightly, this provides an interesting cloud in the water through which a tiny piece of paste on a size 20 hook is presented. Small fish will often feed with abandon on these offerings, and their frenzied activity brings along better sized specimens.

Casting with paste

Because paste is a very soft bait if properly mixed, great care must be taken when casting. While overhead casts can be made without paste and hook parting company, in most situations a sideways cast is preferable. To ensure that the paste remains on the hook, the cast must be a smooth one: the least jerk and the bait will either fly off or partially dislodge itself from the hook. Most trouble arises when casting into wind when a more powerful cast is required. This should not deter the

168

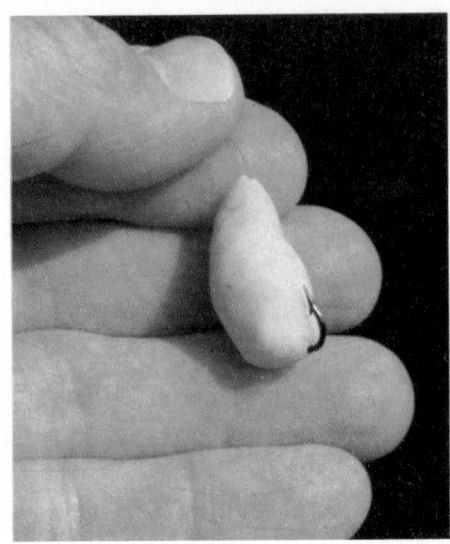

Above: *Ledgering breadcrust for chub.*
Left: *Balanced crust—a tough, castable bait.*
Right: *Floating crust for carp or big chub.*
Below: *Breadpaste on the hook. It can be given interesting colour (and perhaps scent) by the addition of custard powder or dye.*

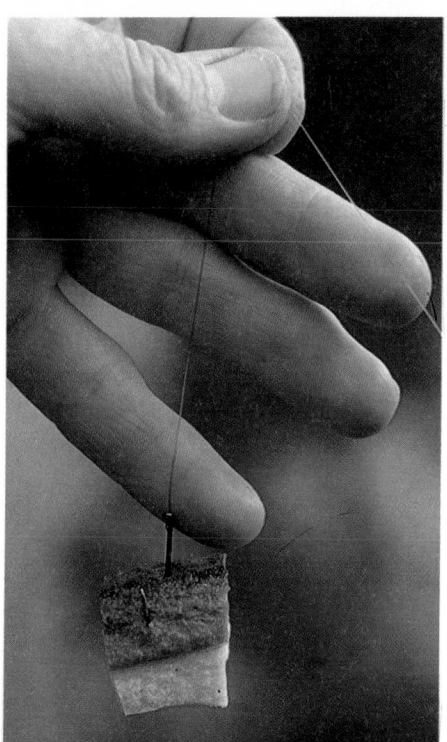

would-be paste fisherman, however. A powerful cast does not necessarily mean a jerky one. Keep it smooth and no trouble will arise. Smooth cast or not, the hook must be the same size as the bait; if it is not this will only encourage the paste to come adrift. It is probably safe to say that it is the problem of keeping paste on the hook which stops so many anglers from using it.

Balanced crust

One very effective, yet comparatively little-used bait is balanced crust. This comprises a carefully judged mixture of bread crust and paste. Mainly a stillwater bait, balanced crust is popular for carp fishing over mud or weed.

It is most important to get the right proportions of the ingredients. If properly balanced, the bait takes a minute or two to sink and, when it does, sinks slowly, finally coming to rest on the surface of the mud or silkweed without actually sinking into it. When the bait does settle, the line should emerge from underneath, thus making it almost impossible for a fish to touch it with its lips as it takes in or investigates the bait by mouthing it.

To make balanced crust, a piece of crust is taken from a new loaf and placed on the bend of the hook. The paste—made up to the consistency described earlier—is then moulded round the hook shank. Too much paste and the bait will sink too quickly and may become partially submerged into the mud or weed; too little paste and it will float.

Balanced crust is a 'big fish' bait and calls for big hooks to match, ranging from 2 to 10. For carp 2, 4 and 6 are suitable; tench, bream and chub need size 8, roach size 10. Should fish be biting shyly, 10s will suffice for all species with the exception of carp. The hook size should be such that the point and part of the bend protrude from the crust, with the paste added until it is level with the top of the shank.

Balanced crust is a fairly tough bait and quite powerful casts can be made using the minimum of lead. Providing the paste is mixed correctly, and the hook is large enough, it will withstand an overhead cast.

ASK THE EXPERT

The paste I mix often goes lumpy and sticky. Am I using the wrong bread?

All kinds of bread make reasonable paste providing the loaves used are old and stale enough. Set aside a few slices on Wednesday, ready for the weekend. If you forget, and have only fresh bread to hand, you can render it dry by baking it in the oven until it becomes fairly hard. Don't overdo it or it will go brown.

Will nothing but white bread paste attract the fish?

On the contrary, in very clear water fish will sometimes shy away from white paste, but feed on yellow or pink. I have never had success, though, with brown bread pastes.

What is balanced crust, and why should it do more than simple paste?

In balanced crust the buoyancy of the crust is countered by the heavy paste resulting in a bait that *just* sinks. There are occasions when paste would sink into the bottom silt or weed and be lost from sight of the fish. A balanced crust settles lightly into the silt where it can be clearly seen.

I am always worried that the paste has come off my hook in the water. What can I do?

There is no need to worry. If the bait stays intact during the cast, it will remain so until you retrieve: *then* bread and hook separate.

Can I store paste in the fridge?

It can be stored for a few days if necessary, but for the price of a few slices of bread it is always worthwhile to mix fresh paste for the hook-baits. Use the stored bait for the small, moulded balls of loose feed.

Groundbait

Knowing where to place your groundbait is part of the secret of successful coarse fishing. There is a wide range to choose from, but making your own is cheaper and can achieve better results

Groundbait is put into a swim to attract and hold fish and is very useful, if not essential, in producing results in most kinds of coarse fishing. Made-up groundbaits range from heavy mixtures, which sink to the bottom rapidly in a fast current, to 'cloudbait', which make the water attractive to fish and are used in slow currents or stillwater. More simply, groundbait can be samples of the hookbait thrown in loose—worms, maggots, casters, hemp, and others, or combinations of these, are commonly used.

Making your own groundbait

Bags of dry groundbait, mixed and ready for use, can be bought from tackle dealers but, unless one buys in bulk, it is generally cheaper to mix your own. You can then make up groundbait to suit differing water conditions and your own personal preferences.

The basis of most groundbait mixtures is stale bread, prepared by breaking it up or mincing and then soaking it in water for an hour or two, or overnight if very hard. When soaked, drain it as much as possible and make into a smooth paste. This can be made into small balls for throwing into the swim. Numerous ingredients can be added to the basic mix and their use is to some extent determined by the type of fish sought and the water conditions. For example, bran, semolina, chicken meal, sausage rusk, barley meal, boiled and mashed potato,

CHEESE

POTATO

MAGGOT PIE

PEARL BARLEY

WHEAT

CASTERS

TROUT PELLETS

FLOUR

CUSTARD POWDER

SEMOLINA

BRAN

clay, peat, crushed egg shells, samples of the hookbait, and other additives are used. These substances are especially useful in extremely fast water and when hook-bait samples are needed on the bottom. The extra weight takes the groundbait to the bottom before it is washed away.

Cloudbait for slow water

In a slow flowing water, light cloudbait can prove effective. This is prepared by cutting bread into thick slices and allowing it to dry out. To speed the process heat the bread in a domestic oven, then crush the dry crisp slices to a fine powder and sieve out all lumps. At the waterside the powder is dampened to the preferred consistency and made into small balls for throwing into the area to be fished. As they sink slowly these will break up and cloud the water. This effect can be heightened by using milk instead of water. The addition of semolina will improve the mix when wet and bind it for lobbing into a distant swim.

It is well worth experimenting with both flavouring and colouring for groundbaits. Some fishes find added honey, for example, very attractive. Flavour can be introduced in the form of oils of aniseed, lavender, fennel, verbena, pilchard and others. Powdered egg and milk are also useful. Other additives will enhance both flavour and colour. Among these are blancmange and custard powder, flour, sausage rusk, crushed biscuits and hempseed. Fishing can sometimes be improved by colouring the groundbait to contrast with the hookbait.

Tasty 'maggot pie'

'Maggot pies', probably first used by Norfolk anglers for ground-

The range of foodstuffs you can add to basic homemade groundbait – stale bread soaked in water, thoroughly drained and stirred into a thick paste – is a matter of personal preference. Using some of the common additives shown below can improve your fishing, and with experience you can adapt your groundbait to suit the species sought and different water conditions. As well as using some of these groundbaits as hookbaits, try mixing a more exotic 'cocktail' bait such as worm tipped with caster – particularly deadly with bream.

MAGGOTS

BROKEN BISCUITS

SAUSAGE MEAT

HEMP SEEDS

TROUT PELLETS

CRUSHED HEMP

RICE

SWEET CORN

PASTA

TARES

BREAD CRUMBS

baiting a swim when ledgering, are based on a cloudbait mixture (either bought or made up), which is poured into a large flat vessel at the water's edge and wetted to the required consistency. Feeder maggots are then added and orange-sized balls are made and thrown into the swim. If expense is no trouble, the mix can be made heavier for fast flowing water by the addition of boiled mashed potatoes. In general, about 1lb of potatoes is used to 4lb of cloudbait. For a long day's fishing, or a big match, make about 10lb of the groundbait and add a half a gallon of feeder maggots. For very fast water it may be necessary to add clay or even pebbles.

'Black Magic' is the name given to a dark groundbait. It is prepared by working in a proportion of lawn peat to the bread. The peat should be dried and sieved finely before mixing, and the final groundbait mixture should be dampened at the water's edge as needed.

Liquid groundbait
A liquid groundbait, unusual yet sometimes effective when fishing lake margins with floating crust for carp, can be made from well soaked bread mashed and mixed with water or milk. This is dilute enough to simply pour into the water.

Trout pellets, which are used to feed and fatten fishery bred trout, are rich in protein and send trout into a frenzy at feeding time! Most fish will take the pellets, but crushed

Below: With well placed groundbait, fish will remain in the hookbait area.
Right: Indiscriminate groundbaiting is bad fishing. It must first attract fish then hold them. Correct positioning is determined by water flow and depth. Your hookbait must always be placed in the action zone.

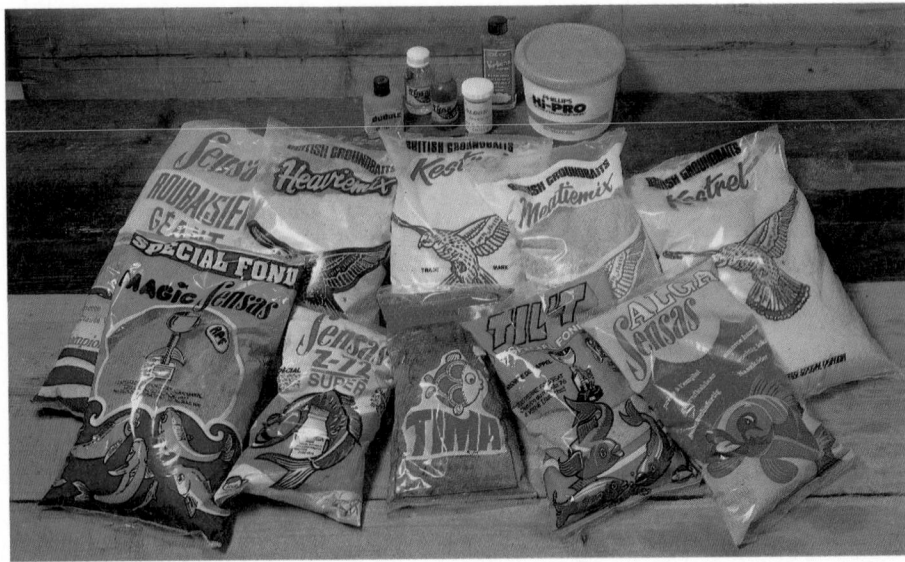

Above: *A selection of commercial groundbait including the heavy mixtures which sink to the bottom. The bottles at the back contain flavourings and dyes.*

Below: *Adding sausage meat to close up the end of a swimfeeder containing sweetcorn — an effective groundbait for attracting carp, tench and bream.*

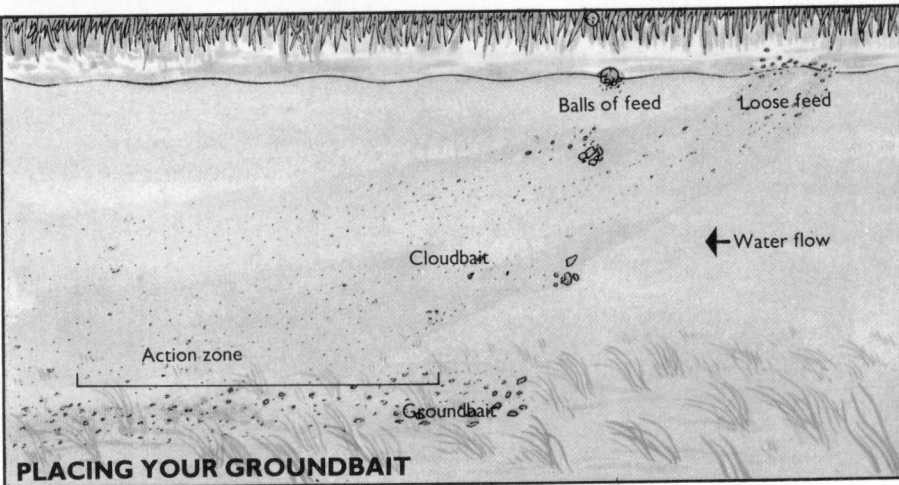

PLACING YOUR GROUNDBAIT

Balls of feed   Loose feed

Cloudbait   ←Water flow

Action zone

Groundbait

172

and mixed with breadcrumbs they make an excellent high protein groundbait that has been successful with carp and tench.

Luncheon meat is a highly successful hookbait for chub and barbel, and groundbait for use with it should contain meat. Sausage meat works well enough, but minced meat is better. Either can be used on its own or added to an ordinary groundbait.

Double groundbaiting

Most anglers bait only one area from any one bank position. But baiting two separate areas, one close in and one far out, is an interesting and effective method of hedging your bets when fishing larger waters.

The diagram at the bottom of this page shows how this technique can be applied to a slow, wide river. For much of the season, roach and dace shoals occupy the margins alongside the shelf, but bream are to be found far out in the deep middle section. By double groundbaiting, you go after either roach and dace or bream, whichever produces the best bites.

For a session starting early in the morning, a sensible plan would be to rig up both ledger and float rods, but first to ledger the middle for bream over a groundbait carpet of cereal and hookbaits. At the same time the near swim, just two rod lengths out, should be loose fed with casters. After an hour or so, if the bream prove uncooperative, you could then switch to the float rod and trot down for roach or dace. You would now be fishing a swim which had been regularly fed without any disturbance—something which gives a shoal confidence. Moreover, a swim which has been fed slowly will often produce fish for much longer.

Top: *A large-cupped catapult is useful for throwing loosely bound and moulded groundbait out to the exact spot where it is needed – keep the area as small as you can.*
Above: *Groundbaiting with sweetcorn.*
Below: *Groundbaiting two separate areas – one close in, the other far out.*

ASK THE EXPERT

What's the difference between groundbaiting and prebaiting?
Strictly speaking, prebaiting refers to groundbaiting some time – hours or even days – before fishing. This is to 'educate' your fish into accepting your bait. Exactly when to prebait depends on the species sought and the water you are fishing. Baiting up a swim, for example, several days in advance, can be effective with bream, tench or carp.

Can you groundbait too much?
Yes, especially on heavily fished waters. Before starting to groundbait, look and see if there is evidence of waste groundbait lying around as this will probably indicate recent groundbaiting. If a water is already heavily groundbaited, then the fish will not accept more. Indeed, in heavily groundbaited waters, feeding patterns can be seriously disrupted and the wary fish will wait until dark before venturing out to feed on the bait left during the day's fishing.

What's the difference between an open-ended swimfeeder and a blockend?
Swimfeeders and blockends are peforated plastic cylinders 2-3in long and 1in in diameter. The open-ended swimfeeder is used mainly in conjunction with cereal groundbaits. The blockend, on the other hand, has closed ends and usually contains maggots and casters. When packed with maggots, a blockend empties slowly, whereas an open-ended feeder releases its contents as soon as the groundbait plug at either end is washed away. In general, a blockend is used in faster flowing water.

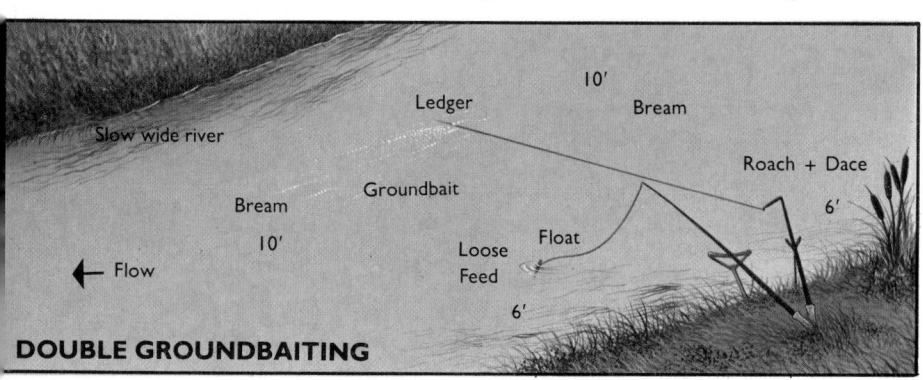

DOUBLE GROUNDBAITING

Slow wide river

Ledger 10'
Bream

Roach + Dace
6'

Bream Groundbait
10'

Float
Loose Feed
6'

← Flow

Deadbaits

The accelerating trend away from livebaiting has resulted in a wider variety of deadbaits being used, with more imagination, by anglers concentrating on more species than simply the pike

The gradual acceptance of dead fish as a highly successful pike fishing bait during the late 1950s will be recorded by angling historians as a fortunate turn of fate. Prior to this, pike fishing took place with a live bait, which meant catching and conveying fish until they could be mounted and used on snap-tackle mounts—a method which entailed considerable inconvenience for both fish and fishermen.

Against this style was a growing lobby of anti-blood sport agitators who were pressing for prosecutions against those who used live fish, alleging cruelty when hooks were mounted into them. River Boards, strengthened by new legislation, were introducing bye-laws prohibiting the use of livebaits because of the risk of spreading disease where baits were transported and used in strange waters. Finally, conservationists were raising their voices at the number of immature fish taken and used for livebaits, stressing that this denuded waters of future breeding stock.

Deadbaits are just as successful as livebaits—at times even more so—and there can be no element of cruelty in mounting them for fishing. They can be easily carried, and need not be freshwater fish, thus silencing the conservationist objections. The angler also has a choice in the size of bait, from a small sprat weighing ounces, to a large mackerel weighing over a pound. Certain freshwater fisheries allow a limited number of fish to be removed as baits, and where this is legal, naturally they may be killed and used to augment the variety.

Freshwater crayfish are rightly regarded by chub specialists as a first-class deadbait. Either the whole creature or its succulent tail section makes a deadly offering. Un-

fortunately they are difficult to find but many inhabit the clear chalk-streams of the south of England. Fresh bait is essential before you can catch crayfish: offal from a butchers is as good as any. Tie it to the bottom of a weighted dropnet, which can then be lowered close to bridge pilings or lock gates. If the banks are rocky, so much the better as crays like nothing better than a deep dark hole. The net is allowed to rest for about 15 minutes and then brought swiftly to the surface. If you use a deepish net there is less chance of your catch getting out during the journey to the surface.

Provided they are frozen directly after capture, crayfish will remain in perfect condition for a long time. You can preserve them, too, in a formalin-water-glycerine mix and a screw top air tight jar. Pack them head downwards in the jar.

Kept in preservatives the bait obviously takes on a most unnatural smell. This can be reduced by running cold water over them for several hours before use, then dipping them in pilchard oil.

Keep deadbaits frozen

All deadbaits are best deep frozen until required, and they should be graded into species and according to size, then bagged and frozen in small batches so that enough for a day's fishing can be removed and defrosted with the minimum inconvenience and waste. Time and trouble spent in freezing each fish straight away will pay when it comes to mounting the bait, and during casting, when twisted fish can often affect both the distance and the accuracy.

Fishing with static deadbaits is by far the most common technique, and it requires a rod soft enough in its action to cast a dead weight over a

Above: *Older pike with less speed often rely on scavenging for carrion. So simulating life in your deadbait is not always necessary.*

long distance. Fast-taper, tip-actioned rods will snatch the bait from its hook in casting. Whether a multiplying reel or a fixed-spool is used is largely a matter of preference and cost. But it is worth remembering that heavy baits, constantly reeled in and cast during the day, impose a great strain on the line: and the multiplier has fewer line angles along the rod.

Match the line to the rod

The weight of the line used in deadbaiting is equally important, and care should be taken to match it to the rod. Lines that are too thick strain the rod and restrict casting distances: those that are too light will strain and are liable to suddenly snap during the cast.

Unlike livebaiting, the majority of deadbaits are fished on, or close to the bottom. If ledgering is adopted as the style of fishing then there will

be little problem with end tackle —the weight of the bait will rule out the need for a large supply of ledger leads, stop beads and so on. But many anglers prefer to use a float, maintaining that with it they can see exactly where the bait is lying and note its slightest movement. A further argument for float fishing a deadbait is that any drift across the surface will ultimately move the bait, and this slow movement can often be used with advantage.

Naturally, when a float is used, it must be capable of sliding up the line, with a stop knot (a short length of nylon tied with several overhand loops) fixed on to the line to check the float at the correct depth, and a small lead fixed above the trace to cock and prevent the float jamming below the surface after it has been cast. Unless the intention is to allow the bait to drift, then the smaller the float the better.

There are innumerable deadbait hook rigs which can be used, some with four or five treble hooks that take time and patience to mount.

Generally, the fewer hooks the better. Fine-wire trebles, sharpened and checked for temper, can easily be mounted on to cabled Alasticum. Their size should match the bait being used because small trebles combined with a large bait obviously reduce the chance of hooking on the strike, and large trebles on a small bait make the whole rig cumbersome.

Probably the most popular rig is the deadbait snap-tackle. Two trebles, equal in size, are mounted on to a trace, their spacing varying according to the size of bait used. One treble is mounted close to the tail, the other into the side in front of the dorsal fin. The trace is then fed under the gill cover and out through the mouth, and tied to the line through the medium of a swivel. If extra-long-distance casts are to be made, then three or four turns of nylon round the body will help to prevent it breaking away from the hooks during the cast.

The alternative method of mounting is with the end treble behind the gill and the second in the side, level with the dorsal fin. The trace is then threaded, with a baiting needle, through the flesh and out through the tail, after which a swivel can be mounted and the line tied to it. The advantage of mounting in this way is that the bait will travel head-first and not backwards, as can happen with the tail-first method.

A lifelike drifting rig

A useful drifting deadbait rig is made by securing a split ring into the eye of a treble. To this is attached a short length of trace that terminates with a similar-sized treble and another separate length of trace, which finishes with the link swivel for attaching the reel line. The bait is mounted with one hook of the end treble through both lips, and two hooks of the split-ringed treble through the back of the fish at the dorsal fin. Mounted in this way, the bait hangs like a livebait, and when fished in mid-water moves freely with any surface drift.

Carrying deadbait rigs needs care if a mess is to be avoided. Barrie Rickards solved the problem with his balsawood log. This cylinder of

How should a fish, intended for deadbait, be killed?
A baiting needle pricked into the back of the head kills a fish quickly and does not damage it. Where the fish has no teeth, another swift resort is to put a finger into its mouth and get sufficient grip to break the spinal cord.

What is the best way of carrying deadbaits in hot weather?
Insulated carrying boxes have largely solved this problem. If you put ice cubes in the bottom of the box, the baits remain thoroughly cold. Small deadbaits may also be kept in a vacuum flask.

What is the correct solution of formaldehyde for preserving baits?
One teaspoon of Formalin in one pint of water will do the job. Remember that you are dealing with a poison, so lock it safely away as soon as you have finished with it.

What species are likely to take freshwater mussels?
Carp and barbel are particularly fond of them, though you may experience lucky bites from other species.

Do saltwater sandeels make a useful freshwater deadbait?
They have been used successfully by pike fishermen, and there is no reason why they should not attract other species. Even inland, most good tackle shops sell packets of sandeels. The taint of salt in no way deters a coarse fish from showing interest in a bait, whether or not it would make a regular habit of eating saltwater fish meat.

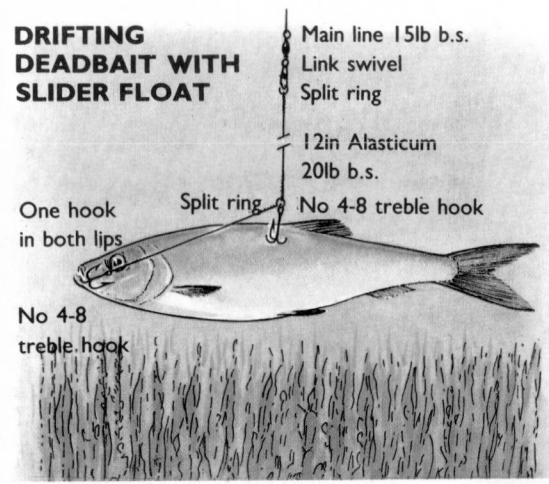

DRIFTING DEADBAIT WITH SLIDER FLOAT

Main line 15lb b.s.

Link swivel

Split ring

12in Alasticum 20lb b.s.

Split ring

No 4-8 treble hook

One hook in both lips

No 4-8 treble hook

Left: *This rig can be drifted a foot or so above the bottom, keeping the fish horizontal and lifelike. Mackerel are best for this method as they stay rigid.*

Right: *Two methods of mounting herring on trebles for pike fishing.*

Below: *Known as Barrie Rickard's Balsa Log, this was the famous angler's original idea for safe and efficient storage of traces. Kept in a tin or box, it prevents hooks tangling with other gear and speeds preparation at the waterside.*

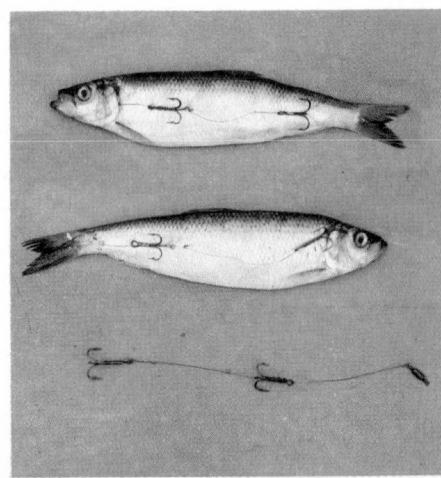

soft wood with end pieces allows trebles and traces to be safely secured, and when slid into an empty tin, will not snag other items of tackle. Baits themselves are best put in leak-proof Tupperware boxes.

A deadbait is only as successful as its angler allows. Cast carelessly into the water in the hope that it will be discovered, it is generally unproductive. The water should be studied, plumbed if possible, and varying depths noted on a simple sketch chart. Items of cover—lily and weedbeds, heavy rush and flag-lined banks—are worth special attention, even though some tackle may be lost.

One method worth using over submerged weedbeds is to inflate the belly of a whole fish with a little air, using a hypodermic syringe. A very small amount is needed to make it float just 3in or so above the bottom. To ensure that just enough air has been injected, drop the bait into water at your feet and watch for its position against the bed. An even better method is to inject pilchard oil as well, with the hypodermic, at various spots along the bait's body, just below the skin. The oil will soon seep out and form an attractive slick.

Although most deadbait fishing is regarded as a static, or possibly a drifting style, dead fish also make excellent 'wobbler' lures. They have all the attraction of spinners plus an ease of casting that puts long distances within range. An added bonus is the cost of wobble baits; they can be used as an alternative to expensive spinners.

Giving a deadbait its 'wobble'

Naturally, wobbled baits must be mounted so that they can be retrieved head first through the water, and the simple snap-tackle rig outlined earlier, modified by mounting it so that the tail section is pulled forward into a curve, will provide an ideal slow-wobble and combined twist. To help keep it down on the bottom, use a thin length of lead or zinc pushed into the mouth and passed into the stomach of the bait.

Once in place, the bait can be given a curve and the shape will be retained by the metal strip.

After casting, the bait should be allowed to sink to the bottom before the retrieve begins. Turning the reel in a succession of slow turns with a stop every few seconds will cause the bait to adopt a rise and fall pattern that few fish can resist. The strike must be immediate, and no time allowed for turning as when fishing a stationary deadbait.

Sweetcorn

Lightly cooked, thawed from the deep-freeze or straight from a can, sweetcorn makes a costly groundbait, but a deadly hook-bait for carp, tench, chub, barbel and many other coarse fish

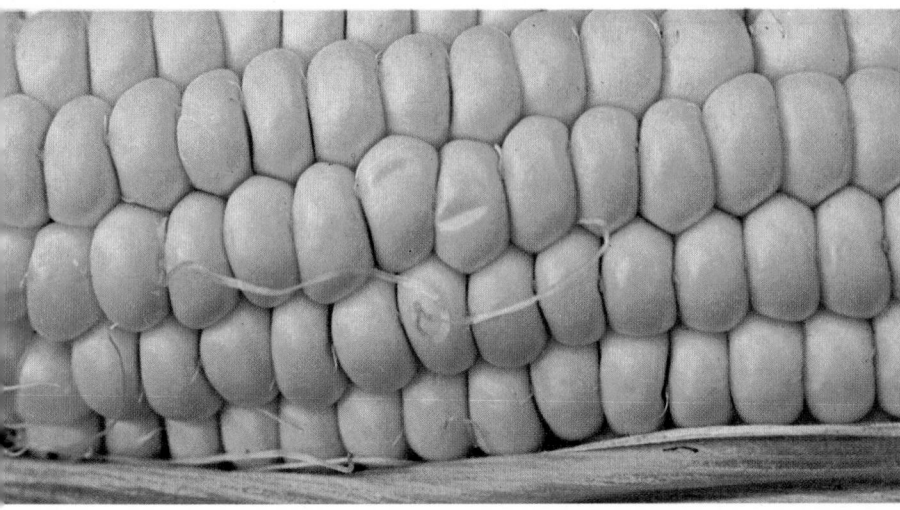

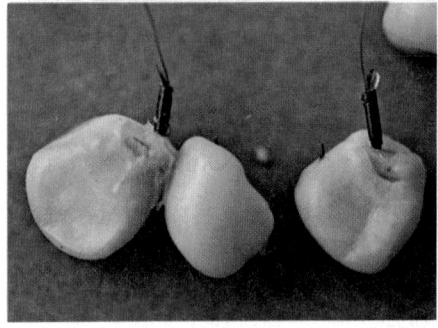

Top: *Copious prebaiting on a large still-water. Hotspots should be carpeted with grains.*
Above: *One or as many as four grains can be hooked on eyed or spade-eyed hooks.*

Among big fish enthusiasts, as well as the match angling fraternity, particle baits have been much in vogue for the past five or six years. But there is nothing new about them. Some, like maggots, casters, hemp, and boiled wheat, have been used for decades. But sweetcorn is relatively new (at least in Britain) and has had a great impact on the big fish scene.

Carp fishing specialists began to experiment with this deadly bait in the early 1970s, although there is little doubt that other enterprising anglers used it long before. The author, for one, caught tench on sweetcorn in the early 1960s, and it is very unlikely that he was the first. Certainly American anglers used corn long before us.

Not only carp take corn

Carp are particularly attracted to sweetcorn, but there are several other fish for which it is equally effective. Other than the predators, most fish, including tench, rudd, roach, bream, chub, dace and barbel, can be 'educated' to take it readily.

Sweetcorn's greatest attractions are its availability and its convenience. In its ready-to-use, canned form, it can be put on the hook without any preparation. Alternatively, you can buy fresh or frozen corn which is just as good after a little preparation. Whole corn-on-the-cob needs cooking and de-cobbing, while frozen loose corn needs boiling for a few minutes to soften it. But if you intend pre-baiting with large quantities, you can make a significant saving by buying bulk and boiling up as required.

Nevertheless, the canned corn is still the most popular form, but do give the environment a thought before taking cans to the waterside. It is more convenient and less anti-social to open the can at home and empty the corn into a plastic bait box or other container. In fact, there are now a few environmentally conscious clubs that ban cans of all types on the river banks and punish infringements with expulsion.

Sweetcorn keeps quite well, but in hot weather treat it like maggots and keep it in the shade if possible. Drain off the 'juice' and give the corn a quick rinse under the tap before putting it in your bait box, for it becomes sticky and slimy in hot weather. Removing the juice does

not detract from its effectiveness as a bait. Corn can be frozen after use, too; it is expensive, so do not waste. With care, it can even be re-frozen.

Sweetcorn grains range in size from that a match-head to that of a large pea. So all manner of bait sizes and hooks can be used—from a single small grain on a No 18 to six or seven large grains hiding a No 4 or No 2 carp hook. Compared with other particle baits, few grains are needed to cover the hook.

It pays to use eyed hooks or spade-ends with a prominent spade. These help to keep the corn on the shank. With whipped-to nylon hooks there is always a risk of the corn sliding up the line, resulting in false bites and snagged hooks. Some anglers favour gilt or gold hooks, but the author has found them no better and uses bronzed, eyed hooks.

The big question with corn is how much free bait to introduce into a swim. This is a very controversial subject, and the views of experts vary, particularly when it comes to 'educating' carp and tench in stillwaters. The general plan, however, is to encourage big fish to feed intensively over a small area.

ASK THE EXPERT

Has sweetcorn every caught roach?
Indeed it has, and big ones too. It is rare to catch roach of less than half a pound on corn—you are likely to need a landing net.

Which species of carp take corn?
All of them have, at some time or other, fallen to one or more grains. Even the smaller crucians seem to have a sweetcorn tooth!

Is ledgering any more or less effective than float fishing?
In choosing a method, the deciding factor is either the range at which the fish are to be fished, or the strength of current. In this respect, corn is no different from any other bait.

How should I use sweetcorn as part of a cocktail bait?
One interesting combination is of sweetcorn with a small piece of crust. The two together prevent the bait from sinking into bottom mud.

How long will leftovers keep?
If you put residual sweetcorn into a polythene bag and keep it in the deep-freeze, it will still be usable several weeks later.

What sort of bites can I expect?
In my experience, very positive bites result from a sweetcorn bait. This is because it is a relative newcomer, and the majority of fish have yet to grow suspicious of it.

Some anglers disdain to use frozen corn and swear by the tinned variety. Is there any great difference?
The only real advantage that tinned corn has over frozen is that it is more convenient, though more expensive.

Approaching the water

Vary your approach with the size of the water. In a small lake of one or two acres, the fish can probably be educated by baiting-up an area of 10 square yards every day for a couple of weeks.

In larger lakes and pits, scatter corn finely over wide areas to accustom the fish to it, then select a hotspot of a few square yards and carpet it with corn. But in both large and small lakes, you will have to modify these general guidelines to take account of the fish population, both of the species you are after and the unwanted species that also like corn. How much modification is a matter of choice.

One way of attracting fish into a baited swim, while at the same time reducing expense, is to use ordinary bread or cereal groundbait. This method is particularly good on large expanses of water and involves laying a trail to the baited area. A small patch of this hotspot is liberally laced with sweetcorn while groundbait is thrown out in a line extending for several yards. In theory, hungry fish will follow the trail of groundbait and light on the sweetcorn.

If this prebaiting pattern is repeated over several days, the fish will become accustomed to feeding in one small area and your chances of making a bumper catch are greatly improved.

For carp, the more corn you introduce, the more frenziedly will the fish feed. Of course, there are practical (and financial) limits and it is possible to overdo the baiting-up. To start with, the carp will move around like vacuum cleaners, mopping up the corn wherever it is thickest, but then suddenly stop. The whole of your object is to get the carp to pick up your bit of sweetcorn, not the five million other pieces in the swim! The limit, after which more corn has a negative effect, has to be found by trial and error. There are no general rules that apply to all waters.

The most important consideration is the number of smaller fish present. For instance, if carp are the chosen quarry, and the water has a better than average tench population, it is unlikely the carp will ever have a chance of finding more than an odd particle; unless you prebait with large quantities of sweetcorn. Under these circumstances, it will probably prove beneficial to introduce a couple of marked loafs into the swim—to over-fill the tench and give the carp a better chance of finding the sweetcorn.

Things are a little simpler on running waters. In these, the familiarization period appears to be much shorter. There have been several occasions when barbel and chub have accepted corn within minutes of it being introduced to a virgin river, and a tinful, trickled in at regular intervals, is generally adequate for a six-hour session. The barbel specialist therefore needs much less corn than his carp-fishing counterpart.

When river fishing for barbel, it is always useful to take along a tin of cooked hempseed. Few baits have the holding power of hemp and once a shoal of barbel take an interest in loose-fed hempseed they are loath to leave the vicinity.

Having caught their attention, the way to change the feeding habits of the bigger fish is to introduce half a dozen grains of sweetcorn every few minutes along with the hempseed. Three grains of sweetcorn will conceal quite a big hook, so your chances are enhanced of landing the real specimens.

The other bonus in rivers is that nuisance fish like bleak and gudgeon are not the plague they are when fishing bunches of maggots, block-feeder style. Corn sinks quickly through the bleak shoals, and gudgeon do not seem to care for it.

Finally, a couple of tips from expert specimen hunter Kevin Clifford. When fishing for carp over a mud or soft weed-covered bottom the bait should sink very slowly so that it does not become buried. This is done by substituting a piece of yellow expanded polystyrene for a grain of corn in a group of three or four particles.

The second tip is a way of throwing 'free' corn a long distance out but still concentrated into a small area. Store ice-cubes of sweetcorn in a wide-mouthed vacuum flask and catapult to the chosen spot in the swim when needed.

Seedbaits

Seeds as bait are cheap, easy to prepare and have accounted for some fine fish. Apart from sweetcorn, tares and wheat, rice and hempseed have achieved popularity with coarse fishermen

Seed baits are apparently baits of fad and fashion. Those in current vogue with non-specialist anglers are sweetcorn, tares and as an enticer or feed-bait, hempseed.

Most seeds will tempt fish and most are prepared for the hook in a similar way. It pays to soak seeds overnight in cold water after first washing the hard grains. Then they are placed in a saucepan and again covered with water which is brought to the boil and left to simmer gently for a particular length of time, decided by the kind of seed.

Correct timing is very important. Under-cooked seed baits are too hard for any fish to mouth. Over-cooked, they become too mushy to use at all. So do not just put them into a pot and leave them. They must, as in all *cordon bleu* culinary arts, have close attention.

Some anglers think that this method is too vigorous a way of preparing seed. There are three alternatives. One is simply to soak for a much longer period of time. Another is to casserole your bait instead of boiling and the other is to cook the seeds in a vacuum flask. With the flask method, however, beware of putting in too many seeds—two-thirds full is ample —before pouring boiling water over them. All seed baits swell considerably in preparation and an over-full flask is liable to explode.

Seed baits are best cooked just before you set off to fish. Hempseed, in particular, is ready for use as both groundbait and hookbait by the time an angler has carried it to the waterside in a vaccuum flask and set up his tackle. Don't throw away the water left in the flask—mix it with a cereal groundbait so that its scent complements the bait.

Groundbaiting is best done by mixing a few grains of hemp with the well scented cereal, then introducing the mixture at frequent intervals. This method invariably produces an earlier response than simply feeding with loose handfuls of bait.

Seed baits are enjoying renewed popularity after a decline during the past decade. Their re-emergence is due mainly to the restless search by carp anglers for new baits. Anglers like Ron Felton, Bill Walkden, Gerry Savage and Kevin Clifford have been using dozens of types of exotic-sounding seeds.

Once banned because of its amazing success, hempseed is once again a popular and deadly match bait.

Cheese

Strongly scented and easily moulded to the hook or mixed with cheaper ingredients as a groundbait, cheese is attractive to most non-predators and even, now and then, to perch and pike

For most purposes Cheddar cheese makes an excellent bait—but it must be fresh. On occasion, softer cheeses such as Stilton or Danish Blue are also very good.

Understanding wives and mothers do not object to anglers removing small pieces of stale cheese, but taking the fresh Cheddar may raise a few eyebrows. Removal of the Stilton or Danish Blue is apt to put a definite strain on any relationship.

The thoughtful angler makes his own arrangements to purchase cheese before he goes fishing. But however you obtain it, it is well worth trying this versatile bait.

Fresh Cheddar can easily be moulded into a putty-like consistency. This should be done as and when needed, the cheese being flattened between the finger and thumb and then folded around the hook and shaped firmly in place.

Chub and barbel
Traditionally, cheese is an excellent barbel and chub bait. It also takes good roach and dace. Much of its effectiveness depends on the fact that the flavour drifts down on the current, awakening the olfactory responses of distant fish and bringing them up to the hook. For this reason, cheese is more effective when used in rivers and streams than in stillwater, and clearly the stronger the flavour the better the attraction. This is not to suggest that cheese will not catch fish in lakes but merely to imply that stillwater fish are less likely to pick up the scent.

For chub or barbel, walnut-size pieces on sizes 4, 6, or 8 are about right. In slow or sluggish waters this can be used on the bottom without using any weights. In faster water, however, it is necessary to use a ledger lead such as an Arlesey bomb to hold the bait down, once in position. A few smaller lumps of cheese should be thrown into or upstream of the swim at intervals during fishing. Groundbait too should be liberally laced with cheese powder as this helps to hold shoals in the area of the hookbait.

If the angler has been careful to work unobtrusively, and provided he has chosen his swim well, chub and barbel will often take a cheese bait within a few minutes of it being cast into position. Should it not be taken soon, it still has the advantage that it holds to the hook well and does not need retrieving to check if it is still there.

For roach or dace, pieces the size of peas on size 10 to 14 hooks are used. In suitable swims a ledger might be used but the favoured practice is to swim the stream with standard float-fishing tackle. Again bites are usually positive. Though durable, cheese is soft enough to allow good hook penetration when the time comes to strike.

The much softer cheeses, such as Stilton and Danish Blue, when mature, are sometimes too soft to be moulded on to the hook. If so, mix the cheese well with a good stiff bread paste. The cheese imparts sufficient flavour to the paste to provide a tasty bait for many species.

Cubes of cheese
As an alternative to moulding the cheese on to the hook, it is possible to cut it into small cubes of a size to suit the hook. The hook is then either pressed firmly into the cube or threaded through it. In either case the hook point must be very close to the surface of the cube, even protruding. Some smaller cubes are thrown into the swim as attractors.

The versatile cheese slice has gained a lot of friends over the last few years. You can use either the white

or yellow variety, cut into slivers, to fish running water where it dances and shimmies through the swim in a most attractive way. It attracts bites from all species of fish—the roach in particular being susceptible to a thin strip of tasty cheese lowered tantalizingly below a lightly shotted stick float.

Different shapes cut from the slices sink and fish quite differently from any other bait, and bites can come at any time during the bait's introduction to the water. A big chub, for example, may appear from nowhere to grab a halfpenny-sized strip of cheese almost as soon as it hits the water.

Sliced cheese is equally effective when used in conjunction with a bread punch. On stillwaters this is an advantage because the shapes don't come into contact with the angler's hands. Lay the slice on a flat surface, press in the punch, and insert the hook lightly. During summer months, crucian carp are spellbound by punched cheese, and very often a tench or two show up.

During the winter, most kinds of cheese lose their impact because the cold water makes them rock hard. This is the time to turn to the various cheese spreads. A little messy to hook during the summer, these soft, creamy cheeses make an ideal winter bait. They are just hard enough to stay on the hook during casting but sufficiently soft to tempt fish.

Try a thumbnail-sized knob of creamy cheese spread the next time you fish for chub in a cold winter spell. It will occasionally produce astounding results.

Perch, pike and trout

Surprisingly, although cheese is regarded as best suited to non-predatory species, it does occasionally take perch, or even pike and trout. There are on record the captures of a 22lb pike and a 10lb 12oz Kennet trout on ledgered cheese. During the early season, when chub and barbel both take fish baits such as minnows, it is sometimes useful to mould the cheese on the hook in the shape of a spinner so that it will revolve as it lies below the ledger. Here, it is necessary to insert a swivel between the ledger and the hook link.

Other predators, such as barbel and chub seeking moving prey may respond to a piece of cheese spinning just off the bottom. The noted Avon angler Bill Warren, who died in April 1978, took more than 200 chub of 5lb-plus from his river—all on cheese paste. If you are fortunate enough to secure a worthwhile trout on cheese it may well make up for the fact that you plundered the best Danish Blue from the fridge before leaving home.

Left to right: Stilton; Danish Blue; Cheddar diced into bait-sized pieces; crusty bread—just the job for a bread/cheese paste mix; grated Cheddar for use in groundbait mixes; cream (or processed) cheese.

What fish can I catch on cheese?
Chub and barbel are the fish most commonly associated with cheese baits, but carp and tench are partial to them on a summer evening.

Should the cheese be mouldy or fresh?
There are two schools of thought on the subject. Some prefer to use fresh cheddar, but a sticky, smelly piece of old Stilton certainly works wonders sometimes. So try both, and reach your own conclusions. If you are going to handle the bait, a mild cheese may 'taint' more readily; a stronger smell might mask the scent of your hands.

Isn't cheese a very expensive bait to use?
On running water, it's true that you can get through a lot of expensive cheese. To reduce your costs, you can mix a paste of bread and cheese and introduce a little as groundbait as well as on your hook.

I have difficulty keeping cheese on my hook when I am long-casting.
A well hooked piece of cheese slice tipped with a maggot casts well and adds an element of movement which the fish appreciate.

Which cheese should I use in stillwater?
If you are going to fish well out, choose a sliced cheese. For close-range fishing, use a nice spreading or soft cheese.

How should I present a cheese bait to catch a specimen carp?
Many big carp have fallen to baits fished either at long range with a ledger or, better still, freelined around marginal weedbeds.

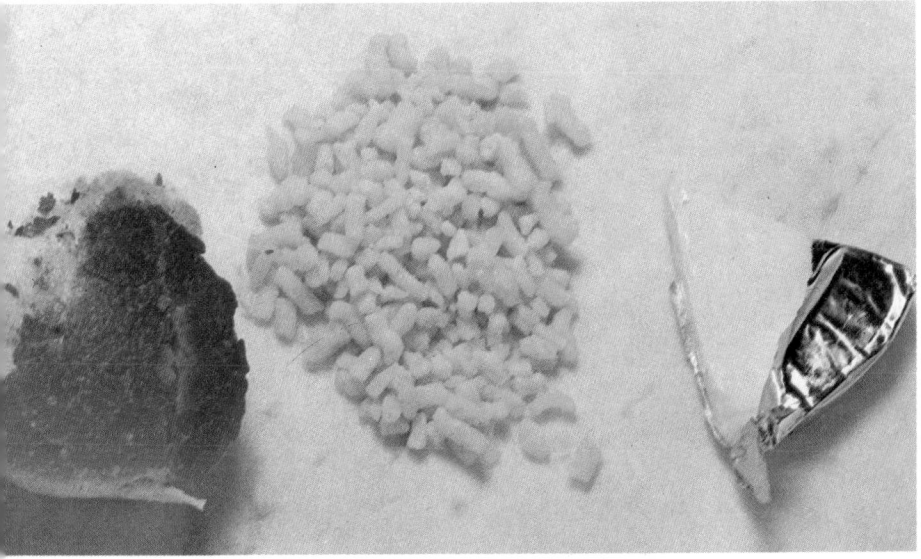

Potato

First popular with specimen carp catchers, potato is now used to take tench, roach, chub and bream. Its big advantage is that while deterring smaller fish, it attracts some really large specimens

Cooked potato, presented in a variety of forms, is favoured as a bait for large carp but is also attractive to bottom-feeders in general and sometimes tench, bream, chub and barbel. The occasional larger roach will take a potato but one of the bait's advantages to the carp fisherman is that smaller fish will usually be deterred by its size and will leave it to the specimens. The attractiveness of potato to large carp is perhaps attributable to its curiosity value and, despite a notorious cautiousness, they will investigate a potential food not normally found in their natural environment if careful groundbaiting is used to allay their suspicions.

Pre-baiting with potatoes is favoured by some anglers, particularly carp catchers. Use a handful of small potatoes thrown into the same swim or swims at the same time every day before a fishing session. A good groundbait can be made up from ordinary or instant potatoes mashed up with scalded bran. This mix, or small par-boiled potatoes similar to the intended hook bait, can be introduced to a swim on several occasions for up to a fortnight before fishing.

Preparation

To prepare the bait, select smallish potatoes—from about large marble to golfball sized. Leave the skins on and boil them for about 15-20 minutes. It is important not to cook them too much for they will fly off the hook on casting or will break up in water if too soft. They should dent slightly under gentle finger pressure when cooked enough. They should then be peeled carefully or scraped before being used on the hook. The peeled and tinned variety make a good substitute and need less preparation as they are already part-cooked.

Ledgering

Ledgering is the usual method for presenting potato to carp. A freelining technique is used, for the bait has its own weight and so does not require leads to assist casting or to get it to the bottom rapidly. Sometimes the weight of the potato will cause it to sink into mud on the bottom where the fish cannot see it. In this case use a slice cut from a potato prepared in the same way. This will lie flat on the bed and if cut large enough it will still deter the smaller fish.

To hook a potato, thread the line through it, using a baiting needle. Better, sink a short piece of plastic tubing through the bait and pass the line through it. This will prevent the line cutting into the potato with the force of the cast, which often has to be a long one. Then tie on a suitably sized hook (some use a barbless model or cut the barb off the regular kind) and pull the hook back into the potato gently so as to prevent fragmenting when casting.

POTATO BAITS

Potato is particularly effective for carp and can be presented whole, chipped, sliced or made into balls. Small new potatoes (fresh or tinned) are ideal, though instant mashed is favoured by some.

Potato slices

Par-boiled potato

Potato chips

Instant potato Granules (or Powder)

OTHER BAITS FROM THE LARDER

Luncheon meat
Only the better quality brands have the right consistency for cutting into cubes and ledgering to barbel and chub.

Semolina and sago
A flavourful groundbait additive which binds together other grain constituents such as rice.

Peas
A groundbait of dried peas makes for profitable fishing with a boiled pea as hookbait.

Bacon rind
The pork rind off uncooked bacon rashers can pass itself of as a worm if it's hooked securely but with a tail left free to wriggle.

Carrots
Small, slimline carrots are reputed to be an excellent spinning bait by those Scottish anglers who use them in place of more orthodox lures.

Bread and cheese
Probably the two most popular baits from your larder. They make reliable ground and hook baits for all coarse fishing.

Effects of casting
To further cushion the effects of casting, leave patches of peel where the point is to penetrate and where it will emerge. Alternatively, use an ingenious method devised in recent years. After tying an eyed hook, the bend is sunk into a round piece of bread crust and then the potato is brought down firmly on to it. This pad of crust will absorb the shock of the cast, which would otherwise jerk the hook back into the potato, possibly breaking it up.

Although a large, eyed hook is preferred by many carp anglers, a hook-to-nylon can also be used by threading the loop through the bait

Isn't casting a problem with such a fragile bait?
Not if the potato has been cooked to the right degree. But always swing the bait out underarm. This will minimize the risk of losing it, and make less splash. When you are after wary specimen fish, you will have to fish from the cover of bushes or below overhanging trees anyway: this itself rules out all but gentle underarm casting.

What size and type of hook is best?
This depends on the size of bait, of course, but use nothing smaller than a No. 8. With the larger potatoes—the size of a golfball—try a No. 2 Goldstrike, or a small treble. Always make sure your hook is as sharp as possible, and don't embed the point.

How do you use chips—and are they really worth trying?
It's always worth trying a variation when carp seem to be losing interest. Hook the chip at one end, making sure it's well impaled. Use a No. 6 or 8—nothing bigger. 'Oven' chips seem to lose their flavour by being refrigerated —but then carp don't object to frozen sweetcorn...

Can potato be used in combination?
Frank Guttfield has had success with potatoes dipped in black treacle. There are plenty of tricks along these lines: honey is certainly one of the best additives for sweet-toothed carp.

Can potato groundbait be used with other hookbaits?
Never overlook a potato-based groundbait. A mix of mash and scalded bran is heavy, and sinks to the bottom quickly without scattering; in this way it's invaluable.

Potato balls made from instant potato mix

Tinned potato in kilner jar

TYING THE HOOK

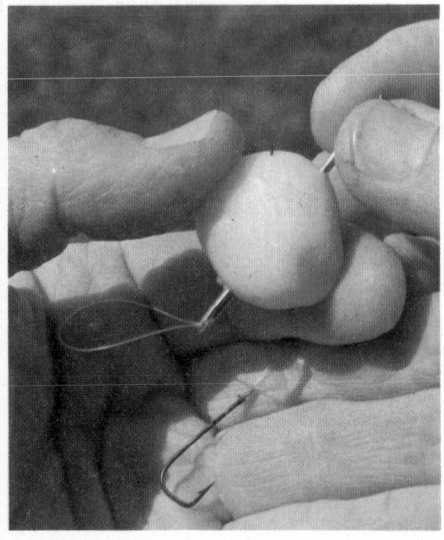

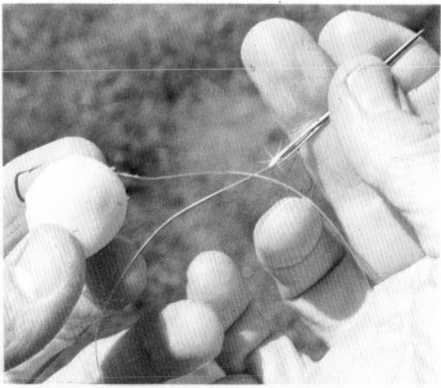

Above: Instead of tying on a hook afterwards, the loop end of the hook-to-nylon is threaded through a potato with a baiting needle. **Top right:** The trace is pulled right through and the hook set gently in the potato with the point exposed. **Right:** Use potatoes the size of golfballs. Here the bait is seen with the hook in position for use.

Small, par-boiled potatoes may be presented in a variety of ways. Try dipping them in a tin of thick black treacle—this is reputedly a recipe for a killer bait.

and then pulling the hook back into the potato.

Remember to take a good supply of par-boiled potatoes on a fishing trip as they will sometimes fly off the hook or break up whatever precautions are taken. The bait must also be changed after taking a fish. Keep the cooked potatoes in water until ready to use on the hook as this prevents them from turning brown. A screw top pickling jar is ideal for this purpose.

Like many baits, the potato is worth experimenting with. Potato chips, lightly fried so as not to be too soft, have been used with some success for carp, although more often in Europe than in this country. A potato paste can be made from mashed potatoes bonded with an additive such as the scalded bran or bread-crumbs used in the ground-bait. The important thing once again is to achieve a consistency that will keep the bait on the hook during casting and while being fished.

Proven carp catcher

All baits—and potatoes are no exception—are subject to fashion and in some cases, mere fad. There are some anglers who stick to one bait for a season or two and then for no apparent reason, switch to something completely different. Of course, there is always room for experiment, but at the same time the most reliable baits always come back again—and potato is nothing if not a proven carp catcher. In any case, it only takes one angler to have a successful session using potato for the news hungry angling press to persuade its readers that potato is the 'new' wonder bait. And with more anglers using it, more fish will be caught.

Fishing with potatoes has accounted for the capture of some of our largest carp and remains among the best methods.

HOOKING YOUR BAIT

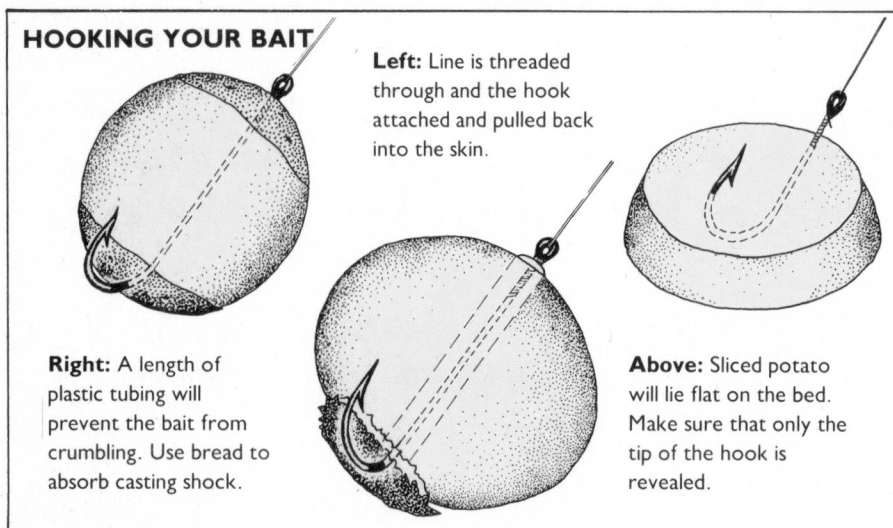

Left: Line is threaded through and the hook attached and pulled back into the skin.

Right: A length of plastic tubing will prevent the bait from crumbling. Use bread to absorb casting shock.

Above: Sliced potato will lie flat on the bed. Make sure that only the tip of the hook is revealed.

Lough Erne system

The Lough Erne system, which straddles Eire and Northern Ireland, is a network of lakes, rivers and streams which offers fabulous sport to suit most angling tastes

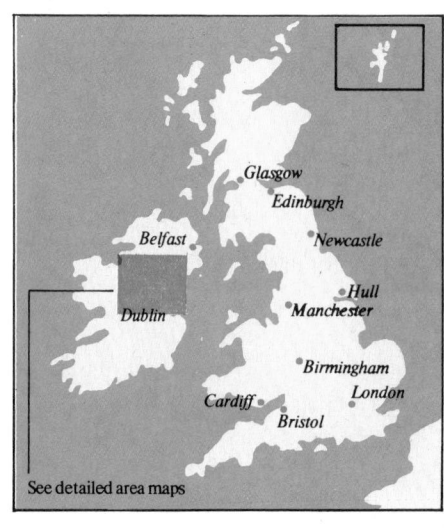

See detailed area maps

Ireland's prime angling is located in the 2,500 square miles of the Erne system—an extensive system of lakes, rivers and streams. It extends south to Dublin, west to the River Shannon, north to Lough Erne, and east to Carlingford. The myriad lakes and rivers are linked to the Boyne system, and many of them are still largely unexploited.

Rules and facilities

Coarse angling in Eire is free. There are no rod licences or close seasons, although statutory fishery boards work to protect salmon and trout. Livebaiting is now prohibited, and no more than two rods may be used at a time. A recent bye-law was passed after the discovery that some anglers had not been returning species in danger of running into short supply, such as pike.

Most lakes have signposted approach roads, or are located alongside main or secondary roads. Car parking is easy, and when an angler wishes to cross fields, a polite request to the owner is rarely refused. The only enemy to the angler is another angler who leaves litter, or carelessly lights fires and leaves gates open, allowing cattle to stray.

The Irish Tourist Board (Bord Fáilte) maintains an advice service for visitors, and maps and advice on bait and techniques are provided by the Inland Fisheries Trust, a semi-state promotion organization offering membership for IR£5 a year. Founded in 1951, the Inland Fisheries Trust has now been merged with other fishery regimes, and consists of a central Fisheries Board and seven regional organizations. Life members of the former Trust re-

tain their right to free fishing, but newcomers must enrol in each separate region of their choice and pay IR£5. The cost of registering in all the regions is IR£35 or a little more though membership of two regions at one time is thought to be ample. Guesthouses catering for

Upper Lough Erne is noted for its coarse fishing. Specimen pike—like the one being displayed proudly here—roach, bream and rudd can be caught but it is usually necessary to fish from a boat.

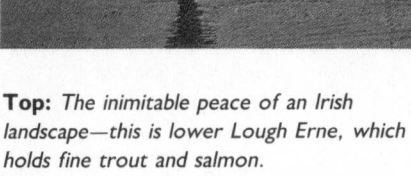

Top: *The inimitable peace of an Irish landscape—this is lower Lough Erne, which holds fine trout and salmon.*
Above: *Lough Allen has good pike fishing.*

visiting anglers can also help with information on where to fish.

Belturbet
Belturbet is a very good centre for coarse fishing and commands a maze of Lough (L) Erne lakes, linking streams, and the main River Erne. Boats are available on adjacent lakes, while the slow flowing River Erne has ample bank facilities, and deep pools containing bream, roach and some pike.

Putiaghan Lake, 2½ miles south, on the Belturbet-Butlers Bridge road, is a first class tench fishery with fish of up to 6lb, and is fished from both stands and boats. North of Belturbet, both Lough Shanncory and L Rout, near Putiaghan, have pike to 10lb, with roach, rudd and perch. Farther south, by Milltown, are L Arden and L Drumany which have good fishing for bream, roach, perch and some pike. Richard Harris, Naughton, Belturbet, can give more details.

The numerous lakes of the Erne system are all within three miles of Butlers Bridge, which is four miles from Cavan town, and on the River

Annalee Derryheen, two miles away, has excellent bream and roach fishing, and bank fishing along the River Annalee offers an abundance of small roach. The upriver stretch near Ballyhaise also has good swims.

Cavan town lies five miles east of the maze of lakes of the Erne system which, together, are known as Lough Oughter. Favourite fishing places are found in Killykeen Forest Park which has good bank fishing for bream, and other waters with large stocks of bream and roach are L Rann, L Killagowan, L Carratraw and L Inchin. L Killymooney in Cavan town has fine tench to 4lb

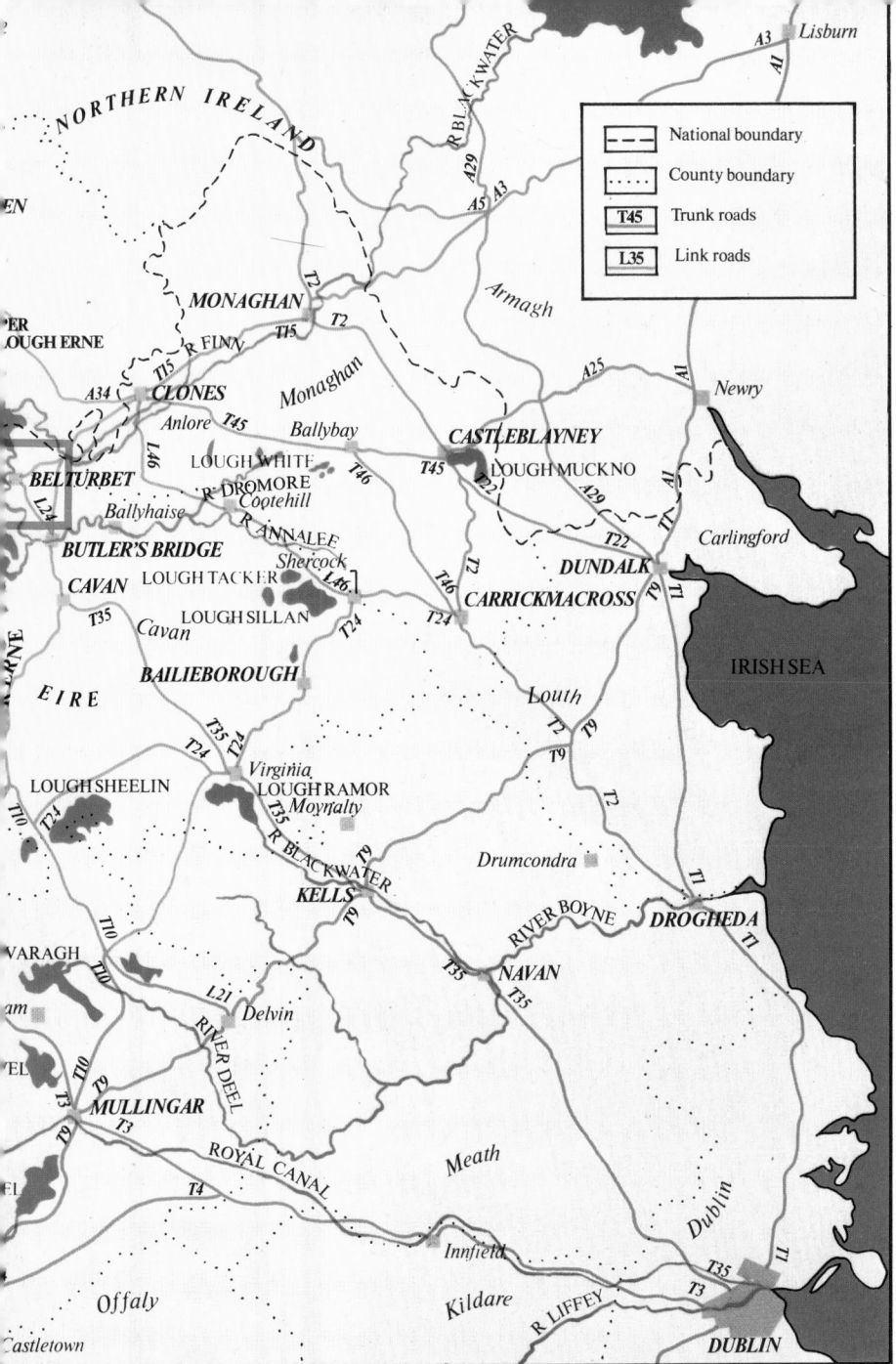

Why is livebait prohibited in Ireland?

It is not actually prohibited—it has simply fallen into disfavour. Live frogs are still being used by some to catch pike and some Specimen Fish Committee medals have been awarded for pike caught on livebaits. The arguments against it have more to do with the shortage of pike than the dislike of cruelty.

What do the Irish mean when they call the pig the fish's worst enemy?

In the small triangle of land between Mountnugent, Kilnaleck and Ballyjamesduff lies the biggest concentration of piggeries in all Europe—72,000 pigs. Slurry from these pig farms runs into the lakes and into many rivers causing over-enrichment of the water that results in thick green algae. Most lakes are now at risk and many rivers are grossly polluted. In Lough Sheelin there is a scheme for removing slurry from the catchment area and spreading it on the land. The Irish government has promised to remove 25 million gallons a year for two years.

Why are pike in short supply in Ireland?

Pike stocks are threatened both in the Republic and in Northern Ireland by irresponsible fishing. Visitors from Europe are largely to blame, for they feel able to disregard the byelaws restricting each angler to two rods. Tourists with up to six or seven rods laid out in front of them scorn threats of prosecution because they know they will be flying off with a freezerful of pike before the week is out. The Continental liking for pike as a food means few are returned to the water.

and bream to 3lb. Mrs B O'Hanlon, St Martin's, Creghan, Co Cavan, can give further details.

Killashandra, two miles from L Oughter, offers the same fishing as the other towns mentioned. In addition, there are L Green in the town providing good tench, L Tullyguide which is a good bream water, and L Derreskit and L Dunaweel, both good for bream and roach. Contact Matty Gaffney in Killashandra, for information.

Source of the Erne

Lough Gowna is a big dispersed lake of 1,000 acres on the Cavan-Longford border. Primarily a coarse fish water, it also holds brown trout and pike, and fishing is excellent, although algae growth is sometimes troublesome. Arvagh, within three miles, is where the Erne flow starts. Lough Garty has limited bank facilities on 500 acres, and there is good roach fishing in L Lisney and the River Erne at Sallachan Bridge and Iron Bridge. Lough Blue Gate is good for roach and bream. Additional information can be obtained from Jimmy Sloan at Lough Gowna Post Office, Co Cavan.

In Co Monaghan, Clones has unlimited bank space on the River Finn, chiefly near Anlore, four miles east at Annie's Bridge. Here the river is fast flowing and weedy in places and holds many roach and rudd. Five small lakes in the area might be worth exploring, but no boats are available. For further details, contact Mrs A Woods, Clones, Co Monaghan.

River Dromore

Cootehill, Baileborough, Shercock and Ballybay form a triangle covering 60 square miles. In Cootehill, there is good fishing on the River Dromore flowing from Ballybay, and excellent bream and roach fishing in L White, at Baird's Shore, near Ballybay. Other lakes are L Black and L Dromore, both of 200 acres, L Inner and L Tacker, L Mullanarry and L Corkeeran, which have good roach fishing, and L Lisnalong which has just one boat. Nearer Cootehill, L Killyudran is good for bream and roach, and L Drumlona is good for bream and pike.

Bailieborough has L Church of 150 acres with adequate bank facilities and four boats, as well as L Castle, L Skeagh, L Drumkerry, and L Galbolie. Lough Skillan, 800 acres, is alongside Shercock with fair pike and bream, seven boats available and bank space for 60 rods. For further information contact B Grennan, The Beeches, Cootehill, or M Brady, Bailieborough, Co Cavan.

Monaghan town is a good centre for fishing the Ballybay area which has the Dromore River and six lakes. They are all good for bream, rudd and perch, but no boats are available. Lough Major, 800 acres, is largely reserved for trout, although restricted coarse fishing is permitted, while L Mullarney and L White provide good bream. For further details contact McCaughery, at 1 Highfield Close, Killygoan, Co Monaghan or G Maguire in Ballybay. Carrickmacross: has many lakes L Monalty, a shallow, weedy lake, has first class bream, rudd and rudd/bream hybrids, and nearby L Corcrin has bream. In the town, L Lisaniske is also good for bream, while Rahan's Lake, with fishing stands, provides good bream and pike. Contact Tom Ward, Coolfore, Carrickmacross, Co Monaghan, for further details.

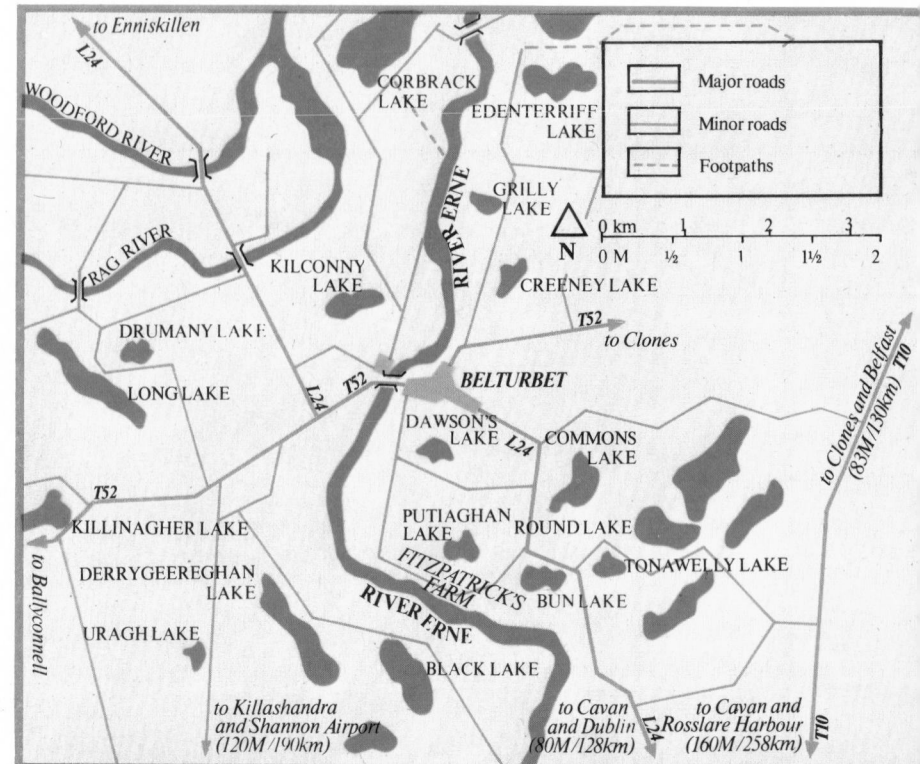

River Woodford

Baillinamore, Carrigallen and Ballyconnel form another triangle west of the Erne system proper. The River Woodford, slow moving near Ballyconnel, has high quality fishing for pike, bream, roach, perch and some rudd. Lough Cranaghan, 50 acres and Lough Clonty, near Ardlougher, have good fishing but limited bank space.

Roach fishing on the slow-flowing River Erne in Belturbet, shown on our detail map of the Belturbet area (top). There are good bank facilities and deep pools holding bream.

At Carrigallen, the little-fished Lough Glasshouse, 100 acres, is worth exploring by boat, and both Lough Rockfield and Lough Galladoo are believed to hold roach and other coarse species.

Norfolk

Dismissed by many as flat and boring, Norfolk nevertheless offers the angler more varied and accessible fishing than perhaps any other county in England in a wide range of unspoilt settings

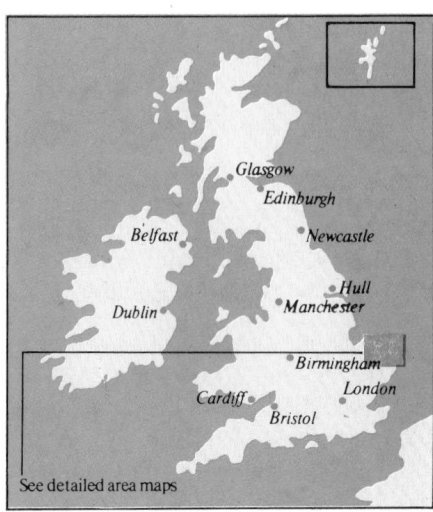

See detailed area maps

Left: *Dave Plummer lovingly holds a magnificent 16lb 8oz pike caught on the River Waveney, which meanders along the Norfolk-Suffolk border. The region is famous for its fine pike, roach and bream.*

Three major river systems feed the Broads—the Bure, Wensum and Yare, each with tidal stretches, and two tidal rivers, the Ant and Thurne. There are also numerous gravel pit complexes plus natural and man-made lakes, meres, ponds and minor rivers.

The River Wensum runs crystal-clear from its source above Fakenham along a 30-mile course to Norwich. It has 2lb roach, large dace, and chub to over 6lb, with perch, a few bream, a good head of native brown trout, and pike in plenty.

Fishing starts at Fakenham, where the local club controls a two-

mile length. Trout day tickets and coarse day tickets are obtainable from local tackle shops.

Wensum roach

From Guist downstream, the LAA controls some good roach fishing at North Elmham with tickets from G Fisher, 10 Memorial Cottages, Norwich (Tel 404289).

There is more day-ticket fishing four miles downstream at Swanton Morley with day tickets available from the bailiff of Morley Fisheries. These give access to excellent coarse fishing in the river and in three gravel pits.

At Lyng, the Dereham and District AA sells day tickets for a short length of the river, while on the opposite bank a little farther upstream, the LAA has a length, and another at Lenwade Common—both with good roach fishing.

Below Lenwade much of the fishing is private, except for a free stretch at Ringland Bridge, and around the sluice pool at Costessey where the AWA introduced some barbel a few years back. All the fishing from here downstream to Hellesdon is private except for a short length opposite Drayton Green Lanes where AWA day tickets at 70p are issued. Downstream from Hellesdon to Norwich, much of the Wensum comes into the city boundaries and is free fishing. At New Mills the river becomes tidal and offers excellent free sport for roach, bream and pike. Eventually, after flowing close to Thorpe Station and beneath Carrow Road Bridge, the Wensum joins up with the Yare.

The Yare is in two parts—the upper reaches, clear, weedy and shallow, hold specimen dace, roach, perch and chub, and the deep, wide, tidal reaches below Norwich hold good stocks of roach and bream.

The 10-mile stretch from Bawburgh to Norwich offers excellent roach, dace and chub fishing controlled by the AWA at 70p per day, with a fair amount of free fishing on available common land in the Earlham-to-Keswick reach.

At Trowse, the Yare becomes tidal and the fishing is free wherever there is access. The AWA controls access at Buckenham Ferry, reached by the Beauchamp Arms roadway, Cantley reached via the Red House Hotel grounds, and at Langley.

Between Strumpshaw and Buckenham on the southern bank, two dykes lead to Rockland Broad, an excellent fishery of about 50 acres. It is mostly shallow, 2–6ft, but is 12ft deep at the junction of the shore dyke. Roach and bream fishing is good, and pike are plentiful in winter. Downstream from Langley, after Reedham Ferry, the new cut joins the Yare and the Waveney, which flow two miles apart at this point but gradually run together to Breydon Water and on to Great Yarmouth.

Superb tidal Thurne

Just five miles long, the tidal Thurne is a superb fishery, containing large quantities of roach and bream, particularly in the Potter Heigham-to-Martham reaches. The river links (via Candle Dyke) the Bure to Hickling Broad, Heigham Sounds and Horsey Mere.

Boats can be hired at Hickling or Great Yarmouth and, from these points, taken anywhere along the Thurne and on to the Broads. There is also extensive free fishing along the Thurne from Martham, through Potter Heigham and to where the Thurne enters the Bure.

Although the Ant has a short non-tidal stretch, the river is not of importance to anglers until it reaches Wayford Bridge over which runs the A149 Stalham road. The flow here is of medium pace, and the river is inhabited by roach, bream and pike, as in most of its length. Fishing is free wherever the banks are accessible.

Downstream from Wayford, the Ant enters Barton Broad—a huge area of shallow water offering good bream fishing, with pike in winter. The Ant then flows out of the Broad's southern end, through Irstead Shoals, where the flow can be strong at times, and downstream through How Hill, Johnson Street,

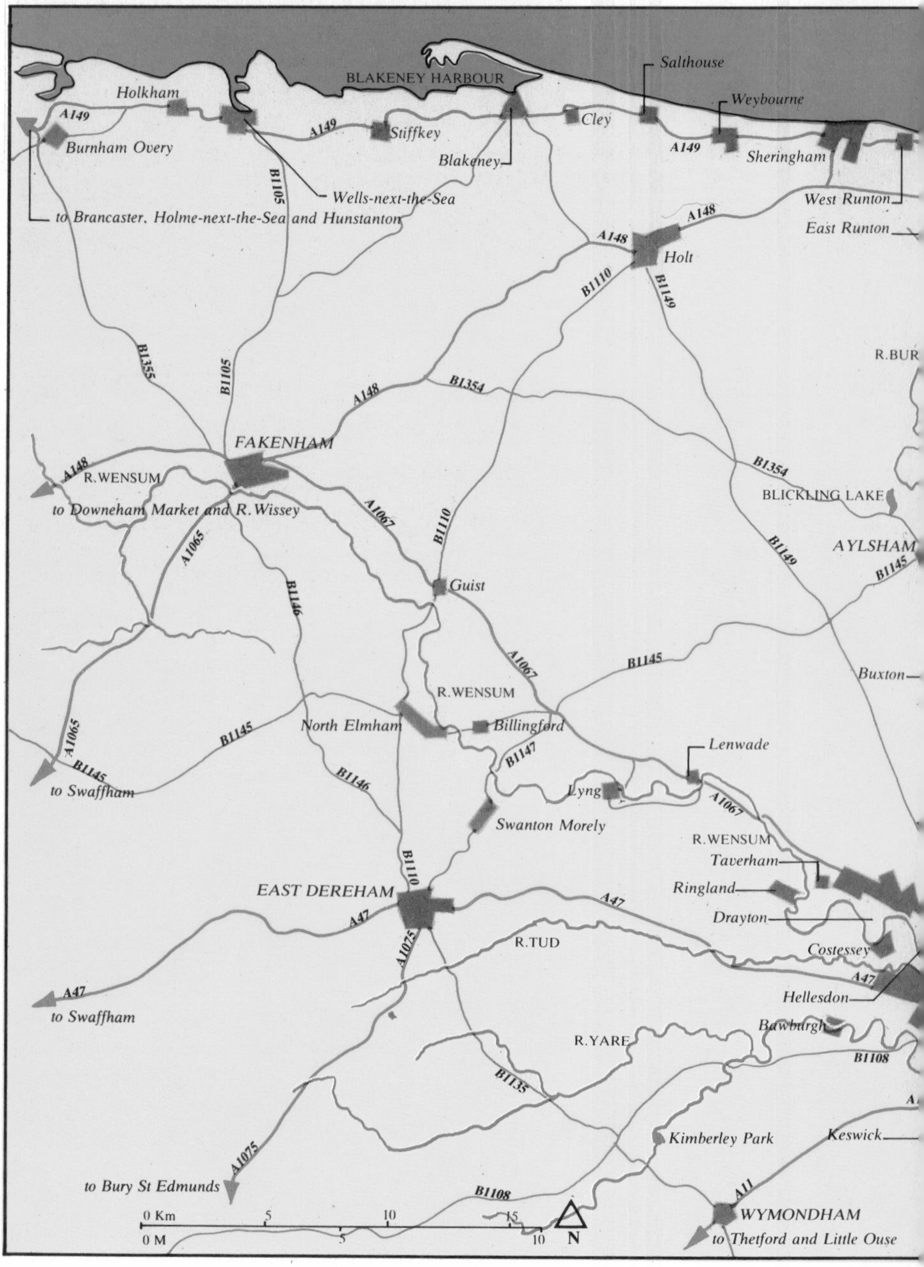

190

to Ludham Bridge. The AWA controls sections of free bank fishing on these reaches, which are extremely good winter and autumn venues. Half a mile below Ludham, the Ant joins the Bure.

River Bure

For most of its length, the Bure is tidal, deep and fast, and holds good roach, dace, and bream in its upper reaches. It connects with several Broads, and with the Thurne and Ant as it flows to Great Yarmouth.

Fishing in much of the upper Bure has deteriorated though roach over 2lb and bream over 6lb are taken

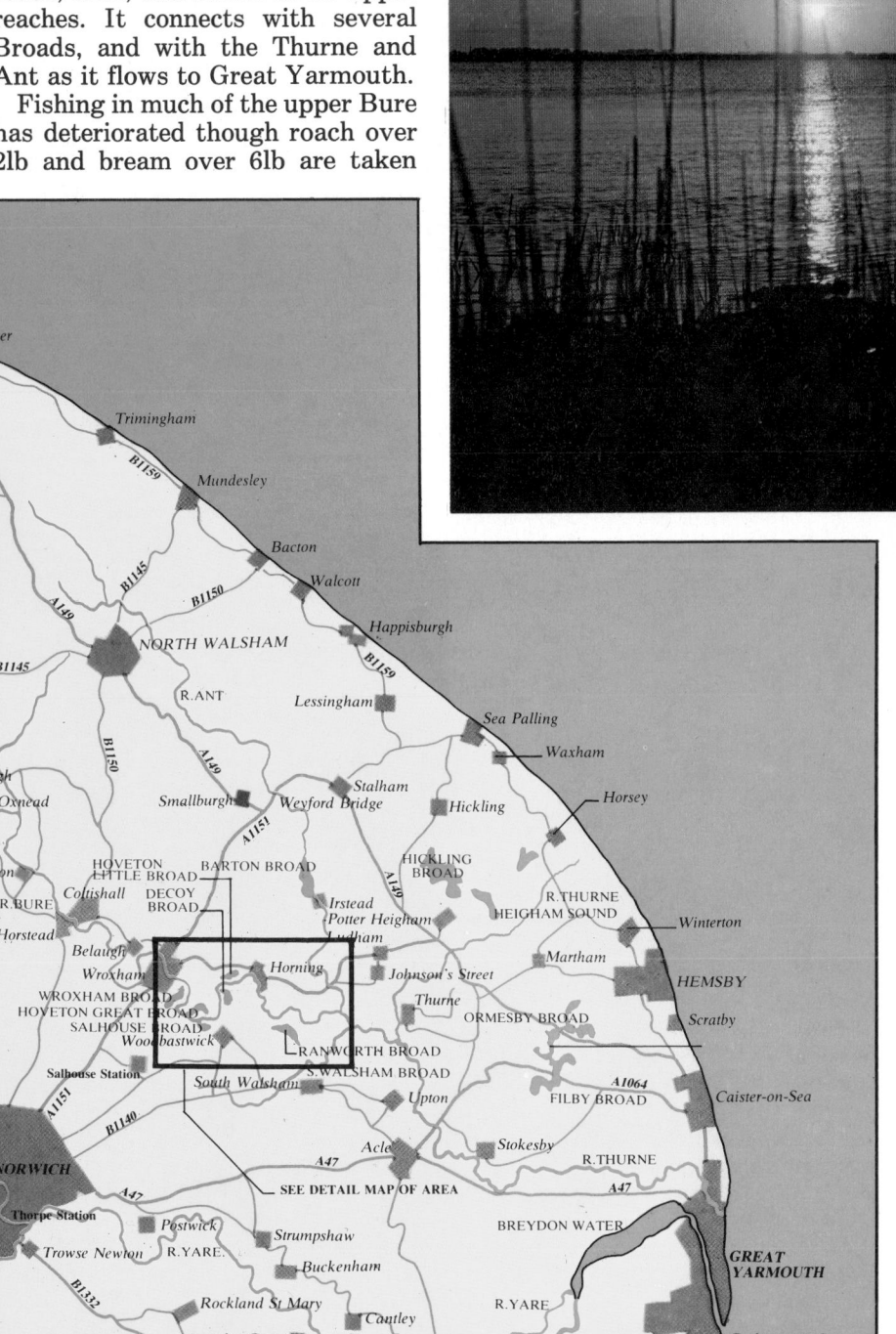

Above left: *Blakeney harbour is typical of the wild, open North Norfolk coastline—ideal for estuary fishing.* **Above:** *Sunset over Hickling Broad, haunt of pike and bream.*

each season, together with the occasional trout and pike.

The Bure becomes tidal at Horstead Mill pool, and from this point the fishing is free. Good locations are at Coltishall, Belaugh and Wroxham, where quality bream and roach are to be found, with perch, rudd and numerous pike, some very large. The flow is not strong, but the Bure gathers pace and depth as it flows through Woodbastwick Marshes and on to Horning, a good winter fishing location.

The AWA controls access to free fishing at Woodbastwick, South Walsham and Upton—and again, much farther downstream, at Acle and Burgh Marshes, where the flow is incredibly strong and ledgering is the only method of fishing. Access to these lower reaches is from the main Stokesby road.

Several miles downstream, the Bure reaches Great Yarmouth. Few anglers fish these last few miles

191

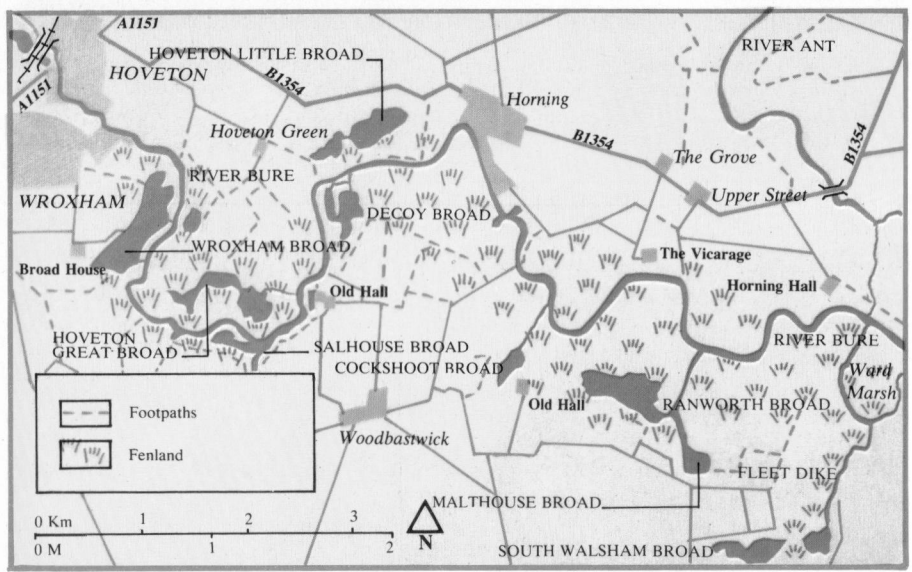

Above left: *Bringing a trout to the net on a stretch of the Upper Bure.* **Above:** *Fishing for bream on the River Ant.* **Left:** *Detailed map of the Broads, north-east of Norwich.*
Right: *Bridge Pool at Lyng, on the River Wensum, noted for its excellent roach.*
Below right: *Set in the grounds of Holkham Hall—Holkam Lake, a day-ticket water.*

because of the salt tides, particularly likely during the winter months.

The Broads
Between Wroxham and Acle, the River Bure feeds many publicly accessible Broads: Wroxham, Salhouse, Decoy, Ranworth, and South Walsham Broad.

Wroxham Broad, with over 100 acres of water of 2ft-10ft deep, has good roach fishing, and numerous bream and good pike in winter. Salhouse Broad offers similar fishing, but is not so deep. Boats are hired at Wroxham, or one can bank-fish by taking the road from

192

Salhouse village.

Decoy Broad is an enclosed water reserved for Norwich and District AA members. Boats for fishing are available on day tickets. This large Broad, with depths from 3–12ft, offers superlative summer fishing for sizeable bream, some roach and tench, and good pike in winter.

Ranworth Broad consists of an outer part which offers free fishing, and a large, shallow, inner Broad, also controlled by Norwich and District AA, which offers fishing from June 16 to September 31 and from March 1-14. Summer fishing produces good bags of roach and

bream, with big pike during the last fortnight of the season.

South Walsham Broad also has two parts: the inner Broad strictly private, the outer Broad offering free fishing. Roach and bream sport is good during summer and autumn, but winter fishing is variable.

The Great Ouse Relief Channel and the Cut Off Channel—deep man-made drains cut between high flood banks—relieve the Great Ouse of much of its flood water and provide high quality coarse fishing. They abound with roach and bream, and also offer pike and zander. The Relief Channel is the larger stretch, being over 100 yards wide in many places and 11 miles long, stretching from Denver Sluice to King's Lynn.

The Cut-Off Channel stretches from Denver to Mildenhall, but accessible fishing is limited to the Denver to West Dereham stretch on both banks. You must ask about day tickets covering fishing on both channels, available from the local tackle shops.

Swingtips and quivertips

With the vast array of rod tip bite indicators now available it is hardly surprising that the average angler is left baffled about which to choose. Here we suggest some guidelines

Left: *A swingtip in action on a ledger rod. It can reduce casting length and efficiency.*
Above: *The target shield is a sheet of gridded plastic against which the movements of a tip indicator are more easily seen.*

Pendulum effect

A common fault is that many swingtips are too short. A swingtip of less than 6in in length just cannot do its job properly, as, within practical limits, the longer a swingtip is, the easier it is to obtain a 'pendulum' effect and less effort is required by a fish to produce a detectable movement.

The swingtip does have its drawbacks however. First, and most importantly, it reduces the length of the cast since the energy required to overcome the swingtip's tendency to drop and wag during casting detracts from the force of the cast. Secondly, the resistance of a swingtip increases immediately following a bite, when it is lifted and more of its weight bears directly on the line. Third, it cannot be used when fishing a river or when the wind is really high. Stiff rubber links or weights added to the tip are favoured by many anglers to beat these conditions, but although many have used them successfully, they do have a tendency to counteract some of the tip's effectiveness.

Ledgering was once considered the lazy man's method, a crude, last resort for most anglers. But the invention of effective bite indicators has changed all this. The swingtip in particular has brought that vital touch of refinement to the method. Anglers such as the late Fred Foster have developed into an art form.

Since Jack Clayton first introduced the swingtip to Lincolnshire waters, a host of bite indicators have been invented and sold. Many are efficient, others can only be described as wierd and wonderful—and are often unjustifiably expensive.

Three kinds of indicator

The wide range of bite indicators available to today's angler can be divided into three main categories—swingtips, quivertips (including donkey tops), and butt indicators. Some indicators are dealt with in the zander fishing article on pp 100-111 and this article deals with swingtips and quivertips.

The swingtip is probably the most efficient indicator of them all. It is a piece of cane or light metal, with rings for the line to pass through, which is attached to the rod end by a flexible piece of plastic or rubber.

Virtually weightless action

Nevertheless, given reasonable conditions and no need for long casting, the swingtip is the most sensitive indicator. It is virtually weightless as far as the fish is concerned, and is in direct line of contact with the ledger weight. Only in windy conditions and running waters do the quivertip, or donkey top, really come into their own as indicators.

The quivertip and donkey top are basically the same, except that the donkey top is spliced into the rod tip, while the quivertip is screwed on. Both consist of a piece of solid glassfibre, with a fine, flexible tip, gradually thickening in section towards the base and, naturally, becoming less flexible.

Fished in a river, the flexible quivertip absorbs the force of the current on the line, bending slightly to do so. If a fish moves the bait, it alters the balance of forces between the current and the quivertip so altering the quivertip's position to register a bite.

Increased resistance

The basic drawback of the quivertip is that as tension in the line increases, the tip pulls over, increasing resistance. A great advantage that it has over the swingtip is that casting is virtually unimpaired. There is no evidence of drag on the line once the cast is underway, as the quivertip remains straight and therefore exerts minimum friction on the line.

As quivertips are detachable, they come in different lengths of various thicknesses. For close-range ledgering on a lake or a river with little flow, a short, thin tip is far more effective than the bigger version. The opposite is true when you are trying to fish a heavy swimfeeder at long range on a fast-flowing river, such as the Severn or Trent. A useful pointer when selecting the right tip for the conditions is that the force of the current on the line should result

Right: *A stockist's typical range of swingtips, quivertips and springtips grouped according to manufacturer. Right of centre is the weighted swingtip adopted by some anglers to counteract wind or current. Some believe it impairs sensitivity.*

194

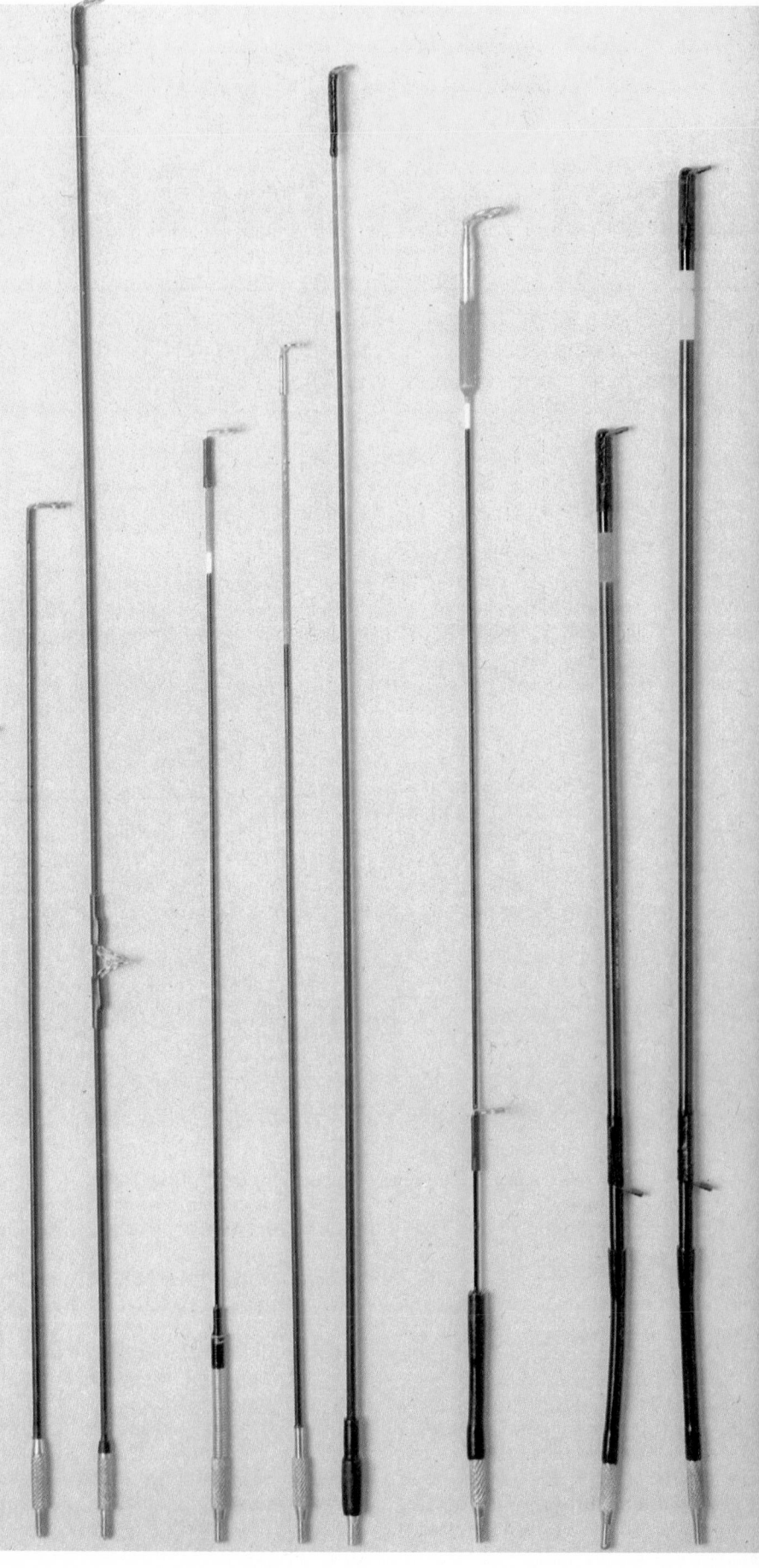

Above: *Swingtip set to register a bite.*
Inset: *The qivertip under tension. It is ideal for fishing close-to in still ponds.*

in the tip bending to approximately 30 degrees, any more than this requires a stronger tip, any less a finer, weaker one.

Even so, it has great value, particularly on rivers with a heavy flow, such as the Severn. One revolutionary version of the swingtip is even better in rough conditions than the quivertip. It was designed by Eric Antill, an engineer. While the majority of anglers use heavyweight swingtips purely to beat windy conditions, Eric realized that weight in the swingtip could be a positive advantage—even in still conditions.

He made his swingtip out of brass rod which he threaded inside so that additional weights could be screwed in, even though bite indicators are traditionally as light and sensitve as possible. In Eric's rig, however, the weight of the swingtip was balanced against the ledger weight, with the swingtip being slightly heavier.

Irresistible action

The result was that once cast out, the heavy tip made the ledger lead 'creep' along the bottom, giving an action to the bait which was often irresistible. Furthermore, the balance between ledger weight and swingtip was such that any interference with the bait registered as a bite despite the weight of the tip.

Eric's idea has never gone much further, although we have proved that it worked. In particular, he had one or two wins under gale-force conditions when conventional swing-tipping was virtually impossible.

Springtips

A fairly recent indicator proving increasingly popular among ledger anglers, is the springtip. Obtainable at most tackle shops, matchmen in particular have found it an ideal compromise between the floppy swingtip, and the fairly rigid quivertip. Whereas a swingtip hangs at 90 degrees to the rod, (and therefore reduces the casting range) a spring-tip remains in line with the rod throughout the cast, limiting friction and increasing the range.

Once a fish pulls a springtip, the resistance does not increase as it does with a quivertip. In fact the opposite is true: the spring simply collapses, resulting in more confident takes and fewer missed bites.

Effective as a springtip may be, it too has its limitations and the thoughtful angler will travel equipped with all three types of tip to meet any situation that arises.

ASK THE EXPERT

How do I know whether to select a swingtip or a quivertip?
Generally speaking, a swingtip is for use on stillwaters with little or no flow, whereas a quivertip is more effective on moving water.

How can I prevent my swingtip blowing about in the wind?
In strong wind you should resort to a springtip, but otherwise you can shelter the tip with a target board. This transparent perspex windbreak screws into a bankstick and protects the tip from the worst of the wind. It is also marked off in segments to show up the difference between dips caused by the wind and out-of-the-ordinary movements which could signal a biting fish.

How long should a swingtip be?
Although for bream fishing you can go up to as much as 12in, the ideal length is usually 9in.

How should I position my rod when I am quivertipping a river?
Point your rod slightly upstream, so that the line is at right angles to the tip.

Why is there a need for quivertips of varying diameter?
The different thicknesses cope with different conditions of flow. The stronger the flow, the thicker the diameter needs to be.

Will a quivertip work on a normal 12ft float rod?
It's better to use a much shorter ledger rod, as the farther away the tip is from you, the more difficult it is to see the bites.

Float rods

Fishing with float tackle has evolved into a complicated science and the conscientious angler can take full advantage of modern developments in the manufacture of float rods

Rods for float fishing should be 12-13ft long, able to handle lines of 3-5lb b.s., and have a slow action. Other types of coarse fishing rod may be used: the specimen hunter, for example, may find a light carp rod best when float fishing for tench or carp in weedy conditions and with the expectation of a big fish. The beginner will often use a glassfibre spinning rod because it is cheap,

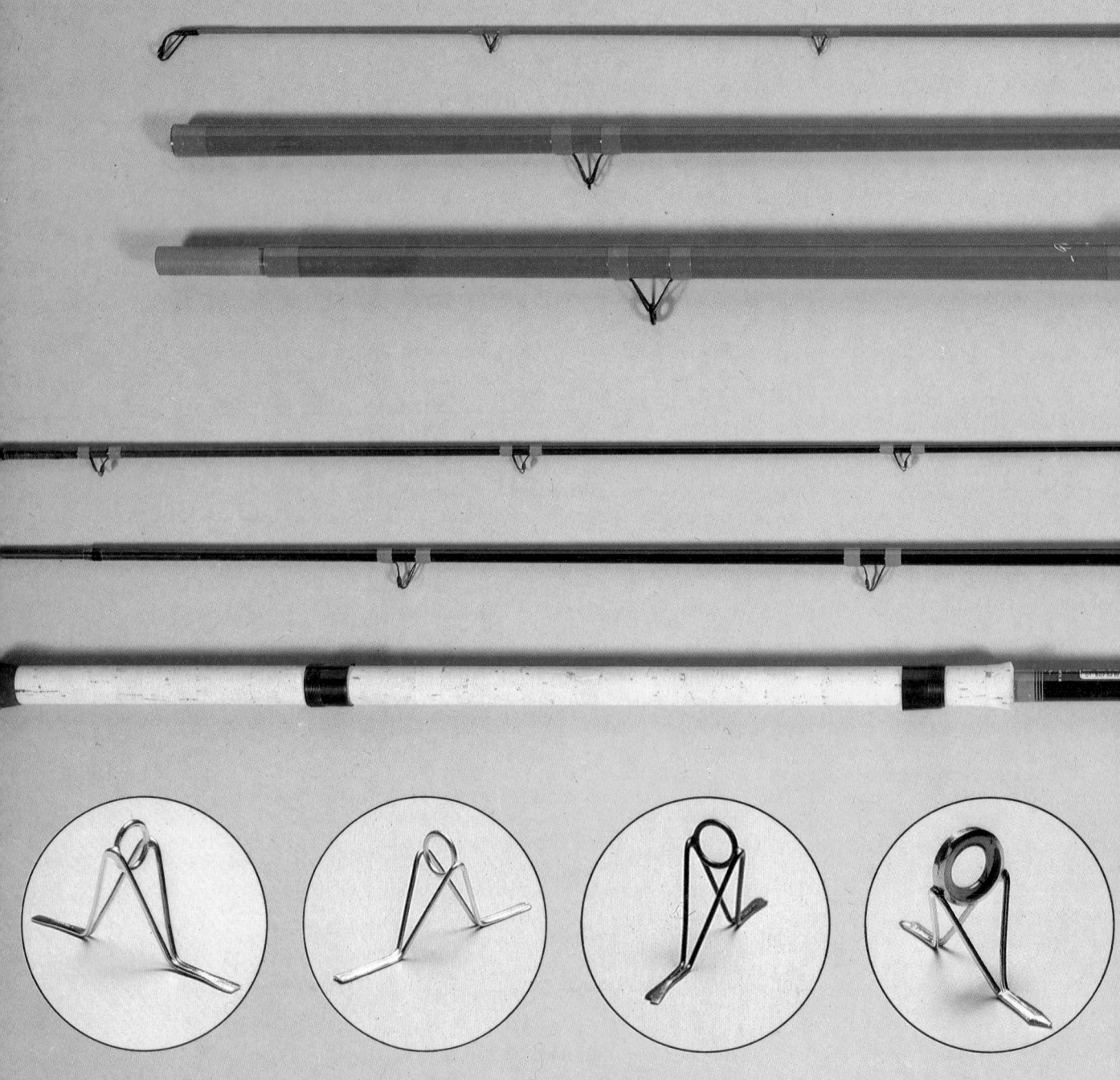

Bright chrome 'stand off' intermediate.

Satin chrome 'stand off' intermediate.

Black chrome 'stand off' intermediate.

Bright chrome intermediate lined with 'Aqualite'.

adaptable and sturdy. But the term 'float rod' is usually applied to the longer rods used for general and match fishing.

These two uses have resulted in the development of two distinct kinds of float rod: slow-action rods, which bend along much of their length when playing a fish or casting; and fast-action rods, usually rigid to within 25 per cent of their length with the action concentrated in the tip.

General-purpose float rods are slower in action than match rods and have stronger tips, usually made of glassfibre and 2½-3mm in diameter. The tip of a match rod is nearer 2½mm in diameter to allow their use with lines of 1½-2lb b.s. In addition, the match rod is usually stiffer in the butt to give quicker

These two masterpieces could never have been envisaged in the bad old days of heavy, sluggish float rods. The top rod is a 'Fibatube' 12ft hollow glassfibre match rod. Like most modern match rods, it has a fast tip action and the high 'stand off' rings are effective in preventing wet line clinging to the rod. The bottom rod is a 'Graphlex' GXL made by Don's of Edmonton: a 13ft match rod with a fast tip action constructed, unusually, of carbonfibre all the way through.

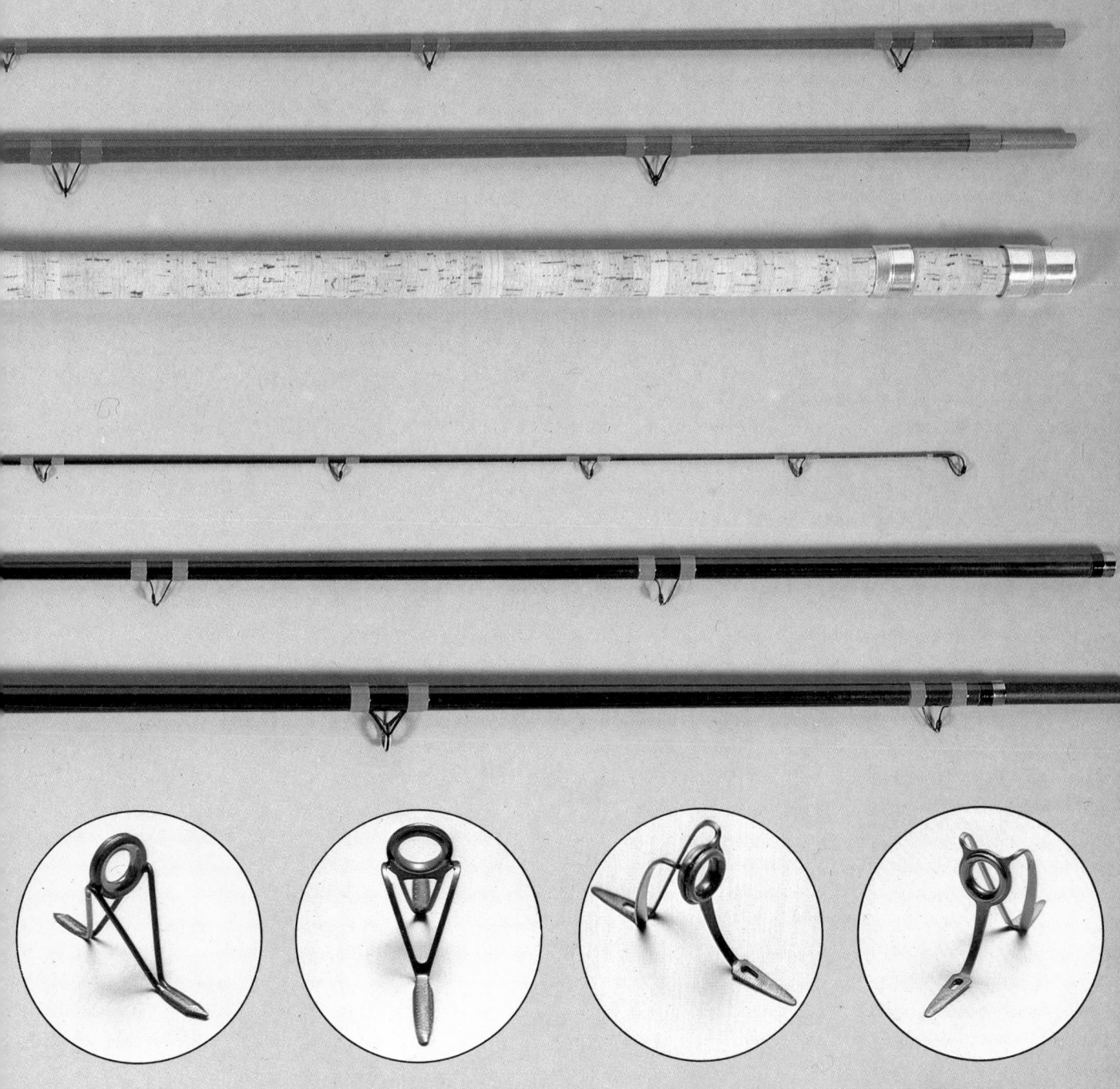

Black chrome intermediate lined with 'Aqualite'.

'Seymo' 3 leg intermediate, aluminium oxide lined.

'Fuji' 3 leg intermediate, aluminium oxide lined.

'Fuji' intermediate lined with silicon carbide.

197

striking. Fish control, however, is more difficult with a stiffer rod, but as a rule, matchmen are not pursuing large fish. There are exceptions to this, such as on the Severn where matches are won with good sized chub and barbel. These fish demand a stronger rod than that used by the average match fisherman.

Match rod development

Due to the changing demands of match fishing, the match rod is constantly being developed. Different areas of fishing call for different actions so there are variations in the type of rod in use.

Most float rods today are made of tubular glassfibre, though carbonfibre rods are increasingly popular.

Float rods are usually equipped with cork handles fitted with sliding rings for holding the reel. This keeps the weight to a minimum.

With a threaded tip ring fitted, the float rod may be used with various screw attachments, such as a swing tip for ledgering. Care should be taken, however, to ensure that the tip of the rod will stand up to the casting weight.

A rod of this description is also suited to long trotting, when float tackle is allowed to trot down with the current of a river or stream and the fish are hooked and played some way downstream from the angler.

Specimen hunters tend to use the longer, lighter ledgering rods—those designed by Peter Stone, for example—since they are capable of casting tackle long distances and controlling heavy fish.

Above right: *Roach pole fishing is now coming back with a vengeance. It is a very sensitive method of taking small coarse fish and demands a particular expertise. Here Peter Ward is attaching a section of a Shakespeare roach pole before fishing.*
Right: *Peter Ward demonstrates two types of float rod. In his right hand he holds a 13ft tip-action match rod and in his left a 13ft soft-action float rod.*
Far right: *Swing or quiver tips are attached to rod tips by being screwed into specially designed top rings (top). Roach pole tip showing the method of attaching the alloy crook and the elastic shock absorber (centre). Playing a winter chub caught on float tackle in fast water (bottom).*

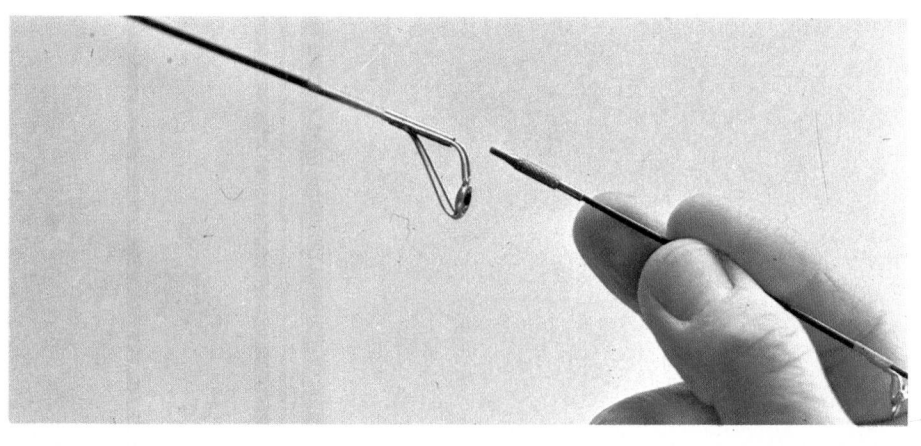

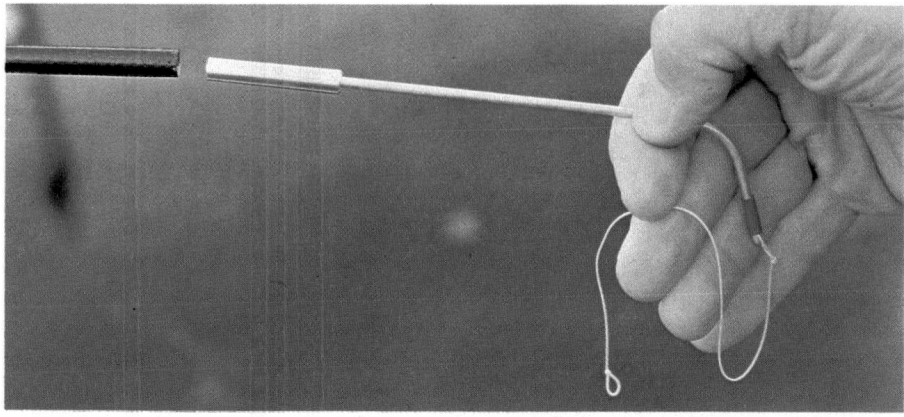

What should I look for in a float rod?

If you are a beginner you should be able to buy a reasonable, hollow glass float rod quite cheaply. For the more advanced fisherman where the rod will be held for long periods the lighter carbonfibre rod is more suitable. It may cost you more initially but it will save re-equipping at a later date. Whatever you decide make sure you buy a float rod suitable for the kind of fishing you intend to do.

How long should my float rod be?

Most children can handle a rod 10-11ft in length if it is reasonably light and robust. Most of the rods used by experienced or match fishermen are 12-13ft long. Rods shorter than 10ft in length are difficult to use with float tackle and are not recommended.

What points should I look for when buying a pole?

When you have decided what length of pole you want you should test its weight, its stiffness and balance. It should be stiff throughout its length and as light as possible. The carbonfibre models are better in this respect. It should be able to take a range of attachments, and to accommodate these the fine tips which are usually fitted can be pushed out from the tip of the pole.

How can I protect my float rod or pole?

Most damage to fishing rods is caused in transit. As float rods are usually made of thin walled glass or carbon they can be damaged very easily. A rod tube or rod holdall can be an invaluable investment. Most poles are made so that the pieces fit inside each other, so additional protection is not necessary.

Fixed-spool reel

No other piece of tackle has revolutionized the art of angling quite as much as the fixed-spool reel. Knowing how to handle it properly can save time and effort and improve your fishing

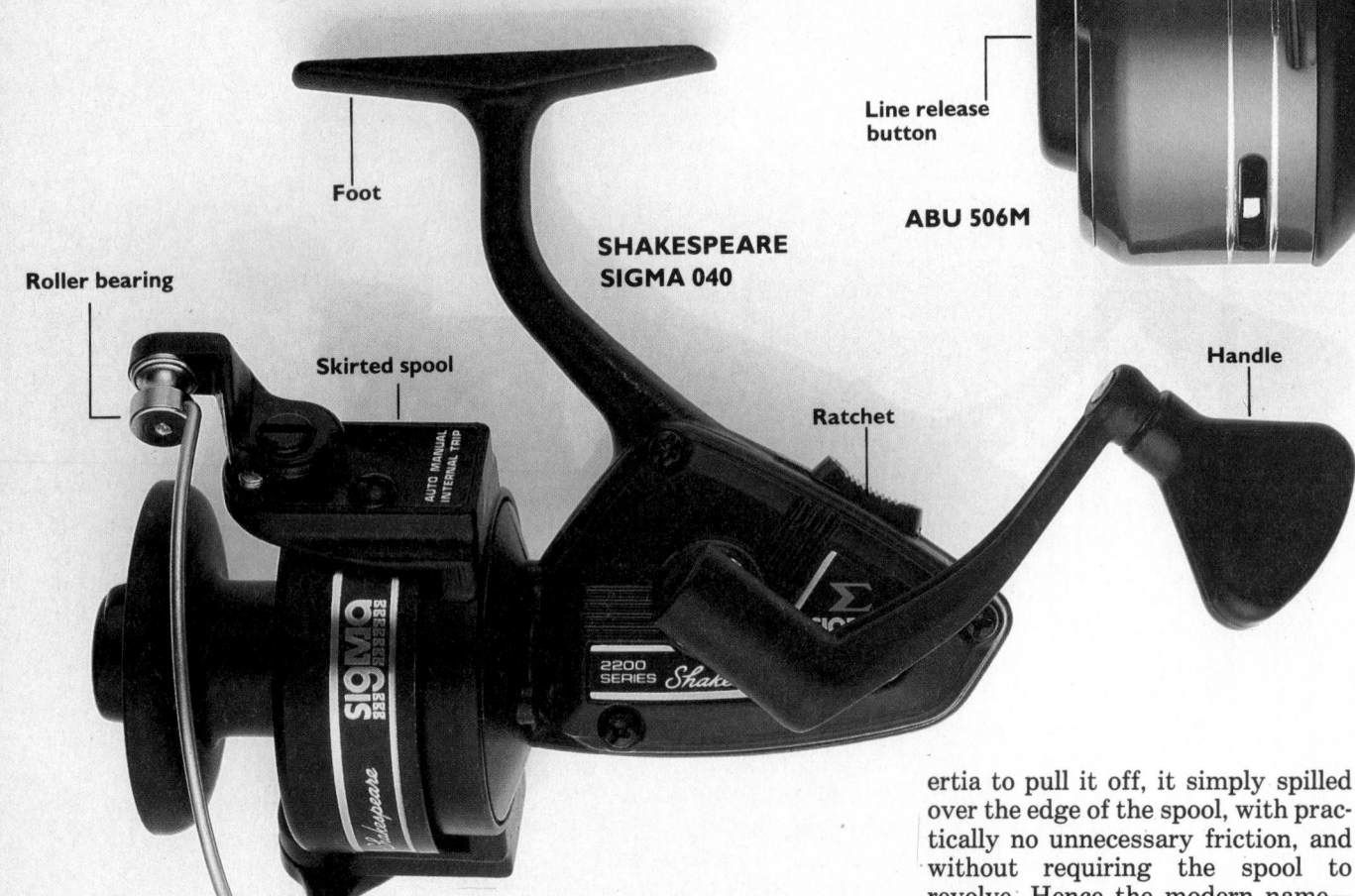

Oscillating spool

Winding cap cover

Line release button

ABU 506M

Foot

SHAKESPEARE SIGMA 040

Roller bearing

Skirted spool

Ratchet

Handle

The modern fixed-spool reel is a masterpiece of engineering design. It has banished one of the angler's oldest problems, that of casting to the required spot, and has doubled, or even trebled the distances over which the average angler can hope to cast accurately. At the same time, it has reduced the problem of tangled line to a minimum.

Despite this, we still occasionally hear the reel's critics bemoaning the fact that it has taken the skill out of casting. Even if this were wholly true, it would be no more a cause for regret than the fact that the washing machine has taken the drudgery out of washing day.

The first fixed-spool reel was patented by Alfred Illingworth in 1905. It incorporated all the basic principles of the modern reel, which still hold good today. The line spool was fixed with its axis at right angles to the direction of casting. When line was released, as long as the tackle provided the necessary in-

ertia to pull it off, it simply spilled over the edge of the spool, with practically no unnecessary friction, and without requiring the spool to revolve. Hence the modern name—fixed-spool.

Line was retrieved simply by hooking it onto a primitive bale-arm, which revolved around the fixed-spool, laying line back when the reel handle was turned.

Slipping clutches

To provide the faster retrieval desired for spinning, Illingworth geared the reel handle to the bale-arm to provide a retrieval ratio of approximately 3:1. The fixed-spool reel has come a long way since those days, and, not long after Ill-

Auto syncro-drag

ABU+

Shakespeare Sigma 2200

The three fixed-spool reels shown here represent the results of the efforts of the manufacturers to solve the problem of casting line at right angles to the spool. The Sigma range has the skirted spool which prevents loops in the line from tangling around the spindle. This is a problem which can occur just after a cast (before the arm is closed), or when ledgering with the arm open when the wind can pick loops off the spool.

Abu 506

This Swedish reel has taken the concept a stage further with its completely closed face. There is no bale arm to operate manually. Line is released for casting by the pressure of a finger on the face of the boss on the front of the reel. Line recovery is engaged immediately by a turn of the handle. For match fishing. when terminal tackle must be out of the water for as little time as possible, this kind of action is ideal.

Mitchell 300A

This range of French reels, all noted for their quality and precision, does not have a skirted spool, but the design of the spool rims aids clean recovery of line. The amount of line a spool can accommodate depends upon the diameter of the line. Many other models of fixed-spool reels can be changed from right-to-left-hand wind by unscrewing the handle and attaching it on the other side of the reel body

MITCHELL 300A

Bale arm

Unskirted spool

Tension nut

RATIO 4.2:1 CAPACITY : TEST/YDS 7/380

MITC 300A

Ratchet

Spool release button

Bale arm trip

ingworth's first reel, slipping clutches and crosswind reels were developed, although these only entered the market in the early 1930s, not really coming into common usage until after the war.

Now it is possible to buy such reels with a wide variety of retrieval ratios suitable for every possible kind of fishing. All have adjustable clutch mechanisms, a reciprocating reel movement which provides even laying of line, and in some cases a crosswind action to prevent the line from jamming.

To be effective, such a reel must be properly used. Most manufacturers' instructions today refer to the loading capacity of the various spools, which varies with the b.s. of the line required. Many manufacturers provide a spare spool, and since most spools are quickly detachable the angler can change spool and line in a moment.

Loading the spool

When loading the spool it must be borne in mind that the rotary action of the bale-arm around the spool im-

parts twist to the line, and that over a hundred yards of line this becomes considerable, especially when medium-weight lines, which are fairly springy, are employed.

This twist in the line is largely responsible for the manner in which the monofilament lines often tend to spring off the spool. To prevent twist it is recommended that the line be pulled off the manufacturer's spool not by letting it turn on a pencil as you wind, but over the flange of the manufacturer's spool in much the same way as the line spills over the edge of the fixed-spool itself. Since pulling line off and laying it on both impart twist to the line, the tactic is to impart opposite twist to the line as the bale-arm lays it on to the spool.

When the slipping clutch is set, this must be done so that if a dangerous strain is put on your line, the clutch will slip before the line breaks. This also implies that you must select a line b.s. suitable for the rod you intend to use. If, for example, your line is of 20lb b.s. and you set the clutch at, say, 18lb, you have a margin of safety of roughly 2lb. However, if you are using a rod of a ½lb test curve there is considerable danger that you will already have strained or damaged, or even broken your rod before the clutch will start to slip. To allow this to happen is clearly absurd, and so lines must be selected to suit the rod. If you must use heavy lines on a light rod you would be better to set the clutch to give when the rod is entering the test curve position, or somewhat before.

Long trotting

Long trotting is a fishing method for which many anglers prefer an ordinary centrepin reel, but this does not mean that they cannot practice it perfectly well with a fixed-spool reel. The technique is to take up slack after casting, and then open the bale-arm so that as the float drifts down through the swim it pulls line off the spool freely. If line is running out too freely, the extended finger comes into play, not on the spool, but close by it so that line in slipping off brushes against the

finger, the friction slowing the rate of flow. When the float disappears, the finger is clamped hard on the reel spool, stopping the line flow at the same time as the rod is raised swiftly to strike.

One of the minor problems of the fixed-spool reel is that line occasionally springs off the spool without warning. Sometimes this is due to the wind, sometimes to

twisted line, and sometimes to overloading. Whatever the cause, this has been the subject of criticism by anglers fishing with fine tackle over long distances. Others complain that for long trotting it does not give instant control.

The closed-face reel was designed to overcome these problems and to provide easier reel control. This kind of reel is closely related to the fixed-

CLEANING A FIXED-SPOOL REEL

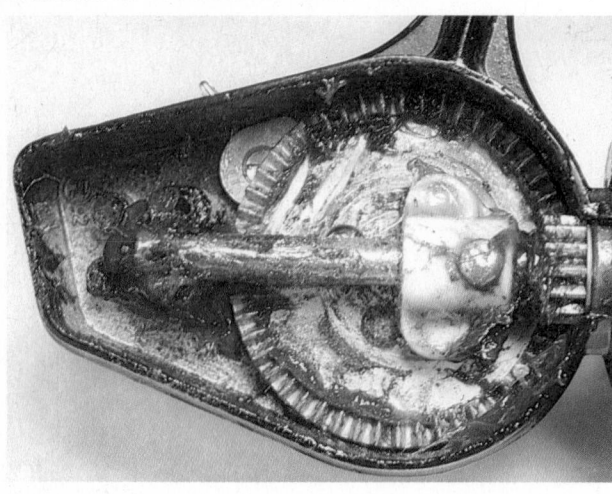

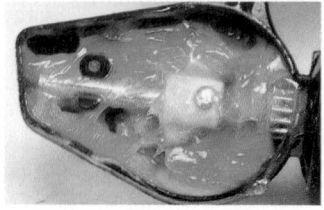

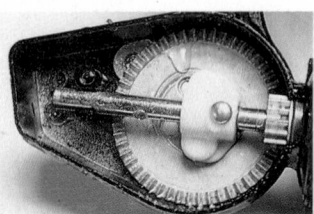

Left: A reel badly needing a clean. **Above:** Swarfega is liberally brushed on to break up the dirt. **Above right:** The reel is washed with water and then shaken or dried near heat. **Right:** The reel repacked with a proprietary grease.

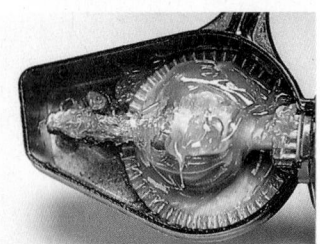

Casting for char in the late evening. The fixed-spool reel has meant that the angler is now able to cast over very long distances with accuracy.

spool and works on the same principle in that the drum itself remains stationary.

The same problems of casting light weights are involved, and as the line spirals off the drum and out through the vent of the reel face the friction is slightly greater.

Most closed-face reels are sold with line of about 6lb b.s. already wound on. The optimum b.s. for these reels should be 15lb of monofilament. Do not use braided line. It tends to bunch and pile up inside the reel facing, wasting line and fishing time.

Fixed-spool v. closed-face

Opinions differ as to whether this reel is better than the fixed-spool, but many anglers prefer the closed-face reel's simpler mechanism. Instead of a bale-arm, a rotating metal cap fits over the spool. This carries a retractable metal stud against which line is trapped. A second metal case over the stud prevents line slipping over the top of it. The inner case revolves when the reel handle is turned and the stud acts exactly like the bale-arm, laying line evenly on the reciprocating inner spool. The stud is linked to a release catch. Pressure on this retracts the stud, allowing the line to run out.

The casting action is very similar to that of the fixed-spool reel.

However, instead of having to hold the line across a crooked finger and manually releasing it, the thumb button or front-plate catch is pressed to free the line.

Like the fixed-spool reel, the closed-face model has an adjustable clutch mechanism, although in most cases this operates on the winding handle rather than the spool itself. The result is much the same. It also has an anti-reverse button, like the fixed-spool reel.

The different gear ratios offered by many fixed-spool and closed-face reels are intended to cater for the varying needs of the specialist. For most purposes, a ratio of about 4:1 is most suitable (depending on the diameter of the spool, which differs according to the manufacturer). A 4:1 ratio reel provides a retrieval rate of about 18—22in for a single turn of the handle. (An ordinary centrepin reel with a 3½in diameter, by comparison, retrieves about 12in per turn.)

Anglers who do a lot of spinning prefer 3:1, giving a retrieval of 14-16in per turn. This enables them to spin at a steady rate and helps avoid the mistake of spinning too fast. Match anglers, however, prefer 5:1 because it gets the line back quickly in readiness for the next cast. Some even use 6:1, bringing in 28-33in of line per turn. But at this rate there is a greater tendency for the maggot to spin through the water and twist the line over much.

These high ratios are primarily intended for the carp and bass angler concerned with fish that suddenly swim in towards him at a rate which allows slack line to develop. At 2½ft retrieval rate, the angler can get line in as fast as the fish swims.

So, fixed-spool or closed face, this style of reel has certainly solved many of the purely mechanical casting problems once faced by anglers. It will not cure clumsy casting, and it will not help catch fish if the angler casts to the wrong places. Nevertheless, used properly and in conjunction with watercraft and other basic angling skills, investment in one of the reels, or both types, is certainly worthwhile. Careful handling of the reel will be repaid by years of use.

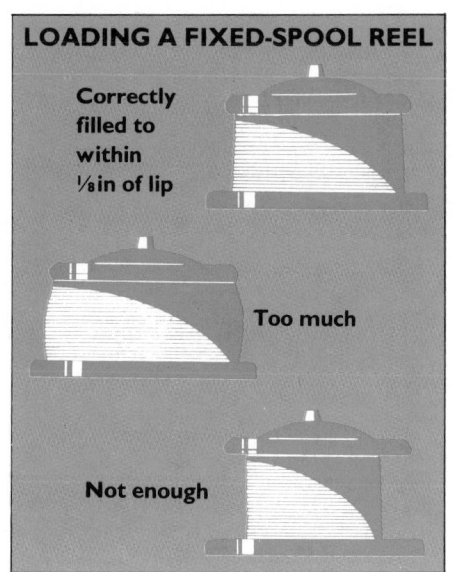

LOADING A FIXED-SPOOL REEL

Correctly filled to within ⅛in of lip

Too much

Not enough

ASK THE EXPERT

Is it better to hold the reel neck between first and second finger or between second and third?
The important thing is that you can reach forward with the index finger and touch the lip of the spool to check it, or reach the finger forward sufficiently to lay line over it. Small boys may find that to do this comfortably they must hold the neck between second and third or even third and fourth finger. Do what is comfortable and effective for you.

What sort of cast is best suited to the fixed-spool or closed-face reel?
For bottom-fishing with finesse, use the underhand lob as often as possible; this gives an accurate cast and a near-silent entry. For spinning or ledgering at a distance, the overhand or sidecast may be equally effective.

Is it wise to backwind on a fixed-spool or on a closed-face reel?
For anything other than very fine fishing it is neither wise nor necessary. If the clutch is set to suit the b.s. of the line and the test curve of the rod, the anti-reverse button is usually engaged to *prevent* backwinding. Backwinding imparts extra twist, and anyway, the clutch is designed to take up any sudden shocks caused by a fighting fish or a strike. However, with lines of up to 2lb b.s., the slipping clutch is rarely sensitive enough to cope, and the danger of a break is increased. So match anglers often do without the anti-reverse button and depend on handle contact with the fish, backwinding if necessary.

Nylon line

Popular with both freshwater and sea fishermen, nylon line is strong, long lasting and dependable. But it does have its drawbacks and needs to be handled with care

Fishing line is one of the most sophisticated and important items of tackle. For many years anglers had to use lines of such materials as braided flax or silk, with a hook link of gut made from the stretched silk-glands of the silkworm. No other material suitable for a hook line could be made in sufficient lengths for use as a continuous line, and no material which was made in lengths of over about 15 yards was fine or strong enough. The invention of nylon in the 1930s and its subsequent development gave anglers a tool suited to the job.

Artificial silk
An angler writing in 1949, having tried the 'new' line for the first time, said that the monofilament he had bought had increased his casting distances amazingly. It had enabled him to catch 34 perch up to 2lb using spinners tied to 5½lb b.s. nylon.

Nylon was first developed as an artificial silk, imitating its molecular structure, but capable of manufacture in much greater quantities than could be produced by the silkworm.

This was achieved by joining simple molecules into long 'chains'. The addition of other elements can be used to change the structure of the nylon, so producing different physical properties.

Monofilament line
Nylon monofilament line, the kind used by most anglers, is manufactured by first drawing the nylon into a thread while in a semi-molten state and then straightening out the molecular chains by drawing it out a second time. Its value to the angler lies in its great strength, fineness, and resistance to kinking. All these qualities are supplemented by nylon's natural elasticity.

Nylon line has the property of absorbing between 3 and 13 per cent of its own weight of water. This has the effect of decreasing the breaking strain, in some cases by 10 per cent.

Another advantage is that it deteriorates very slowly, if at all, even with frequent use. There used to be a suspicion that if not stored in the dark, nylon tended to weaken quickly because of the ultra-violet

rays in daylight. Certainly the lower breaking strains of line, up to about 3lb, were likely to snap very easily after a season's fishing. But it is debatable whether this was due to continued strain or ultra-violet light. Another boon to anglers is that nylon line does not need stripping off the reel and drying after use, a tiresome chore for users of silk.

It should be mentioned that the elasticity which aids strength also has a definite disadvantage in that a strike is softened by the line stretching, especially if it is of low breaking strain. This must be borne in mind and a strike over long distance made correspondingly forceful if the fish is not to be missed. Braided nylon, which stretches less, is sometimes used in sea fishing to overcome this difficulty.

Camouflage
Manufacturers claim that their clear nylon lines are virtually invisible in water, but even so, camouflaged varieties in blue, green or brown can be bought. Some enthusiasts even dye their lines themselves to match water conditions.

Spools of nylon monofilament come in lengths of up to 100 metres, but when they are received from the suppliers the spools are not separated. This enables anglers to buy lengths of line in multiples of 100 metres.

When nylon is retrieved onto the spool under pressure, as when playing a large fish or drawing a heavy

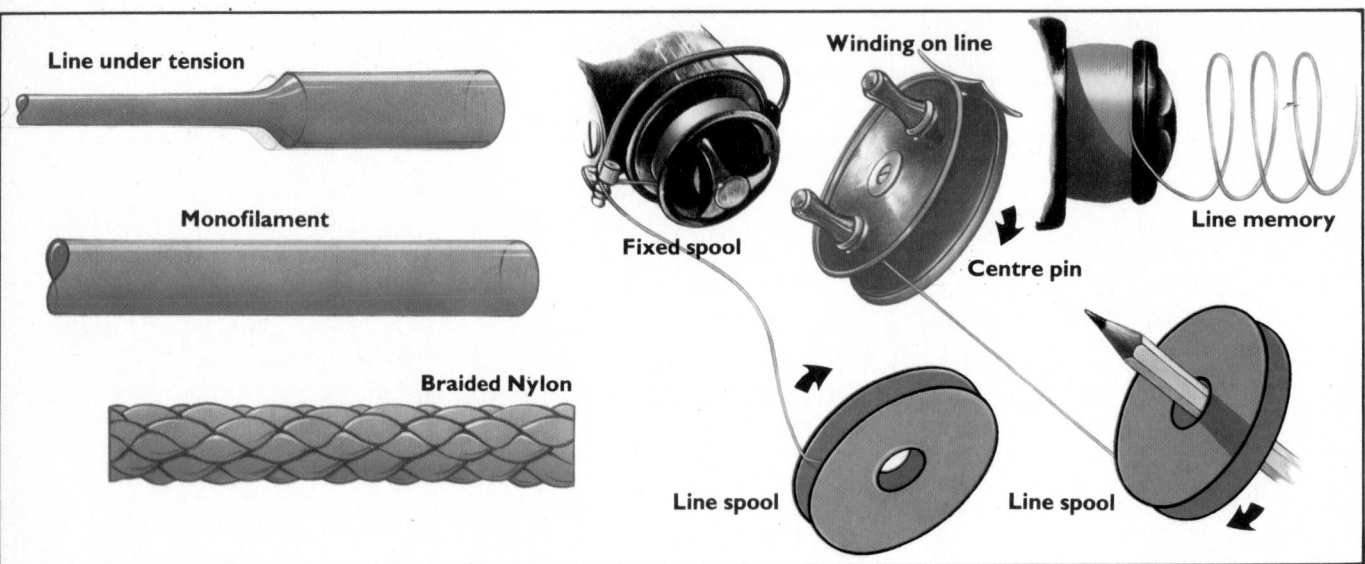

Line under tension

Monofilament

Braided Nylon

Fixed spool

Winding on line

Centre pin

Line memory

Line spool

Line spool

specimen up through perhaps 30 fathoms of heavy sea, it winds back very tightly, especially with a multiplier reel. After fishing, the line should be wound at normal speed on-to another reel, for if left on the first it can distort the spool and ruin the reel. It is also worthwhile to wind off your line occasionally and then wind it back onto the spool, making sure that it is distributed evenly. When tying hooks directly to your nylon, be careful to remember that one of the properties of nylon is that the old-fashioned 'granny knot' will not hold. A good knot for tying hooks to nylon is the half-blood.

Discarded line
As with nylon line's elasticity, its resistance to decay has a serious drawback. Hook lengths, 'bird's nests' and odd lengths of unwanted line are frequently thrown away or left at the waterside after fishing.

Before the invention of nylon line, a fish of this size and weight could not have been caught with a rod.

These coils and loops can easily become entangled in birds' feet, especially as they will often in-vestigate the remnants of bait that anglers also leave nearby. Birds are even hooked occasionally on discard-ed tackle. The consequences of careless jettisoning of line are all too often fatal for birds and so it should be taken home and disposed of.

It is always advisable to fill your spool with line, especially if the reel is of the fixed-spool variety, for this will mean that line flows off more easily when casting and will be more rapidly retrieved on account of the increased diameter of the loaded spool. When sea fishing, and to some extent for freshwater fishing, it is also advisable to have a good reserve of line on the spool in case a fish should make a long run, taking a good proportion of your line. A fish can easily be lost through lack of line on which the angler can play it. Backing lines, available from tackle dealers, are used to pad out the spool, on a fixed-spool reel to within ⅛in of the rim.

ASK THE EXPERT

How can white line be dyed at home?
Dylon hot-water dye is the answer — but don't plunge line into boiling water. Boil up the dye, let it cool, then immerse your coil of line. Be sure it's dry before winding on to a reel.

Can floatants be used on monofilament?
Anglers floating bread across a lake often grease up with a floatant like Mucilin. Pike anglers, too, grease the section of line between two floats used in tandem with a bung-float. But some people complain that nylon takes *too long* to sink, and use a sinking agent on fly leaders to get a fly down fast. Both fluids are easy to apply but difficult to remove thoroughly, so keep treated lines separate. Agents may cause deterioration over long periods.

What is fly line made of if not nylon?
Leaders are nylon. The rest of a fly line usually consists of a nylon (not monofil) core coated with plastic.

If braided nylon doesn't stretch, why doesn't it take over from monofilament?
At present, it is much thicker; the sea reels on which it is used are monsters compared with the coarse fisherman's. Until thickness is brought down, the short lengths that can be stored on any reel will limit its usefulness.

Is there any remedy for kinking?
Yes, throw the line away and buy a new one! Nothing will restore damaged line.

Knots

For every angling occasion there is a wide range of knots to choose from. Knowing which knot to use and when is an indispensible skill which every angler should master

Forty years ago you might have seen an angler attaching a hook with deceptive ease. He would have been using cotton, silk or flax lines with a short gut cast. A clove hitch in rope or yarn can be quite loose but, strained, it tightens upon itself and holds fast. Nylon lines are far more elastic, flexible and slippery than the older fibres and an untightened nylon knot, especially if not designed for this material, will begin to slip as soon as strain is exerted upon it.

With the advent of nylon monofilament and braided lines, many anglers had trouble with knots coming adrift, but the manufacturers soon designed several basic knots and loops for attaching hooks, for interconnections and for joining two lines of different thickness (with or without droppers). Anglers played some part in developing and making up knots for this exciting new material and now hardly anything else is used for fishing lines.

Choice of knots

For each occasion there is a choice of knot. The angler selects not merely for strength but also for ease of tying at a particular moment. For example, towards evening, in half-light, you could still manage a tucked half blood or a blood bight but might hesitate to try a two-circle turle or a dropper knot. In considering the knot-strength it is also essential to take account of the difference between the dry breaking strain of the line quoted by the manufacturer and the actual, wet breaking strain (b.s.) of the nylon in water. Something like a 10 per cent loss should be allowed for and since the knot is the weakest link in the tackle, the number of knots should be the fewest possible.

The specimen hunter prefers to

have only one such weak link. He slips floats, shots and other attachments straight on to the reel line, fastening his hook at the bottom. Not for him the minor pleasure of catching small fish: he puts all his hopes on having the right bait in the right place at the right time so that when his big fish does take the bait the chances of loss are minimized.

But this is not a typical fishing situation. Trout anglers find it necessary to use casts that taper from a high breaking strain and diameter down to the finest one suitable for the water being fished. To make up such a cast, three, four, or even five dropper knots are required, although only one knot may actually have a dropper attached. Such knots must be very carefully tied and tested if the angler is to have real confidence in his tackle when a big trout takes.

Match fishermen also have to come to terms with many-knotted tackle. They need to catch as many

Knots can be the weak link in your tackle. A good fish may be lost if this Grey Wulff is not tied correctly to the leader.

KNOTS FOR HOOKS, SWIVELS, SPINNERS, ETC.

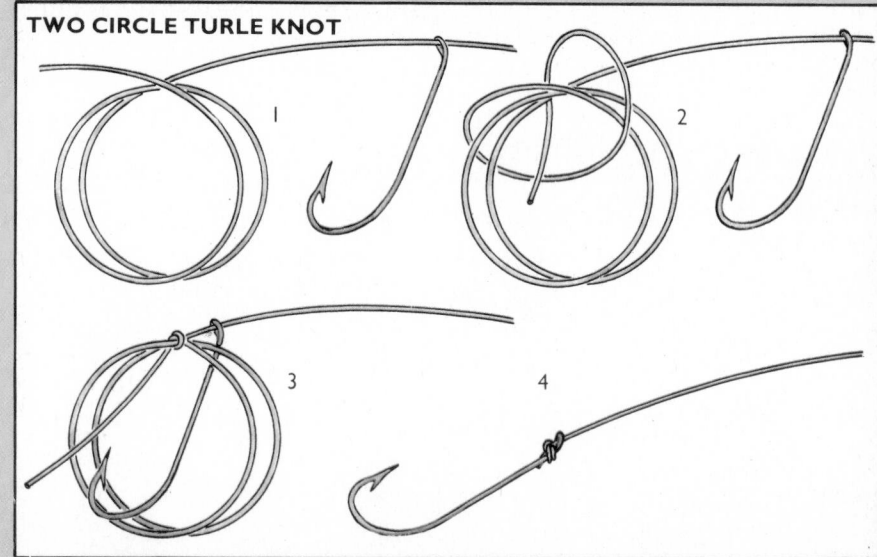

TWO CIRCLE TURLE KNOT

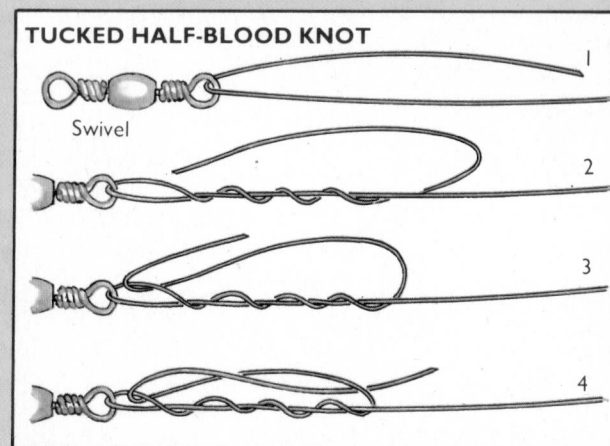

TUCKED HALF-BLOOD KNOT

Swivel

Above: 1 Thread hook up cast, make circle, over lay with another. **2** Push ends through loops, forming a slip knot. **3** Tighten, push hook and working end through circles. **4** Pull tight, snip off free end.
Right: 1 End through eye. **2** Twist four times round line. **3** and **4** Pass end through main loop, pull taut then snip off the end.

Right: 1 Pass the line through the eye and lay along the shank. 2 Make eight turns over the loop so formed, passing end through loop. 3 Pull taut, snipping off the loose end.

Below: 1 Lay a loop along the shank, holding hook. 2 Make a turn round the shank over end of hook. 3 Make a further turn, crossing firmly over first. 4 Add five or more successive turns along the shank towards the point. 5 Pull through.

DOMHOF KNOT

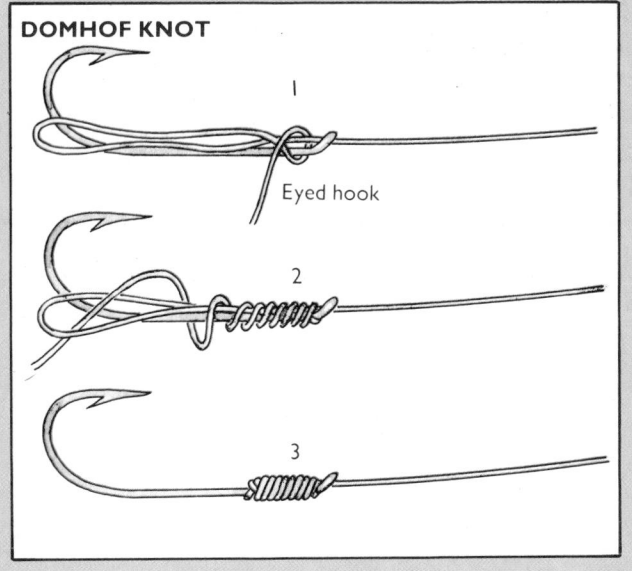

Eyed hook

WHIPPING KNOT (SPADE END)

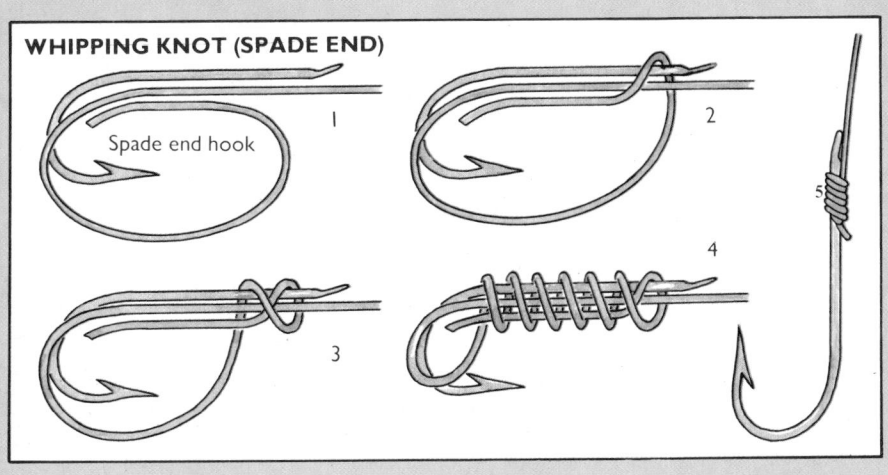

Spade end hook

Which is the best knot for fastening a swivel or spinner to a line?

The tucked half blood is reliable, neat and doesn't create much disturbance in the water. Some anglers prefer to use a loop threaded through the eye and then pass the swivel or spinner through the loop; this is quicker if you have to keep changing spinners.

I find the water knot attaching my cast cuts a wake through the water as I retrieve a fly. Is there a more satisfactory join?

The double four loop blood is tidier than the water knot and many fly fishermen prefer it for this reason. The water knot is easier to tie, though, in failing light.

How should I attach spade-end hooks to the end of a line?

Whipping is probably best for either tanged or spade-end hooks: it's difficult to learn, but it's surprising how quickly you can tie it at the waterside once you get the hang of it.

What knot do you recommend for eyed hooks at sea?

The Domhof is very reliable, and although the fly fisherman finds it too bulky at the end of a cast, it's fine for sea work.

What's the best way to tie up a boat?

It's impossible to say: using a mooring pin or short post, the delightfully simple two half-hitches work, but tying up to a beam above your head calls for a rolling hitch. The knots needed by a boat user almost equal those needed by the fisherman. Get hold of a sailor's primer on the subject.

fish as possible, big, small or indifferent, in the alloted time and swim. Should the day begin with small roach or bleak, ultra-fine float tackes may be needed but when a neighbour lands (or maybe loses) a 2lb bream, the match man must be prepared to switch tackles at a moment's notice. In order not to waste valuable time, he usually carries a number of casts of different breaking strains and shotting, with floats for different purposes made up ready on his cast winders. These generally have a loop at the top: with a similar loop at the end of the reel-line, he can substitute the whole cast and be fishing again in minutes.

Anglers fishing in snag ridden waters will use several knots on the line. The main cast with floats and shots may be on 4lb line, but the final 18in of hook-line will be attached with 2lb or 3lb line. In the event of a bad obstruction on the bottom, only the hook line will be lost.

The knots illustrated have now withstood the test of time and can be relied upon for all nylon lines, braided, twisted or monofilament. It is important to make them up properly and to give them a quick test before use, by holding the hook between finger and thumb and giving the nylon a sharp pull.

Whipping—reliable for nylon

The whipping that is illustrated deserves special mention because it is the traditional method used by sailors to whip rope ends but, provided at least five turns are made, it is completely reliable for nylon. It may look difficult but it is easier to tie than to describe or illustrate. A little practice with a piece of string whipped on a pencil stem will soon bring confidence. When using this whipping on a spade-end hook, nimble fingers and good eyesight are valuable assets. Early attempts should be tested by inserting the hook-point into a piece of wood and giving the free end of the line a couple of pulls.

The water knot is a development of the double overhand loop. Instead of forming the knot on the bight of line to make a loop, it is made on the married shorter ends of the two lines to be fastened.

KNOTS FOR FORMING LOOPS

BLOOD BIGHT

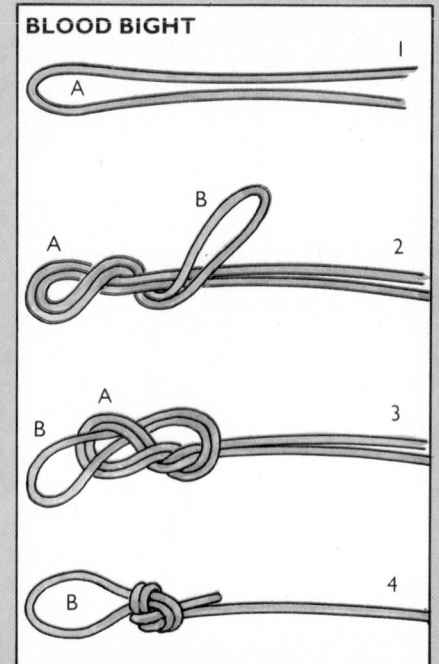

Above: Blood bight, a simple knot tied in four stages and used to make loops in fly fishing leaders and sea fishing.

Right: The Universal Loop. A popular knot with freshwater anglers for tying snoods. Double a length of line, wind round three times, then pass the loop through the eye of the hook, wind round and pull through.

DOUBLE OVERHAND LOOP

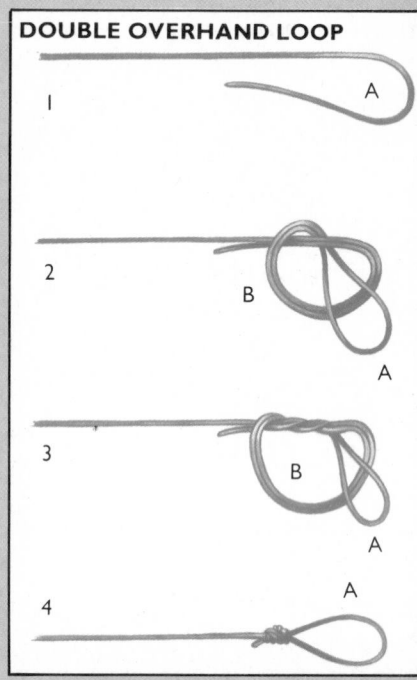

Above: Form two knots A and B and pass A through B. Twist A around line and through B again, working knot tight.

UNIVERSAL

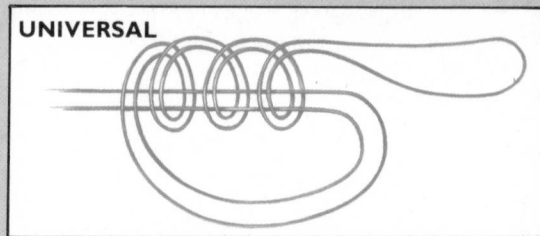

FIGURE OF EIGHT

LOOP TO LOOP

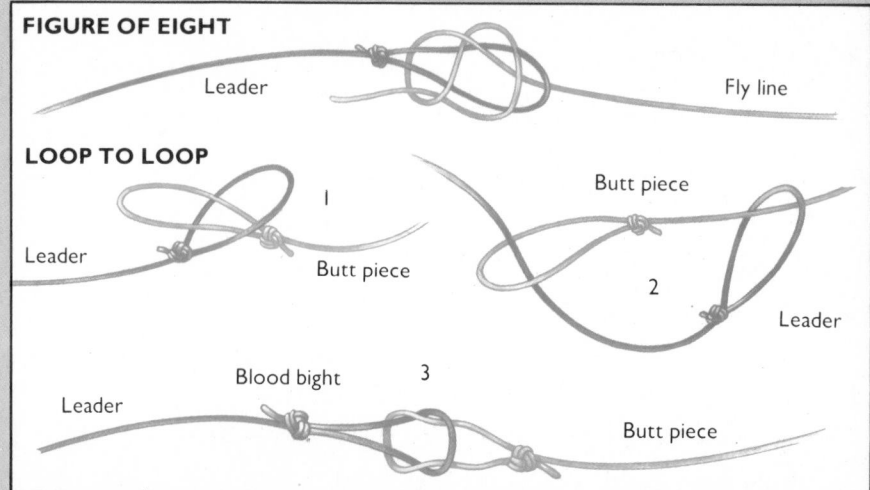

Top: The figure of eight knot will not jam as an overhand knot tends to.

Above: When tying loops make sure they are long—they will cause less jamming.

DROPPER KNOTS AND KNOTS FOR JOINING LENGTHS OF LINE

DOUBLE FOUR LOOP BLOODKNOT

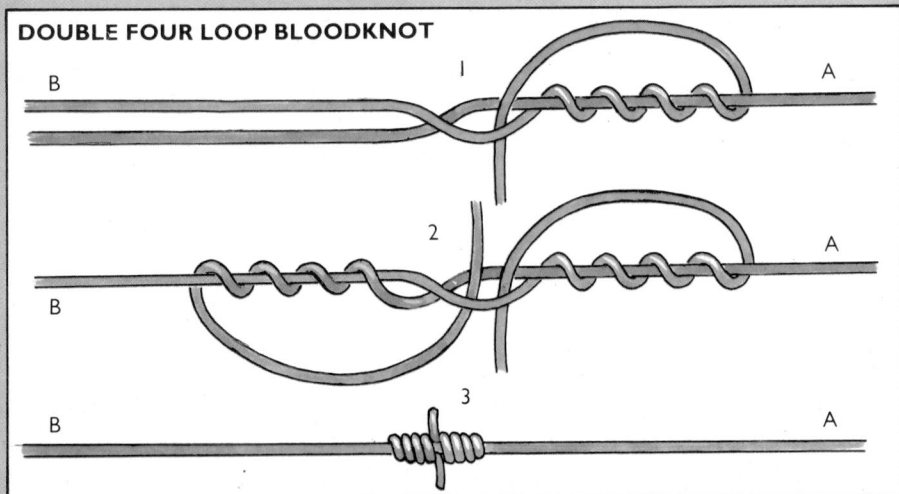

Left: Dropper or Double Four Loop bloodknot. Similar to the blood loop dropper knot, this ties two strands of nylon together neatly. **Below:** The Water Knot is useful for tying a leader containing one or more droppers. **1** Hold the ends so that there is an overlap. Draw the two ends together to form a loop. **2** Pull the right hand end through the loop from behind making an overhand knot. **3** Repeat this four times, then pull tight.

When used for making a dropper, the fly is fastened to the stalk which runs towards the rod. Because the lie of the dropper opposes the pull of the line, the fly will stand out from the leader.

BLOOD LOOP DROPPER

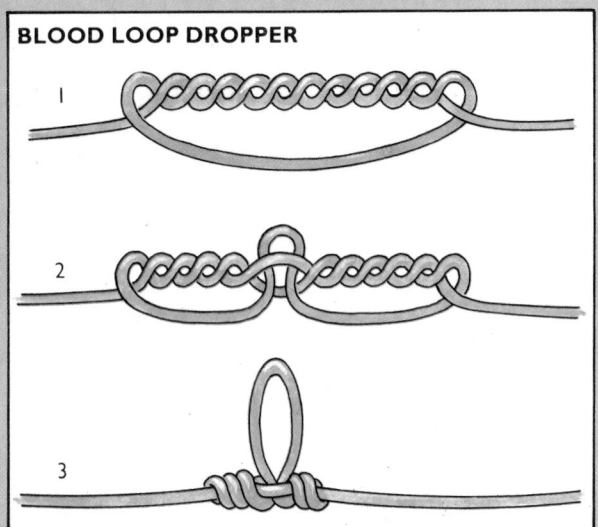

WATER KNOT

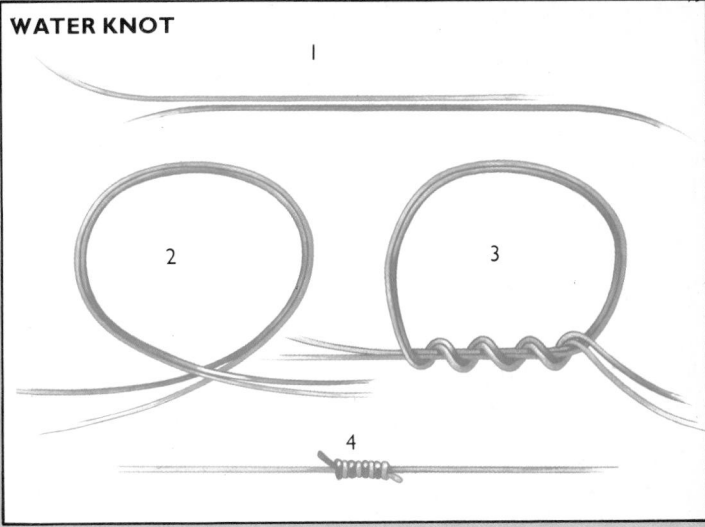

Above: Blood Loop Dropper Knot. **1** Form a circle with long overlapping ends, twist the ends round the circle, making ten smaller ones. **2** Enlarge the centre and push original circle back through. **3** Pull on the ends to tighten, holding finger in loop to prevent it slipping.

Right: Universal Knot, a popular, all-purpose knot. The loose ends may be cut off or one end left loose to make a dropper. Leader Knots and Heavy Duty Leader Knots are useful when beachcasting. After tying, all knots should be wetted before slowly tightening.

UNIVERSAL

LEADER KNOT

HEAVY DUTY LEADER KNOT

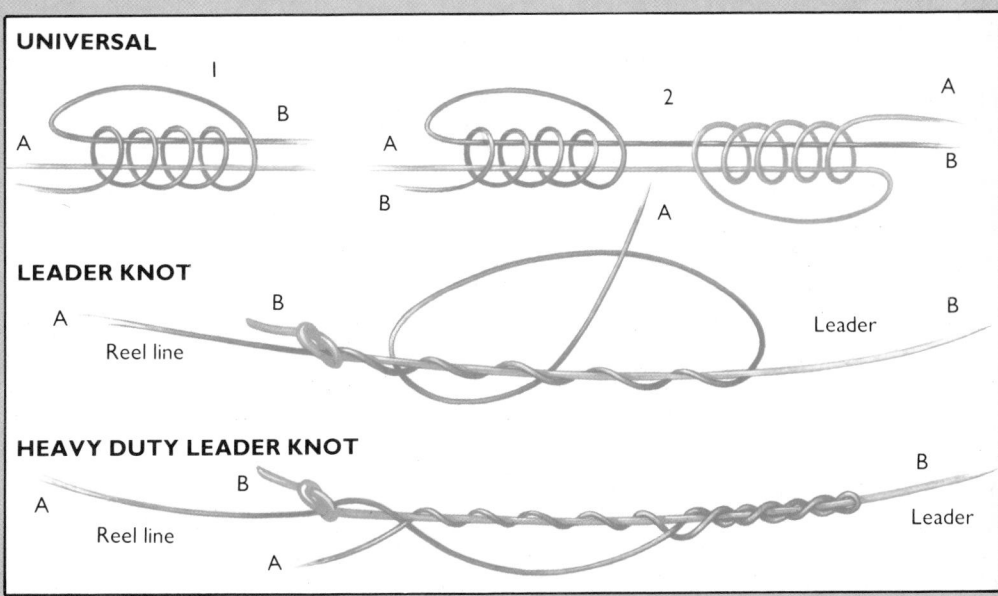

Freshwater hooks

The best fish are never the ones that are caught, but those that got away. This needn't be so, though, if you take the time and trouble to select the right kind of hook for the fish you want

Hooks are the most important items of an angler's tackle and yet, all too often, they are not chosen with enough care. Admittedly the range of hooks available is bewildering to the beginner, but in order to enjoy consistent success a reliable hook is indispensable.

Categories of hooks
Freshwater hooks fall into three categories: eyed, spade-end and

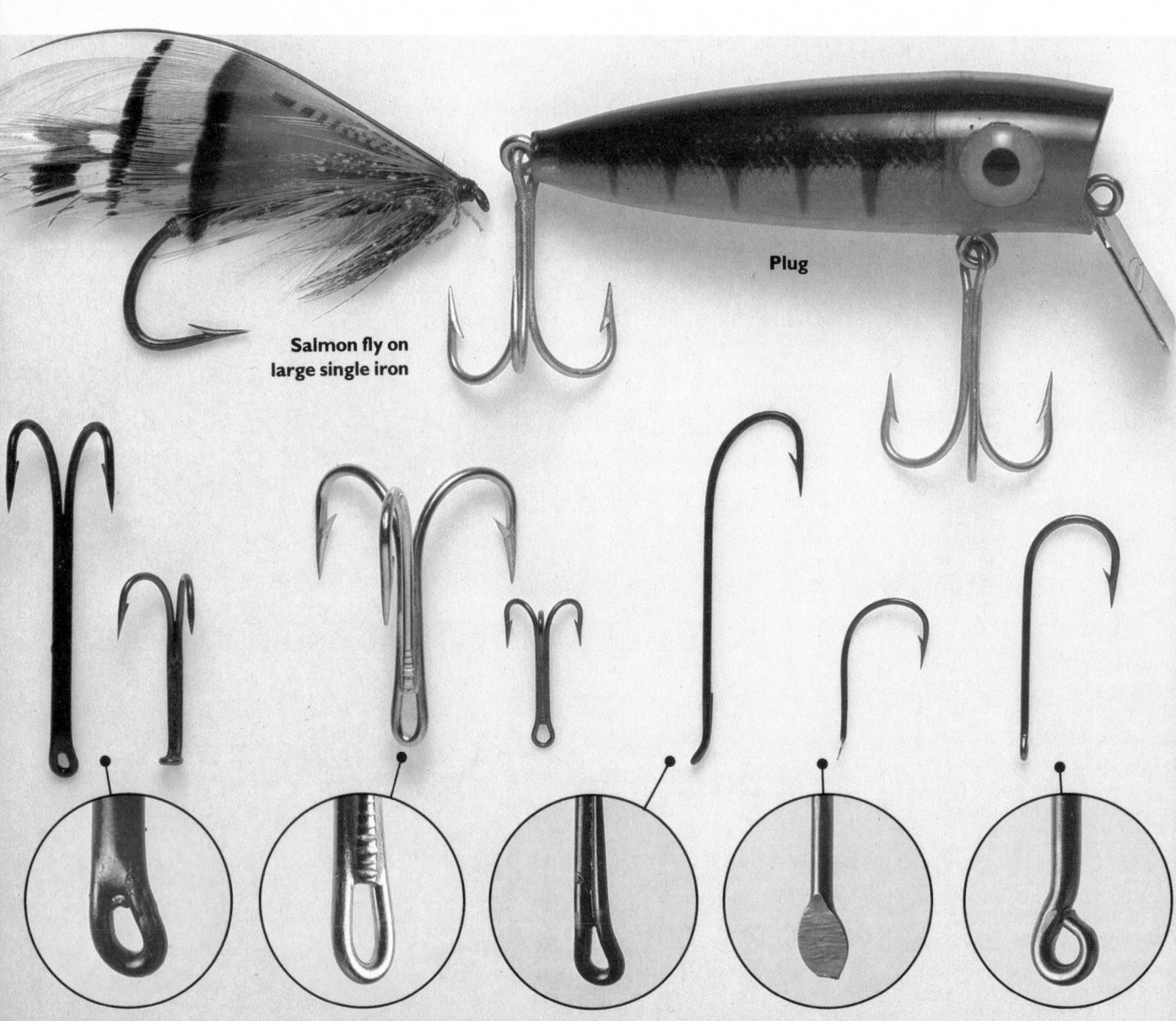

Salmon fly on
large single iron

Plug

Double eye
A double hook. This hook has a japanned finish, which gives it good protection against rusting.

Needle or oblong eye
Needle eyes such as this are often used by anglers who wish to make up neat traces for pike fishing

Looped eye
A typical looped eye. This is the type of eye which is widely used on low water single salmon hooks.

Spade end
Also known as the flatted shank, this hook is useful where a neat junction of hook to nylon is required.

Tapered eye
A tapered eye on a hook with a bronzed finish. Bronzing is generally better than japanning.

ready tied to nylon. The first are tied to the line by the angler, who can use a variety of knots. The important thing is to be sure the knot holds, as this can easily be the weak point in your tackle which will fail when most needed. Spade-end hooks, as the name suggests, are flattened at the top end and are whipped to nylon using the method illustrated or some other reliable method. Ready tied hooks are bought already whipped to a short length of line, nowadays nylon.

There are many variations as to bend, length of shank and so on, but these are mainly variations on the three main kinds of hook. Double and treble hooks are mounted on plugs and spinners for pike, perch, chub, trout, salmon and zander. Stewart tackles comprise two single hooks set a couple of inches apart.

There is a further category of hook, the gorge hook, whose use is illegal in Britain. This is simply a straight hook, pointed at both ends. Inserted sideways in deadbait and when swallowed by a fish it becomes firmly lodged in the stomach.

The basic requirements

The essential requirements of a hook are the same for all kinds. It should be well-tempered and thin in the body (or 'wire'); the point and barb should be sharp; the barb, set close to the point, should not be at too great an angle from the body.

The thickness of the 'wire' is very important. The weight of a thick hook can cause a bait, especially a

1 The Limerick bend. Note the rather sharp angle of the bend.

2 Often used with lobworm bait, the round bend has a wide 'gape'.

3 The Viking is simply a Mustad trade name for one of their hooks.

4 The Sproat bend is similar to the Limerick but rounder in shape.

5 Crystal bend, used mainly with maggots.
6 The Sneck bend is squarer than most.

Barbless point
Though demanding a tight line, barbless points make unhooking easier.

Hollow point
Note how straight the outer edge is in comparison with the other hooks.

Curved-in point
The point of this hook curves inwards towards the shank.

Dublin point
This one curves outwards, away from the shank of the hook.

Turned-down eye
See turned-up eye.

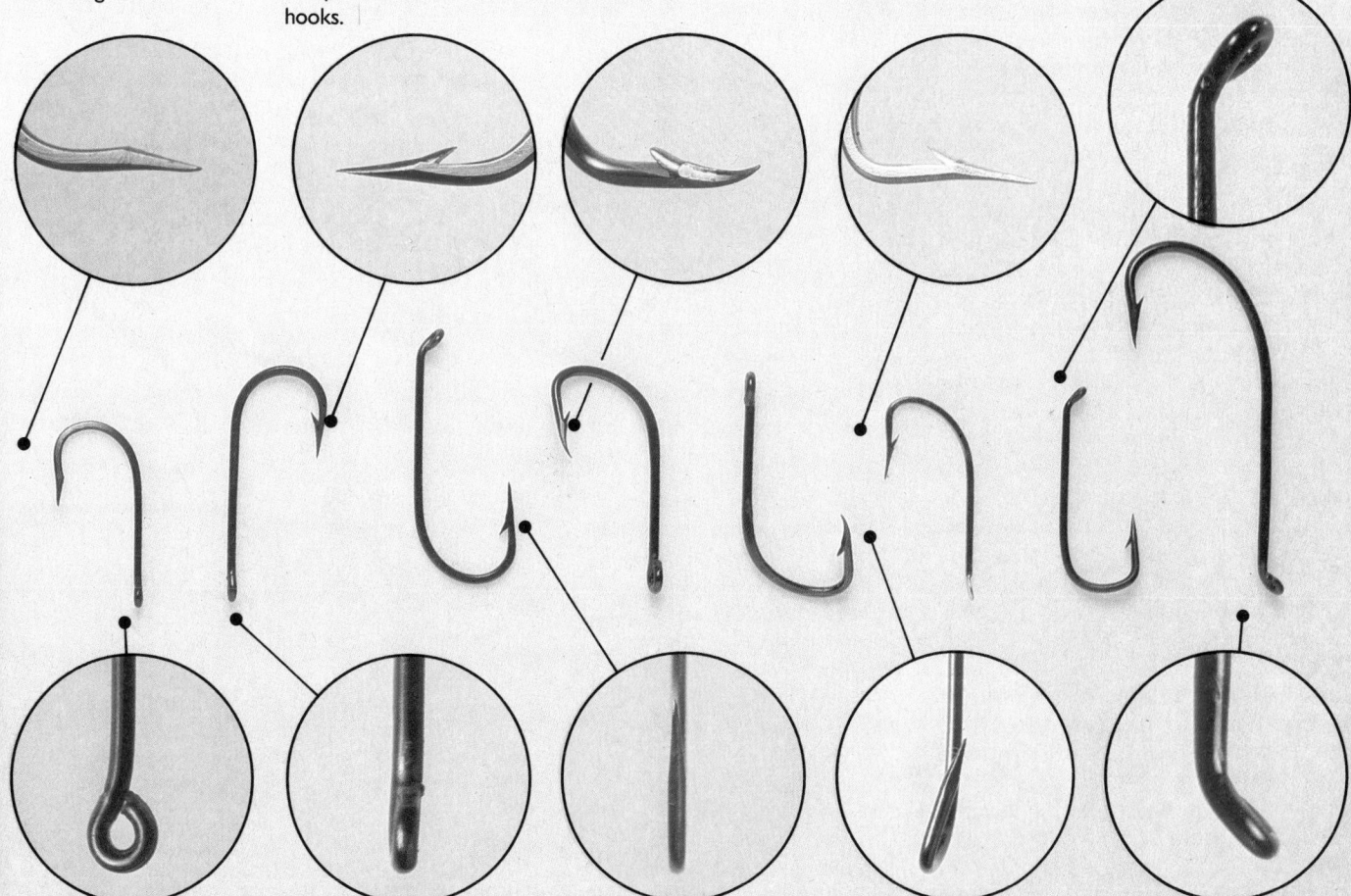

Ball eye
When using ball eye hooks, make sure that the ball is closed or the hook may leave the line.

Straight eye
A Viking hook with a straight eye (also known as a ring eye). The eye is set in line with the shank.

Straight bend
A straight bend. Note how the point runs parallel to the shank of the hook; this is not always the case.

Kirbed bend
The point is offset to the right with the hook held bend downwards and the point facing you.

Turned-up eye
A turned-up, as opposed to a turned-down, eye is turned away from the point.

light one such as maggot or caster, to sink too quickly when 'freelining' — using no float but allowing the bait to sink naturally down to the fish. An additional disadvantage of a hook that is too thick is that it can burst a bait instead of entering it cleanly.

Before using a hook, test the temper of the wire. Under pressure it should bend but not remain bent, and it certainly should not snap. To test it, hold the hook by the shank and pull just above the point with pliers.

Barbs

The barb is most often the trouble-spot in a hook. Most are cut too deep (stand out too far from the body), which causes weakness at that point. This, coupled with the common fault of the barb being set too far from the point, means that undue force is required to drive home both point and barb, sometimes causing the line to break. If the strike is less forceful a hook of this sort will not fully penetrate the fish's skin, particularly if it is a hard-boned and tough-skinned species like the pike, perch or barbel. A big deeply-cut barb may look effective but is not.

The eyes on eyed hooks should be examined. The size of the eye will depend on the gauge of the hook but always try to pick one which will just take the thickness of the line you intend to use — there is no point in having a gaping, obtrusive eye which causes the hook to hang from the line at an odd angle.

Shanks

The length of the shank is important where some baits are concerned. For crust, paste, lobworms and sweetcorn a long shank is best; for maggots a short one. For casters, the variety with a long shank known as a 'caster hook', is favoured. It should be remembered, however, that the longer the shank relative to the eye, the smaller will be the angle of penetration. This means that the hook will penetrate more easily but to a lesser depth. With short-shanked hooks it takes a stronger strike but the hook

212

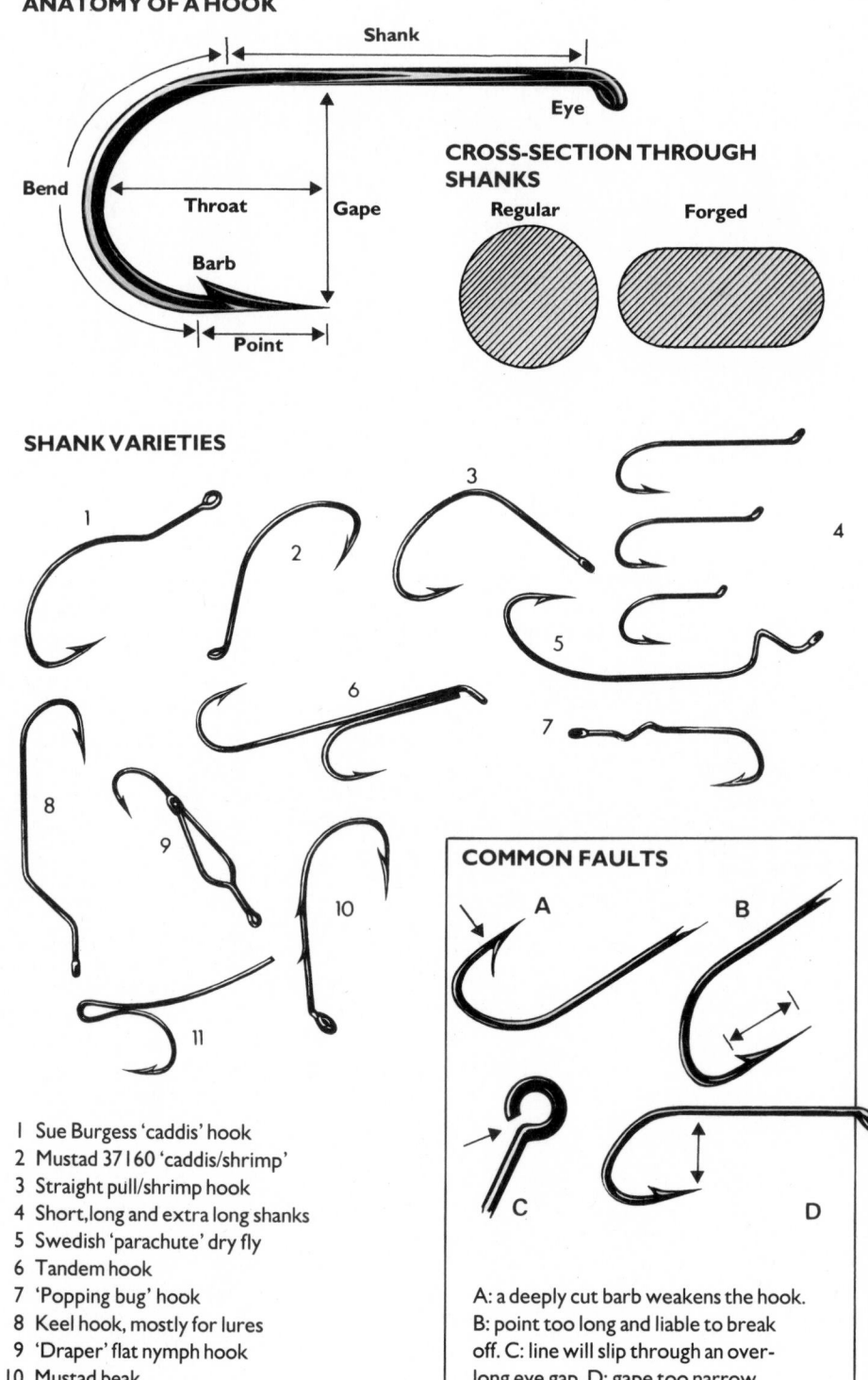

ANATOMY OF A HOOK

Shank

Eye

Bend

Throat

Gape

Barb

Point

CROSS-SECTION THROUGH SHANKS

Regular

Forged

SHANK VARIETIES

1   Sue Burgess 'caddis' hook
2   Mustad 37160 'caddis/shrimp'
3   Straight pull/shrimp hook
4   Short, long and extra long shanks
5   Swedish 'parachute' dry fly
6   Tandem hook
7   'Popping bug' hook
8   Keel hook, mostly for lures
9   'Draper' flat nymph hook
10 Mustad beak
11 Yorkshire flybody

COMMON FAULTS

A

B

C

D

A: a deeply cut barb weakens the hook. B: point too long and liable to break off. C: line will slip through an over-long eye gap. D: gape too narrow.

will drive home deeper.

Hooks to nylon should always be treated with caution. First, see whether the whipping reaches the top of the shank. On some hooks it is too short, causing the hook to turn over when making contact with a fish and preventing proper penetration.

Make sure that there is sufficient varnish on the whipping, as if there is too little the whipping may fall apart (eyed and spade end hooks do not require varnished whipping). Check the loop at the end of the trace. If it is not straight it has been tied badly and may be unreliable.

KNOTS

Universal

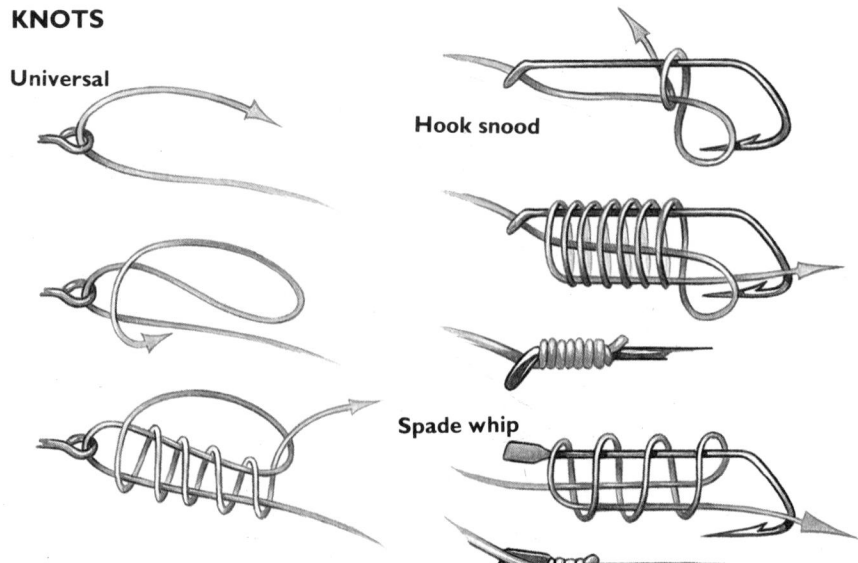

Hook snood

Spade whip

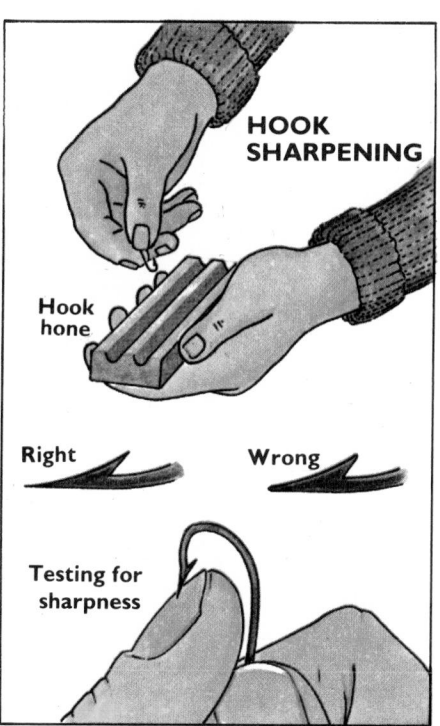

HOOK SHARPENING

Hook hone

Right Wrong

Testing for sharpness

HOOKS AND BAIT

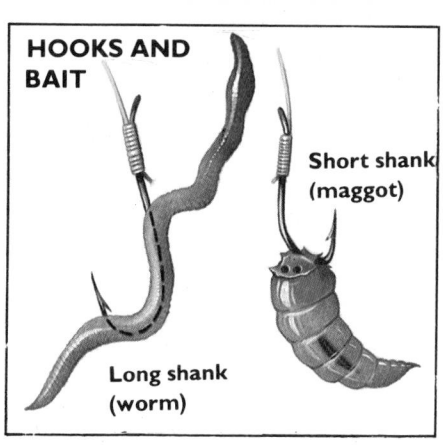

Short shank (maggot)

Long shank (worm)

Above: *The recommended types of knots and whipping used for tying freshwater hooks to nylon monofilament line.*
Left: *A blunt point can be sharpened on a carborundum stone, which every angler should carry when fishing. The sharpening motion should be from the point towards the bend.*
Below left: *Use a hook with a round bend and a long shank for worms, and a hook with a crystal bend and a short shank for maggots.*

Sizes and patterns

The size of hooks is indicated by even numbers on a scale from 2 to 30, the lower the number the larger the hook. A number 2 is about ¾in long, a 12 is ³/₈in and a 20 is ¹/₈in. Hook sizes, unfortunately, are not yet standardized. The 'Goldstrike', for example, is one size bigger than most other brands.

The angler will sometimes use a different pattern of hook to suit particular circumstances. The 'Crystal' is a combination of curved and angular, which requires little force to drive home but which, because of its sharp bend, is weakened and not recommended for strong, fighting fish such as carp or tench. The 'Round Bend' has a curve with plenty of 'gape', and is preferred for use with lobworms by many anglers.

The famous 'Model Perfect' hook, which was developed by Allcocks, had a round bend and an off-set point with wonderful holding power. Many modern hooks are based on the design of this classic hook.

ASK THE EXPERT

Why are there so many different kinds of hooks?
Because the various species of fish have different-shaped mouths. A skate, for instance, has large flat teeth for crushing its food. A carp, on the other hand, has no 'ordinary' teeth, but plates and throat teeth and a protrusible mouth, while a cod has a very large mouth with hard-to-penetrate rubbery lips. Hooks must be designed to cope with these differences.

Why are sea hooks usually larger than those for coarse fishing?
Most sea fish are larger and, pound for pound, stronger than the average roach, dace, bream or other freshwater fish. Hooks for use by sea anglers therefore have to be bigger and stronger.

Why do some anglers use barbless hooks?
Barbless hooks originally came into use because they made for easier unhooking than barbed hooks. It was at first assumed that, having no barb, these hooks would be liable to become dislodged if the line were allowed to slacken during playing, and that the resulting need for 'tight lines' would lead to greater angling skills. It has since been found, however, that fish find it more difficult to dislodge a barbless hook, possibly because it makes a smaller and cleaner hole.

Is it possible to catch fish with a rod and line but no hook?
Have you ever tried 'babbing' for eels with a length of wool in place of your hook link? The bait — a piece of sausage meat for instance — is threaded on to the wool, and any eel that's tempted to try for it quite literally ties itself in knots!. It's an old and well tried method — and you don't need a hook!

Swimfeeders

An established part of ledgering is tempting fish to the spot where you are fishing with groundbait or samples of the hookbait. Swimfeeders enable you to do that with accuracy

Swimfeeders and blockends are perforated plastic cylinders, approximately 2-3in long and 1in diameter. Swimfeeders are open at both ends and are used mainly for groundbaiting with cereal or cereal mixed with samples of the hookbait—maggots, casters, worms, and in recent years, sweetcorn. Used in rivers by bream and chub fishermen, a swimfeeder is particularly effective. Blockends have closed ends and are usually packed with either maggots or casters.

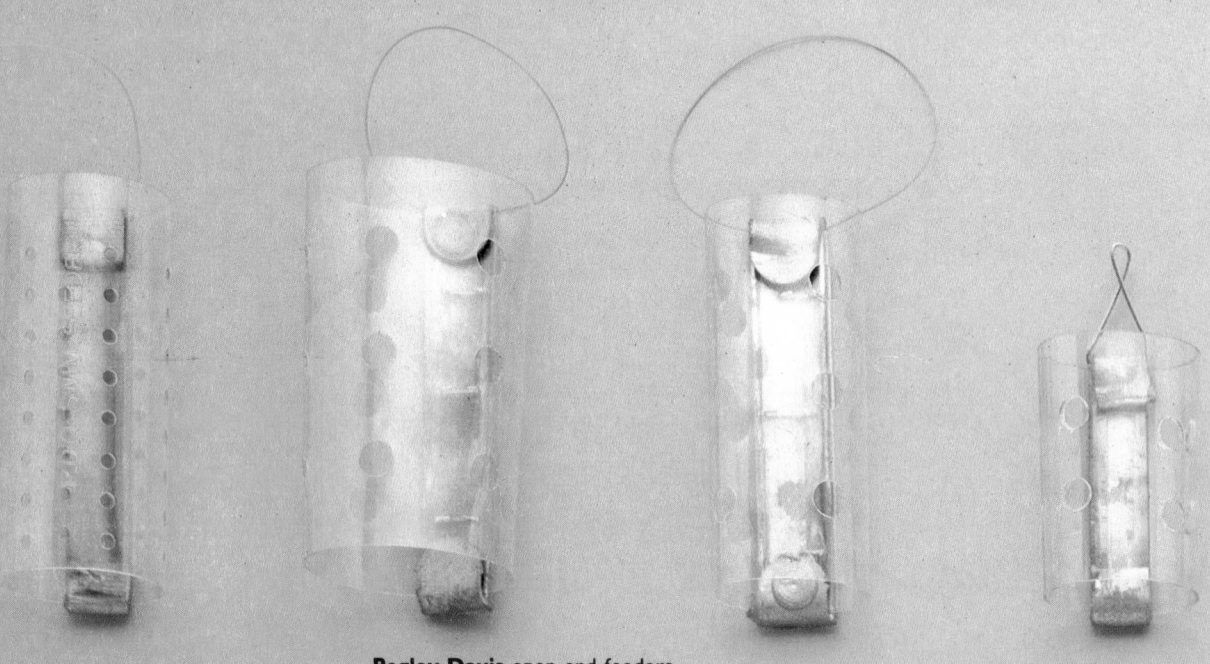

Pegley-Davis open end feeders

Open-ended swimfeeders are used mainly with cereal groundbaits. Blockend feeders have closed ends and are used with maggots and casters. Both types of feeder have a strip of lead running through the centre: this might make them heavy and clumsy. The greatly refined Drennan 'Feederlink' does away with this strip of lead, substituting instead a strip of nylon with swan shot at one end. Swivel feeders reduce tangling of the line close to the feeder.

Hobby Crafts swivel feeders

ATTACHING SWIMFEEDERS
With feeders which have swivel attachments, the main line is passed through the swivel and a split shot, ledger stop or swivel is used to keep the feeder at the required distance from the hook. Feeders with wire or nylon loop attachments can be attached to the line with swivels.

The shape and size of both blockends and swimfeeders is important. A blockend with cone-shaped ends (like the Drennan Feederlink), for example, will cast further and more easily, resulting, in some situations, in a bigger and better catch. A large feeder is usually better than a small one when attempting to hold a large shoal of chub or bream in a swim, but when seeking specimen roach in a small, shallow river a small feeder is probably better.

Swimfeeders and blockends come in many different shapes, each designed for a specific use. Some are cone-shaped, some short but stout, some long and stout, some short and thin. Some models set up considerable resistance when retrieved, which in stillwaters particularly can have an adverse effect on both fish and tackle. The Drennan Feederlink, on the other hand, with its cone-shaped ends, cuts through the water more cleanly and reduces resistance to a minimum.

Past deficiencies

Until just a few years ago most swimfeeders and blockends were big and crude, with a large strip of lead attached to one side. Since no adjustment to the lead was possible in running water, the angler was placed at a considerable disadvantage. And because of the strip of lead, feeders were too heavy and clumsy for stillwater fishing.

Experiments with blockends began several years ago when two Oxford anglers, Fred Towns and John Everard, ran a length of nylon through the centre of a small plastic container of the type in which screws and nails used to be sold. Holes were made with a small file heated over a gas or electric ring, and swan shots (SSG) attached to the end of the nylon. The line was then passed through a swivel which was tied to the other end of the nylon.

With this new-style feeder, casting was found to be both easier and more accurate, with less resistance in running water. Another important feature of this feeder was that the weight was adjustable. If insufficient weight is

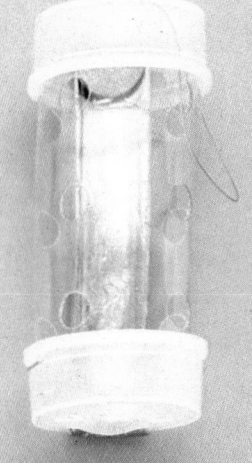
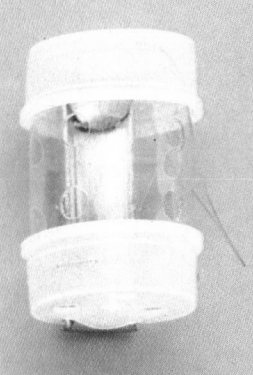

Thamesly block end feeders

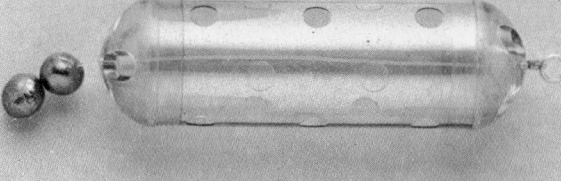

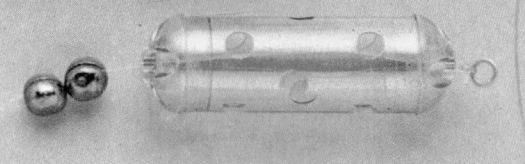

Peter Drennan 'Feederlink'

USING SWIMFEEDERS

Always cast downstream when using a swimfeeder, so that if the current rolls it up against a rock it will not get trapped. If you cast upstream and it gets tucked behind a rock, the rock will be between you and the feeder and you may not be able to pull it free.

used in rivers a feeder will roll, which in most situations defeats its object. By adding or subtracting shots, the weight could be adjusted to just hold the bottom, or roll at whatever speed the angler considered necessary.

Modern developments

The idea of passing a length of nylon through the centre of a plastic cylinder was taken further by Oxford tackle manufacturer Peter Drennan, who produced the now famous Drennan Feederlink. The 'blockends' were a vast improvement on what had previously been a simple 'chuck it and chance it' method, and today are used widely throughout the country.

After passing the main line through the swivel, the feeder is stopped at the required distance from the hook by either a split shot, ledger stop, or swivel. One of the best methods is to take a length of monofilament the required length of the tail (the distance between hook and feeder) and on one end attach the hook, on the other a swivel. Push the main line through the swivel on the feeder and tie it to the swivel on the tail. The feeder now rests against the swivel. This arrangement results in less tangling of the line close to the feeder.

When retrieving in stillwaters, the feeder should be wound in slowly with the rod tip kept low so it does not bounce across the surface. If retrieved quickly, tangling will occur. This is especially true of fast-retrieve reels.

When a fish picks up the bait, the line should pull through the ring or swivel. If it does not, do not worry, for when empty, providing the minimum of weight is used, little resistance will be felt by the fish.

In running water, feeders are fished either stationary or allowed to roll along the bottom according to the whim of the angler—or fish. In fast water, the stationary method is usually adopted to avoid the contents being scattered. Only in water of moderate flow—and then not in every situation—should the feeder be allowed to roll or move.

In stillwaters, cast the feeder into the same spot every time: if you do

216

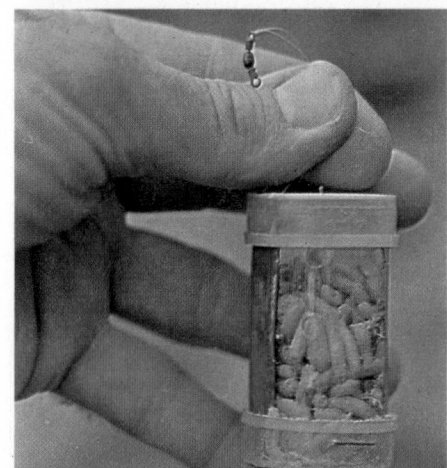

Above: *Filling a blockend swimfeeder with uncoloured maggots.*
Left: *The maggot-filled blockend is ready to be attached to the line by the use of a swivel. The lead strip acts as a ledger weight. The blockend should be cast as soon as it is filled to prevent the maggots dispersing before or during the cast.*
Below: *Swimfeeders are plastic tubes with holes through which maggots can wriggle. Groundbait is used to plug the ends until it crumbles and allows the maggots to emerge near the baited hook.*
Bottom: *A blockend swimfeeder packed with groundbait and maggots was used to tempt this fine tench.*

SWIMFEEDER

Groundbait and maggots

Maggot bait

Above: *Bait droppers come in various designs, all working on the principle of getting samples of the hookbait down to where the fish are feeding instead of being allowed to sink naturally as when using a swimfeeder or blockend. It is usually necessary to use another rod to cast out the bait dropper: this prevents tangling and allows you to position the bait dropper precisely.*

Right: *The bait dropper incorporates a container with a lid held in place by a metal rod attached to a weighted plunger. The container is packed with maggots and cast out; when the weighted plunger touches the bottom the lid is released and the maggots are deposited in the correct place. The hookbait is cast nearby.*

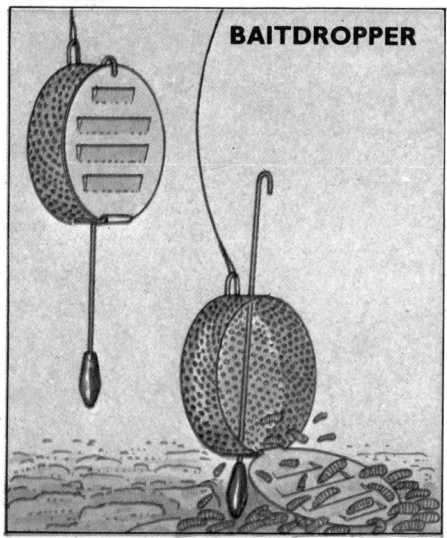

BAITDROPPER

How much does a Drennan Feederlink hold?
There are three sizes of Drennan Feederlink: the largest takes 90-100 maggots; the medium one holds 30-40 and the smallest 15-20.

How do I know what size to use?
This depends largely (but not wholly) on the species you are after and the nature of the water you are fishing. For tench in gravel pits, the medium-size Drennan feeder is best, but for bream and chub—especially where quantity is more important than specimen-sized fish—the larger the better.

If I am making a blockend, is the size of the holes important?
Yes. On the Drennan models, the holes are based on the size of good quality shop-bought maggots, enabling them to escape easily in still or running water.

Can a blockend be changed to a swimfeeder?
Dismantle a Feederlink and discard the removeable cap. Pass nylon, preferably a new piece, back through and pinch on, say, two swan shots. Pull tight so that the shots rest inside the feeder against the remaining cap. Attach a swivel to the other end of the nylon and you have a swimfeeder.

What are the guidelines on tail-length?
At most times, 15in is about right. But when fish are taking 'on the drop'—as the bait falls through the water—a longer tail of up to 3ft is appropriate. Conversely, in cold water when fish are sluggish a 10in tail often brings better results.

not, the contents will be scattered around like a rolling feeder in rivers. Accurate casting is essential. It is also important when casting to keep the line straight, especially in a side wind. As the feeder is punched forward, bring the top of the rod down to eye level then, as the feeder hits the surface, quickly thrust the top under the water to a depth of three feet. The feeder is allowed to sink on a slack line. Should it sink on a tight line, it will fall out and away from the swim.

Overhead casts
Whether fishing still or running water, overhead casts are recommended. When packed with bait, a feeder is heavy and can be cast considerable distances. Weight makes for accurate casting too.

In gravel pits, a blockend is ex-tremely effective when seeking tench and bream. By ensuring the feeder lands in the same spot every time, a hotspot is quickly formed and the fish, once they discover the bed of maggots and casters, will re-main in the area for a considerable time mopping up the loose feed. On the other hand, this may result in minute bites which though difficult to see, are often easy to hook.

Swimfeeders and blockends can be used to catch a variety of fish. The swimfeeder is especially effective for bream, barbel, roach and chub, where a cereal groundbait is neces-sary; the blockend when fishing maggots for tench, bream, roach and barbel.

Swimfeeders and blockends are normally used only when ledgering, only rarely are they used in conjunc-tion with a float.

Rod rests

Not long ago a rod rest was thought of as the sign of a lazy angler. Nowadays sophisticated angling styles have made a rest an essential part of the angler's equipment

Until recently a rod rest was a length of stick with a forked end, often cut from a hedge by the water and sometimes referred to by the term 'idleback'. Its best use was as a support for the rod while eating a snack, but today any attempt at ledgering, swing tip work, or laying-on is certainly pointless without a firm base on which the rod can be securely cradled.

Strength, lightness, adaptability and simplicity are the four essentials of a good rod rest. Strength sufficient to penetrate deeply a hard bank or gravel pit edge so that the rod will be firmly held, especially in a wind, suggests the use of a metal support. But when one considers that two sets (four rests) may have to be carried, lightness prohibits the use of thick steel or iron bars.

Various kinds of thin, light alloy rod rests are available in the shops, but most are likely to bend if full body pressure is applied to drive them into the ground. Better models are thick, hollow, well pointed, and without a seam or join along the side through which water can seep and leak over tackle or the angler.

One or two models, made from a hard metal and shaped into a 'T' or 'I' section, have recently appeared on the market. They are remarkably strong and by virtue of their shape are easy to mount into the bank. But they do cost a lot more than the average rest and are just as likely to be left behind as their cheaper counterparts. One suggestion for the forgetful angler is to paint a part of the rest a bright colour to act as a visual reminder.

Adaptability includes adjustable length and several angles of use apart from the upright position. Telescopic rests that can be held open to the required length by a thumbscrew are popular, but rather more delicate than the one-piece variety. Unfortunately, they tend to collect water and mud in the hollow section, to the detriment of rod bags or hold-alls.

There are a few rests that have adjustable heads, but most have vertical grips for holding the rod. A model with an inclined head is available, however, which can support a rod with the tip pointing downwards for swing-tip ledgering.

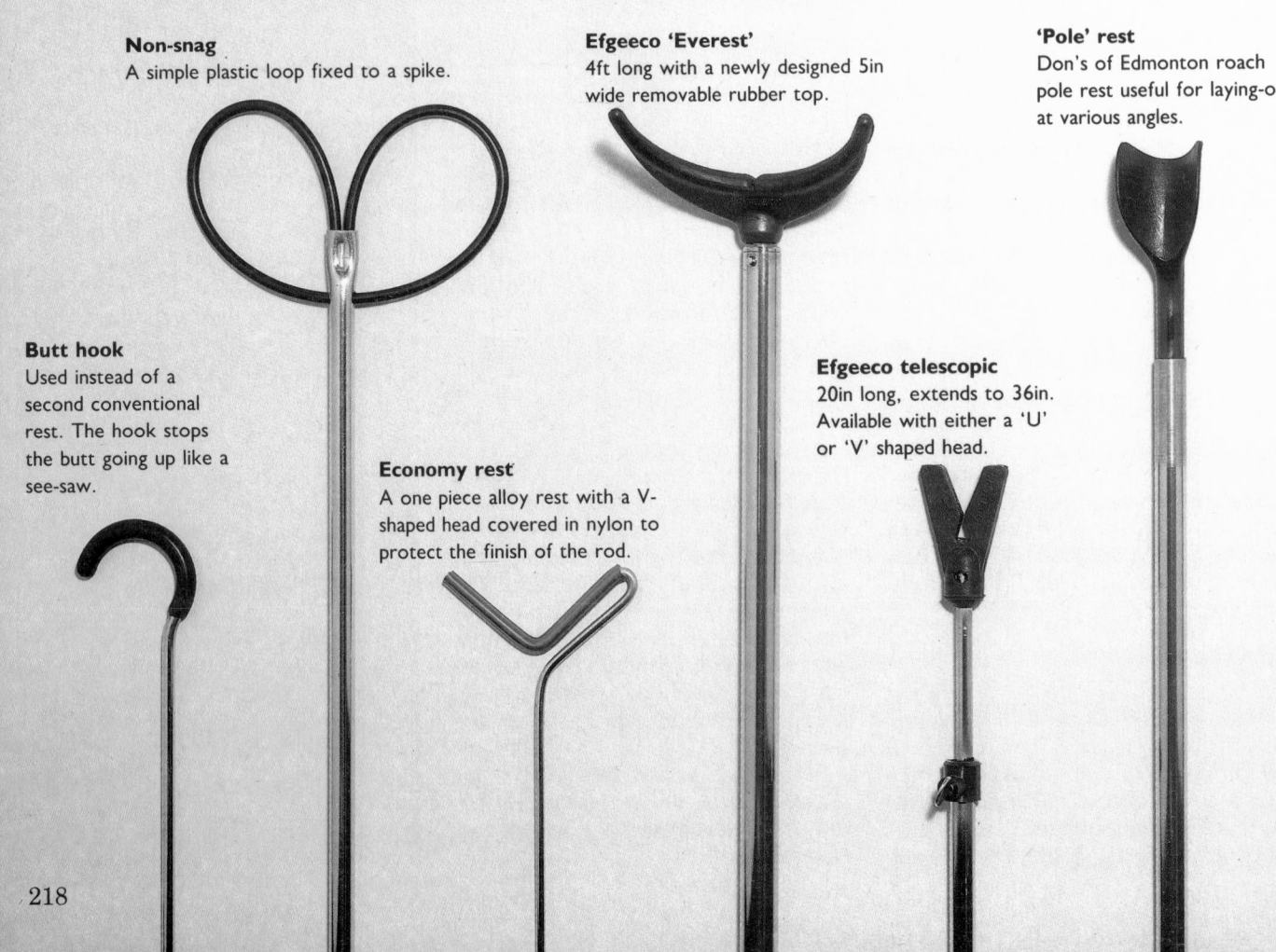

Non-snag
A simple plastic loop fixed to a spike.

Efgeeco 'Everest'
4ft long with a newly designed 5in wide removable rubber top.

'Pole' rest
Don's of Edmonton roach pole rest useful for laying-on at various angles.

Butt hook
Used instead of a second conventional rest. The hook stops the butt going up like a see-saw.

Economy rest
A one piece alloy rest with a V-shaped head covered in nylon to protect the finish of the rod.

Efgeeco telescopic
20in long, extends to 36in. Available with either a 'U' or 'V' shaped head.

Simplicity is essential at the head. The rod should sit lightly but firmly in the support, and there should be a gap so that the line can run smoothly when a fish takes. The usual 'U' and 'V' shapes are particularly likely to trap a line below the rod, and more than one good run has stopped short because of this.

Two specialized rests are worth mentioning. The roach pole is usually associated with hand held, small fish tactics. But it is equally useful for laying-on, the tight line between rod tip and hook resulting in good hooking. To enable the pole angler to lay-on in moving water at various angles through the swim a multi-notched head can be used that allows the rod to be shifted, fan wise, until the whole swim has been worked. This special rest can be cut by the average handyman from off-cuts of marine plywood mounted on-

to a flattened metal stake. Naturally the wooden notches in which the rod will rest must be lined with foam or rubber to protect the rod varnish.

Rod rests on which bite indicators are incorporated are expensive, but usually possess a very firm metal shaft for driving into the ground. Even if the indicator is not being used, they are good value by virtue of their rugged construction. When used with the bite indicator mechanism they should be sunk deeply into

the bank—otherwise wind vibration can set off the alarm signal.

Setting rod rests demands a little thought. They should be well spread, giving maximum support to the rod itself. Mounted too closely together the rod will vibrate in any reasonable wind, leading to false bites registering at the indicator or float tip. Where the bank is extra hard, preventing a good vertical push into the ground, try to set the rests at right angles to each other.

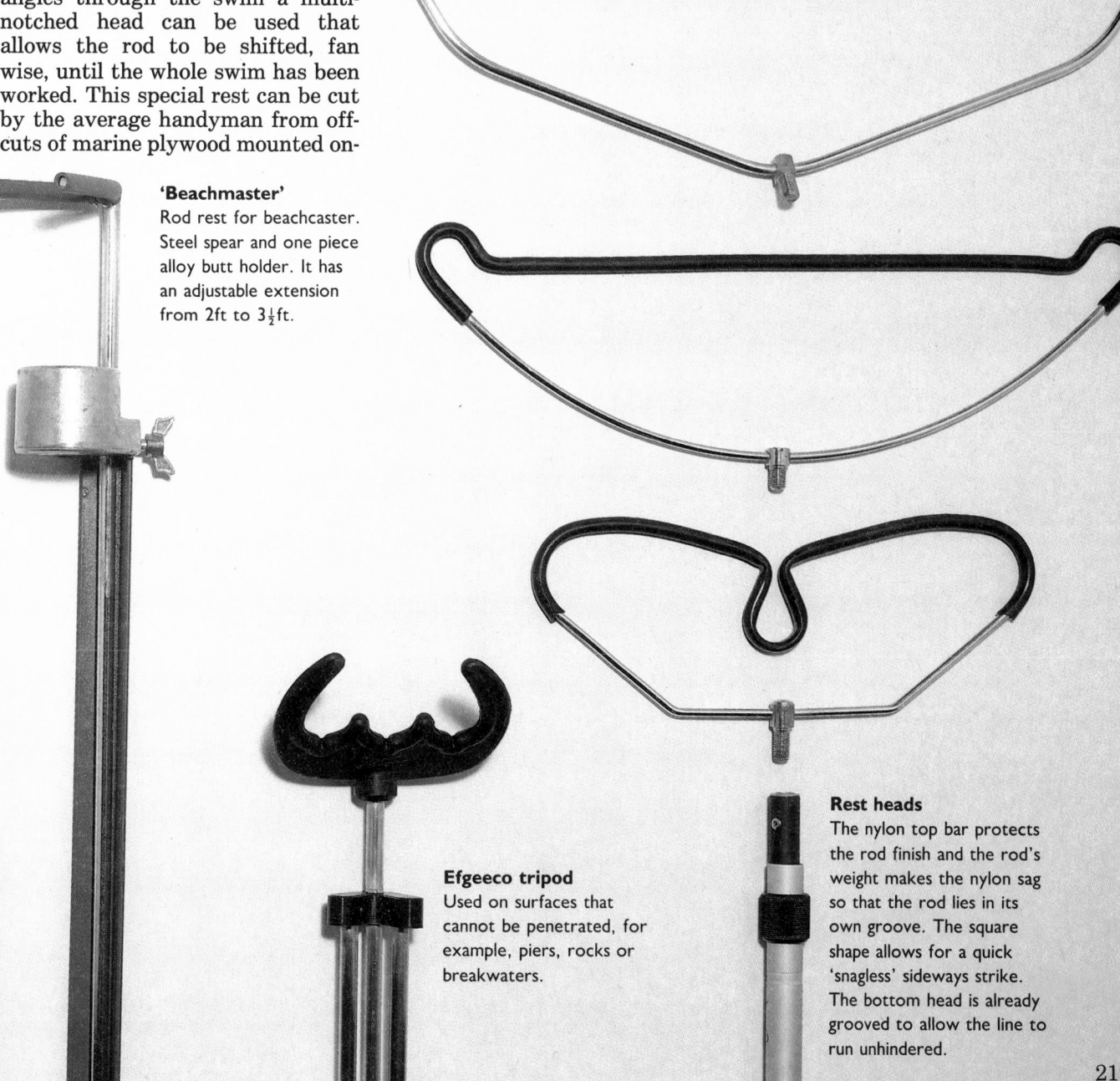

'Beachmaster'
Rod rest for beachcaster. Steel spear and one piece alloy butt holder. It has an adjustable extension from 2ft to 3½ft.

Efgeeco tripod
Used on surfaces that cannot be penetrated, for example, piers, rocks or breakwaters.

Rest heads
The nylon top bar protects the rod finish and the rod's weight makes the nylon sag so that the rod lies in its own groove. The square shape allows for a quick 'snagless' sideways strike. The bottom head is already grooved to allow the line to run unhindered.

219

Spinning rods

The range of rods which fall within the one category begins with the small, handy wand used by a roving fisherman on tiny streams to weapons capable of landing a salmon

Spinning rods may usually be classified by the weights they can cast and the line strengths the rod can handle, their basic function being to cast a lure and to control a hooked fish.

As a general rule, the lighter the lure or spinner to be cast, the lighter and shorter the rod. In general also, the lighter the lure, the finer will be the line used with it. This is because the heavier and thicker the line the more weight is required in the lure to overcome the drag of the line, which is to be avoided especially when long casts are needed.

Most rods designed for use with the lighter spinning lure (up to ½oz)

are 6-8ft long and are teamed with fixed-spool reels and relatively light lines of 4-8lb b.s. Rods for the heavier lures are more often 8-10½ft long and may be used with fixed-spool or multiplier reels loaded with lines up to 20lb b.s. These heavier spinning rods are very often used with two hands when casting and so have naturally been referred to as double-handed.

In addition to the standard patterns of spinning rods, there is a special type which originated in the US and is known as a 'baitcasting' rod. This rod, designed to be used in conjunction with a multiplier, features a pistol-grip, cranked han-

dle to allow the fisherman to cast and control the reel using one hand. It is made with a one-piece top 5-6ft long, and the reel is mounted on top of the rod. This arrangement enables accurate casting but has the disadvantage that long-distance casts are not possible.

Baitcasting rods
These outfits are used extensively in America for freshwater black bass fishing, but are not popular in Britain as they are best used with plug baits which, by contrast with spinners, spoons, Devon minnows and similar lures, have not yet gained wide acceptance here. Baitcasting rods also require a fairly heavy plug or lure to cast well and it is still more usual in Britain to use longer rods in this situation.

For light spinning for trout, sea trout, perch and pike, a rod of 7-8ft long, capable of casting up to ¾oz, makes a good all-round tool when coupled with a small-to-medium fixed-spool reel carrying line of 4-8lb b.s. depending on the type of

Spinning rods (from top to bottom): the Abu Caster—6ft long and suited to weights of less than ½oz; the medium-weight Fibatube 9ft Special; the Shakespeare 1570–270—8ft 10in of powerful action.

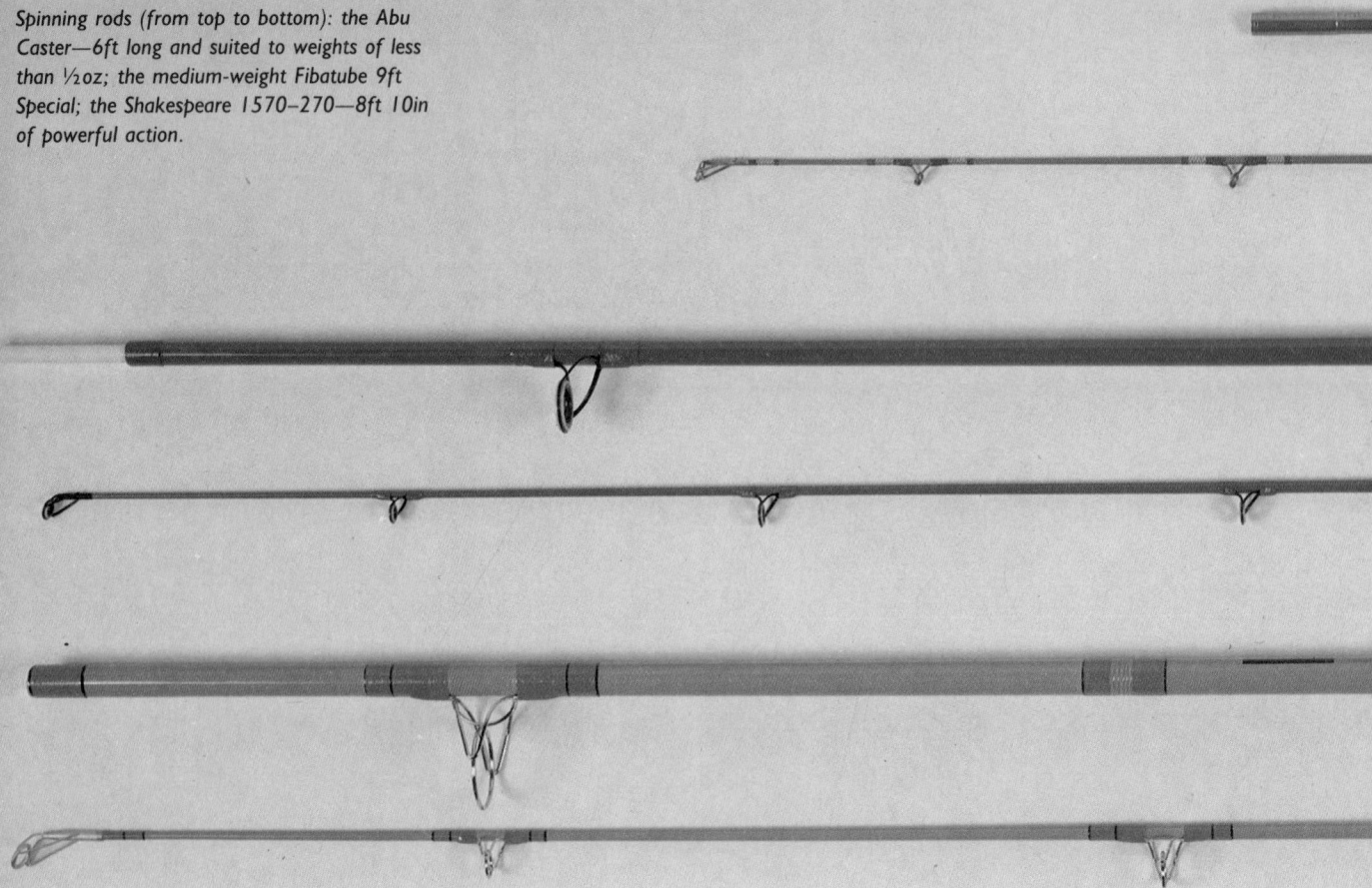

fishing. This pattern of rod is usually made of hollow glassfibre, with cheaper rods in solid glass.

A cork handle about 18in long, fitted with a screw winch-fitting to hold the reel securely is the basis of all spinning rods. The size of rod rings should be graduated to aid casting by ensuring smooth line flow from the spool.

A rod suitable for heavier types of lures in the ½-1oz range should be 8½-9ft long. The handle should be about 24in long, with a screw winch-fitting about 14in from the bottom of the handle when used with a fixed-spool reel, and 2-3in higher with a multiplier. This substitution of lines of 9-15lb b.s. makes the outfit suitable for the heavier types of freshwater spinning—salmon and pike—and for lighter saltwater spinning for bass, pollack, mackerel and other species.

Heavy-duty spinning rods
The heaviest patterns of rod are required for spinning with deadbaits for salmon and large pike in very un-favourable water conditions. The deadbaits can weigh up to 4oz, and lines up to 20lb b.s. are needed.

A rod capable of handling heavy lures and leads should be 9½-10ft long and fairly strong, with a test curve of 1½-2¼lb. This type of rod is very often used with a multiplier, for heavy spinning. The handles are usually 24-28in long.

Greenheart rods
The design of spinning rods has altered considerably over the past 50 years. The original rods were heavy and long, and made for salmon spinning. They were usually of greenheart (a special type of hardwood), or built cane. The centrepin reel used with these rods required them to be slow in action to assist the revolving drum to accelerate evenly and allow line to flow off without jamming.

With the introduction of the fixed-spool reel, rod action could be improved. They could be faster in action, as well as lighter. The fixed-spool reel could casts lighter baits

and, because the spool of the reel did not revolve, the line did not jam or overrun, making casting easier.

The multiplier became popular at about the same time, and was an improvement over the centrepin so far as casting was concerned. However, it is only in the last 10 years or so that the multiplier's braking systems for casting have been developed enough to allow rod-makers to match them with the lighter, faster-actioned rods now favoured. The latest material to be used in spinning rods is carbonfibre. These rods are expensive, but perform well.

Prices for the various types of spinning rod vary considerably, depending on the quality of the materials and workmanship. A good tubular glass rod by a reputable maker costs from £25-£50 while imported rods may be bought for as little as £10.

For anglers who only use a spinning rod on the odd occasion each

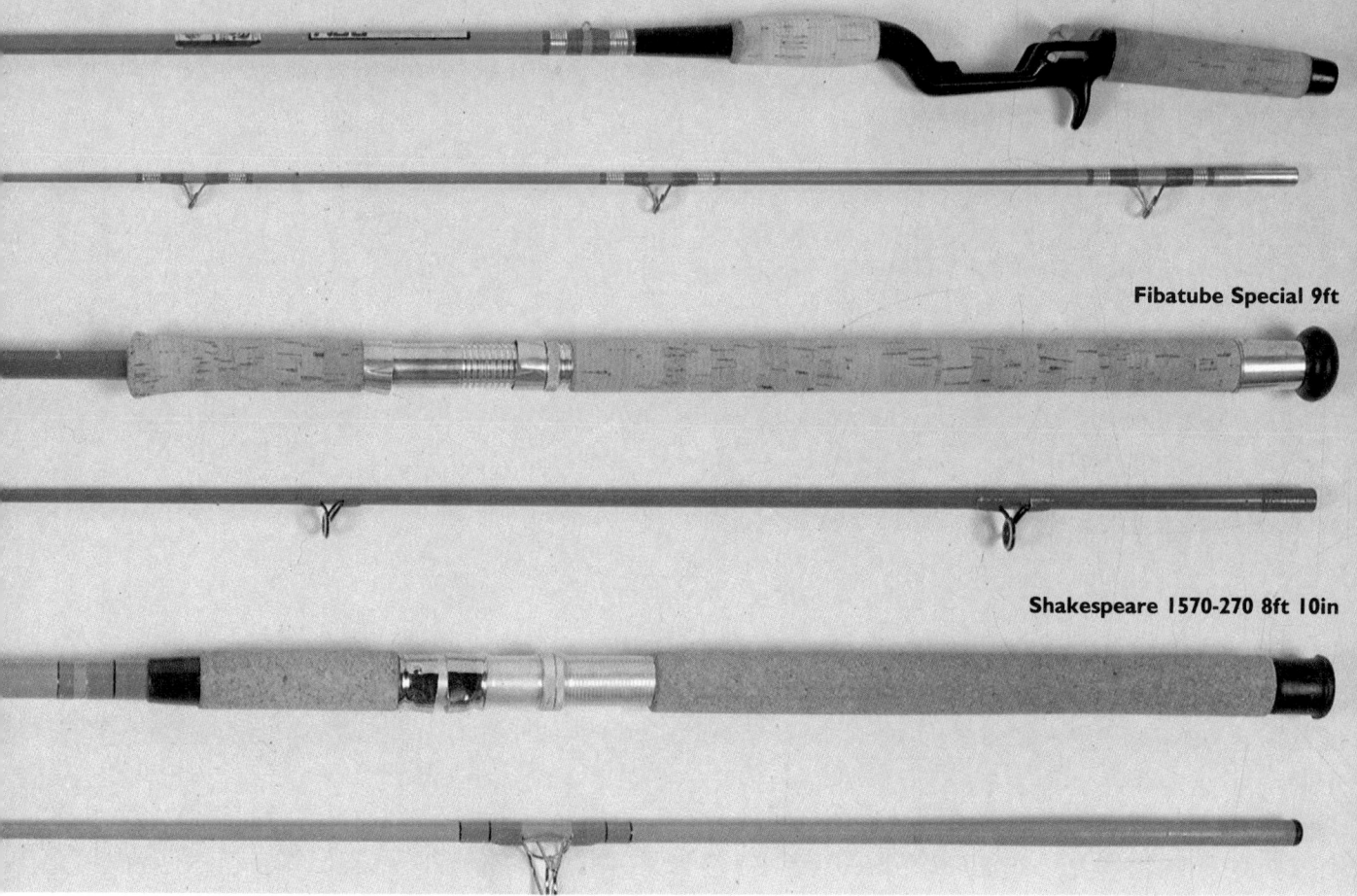

Abu Caster 6ft

Fibatube Special 9ft

Shakespeare 1570-270 8ft 10in

Centrepins and multipliers

Fixed-spool reels are appropriate for light-tackle fishing, but when using some specialized techniques and for big-game fishing centrepins and multipliers may be essential

A centrepin is a reel acting as a line reservoir with its axis at right angles to the rod. Good centrepins consist of a flanged drum, machined to very fine tolerances, which revolves freely on a precision-engineered steel axle. Many models have appeared over the years, ranging from the cheap and simple kind in Bakelite to the comparatively expensive models manufactured from stainless steel or enamelled metal. Wooden models have also been produced, but are now not so common.

The centrepin is simple in construction, and—by virtue of this—reliable, as well as being easy to operate and to maintain. Once the use of the centrepin has been mastered many anglers prefer it to the fixed-spool reel.

Trotting

The centrepin is used mainly for 'trotting'—allowing the river's current to carry float-tackle smoothly downstream, allowing the bait to cover long stretches of water at one cast. It is with this method that the free-running centrepin drum is put to best advantage. To recover line quickly, the drum is given a series of taps with all four fingers in a practice called 'batting'.

The diameter of the reel can vary, but most are between 3½in and 4½in. The drum's diameter will be

Reel foot

Spool

Ratchet

Reel foot

Backplate

Line guard

Drag control

Reel foot

Spool

Handle

Spool release clip

Line guide

Ratchet spring

Ratchet panel (off)

Drag tensioner

Ratchet cog

AVON ROYAL SUPREME III CENTREPIN

A freshwater reel, mainly used for long trotting and swimming the stream. Extremely free-running, centrepins enable the bait to be carried smoothly downstream. Though simple in design, centrepins are more difficult to use than the more popular fixed-spool reel. The large drum allows fast, smooth retrieval.

almost as large, and the larger the drum the more rapid will be the line recovery. Most centrepins have a line guard and optional ratchet, while some also have a drag mechanism. An exposed smooth rim, which allows finger-pressure to be applied to control the line when casting or playing a fish, is a valuable feature. Many of the older centrepin reels are now very much in demand for their fine, free action.

Although the centrepin is still used —and indeed has made a come-back in recent years—its popularity suffered greatly when the fixed-spool reel was introduced 40 years ago. This reel permits almost effortless long casting, because the drum is parallel to the rod. To achieve similar distances with a centrepin is a satisfying accomplishment. Nevertheless, the centrepin is still unrivalled in two circumstances. In water where the fishing is virtually under the rod end and there are likely to be big fish which go off at high

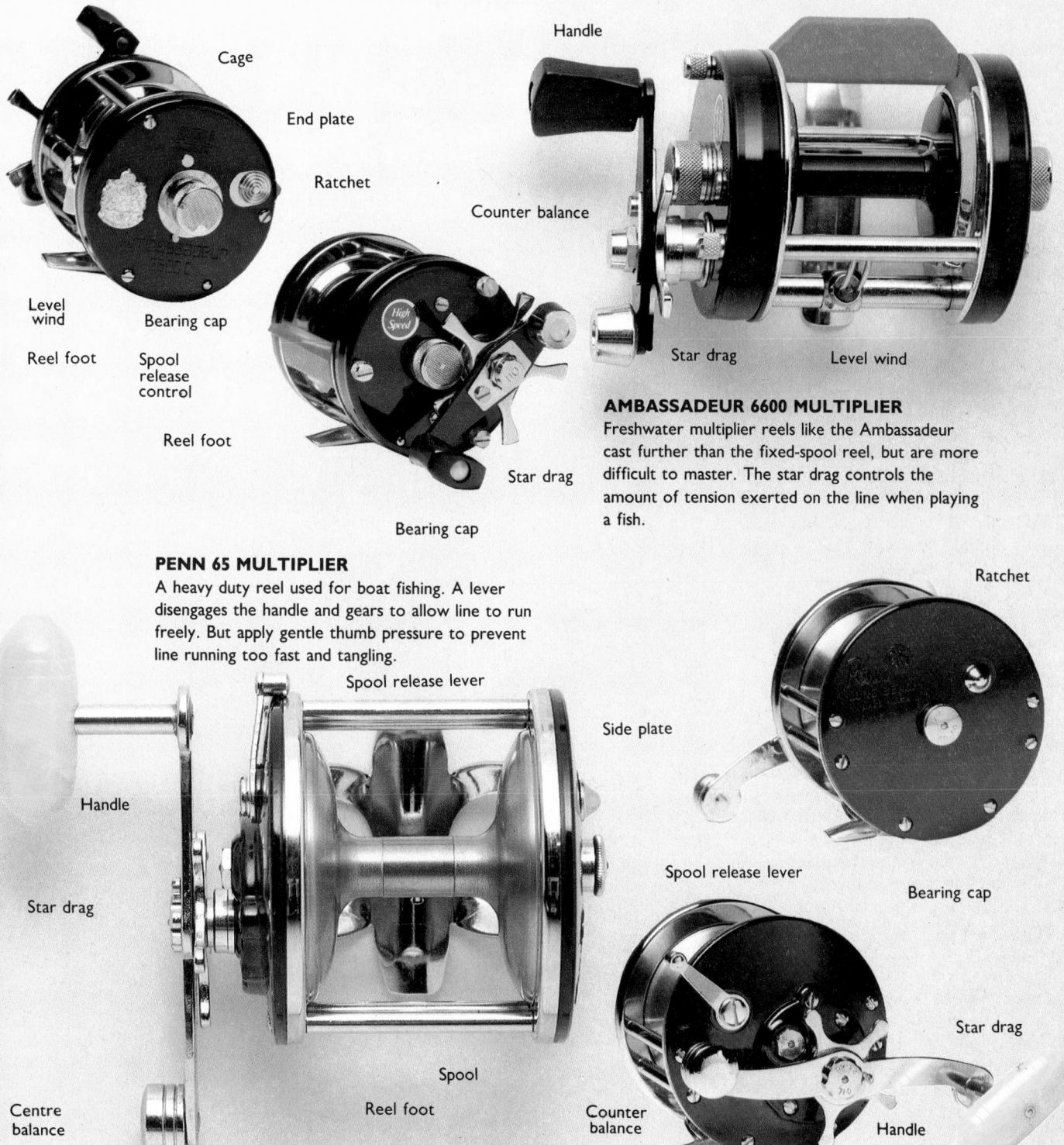

Cage

End plate

Ratchet

Handle

Counter balance

Level wind

Reel foot

Bearing cap

Spool release control

Reel foot

Star drag

High Speed

Bearing cap

Star drag

Level wind

AMBASSADEUR 6600 MULTIPLIER
Freshwater multiplier reels like the Ambassadeur cast further than the fixed-spool reel, but are more difficult to master. The star drag controls the amount of tension exerted on the line when playing a fish.

PENN 65 MULTIPLIER
A heavy duty reel used for boat fishing. A lever disengages the handle and gears to allow line to run freely. But apply gentle thumb pressure to prevent line running too fast and tangling.

Spool release lever

Ratchet

Side plate

Handle

Spool release lever

Bearing cap

Star drag

Star drag

Centre balance

Spool

Reel foot

Counter balance

Handle

speed, such as carp; and where the fishing is close-in.

The centrepin scores in both conditions for the same reason—the perfect control which can be exercised by the thumb on the drum of the reel. A point in favour of this method is that the alternative—using the slipping clutch of a fixed-spool reel—was not designed for use with the fine lines normally used by the matchman.

In 1977 a centrepin reel for fly fishing, made entirely of carbon fibre, made its appearance. This, the 'Line-Shooter', is a big reel with a wide drum and exposed rim, allowing rapid line recovery by winding or 'batting'. It is also the lightest centrepin reel ever made, weighing only 5oz. The ratchet is optional and, by contrast with many other models, is reasonably quiet. It also incorporates an extremely sensitive drag control. Although built as a fly reel it has found favour with coarse fishermen, who use it for trotting. For this, the drag should be set so that the reel revolves with the current's pull. For 'laying-on' (float fishing but with about 18in of line on the bottom, which gives a clear bite indication) or 'stret-pegging' (again setting the float higher than the depth of the water and casting the tackle into a groundbaited area) the setting should not allow the line to pay out too freely and so tangle.

The multiplier reel

The multiplier is essentially a reel with a small-diameter drum geared to a ratio of 3 or 4:1 so that line is retrieved rapidly by winding. Models with automatic gears are available, but are far more expensive. These have ratios of about 2½ and 4½:1. As with the fixed-spool reel, there is a wide variety.

To the beginner the multiplier may appear complicated. But you should become familiar with its star-drag, brake and other parts before going fishing with it. Most multipliers are right-handed and cannot be adapted for left-handers.

The main problem with the multiplier reel is that of the line over-running and tangling into 'bird's nests'. To reduce the possibility of this, whether when

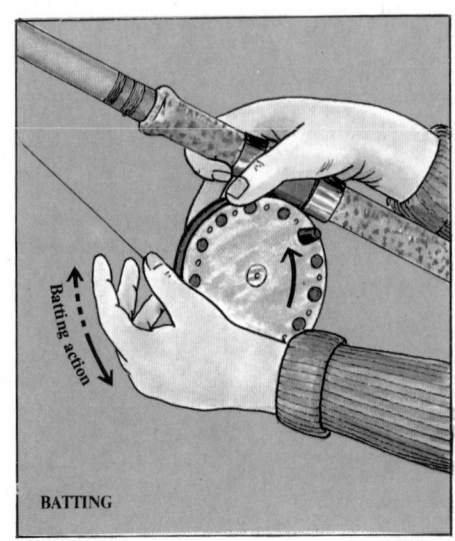

BATTING

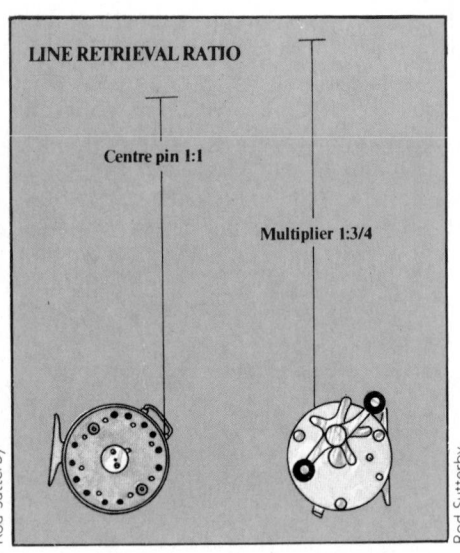

LINE RETRIEVAL RATIO

Centre pin 1:1

Multiplier 1:3/4

Above: *By giving the side of the reel a series of taps on the side with four fingers, you can recover line more quickly than winding.*
Above right: *Line retrieval. The centrepin (1:1) compared with the multiplier (1:3/4).*

Below: *Pike fishing on Loch Lomond using a multiplier. The advantage of a multiplier is that the adjustable drag can apply tension on a running fish, especially useful when a big fish is running towards you.*

A rare wooden starback centrepin reel, used for deep sea fishing in the Shetlands.

lowering the bait over the side of a boat and down to the sea-bed or casting up to 100 yards from the shore, the thumb must rest gently on the line as it pays out. Various devices have been incorporated by manufacturers in some of their models to overcome this difficulty. These include spool tensioners, centrifugal govenors, oil 'drag' retarders and 'lift' and 'brake' gadgets, but bird's nests can be avoided by the angler if he learns how to use his reel properly.

The more expensive multipliers have ball bearings set in both end-plates. Leading from one spindle is a governing mechanism, usually consisting of fibre blocks, which are thrown outwards by centrifugal force, thus acting as a brake when the bait hits the water. To stop the line from running with the weight while casting, a manual brake on the side of the reel can be employed. Another feature of superior reels is a 'line-spreader', which ensures the even distribution of line on recovery.

The mechanism of the freshwater multiplier is extremely delicate, and sand, dust, and, worse still, saltwater, are to be avoided at all costs. The heavier saltwater models still need to be kept clean and oiled, but they are usually rust-proof. Unlike other reels, which are fixed to the underside of the rod handle, the multiplier is used with the rod reversed and the reel uppermost.

Maintenance

It is essential after each outing to rinse the reel thoroughly in freshwater and, after drying it, to apply a recommended lubricant, especially if the reel is not to be used again for some time. Periodical inspection is also advisable, for sand or grit in the gears can wreak havoc and a jammed reel while playing a strong fish is an event no angler wants to experience.

The multiplier used in pike fishing will, with practice, allow baits, spinners and plugs to be cast as far as with a fixed-spool model. As a bonus, playing fish on a drum reel, which demands special skills, can be a real delight.

Can you still buy new centrepin reels?
Yes. In fact only recently the Allcock Aerial, which many anglers consider the finest reel of its kind ever made, was re-introduced to the market.

Is it difficult to learn to cast with a centrepin reel?
Despite their simple appearance centrepins are more difficult to master than the fixed-spool reel. Buy a fixed-spool reel first, master its use thoroughly and when casting has become effortless, try using a centrepin. If you are able to get an expert to teach you, so much the better, but with practice proficiency should not be too long in coming.

Is the centrepin only used for trotting?
Yes, although a few anglers use them in stillwaters. For ledgering, a fixed-spool is essential.

At the end of the season, should I empty the reel before storing it away?
Never put a reel—of any kind—away for long periods loaded with line. For the amount nylon costs these days, it's not worth saving the line you remove, either. Especially with light line, strip it off and start afresh the next season.

Is there any other maintenance work to be done on a centrepin reel?
After every fishing trip, wipe the reel down and dry it. Saltwater centrepins are particularly prone to corrosion. Once a month, remove the side plate and inspect: unless you check regularly for grit, and use 3-in-1 oil to grease the spindle, the reel may let you down.

Plugs

Here's a bait which resembles a fish or insect or waterside creature ready equipped with spinning mount, hooks and a lifelike movement to attract the shyest predator

The best description of a plug is a cross between a spinner and a dead-bait. In shape it resembles a dead fish with hooks ready-set. In use it is retrieved in much the same way as a spinner. But a plug possesses advantages that neither spinner nor dead-bait have—it can be made to work with innumerable variations on a straight retrieve at any of many

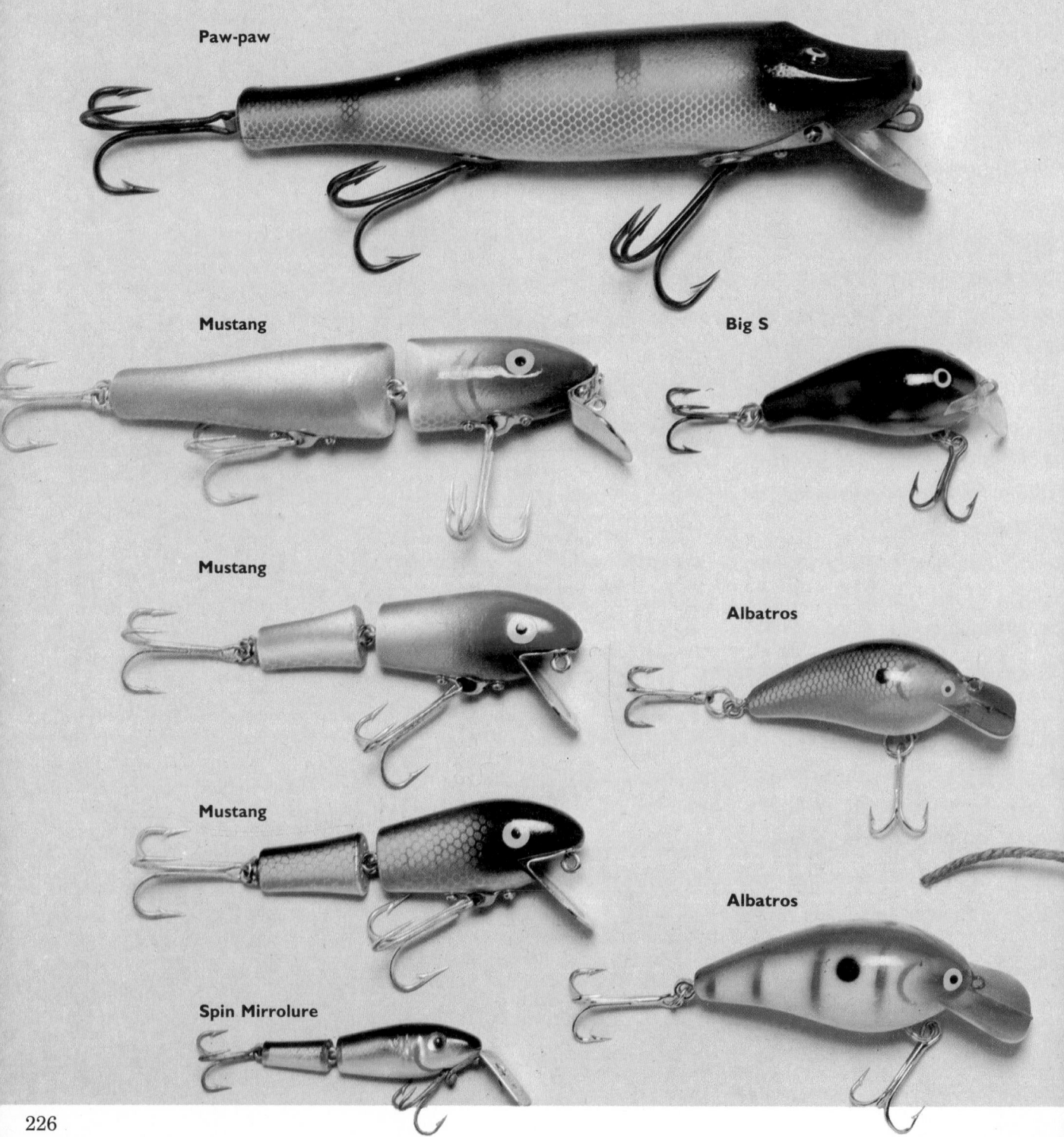

Paw-paw

Mustang

Big S

Mustang

Albatros

Mustang

Albatros

Spin Mirrolure

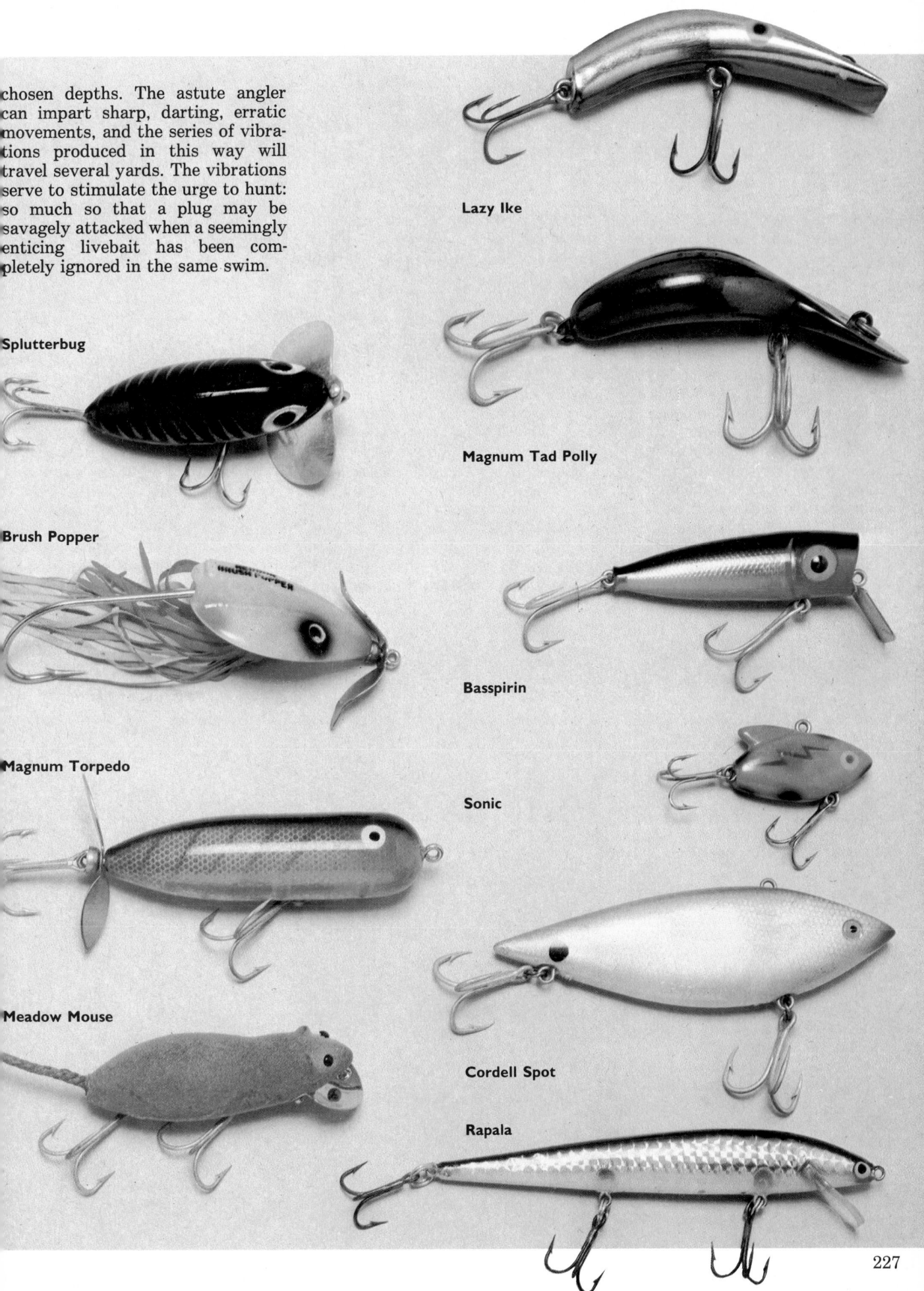

chosen depths. The astute angler can impart sharp, darting, erratic movements, and the series of vibrations produced in this way will travel several yards. The vibrations serve to stimulate the urge to hunt: so much so that a plug may be savagely attacked when a seemingly enticing livebait has been completely ignored in the same swim.

Lazy Ike

Splutterbug

Magnum Tad Polly

Brush Popper

Basspirin

Magnum Torpedo

Sonic

Meadow Mouse

Cordell Spot

Rapala

Plugs fall into four general categories that coincide with the depth at which they should work. There are surface lures, floating divers, sinkers, and deep divers. Their shape, especially at the nose, often gives a clue to their working use. But it is left to the angler to actually get the best action from them when he is fishing.

Kinds of plug

Floating plugs are light, usually made from wood, and have a 'V'-shaped wedge inserted in the nose. There are models made to represent mice, and one has broad arms, or sweeps, that vibrate backwards and forwards during the retrieve; they are intended to represent a surface-swimming fish in distress—rather in the fashion of one with swimbladder trouble.

They should be cast close to the bank, under overhanging trees and bushes and retrieved alternately fast and slow, causing them to dive a few inches under the surface, then pop up to the top. The bow wave caused by this sudden dive is probably the lure's main attraction.

Floating divers are the most versatile of all plugs. They have lighweight bodies with a medium-sized diving nose (or lip) set into the head. After being cast, they will lie on the surface, only diving when the angler commences the retrieve. The faster the motion, the deeper they will dive—short, hard turns on the reel and then a few seconds with the handle stationary, produce a series of swoops and rises that few fish can resist. They have an added advantage in snaggy waters. By stopping the retrieve when an underwater obstruction is reached, the plug is allowed to float up, and can be coaxed gently past the danger area before continuing with the normal dive and rise action.

One floating plug—if it can be called a plug at all—is particularly successful with pike and chub: the artificial frog. This green-painted moulding, complete with realistically supple legs, often has a small diving vane around the mouth and is worked across or just below the surface of the water. As with all floating plugs, the take consists of a

228

massive swirl as the fish lunges forward. The savage pull that follows can easily catch the unwary angler off guard and break his line. For this reason it is important to concentrate and anticipate a take at any time—even when the line is right at your feet. Often, a big fish will follow the surface vibration several yards and only attack just before the plug is lifted clear of the water.

Sinking plugs

Sinking plugs are for very deep gravel pits and reservoirs where the lure has to sink some way before it can be fished usefully. In order to find and keep the 'taking' depth, the count-down method should be used. After the lure has hit the water, the angler counts from, say, one to six, then starts his retrieve. On the next cast, he may count to seven, then eight on the following casts—and so on until a fish is taken. This will probably be the taking depth, and future casts should be allowed the

same time before retrieve begins.

Few plugs in this category have a diving vane, all are heavy, and some models have a metal ball sealed into a cavity in the body. When the retrieve begins, the action of the plug under the water causes this ball to rattle, making vibrations that are highly attractive to predators.

Deep divers

The last selection of plugs, the deep divers, are easily recognized by the extra large metal vane set into the head. This broad lip sets up drag against the water when the retrieve starts and causes the plug to dive quickly, at a sharp angle. As with sinkers, the count-down method is the best when exploring a water.

The colour range of plugs displayed in a tackle shop can be quite staggering. But action is more important than colour in a plug, and generally those with green, yellow and a little red coincide with the natural colours of fish and appear to

be the most acceptable.

Most important of all is the construction of the plug. Hooks should be neither so large that they dwarf the body, nor so small that they will fail to set into the jaws of a fish on striking. The best hooks are made from fine wire, with well-defined barbs. Most of them are mounted into the body by screw eyes or metal bands secured with screws. These should be most carefully checked, and, if they appear loose, should be removed and re-set with a little Araldite glue to hold them firm. The eye-loop at the head, to which the trace will be mounted, should also be carefully looked at to ensure that it is firmly closed, otherwise the trace will slip free from it during a cast.

One naturally thinks of pike fishing in connection with plugs, and most of the sinking and deep-diving models will take good fish. Size does not seem important where pike are concerned—4 and 5in double-bodied plugs that simulate the flowing movements of a swimming fish, down to tiny 1½in minnow imitations, will all produce results. Perch take a running plug, too, especially in reservoirs and gravel pits. Their large, 'telescopic' mouths are perfectly capable of tackling the large lure intended for a pike. Chub are appreciative of surface plugs that can be persuaded to make a large disturbance on top of the water—especially the more gaudy, tassel-embellished models. Shallow divers of the minnow size are worth a trial during the winter months.

Unfortunately, the vibrations produced by a plug can, on occasions, make predators bolt for cover. However incomprehensible the response is, it calls for an immediate switch to spinner or deadbait.

But there are few fish that have not, at some time or other, fallen for a plug—particularly in the early part of season, a period when many of the old adult stock have turned cannibal.

Left: *Although this long, articulated plug does not much resemble a fish in our eyes, its movement was patently able to trigger off the hunting instinct in this handsome East Anglian pike.*

Below: *Stored like this, a large array of artificial lures can be examined at a glance and an appropriate bait selected. Multiple trebles easily become entangled with each other if they are not stored carefully.*

How do I begin to choose from among all the plugs available in the shops?
The most important criterion is depth of water. If you plan to fish a shallow, snaggy water, you must choose a floating plug. The deeper the water, the bigger and more angled the diving vane needs to be.

Is the colour of a plug important?
Colour is often a stimulus to feed, but its importance in plug fishing is negligible compared with the realism of its action and the depth at which it is fished.

For pike fishing, should I attach a wire trace to my plug?
A wire trace is always a good idea when dealing with pike, but it is less important for plugs than with live or deadbaits.

Is an anti-kink vane necessary?
No. A plug does not spin in the water as it is retrieved, so problems with kinking line should never arise.

What advantages does a double-jointed plug have over a one-piece design?
The action of an articulated plug is rather different, as it not only dives and vibrates but also 'waggles' in the water. This movement is particularly attractive to heavyweight pike.

Will non-predatory fish ever accept a plug?
All fish are predatory to some extent or at some stage in their development. Most species will snap at a passing plug. Perhaps the non-predators are spurred by an instinct to protect their 'territory' from an interloper.

Spinners

Fishing with a whirling, seductively flashing spinner can be a deadly way of catching predatory fish—but the variety of spinners on the market is overwhelming

A spinner can be defined as an artificial lure that comprises a blade or body which rotates quickly about a straight line axis consisting often of a wire bar. Spoons, in contrast, have a wobbly retrieve and do not usually spin. Plugs are artificial fish-like objects, made of various materials, which wobble on retrieve. These distinctions are not clear-cut, and it

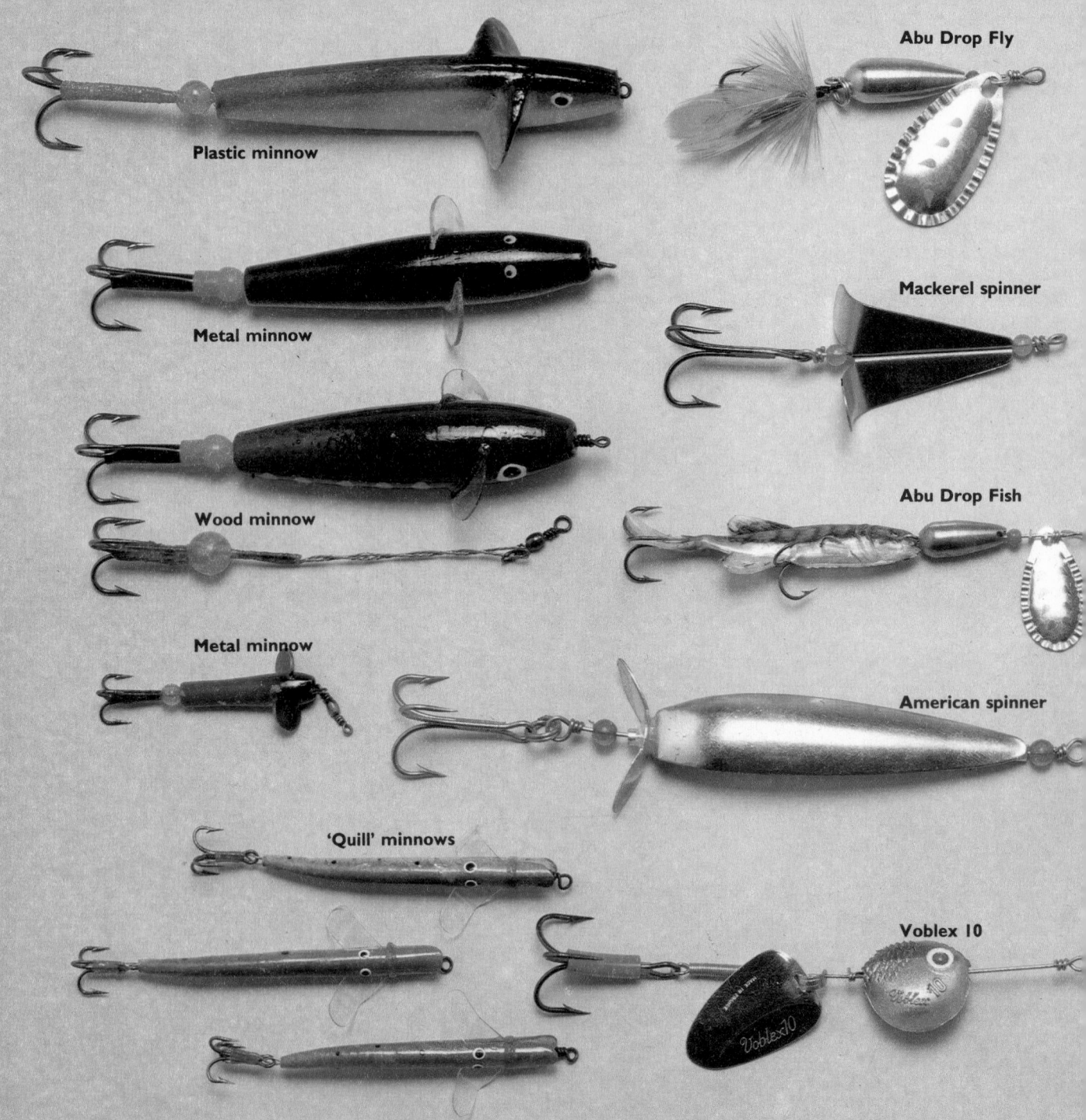

Plastic minnow

Abu Drop Fly

Metal minnow

Mackerel spinner

Wood minnow

Abu Drop Fish

Metal minnow

American spinner

'Quill' minnows

Voblex 10

is possible to buy, or make, spinners that are headed by a sizeable body and are therefore halfway between spinners and plugs (such as the famous Voblex), and spinners with so much hair or feather that they approach flies in construction, but with the added flash of a small rotating blade. There is great scope for inventiveness among anglers and many new combinations are possible, if not many new basic designs.

There are five basic kinds of spinner—artifical minnows, wagtails, mackerel spinners, fly spoons, and barspoons. It is unfortunate that the last two incorporate the word 'spoon' in their names, for they are in fact spinners with a straight axis around which the blade spins.

Artificial minnows

Of all the kinds of spinners, artificial minnows most closely represent fish, both still and on the move. The body, made of either wood, plastic or metal, is round in cross section, minnow-like in profile, and has a hole along its length through which a metal bar or wire trace passes. At the tail is a treble hook and at the

Intrepid Flectolite

Abu Drop Flex

Mepps Aglia Longue

Mepps Black Fury

Normark Vibrax

Daiwa

Veltic 6

Ondex 6

Mepps Aglia

Abu Reflex

Abu Droppen

head a swivel which can be attached to the reel line or, if fishing for pike, to a wire trace link swivel. Generally, the swivel at the head has a smaller overall diameter than the hole through the middle of the lure so that on the take the fish tends to blow the lure up the line, giving itself nothing to lever against as it tries to throw the hook. This is an excellent feature of the design which is occasionally incorporated in such other lures as plugs.

The head of the minnow has a pair of vanes which cause it to rotate. Some makes have adjustable vanes so that the spin can be reversed, and line twist reduced.

A variation on the minnow theme is the quill minnow, a superb lure for fishing for trout in hill streams. The whole body of the quill minnow rotates, often including the bar wire through its middle, so that the swivel has to work well to avoid line twist, and an anti-kink vane is usually necessary. These lures normally have up to three sets of treble hooks and since many hill trout take the spinner crossways, this is an advantage despite the tendency of the lure to become hooked up in rocks or weeds and other snags.

Wagtail movement
Wagtails look more lifelike when moving than when still. They usually have a head complete with eyes, spinning vanes, a swivel and tube-like body hidden inside two long rubber flaps which are pointed at the tail end, close to the treble hook. The name comes from these loose, flapping strips of rubber. All this detail disappears, however, when the whole body rotates quickly and, other than in body softness, the wagtail probably differs little from the various minnows. Wagtails can be made to quite large sizes and with a slow spin. This can occasionally be an advantage over commercial minnows. Like minnows, wagtails are mostly used when fishing for salmon, sea trout and trout, but can be very effective for pike.

Mackerel spinners
Mackerel spinners are superb lures for any predatory fish. They do not work well if more than 2½in long, but most commercial ones are 2in or less. They have a tube around the axial wire, and this tube is brazed to a triangular-shaped plate that has the spinning vanes at the rear, near the treble hook. Mackerel spinners can be retrieved in very shallow water and with extreme slowness at any depth. For catching large numbers of perch and pike they are perhaps the best lures ever designed, and should be fished on lines of 6-8lb b.s. to obtain the best casting results from their aerodynamic shape. Mackerel spinners have advantages over other spinners, as they are very cheap and nearly indestructible but they are not easy to make unless you dispense with the tube and make do with a couple of bent eyes at the front and at the back of the blade.

Fly spoons
Fly spoons, as their name implies, have traditionally been used for game fish, but are very effective for chub and perch on small streams. They are small, twinkling lures, most of which spin rather than wobble, and are essentially spinners for short casts on light tackle of 2-6lb b.s. monofilament lines. They can even be fished on fly tackle with fly lines. This is probably how they originated but today it is unusual to see them fished in this way. Many fly spoons are constructed with a

Removing a Colorado Spoon from a pike's mouth. The Colorado Spoon is misnamed: it is actually a spinner, the blade revolving around a central axis. The red wool tag provides an aiming point for predatory fish.

QUILL MINNOW

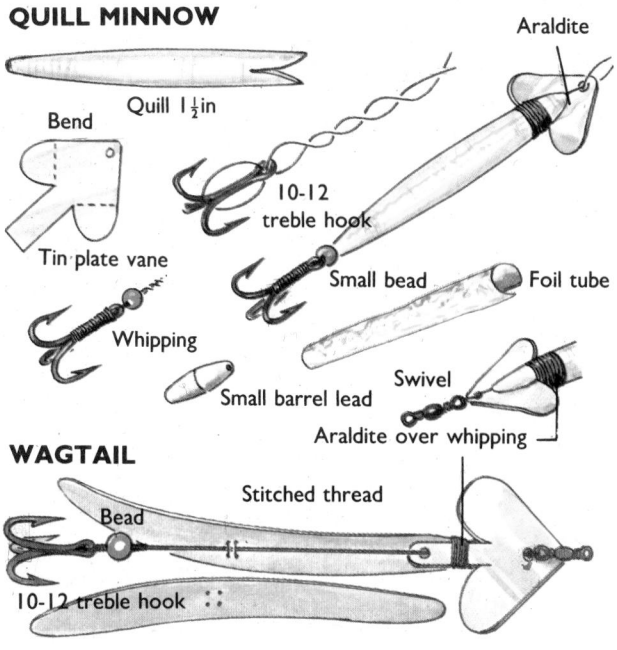

Quill 1½in

Bend

Tin plate vane

Whipping

Small barrel lead

10-12 treble hook

Small bead

Foil tube

Swivel

Araldite over whipping

Araldite

WAGTAIL

Bead

Stitched thread

10-12 treble hook

Left: *A home-made quill minnow, identical in action to the Devon minnow. A goose quill is used, to which is glued and whipped a piece of metal cut in the right shape. A triple hook with a bead at its eye is whipped to Alasticum wire and threaded through the quill. A small lead weight is drawn down the quill and a swivel is attached, and the body of the minnow covered with foil.*
Below left: *Wagtails look unnatural when seen out of the water, but in action they work in a lifelike manner. One side piece is removed to illustrate the wagtail's structure.*

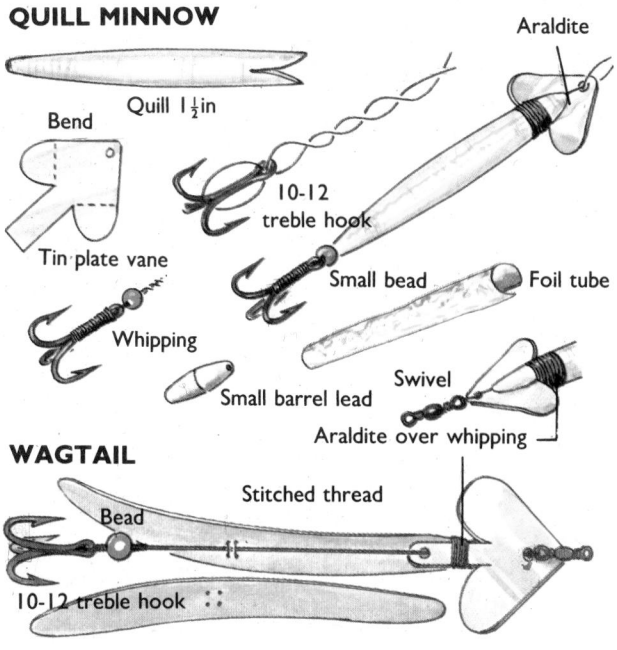

spinner blade attached at only one end to a split ring connecting two swivels. A treble hook is attached to the other end of one swivel and the reel line to the opposite end of the other swivel.

Barspoons

Barspoons are in fact more correctly classified as spinners since they have a straight axis of wire around which the blade, attached at one end, rotates with a strong vibration. Weight is added to the bar, just behind the spinning blade, and this weight can be made to look like a body and can be painted different colours. Bar spoons are among the most versatile of lures and all except the very heavy ones are retrievable even when you are fishing in very shallow-water conditions.

Heavy barspoons, however, can be cast a long way, and many can be fished very deep and slow. Making your own is easy provided you attach the blade to the bar with a separate link, rather than passing the bar through a hole in the blade. Among the most popular commercially made barspoons are Ondex, Veltic and Mepps.

A change in the blade shape has given rise to some classic lures: the Vibro has the end away from the bar pointed quite sharply, and the result is a spinner which vibrates very strongly. The kidney spoon has a

kidney-shaped blade which gives a pulsating spinning action.

Perhaps in a category of its own is the Colorado which has a spoon-shaped blade attached at both ends. It spins about a bar axis by means of spinning vanes at the head end. It is one of the oldest lures available, and in its smaller sizes can be extremely effective for perch.

Do-it-yourself enthusiasts can have a field day with spinners. Spinner blades are lighter than most spoon blades and they can be easily cut with tin snips. Even plastic blades can be used successfully. All you need are lengths of wire, round-headed long-nosed pliers to bend the wire into terminal loops, and the ability to cut various weights of metal sheet into blades that can be beaten to the required curve.

Anti-kink vanes

There is one more thing the spinning angler needs—anti-kink vanes to prevent line twist. Half moon leads which can be clamped to the reel line or trace are amongst the best. They range in size from minute to very large and for really heavy spinning they can always be used in multiples. Many more anti-kink devices are available, and it is wise to try them all, but make sure they are firmly fixed to the line or trace, otherwise you may well find that they are totally ineffective.

Can I make my own spinners?
Easily! The easiest is made from a dessert spoon. Drill a hole at each end and attach a hook to one, by means of a split ring, and a swivel to the other. Cheap, simple—but effective.

Are coloured spinners better than plain ones?
No one can answer this age old question categorically, but most fish will show a preference for certain colours under certain conditions.

How can I spin in really deep water?
Either allow a heavy spoon to hit the bottom before retrieving, or add weight to the line 2ft above the spinner.

Should any effort be made to conceal a spinner's hooks?
Many designs have red wool tied around the hook, but its effectiveness is questionable. Most likely the predator goes for the spinner either because it's hungry or provoked.

Is the size of fish caught related to the size of spinner?
Generally speaking yes. One of the exceptions I've recorded was a 6in perch which took a 3in spinner.

Do non-predatory fish ever fall to spinners?
Carp, bream and roach have all been known to take small barspoons, but probably did so more out of aggravation than a need to feed.

The water I fish is so weedy that it robs me continually of spinners. What should I do?
Try a floating plug with an adjustable diving vane. Or buy a spinner which calls itself 'weedless'.

Freshwater traces

How the traces currently in use by freshwater anglers came by their format and popularity; how and when they should be used; and how they can cut down on your number of lost fish

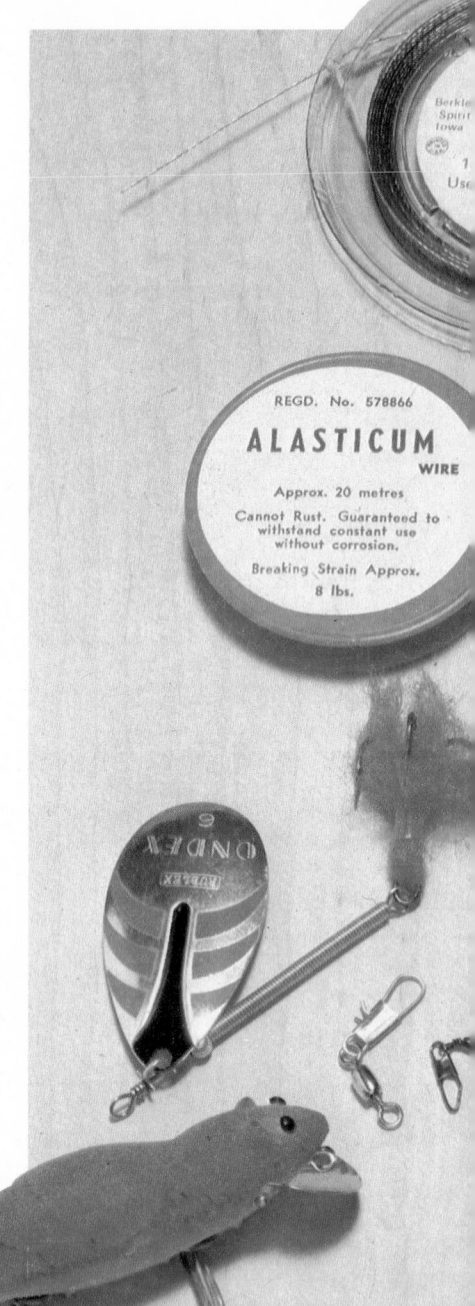

To fish for any species of fish possessed of strong jaws and sharp teeth without making use of a special trace is to ask for disaster. Nylon lines, in any of their present forms, may be strong, but they cannot resist direct chafing and cutting from an abrasive surface, especially if they have been stretched.

For many years the only solution for the angler was to use gimp, a soft fine wire which was either plaited or twisted around a silk or flax core, and sold ready mounted with swivels and hooks as traces or snap tackle. At best gimp was successful the first time it was used. After that, however, the action of water on the wire quickly caused rotting and corrosion, particularly because of the centre core's tendency to remain damp no matter how carefully the angler attempted to dry his tackle.

The first breakthrough in trace material came with the marketing of a trace wire under the trade name of Alasticum. This thin, supple, dark-coloured wire, available in several breaking strains, was rust- and corrosion-proofed and possessed the added virtue of stretching before it finally parted—a symptom that could easily be recognized.

The only drawback—the fact that it kinked, thus causing a localized weakness—was discovered some years later. This was then overcome by cabling or twisting together several strands—usually three—to form a stiffer, less fragile trace.

Ready-twisted Alasticum cable may now be purchased from tackle shops although many anglers still prefer to twist their own. It is a simple job, requiring three equal lengths of single Alasticum with the

ASSEMBLING A SPINNING TRACE

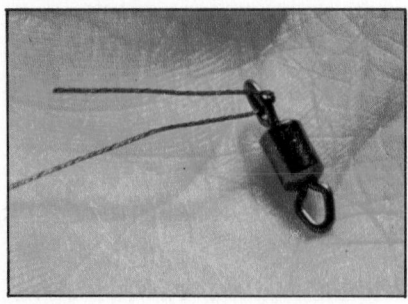

Pass the trace wire through the eye of the swivel and bend back a length of about 1in.

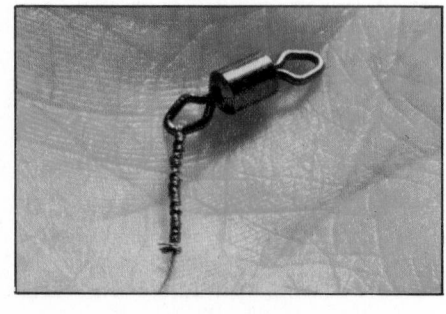

Twist the strands together until they lie in a flat cord. Cut off any loose ends, being careful not to nick the main line.

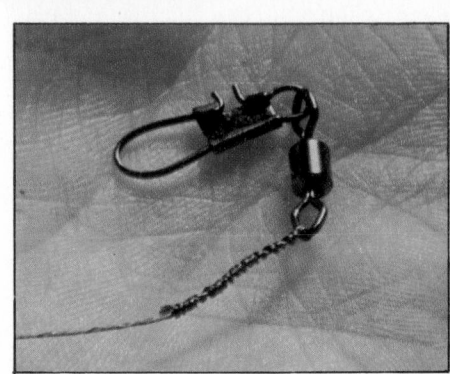

Repeat the process at the other end, using a link swivel. The 'safety pin' type are to be preferred.

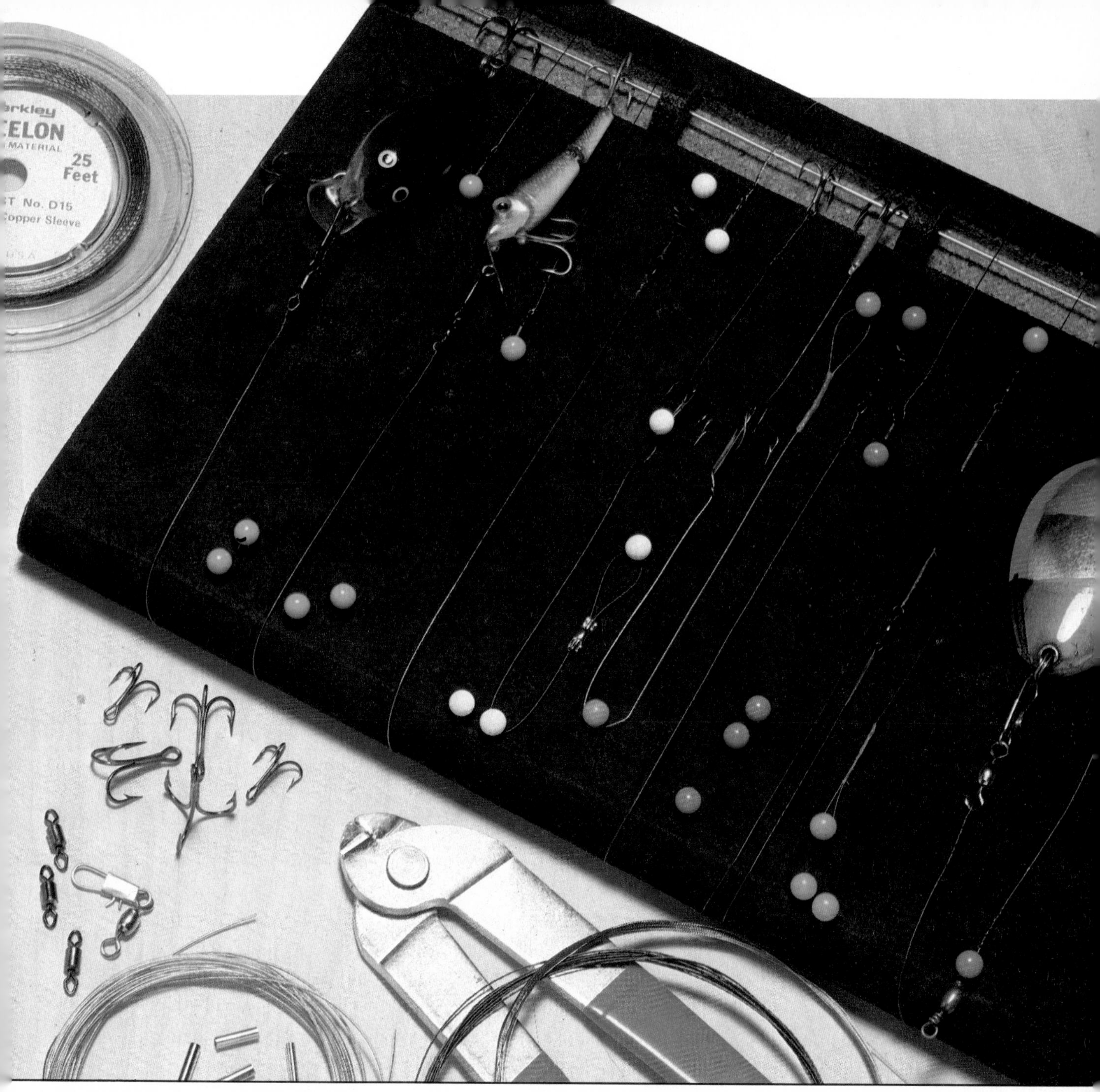

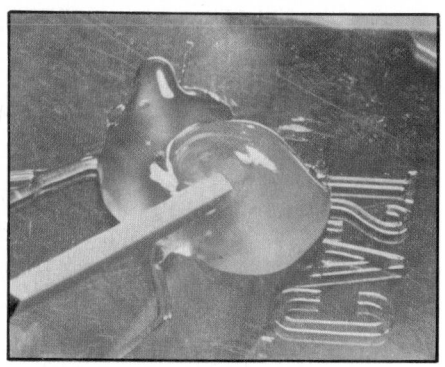

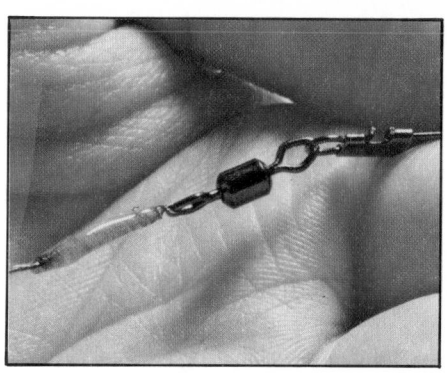

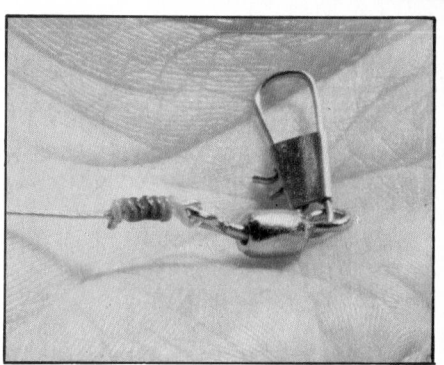

(Optional) Mix Araldite and its hardener in equal proportions, following the manufacturer's instructions, and. . .

. . . coat the twisted joints above the swivel eyes, taking care not to get glue on the actual swivel.

Using plastic coated wires, an alternative is to melt the coating so as to bond the strands.

same breaking strain. They should be held tightly at one end with a pair of artery forceps or pliers, well above the ground—over the well of a staircase is ideal—and a suitable weight attached to the other end. The weight is slowly twisted, turning the strands together, and when firmly formed the cable can be cut into suitable lengths. Take care not to overtighten during the twisting process otherwise stretching and subsequent weakening will occur.

Easy trace-making

Trace making is simplicity itself, and an amount sufficient to last the angler the best part of a season can be made at the dining table in an hour or so. An 8in-length of cabled Alasticum should be cut with a sharp pair of pliers or wire cutters, and a swivel should be threaded onto one end. The cable should be doubled back with an inch of overlap, and the overlap twisted around the main part until it lies flat. Trim off any loose pieces. To the other end a link swivel should be threaded and secured in exactly the same way. For added safety a smear of Araldite or similar glue can be rubbed along the twisted joints, taking care not to allow any to set on the swivel parts. Once dry, rub with an oiled piece of cloth before storing.

For heavy sea fishing a steel-cabled wire trace, plastic-covered to be corrosion-proof, is available in varying b.s. In sizes up to 20lb b.s., it is also suitable for freshwater fishing where extra-large baits are to be cast in very large waters—for example in Scottish lochs.

This plastic-covered wire trace is ready spooled, and necessary lengths can be cut and traces made in the same way as described for Alasticum. Allow sufficient overlap for joining swivels, hooks and other additions and after securing the ends by twisting, the plastic coating can be gently heated with a match or lighter flame to melt and bond it.

A stronger and more secure method of finishing, although a lot more visible and cumbersome in freshwater, is to use crimps or brass sleeves that can be slid onto the trace and over the ends to be secured. These are then gently

236

TRACE MAKING USING CRIMPS OR WHIPPING

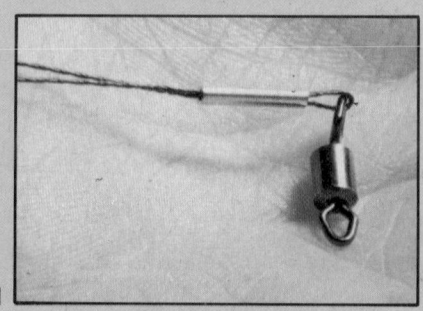

1 Slide a suitable diameter of crimp up the trace length. Pass the wire through the swivel eye and bend back as before.

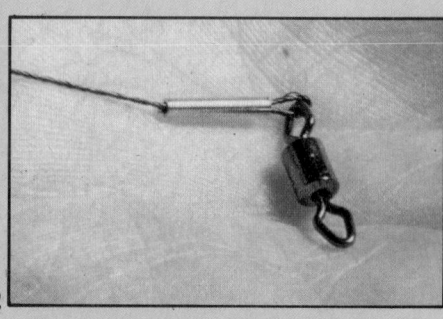

2 Slide crimp down trapping both ends. Trim loose ends as close to crimp as possible to protect your fingers as you work.

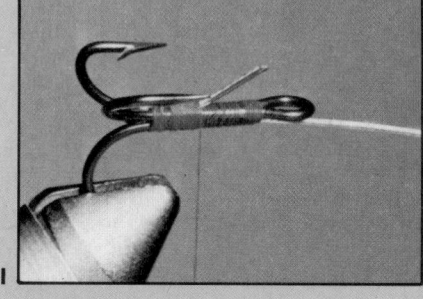

1 For deadbait traces, treble hooks are attached by whipping. It is useful if you own a fly tying vice.

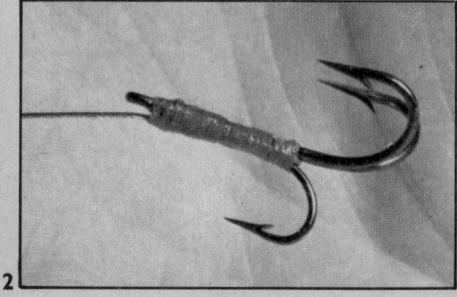

2 The special trebles used for this purpose. Apply varnish or super-glue to the whipping.

crimped with the cutting edge of a pair of pliers, or a crimping tool.

Excellent though the coating on these steel traces may be, they still wear and chip with use, especially when used for ledgering over rock and gravel beds. After use they will benefit from a wipe over with an oiled cloth, particularly at the point where swivel or hook eye are looped. Discard any suspect trace length.

Storing and carrying traces made from steel wire is difficult. There is a natural tendency for them to spring apart when wound into a coil and this can only be prevented by fixing them firmly with pins into a sheet of cork, or around a block of polystyrene. Large mapping pins make ideal mounts, and have the advantage of coloured heads, so that colour-coding can indicate various b.s. and hook and swivel sizes.

For the majority of freshwater fishing, wire traces are only necessary for four species of fish—pike, zander, catfish and eels.

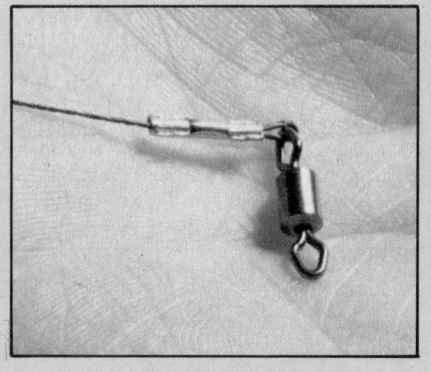

3 Using crimping pliers, make two crimps in the sleeve. You may use the cutting notch on ordinary pliers, but with care.

4 The finished article. Never attempt such jobs at the waterside, but prepare several traces in advance of fishing.

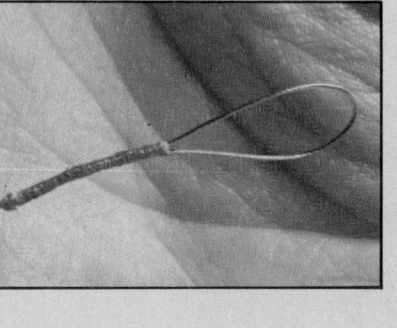

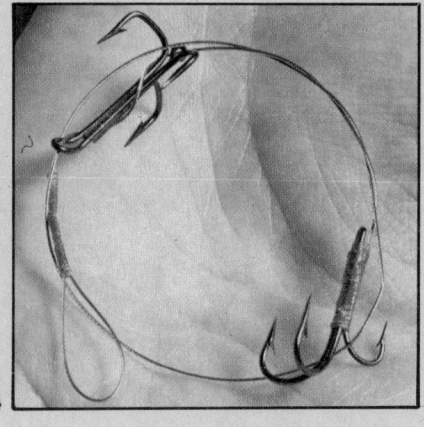

3 A loop or swivel can be added. A loop is formed by twisting, and then whipped.
4 Trace with fixed and moveable treble.

Not all anglers agree on their use for all these. Many successful specimen eel hunters prefer the suppleness of a thick trace line.

A common method of spinning for pike is to mount a light plug or spinner direct to a 6-8lb line and roam a length of water casting to a variety of swims. Nine times out of ten, fish caught in this way are lightly hooked, so that the line is never in danger of being severed by a pike's teeth. Occasionally, however, a bigger-than-average fish engulfs the spinner and becomes deep-hooked. This is highly unpleasant, so it is far better to use a light wire trace whenever spinning for pike, regardless of the kind of lure.

Under no circumstances should a deadbait be used for pike without a wire trace. No matter how soon after the take the angler strikes, it is inevitable that some fish will be deeply hooked and it is equally inevitable that some will sever the line. The result for the pike is not pleasant.

What length of wire trace would you recommend for pike or zander?
Eight inches is usually more than enough. The days of using gorge tackle for pike are thankfully gone and most fish are now hooked in the mouth, not in the throat.

Can these traces be stored in ordinary hook packets?
Better not. Alasticum wire is very springy and easily uncoils, so it would be much more advisable to store it on blocks of cork, balsa or polystyrene.

Would ordinary fuse wire make a good trace?
No. Once kinked it becomes very weak. Alasticum will never let you down if you treat it correctly. Even that can kink and when it does, discard it. Weaknesses show up at the most crucial times if you leave it to the fish to find them out.

How can I avoid kinks in my wire trace when spinning?
The use of a swivel and an anti-kink vane should be sufficient to prevent kinks in both the trace and the main line.

Won't a wire trace deter a specimen catfish from taking the bait?
The number of bites you get may be reduced with a wire trace, but on balance your overall catch-rate should improve. A big cat has formidable jaws and can make light work of a nylon trace.

Spinning flights

Whole deadbaits can be hard won or expensive to buy. It's worth mounting them in such a way as to get the most lively action while protecting your line from kinking and strain

A deadbait mounted on to a spinning flight and sensibly fished is every bit as effective and productive as a big, shiny, artificial lure. Add to efficiency versatility and cheapness —most spinning flights can be made on the kitchen table—and the arguments in favour of their use are thoroughly convincing.

Spinning flights are designed to impart a pure spinning action to the lure, not a wobble or side swoop.

This spinning action can be achieved in three ways: by vanes made from metal, or by plastic set at the head of the fish, or by mounting a series of hooks that will give a twist or kink to the body of a fish, causing it to spin as it is retrieved. The bigger the lure the slower the rate of spin will tend to be, a fact often to the angler's advantage.

Pickled fish are best

Most small fish can be used with a spinning flight, although anglers usually chose silver coloured varieties, and those with a thin, or torpedo shape. Sprats, herrings and small trout from the fishmongers can be used fresh or from the deep-freeze, as can roach, bleak and dace. But fresh or frozen fish are likely to

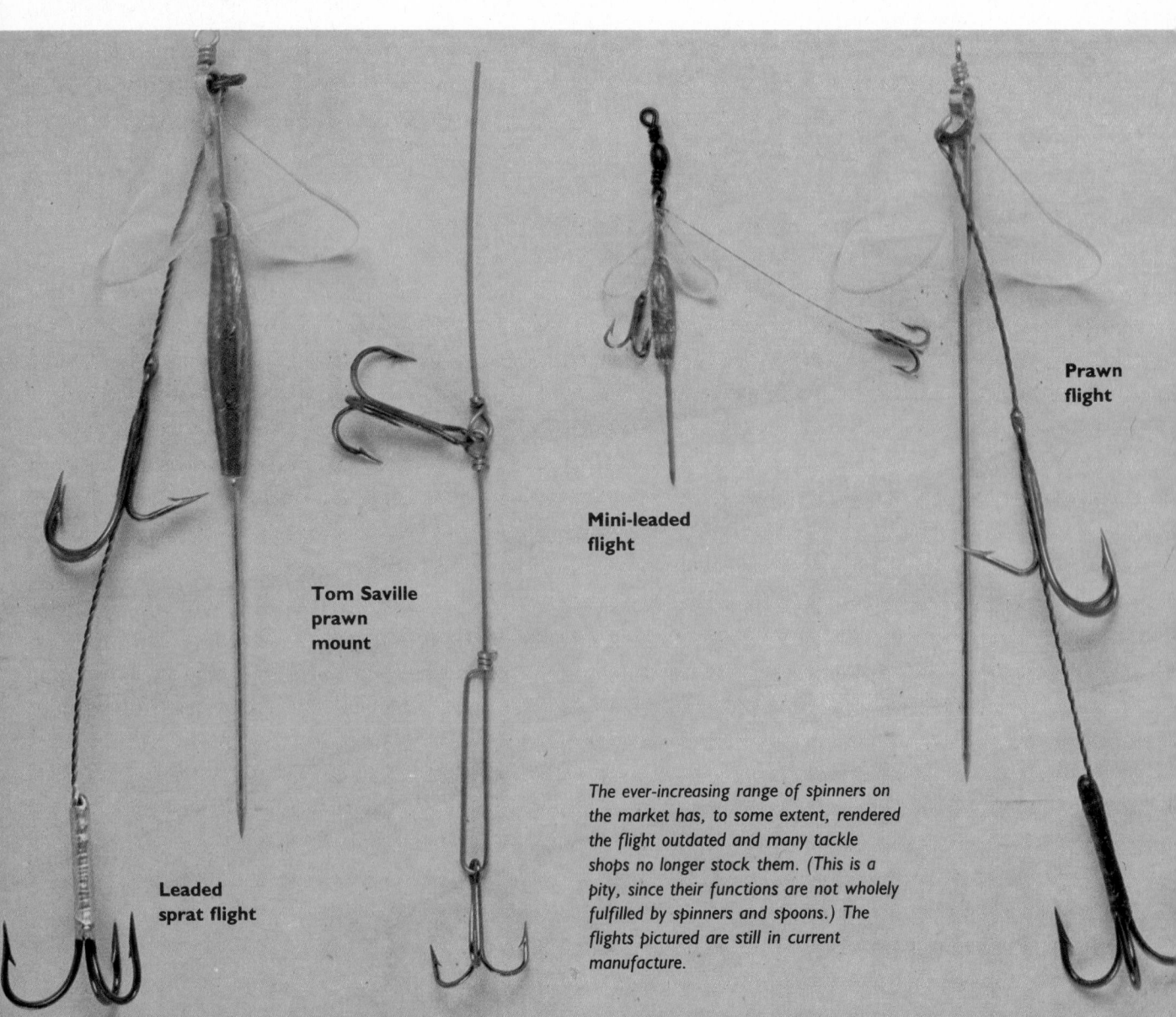

Leaded
sprat flight

Tom Saville
prawn
mount

Mini-leaded
flight

Prawn
flight

The ever-increasing range of spinners on the market has, to some extent, rendered the flight outdated and many tackle shops no longer stock them. (This is a pity, since their functions are not wholly fulfilled by spinners and spoons.) The flights pictured are still in current manufacture.

Above: *Spinning for pike with sprat—a sturdy bait which stays intact—mounted on a spinning flight.*

split and break up with repeated casting, and preserved baits which have been pickled in a formaldehyde solution are tougher and better able to withstand repeated use. Any taint can be concealed with a little pilchard oil wiped on to the mounted bait before spinning commences.

Small bleak, dace and sprats can be mounted on to a sprat flight in a matter of seconds. This flight has a metal pin with a lead weight attached, which is pushed into the mouth of the fish. When it is fully home, the head will rest into the curved vanes which provide the spinning action. The body is held in place by one flight of two treble hooks, which are pushed into the side of the fish. These hooks must be mounted flat against the body, and no attempt should be made to bend the fish in any way—it would prevent spin and produce a wobble instead. The baited flight should be attached to the line by means of a swivel.

If after constant fishing, no response has been observed, then is the time for a little bending. By repositioning the bottom treble an inch or so, the tail of the fish will bend in slightly, and when retrieved a peculiar mixture of spins and wobbles is achieved. However unnatural this may appear to the angler, a predator sees only a fish in distress, often resulting in a savage take. The

fine balance between a wobble and a spin may require a little repositioning of the hooks but based on results, it is often time well spent.

If an unweighted flight for a small fish is required, then a prawn flight, used by salmon anglers, is appropriate. The flight consists of the same arrangement of vanes and trebles as a sprat flight, but there is no lead attached to the pin.

Both the prawn and sprat flight can easily be made by the enterprising angler from sheet plastic, Alasticum and brass wire, together with the necessary trebles. Indeed, the rig can be 'scaled-up' to suit small roach and herrings. Nevertheless, the prices charged in a tackle shop are not high.

A better rig for larger fish is the Archer flight. At the top of the body pin are two hinged metal vanes that open outwards and clamp back into place once the head of the bait is in position, holding it firmly and providing extra protection against the flesh breaking up during a cast. Two flights of hooks are provided: one flight with two hooks is mounted into the body, the other, designed to lie on the opposite side of the fish, either hanging freely ('a flying tre-

Landing nets

To the basic angling essentials—rod, reel, line and hook—add one other: the landing net. This piece of equipment is vital if you wish to take fish consistently

Watching the expert match angler swinging small fish directly to his hand, a beginner might be misled into thinking all fish can be landed like this. A quick glance at the bankside equipment, however, should dispel the thought at once. There will certainly be a landing net made up, in position, and ready to hand. When the match man merely *feels* a fish of better proportions he gently subdues it, and reaching at once for the landing net, gets the fish ashore.

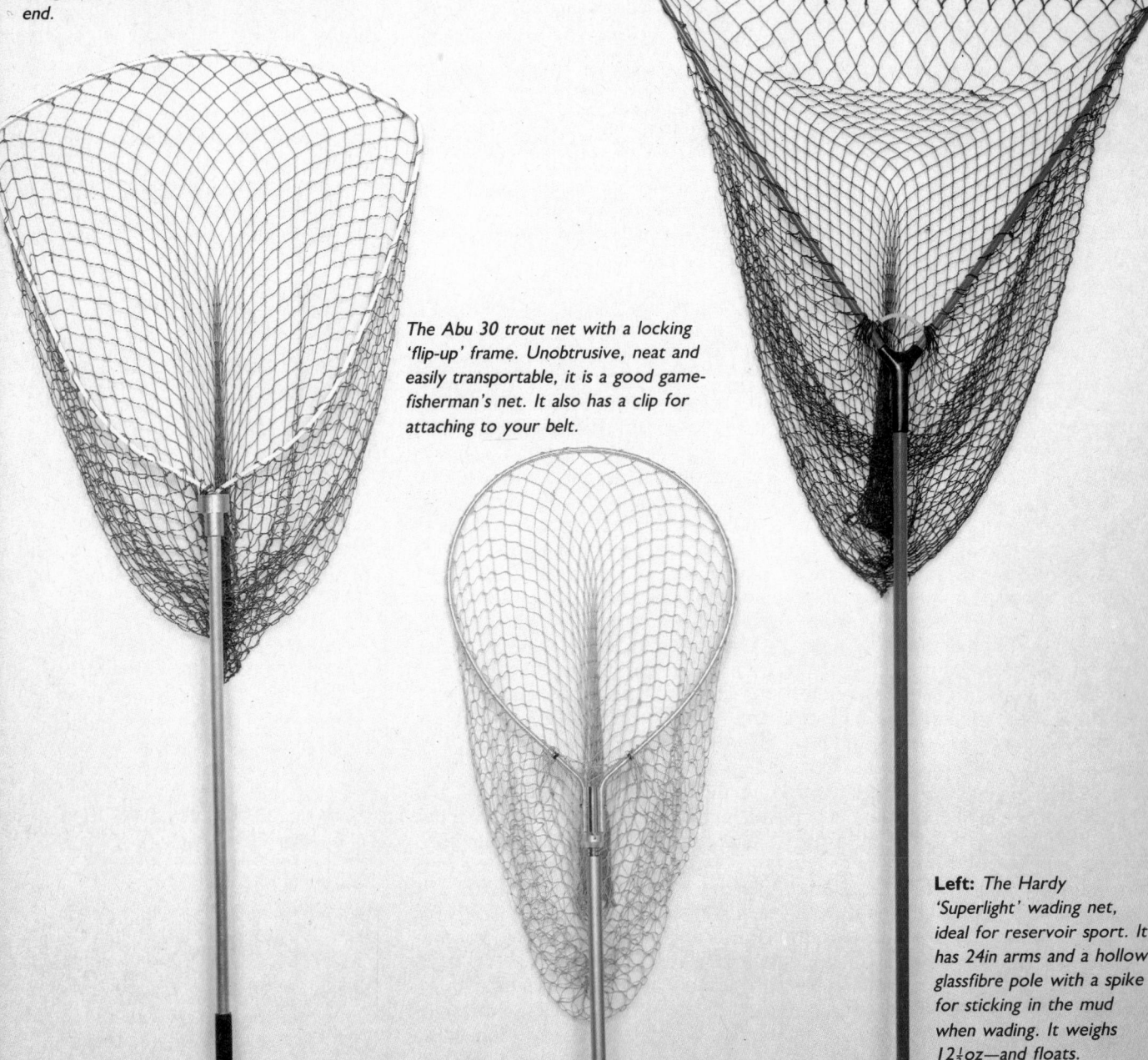

Below: *The 'Albatross' net by Wilco Sports. This landing net has a rigid, non-collapsible bow-shaped frame which slides along the pole and locks into place at the end.*

The Abu 30 trout net with a locking 'flip-up' frame. Unobtrusive, neat and easily transportable, it is a good game-fisherman's net. It also has a clip for attaching to your belt.

Left: *The Hardy 'Superlight' wading net, ideal for reservoir sport. It has 24in arms and a hollow glassfibre pole with a spike for sticking in the mud when wading. It weighs 12½oz—and floats.*

He does this because he knows that the fine lines (of about 1lb b.s.) necessary to take the shy fish he seeks are capable of dealing with fish up to several pounds when gently played, and *while in the water*. To attempt to lift them bodily places the dead weight directly on the fine line, and if this doesn't break at once, there is every chance of a light hook hold giving way.

Even with sea and game angling the same principle holds good too. Most competent anglers can subdue fish up to 20lb or so on lines of half that b.s. so long as they are submerged. To lift them clear, the use of a net is essential.

The beginner, already spending large sums on the basic rod and reel, and attracted by a host of highly coloured floats and gadgets (which catch more anglers than fish) may be tempted to do without a landing net. But floats can be home-made for next to nothing and it would be wise to save money on floats and to buy a landing net, which is as essential as the rod, reel, line and hook.

A landing net comprises a bag-like net; a triangular or circular metal frame, which can be folded for easy storage and transport; and a 4ft

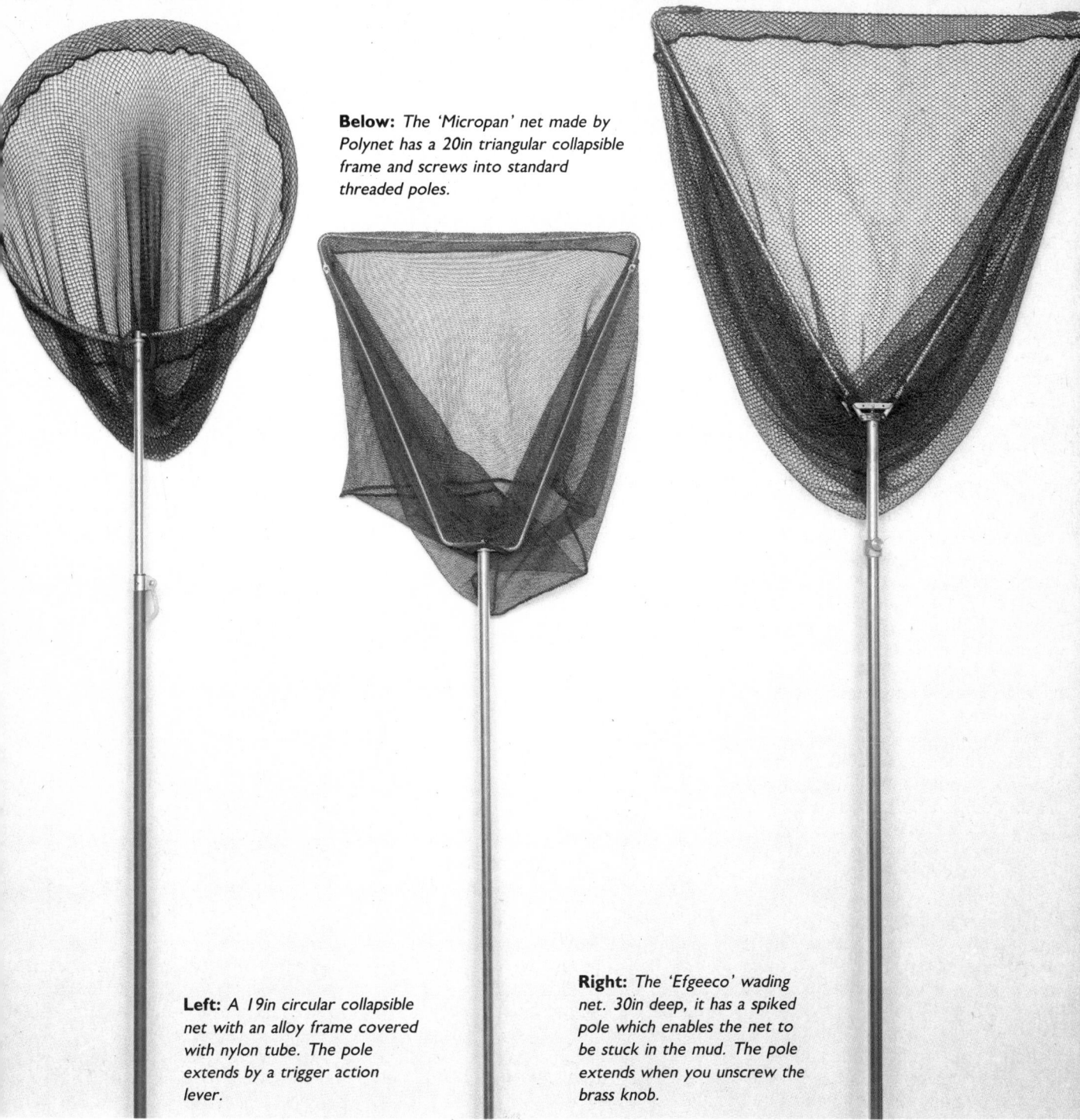

Below: *The 'Micropan' net made by Polynet has a 20in triangular collapsible frame and screws into standard threaded poles.*

Left: *A 19in circular collapsible net with an alloy frame covered with nylon tube. The pole extends by a trigger action lever.*

Right: *The 'Efgeeco' wading net. 30in deep, it has a spiked pole which enables the net to be stuck in the mud. The pole extends when you unscrew the brass knob.*

241

handle with a screw thread at one end for attaching frame and net.

The net and frame can usually be purchased for the price of a few days' bait, and for both a minimum width of 18in is strongly recommended. A 1in diameter cane or even a broom-handle can be fitted with a brass screw fitting at one end to provide a serviceable handle at little cost. Such a net will see the novice through several years of his apprenticeship in the art of fishing. It will cope with roach, rudd, dace, bream and tench, as well as the odd jack pike. When the angler is prepared to spend more, he can graduate to refinements which suit the kind of fishing in which he specializes.

The extending handle
One valuable refinement is an extending handle which is very useful when fishing from banks several feet above the water's surface, or when fishing over extensive reed fringes. These handles are usually telescopic and can be obtained in metal or glassfibre. They should be matt-painted in dark green to prevent glare, and it is essential to test the locking device to ensure that the handle will not close or extend except when needed. More important still, check that the two halves cannot separate during use. A treaded rubber or plastic non-slip sleeve grip is a useful addition. Some anglers also like to have a spear fitted on the end of the handle to allow the net to be stuck firmly upright in the bank, or used as a staff when wading in shallow water.

It is helpful to fit the landing net handle with a cord sling which enables it to be carried hitched over the shoulder. This leaves both hands free when, for example, moving pitches during a roving match, and leaves the angler uncluttered.

Collapsible folding nets
Collapsible folding nets are useful, all-purpose tools. They are usually based on a triangular shape with two metal arms set at an angle. The open end of the triangle consists of a strong cord. When folded back for carrying or storage, the frame arms lie snugly along the net handle, and a flick of the wrist splays them out,

242

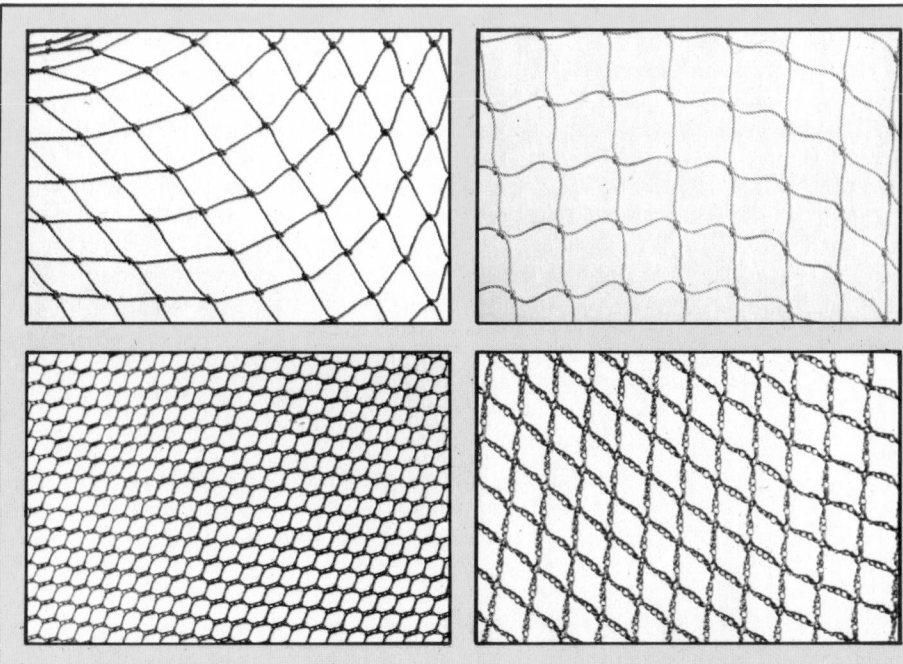

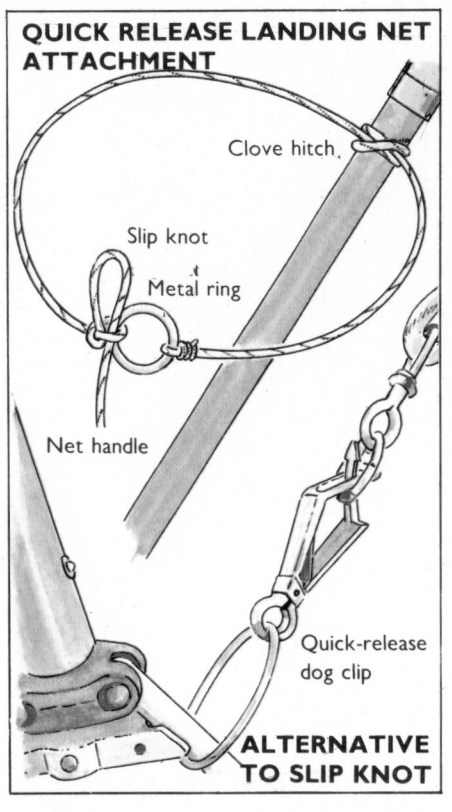

QUICK RELEASE LANDING NET ATTACHMENT

Clove hitch
Slip knot
Metal ring
Net handle
Quick-release dog clip
ALTERNATIVE TO SLIP KNOT

opening the net for use. In conjunction with a spring-operated telescopic handle, this kind of net offers versatility, especially to the trout angler, who clips the net to his belt when wading. A rugged clip is necessary, however, because it is all too easy to lose such a net when scrambling through foliage or among tall reed margins. A positive locking device, easily released with a spring-operated catch, is ideal, but regrettably, few manufactured nets incorporate such a device.

Specimen hunters, especially when seeking carp, need much larger nets than those so far described. Now that big trout are becoming

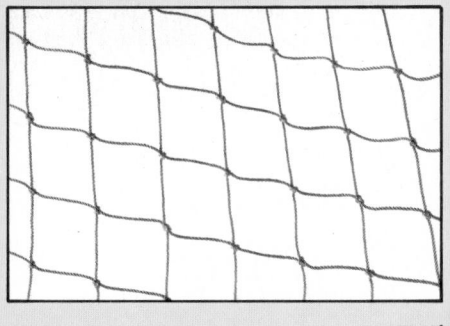

Left: *An assortment of the kinds of net meshes you will find on the market today. Wide-meshed netting is out of favour at the moment for a number of reasons: it allows small fish to slip through, and fish are often caught by their gills when they are being removed from the net. Barbel in particular suffer: they have a large serrated first spine on the dorsal fin and this tangles with wide-mesh netting. Clearing this can take time and damage the dorsal fin. Knotless mesh is much preferred by conservationists because it causes less damage to the scales, skin and slime layers of the fish, and if they have been handled carefully, they can be returned to the water none the worse for their experience.*

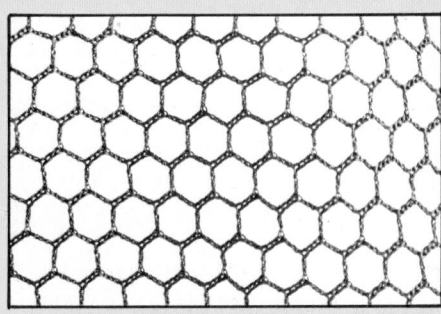

ASK THE EXPERT

What can I do if I forget to bring a landing net?
Where there are no obliging anglers around who will net your fish for you, look for a lightly sloping bank or beach. Work hooked fish towards it and beach them: make sure the fish is thoroughly beaten, then bring its head up and draw it quickly across the surface in one movement of the rod so that the momentum strands it on the bank. Then pounce.

Is a net vital for boat fishing?
Unless you are sea fishing or salmon fishing, where a gaff or tailer is used, a net is even more necessary than on shore. You cannot beach your fish when you are afloat, and if you lean over the side you may capsize.

What net is best for trout fishing?
Many trout fisherman buy one with a 4ft handle and a spike on the end. When wading they can then stick the spike in the bottom so that the net stands within reach. Some anglers like a net which clips on over the shoulder while others prefer a collapsible net with telescopic handle which clips to a belt until needed. For all purposes, the mouth of the net should be big and the handle made of light glassfibre or plastic that floats if dropped.

I often fish with one dropper fly and one tail fly. If I were to take trout on both, how could I net them?
Fortunately the two hooked fish tend to fight each other, often to exhaustion, in which case it's fairly easy to net the *dropper* fish first, then hand line the tail fish towards you and net this too. If you are with someone, it may be quicker for your companion to net the second fish.

Far left: *A loop-knot and clove-hitch can be used to attach one's landing net to a belt. Another quick-release method is to use a dog-clip. Portability and ease of access are essential here.*
Left: *Bill Chillingworth with a large pike in his capacious landing net.*
Above: *A bream being drawn properly into the waiting, submerged net.*

more and more easily available, the trout angler too must give thought to the size of his net. The days when pike were automatically gaffed and killed have fortunately gone, and the keen pike angler nowadays carries a net suitable for landing the big ones in order to return them alive.

The pioneers of 30 years ago had

no alternative but to make up their own monster landing nets. Bicycle wheels, barrel hoops, bamboo hoops and even window frames were pressed into service to make nets big enough for large carp. The modern specimen hunter has several manufactured alternatives at his disposal. Most are constructed on the triangular principle of the collapsible net.

For the specimen hunter, a 3ft-wide net frame with 4ft-deep net is not too large. This angler must remember to drag the net ashore rather than lift it, since a fish of 30lb or so would exert a tremendous leverage at the end of a 4ft handle. Any attempt to lift a fish without

Forceps and disgorgers

If you like to picture yourself as a humane fisherman, you must carry the equipment to unhook catches quickly, cleanly and with a good chance of returning fish to the water unharmed

Of the many tackle items that the angler will invest in, disgorgers, gags, forceps and pliers will be the cheapest, most essential, and generally the most easily mislaid. These simple pieces of equipment enable him to remove a deeply embedded hook and are vital to fish life and fisherman alike. They are important time savers too. There is a bewildering array on sale.

Despite their usefulness, the angler should be aware that, in many situations, these tools only become necessary because of bad fishing techniques and that deep-hooking can often be avoided.

Of course there are times when a fish bolts the bait with such speed that throat or cheek hooking is unavoidable, but many such cases could be avoided if proper attention were paid to the rod, with the angler close at hand and not several yards

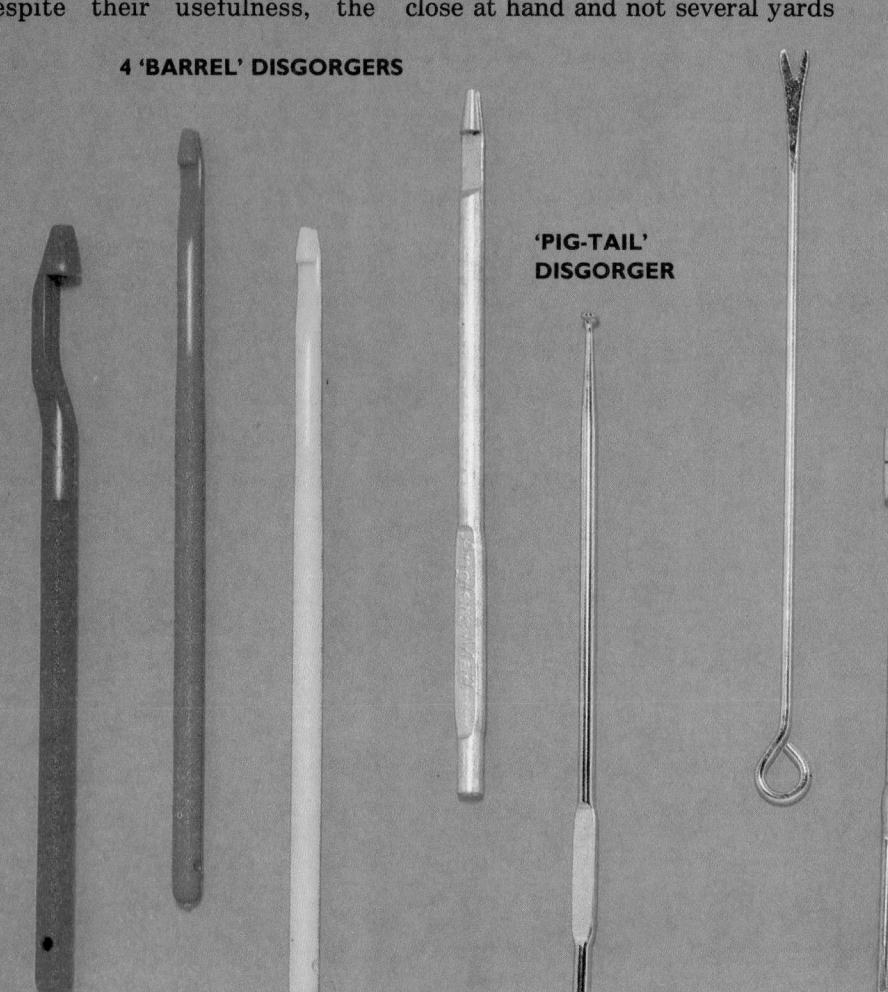

4 'BARREL' DISGORGERS

'PIG-TAIL' DISGORGER

4 'FORK' DISGORGERS

244

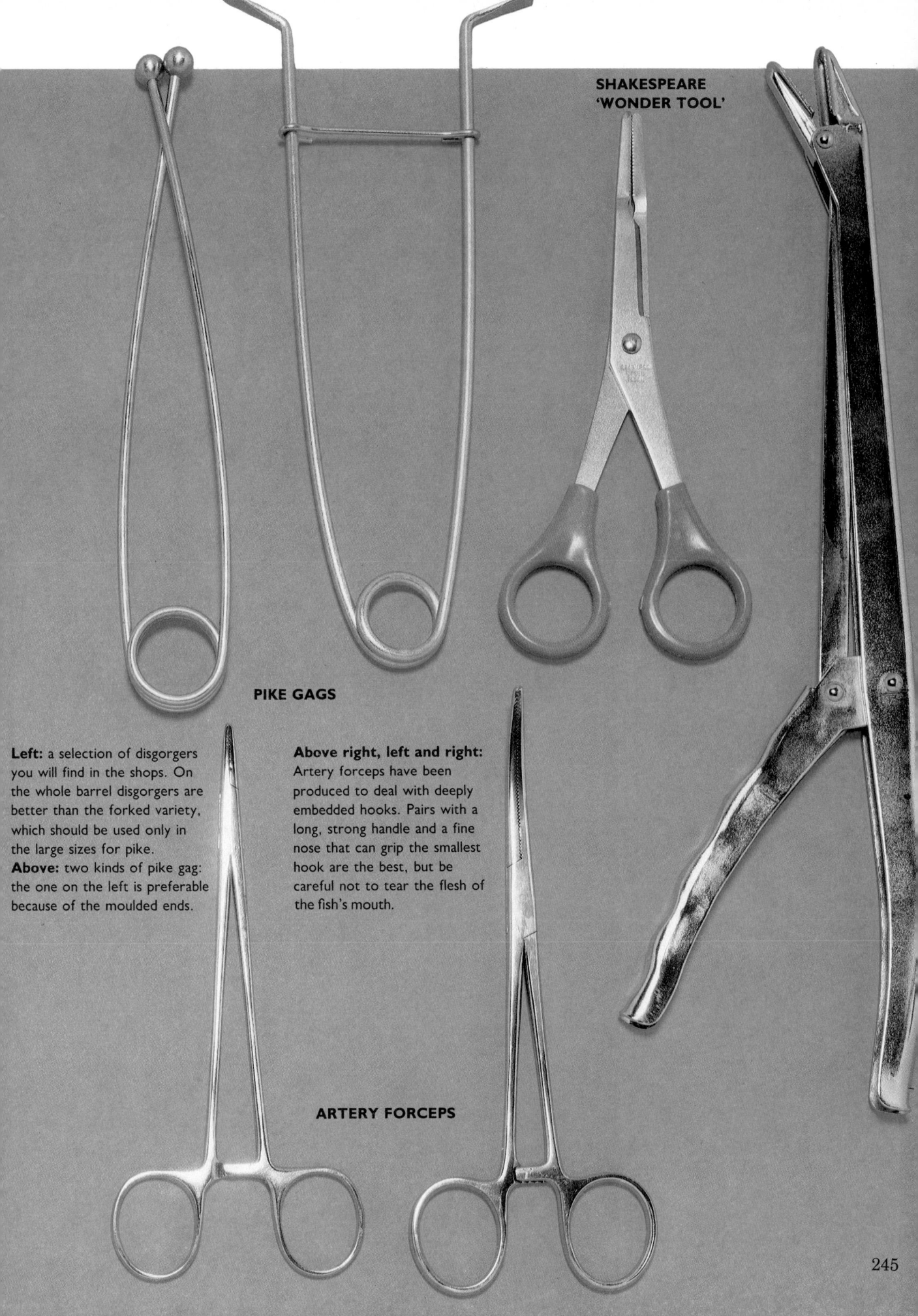

SHAKESPEARE 'WONDER TOOL'

PIKE GAGS

Left: a selection of disgorgers you will find in the shops. On the whole barrel disgorgers are better than the forked variety, which should be used only in the large sizes for pike.
Above: two kinds of pike gag: the one on the left is preferable because of the moulded ends.

Above right, left and right: Artery forceps have been produced to deal with deeply embedded hooks. Pairs with a long, strong handle and a fine nose that can grip the smallest hook are the best, but be careful not to tear the flesh of the fish's mouth.

ARTERY FORCEPS

245

away from it. A small hook is another cause of deephooking.

A rank barb—one that protrudes too far from the body of the hook—can cause further disgorging problems, and each hook that is tied to the line should be inspected and a few strokes of a file or sharpening stone used to remove excess metal. Badly tempered or soft hooks that straighten under pressure can also present difficulties: a few seconds should be spent in examining hooks. Reject any that distort when flexed against the thumb nail.

It is in the realm of pike fishing where most unnecessary disgorging is seen. Reasons for it include bad timing of the strike ('give him a few seconds more to make sure he has really taken it'), and the use of fancy dead-bait rigs that are reminiscent of gorge tackle.

If all these precautions have been observed and the angler is still presented with a deeply hooked fish, quick action with the correct unhooking aid will prevent a death.

Disgorgers

Many anglers wrongly believe that one type of disgorger will release a hook from any fish. At least two types will be required depending on where the hook has lodged and on the type of hook being used. Where the hook is deep inside the mouth, but still visible, then the straight-forward flattened 'V'-shaped disgorger, with a long handle, may be used to ease the barb back through the skin. Where the hook is deep and cannot be seen, a disgorger with some sort of loop or ring will be necessary. This can be slid down the line to the bend of the hook.

Several of the ring and guide types are available, but most fail in practice either because they do not slip easily onto the line, or more generally because they jam at the eye or spade of the hook. Only one type will slide onto the line and ride easily onto the bend of the hook, and that is the simplest design of them all—the open wire loop or 'pigtail'.

Simply sliding the disgorger down the line and blindly stabbing with it will, in many instances, push the barb further into the flesh. The easiest method—and the safest for

the fish—is to support the creature with one hand gently but firmly behind the gills. If it is too large, lay it along the bank with the head raised against a tackle box or rod handle. Hold taut the line leading into the mouth, put the disgorger onto the line, slide it down and ease it over the eye or spade of the hook and onto the bend. Press directly downwards until the hook moves freely and withdraw from the mouth—still supported in the disgorger—taking special care not to catch it against the tongue.

The disgorger is ridiculously easy to lose, but there are two things you can do to reduce the number that you mislay. One is to tie the handle by a piece of thin, strong line to your jacket lapel or through a buttonhole. The other is to paint the whole object either bright red or yellow, preferably with luminous paint. This also makes the business end easier to see inside a fishes mouth.

A lost disgorger can be replaced, in an emergency, by a small, forked twig or a twig into which a groove has been cut or filed.

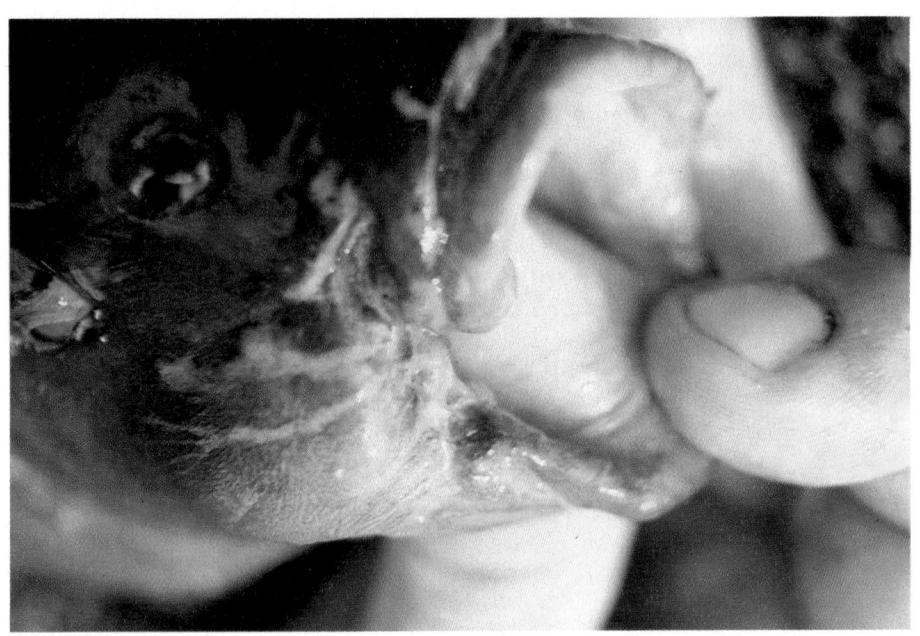

ASK THE EXPERT

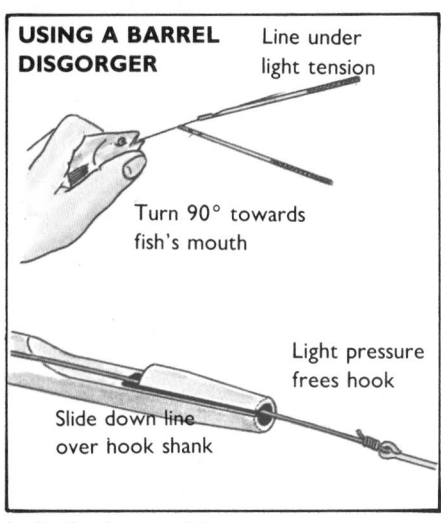

USING A BARREL DISGORGER

Line under light tension

Turn 90° towards fish's mouth

Light pressure frees hook

Slide down line over hook shank

Left: *Careful use of forceps.*
Top: *This is what results from not having the right tools to hand. This tench's mouth has been mangled by cack-handed unhooking.*
Above: *A barrel disgorger runs down the line to dislodge an eyed or spade-end shank hook.*

Forceps

Within the last few years, medical artery forceps have become popular as a means of releasing a deeply-embedded hook, and several firms have produced them specifically for the angler. They are useful, but like most pieces of equipment, they have their limitations.

Some fish have a relatively small mouth opening even though the actual mouth cavity is quite large. The width of a pair of forceps, particularly when they are open, can block the view of the mouth, and if they are opened widely, can cause actual damage. It is all too easy to grasp a portion of flesh, together with the hook, and tear it in the process of unhooking. For fish with bony or leathery mouths, therefore, artery forceps are an efficient means of freeing most hooks. Even so, the very large treble hooks used, for example in pike fishing, need a lot of leverage, and forceps are not always adequate. Choose a pair with strong, long handles and a fine nose that can grip very small hooks.

Pliers are infinitely better for removing treble hooks than either forceps or disgorgers—even the king-sized, foot-long models sold as 'pike disgorgers'. Obviously, those with a long and narrow nose are best, and stainless metal preferable to cheap tools that rust. There is at least one pair on the market that are especially designed for this heavy work on large and 'toothy' fish.

Like disgorgers, forceps are best tied to the jacket with a length of line and not clipped on to a lapel.

Gags

These are usually thought of as pike disgorging aids, and there is no doubt that they beome essential where large pike have been deeply hooked. But their use is not appropriate with small fish. In fact, considerable damage can be caused to both mouth and tongue where gags are forced in.

Is there any way of preventing fish swallowing my bait?
You will never prevent it entirely, but striking sooner reduces the incidence of deeply hooked fish.

Wouldn't a larger hook stop them taking it down too far?
Of course it would, but it would almost certainly reduce the number of bites you get as well.

Are barbless hooks easier or more difficult to remove with a disgorger?
Unquestionably they are easier to remove and are therefore the least damaging, most humane, hook of all. Fish are returned after one small, quick operation, no worse for having been caught.

I'm forever dropping my disgorger in the river. Are floating ones sold?
There is a floating one on the market, but I find a small pike bung slid over the barrel of the disgorger prevents it sinking.

So which is the best, all-round disgorger to buy?
For normal coarse fishing, the 'pigtail' disgorger is functional. The specimen hunter or pike enthusiast will probably go for forceps. Peter Drennan has recently brought out an excellent plastic disgorger which compared with the aluminium ones does reduce damage to fish.

Why do matchmen swear by long-shanked hooks?
Long-shanks do reduce the need for a disgorger and are therefore a godsend to match anglers. A fish may be quite deeply hooked and yet the hook can be removed easily with the hands.

Keepnets

Before the introduction of keepnets matchmen would fling their catch on the bank to be collected at the end of the match. Today, keepnets provide a humane alternative

Most modern coarse-species anglers use keepnets whether for specimen hunting, pleasure angling, or competition fishing. The match-man obviously needs to weigh in his catch at the end of the match to establish who wins the prize. The keepnet enables him to do so without killing the fish. Pleasure anglers once used to return fish as soon as they were unhooked. Nowadays we often carry a camera and record the catch in photographs. The keepnet enables us to do this with no damage to the fish. Specimen hunters often keep a very detailed log of their catches, recording weight, girth and length and other details. They too find the keepnet a valuable accessory.

The important thing about these differing groups of anglers is that they all return their catch alive as soon as possible. All are strongly conservation minded, not only carrying out the law with regard to immature fish, but returning also the big ones which, a couple of decades ago, would probably have finished up in glass cases.

Introduction of the keepnet

The match fisherman was responsible for the introduction of the keepnet. Before its arrival, every fish caught during a contest was thrown on the bank to be collected and weighed when fishing ceased. The drain on the fish population, even in the best-stocked waters, eventually led to the use of a net to keep fish alive for the duration of the match. Although those early nets were small and made from heavy twine, they were of vital importance.

Today's nets are available in a vast choice of sizes. Naturally, the bigger the net, the less risk of damage to fish through overcrowding. Although most anglers favour a round net, there is a distinct advantage in using a rectangular one when shallow waters are fished. These models will allow a greater area to remain submerged, thus providing more water space for their inhabitants.

In many areas Water Authorities now specify the minimum size of keepnets to be used in their waters. Where the Water Authorities fail to do so, most of the larger and forward-thinking clubs themselves specify minimum keepnet sizes to be used by their members. Some clubs go even further and specify how many fish of each species may be kept in the net. A dozen roach in a net 6ft long with 18in hoops would seem to be in no danger, but a dozen bream, or even carp or pike, would suffer. Bream are especially vulnerable to overcrowding as their narrow body cross-section causes those at the bottom of the net to be forced on their sides and crushed if they are overcrowded. They are also the most sought-after quarry of the competition fisherman.

Vulnerable species

Barbel and carp are also vulnerable to keepnets because both species bear large serrated-edged spines on the dorsal and anal fins, and these often tend to tangle in the mesh during movement, resulting in considerable damage if the fish struggle to free themselves.

The organized match-angling world is also very concerned with this problem. To prevent overcrowding in certain well-organized matches the stewards are required to patrol the bank at regular inter-

GUDGEON MESH (same size)

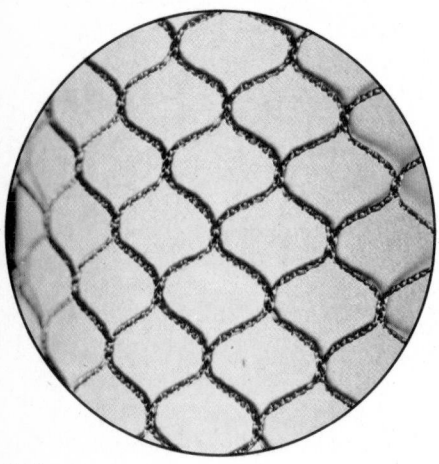

MINNOW MESH (same size)

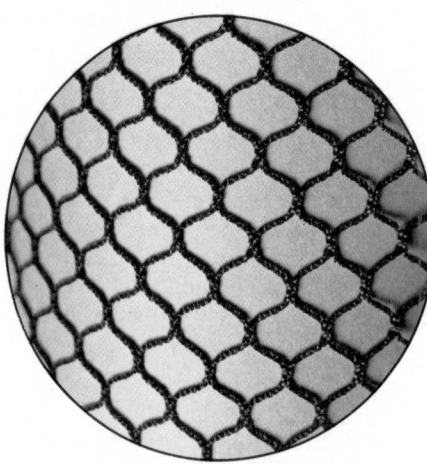

Today keepnets are made with a variety of mesh sizes. Pictured are three kinds of mesh manufactured by Steadefast. From left to right: gudgeon mesh, minnow mesh and micromesh. Steadefast also produce a superfine mesh. Their keepnets range from 5ft-12ft long, and have differing widths.

MICROMESH (same size)

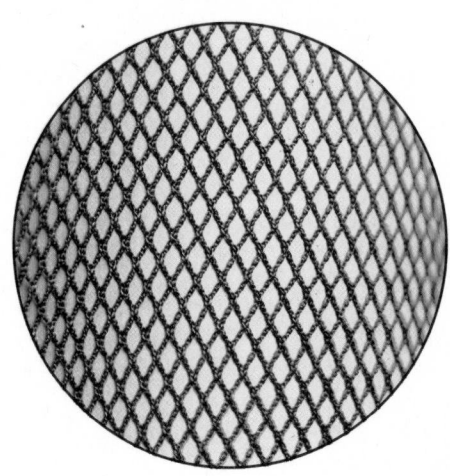

vals to individually weigh the big fish and record the contents. When you consider that a match champion may take several pounds of fish in the course of the match, it requires little imagination to appreciate the suffering to fish which could arise in a single match.

Keepnets vary a great deal according to their specific function. The match angler's net is likely to be about 8 or 10ft long, with hoops of at least 15 or 18in. His specimen-hunting counterpart will probably use a far larger net which may be anything up to 12ft long with hoops up to 3ft in diameter to accommodate larger fish.

Spacing rings

Spacing rings, to provide support and strengthen the net, are manufactured either from galvanized wire or plastic. Wire rings are joined by brass ferrules that have an annoying habit of pulling apart. They can be glued with Araldite or soldered, but will always be suspect. Plastic rings rarely break and being soft reduce the chance of damage to fish. But being pliable they tend to become oval-shaped and thus crowd fish together. They are also lighter than wire, which may cause smaller nets to roll in a strong current, but adding a stone in the base of the net will hold it down.

However big the net, it cannot do its job if it is badly placed in the water. If the net is not properly extended, 10ft of netting is of little value, and hoops of 2ft diameter are useless in 18in of water. They are usually attached by a screw fitting to a bank stick conveniently placed to allow the angler easy access to the open end. They can also be prevented from collapsing with the aid of mesh-spreaders which attach to the rings and hold them apart.

The ring at the neck, into which the bankstick is mounted, is important. Many models have a very small ring, which makes it more difficult to slide a fish into the bag of the net. Choose the net with the biggest plastic-coated ring possible, so that if a fish is dropped against it there will be less risk of injury. Some rings have a dent or curve so that a rod can be rested across the net

while the angler unhooks a fish—an advantage if the net is firmly fixed in the river bed.

Nylon netting has long been available in several mesh sizes, from 'minnow' upwards, and if machined in a tubular run will be free of knots. This means that the only stitching should be at the base and neck rings—both weak areas that must be examined even in a new net. A recent introduction and improvement on the nylon mesh is micromesh, a soft nylon material with extremely small holes that is reported to cause little or no damage to fish. A few clubs and authorities are already insisting on its use in an effort to reduce the incidence of disease. Micromesh is expensive, but has a long life and dries quickly.

Maintenance

Regular maintenance is needed if a keepnet is to remain efficient. Although mesh may be advertized as 'rot-proof' it is still liable to strain, especially if a large weight of fish is lifted awkwardly. Check the

Above: *A huge keepnet was needed for this haul—over 100lb of roach! Impressive though the catch may be, it must harm the fish.* **Below:** *You may have to use an extending landing-net handle to push the keepnet to its full extension.*

ASK THE EXPERT

Won't pike eat their way out of a keepnet?

You're more likely to find them trying to eat their way in, in pursuit of its occupants. Many a pike has been lifted from the water with its teeth entangled in the mesh of a keepnet.

Even if the mesh doesn't remove scales, can't it damage fish by removing their protective slime?

It can if you lift fish out from the water and allow them to flap around inside. Unless you are photographing, try to return them without doing so.

What's the point of using a keepnet if I'm not going to lift it clear of the water?

The main purpose is to prevent captured fish rejoining the shoal and 'spooking' them—in much the same way as a lost fish can do.

Sometimes a fish or two dies in the net, How can I prevent this?

The main reason for mortalities in a keepnet is deep-hooking. A good rule is to return any fish to the water if you have had to use a disgorger.

On canals I find that the wash of passing boats makes my net fold over.

At the bottom of the net you will find a ring. Peg this into the banking so that several rings are submerged. Then your net will remain firmly in place.

What are the chief points to look for in buying a net?

A good net has a large opening ring, well spaced plastic rings throughout, and is a generous length. If you are going to fish small-fish waters such as canals, choose a minnow- or micro-mesh netting.

base of the net for signs of fraying, and replace it at once if need be.

Fish slime, allowed to accumulate with repeated use, can work its way into the mesh, stiffening the net to such an extent that it will have the effect of glass paper on fish scales. Washing the keepnet in clean cold water and thoroughly drying it after each outing will prevent this and leave the net more wholesome to handle in the future.

Remember that fish naturally face the current, so the net should lie parallel to the bank, the mouth facing upstream. Provided the net is long enough, there should be no difficulty in arranging this. The mouth should lie close to the angler.

Most damage to keepnets occurs when they are lifted with their contents at the end of the day. Grabb-

ing the neck ring and pulling will eventually split open the bottom. The correct method is to retrieve the net hand over hand by the spacing rings, and then lift it, holding the bottom and the gathered rings in separate hands. Better quality nets have a small ring attached at the base with which to hold and lift.

Once onto the bank, avoid tipping the net on its side and shaking the fish free. This will dash them against the mesh, removing scales and ripping fins. Instead, collapse the net so that hands can be inserted, and lift out fish individually. After weighing or photographing, they should be returned to the water immediately, not re-netted—a practice that can cause further abrasions if the fish are tipped back using the net as a shute.

Place, not drop, fish in the keepnet

Swivels

While a twisted line cannot be completely eradicated by a swivel—even when used in conjunction with an anti-kink weight or vane—it may save you the catch of a lifetime

One of the most useful, but most neglected accessories for the angler is the swivel. It is primarily used to prevent fishing line from becoming twisted, and whether the angler employs any of the various forms of spinning, or merely retrieves a dead-bait, the turning action of the bait spiralling through the water will be transferred to the line. If monofilament is allowed to twist, it begins to kink, and at best becomes a tangled mess—at worst the line weakens so badly that it will most likely break at the first strain.

The only preventative is the use of one or more efficient swivels mounted between the line and lure, working in conjunction with an anti-kink weight or vane. Such devices are attached to the reel line by means of a bloodknot or grinner knot. But efficiency is difficult to achieve in a swivel. Early traces had

two, three or more swivels, operating on the principle that the more that were added, the better the chance of at least one working. Those early mechanisms were in the form of an open, oblong box with eyes mounted through each end. A little corrosion or rust plus an accumulation of grit and mud quickly impaired their efficiency.

Different types of swivel

Today, the angler has the choice of several types of swivel, all working on the same basic principle but with varying refinements. The plain barrel swivel is the most popular and probably the tackle dealer's best seller especially since many anglers simply ask for 'a swivel' and leave the choice to the assistant. Its construction is simple, with two eyes (through which trace and line are mounted) allowed to revolve in-

dependently on their separate beads of metal carefully shaped to fit the inside of the barrel. The free rotation of the eyes depends on tolerances left when the thin metal is compressed during machining; nine times out of ten, the tolerances are adequate and the swivel revolves freely. The tenth case is where trouble sets in, and before leaving the shop it is worth checking each swivel that is purchased, and again before fishing.

An improvement on the plain barrel is the American Berkley swivel. It differs only in that a good grade of metal is used and the eyes are flattened slghtly at the terminal ends to ensure that trace and line stay in place, free from a natural tendency to pull to either side when an unequal strain is applied. An improvement in efficiency which costs little more, is the Hardy ball-bearing swivel. Again, there is the barrel type of construction but with exacting tolerances and incorporating small ball-races that ensure that the eyed pieces revolve freely.

One swivel remains in this category—the Diamond swivel, in which the loops are not round but diamond-shaped and are fastened by means of an expanded link. Usually manufactured from fine steel, they appear rather flimsy, but in fact are

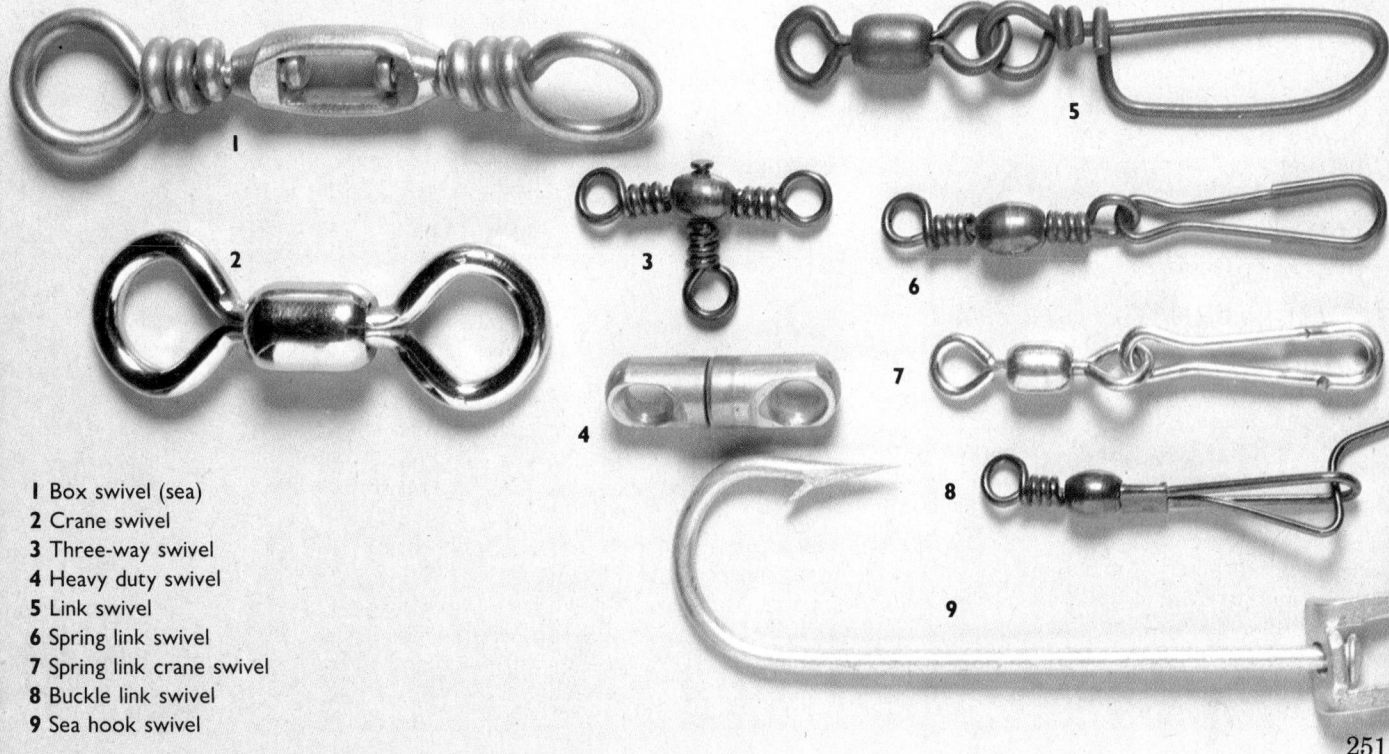

1 Box swivel (sea)
2 Crane swivel
3 Three-way swivel
4 Heavy duty swivel
5 Link swivel
6 Spring link swivel
7 Spring link crane swivel
8 Buckle link swivel
9 Sea hook swivel

How are swivels sized?

In exactly the same way as hooks. The smallest is a freshwater swivel designated 18, and the largest a sea-going 8/0. Swivels for really big game fishing are not given a number: those used for broadbill, swordfish, and shark weighing 2,000lb and more, are handcrafted and extremely expensive.

How many swivels should be incorporated into a shark trace?

A 12ft trace should have at least two—one at the midway point and the other connecting the wire to the reel line.

Can I troll with line running through the centre of a streamlined lead?

No. This causes twisting and kinking. Always use a weight, preferably swivelled so that its centre hangs below the level of the line.

What is a Deal swivel boom?

It is a box-type swivel with a 6in wire boom standing at right angles to the body. It is used as a paternoster, or as the basis of a flying-collar long-trace rig used by pollacking boat anglers. The idea itself is an old one although Deals have largely fallen into disuse.

Is it true that I can use a spinner to take twist out of a line?

In theory it is possible to reverse the spinning vane on some Devon minnows so that they spin in the opposite direction to any twist in the line. Trailing, then retrieving a line across a field of grass is also reputed to remove twist. In practice, however, it is a better idea to throw away twisted line in case indetectable weaknesses have already developed.

equal in strength to other types. They are considerably lighter and rarely jam.

Swivels for freshwater fishing are usually made of brass or blued steel, and if you have any choice it is better to purchase the steel ones because they are harder and last longer before wearing out. Brass, a much softer metal, suffers from wear and tear quite quickly. Neither brass nor ordinary steel are used in sea swivels as salt water is particularly corrosive to these metals, and stainless steel is now more commonly used.

Sea water is very abrasive too, because of the particles of sand suspended in it, so the rather open construction of a barrel swivel will allow sand to enter and cause damage to the moving parts. This is not very important if the swivels are bought cheaply and thrown away after use, as is often the case with sea anglers who fish for the smaller, weaker species around our coastline, so that it is not too serious if a swivel jams.

Matters can be very different if you are fishing for big conger eels, skate, or shark. And the angler who is lucky enough to fish for such hard-fighting, powerful species as marlin, or broadbill swordfish, or the very biggest sharks, should never use anything but the very best tackle, —including swivels which are engineering marvels.

These swivels are made of stainless steel or a really hard alloy not affected by sea water. All moving parts are machined to very fine tolerances, so that it is almost impossible for abrasive particles to enter and will probably be grease-filled as a further protection. Miniature ball-races can be built in to ensure the smoothest possible rotation by minimizing friction, and modern developments have produced swivels which are far in advance of the simple barrel-type device.

Ball-bearing swivels

Ball-bearing swivels are now being manufactured in England. They bring a new dimension to fishing for the larger species. High quality ball bearings locked into a machined cage of stainless steel ensure that

the swivel will not jam, no matter how much pressure is applied. It is the perfect link between reel line and trace when dealing with tough fighters like conger, common skate, porbeagle and mako shark. All that is needed to keep the swivel in first class working order is a drop of sewing machine oil applied periodically through the gap between body and turning eye. This eye is big enough to accept the tough wire needed to combat powerful jaws and teeth.

Pirk fishing over deep water wrecks and, to a lesser extent, snaggy reefs can take a heavy toll of end tackle. With 20-26oz pirks costing up to £5, it is also expensive. A recent solution to the problem is a 'positive poundage link', which can be positioned between the body of the pirk and the treble hook. When a hang-up occurs, the link will open under pressure so that only the hook is lost.

The links (which can be swivelled with the aid of split rings) are available in 15, 25 and 45lb breaking strains. The accurate breaking out

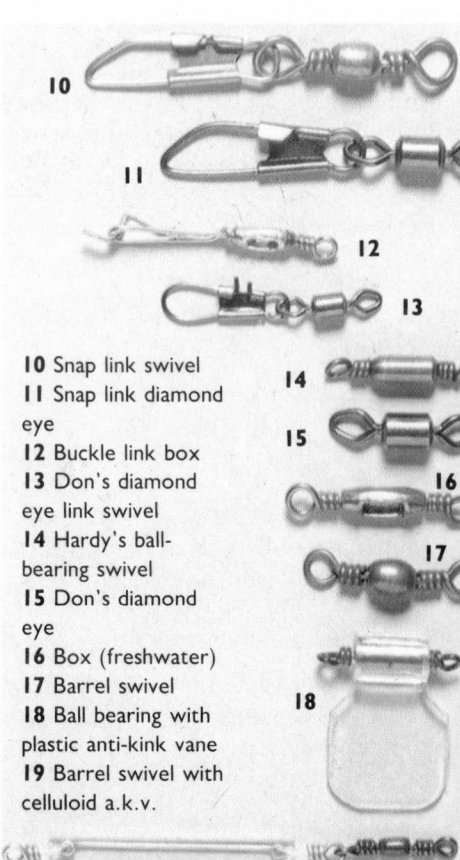

10 Snap link swivel
11 Snap link diamond eye
12 Buckle link box
13 Don's diamond eye link swivel
14 Hardy's ball-bearing swivel
15 Don's diamond eye
16 Box (freshwater)
17 Barrel swivel
18 Ball bearing with plastic anti-kink vane
19 Barrel swivel with celluloid a.k.v.

ANTI-KINK VANES AND LEADS

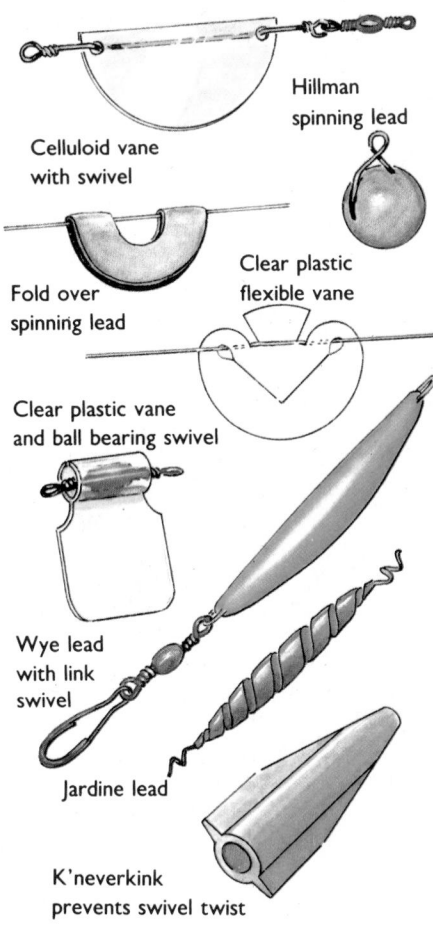

Celluloid vane with swivel

Hillman spinning lead

Fold over spinning lead

Clear plastic flexible vane

Clear plastic vane and ball bearing swivel

Wye lead with link swivel

Jardine lead

K'neverkink prevents swivel twist

An assorted collection of anti-kink vanes and leads. The anti-kink vane is designed to complement the ball-bearing swivel.

pressure of the link is achieved by carefully balancing tensile strength in the steel wire to the radius of the hook circlet.

Three-way swivels and link-swivels

The three-way swivel is most frequently used in forming the float paternoster for fishing a livebait. Constructed in the barrel style with an extension eye standing out from its side, it is prone to distortion and weakness if the bait gets caught and extreme pressure is applied as the angler pulls to break free. The only precaution against this weakness is being able to recognize it and replace the swivel immediately.

Link swivels are a means of quickly attaching (or detaching) a lure to a trace, or to a line. Ideally they should be simple to open and close —even with wet, cold hands—and

strong enough to grip without completely collapsing when extreme pressure is applied.

Plain link swivels with two overlapping half-clips seem to find greatest favour among anglers, despite the fact that they are difficult to open when needed and often slip open without warning to shed either lure or trace during use. An improvement is the safety-pin link, where an open steel loop doubles back to fasten—as the name suggests—into a metal clip. Providing the clip is secure and there is sufficient overlap on the pin to fit snugly into it, this is a safer and more convenient unit than the plain link.

At first sight the diamond-link looks a flimsy affair of a single wire loop doubling back to clip over itself. But in practice it is strong, simple and easy to clean.

How many swivels to use?

How many swivels should be used when fishing? Generally, the fewer the better; every swivel requires a join either to the line or cast, which weakens it. On most occasions just one is enough, provided that is has been properly maintained and is used with an efficient anti-kink vane. But there are arguable exceptions to this rule. Some would say that the choice depends upon the length of the trace: a short trace needing two swivels, one at each end, while a longer trace needs another built in about the mid-point. In eel-fishing, too, multiple swivels are necessary.

Eels have the habit of spinning in the water, causing severe line twist. Because they also have sharp teeth, it is advisable to make up a number of short fine wire traces, with the hook at one end and a swivel at the other. If you slip a ledger weight on to the reel line before tying the hook link on, the swivel acts as the stop and prevents the lead slipping down to the hook.

Anti-kink devices

Anti-kink devices either attach to the line in the form of a vane, which is designed to hold it and prevent it turning, or by means of a weight clipped to the line and intended to hold it from revolving. Celluloid or plastic vanes fastened to the line

work well in principle, but wear slightly after repeated use, allowing the line to turn after all. An improvement is the Kneverkink, a finned tube that fits on to the line and slides on to one eye of the swivel, holding it and making sure that the other parts turn. Last, and probably best of all, is the anti-kink vane designed specifically to complement the ball-bearing swivel, clipping on to its barrel and really making sure that it remains stationary.

Necessity of having casting-weight

As for anti-kink weights, since some spinners are too light for efficient casting, the lead added to prevent line-twist also contributes the extra weight needed.

The simple half moon lead folds over the leader and is squeezed firmly into position. The Jardine spiral weight twists on to the line—fine in principle, but prone to untwist at the most inopportune moments. The Hillman lead is a round bullet with a wire clip that fastens to the eye of the swivel above the trace attachment; highly efficient if it were not inclined to catch on every patch of weed, clog up and bring everything to a standstill. The boat-shaped Wye lead, with a wire loop for attaching to the line and a swivel mounted to its other end to take the trace, is also an efficient item but inclined to snag on the bottom or in weed. The answer is to use the anti-kink device best suited to the water—plastic vanes for weeded and shallow areas, leads for deep, clear water.

Maintenance

Whichever swivel you choosen and use, these small pieces of your tackle should be treated with care. Keep them separate from the rest of your equipment and do not allow them to rattle about loose, in case they become damaged. Some anglers keep their swivels in a small box or tin lined with felt and apply an occasional squirt of oil, which stops the steel items from rusting and keeps them spinning freely. Check swivels over regularly, and if they show the slightest sign of sticking, throw them away. A swivel that is not working properly may lose you the fish of a lifetime.

Weighing-in scales

Major contests with big prizes at stake rely on precision equipment accurate to fractions of a dram. The lone angler, checking a catch out of mere interest, needs something quite different

Having caught a large bag of fish or one substantial specimen, the successful angler will want to weigh his catch. There are many types of scales that can be purchased, some of them bulky, some pocket-sized.

There are four kinds of scales: the clock or dial type, the pan design, the beam design and spring balance. The clock or dial type is the most popular for competition use and can also be purchased in handsets. The pan type is usually preferred by sea anglers as they do not usually have to worry about weighing-in live fish.

The beam type are the most accurate and will weigh to a single dram. Because of their weight and problems of carrying, they are less popular with clubs. Beam scales can

be transported along the bank during matches and are ideal for weighing small specimens accurately, but two scalesmen are needed. The pocket spring balance is carried by many individual anglers.

When weighing live fish, great care should be take to cause as little harm to the fish as possible. Most clock or dial scales now have a plastic-covered wire basket with a loose-fitting lid in which to place the fish. Before even beginning to fish, the scales should be set up on their tripod and adjusted by using the small screw on the clock. The scalesman should check that all is completely ready before asking the angler to take the fish from the water for weighing.

Keepnet considerations
When fish are lifted in a keepnet, they should never be tipped down the net into the basket of the scales. Sliding over the mesh will remove their protective slime and possibly their scales. While the keepnet is still in the water the fish can be fed down to the top ring by lifting the bottom of the net from the water; all the fish will then be trapped in the top of the net which can then be lifted from the water and the fish gently turned into the basket. After weighing, the basket containing the fish can be placed in the water so that the fish are free to swim away when they have recovered. Any specimen fish can be retained for separate weighing.

the fish should be tipped into the folded keepnet and the net then lowered into the water and the fish allowed to escape.

At a match event, as the scalesman moves along between anglers, he should reset the scales before recording each weight. In matches where more than one set of scales are used, all the scales should be checked for accuracy before the match by one of the organizers. This is important, as, in any disputes, the match organizer must be able to certify that all the scales were reading the same.

In addition to such precautions, it is important that all scales should be returned to the makers once a year for their accuracy to be checked. Reputable manufacturers will ask purchasers to return their scales at least once every 12 months. It is also most important that scales used to weigh specimen fish, or possible record contenders, should be accurate and reliable.

Should a dispute arise or a protest be lodged during a match, it is the scalesman's job to reweigh catches and to advise all the anglers immediately that there has been an objection. You cannot weigh catches after they have been returned!

Record Committee's rules
Should a possible record fish be captured it is most important that the angler should follow the rules laid down by the British Record (rod-caught) Fish Committee. When record claims are made, the Committee's rules state that scales or steelyards must be used which can be tested on behalf of the Committee. The Committee also states that scales should be regularly tested by the Weights and Measures Department. Certificates from the Department must also be produced with record claims which certify to the accuracy of the scales used to weigh the fish. Claims for small species of which the weights are always below 1lb must be submitted in grammes.

Before rewarding any record claim with recognition, the Committee checks not only on the accuracy of the weighing but also on the technique used for the catch and on the identification of the fish species.

Far left: *The zinc pan on this simple beam scale affords fish little protection.*
Top centre: *Efficient, accurate dial scale; the mesh of the basket is plastic-coated.*
Centre: *Modern pan scales: accurate, but the fish can jump out of the pan.*
Above: *A spring balance: portable, convenient, but not very accurate.*

Scales for specimen hunters
The handset clock scales or spring balances are those preferred by the specimen hunter and other individual anglers. Many of these handsets now have a polymesh net supplied with them for weighing the fish and these nets should be wet when used, as a dry net will harm the fish.

When weighing live fish it is also advisable, where possible, to set the scales up over grass. Fish do jump out of scales, and grass is better than gravel. When returning the fish in a place where the bank is too high to place the basket into the water,

Catapults and bait throwers

The principle is simple—to throw loosefeed accurately into a distant swim. But to maximize power and accuracy, these simple items have evolved into quite sophisticated tools

The best groundbait in the world is useless unless it can be accurately placed into the swim that the angler is fishing. Where his selected swim is close in to the bank he is sitting on, it is a simple matter to estimate the speed of the stream and then throw the bait, by hand, towards the head of the swim so that it will be carried down into it. But where the swim is some distance away—under the opposite bank for instance—difficulties will arise, more especially if the groundbait cannot be pressed into a heavy ball. For these the catapult is an excellent solution.

The fishing catapult has made its appearance as an angling aid in the last few years and is now available in various designs, both good and bad. The good points should be checked carefully before the item is purchased. It naturally follows that the bigger the model the greater will be the force that can be applied as the bait is released. Weak, spindle-type forks of wire or thin plastic will soon bend and snap, and they should be rejected. Look for a heavy plastic, one-piece moulding, preferably with a shaped hand-grip that is well below the fork. If the handle is too short, there is a risk that you will receive a painful blow on the hand each time you let go of the pouch.

Right shape for accuracy

Too big is better than too small, and this particularly applies to the spacing of the forks themselves. A large 'U'-shape, with the ends of the forks turning slightly outwards will give the greatest accuracy. The elastic should be secured through holes at the fork ends, either by a large knot (which makes for easy replacement) or by crimped metal tubes. The elastic should be soft and able to return to its original length after stretching. Before buying elastic flex it once or twice to ensure that its pull is within your capability. The cup into which the bait is placed should be rigid and have a large,

well-shaped flange at the rear which enables you to keep a firm grip when it is pulled back.

While most anglers are well aware of what a catapult can do, it is sensible to know its limitations before starting to use one. It cannot place large amounts of groundbait at any one time, nor can it manage very heavy baits such as saturated and stiffened cereals with any degree of accuracy. It will not cope with extremely light cereal baits—the spring of the elastic and forward propulsion make it break up in mid-air and scatter over a wide area. It is most successful with pellet and grain baits, which include maggots, casters, hemp, wheat, tares and so on. These should be kept damp or, in the case of cereals, wet. This will provide the weight and 'cling' needed to keep the bait intact.

Judging the speed of the current

To place the bait accurately, the angler must be able to judge the speed of the current where the bait is finally to land. If this is against the opposite bank, then check the speed of the current against the bank you are fishing from. Many anglers make the mistake of estimating the speed of the current from the faster-flowing mid-river swims, which results in the groundbait being placed too far upstream.

The purpose, once the cup of the catapult is loaded, is to drop the bait into the swim by means of a gentle curve through the air. Firing the bait straight will cause a big surface disturbance and make the groundbait break up. The curving type of delivery applies especially if the opposite bank is tree-lined; by lobbing the bait through the air, it will drop through the overhanging branches and fall naturally into the swim.

The Black Widow catapult, which is strung with such powerful rubber that a rigid wrist brace is added for extra leverage. It is of particular interest to carp specialists wanting to put out groundbait with pinpoint accuracy over long distances.

ASK THE EXPERT

How can I keep groundbait from breaking up in mid-air?
The easy answer is to mix it to a much stiffer consistency. But often the problem lies in the number of maggots you are trying to compress into the feed. Casters bound together with groundbait—even in a much softer mix—rarely break up when catapulted.

Which is better—the circular, three-point catapult or the simple forked one?
The circular type was quite popular three or four years ago, but has largely disappeared from the fishing scene. It was designed to overcome deficiencies in the design of pouches, and since these faults were ironed out the three-point has become obsolete.

Have swimfeeders rendered the catapult obsolete?
No. The swimfeeder cannot be used in conjunction with a float rig. A bait catapult is intended primarily to complement float fishing tackle.

Can I make a simple bait catapult?
What small boy hasn't made a catapult? It is simplicity itself to cut a two-leg fork from a tree; the elastic can be bought in a tackle shop; and for stiff groundbait mixes, a strip of leather is all you need for the pouch.

Don't the silhouette and movement of an angler standing to use a bait thrower frighten fish away?
Yes, they could well do. This probably explains why the thrower is not a very popular item of tackle. A catapult fulfills the same function but can be used from a sitting position and without much arm movement.'

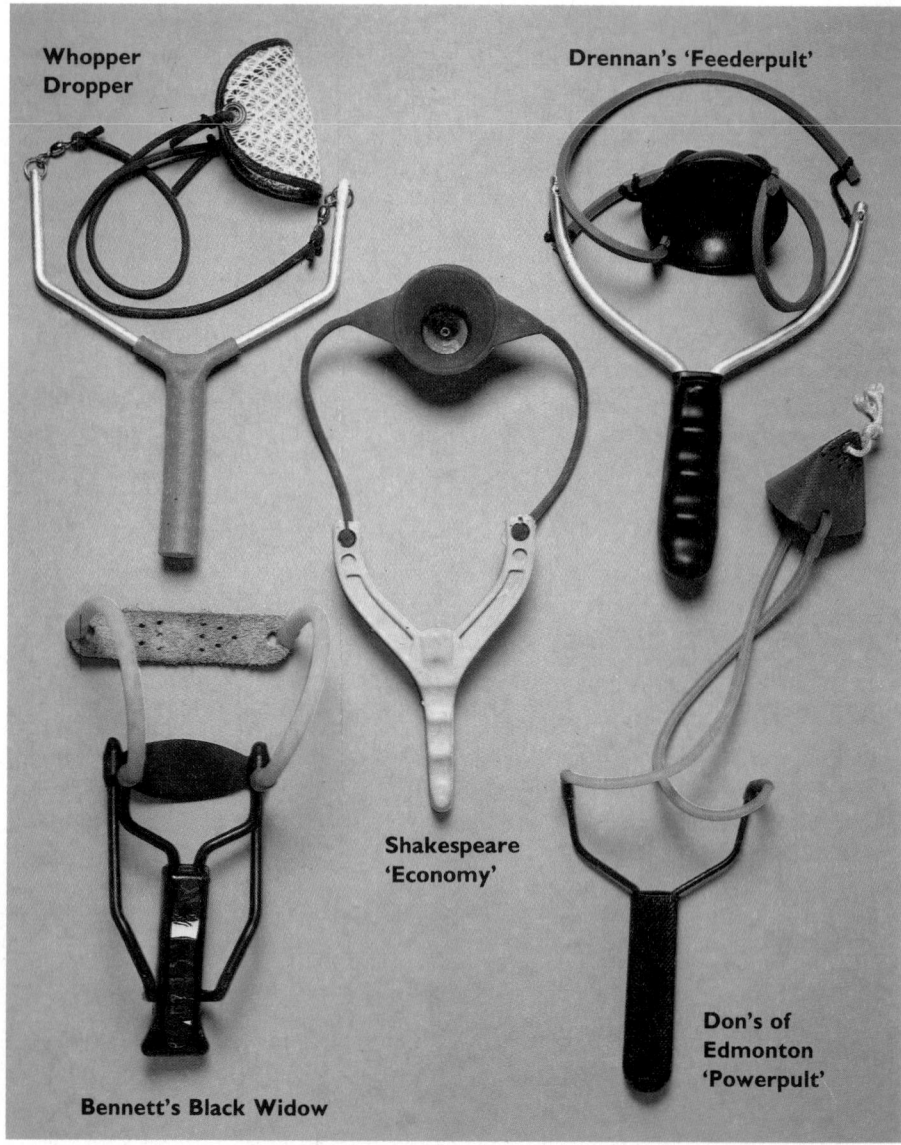

Whopper Dropper

Drennan's 'Feederpult'

Shakespeare 'Economy'

Bennett's Black Widow

Don's of Edmonton 'Powerpult'

A final word of warning concerns the temptation to hold the catapult at face level and to sight along the elastic and through the fork. Should the elastic break or pull free (and this happens) the result can only be face or eye injuries. It is essential to keep the cup with its load well down below the face and to keep the forks on a level with it. Then if anything should break, only the body will receive the impact.

The bait thrower is a simple tool usually consisting of a short stick with a metal cut-away cup mounted on to the end. Groundbait is loaded into this cup and the thrower held in the hand with its high back facing the angler. A quick forward flick and the bait is propelled out into the swim. This is a straightforward way

A variety of catapults showing the different cups available for such differing groundbaits as maggots, dough, particle baits, potatoes, breadpaste, black magic and high protein.

of throwing heavy groundbait over a considerable distance, governed by the length of stick that is used. In general terms, the longer the stick of the bait thrower the farther the bait will travel.

A bait thrower can easily be made from a small tin, its top completely removed. The side of the tin is cut away with a pair of tinsnips, leaving the high back which stops bait from spilling over the angler during the throw. The tin is secured on to a length of ¾in dowling, 2-2½ft long, and the tin itself given two or three coats of paint to prevent rusting.

Gravel pits

Hidden beneath the surface of many gravel pits lies a rotting landscape of dead trees, ditches and weed. Find these and you will have found the larders and lairs of all the pit species

Faced with a vast acreage of gravel pit, with no indication as to depth or character, no angler can decide where to fish without some reconnaissance. When no currents or slacks give a picture, one has to consider other factors—depth, movement of water by wind, temperature fluctuations, plant life and underwater structures.

Only areas within casting range can be charted and it takes time to plumb a big gravel pit. But by counting down a lead until it touches the bottom (timing it with the second hand of a watch is likely to prove more accurate), deeps, shallows, reefs, drop-offs and other features can be located. The nature of the bottom can also be discovered by 'feeling' the lead on the retrieve, and by studying anything clinging to the lead as you pull it out.

Reed or rush margins, lily-pad holes, and soft weed beds all indicate the presence of fish. The weedbed may be a dense patch of milfoil, hornwort, or Canadian pondweed, and it pays to use a hook attached to the lead to bring some back for study. Weed frequently indicates tench, bream, roach or rudd, and while it is not advisable to fish directly into it, fish may be drawn from it towards groundbait.

Lily beds for food and shelter

Lily beds are also potential fish holders and in many gravel pits are the only recognized fish spots. They grow only in comparatively shallow water and offer food, shade and shelter for foraging fish, so the deep water surrounding them often remains fishless.

Giant reed mace, Norfolk rush and bulrush beds are also good fish-holding spots, and rudd in particular haunt them for days, while bream and tench seek their shelter in hot weather. Round-stemmed bulrush beds grow on gravel bottoms and are good hunting grounds for perch and tench. Tench love mud, yet will often patrol a hard bottom, where they eat snails, small mussels and caddis grubs.

In hot weather there are tench like this one to be tempted from their shelter among the cooler bankside rushbeds.

259

Old and well-established pits often silt up, and muddy areas located with a plummet usually indicate tench. The digging tench, unlike the hard-bottom dweller, stays put more and responds well to groundbait or to loose feeding.

Other likely holding spots are little bays or inlets, or steep banks where bushes and trees overhang. Pike often ambush there and are almost certainly in residence when small fish are seen to leave the water in a silver shower.

Wind direction plays an important part in fish movements, and the case for fishing into the wind has often been proven. Surface food blown across the water causes fish to accumulate on the windward side.

Small fish dimpling the surface, grebes diving continually in a certain spot, and splashy rises to surface flies all indicate fish. Any prolonged activity may attract pike.

Boat fishing
Although much knowledge can be gained from the bank, to read a big pit well, a boat is essential. Bankside observation cannot reveal the underwater structure of out-of-reach areas, and at best only shelves near the bank, depth changes and other structures can be charted. By rowing round the pit and sounding the bottom with a long pole or plumb line, however, you can assess the underwater structure fairly well.

With a boat, you can also investigate scum lanes—oily surface strips that remain calm in a ripple.

Top left: *Study local pit workings for future reference, but remember that it may take years for many of the fish food sources to establish themselves.*
Above: *The regular lines along which a pit is worked can be of help to the angler who can remember or detect which way the ridges run.*
Left: *A strong wind blowing in a steady direction washes fish food towards the windward bank—though casting can be awkward and fishing less comfortable.*
Top right: *Ray Mumford nets a 14lb pit pike.*
Right: *Carp fishing in a Kent gravel pit near Dartford. Carp of over 40lb have been taken from the Hertfordshire pit pictured below.*

The reservoir angler uses these to find trout, the pit angler pike.

Many gravel pits were dug dry and did not fill with water for several years. Trees and shrubs grew, and later, when the pits were filled, there were large areas holding submerged or partly submerged trees. The water killed them, but they remained hard, in some cases as if petrified. These trunks, together with fallen branches, provide cover for many species of fish.

When searching for underwater structures from a boat, any indication of a stump or underwater tree should be investigated. The bottom there may be littered with snags, but it is an undeniable fact that these areas are fish larders and sanctuaries. How to fish them is a problem, but such fish as rudd, roach, perch, pike—and occasionally bream and tench—can be taken just off the bottom, a little away from the snags. Never ignore these places.

Anchor the boat and watch for

Is it possible to fish gravel pits while they are being worked?
Permission is not readily granted as a rule, but experience shows that plant, insect and fish life are developing in many forms before work is completed.

Is there a period during the year when pits fish better than at other times?
It depends what kind of fish you are after. Tench feed avidly during the summer, so do bream. Both species tend to become semi-dormant in pits after September. But roach, rudd, perch and pike remain fairly active all year round, and November seems to be the best month for pike and perch.

Do many gravel pits contain eels, and if so what's the best bait for them?
Most do, but those close to river courses seem to hold larger numbers. Baits include small dead fish, fish bits, prawns, mussels and worms.

Does the average pit have 'big-fish' potential?
Over a long period, perch and rudd stocks tend to increase to such an extent that there are too many small ones to merit specimen fishing. So a relatively new gravel pit may be more profitable for the specimen hunter.

What's the best time of day for gravel pit tench?
There's no clearcut answer: the night and early mornings have accounted for specimen tench, but another day they'll refuse to feed until 11am. 'Fish early, fish late' does not always apply. Subtle changes in temperature, light, and wind direction affect the behaviour of tench differently from one pit to the next.

Above: *Fish-eating birds, scum lanes, and hunted fish leaping clear of the water are just a few of the tell-tale signs a really observant angler can use to his advantage.*

movements near the surface. See the terns swoop and grab small fish, and the heron perched on one of the emergent stumps. They are there because they have seen fish.

Many gravel pits have underwater banks and channels running in the same direction. Locate them and mark them well so that you can follow one or the other and not cross over. Fish tend to lie either over the banks or in the channel—temperature and food availability being two of the obvious reasons for this —although on occasion they swap from one place to the other. Drifting for pike with dead baits or lures along, say, a channel, is critical to within a few feet, and if the pike are in the channel there is no point in drift-fishing the banks.

Information about the pit bottom can be easily obtained by using a transistorized sonar unit. Many are available today, and some even chart the bottom on paper as the boat proceeds. This type is not strictly necessary for gravel pits, and simple units which give the exact depth on a rotating dial are quite adequate.

It takes a while to be able to read what the unit is saying, but once mastered, you will be able to recognize mud, weed, branches, rocks, hard gravel, ledges, drop-offs, deep holes, and the exact depth.

Locating the shoals

The permanent reading at zero represents the surface, while the movable signal, shown at various places on the dial as the boat proceeds, indicates the bottom. Little blips between zero and bottom indicate fish or fish shoals. Do not imagine, however, that you can get a very *direct* reading of fish location from the sonar unit. Rather it enables you, once you have learnt to translate the signals, to transcribe a picture of the underwater topography, which in turn will help you locate the shoals.

The unit gives the strongest signals on a bottom of gravel or hard clay. Such signals are very clear at a depth of around 40ft, but at greater depths, up to 80ft, you need to turn up the 'gain' or power.

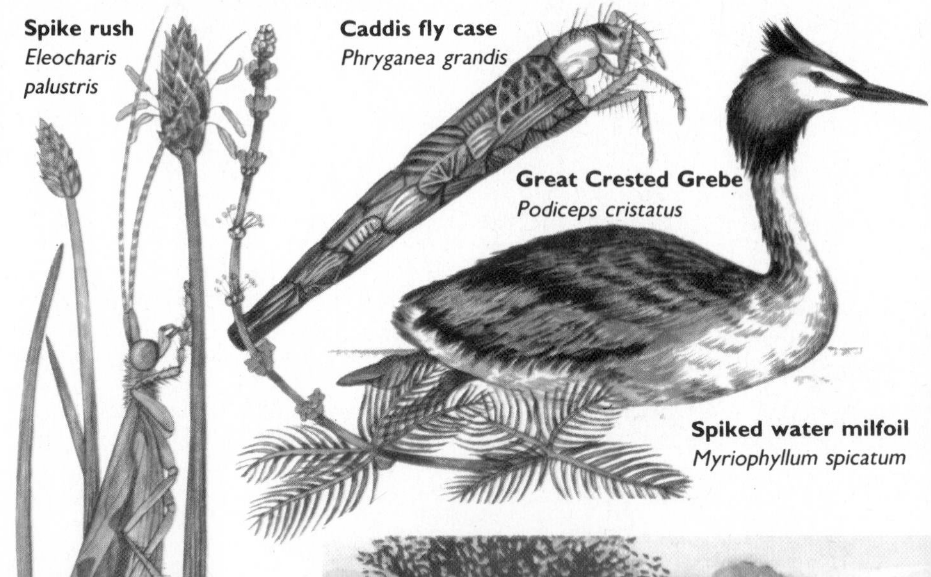

Spike rush
Eleocharis palustris

Caddis fly case
Phryganea grandis

Great Crested Grebe
Podiceps cristatus

Spiked water milfoil
Myriophyllum spicatum

Caddis fly
Phryganea grandis

Glutinous snail
Myxas glutinosa

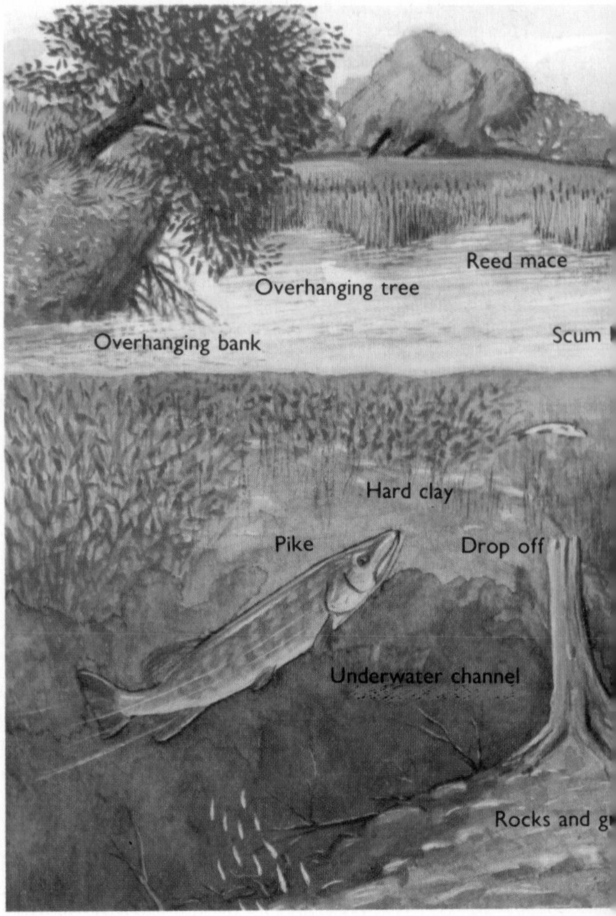

Above: *Plant, insect and bird life to be found in and near flooded pits.*
Right: *Cross-section of a gravel pit showing underwater and bankside weed, rotting vegetation, wildlife and submerged trees.*

Reed mace

Overhanging tree

Overhanging bank

Scum

Hard clay

Pike

Drop off

Underwater channel

Rocks and g

If you then move over a bottom of mud and decayed vegetation, the clear, distinct signals will disappear at times. This does not mean that you have suddenly come to very deep water—the dial would have shown the drop-off with a wide band of signals—but that the mud and vegetation have absorbed the sound waves, making them disappear.

Over a gravelly bottom with weeds, the signal unit will transmit many thin signals, which climb towards the zero point as the boat approaches and return towards the bottom point as the boat leaves the weeds. The same signals will register as your boat approaches or leaves trees or bushes. You can use these signals to steer your boat along the edge of weedbeds.

Sudden changes in depth

The unit also registers sudden changes in depth, for example where there is an underwater cliff, or a submerged tree. In either case the unit will give two readings, at the highest point and at the bottom, but an underwater tree gives weaker signals than does a reef or an underwater cliff. It is possible to mistake a tree for a shoal of fish. If you are not sure, anchor your boat bow and stern so that it cannot move, and take further readings. Constant signals indicate a tree, while intermittent signals indicate fish.

The sonar unit itself is simple to operate. There is a transducer and a dial. The transducer is hung over the boatside into the water and the unit switched on. As the dial rotates, a red light shows at zero and at the bottom. Some adjustment is needed to ensure that the dial is recording correctly and only experience will tell you if you are using too much or too little gain.

There is no doubt that transistorized sonar units make the reading of big gravel pits much easier. They never lie and always record accurately. It is more or less certain that if an angler has the ability to read the signals, he will also be able to read the water.

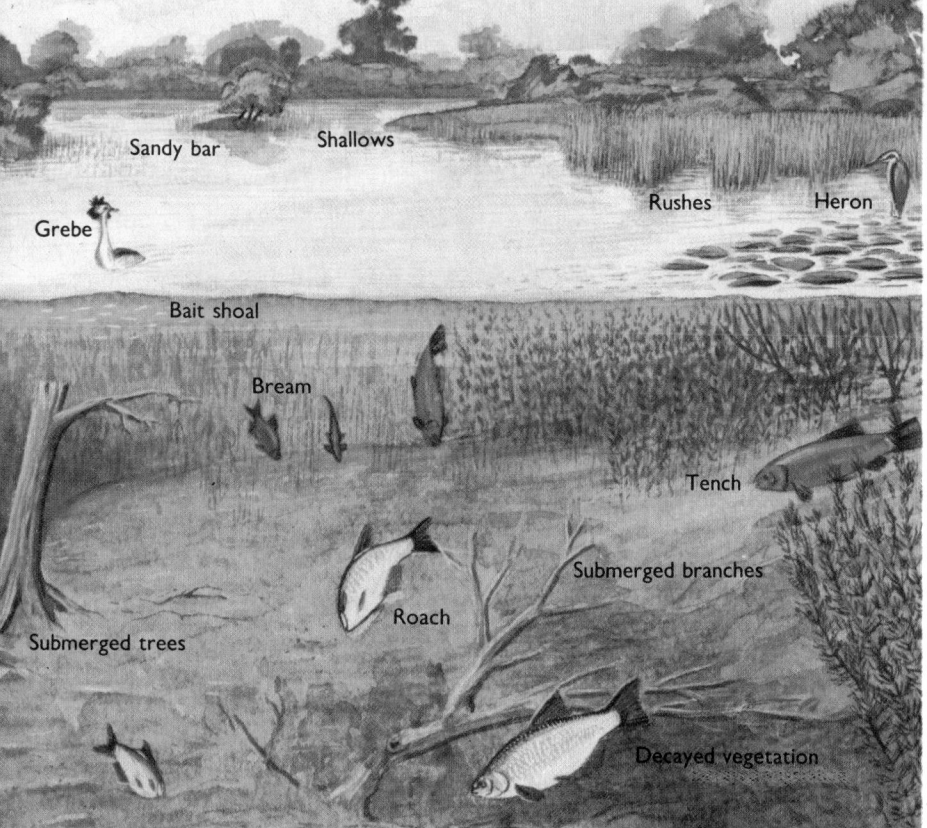

Summer lakes

A good knowledge of the habits of fish, and the tell-tale signs that betray their presence, can mean the difference between success and failure when fishing lakes in summer

Perhaps the most beautiful sight to an angler's eye is a peaceful summer lake with the sun high above the water, enriching the colours of the surrounding herbage. Such a setting is always full of promise, but the keen angler will want to know much more — a beautiful environment does not mean that fish will be caught.

No two lakes are the same. Not only do the depth, extent and clarity vary from lake to lake, but so do plant life, food and fish.

Reading the water

Shallow lakes are the easiest to read, and often abound in food and large fish. Almost every square inch of the bottom of a silty, shallow lake will be rich in bloodworms (the larvae of the midge), on which nearly every species, except pike, feeds. Both tench and carp are avid silt-sifters and consume larvae in vast quantities, as, to a lesser extent, do rudd and roach. Large patches of big bubbles, seen anywhere in the lake, indicate a feeding carp, while smaller effervescent bubbles betray tench.

Try to match any bubbles with the species suspected. Although most species can be recognised by the bubbles they send up while feeding, one fish often makes this guessing game much harder — the eel, which can create about every kind of bubble. Usually, though, a very large patch of frothy bubbles, which does not move or reappear, gives away an eel as it twists and burrows into the silt to feed on bloodworms or merely to hole up and rest after a good meal.

What to look for

Even during a hot summer's day, fish activity can be seen somewhere on small lakes, especially in marginal

Above: *Lily patches provide plenty of cover for carp and tench.*
Left: *Lakes with clear water are best fished at night, but where the water is coloured the fish will move about and feed freely during the day.*

Below left: *The silty bottoms of shallow lakes abound in bloodworms.*
Below: *Wind wil blow hatching nymphs towards the windward shore, and fish that feed on them will follow, so heed the old advice and fish 'into the wind'.*

What effect does rain have on summer lake fishing?

Apart from the discomfort it causes the angler, it doesn't in general have any adverse effects on your chances of a good catch. In shallow lakes, however, the drumming sound caused by prolonged heavy rain is thought to upset deep-sided fish such as bream and put them off feeding. In overcast conditions, a sudden change in atmospheric pressure or the approach of a thunderstorm can also affect the behaviour of fish — often to the benefit of the angler. Some fish, in particular tench and eels, may become more active in this kind of weather.

How can you tell if there are fish in a lake?

A quiet approach, keeping behind cover, and a sprinkling of breadcrumbs or maggots, should soon tell you! But if the water holds plenty of weed growth and insect life is abundant, the chances are that there are fish there.

What is the best way to begin fishing on an unfamilier lake?

The first thing to do is to control the urge to put your tackle up and start fishing. Sit and look hard at the water surface, the edges, the likely lilypads, and watch for rises. A half-hour's study is worth a day of chuck-it-and-chance-it.

Do rising bubbles always mean feeding fish?

No. In some hot conditions, rotting weeds and leaves can release bubbles of marsh gas. So if the bubbles keep rising from exactly the same spot it is probably not a hungry tench.

Do polarized glasses help?

Very much. They enable you to see beneath the surface by filtering out the rays of light reflected from the water.

plant life, such as lilies, reeds, or patches of broad-leaved potamogeton. Look for lily stalks 'knocking' as a large carp or tench moves lazily beneath, sucking in water snails, or their eggs, which adhere to the underside of the pads.

Sudden splashing from a rudd as it leaps clear of the water may indicate a hunting pike. Pike anglers should also note any undercut banks where predators might hole up. A fallen tree or a mass of tangled roots pushing out into the water create a natural lie. And pike will pounce from the edge of reedmace and rushbeds whose stalks are cover enough to hide them from their prey. On a larger lake, pike anglers need to carry out a methodical mapping of the bed by plumbing its contours. Pike lie in fall-offs and indentations, and launch ambushes from behind underwater obstructions often invisible from the bank.

If bream are thought to be present, watch carefully for movements as the shoal meanders slowly beneath lilies or potamogeton. Stalks which move when there is no wind, or small ripples from the pads, are the pointers to look for, as is the occasional stream of bubbles as a bream dives into the bottom layer of silt or silkweed to feed. If surface weed is sparse, search for disturbed water where the colour is darker than elsewhere, or where small patches of bubbles rise to the surface when the rest of the lake has none.

Observation with binoculars of where the shoals gather for their evening or morning feed may provide a basis for your fishing, as bream take advantage of the poor light to enter shallower marginal waters in search of food. On some lakes the reverse may happen, with bream feeding during daylight betraying their presence by gently moving the marginal reeds. A bait on the edge of the margins will often take them.

Feeding patterns

Working out feeding patterns in huge lakes is not easy. In any case, they do not necessarily apply to similar water, even an adjacent lake.

On many lakes feeding patterns are evident only during low light, as at dawn or dusk, or when the sky is heavily overcast before a storm. But

in other lakes, particularly very weedy waters, feeding can be seen almost any time of the day. To read any new water you need to spend as much free time there as possible, just looking. Close and consistent observation will tell you what fish are present, on what they feed, and, most important, when and where.

When water and air temperatures continually fluctuate, patterns of fish movements may change daily. In very warm conditions carp may be

seen moving — sometimes quite quickly — all over the lake, jumping, bubbling, and bow-waving across the water. but if prolonged heavy rain chills the water, you may not see the slightest sign of fish. So try to explore new waters during periods of settled weather, preferably when the sun is well up.

Beware of splashy rises during full sun up for they are usually made by small fish rather than specimens. Big fish make surprisingly little

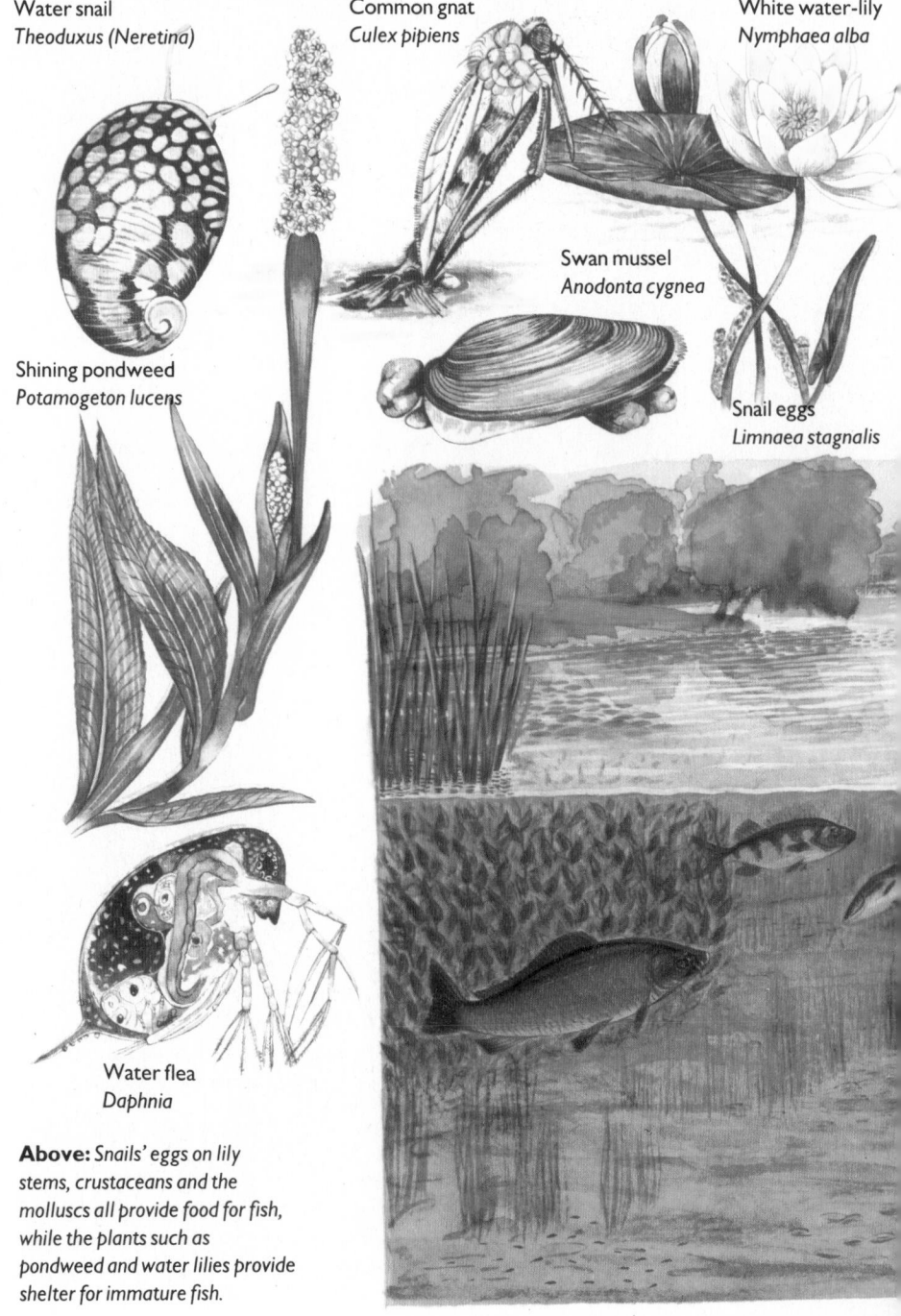

Water snail
Theoduxus (Neretina)

Shining pondweed
Potamogeton lucens

Common gnat
Culex pipiens

Swan mussel
Anodonta cygnea

White water-lily
Nymphaea alba

Snail eggs
Limnaea stagnalis

Water flea
Daphnia

Above: *Snails' eggs on lily stems, crustaceans and the molluscs all provide food for fish, while the plants such as pondweed and water lilies provide shelter for immature fish.*

Above: *This fine mirror carp, weighing 17lb 9oz made for a patch of scum after breaking through a bed of water lilies. It eventually wallowed in as a dead weight, weed and all.*

Below: *The summer lake and some typical examples of the kind of feeding grounds where fish will congregate. Placing your bait in the right swim is essential.*

movement when swimming through surface weed because unless they are preoccupied in their feeding on bottom buried baits, such as blood-worms, they need only move casually to sip in a variety of creatures. Water snails, water boatmen, damselfly nymphs, water lice, freshwater shrimps, caddis grubs and slow movers like pea mussels and even swan mussels are taken like this.

As the sun goes down, you may notice rudd and roach 'priming' on the surface stimulated by the evening hatch of midges and other aquatic flies. Surface species feed heavily on pupae or nymphs, and during a prolific hatch, when millions of nymphs shed their cases to become airborne flies, activity can be seen all over the lake. Then, some of the largest and wiliest roach and rudd, which were impossible to locate all day, will, for the duration of the hatch, fall to the coarse angler with a fly rod. Alternatively, breadflake fished hard on the bottom may still work as darkness falls.

Clue to specimen tench

It is thought that only carp have pharyngeal teeth powerful enough to crush a small swan mussel for the succulent meat it contains, but tench and bream will take mussel bait, and roach and rudd have been known to take them whole, de-shelled. Perhaps fish have a method for opening their clam-like shells. In lakes where swan mussels grow large, one usually finds that the bigger fish, like carp and tench, reach specimen proportions. Is it coincidence?

The smallest form of life relevant to fishing summer lakes, which moves around with the warm surface-layers directed by the wind, is daphnia, or water fleas. During warm conditions these crustaceans can multiply very quickly to form vast clouds of protein-packed food, varying in colour from grey to a shade of brick dust. All surface species feed heavily on daphnia, but so do tench and carp in very shallow waters. In lakes thickly clouded with daphnia, tench in particular can become so preoccupied with feeding that they totally ignore other food, including baits.

In windy conditions, daphnia are more responsible for movement of

267

When there is little or no wind, watch for the movement of weed stalks or lily pads which betrays the presence of fish moving amongst them.

the smaller species than any other food, and the old advice to fish into the wind is well founded. Wind direction is also important when nymphs are hatching, because they will drift in their thousands, with the surface scum, to the windward shore.

With large or huge lakes, much of this water-craft still applies, except that fish locations and movements are much harder to discover. Bream, especially, are known to roam over the entire water within 24 hours, resting and feeding.

Baits

Baits are only a small part of the angler's involvement with summer lakes until all the homework has been done. It is useless offering a good bait to fish which are not present in the

swim, so all elements must be considered — wind direction, weed growth (bottom and surface), water clarity, and the species to be found.

In lakes that seem barren of surface weed, marginal weed growths are always frequented by some species. Carp and tench, especially, love to patrol along sedges or reed mace for damselfly larvae, snails and caddis, which live in the reed stems. At first glance, even with crystal clear water, there does not appear to be much food to sustain large fish, but all species, except predators, consume vast quantities of tiny food items. Only baits such as large protein 'specials', breadflakes, and others, give the fish a quantity of food in a single mouthful, which is why big baits often lose their effectiveness once fish are wary of them. Then, small particle baits, which are much closer in size to a fish's everyday food are more effective.

Where and when to fish

As a general guideline — if you are fishing a clear lake you will usually do better to fish at night when fish are less wary, while in coloured water fish will move and feed during daylight.

Even very large waters will, after several hours spent just watching and learning, seem far more satisfying when you have several good reasons for choosing a certain swim, and not just any spot because it looks attractive or the bankside shrubbery has been cleared away.

If you settle in a swim where the fish have stopped feeding, think about the situation. Has the shoal moved on to a deeper area as the sun penetrated the water? Or is it simply that the shoal has had enough and retreated beneath a nearby lily patch? There are always questions to ask when bites are not forthcoming, and the answer often lies in what happens along the marginal weed growths and beneath the surface.

Lay-bys and eddies

Fishing lay-bys and eddies pose complex problems when you first tackle them and change in character at different times of the year—but they can be remarkably productive of fish

Above: *A lay-by on the River Thames.*
Left: *Chub, like the 4¾lb beauty pictured here, favour lay-bys with a steady flow.*
Below: *A good Thames barbel—usually they are found close to lay-bys, not in them.*

Over the years I have found that lay-by, swims regularly produce specimen fish. Much of my experience has centred on the Dorset Stour, Thames, Kennet, Hampshire Avon, and Great Ouse, but, swims up and down the country are just as productive.

This type of swim is at its best during the winter season after or during floods, when the contrast is most sharp between the main flow and the sheltered lay-by. About 70 per cent of my river fishing is done between December and March.

Sometimes, it is difficult to distinguish between a lay-by and an eddy. Some lay-bys are also eddies, or can be at certain times of the year. At normal winter level, with a steady flow, a small lay-by makes an ideal chub lie, but when the winter rains push the level up a couple of feet the stronger current creates a boiling eddy as it hits the bank. This is likely to send the chub elsewhere. In bigger lay-bys, changing water levels may turn part of the lay-by into an eddy while the remainder of the swim may still remain a suitable environment for the fish.

As well as the 'normal' type of lay-by which consists of a natural indentation cut along the bank, there are other features that have a similar effect on the flow of water and therefore harbour big fish. A fallen, submerged tree, for example, will gradually collect rubbish around it to form, in time, a fairly solid raft: it may even get silted up. This will result in a nice pocket of water close to the bank with a much reduced flow. The fishing here is even better than in a normal lay-by swim since the submerged tree and the rubbish raft can provide both fish and angler with generous cover.

I can also remember several productive winter chub holts on the Great Ouse where we used to take them from an 'artifical' slack, or lay-by, produced by moored cabin cruisers. When the river was at its normal winter level, the chub would be found between the offside of the boat and the main flow. But in high water, they tended to drop back downstream and tuck in close behind the boat and the bank where the flow was reduced.

Pike, roach and chub are regularly found in lay-bys. Look for a lay-by, without counter-current or eddies, that has a slow, steady flow. In highly coloured floodwater, big roach hole up in dead slack lay-bys. Small fish of most species spend time out of the main flow. That is why big pike are never far away.

A sight to gladden the angler's heart—a mill pool on the River Yare at Trowse, crammed with fish-rich features. Note the eddy at the edge of the lily bed, the bank supports and the overhanging trees.

Lay-bys with undercut banks, underwater snags, or tree roots attract big chub—the perfect setting for those stories of a 25lb pike grabbing a four-and-a-half pound chub as it is being played!

Barbel are usually found close to lay-bys rather than in them. A few specific examples illustrate that other big fish also favour lay-bys with a steady, even flow, but prefer to intercept their food on the edge adjoining the stronger main current. The two exceptions are pike and

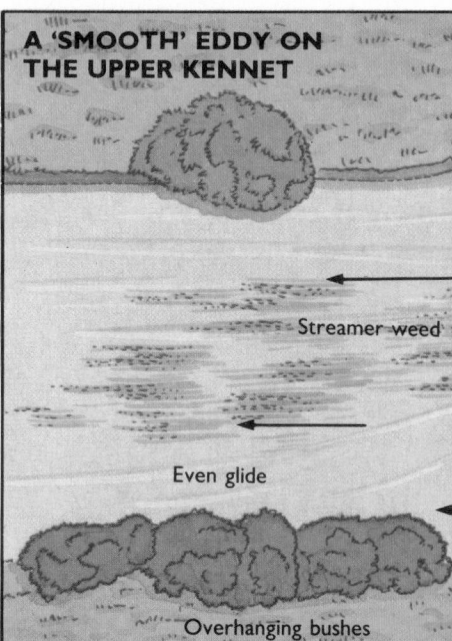

A 'SMOOTH' EDDY ON THE UPPER KENNET

Streamer weed

Even glide

Overhanging bushes

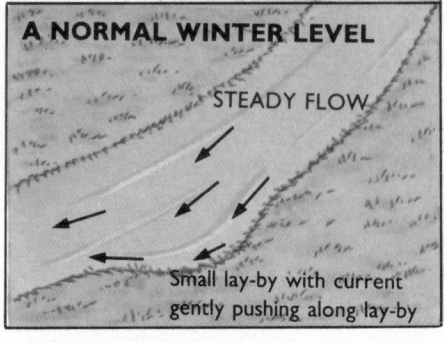

A NORMAL WINTER LEVEL

STEADY FLOW

Small lay-by with current gently pushing along lay-by

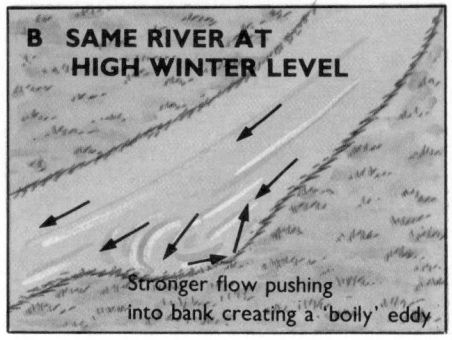

B SAME RIVER AT HIGH WINTER LEVEL

Stronger flow pushing into bank creating a 'boily' eddy

chub, which often hunt their food from under the angler's feet.

There is one kind of lay-by that I have hardly ever found productive. On several of my favourite stretches of the Thames and Dorset Stour there are some *very deep* lay-bys where the bank drops away almost vertically into water very much deeper than elsewhere—12-14ft within a few feet of the bank. These deep lay-bys look very attractive but nearly always result in blanks —even when the water is very cold and good results could be expected. Strong undercurrents may account for these 'exceptions to the rule'. Or perhaps I have simply failed to master the situation.

A far-bank chub lay-by on the middle reaches of the Great Ouse is overhung by a large willow. The river is 30 yards wide and the swim is reached by upstream ledgering. At the downstream end of the lay-by is a cabbage patch, and behind it chub lie up in 8ft of slackish water among tree roots.

Are lay-bys more productive at one particular time of year?
They are chiefly winter haunts when there is plenty of water. In summer they are often dead, without flow, too shallow and often solid with weed.

Which species favour lay-bys?
Under some conditions, nearly every river species, big or small, can be found there. Chub, roach, perch, pike and barbel are all regular inhabitants. Pike and roach are probably the most frequent visitors.

Can I fish for lay-by roach and pike at the same time?
Absolutely! A light ledger rig is used for the roach at the downstream end of the lay-by, with a herring or other deadbait anchored at the upstream end or close in under your feet, for the pike. This is probably the most exciting form of river fishing!

Can cattle-drinks be classified as lay-bys?
Cattle drinks shelve gradually, whereas lay-bys are often undercut or drop away steeply. This means that fish may often be found close to the bank in a lay-by but will be farther out—much closer to the main flow—in a drink.

Is there a 'best' method to adopt?
Float, ledger or freeline can all be effective. You will often be amazed how little lead you need to hold bottom in these slacker swims—even when the river is running bank-high.

Do any river species spend long periods *inside* eddies?
The dace and minnow—neither of them an absorbing prospect for the big fish enthusiast—are the only exceptions to the rule: eddies don't normally hold fish for very long.

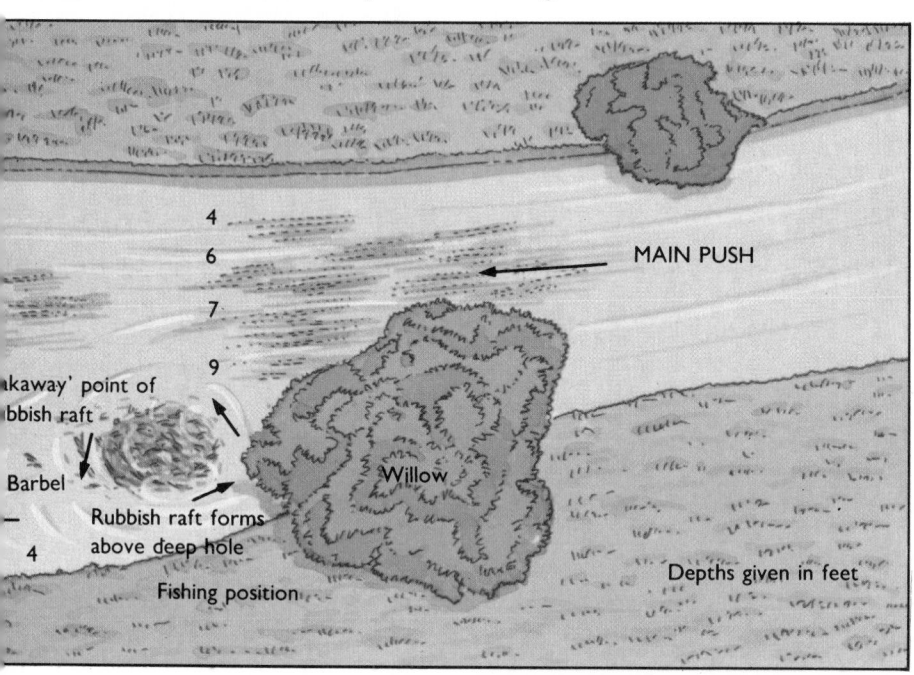

4
6
7
9

akaway' point of bbish raft

Barbel

Rubbish raft forms above deep hole

4

Fishing position

MAIN PUSH

Willow

Depths given in feet

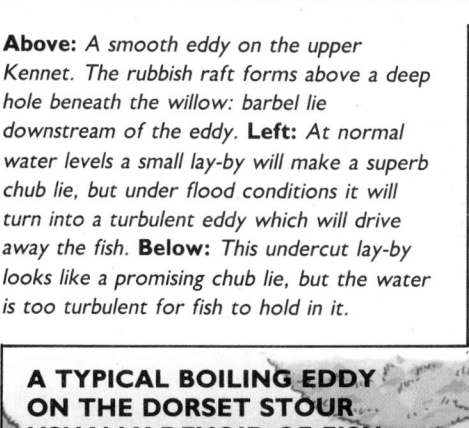

Above: *A smooth eddy on the upper Kennet. The rubbish raft forms above a deep hole beneath the willow: barbel lie downstream of the eddy.* **Left:** *At normal water levels a small lay-by will make a superb chub lie, but under flood conditions it will turn into a turbulent eddy which will drive away the fish.* **Below:** *This undercut lay-by looks like a promising chub lie, but the water is too turbulent for fish to hold in it.*

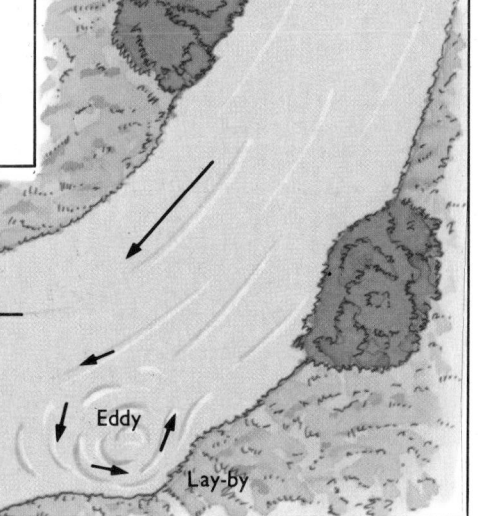

A TYPICAL BOILING EDDY ON THE DORSET STOUR USUALLY DEVOID OF FISH

Eddy

Lay-by

Stour lay-bys

A long lay-by on a straight stretch of the Dorset Stour is much less sheltered. In high water an eddy forms at the upstream end and, although pike continue to be found all along the inner lay-by, the great majority of roach to take advantage of this interruption to the flow are found on the edge of the lay-by. Chub are taken downstream, from the very end of the lay-by, in front of overhanging hawthorn bushes. The water there is 6ft deep and quite unaffected by the turbulence of the main flow washing abruptly into the lay-by.

An ideal pike lay-by is found on a similar stretch of the same river. The lay-by is deeper than the rest of the river bed, which grows shallower in mid-river. The deepest hole (9ft) harbours big chub, but in front of the submerged trees which project out from the back of the lay-by, pike find ample cover for their ambushes. They are not directly enjoying the shelter of the lay-by, but are lying on its verge, positioned to take prey from the passing main flow.

In a very small lay-by on the upper Thames, the effects of high water make the bank's indentation a hostile environment for any fish. But barbel are found in large numbers on the edge, and not the middle of the eddy that forms there. The swirl is so powerful that the gravel bottom has silted up completely at the rear of the swim. Chub gather on the opposite bank in the shelter of some big willow trees. Their feeding may well be affected by the lay-by's interruption to the river's pattern.

Eddies and lay-bys have one thing in common: big fish are found in them comparatively rarely, although they are often found very close by. Some think this is a sweeping generalisation. But after many years of attempting to conjure fish out of a wide variety of eddies, I reject much of what is written about eddy-fishing. Nevertheless, an eddy is a most significant pointer for the specimen hunter. He needs to know how to identify the dozens of different kinds of eddies, and to anticipate just where his fish will be in relation to them.

Eddies

A wide variety of underwater factors can cause an eddy. But whatever it is that suddenly deflects the flow, it results in passing particles of food slowing down in the current so that fish are able to take them more easily. The illustrated swim on the upper Kennet affords a useful eddy that neither boils nor spins. In time of high water and flooding, the effect of eddies on passing food is exaggerated. But fish avoid being tossed and twirled in turbulent water, so that roach, perch, chub, bream and barbel position themselves close-by, where the eddy begins to attain an equilibrium. 'Reading' the exact spot requires a lot of practice. But there are eddies almost devoid of fish. In the swim on the Dorset Stour, for example, the undercut lay-by seems to promise big chub, but the boiling holes at this elbow are in fact, far too turbulent to contain fish.

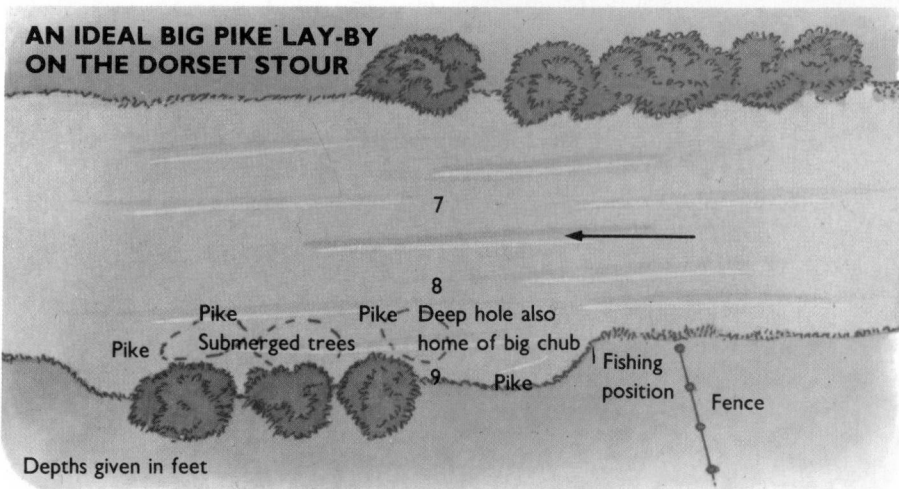

AN IDEAL BIG PIKE LAY-BY ON THE DORSET STOUR

7

8

Pike   Pike   Deep hole also home of big chub

Pike   Submerged trees

9   Pike   Fishing position

Fence

Depths given in feet

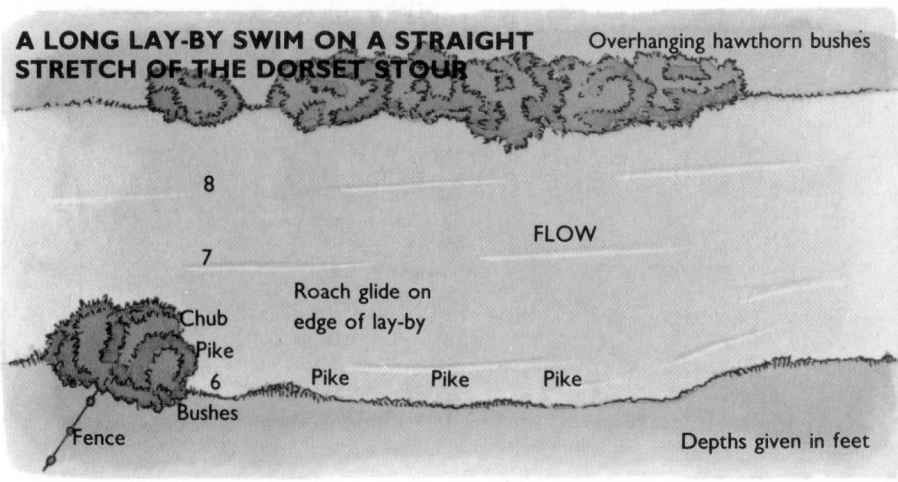

A LONG LAY-BY SWIM ON A STRAIGHT STRETCH OF THE DORSET STOUR   Overhanging hawthorn bushes

8

FLOW

7

Roach glide on edge of lay-by

Chub

Pike

Pike   Pike   Pike

6

Bushes

Fence

Depths given in feet

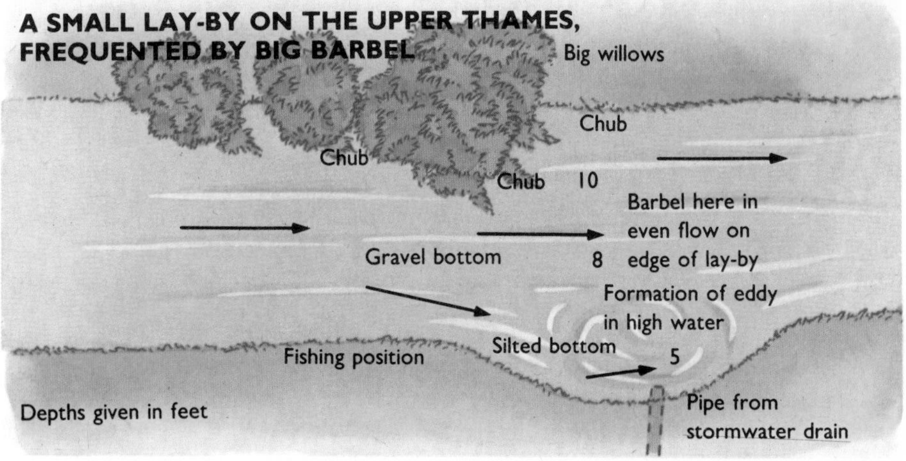

A SMALL LAY-BY ON THE UPPER THAMES, FREQUENTED BY BIG BARBEL

Big willows

Chub

Chub

Chub 10

Barbel here in even flow on edge of lay-by

Gravel bottom 8

Formation of eddy in high water

Fishing position   Silted bottom   5

Depths given in feet

Pipe from stormwater drain

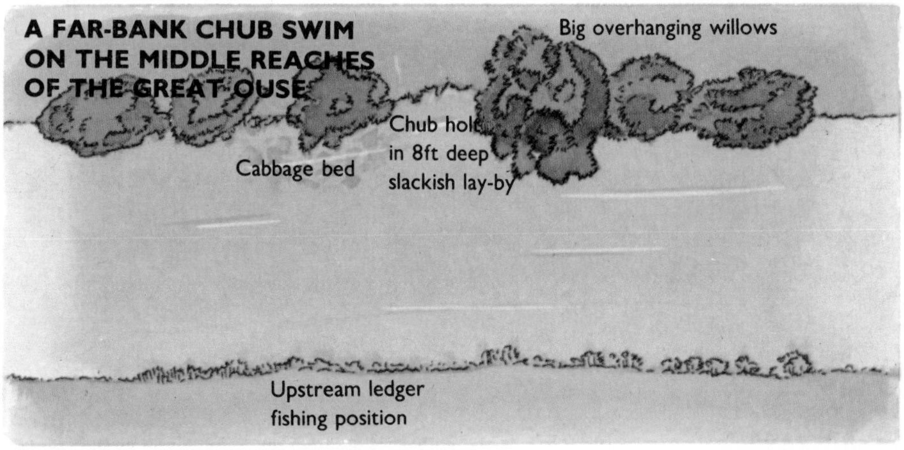

A FAR-BANK CHUB SWIM ON THE MIDDLE REACHES OF THE GREAT OUSE

Big overhanging willows

Chub hold in 8ft deep slackish lay-by

Cabbage bed

Upstream ledger fishing position

Above: *An inviting lay-by on the Wensum at Costessey in Norfolk.* **Left:** *Frank Guttfield's 'ideal pike lie'.* **Bottom left:** *Another lay-by on the Stour: pike are found close in all along the nearbank lay-by; chub lie up at its downstream end and roach glide on its edge.* **Top right:** *An upper Thames lay-by.* **Above right:** *This lay-by on the middle reaches of the Great Ouse is a fine chub holt.* **Bottom right:** *Some of the foods likely to be found in the calm of a lay-by.*

'Dustbin' fishing

An eddy is a natural dustbin as well as a larder. To avoid this vortex of rubbish, fish keep out of the thick of an eddy. However, floating rafts of rubbish can provide an excellent indicator of where the fish will be. The point where bits of the raft break away are likely hotspots, for the same is probably happening under the water to food particles which, swept along by the current, adhere to the rubbish.

Fishing lay-bys may be too complex and problem-prone for them to become your favourite kind of swim. But they certainly provide a challenge, and can be looked on as preparation for the even bigger challenge of a weirpool—a wild mass of eddies with its own distinctive character and fish population.

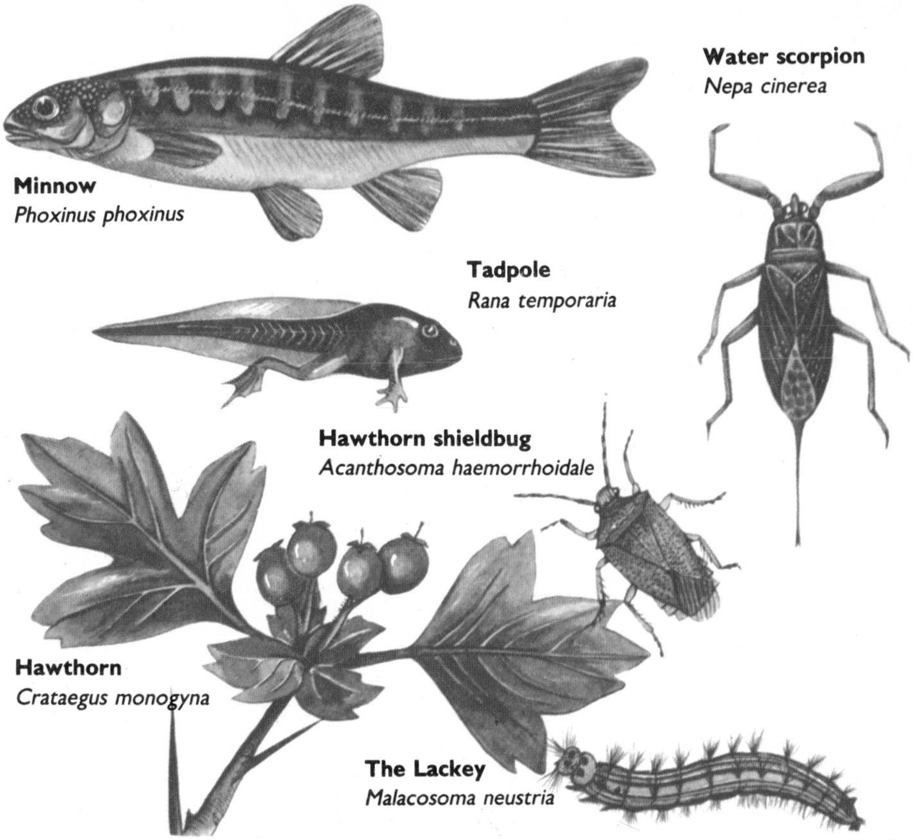

Minnow
Phoxinus phoxinus

Water scorpion
Nepa cinerea

Tadpole
Rana temporaria

Hawthorn shieldbug
Acanthosoma haemorrhoidale

Hawthorn
Crataegus monogyna

The Lackey
Malacosoma neustria

273

Hot-spots

The angler seeking a hotspot has been likened to the burglar looking for an open window: once he has found it, there are rich pickings to be had with the greatest of ease

The expression 'hotspot' became an in-word with specimen-hunters in the mid-1930s and has since become more widely used. If anything, it is now too widely used, and often in the wrong context. Unfortunately, too, the hotspot era has brought with it the problem of 'swim-jumpers', who watch successful anglers then 'beat them to it'. Ironically, the hotspots in those swims are often wasted by these fellows as they are not aware of the existence of them.

Know your hotspots

So what is a hotspot? Basically, it is a comparatively small area in a big-fish swim that for a variety of reasons (known and unknown) is highly productive.

Many people confuse swims or fishing positions with hotspots, and kid themselves that they are halfway to success because they have chosen a swim known to produce big fish. The most important point is to know precisely *where* in that swim to locate the fish, and pinpointing the fish is not easy when a lot of water is within easy range of most fishing positions.

In my experience there are three types of hotspot. First, the 'natural' hotspot, where fish (several species perhaps) concentrate and feed consistently. Natural hotspots probably occur more frequently on small or medium sized rivers than on large stillwaters or wide rivers and drains.

The second type is the hotspot where fish will often stop-off or congregate to feed after mild encouragement from the angler. This type occurs in many kinds of water, both still and flowing.

The third type is what I call an 'artificial' hotspot, which is almost entirely created by the angler. A good example is the hotspot produc-

POINTS TO WATCH
Variations of current—there may be a perch at the tail of an eddy, where the current slows down.

Channels among weedbeds—often part of the natural patrol routes followed daily by some species. Judicious freebaiting works wonders.

Tuck-ins and lay-bys—where fish may pull over to rest or eat.

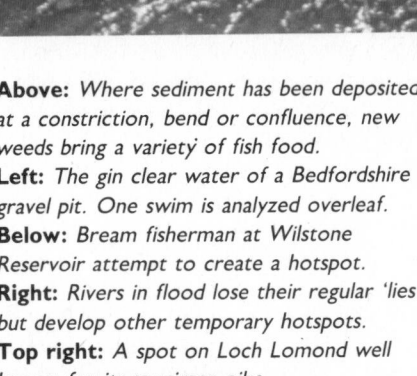

Above: *Where sediment has been deposited at a constriction, bend or confluence, new weeds bring a variety of fish food.*
Left: *The gin clear water of a Bedfordshire gravel pit. One swim is analyzed overleaf.*
Below: *Bream fisherman at Wilstone Reservoir attempt to create a hotspot.*
Right: *Rivers in flood lose their regular 'lies' but develop other temporary hotspots.*
Top right: *A spot on Loch Lomond well known for its specimen pike.*

ASK THE EXPERT

What is the precise definition of a hotspot?

There is no precise definition. Generally speaking, hotspots are small, highly productive areas, usually a few square feet, found within a swim. In most cases the reason why a hotspot is rich in fish is not fully understood.

Is there an easy way of locating them?

No. Only experience will enable you to recognize a hotspot. But you can begin by studying a chosen water and systematically exploring it and recording what you see. The advice of an older, more experienced angler who knows the water well also helps. But learning where a hotspot is within a new stretch of water will take time.

Is finding a hotspot the key to successful fishing?

For the novice it is far more important perfecting basic angling skills rather than spending time trying to find a perfect place to fish. With experience, the angler develops an instinct which enables him to track down hotspots. But because access to them is often through a window of a few square feet, accurate casting is essential in order to exploit it. So rather than spending a great deal of time trying to find an elusive hotspot, the novice is best advised to first learn those techniques which will help him exploit a hotspot when he finds one.

Are hotspots to be found in every type of coarse fishing water?

From the smallest stream to the widest river, in the tiniest pond and on the largest reservoir, anglers note patches of water which they consider 'hotspots'. But hotpots are most often associated with lakes and pits.

ed when bream fishing in a large reservoir. The angler may have only a scant knowledge of the patrolling breams' routes, which cover many hundreds of square yards of water, but by regular and/or heavy ground-baiting the bream are 'educated' to feed in a particular area. In this case the hotspot may be several square yards in area, but in relation to the overall size of the water it is still comparatively tiny.

There are numerous pointers to hotspots, or rather swims *containing* them, and these are covered in other 'Reading the Water' articles. But hotspots themselves cannot be described in general terms. The best way to explain them is to examine a couple of examples.

Example 1 shows a typical gin-clear Bedforshire clay pit, where the water can be read by climbing the bankside trees. This pit is a good water for summer tench, with natural patrol routes through the weed-free channels into the more open water. Tench could be encouraged to stop and feed in certain hotspots by the careful and selective use of free bait.

It was comparatively rare for tench to accept a bait presented in the open central part of the swim. During the day, they favoured the security and shelter of the submerged tree stumps among the weed. Thus, daytime hotspots tended to be on the very edge of the weedbeds causing problems of snagging for the angler.

On warms nights, the tench would venture closer in and root around the rushes for food in 1-3ft of water, so the edge of the rushes became the new night hotspot. But the bait had to be fished very close to them, as the tench would not stop long in the clear, central channel.

On hard-fished lakes like this, fish prefer to feed in areas close to the shelter of weedbeds or underwater snags, so it is hardly surprising that hotspots are often close by.

Example 2 shows a 'natural' hotspot on a small river on the higher reaches of the Great Ouse where the river is only 5-7 yards wide.

At the river's normal winter level, the depth of the swim varied from 7-9ft, and the total extent of the

swim was 18 yards. There were three natural hotspots for three species —chub, roach, and perch. It was not a case of an isolated red-letter day when the swim turned up trumps: by careful positioning and fishing all three species can be caught.

It would have taken an idiot not to identify the big chub hotspot in the

downstream sector of the swim, tight to the near bank. There, the deep undercut had a depth of 6-7ft and there were natural arches formed by small hawthorn bushes. Moreover, about halfway along, there was a lovely 'tuck-in' or lay-by—possibly the result of a large willow being pulled out years before.

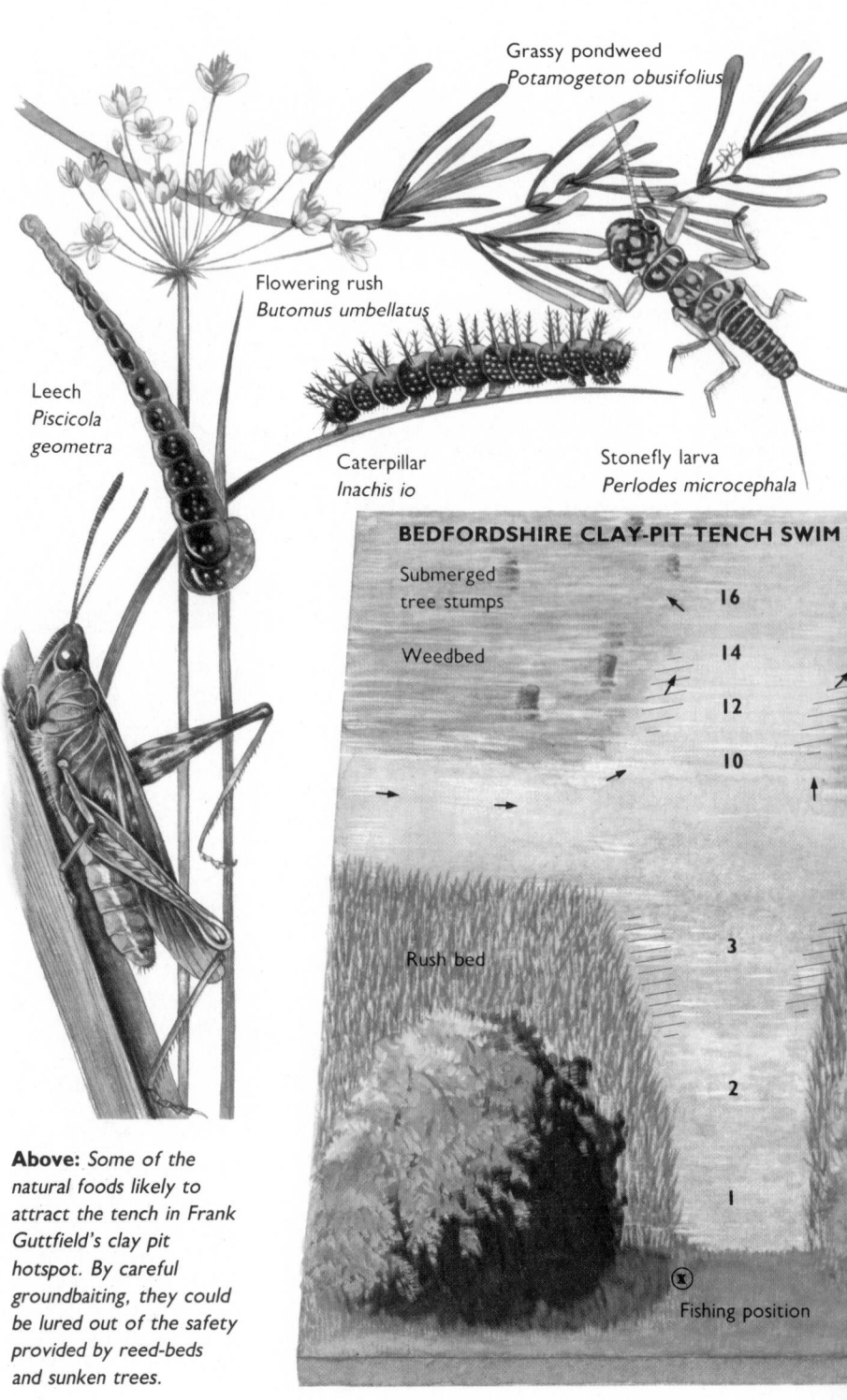

Grassy pondweed
Potamogeton obusifolius

Flowering rush
Butomus umbellatus

Leech
Piscicola geometra

Caterpillar
Inachis io

Stonefly larva
Perlodes microcephala

BEDFORDSHIRE CLAY-PIT TENCH SWIM

Submerged tree stumps

Weedbed

Rush bed

16

14

12

10

3

2

1

Fishing position

Above: *Some of the natural foods likely to attract the tench in Frank Guttfield's clay pit hotspot. By careful groundbaiting, they could be lured out of the safety provided by reed-beds and sunken trees.*

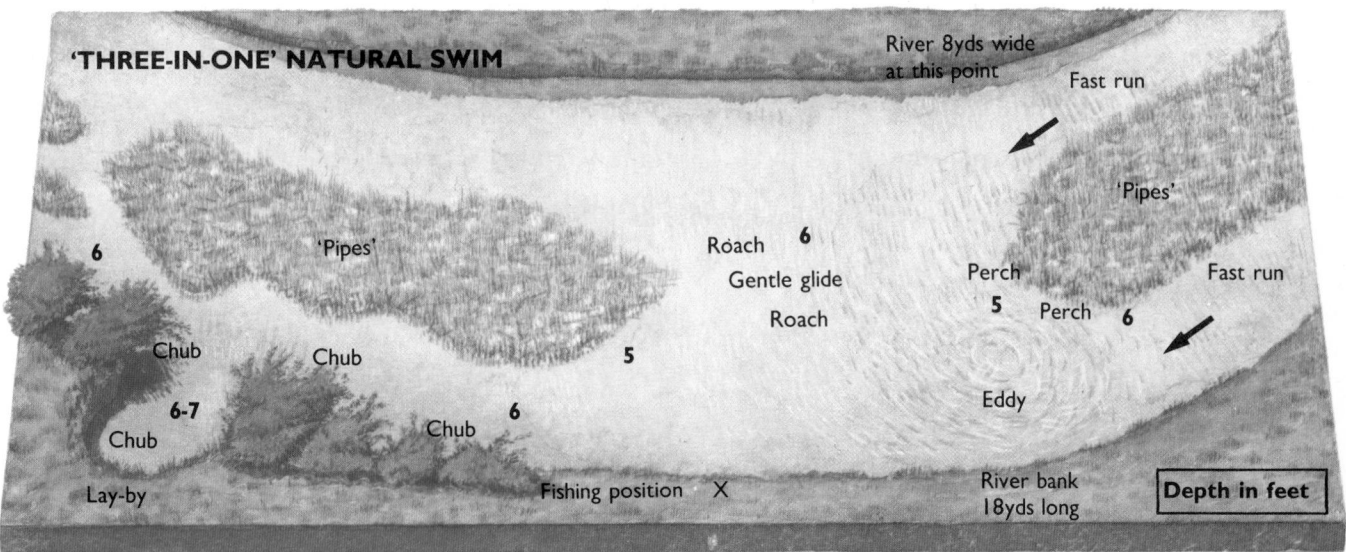

'THREE-IN-ONE' NATURAL SWIM

River 8yds wide at this point

Fast run

'Pipes'

Fast run

'Pipes'

6

Roach **6**

Gentle glide

Perch

Perch

Roach

5

Perch **6**

Chub

Chub

5

6-7

6

Eddy

Chub

Chub

Lay-by

Fishing position X

River bank 18yds long

Depth in feet

Above: *Three hotspots for three species—chub, roach and perch—could be reached from the one position on this river bend.*
Right: *An 85lb bag of pike taken in just three hours from the Dee—a river rich in pike, as well as salmon.*
Below: *A section of the Bedfordshire gravel pit described by Frank Guttfield.*

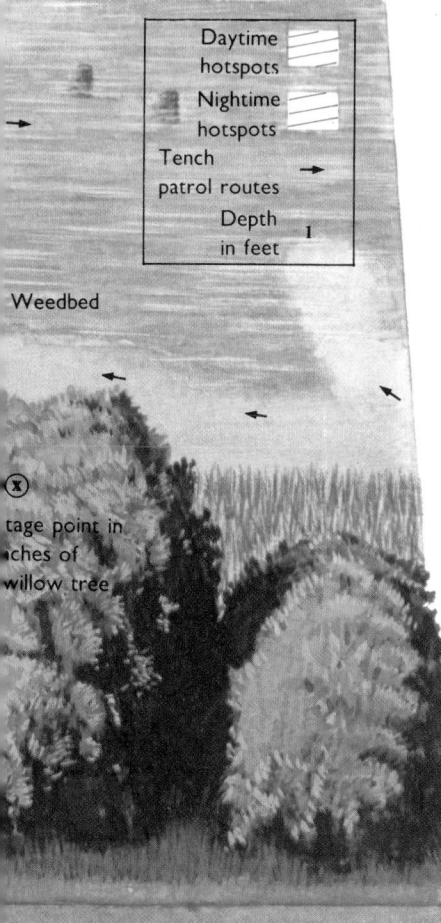

Daytime hotspots

Nightime hotspots

Tench patrol routes

Depth in feet   1

Weedbed

X

tage point in ches of willow tree

A certain chub holt. This hotspot always contained a few chub, perhaps just three or four, but they were invariably a good size.

In summer, Ouse perch tend to disperse, but in winter they group in small shoals, and never seem too far from the beds of 'pipes' left by bulrushes when they die back.

River perch seem to like a clean bottom and bulrushes usually grow in gravel. It was hardly surprising, therefore, to find the perch hotspot between the eddy on my own bank of the river and the edge of the bulrush pipe bed.

Current slowed down

Although the perch were slightly upstream, it was easy to present them with float-fished worm for the eddy slowed down the current in the hotspot. So, with much of the line kept off the water, fishing those few square feet of rich territory was more like canal fishing than normal river sport.

It is interesting that, although the eddy itself looked attractive, the perch never seemed to venture into it. The only species that seemed to stay there were minnows—another reason for the predatory perch being close by and willing to bite.

The perch lie tails off into a shortish glide about 6 yards long and with an even depth of 5-6ft. This, the 'heart' of the swim, was favoured by the roach.

For roach, it is most important to analyze the surface—it should be silky smooth and steady in flow. It can even be fast, but it must not have the slightest hint of turbulence. This glide was beautifully smooth and its bottom clean, except for an inch or so of silt. It was ideal for trotting except when the river was running fast, when a ledgered bait was more practical.

These two examples should have shown you the sort of features which make one place in a swim a hotspot and not another. Once you have found it, catching those elusive specimens is that much easier.

Bob Jackson with a 5lb chub taken from a deep hole in the river bed: detecting the hotspot did not diminish his skill in catching the fish.

Lake margins

Heavy plant growth at the edges of lakes often promises rich catches—but can be frustrating. Learning how to read the margins of lakes clearly will double your effectiveness

I first realized that it was possible to read lake margins in the early 1950s. One facinating summer's study led me to believe that all species of lake fish spend a great deal of time in the marginal shelter. Carp fishing was becoming recognized as a worth-while pursuit and 'margin fishing' was soon to be developed by Dick Walker. His object was to present a surface crust immediately below the rod tip, close to the bank, so that no line lay on the water to worry the carp. It was simple, and like many simple methods, highly efficient.

Tench studies
At that time I was studying the behaviour of tench throughout the season, and found myself reading the lake margins for signs of them. By watching the rush stems I was able to recognize the difference bet-ween the activities of feeding tench and those of cruising rudd.

When the baited swim stopped producing tench, and as the sun rose higher, I noticed activity in the thick marginal rushes and when single stems bent towards the water, fish of several pounds were clearly responsible. During the heat of the day I fished the thick margins with small baits and caught tench at in-tervals until evening.

Food-bearing rushes
There was no other indication except for the occasional 'kissing' noise in the thick rush beds and, while eels make such noises and barbel make similar sounds in streamer weed, I had a hunch that tench were sucking food from the rush stems. Also, their continual brushing against the rushes possibly had the function of dislodging food from the stems. I am convinced that tench do not like strong sunlight and that they retire to the shelter of marginal rushes to feed once the sun is high. My marginal catches bear this out and, today, presenting a slowly sinking bait is as deadly a method as any for daytime tench fishing.

When I was catching these marginal tench, big rudd put in an appearance from time to time and their near-surface flips and swirls were easily distinguishable from the more determined delvings of tench.

As I have learned since, bream often behave in a similar way. One dense bed of giant reed-mace on a large lake has yielded countless bream over 6lb since I realized that they were making regular trips into the thicket. There were defined paths—channels just wide enough to permit the passage of a fish, and fur-ther exploration with a boat showed

Left: *Fishing thick margins with small baits can produce big tench.*
Above: *Heavy bankside growth houses insects which fall into the margins. Caterpillars and grubs are of most interest to surface feeding fish.*

a wide, clear area in what appeared to be a completely over-grown margin. This area was sheltered from the wind, fairly deep, teeming with snails and other small creatures, and those bream had little cause to investigate a heavily baited swim nearby. Their main food source was obviously to be found in the margins.

This lake afforded many similar areas. Each had narrow channels leading into a clearing where the rushes thinned out and almost completely disappeared. On other bream waters since then, those narrow channels have been an absolute give-away. There is no guarantee though that all bream waters possess such obvious characteristics.

Sweet Flag
Acorus calamus

Broad-bodied Libellula dragonfly
Libellula depressa

Shore Weed
Littordla uniflora

Green Hydra
Hydra viridis
Hygrotus sp.

Left: *Some of the plants and insects you should look for: beetles, dragon-flies and eggs deposited on weeds and rushes make for good fishing.*

Reedmace

Bream

Channel

Surface disturbance

Uproo

Rudd

Carp

Tench

Right: *When you know what to look for you can pinpoint the presence of fish with accuracy. Uprooted reedmace, for example, means snuffling carp; narrow channels leading to clearings suggest bream; surface disturbance could be rudd.*

280

Above: *This daytime angler may well discard groundbait at the end of the day, baiting-up the margins conveniently for the knowledgeable and cautious night angler.*

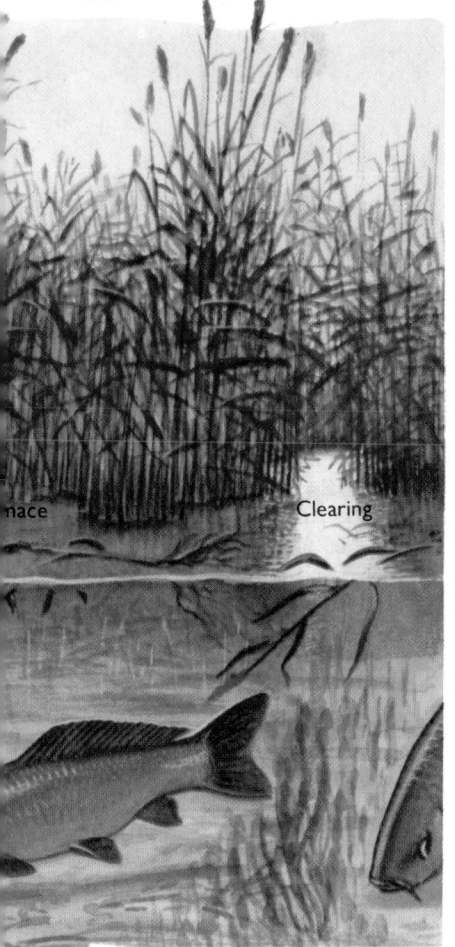

face

Clearing

Marginal carp signs are even easier to read. Where large numbers of big carp are present, the reeds sway and shudder as big fish move close to them. There are also areas where their constant foraging has completely uprooted the reeds. If you see them uprooted and lying on the surface, close to intense fish activity in the thicket, big carp are working the area. Swans and other water fowl probably dislodge rushes too, but I believe carp to be responsible for most of the uprooting that I have seen.

Sure signs of carp
I was told that no carp existed in a certain lake and I was puzzled by the uprooted rushes. I later heard that carp *were* present but that they were never caught. However, only the open water had been fished. I could not wait to get a bait into those ripped-up, marginal reeds and at the first attempt extracted three carp and lost two more. There was nothing magical about it: the rushes were simply the logical spot to fish.

Marginal reeds and rushes bent and broken during the summer offer a further indication of big fish. Later in the year, when the stems weaken, green bulrushes fold over and die off, but where healthy plants appear suddenly flattened (and it is not the work of a dog, otter or swan) big fish

may be responsible. I have actually seen Norfolk rush stems collapse at the water line when carp have been active, and a late spawning drive will have this spectacular effect.

If doubt remains regarding the cause of the uprootings, and time is on the angler's side, there is a simple ruse to employ. Fish, whether they be carp, bream or tench, having caused marginal plants to flatten or uproot, may be assumed to be feeding, and bait introduced to the margin can be watched for several days to make sure.

Baits for bream
The bait should be in the form of big hook samples—pieces of well pinched bread flake, small potatoes or any other easily visible portions. In shallow margins these food items show up well and, in the absence of swans, it may be assumed that it is big fish that are responsible if they disappear.

Soft groundbait or meal, sweetcorn and other small particle baits, may well disappear overnight, but there is no guarantee regarding size of the fish responsible. Drifting shoals of rudd are capable of clearing up a great deal of 'small' food as indeed are skimmer bream. It usually takes a big fish to clear up a 'potato patch', and if small half-cooked potatoes are taken, it is usually a sign that carp are present.

Big bream shoals tend to follow a defined course around a large lake and, although they do not always venture into the very shallow water in search of natural food, they may well be encouraged to do so if the area is baited. By taking careful note of their timing it is sometimes possible to be present with a hookbait in place ready for their subsequent visits. It does not always work (and it cannot be expected to immediately), but a careful study of the margins over a period of weeks may well bring about the catch of a lifetime. I once caught three bream over 8lb in three casts as a result of such a study. They came from marginal water no more than two feet deep and their backs were out of the water as they foraged.

Pike, too, love the margins, but a pike quietly awaiting its prey does little to betray its presence until it strikes out at a passing fish. Then there is no mistake. The whole area often explodes with action and the marginal plants may be seen to shudder and sway as the pike returns to eat its meal. Pike anglers often fish the edges from a boat, and it is common practice to beat the rushes with paddles before fishing livebaits in open water. Pike do not stay in the margins when the wind is high and waves are lapping the shore. Then they are more likely to be found in open water. It has been suggested that they feel some kind of discomfort in the swaying rushes.

When there is no sign of fish in the near-bank rushes, it makes sense to use the wind to advantage and, from a boat anchored well out, toss in some loose crusts and let them drift naturally to the edge. Tossing them in directly from the bank may work, but usually takes longer. Drifting crusts are often attacked by rudd very quickly and the noise they make sometimes causes carp to move out and investigate.

Tench and bream also investigate marginal disturbance. I once watched a big tench cruising slowly around a floating crust while rudd continued their attacks. Finally, it pushed it right into the marginal thicket. The crust disappeared with a carp-like slurp. In some waters it is not at all unusual to watch tench rise slowly from the depths to suck in large chunks of floating crust. Through polarized lenses I have watched bream take slowly sinking portions, broken off a larger piece by surface-feeding rudd.

Although we tend to think of rushes and reeds at the mention of margins, there are, of course, many where no plant life grows at all. The dam ends of some traditional lakes and reservoirs are deep and usually free from obstructions. Where there are structures of any kind, perch are likely to gather, and one way of 'exploring' these areas is to spin with small vibrating spoons or spinners. Perch will come up from the depths to investigate the source of these vibrations and although this does not always result in positive takes, these 'follows' prove that the fish are indeed there.

The last kind of margin to be considered is the swampy area that cannot be reached from the bank. It is overgrown with vegetation that has encroached over the swamp and into the lake itself. Many such areas exist in Ireland, but only boats or jetties give access to them. Attempts to wade or cast to them only scare the fish away and spoil a wonderful opportunity, for many of these margins hold fish in large numbers.

Many fish, tench in particular, do not venture out from under the vast cover of tangled branches and herbage. Their retreat may lie several feet back in a jungle of greenery. I have swum into one such thicket and found water, some four feet deep, going back three yards from the apparent bank line. These areas must be approached silently and with care. Anchors should be lowered quietly and casts made from long range. Light groundbait thrown first on top of the cover so that it trickles through, and later into the water at the bank line, should bring fish out to feed.

Right: An 18lb mirror carp taken from thick margins. **Below:** Reedbeds may hold predatory fish. **Below right:** Carp of over 40lb have been taken from under these yellow lilies on a lake in Hertfordshire. **Below far right:** Plants standing in water are natural larders.

ASK THE EXPERT

Do fish inhabit shallows where there are no rushes or reeds?
Most species investigate marginal weeds at some time—most often at night. Tench of over 5lb have been taken from weedy margins after dark on big baits fished only a rod's length from banks with no standing plants whatsoever.

What's the right tackle for fishing margins?
Generally, margins are unsuited to traditional float fishing. A simple, freelined, leadless rig is best for large baits like lobworms, paste or flake: the bait gives you casting weight and there's less chance of snagging. A small self-cocking float tackle is useful for small baits close to rush stems, where depth permits.

Can't the natural food in lake margins be put to use as bait?
Yes indeed! Mussels, caddis grubs and water snails are ideal. Use mussels whole or in snippets. Caddis grubs are small and need small hooks. Both baits should be removed from their shell or casing, but snails may be used whole.

Where shallows are overgrown, should I clear a swim?
It's often essential, but confine yourself to a small area. Dragging operations may well attract tench, but they tend to leave again once the mud has cleared, especially in hot weather.

Which hours of the day are most productive?
If, like most anglers, you settle down for about four hours fishing in any one day, make it the first four hours of daylight, starting from the moment when you can first see your bait hit the water.

SEA FISHING

FOR MANY freshwater anglers, sea fishing tackle is considered heavy and clumsy, with none of the 'feel' and finesse that is associated with fishing for the wary roach, carp and so on. But while these accusations once had some validity, when thick cuttyhunk line and matching, massive rods and reels were the order of the day, the advent of glassfibre and carbonfibre coupled with nylon monofilment line enabled the tackle manufacturers to market gear that *pro rata* with freshwater fishing is comparable tackle.

The sea provides its own dictates in many areas of the sport. All freshwater and game species of fish have their seasons and these have been ratified by law into statutory close periods when the angler may not seek them and it is illegal to fish. However, the saltwater species provide their own seasons because they migrate to warmer or colder waters when the reproduction cycle drives them; the result is that they are just not present at well understood times. This and other migratory movements are recognised and the experienced sea angler seeking certain species times his outings accordingly.

In the sea the freshwater angler's technique of float, ledger and paternoster are mirrored but they have their own refinements, one major difference being that water conditions, depth, tides, state of the sea, all provide much sterner tests of both fisherman and his tackle, and the tackle rigs have to be assembled accordingly.

This section of the book covers a very broad range of species, tackles and baits and it includes descriptions of two major sea angling centres. Of all the places where prime saltwater fishing is to be found, the south-west coast of England stands supreme. The reasons are a combination of an ideal seabed, with ideal marks of sand and rock pinnacles, the proximity of the open Atlantic where because of its latitude the water is warmer than the rest of Britain's surrounding seas. The biggest threat to fishing here is the weather since the prevailing westerlies are liable to turn into gales which can become very fierce.

The area of the south west also has a large number of wrecks, some from a hundred or more years ago but many others are from the two World Wars, evidence of the desperate days when Britain's lifeline was the Merchant Navy, now so sadly depleted, but then its crews defied the terrors of the torpedo attacks from U-boats for week after week in order to keep hungry stomachs fed and to

bring much-needed munitions across the Atlantic. Stark evidence of wartime came to me one day while fishing a couple of dozen miles out from Newhaven, Sussex. The anchor went down and just would not hold, the boat slowly drifting westwards with the tide, taking us away from the rough ground where fish were known to feed. So the rope was hauled in and as the anchor came to the surface I saw the reason why it would not hold, one tine was embedded in the empty mouth of a 3in brass shellcase, well corroded. Once released and down again, the anchor held perfectly once we had found the mark.

The second area covered here is Eire's coast whose prolific seas have long been noted for giving fine sport and yielding outstanding specimens. There are, too, places where even in the worst of weather the boat angler can ply his trade in reasonable comfort and with the expectation of good fish. Here again I can confirm the excellence of the seas off Southern Ireland, having taken good-sized blue shark from the deep, rough waters over the wreck of the *Lusitania* 300 fathoms below; cod from the sheltered waters of Cobh; very edible fighting bass from the storm beaches near Waterford, and equally tasty and powerful skate and huss from the myriad islands dotting Westport Bay.

But the waters of Ireland and England's south west are but two areas. The whole of Britain's rugged and beautifully varied coastline offers the sea fisherman anything he needs in terms of sporting fish, except of course those exotic big game fish found in tropical and sub-tropical seas. There was even a period of tunny fishing found off the Yorkshire coast in the 1930s, as is evidenced by that 851lb entry in the British Record Fish Committee's lists. But Mitchell Henry's huge 1933 fish was one of the last of its species, their numbers dwindled and they are no longer seen in British waters.

After discussing the majority of the saltwater species found in British waters there are three features which concentrate on the two most widely practised styles of sea fishing, that of off-shore fishing and its attendant wreck fishing. The latter is probably the most exciting kind of salt water sport outside that of deep-sea big game trolling in the tropics and sub-tropics. The deepwater wrecks offer shelter and food for many large and powerful conger, ballan wrasse, bass, while above them hang swarms of specimen pollack and coalfish. On the fringes of the area big huss (properly called nursehound) and rays lie and shark are often attracted to the area homing in on the oily scents oozing from the baits and hooked fish.

Off-shore fishing is a catch-all description of angling from dinghies close-in and perhaps no more than 100 yards out to large charterboats capable of holding up to ten anglers and steaming anything up to 15-20 miles before either anchoring or drifting.

While not including a section on beachcasting for

those unfortunates who have found through bitter and unpleasant experience that the motions of a wallowing, rolling, jerking charterboat combine to remove all the pleasures of fishing, the beaches, piers and rocks round our coast do offer some fine sea fishing. Each demands its own correct tackle, but baits there are in plenty on rocks and in the sand and mud of the tidal areas. The tackle for beachcasting is quite unlike that for boat work. Casting out some 100 yards from a beach demands a rod, reel and line capable of withstanding the stresses produced by the actions of the angler. The rod is usually 12ft or so, which is totally useless in a boat, where the line and terminal tackle is lowered over the side and allowed to drop to the seabed under the control of the thumb on the spool. One most important warning for rock anglers is that on no occasion should they wear smooth-soled wellingtons. A slip on weed-covered and slimy rock can deposit angler and all his tackle into cold, deep water – and sea-filled waders which act as sea-anchors for the unfortunate wearer are very dangerous things.

Never forget that the sea has many faces, many moods. In the warm of the Mediterranean sun and its shallow waters it is a playground for all, perfectly safe; it is a highway for the world's merchant fleets (and also, unfortunately, for drug smugglers); it is a major sporting venue for all kinds of water sports, fishing being but one. But it can kill: never underrate the ability of the sea to suddenly become ferocious and lethal. Treat it with all the care, respect and vigilance that you give to anything that is capable of snuffing life out without warning.

There is one subject which is rarely given space in any angling publication – sea angling clothing. It is a safe bet that the members of any party of sea anglers heading towards their boat will resemble nothing more than a group of dropouts looking for a night's rough sleep. Of course, the conditions on a boat at sea, with baits being cut up, fish coming inboard with much splashing and thrashing, are not those of a spotless hospital ward. But looking like a tramp is not an essential for the sea fisherman. He needs warm, waterproof clothing and sufficient spare to put on if it turns much colder. The waterproofs must be reliable, for in a strong wind with rain and seawater seeping through to wet the clothing beneath, the body can suffer severe chills.

The sea angler's clothing also includes that which be required to save life. By law and before the necessary insurance can be taken out every charterboat must carry lifejackets for every man aboard, as well as flares. Many experienced sea anglers obtain their own, to the pattern of their choice and wear them as a matter of course. And with safety in mind, any craft going into shipping lanes should wear a proper metallic radar reflector on the highest mast or part of the boat.

Anyone, even the most experienced of sea anglers, can suddenly fall foul of *mal de mer*, especially if he or she is off-colour and below par, suffering from a cold or chill or in some way just not on form. It is believed that Admiral Lord Nelson, of all sailors, suffered from sea sickness every time his ship left harbour, but he fought it with the same determination that he fought Britain's enemies. Those who suffer should take comfort from this knowledge, but at the time I doubt it. There is little serious advice that one can offer, but avoiding food before setting out is certainly wrong. At the first hesitant pangs, fix the eyes on the horizon and keep in the fresh air, away from diesel fumes and old baitboards. Spike Milligan's classic and comic – but horribly accurate–advice is of little help: 'Go and sit under a tree!'

Food is also important. If you are at anchor 15 miles out it is not much use telling your pals that you forgot your sandwiches; someone might take pity but don't rely on it. For many anglers, myself included, sea fishing is a hunger-producing sport. One dodge used by old hands is to anticipate that one or more of the party will suddenly lose interest in eating after the just-anchored boat has carried out its first few wild gyrations.

The world of big game fishing just touches British waters. The conger is not considered a big-game species but for sheer brute strength and ferocity there is not much to beat it except for large shark species. Britain's waters have plenty of big conger, king of all so far being the 109lb 6oz record breaker boated by R. W. Potter while fishing over the famous Eddystone reef off Cornwall. Had that conger been hooked while still partly in its rocky lair it must have defeated all attempts to dislodge it and get it into open water to be played to the boat. Even this monster has been outweighed by conger which have fouled commercial nets, so that weight can well be beaten. For sharks Britain has its share, with a world record porbeagle weighing 465lb, caught by J. Potier in 1976 off Padstowe, Cornwall. Other sharks which made the headlines were a 500lb mako, a 217lb blue and 323lb thresher.

When large-scale trawling is mentioned we cry 'shame!' shock and horror on our faces. And shame it is but the fact is that in a smaller way anglers themselves have also been responsible for the declining fish stocks. Littlehampton, Sussex, used to be the venue for annual black bream festivals. Vast numbers of this beautiful fish were caught but most died in the boats and after being weighed they were thrown back. Those bream were there for breeding purposes. Now the bream are scarce and the festivals no longer take place. The price of fish is now astronomical when compared with the old, tasty and nutritious couple of bobs' worth of fish and chips, now paid for in pounds. So keep only those fish which you need for the table and put all unwanted ones back alive into the sea.

Black bream

Ubiquitous and voracious, with a truly extraordinary sex life, the black bream offers fine sport. Its numbers, however, are declining rapidly and the species is becoming scarce

The black sea bream, *Spondyliosoma cantharus*, is one of those species familiar to the angler but which have been too little studied by biologists. It shares many of the characteristics of the family Sparidae, a group of marine fishes of worldwide distribution in tropical and temperate seas. The moderately deep, fully scaled body, a long dorsal fin with sharp spines, and a shorter anal fin with three strong spines, are common to most sea breams.

By the wheelhouse of the Girl Alison, *John Garlick poses with his record black bream of 6lb 14oz 4dr taken over a wreck off the coast of Devon.*

Where it differs from many others is in its dentition: the teeth are slender and pointed, only those in the outer row being larger and slightly flattened to look like incisors, while those all round the sides of the jaws are pointed and slim. In this relative uniformity, the black bream differs from all the other British breams, which have either large dogteeth in the front of the jaws, or rounded crushing teeth in the sides of the jaws, or, in a few cases, flattened incisors, similar in shape to human front teeth. The variation in the teeth of the sea breams is a fascinating example of adaptation to different kinds of foods and methods of feeding.

Confusion with Ray's bream

There is little chance of an angler confusing the black sea bream with any other species of sea bream, its teeth and its coloration of silver with horizontal dark lines (in breeding fish broad vertical bands and, in particular, a dusky forehead) being distinctive. Curiously, most of the identification problems that I have encountered have involved a quite unrelated fish—Ray's bream *(Brama brama)*, which is a member of the family Bramidae.

Despite its name, Ray's bream is not a sea bream, although it has a superficial resemblance to them, being deep-bodied and fully scaled. It is. however, very thin in the body, and it has no separate spines in its dorsal or anal fins. The tail fin is also deeply forked, too much so to be that of a sea bream. If these points are borne in mind, there should be no confusion, but as Ray's bream is dark-coloured and unfamiliar to most sea anglers, it is not surprising that it is sometimes thought to be a sea bream.

In British waters, the black bream is commonest in the English Channel, the southern Irish Sea, the Bristol Channel, and off South-West Ireland. Elsewhere it occurs fairly regularly, although with declining frequency the farther north and east one goes.

Dramatic decline in black bream

The large numbers of black bream that were formerly taken by anglers in the Channel during the spawning season seems to have resulted in a dramatic decline in numbers of spawning fish. If, as seems to be the case, this is the major spawning area of the species north of Biscay, then the effects will be felt far beyond the eastern Channel, and the species will become increasingly scarce in the North Sea and probably along the rest of the Channel coast.

The black bream spawns in April and May. Its spawning behaviour has been well described and differs in many ways from that of other sea breams. The male makes a nest on the sea bed, usually where fine gravel or coarse shell grit form the surface, by sweeping the finer material away with vigorous side-to-side movements of the tail.

Separate nests may be quite close together, but their spacing probably varies with the size of the area suitable for spawning and the number of males in the breeding population. In dense populations they may be within 3ft of one another, but with lower numbers, common in nature, they are separated by 10ft-30ft of clear ground.

The male's activities

It must be assumed that in crowded conditions the males spend more time defending their territory and nest and that survival and success of the young is lower than in less crowded situations. Normally, the males spend a considerable part of their time, once the nest is made, in pursuing females, sometimes swimming up to 30ft away from the nest in pursuit of a female and attempting to chase it towards the nest.

It is during the frenzy of nest construction and soliciting for a mate that the male's coloration becomes most intense. The normal pale colouring changes to an intense dark violet, almost black, the head being black above the level of the mouth.

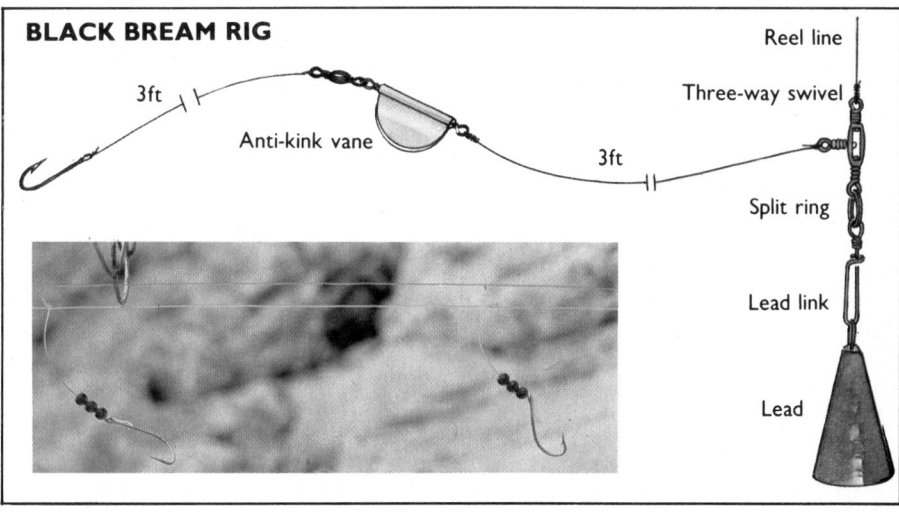

BLACK BREAM RIG

Reel line

Three-way swivel

3ft

Anti-kink vane

3ft

Split ring

Lead link

Lead

A prominent vertical white stripe runs across the back and side, ending at the vent, and there are light flecks on the head, notably one running under the eye. Individual fish vary in coloration, some spawning males being much darker than others. Female colouring too is heightened during spawning, the darkest-coloured females being almost as dark as the lightest males. These specimens may be in the process of, or only just have completed, the sex change described below.

The eggs form a single layer on the bottom of the nest, although where the bottom is irregular, two layers may be found. They form an irregular, light-coloured patch, which is guarded by the male until the eggs hatch in about nine days at 13°C (55.4°F). In addition to keeping predators away from the eggs, the male keeps the nest free of deposited silt by fanning with its tail and fins. In aquarium conditions the nest-

Above: *Driftline for black bream with a single size 4 or 6 hook on a 6ft trace with an anti-kink vane.* **Inset:** *A two-hook bream rig is effective when fishing a shoal.*

guarding male has been observed to attack rays, various flatfishes and rock lobsters, driving them away by continually biting at them.

It has long been known that some sea breams, as well as various other fishes, change sex. This is the case with the black sea bream. The original observations on this subject were made in the Mediterranean but have been more recently confirmed by a French researcher working on the North African coast. He provided confirmation by 'sexing' and measuring the fish caught on a research cruise. He found the numbers of each sex changed with the length of the fish. Mature fish between 7in and 15in (18cm and 38cm) in length comprised 31 males and 196 females. Between 15in and

FISHING FOR BLACK BREAM

Habitat	Baits	Groundbait	Method	Rod	Line	Reel	Weight	Hook	Distribution
Rock beds and reefs	Lug, mussel, sandeel, mackerel, squid and cuttle cut into strips and used singly or as mixed baits	Minced fish offal and bran in open mesh sack attached to anchor cable	Sliding float	8-9ft built to cast approx 2oz 6g	10lb b.s.	Fixed-spool or multiplier	1oz approx	Size 1 down to 6, according to bait	Widely throughout Mediterranean parts of eastern Atlantic. In British waters mainly limited to English Channel, part of the Bristol Channel and the Welsh coastline
Shingle and patches of rocky ground	Lug, mussel, sandeel, mackerel, squid and cuttle cut into strips and used singly or as mixed baits	Mixture of parboiled rice/wheat and mixed 50/50 (by volume) with fine grit	Ledger or paternoster	6ft light boat rod	15lb b.s.	Multiplier	According to tide 1-3oz	Size 1 down to 6, according to bait	
Chalk beds and similar hard broken and rocky ground	Lug, mussel, sandeel, mackerel, squid and cuttle cut into strips and used singly or as mixed baits	Mixture of parboiled rice/wheat and mixed 50/50 (by volume) with fine grit	Ledger	Medium boat rod	18lb b.s.	Multiplier	According to tide 3-6oz	Size 1 down to 6, according to bait	

ASK THE EXPERT

What other fish change sex?

Among British species, the cuckoo and ballan wrasses, the comber and the red sea bream change sex. Few other species have been studied properly, and other wrasses, sea breams and sea perches may also change. Sex changes play an important role in territorial and communal-living fishes and in some tropical species a community living on a wreck may be composed of one dominant male fish, a lot of females and the young. If the male dies, the largest of the females changes sex—ensuring the continuity of the species.

Can overfished fishing grounds recover?

In the 1950s and 1960s the eastern English Channel bream marks were heavily overfished, mature fish being taken right over their spawning grounds. Though catches have declined, there are now fewer fish. Despite attempts by conservationists, the bream have been slow to respond. Netting has also taken its toll. It may never be possible to reduce pressure on the fish population enough for it to reach its former level.

Do many fish eat seaweed?

Surprisingly few. Many fish have been reported to have weed in their stomachs, but only the shore-dwelling shanny and some wrasses actually feed on it.

What limits black bream distribution?

Temperature. The Channel forms the northern edge of the bream's spawning range. Although currents carry it further north it rarely breeds there. Unfortunately, there is evidence that local sea temperatures are slowly falling, so our coast may, in time, lose its bream.

Two fine 3lb bream caught on a 2-hook rig will put on a determined struggle.

21½in (38cm and 55cm) in length he found 31 males and 16 females. Two fish measuring 9.8in and 15.3in (25cm and 39cm) contained both soft roe and hard roe, and were thus bisexual. It seems therefore that the black sea bream is a protogynous hermaphrodite. This means that it starts its mature life as a female and, if it lives long enough, ends up as a functional male.

As its teeth suggest, the black bream is not a specialized feeder. Its fine, sharp teeth allow it to snap up any small soft-bodied animals it encounters. The black bream's diet contains substantial quantities of small crustaceans and fishes, but it does not tackle the larger crustaceans nor to any great extent molluscs, both of which are a prime food for other species of bream. It also eats substantial amounts of seaweed. When feeding, a school usually congregates above a reef with a pronounced crest or on broken reefs where the groundswell causes local currents to sweep up and over the rocks, carrying planktonic organisms or other edible items with it. While actively-feeding fish may systematically work along the ridge, the remainder hang 3 or 4ft or so above it, waiting for chance food to be swept along. Small particles of algae are quickly seized upon, but larger edible items are quickly surrounded and attacked by as many fish as can get a grip on them. This frequently happens with a baited hook, which will be the focus of attention of up to ten fish before the bait is either stripped off or a fish is hooked. This accounts for the frequency with which they are lip-hooked, and also for the 'knocks' and half-bites at the bait that the angler can feel in a calm sea.

British record black bream

The preference of this species for broken ground and reefs no doubt explains why the great majority are taken by boat anglers. Usually only small fish are taken close inshore, but large fish taken from the beach, such as the current shore-caught British record of 4lb 14oz 12dr taken on 25 September 1984 by D Boham fishing the Natural Arch, Alderney, C.I., in relatively deep water and rough ground. The British boat record is held by a fine fish of 6lb 14oz 4dr, caught in September 1977 by John Garlick, from a wreck in 37 fathoms off the Devon coast. Such a fish must be very close to the maximum size of the species and this record may stand for a long time.

Bass

In certain conditions a groundswell mounts in the Atlantic which claws crabs and worms out of our windward beaches with combing surf to feed bass shoals day and night

Surf fishing for bass—supreme sea fish of autumn and the Atlantic surf-strands—is an emotive experience. It is an unfortunate angler who wades into the surf and is not elated by the sounds of the sea and the kaleidoscope of images that surround him. Any fish hooked in these conditions would highlight a day's

Wading out is exhilarating but exhausting—leave strength in reserve for the wade back and know just what the tide is doing.

Left: *'Beyond the third wave'—that's the saying, but the bass angler is really casting beyond the farthermost breaker.*
Above: *A seven-pounder caught on live sandeel on the Skerries Bank.*
Above right: *An angler waiting for the incoming tide to build up.*
Below: *Estuary bassing on light tackle.*

sport; that it should be a bass—a fish strikingly similar to sea trout and salmon—completes the picture.

Such perfection, however, introduces problems of its own. Surf anglers are so intoxicated with their fishing that they attribute to the bass characteristics which it lacks. Bass are said to be exceptional fighters, cunning fish—fish with almost supernatural powers. But they are no more difficult to hook than flounders and pouting.

If there is one lesson to be learnt from surf fishing, it is to accept the superb atmosphere of the surf beach but never imagine that you need to be clever to hook a bass. Surf bass fishing is little different from any other kind of angling.

Good surf conditions depend upon two factors: a groundswell generated over many miles of open sea, and shallow beaches where high and low water marks are distant from each other. In the British Isles this means Atlantic water, and conse-

quently the best surf beaches are in Wales, the West Country and Ireland. They face between south and west and into the eye of the prevailing winds.

The breakers and backwash drive sandeels, crabs, small fishes and worms from the sand and predatory fishes such as bass invade the surf to wolf down the harvest. Bass hunt at all stages of the tide, but on any one beach they tend to follow an established pattern. Sometimes the flood is best; sometimes the ebb, or even slackwater, produces more fish.

Surf and food bring bass
It is difficult to predict when the bass will arrive, how long they will stay, or why they come in the first place. Food is a major factor, but many experienced anglers suspect that there are more subjective reasons: perhaps bass enjoy being in the surf. Whatever the explanation, surf brings the bass close inshore and the abundance of food usually

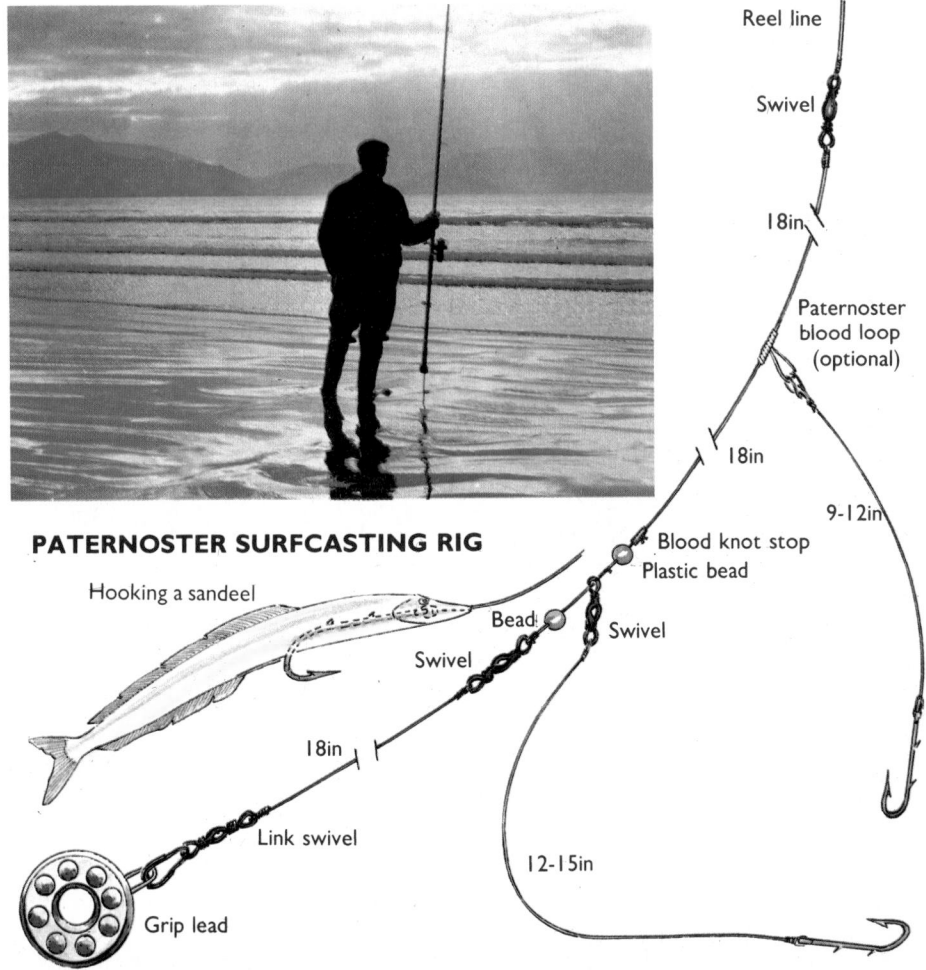

Reel line

Swivel

18in

Paternoster
blood loop
(optional)

18in

9-12in

PATERNOSTER SURFCASTING RIG

Hooking a sandeel

Blood knot stop
Plastic bead

Bead

Swivel

Swivel

18in

12-15in

Link swivel

Grip lead

makes them keen to feed.

Bass are comparatively small fishes, average fighters and, in the open sea at least, not at all tackle-shy. Long distance casting is generally unnecessary, and the water, for all its apparent churning, has little or no lateral current to sweep away the line. Taking all this into account, there is no need for heavy tackle, except when the waves are particularly vicious.

The ideal rod
A medium casting rod, with a small multiplier or fixed-spool reel, is ideal. The main criterion is lightness, because the tackle will be held all day. But it is well to remember that very light tackle —for instance, the 6lb class equipment recommended by some anglers—can be self-defeating. There is always the chance of a very big bass, a tope, a heavy ray; or that floating weeds and seabed rocks will snag the tackle.

Equipment of the 15lb class is ideal for surf bass, although there are occasions when 25lb line is necessary, for not all surf beaches are of clean sand. Some of the very best marks are strewn with rocks, pilings and breakwaters and you need strong tackle to master a hooked fish before it can take the line around the nearest obstruction.

Another advantage of medium weight tackle is its ability to cast 3-4oz sinkers. A heavy sinker carries the baits more slowly so that they remain on the hook during the cast. Anchored firmly in the sand, a 3 or 4oz grip-wired or pyramid sinker helps drive home the hook by pulling the fish up short as it attempts to make off with the fisherman's bait.

Self-contained mobile surf-angler
The movement of the water and the shallowness of the beach require an active form of angling where you wade with the tide. Rod rest tackle boxes and anything not strictly essential have no place in the surf. To fish well you must be self-contained and mobile. Spare hooks and sinkers go into a pocket, baits are kept in a bag suspended from your belt or from a cord around your neck. Waders and waterproof

trousers keep out most of the water. Some anglers use chest-high waders, but they are not necessary and are detrimental in that wading too far and too deep makes for inefficient casting and can be dangerous in rough water.

Wade into the surf to a comfortable depth, load the hook with bait and cast out about 50 yards. Hold the rod, feeling for bites by looping the line over your fingers. Tighten the line at the least sign of a bite. If you miss wait a little longer on the next bite, or hit even faster. It is impossible to predict how bass will take the bait—one day they tear it from the hook, the next they nibble at length. Trial and error is the only way to establish the precise timing of the strike.

Move up and down the beach with the tide, varying the casting distance, and changing baits regularly, for the surf soon washes out the juices and oils. Bass have catholic appetites and will take soft-back and peeler crab, all kinds of marine worms, squid and mussels, but the best offering by far is live sandeel. The wading angler can gather this deadly bait easily by tethering a wooden courge to a length of line which is attached to a sinker weighing a few pounds. This obviates the need to return to dry land to rebait.

A fine wire Aberdeen hook between 2/0 and 4/0 is the best type when offering sandeel, and can also be recommended for other types of bait. A 3ft monofilament trace of about 12lb b.s., rigged as a running ledger is the best terminal rig for live eels. The alternative is a two-hook paternoster with 6-8in snoods.

Never be afraid to bait big for bass: the species has a hinged mouth and a four-pounder is quite capable of engulfing a side of mackerel. Fish in the 10-12lb weight range will happily attack and swallow quite large fish or a whole squid. This is confirmed by many specimen bass that

Top: *A forest of beachcasting rods on Folkestone Beach in Kent, planted in the hope of surf and bass.*
Right: *Des Brennan with two brace of fine bass caught in Finnan's Bay, Co Kerry—a more reliable storm beach.*

292

What length of rod do you recommend for surf beach fishing?
One at least 11ft long which helps keep the reel line above the first row of breakers. It must be capable of throwing 6oz weights and heavier. Estuary shore fishing for bass can be successful with a 10ft double-handed spinning rod which falls into the category of a light beachcaster.

When is the best time to fish?
The majority of bass taken by shore anglers are hooked at dusk, after dark and just as day breaks. An hour's spell at dawn on an incoming tide can be rewarding, too.

How serious is the threat to bass of over-fishing?
Vast quantities of this valuable fish are removed each year from our coastal waters. Some areas where they were common five years ago are now virtually barren. Whitsand Bay off the Cornish coast and Eddystone Reef, Britain's top bass mark, are prime examples. It is not simply the quantity of fish taken, but the use of monofilament gill nets can completely eradicate a shoal so that no stragglers remain to rebuild stocks. Many sea angling clubs in good bass areas are encouraging members to return all fish under 3lb. It may be a small gesture against a background of commercial netting, but it might just ensure a future for this hard-fighting predator.

What type of beach should I look for?
Best are the kind with rocky outcrops divided by clear ground. Reconnoitre the ground at low water, preferably during a spring tide. Then try to drop your bait on to the sand as close to the rocks as possible.

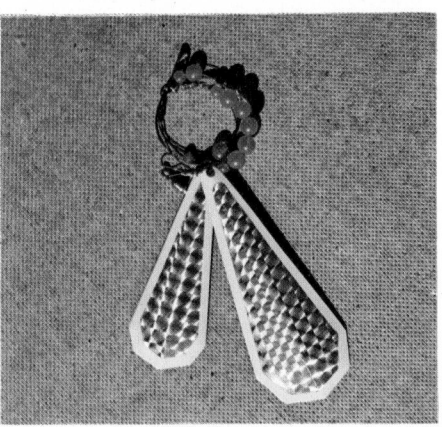

Real and artificial bass baits.
Above left: *Lesser sandeels.*
Above: *Flasher vanes on a trolling rig.*

fall to shore anglers fishing for conger after dark from harbour walls and piers. Cornwall's record bass of nearly 15lb was taken like this. Some baits seem to work better on particular beaches, but King rag or lugworm are universally acceptable. It is good policy to keep the bait moving, so that a lot of ground is covered, and always be keyed up to strike the instant an offer is transmitted to the rod tip. A tight line should be maintained at all times. It is also vitally important to keep in direct contact with a hooked fish—give him slack and chances are you will be bidding him goodbye.

Beaching your fish
On driving the hook home, keep the line tight. Let the fish run if it wants to, for every effort it makes will tire it. Let the waves bring it ashore and wash it on to the hard sand. As the backwash recedes, grab the fish and carry it farther up the beach, taking care not to touch its spines. Those of the dorsal fin are easily seen and avoided, but the knife-edges on the gill covers have slashed many a careless hand.

Dogfish

Born in miniature perfection out of mermaid's purses or into their mother's wake, dogfish grow into spiney scavengers or tiger-spotted hunters and travel under a dozen different names

There are three species of dogfish of interest to anglers fishing British waters—the lesser spotted, greater spotted (also called bull huss) and the spurdog. The black-mouthed dogfish *(Galeus melastomus)* is also found around Britain but in deep water along the Contintental Shelf and it is not an angler's fish.

Lesser spotted dogfish

The lesser spotted dogfish *(Scyliorhinus caniculus)* is one of the commonest elasmobranchii or cartilaginous fishes native to British waters. These fish have a skeleton of cartilage while the majority of fishes have a skeleton of hard bone. Although it possesses a typical fish shape, the lesser spotted dogfish, like its greater spotted relation, is strikingly distinguished from the bony-skeletoned fish by its crescent-shaped mouth. This is situated on the underside of the head, which forces it to turn sideways to attack its prey. Another difference is the lack of an operculum or gill covering. The five gill openings are long slits, situated behind the mouth and slightly forward of the pectoral fin. The upper half of the body is a reddish brown colour covered in hundreds of small black spots with one or two darker blotches. The underside is a creamy white, but when left exposed to the sun after capture large red blotches appear. The skin also differs greatly from bony fish in that, instead of having large overlapping scales, the scales are hundreds of minute pieces of bone embedded in the skin. The angler catching one of these fish should exercise great caution as the skin of the dogfish is extremely rough and can inflict a very painful graze.

The crescent-shaped mouth has small, pointed teeth which bite and tear food. Just in front of the mouth are the very large nostrils which may account for its very strong sense of smell. It certainly needs this faculty as it has very poor eyesight and so seeks its food mainly by scent. In this way it can detect any dead organisms in its vicinity and so act as a scavenger.

As the dogfish is so widely distributed, every angler is bound to catch one sooner or later. The easiest way of extracting the hook without coming to harm is to either subdue the dogfish with a blow on the head or to hold the tail and fold it towards the fish's head, holding the two together, and so immobilizing the fish while the hook is extracted.

Breeding habits

The breeding habits of the lesser spotted dogfish differ greatly from the bony fish in that the dogfish family possess male and female sex organs. In the male fish, part of each pelvic fin is modified as a clasper with which the female eggs are fertilized internally. The female of the species lays her eggs in pairs. These are about 2-2½in long by 2in wide, with four long, curling tendrils—one at each corner. With these tendrils, the female anchors her eggs to growing seaweed or other objects on the seabed.

Egg laying appears to go on throughout most of the year as fish are often caught with these egg capsules about to be laid. It is not unusual to discover such capsules in the boat after landing a female. On opening the capsule it will be found to be similar to a bird's egg in that it contains a yolk and a white. The empty capsules, known as 'purses' are frequently washed up on to beaches after the young have developed. The incubation takes several months and when the fry emerges it is a perfectly formed fish

Below: *Matching pair of lesser-spotted dogfish brought in on a multi-hook rig. Up to three hooks can be baited, but if you start striking big dogs reduce it to two.*

Left: *A noted anchorage for spurdog fishing off Clare Island.*

Above: *Aborted baby spurdog born into a boat after the summer capture of a female. Unlike Scyliorhinidae, spurdog are ovoviviparous shark which develop inside the mother and are born out of her free-swimming and self-reliant.*

about 4in in length. Unlike most other fish which are able to live off their yolk sac for a time, it has to forage immediately for its food.

The lesser spotted dogfish matures at a length of about 24in and a weight of about 1½lb, but rarely exceeds a length of 3ft and a weight of about 2½lb. The British rod-caught record fish weighed 4lb 8oz and was taken from Ayr Pier in Scotland in 1969. The species is abundant all around the coast of the British Isles, and is found in both deep water and in shallow water near the shore. Although it sometimes inhabits water over rocky ground, it favours sandy, gravel or muddy bottoms. Most of its feeding takes place on the bottom, but it will sometimes swim near the surface to steal herrings, sprats and other fish from drift nets, often getting caught itself in the process. The basic diet consists of shrimps, small crabs, hermit crabs, molluscs, and any small or dead fish that come its way.

Greater spotted dogfish

The greater spotted dogfish *(Scyliorhinus stellaris)*, also known as the nurse hound or bull huss, is far less common in British waters than its smaller relative. It is again distributed all around our coasts but is found in numbers only along the South Coast and around Ireland. Generally, it prefers deeper water and a rocky seabed.

Apart from being a larger fish, it differs from the lesser spotted kind in that, as the name suggests, it has bigger, but fewer, black spots on the reddish-brown upper half of the body. It also tends to have a rather broader snout, but neither characteristic is a certain means of distinguishing one species from the other. The only reliable aid to identification lies in the difference between the nostril lobes or flaps. The nostrils of the lesser spotted variety are covered by a single flap, whereas the greater spotted dogfish has a separate flap for each nostril.

The greater size of this species — the record rod-caught fish weighed 22lb 4oz and was caught off Minehead, Somerset, in June 1986 by M Hill — means that it can consume big prey. The greater spotted dogfish has been known to eat fish as large as the thornback ray.

The species mates, eggs being fertilized internally, as does the lesser spotted species. The eggs are larger, measuring 4-5in by 1in, and have long tendrils on each corner by means of which the eggs are secured to the seabed. The newly hatched fry measure about 6½in.

Both species of dogfish can be taken on a very wide range of baits. The stronger the smell of the bait, the better. When fishing from a boat, a sack of rubby dubby tied to the anchor is used to send a strong scent of fish offal down on the tide to attract any dogfish.

The lesser spotted dogfish is a very useful fish for the competition

DEEP WATER

Molluscs

Squid

Dead fish

Hermit crabs

HOOKING A SQUID

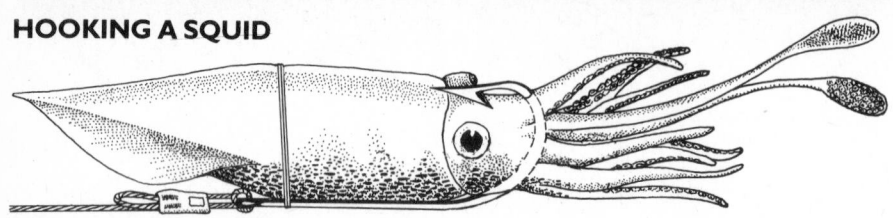

angler as it hunts in packs and can be caught in numbers. If three hooks are used, three fish at one time can sometimes be taken. The bait should not be too large for this fish as it has a smallish mouth. When hooking a fish strip—mackerel or herrings are often used—a piece about 3in in length by 1in in width should be used with a 1/0 hook. On a strong tide a running trace of about 7ft is recommended, while on a slack tide the paternoster rig pays off.

The bite is slow and bouncy, and very distinctive. Do not strike until the fourth or fifth pull in order to ensure that bait and hook have been swallowed. The dogfish is slow-moving and sluggish, and indeed seems incapable of achieving any real speed. Once hooked, this fish's fight is unmistakable. There is a backward pull, followed by a move towards the boat, and this sequence is repeated all the way to the surface. Remember that very often the angler is convinced that he has hooked the fish only to find that it has merely been holding the bait, which it releases on being hauled up.

The spurdog *(Squalus acanthias)* is very numerous in British waters, where specimens up to 21lb 3oz have been caught. It can be easily distinguished by the 'spurs' or spines, in front of each dorsal fin. Great care must be taken when

Above: *Huss feeding in deep, murky water can be taken on ledgered fish strip, or squid if it can be presented in a natural way.* **Bottom:** *More lesser-spotted are found feeding in shallow water though other kinds do also.*

handling the species, as these spurs can inflict severe lacerations.

Also called Picked dogfish or Common spiny dogfish, the spurdog is given to hunting in packs. Meeting up with a pack is either a blessing or a disaster, depending on your point of view: they snatch at just about every kind of bait without the slightest caution. Unlike the bull huss and lesser spotted varieties, the mouth of the spurdog makes very short work of a nylon monofilament trace, so light wire is usually used by specimen hunters.

The fish will often seek its prey close to the shore which gives the beach and rock angler the chance of a good catch. Most of the top action is on cold winter nights during an incoming spring tide, as the fish likes the security of a good depth of water. Among the best places to fish for them is the 18 mile long Chesil Beach on the Dorset coast, and the North Cornish headlands of Trevose and Towan. The British Record shore-caught spurdog of 16lb 12oz was taken as Chesil in 1964.

Shore anglers often make large catches of the lesser spotted

SHALLOW MURKY WATER

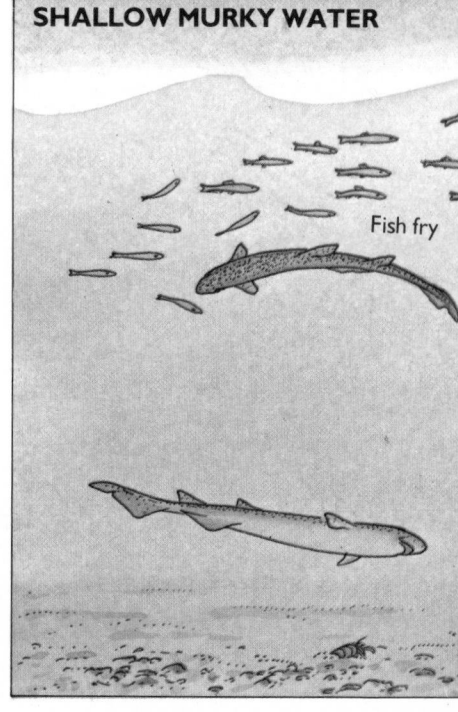

Fish fry

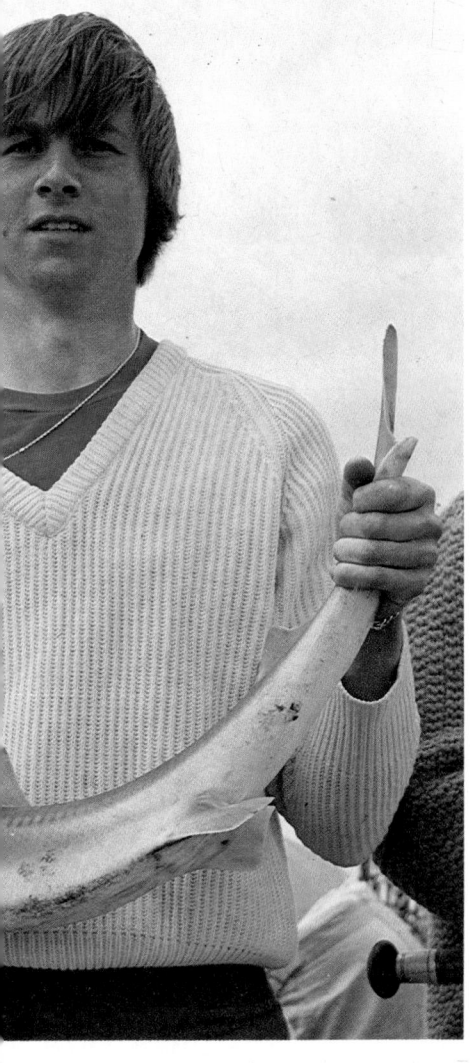

Left and above: *Rough and spined dogfish need very careful, decisive handling to avoid painful grazing or even deep lacerations of the skin. Both these holds are correct.*

Shrimps

Molluscs

dogfish, particularly in the west of Ireland. In shallow water, catches are better after dark than during the daytime, although when the water is coloured there are exceptions to this rule. It would appear from this that the fish does not like strong sunlight, for this perhaps has an adverse effect on its already poor vision.

Bouncy bites

Shore-caught fish behave in exactly the same manner as those taken from a boat, except that the bouncy bite is more pronounced (particularly if the rod stands on a monopod rest), making the angler think something much bigger than a 2lb dogfish has attacked his bait. This can be very irritating to the bass angler after a sporting fish, or to the tope hunter who might have taken considerable pains to cast an immaculately presented mackerel bait a great distance only to have it mutilated by small dogfish.

The greater spotted dogfish, by virtue of its greater size, puts up a much better fight than the smaller variety, although the bite is very similar. Once the strike is made, however, the similarity ends. On a

ASK THE EXPERT

Is day fishing worthwhile from the shore?
Generally speaking night fishing from beaches and rocks accounts for the best fish. But fishing can be equally good in daylight when the sea is very rough and highly coloured.

How can I tell the difference between a smoothhound and a tope?
The answer is in the name 'smoothhound'. While a tope's skin is like sandpaper, the skin of the smoothhound is smooth to the touch.

Are all dogfish members of the same family?
No. The lesser and greater spotted dogfish and the black-mouthed, belong to the *Scyliorhinidae* family. But the smoothhound (*Mustelus mustelus*), often confused with the Stellate smoothhound (*M. asterias*) is of the family *Triakidae,* as is the Stellate. Spurdog, picked dogfish and Blainville's dogfish are members of the separate *Squaloidea* family.

What end rigs are suitable for both bull huss and spurdog?
Bull huss hunt alone, very close to the bottom, so a short ledger trace with an 8/0 hook is correct. Spurdogs usually search in packs near the bottom but higher up at times. For them a two or three-hook paternoster tied from light wire to 6/0 hooks, would be better.

Do dogfish make good eating?
Yes, once you have removed the tough skin. Commercial fishermen make a cut round the fish's body behind the head, before impaling it on a stout nail. Then a sharp pull from the edge of the cut to the tail will remove the skin in one piece.

297

Right: *Beachcasting for dogfish in Clew Bay.*
Below right: *A writhing bull huss. To quieten a dogfish bend its tail round towards it head taking care not to strain the spine.*

strong tide this fish is capable of a short run, and takes full advantage of the flow for this. The jaws are lined with sharp teeth, which the fish often uses to chafe through the nylon hook length and so gain its freedom. For this reason, a short snood of wire is recommended.

Baits

Reliable baits include whole small squid and large fish baits. A whole mackerel, intended for tope, presents no problem to this dogfish. The strike should be delayed to give ample time for the bait to be swallowed, for, as with the smaller dogfish, the great spotted kind has the nasty habit of just hanging on and then letting go at the surface before it is in reach of the gaff. If this happens, lower the bait once more to the seabed for it is not uncommon for the same fish to atack the bait a second time. In one case the same fish—a distinctively marked specimen—was brought to the surface three times within a short space of time, only to swim off each time. It must have tired of the procedure after the third time, for it gave up, and was not caught. Here again, patience is the dogfish hunter's most valuable asset.

FISHING FOR DOGFISH

Methods	Rod	Reel	Reel Line	Terminal Tackle	Hooks	Leads/ Weights	Bait	Groundbait/ Attractor	Habitat	Time of Season	Distribution
Ledger (Boat)	6ft 2in-7ft h/g, 20-30lb test	4/0, 6/0 multiplier	25-35lb	Short wire or heavy m/f trace	4/0-6/0 dogfish: huss up to 10/0	Circular grip	Squid, mackerel or other fishbait	Rubby dubby bag on anchor rope	Universal, but particularly rocky ground	Year round in deepwater, May-November in shallows	Spurdog and Lesser Spotted Dogfish are widespread, Huss, however, are only common in the South-West and off the West Coast of Ireland
Paternoster (Boat)	6ft 2in-7ft h/g, 20-30lb test	4/0 multiplier	25-35lb	M/f trace with hooks on short snoods	2/0, 3/0	Circular grip	Fish strip	Rubby dubby bag on anchor rope			
Beachcasting	12ft h/g beachcaster, or heavy spinning	3/0 or 4/0 multiplier, large fixed-spool	25-35lb	Short wire or m/f trace	4/0	Circular grip	Fish, lugworm, King rag, sandeel	—	Beaches near rocky ground, large harbours, tidal rivers	Mainly May-November but large spurdog in winter	

Dogfish are one of the most common sea species. The boat angler can use either a ledger or a paternoster rig for them, although the latter is inferior for the larger and stronger huss. The beachcaster will normally have most success after dark, but good catches of dogfish and shoaling spurdog are made by day, particularly if the water is well-coloured.

Conger

Massive conger live long lives coiled in harbour walls or cliff crevices as well as in rusting wrecks or among reef pinnacles. So shore and sea anglers have an equal chance of thrilling sport

Conger fishing can be one of the most exciting forms of saltwater angling, whether practised from a boat or from shore. From the beginning of a trip when the bait first enters the water until the first tentative 'knock' on the line, the tension grows—for there is no way of knowing at this stage just how big a fish is mouthing the bait. Next comes the excitement of the strike and playing the fish, for this is no tame, easy-to-catch species. Even when the conger is on the surface of the water there is still the task of finally landing it.

When the angler goes fishing for a species that has a rod-and-line record of 109lb 6oz from a boat, and a shore record of 67lb 1oz, it is obvious that the tackle must be suitable for a large fish.

The choice of reel is most important. A strong multiplier or large centrepin is essential. A rod that will stand the shocks from the lunges of a big fish, yet is flexible enough to play the fish out, is also necessary.

The type of line used will depend on where the conger fishing is done. In shallow water the braided lines are extremely sensitive and give a feel of the movements of the fish.

Playing a conger from a breakwater under the ideal conditions of the build-up to a storm.
Inset: *On a large specimen, the head can be as big as a dog's and just as ferocious.*

CONGER FISHING RIGS

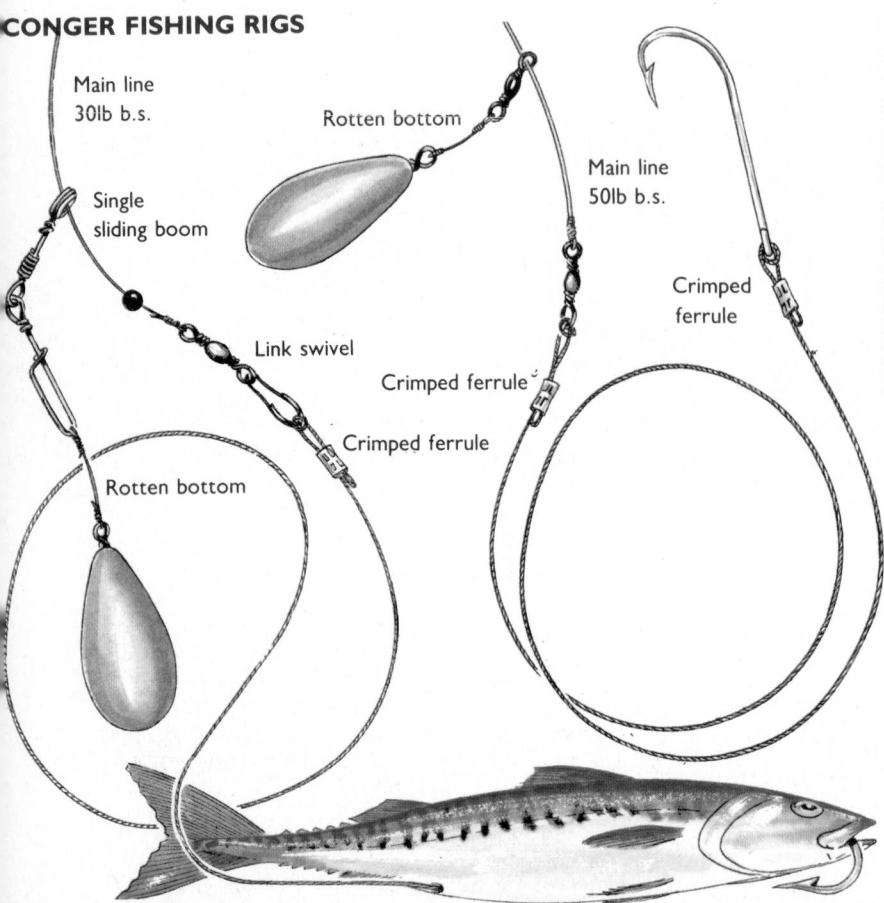

Main line
30lb b.s.

Rotten bottom

Main line
50lb b.s.

Single
sliding boom

Link swivel

Crimped ferrule

Crimped ferrule

Crimped
ferrule

Rotten bottom

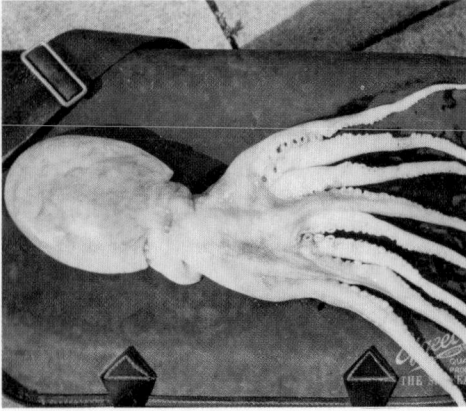

Above: *A whole squid as bait. Unlike other deadbaits, it should not be split open as its ink could repel rather than attract conger.*
Left: *Conger rigs—built for strength.*
Below: *Welsh angler John Reed fights it out with a big conger. A fighting fish must be kept from diving under the keel.*

When used in deep water where a strong current is flowing, braided lines have a tendency to belly away in the water, making it impossible to feel the fish biting. In deep water, such as when wreck fishing, nylon monofilament is the better choice, as it is more resistant to chafing, and less affected by a running tide.

Wire traces are needed, and the stronger the better, to prevent the conger's jaws from biting through the line, and also to grasp firmly when landing the fish. A conger can twist a trace around a gaff and break 60lb wire as if it were cotton thread. The wire trace should therefore be of at least 100lb strength, and about a foot long.

As a large bait is more often used, a size 9/0 or 10/0 hook is needed. The conger is more readily hooked in the jaw with a large hook. With the swivelled hooks, sometimes sold as suitable for conger fishing, the angler may find that the fish ejects the hook with the bait or swallows the bait, together with the hook, deep inside itself.

Shore fishing for conger
Shore fishing for conger produces the best specimens after dark, and autumn evenings can be very productive. The conger is found where there is deep water and a supply of food. Breakwaters, harbour walls, piers, rocky entrances to river mouths—all have produced some fine fish. Fish of over 55lb have been taken from shore marks in the Portland area, and each year sees the landing of fish over 40lb from such marks, particularly in the West Country. Groundbaiting can be very effective, and small pieces of fish will attract the conger to your bait.

Conger tackle
The best tackle when shore fishing for conger is a good rod, a reliable reel loaded with at least 30lb-strength line with a strong wire trace, and a hook at least 6/0 baited with an oily fish bait or squid. A running boom placed on the main line above the trace should have the lead weight attached to it by some lighter line, as this enables the

angler to retrieve the remainder of the tackle if the lead gets jammed in the bottom. This is one of the hazards that conger fishermen have to endure. Wherever this sort of fishing is done—from the shore, over the reefs, or when wrecking—congers and snagging ground go together, and the angler must be prepared for many tackle losses.

When shore fishing, the best results are achieved when the rod is propped up on a rod rest or secured to the side of a wall. The reel should be set on the free spool and the ratchet engaged. The bite of a conger is very gentle—a knocking on the line. When this is observed, leave the rod alone until the line is taken off the reel at a steady rate: then strike the hook home and pump the fish as hard as possible. Try not to give

line, for the fish has a habit of curling its tail around the nearest obstacle, where it is difficult to dislodge. Avoid giving line by keeping full pressure on the fish at all times. When the fish is alongside it should be gaffed as quickly as possible. Most escapes happen here.

Boat fishing for conger

Boat fishing for conger employs similar techniques, but the fish are usually larger. Wreck fishing almost inevitably produces the biggest specimens. It is advisable to leave the locations of these marks to the professional charter skippers who have the equipment to locate the wrecks, and the knowledge to anchor their boats in the right place for anglers to fish into them.

The boat has to be positioned up-

How do you mount a whole fish?
Use a baiting needle to pull the trace right through the bait fish's body until the hook rests in its mouth. Conger always take a fish head-first. Fish weighing about 1lb are best—mackerel, squid, pouting and pollack. They must be fresh and (with the exception of squid) the belly should be slit to add to the attraction. If you get a bite, allow time for the conger to get the whole fish down.

What kind of hook is best for wrecking?
Most conger specialists swear by the Mustad forged-eye Seamaster. Any other might not be strong enough for this brutal work.

Must I buy an 80lb test rod before I can tackle the largest congers?
This weight of rod is quite unnecessary. Specimen hunters use rods of 50lb test. There is even a swing towards 30lb now that really tough carbonfibre/glassfibre blanks have appeared on the market.

What is the best means of bite detection?
When reef fishing, hold the line between forefinger and thumb, and rest the rod on the gunwhale with the reel on 'ratchet'. In wreck fishing, however, you must hold the rod while a bait is on the bottom. Wreck conger hit a bait much more positively, and the rod tip announces them in no uncertain way!

tide, at just the right distance for the baits to reach the fish. A fast-taper 50lb-class boat rod, with 50lb monofilament on a heavy duty multiplier reel is recommended. You can use the same end tackle with a Clement's boom or a large swivel to which the lead weight is attached. This weight is at least 1lb and sometimes has to be heavier if the tide is a strong one. Between the end of the main line and the wire traces, use a strong link swivel which will act as a quick release if the fish is deeply hooked. You should also have spare traces ready.

The bait is either a small whole mackerel or half a very large one. A

fish is only nibbling at the bait, the movement of it away from the conger will cause an even more enthusiastic attack on it.

Get the fish clear off the bottom. In most cases in deep water there is no need to strike as the fish will hook itself as it turns towards the bottom. Quite often the fish will come up quite easily. It is sometimes possible to get the fish halfway to the surface before it realizes that something is wrong and starts to fight.

If the conger dives
Make sure that the clutch on the reel is set correctly to allow line to be taken if the fish dives. When a large conger makes a determined dive for the bottom it is practically impossible to stop it, so give line reluctantly and always be ready to start pumping the fish back up again when you sense it slowing down. This can be very hard work, but the fish must be played out, or there is the chance that it will be too fresh when it reaches the surface and might break free and escape.

There is more chance of controlling a conger just beneath the surface than when it is on top of the water,

and every effort should be made to play the fish out before it gets to the side of the boat. With wreck fishing there is usually a good depth of water beneath the surface, but on many reef marks this is not the case, and the fish will have to be played just below the surface.

The conger should be gaffed either in the lower part of the jaw or beneath the head. Once the gaff has been properly placed, the fish should be lifted smoothly and quickly on board. The angler whose tackle is in the fish should have his reel clutch set in case the fish avoids the gaff and plunges for the bottom again.

There is a great sense of achievement in catching a large conger, and it is a form of angling that has a fanatical following both in this country and on the Continent. The British Conger Club was formed to cater for the enthusiasts and will assist any anglers who wish to try this fascinating sport.

Left: *Hire boats converge on famous conger grounds off the Isle of Lewis.*
Below left: *Sadly, these huge centrepins have become extremely rare.*
Below: *Boated conger remain dangerous for hours. Don't underestimate them.*

small mackerel is baited-up by taking the point of the hook into the mouth and bringing the barbed end out between its eyes. Conger seize a fish-bait head first, so the hook should always be at the head end.

One very useful additional piece of equipment is a body belt or butt-pad with a socket to place the rod butt in when playing and pumping the fish.

When the conger takes
When a bite is felt, it is best to start winding your line in slowly until you feel the weight of the fish. There are two good reasons for doing this. First the line will be tightened ready for the next move, and second, if the

Flounder

The holiday-angler's fish because of the vast numbers scattered in shallow water within easy reach of pier, harbour wall and sandbar. But you can still make an art of catching flounder

The flounder, with its love for shallow water, provides good sport for both shore-based and dinghy anglers, and estuaries and tidal reaches of rivers produce the best bags of this flattie. Most flounder spend the largest part of their lives in brackish water but some ascend rivers right up to freshwater, and it is not uncommon for anglers seeking

roach and bream to encounter them. The best sport, however, is to be found in the shallow water of sheltered estuaries, particularly where there is a seabed of sand and mud with here and there a rocky outcrop. Here, the flounder seeks out its food in the form of marine worms, small crustaceans, larger crustaceans such as the shore crab, soft after just moulting, and small fish —whitebait, sandeels and gobies.

As the flounder does not grow to any great size—3lb is a good specimen—light tackle can be used with confidence. For estuary shore fishing, however, the coarse angler can use his heavy ledger rod or light pike-spinning-rod to good advantage. With this type of rod, a fixed-

How can I keep my bait away from robber crabs?
Incorporate a polystyrene or balsa float into the trace. It should be positioned 5in from the hook and kept in place with small swivels. Sliding floats for the purpose are now sold at most tackle shops.

Which type of lead should I use in shallow estuaries and tidal rivers?
Thin flat leads are best, as they do not plummet through the water and embed themselves in the soft bottom.

Which is best, day or night fishing?
Beach flounder feed quite well after dark, but those in tidal rivers tend not to. The last hour of light, when it coincides with the young flood tide, can be very productive. Tidal river fishing is always at its best during daylight.

Can I fish two hooks with a flounder spoon rig?
Yes. Connect a three-way swivel to the bottom of the spoon with a split ring. A 5in snood can be tied to one eye and a 10in trace to the other.

What is the maximum weight for flounder?
A few of 7lb have been caught commercially in estuary nets, and while there are bound to be bigger fish in the sea, it is difficult to imagine weights beyond 8lb.

Is it true that some flounder have orange spots?
Many do and are often mistaken for plaice. But there are considerable differences between flounder and plaice so there should be no difficulty in identifying them. One caught well out at sea is likely to be a plaice.

spool reel carrying 100-150 yards of 9lb b.s. monofilament line is adequate. It is unwise to use lighter than 9lb line as the centrifugal force created when casting 1-2oz of lead will snap it.

Terminal tackle is best kept simple. A lead of suitable weight for the rod, preferably of the Arlesey bomb type, should be threaded on the line and stopped 2ft up, either with a plastic ledger stop or split shot pinched on the line. A plastic ledger stop is recommended as this has a less adverse effect on the line.

The hook is then tied direct to the end of the line. Hook size depends entirely on the type of bait used. For the smaller varieties of ragworm, a fine wire size 6 or 4 is ideal, as this will not mutilate the worm, while for king ragworm a long-shanked size 1 will do the job best. For the bodies of peeler (soft) crab, size 1/0 is recommended, while the legs and claws can be baited on a size 4. Alternatively, if several legs and claws are going to be used on one hook, a size 2 is better. Lugworm, not so highly rated as ragworm or crab as a bait for this species, can be used on a size 2 or 1 hook.

As an added attraction, a spoon can be used just in front of the hook. The large, white, celluloid type is preferable to heavy metal as it will require less tide or movement to cause it to rotate. This rotation itself arouses the fishes' curiosity but it also stirs up plumes of sand or mud that also spell food to them.

Ledgering for flounder

Ledgering is normally used when the tide is fairly fast-flowing. If, after casting, the tide tends to drag the weight around, do not be dismayed, as the terminal rig will cover more ground when this happens. Flounders, like all flatfish, are very curious, and are attracted to moving objects. Even when the lead drifts close into the shore, do not be in too much of a hurry to recast, for these fish often come to within a few feet of the water's edge.

One problem when using conventional beachcasting gear—an 11 or 12ft hollow-glass rod in conjunction with either a large capacity fixed-spool or multiplier-type reel—is that

it is impossible to cast ultra-light leads, most beachcasters being designed to cast leads in excess of 3oz. If you wish to use light lines, therefore, a shock leader becomes necessary. For maximum casts a heavier lead is necessary.

Slow line recovery

Using a heavier lead will probably prevent the natural movement by tide drag, so it is best if the angler recovers line very slowly, thus giving movement to the terminal tackle. When fishing from open beaches or estuaries with this type of outfit, it is better to use paternoster-type gear than a trace as the extra distance achieved during casting often results in a trace becoming tangled with the main line, limiting distance. In the paternoster rig, two or even three hooks on short snoods are tied direct to dropper loops, which in turn have

been tied to the reel line at varying distances above the weight. The nearest snood ought to be at least 2ft above the lead.

In estuaries where the tide is sluggish, float tackle can be used very successfully with the same type of rod and reel as used for ledgering. Thread a small pike float (preferably the celluloid kind with a hole through the middle) up the line and stop at the required height with a rubber band inserted in the line. Then thread on a drilled bullet, and stop with a split shot 15-20in from the hook tied direct to the line. As line is recovered the rubber band winds through the rod rings while the float slides down to the lead weight. When cast out, the lead will drop to the seabed pulling the line through the centre of the float until it comes up against the rubber stop.

The ideal depth to float fish for flounder is between the seabed and

FLOUNDER FLOAT RIG

Celluloid pike float

Rubber band stop

Bullet shot

15-20in

Left: *Howard Bottrell with really big flounders caught from the River Yealm.*
Above: *Float rig to present a bait 2–6ft off the bottom.*
Right: *Specimen hunter Mike Prichard unhooks an Irish flounder. Quite often the hook is taken right down into the fish's gut.*

2ft off it. Adjust the rubber band so that the hook is fishing at this level. Even so, flounders can be taken 6ft or even more off the bottom. Whether using ledger tackle or float gear, the first tentative plucks of the fish feeding on the bait should be ignored; and the strike only made when the positive pull of the fish moving away with the bait is felt.

Flounder fishing in a dinghy
The flounder's love of sheltered bays and estuaries make it an ideal fish for the angler with his own small dinghy. Here again, to obtain the best sport, a light, lively rod is ideal, and for this light type of fishing the reel can be either centrepin, fixed-spool, or the multiplier type, whichever gives the angler most pleasure. When estuary fishing, anchor on the edge of the main channel. The most productive period will then be on either side of low water. At this time, all the fish that would normally be searching and foraging for food over the now dry mud flats congregate in the deeper water.

Groundbait can be used to good effect. The best materials to use are the ordinary shore crabs of which there is no shortage when estuary fishing. The crabs should be put into a fine mesh string bag—shrimp net-

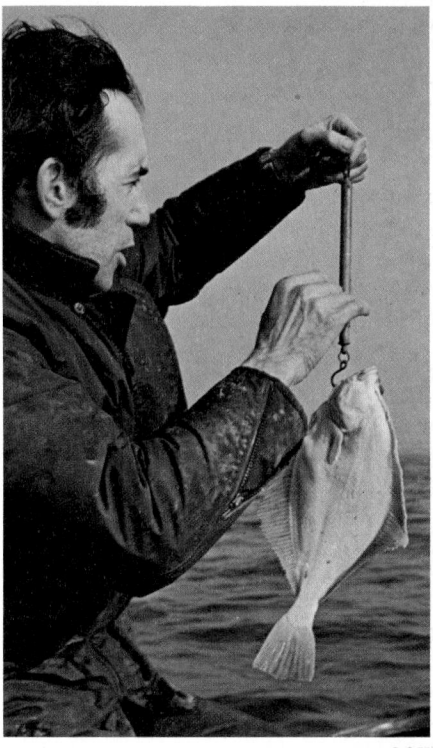

Above: *Two flounder rigs: one the classic spoon, the lower a float rig to keep marauding crabs away from the bait. In tidal reaches this is vital.*
Right: *King rag mounted for flounder fishing in a tidal river.*
Far right: *Eric Pace weighs a specimen flounder caught on a baited spoon.*

ting is ideal—and crushed to a pulp. The bag is then tied to a length of cord together with a heavy lead weight and lowered to the seabed from the bow of the boat. The value of such groundbaiting is proved by the number of caught fish that regurgitate pieces of crushed crabs.

Importance of light line

The boat fisherman may use either ledger or float rig. Whatever he uses, the line should be kept to the lightest possible b.s. as, if the water is clear, the fish may be very wary. On slack tides float fishing is preferred as this will search out a larger area. The float set-up is exactly the same as for beach fishing, indeed the boat angler has the advantage of getting the correct depth more easily. But he must remember to adjust the distance between hook and rubber stop as the tide floods or ebbs.

For ledger fishing, a two- or three-hook trace is preferable, as this gives the angler the chance to experiment with more than one bait at a time. It is not uncommon to catch two, and sometimes even three, fish at a time as flounders invariably move around in small groups. The lead should be as light as possible to keep in contact with the seabed, and the angler should continually raise and lower the rod tip lifting the lead 3 or 4ft from the seabed each time.

Upon feeling a fish take the bait (quite frequently this happens while the rod tip is lifted), the lead should be lowered immediately to the seabed and left undisturbed for two or three minutes to give the fish ample time to swallow the bait. If, after this time, no movement has been felt from below, the rod tip should be gently lifted again, and at the first indication of resistance the strike should be made.

Volunteer flounders

Do not retrieve the tackle, however, if the flounder is missed, but allow it to remain on the bottom, for quite often the missed fish will make a second attack on the bait. Moreover, when retrieving the hooked fish, it is not unusual to see two or three other fish following the captive to the surface. If you unhook and rebait quickly, it is often quite possible to make

contact with these other fish before they leave the area.

Most flounders hooked range from 4oz to 1½lb, but occasional bigger specimens are caught. If you are lucky enough to get one, lift it from the sea into the boat with the aid of a landing net. For their size, flounders are quite good fighters and larger fish will make a spirited dive for the seabed when nearing the surface, so be prepared to let the fish have its head when using light lines.

The best flounder fishing is found in the tidal rivers of the South West of England, where many hundreds of fish over 2½lb are taken between late October and early March. The lower reaches of the River Teign have the justified reputation of being the most productive area. The fish average nearly 2lb in weight, and during the peak fishing period of December and January, one in ten tops 3lb. Bill Stevens of Crediton set the current shore record for the species on the Teign in 1978 with a superb specimen of 5lb 2oz. The great majority of the Teign's fish fall to peeler or softback crab; using any other bait is largely a waste of time. The best catches are made during the flood tide, the hotspots being Gasworks Corner on the Teignmouth side and Charlie's Beach, which is half a mile upstream from Shaldon. Other great West flounder rivers include the Yealm, Tamar, Fowey, and Helford. The Fowey is much fished by dinghy anglers and while good specimens can be expected almost anywhere in the river most regulars concentrate on the sandbars which cross the river near the railway sidings at Golant. Britain's biggest rod-caught flounder of 5lb 11½oz came from this spot in 1956 and was taken on a baited spoon rig, a technique much favoured locally. The tide moves swiftly through the Golant Neck and large spoons weighing up to 8oz are best suited to these waters.

Right: *Last light on the River Yealm—an excellent time to go fishing. The Yealm dries into mudflat at low water with a narrow channel winding through it into which a host of fish must fall back.*
Inset: *Float-caught specimen flounder taken from a wide but sheltered Irish beach.*

Mullet

Mullet shoals are a common sight from the harbours and piers of seaside towns, but their shyness deters many fishermen from tackling this strong, wary, fighting fish

Mullet are probably the most frequently seen and easily observed marine species around our shores. They are strong sporting fish which lend themselves to light-tackle fishing, yet are little fished for except by enthusiastic specialists. Due to the mullet's natural caution and unique feeding habits, myths and legends about their virtual uncatchability abound. Difficult they may be at times, but uncatchable they are certainly not.

Three species of mullet
Three species are found in British waters. The thick-lipped grey mullet is the commonest and is found all round our coasts. It is also the largest, attaining weights in excess of 10lb, but the average size is about 2-4lb and a 5lb mullet is considered a specimen. The thin-lipped grey mullet is smaller on average and has a more localized distribution, being found mostly off the south coast of England, in Cornwall and the Channel Islands. The golden grey mullet is the smallest and scarcest of the three species. Mullet are inshore fish frequenting sheltered beaches, bays and coves, harbours and estuaries.

Left: *Putting out groundbait on estuarial mudflats as the tide begins to flow.*
Below: *Fishing for mullet in a tiny creek in north-west Norfolk—a favourite spot.*

They have considerable tolerance of freshwater and will travel a long way up estuaries, tidal creeks and lagoons, even penetrating for a while into freshwater.

Mullet will be seen from time to time scouring the bottom, sucking and blowing mud and sand as they extract diatoms and other tiny creatures from the waste matter. As their food is available to them virtually everywhere and at almost all times their feeding patterns are unpredictable. Such food is impossible for the angler to imitate, but in places the mullet become used to feeding on other than their natural food and are consequently vulnerable to the angler.

Successful baits
In harbours where trawlers gut their catch or dump waste fish and fish offal, or where fish factories and processing plants pipe their waste into the sea, mullet acquire a taste for fish. In holiday resorts or places where waste food is regularly dumped or near sewer outlets, mullet will again become accustomed to feeding on a mixture of scraps and can be caught on a large variety of such baits as cheese, ham fat and bacon rind. Generally, however, the most frequently used and most successful baits are pieces of fish, bread flake, dough and small harbour

Above: *Lugworm diggers on mudflats. After they have gone and the tide has risen, mullet search their workings for discarded worms.*
Below: *Porridge spiced with pilchard oil—an excellent groundbait mixture.*
Below right: *'Tramlines' made by the top lips of mullet sucking up food.*

SHORE

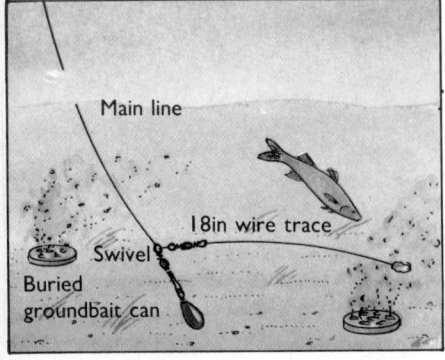

Main line

18in wire trace

Swivel

Buried groundbait can

HARBOUR

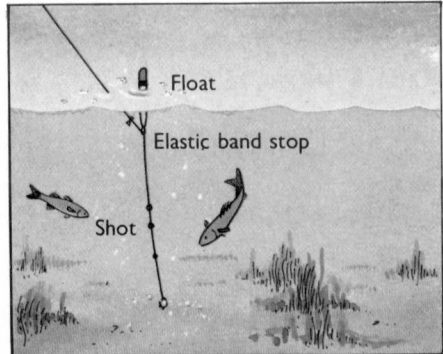

Float

Elastic band stop

Shot

ESTUARY

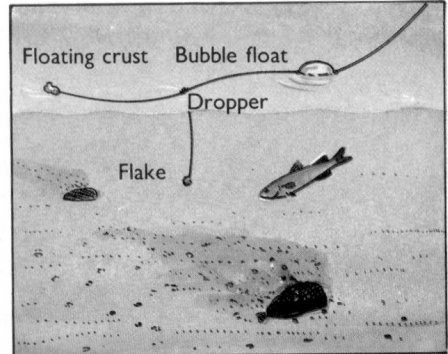

Floating crust   Bubble float

Dropper

Flake

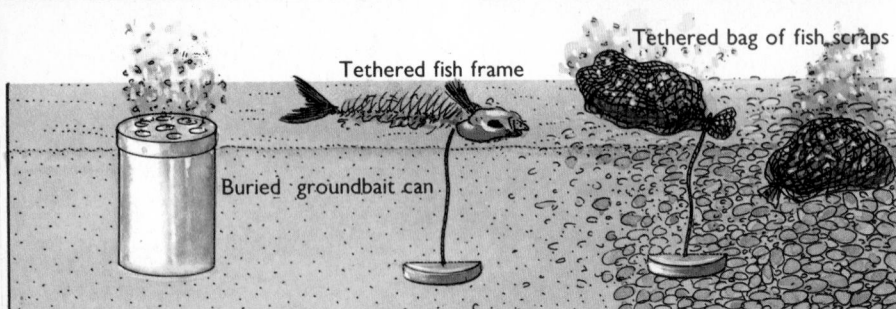

Tethered fish frame

Tethered bag of fish scraps

Buried groundbait can

Above and left: *Groundbait for mullet can be tethered in perforated tins, or anchored. The three illustrations show rigs for shore, harbour and estuary fishing. The terminal tackle and lead for the shore fishing style are exaggerated in size for the sake of clarity.*

Below: *Even with the tide this low, mullet are found in the shallow, muddy water of Maldon on the Essex Blackwater.*

ragworms. These mullet are fished for as soon as they are observed feeding on the waste, and all that is required is to introduce your hookbait without frightening the fish. At other times it may be necessary to groundbait with fish or bread to interest them in food and bring them on to feed.

Groundbaiting
Mullet feeding on their natural food require a very different approach. They must be weaned onto feeding on something which the angler can use as bait. This requires careful planning and patience. Choose places where mullet come to feed on the tide and spend time before moving on. The groundbait such as fish frames or skeletons, bread, or a mash made of fish waste mixed with fish oil, should be spread on the bottom at low water. Mullet like to move around a lot when feeding and will not remain in one spot, so they must be given a choice. Groundbait in three or four different places but ensure that all are within casting range of where you will be fishing. Fish frames should be tethered to the bottom, so that they will not be swept away by the current. No effort should be made to actually fish for the mullet for three or four days

until the fish have become accustomed to and have accepted and started feeding on the groundbait.

Ordinary coarse fishing tackle is ideal for mullet fishing. Indeed, in many ways they are a coarse fisherman's fish, as his techniques, tackle and methods are best suited to catching them. A long flexible rod, a freshwater fixed-spool reel, 5lb b.s. line, hook sizes 8-14, floats, lead shot

and a few Arlesey bombs are all that is required. When the water is not too deep, or mullet are feeding near the surface, float fishing with a fixed float set at the desired depth can be most effective. Sufficient shotting should be used to give the float the least possible positive buoyancy compatible with visibility. Mullet are cautious and the less drag they feel from the float the better.

What length of rod is best for mullet fishing?
A rod of between 9ft and 12ft will suit most shore fishing situations. Coarse rods are perfectly acceptable.

Are mullet drawn to artificial light?
Very much so. Many catches are made on baits offered in the pool of light cast by a dockside lamp. This kind of fishing is usually best in winter when mullet hang around harbours and seem to lose much of their caution.

How can I tell a golden-grey from the thick-lipped?
The cheek and gill cover of the golden-grey mullet has a gold blotch—but this fades soon after death. The pectoral fin on the golden-grey is long and blunt.

Can mullet be 'conditioned' to take only one kind of food?
Fish that live close to food processing outflows will *only* take the food discharged by the pipes. To try and catch them with something different is a waste of time.

What are my chances of catching red mullet?
Better than many suppose. This close relative of the grey is caught regularly off the coast of Cornwall, usually by small-boat anglers bottom fishing over rough ground. It is rarely caught by shore anglers.

Do mullet make good eating?
It depends on where they live. Tidal river fish have a slightly muddy taste and many anglers are put off eating a catch they have made below a sewer outfall. Mullet also have far too many bones to make easy eating.

Floating crust

At times, mullet take floating crust and the bait must then be presented to them on the surface. A controller float is used to give casting weight but a fixed float with all the shot bunched immediately under the float will also work. The float should always be drawn away from the floating crust in case it obstructs or frightens the mullet when it trys to take the bait. On occasion mullet taking surface bread may try to sink it and break it up before actually taking it. In these circumstances, a two-dropper terminal tackle is very useful, as one bait can be fished on the surface and another in the water. When wishing to float fish but at a depth which makes casting either awkward or impossible, a sliding float should be used. A stop in the form of a piece of elastic band which will run through the rod rings without catching may be used to regulate the depth of the bait.

Above: *This fine, thick-lipped grey mullet was hooked from Plymouth Breakwater and 'beached' on to the shelving slabs.*

Paternostering

When fishing from rocks, piers or harbour walls for mullet which are feeding close-in either on the bottom or along the wall or rock face, a one or two-hook paternoster can be used. If the fish are feeding well off the bottom and the depth is ascertained, an elastic band fixed to the line can be used as a gauge. For this kind of fishing the rod should always be held and a finger kept on the line so that the slightest indication of a bite may be felt. Mullet take very gently and may either let go again or strip your bait without signalling a bite unless the rod is hand held.

For the novice, mullet makes the perfect introduction to sea fishing. And with tench, bream or roach tackle, he is likely to do better than the sea angler using heavier gear.

Wrasse

Wrasse find their food and shelter in the recesses of a broken, rocky coast where they may seem within reach but can tantalize any angler trying to winkle them out

Wrasse are not difficult to find around Britain, particularly on the West Coast where the water is slightly warmer and the shore more rocky than elsewhere. But to fish for wrasse successfully, a keen knowledge of the fish and its behaviour are a necessity.

To find a wrasse fishing spot, look for deep water close inshore—at least two fathoms at low tide. Depth does not play a major role, however, as many ballans in the 5-6lb size range have been caught in no more than 3ft of water. A rocky coastline with vertical cliffs, interspersed with sheltered, broken ground where vegetation can grow, is ideal. In such areas a dense population of many kinds of animal, particularly molluscs and other invertebrates, ensures food for the wrasse. Catch one wrasse and, before long, you can expect to hook more.

Wrasse of 7lb can be expected along the coastline of Devon, on the south and north coast of Cornwall and around the Channel Islands. The largest fish, weighing up to 9lb, invariably come from the areas mentioned, but bigger specimens certainly live in the kelp jungles. There is irrefutable evidence of a 10lb 2oz and a 9lb 12oz fish living in the Mevagissey area of Cornwall.

Medium weight tackle may be suitable but it must be of sufficient strength to cope with the difficult

terrain in which these fish live. Wrasse are essentially bottom feeders and by far the best rig is a single hook ledger. This leads to many snags and the loss of terminal gear but such drawbacks have to be accepted as 'all part of the game'. The sliding float is a popular and effective method, but it is essential to swim the bait just above the bottom or over the kelp weed. Float fishing takes the largest specimens, but fish between 2 and 4lb are more common with this method.

Float fishing is certainly the most exciting method as it gives the angler something to watch. Your response to bites can be quick and positive and your bait can be fished over a wider area.

The ideal spot

Imagine a rocky shore with indented gullies, into which the water surges at the pattern of swell and wind. Using float fishing tackle, a bait can be put into the many possible feeding areas along such a shore with far less risk of it becoming snagged than a tethered bait on a cast ledgered rig. Float fishing allows an angler to find a fish rather than expecting it to come out in search of a bait. Furthermore, wrasse can see

Below: *The ragged coasts of the South West harbour ideal spots for wrasse. A short rod is no use for this kind of fishing; it must be at least 9ft, with plenty of butt control.*
Inset: *Dinghy fishing for wrasse in the Salcombe Estuary.*

ASK THE EXPERT

Do wrasse live in tidal rivers?
Large fish have been caught as much as two miles from the open sea in the Dart, Salcombe River and the Fowey, which have very rocky shores hollowed into caverns which provide perfect shelter. Ledgering from a small dinghy anchored close in to the rocks is a popular and productive technique.

What are the best conditions for shore fishing?
When rough water is pounding the shore, wrasse do not move from the shelter of the deep gullies and rock holes. So the calmer the weather, the better the fishing will be. A fine summer's evening during the first two hours of a flood tide is best.

Should I fish two hooks on a ledger trace?
A single is quite sufficient. If you use two, you double the risk of getting caught up. You may put yourself in the unhappy situation of hooking a fish on one and snagging the other during the fight.

What kind of rod do you recommend for rock fishing?
A light 11-12ft beachcaster has enough length and butt power to control a fish hooked among hazardous rocky ledges. (Any rod shorter than 9ft is quite unsuitable.) Team it with a small multiplier or skirted reel loaded with 15lb b.s. monofilament.

Should I offer a crab bait whole or in pieces?
If you are a specimen hunter, the larger the bait the better. A ballan wrasse of 6lb has the power in its jaws to engulf and crush a big crab in seconds: watching them feed in an aquarium is an education.

well, which is yet another reason for choosing a rig that swims a bait to and fro with the current.

When there are clean patches of sand and mud between the rocks, and you know where these are, then it is possible to use a ledger rig. Nevertheless, a rotten-bottom of lesser breaking strain should be used between reel line and lead. Wrasse have a habit of grabbing a bait, then rushing into the nearest weed or broken ground. A pull then results in a lost fish and probably lost terminal tackle as well. With a rotten-bottom, all you should lose when pulling free is the weight.

When float fishing, there are times when the bait should be trotted and times when it should be kept stationary over a known wrasse hole. For trotting, use a free-swimming rig and for stationary holes, a tethered rig (see diagrams). With the latter, the float bobbing up and down with the waves can drop the lead into crevices or thick seaweed,

so a rotten-bottom is again used in order that the rig can be salvaged if it becomes fouled.

An inverted float, which has less friction, is far more efficient on the strike than the conventional hollow stem pike float or fixed bung. Rig the float as a slider to cope with the change in depth as the tide ebbs or flows. A wisp of nylon or a rubber band can be clove-hitched on to the reel line to act as a float stop and means of controlling depth.

Keep your hooks sharp. The lips of a wrasse are rubbery and thickened to prise limpets and other shellfish off the rocks, and it takes a good hook to penetrate them. Probably more fish are lost because of a light hook-hold than for any other reason. Size is not too important—if a wrasse wants the offered bait it will take it—but sizes 3/0 down to 4 are fine for most fish. A stout, carp type short-shanked pattern is best; fine wire hooks tend to bend while being removed, but have much better

A SIMPLE LEDGER RIG

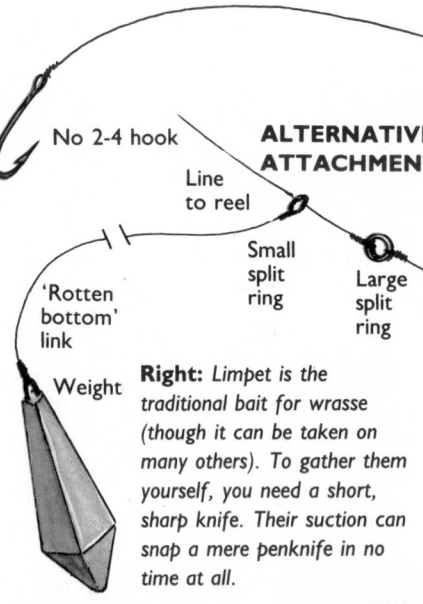

No 2-4 hook

ALTERNATIVE ATTACHMENT

Line to reel

Small split ring

Large split ring

'Rotten bottom' link

Weight

Right: *Limpet is the traditional bait for wrasse (though it can be taken on many others). To gather them yourself, you need a short, sharp knife. Their suction can snap a mere penknife in no time at all.*

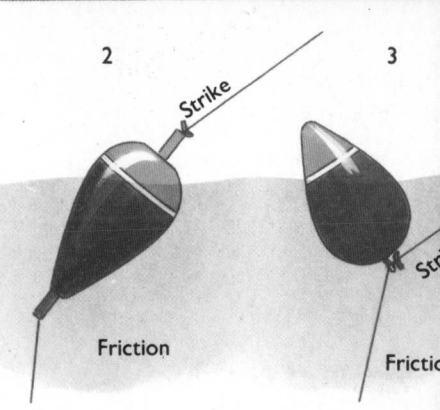

FREE SWIMMING FLOAT

TETHERED FLOAT RIG

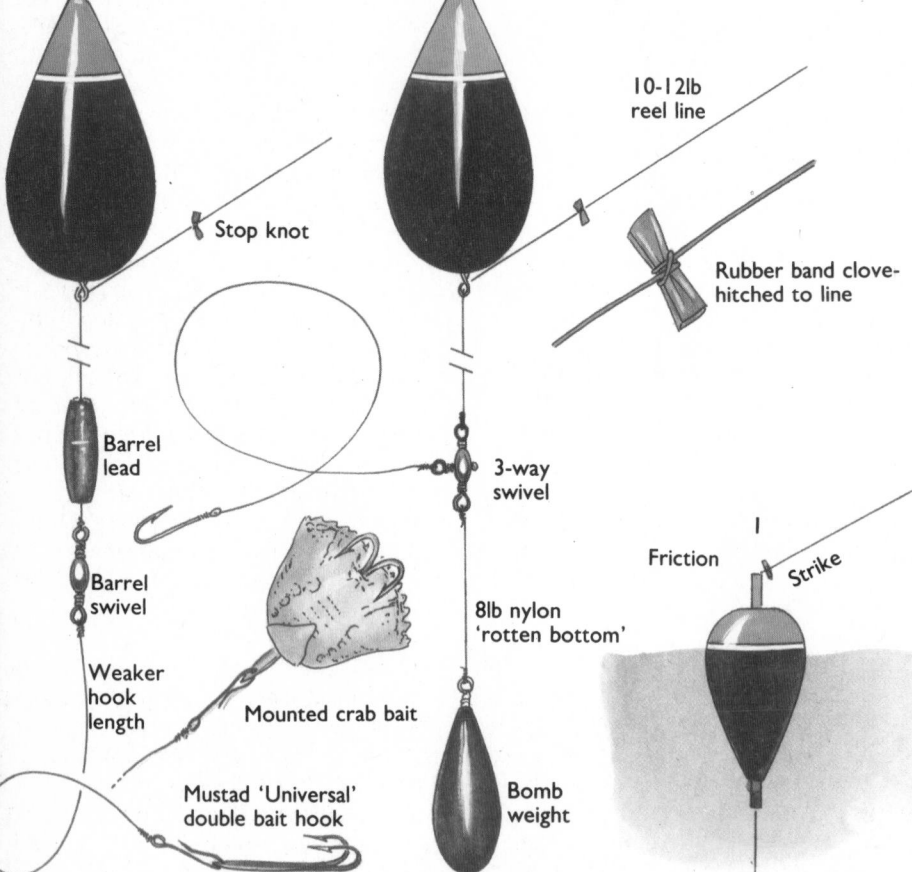

Stop knot

Barrel lead

Barrel swivel

Weaker hook length

Mounted crab bait

Mustad 'Universal' double bait hook

10-12lb reel line

Rubber band clove-hitched to line

3-way swivel

8lb nylon 'rotten bottom'

Bomb weight

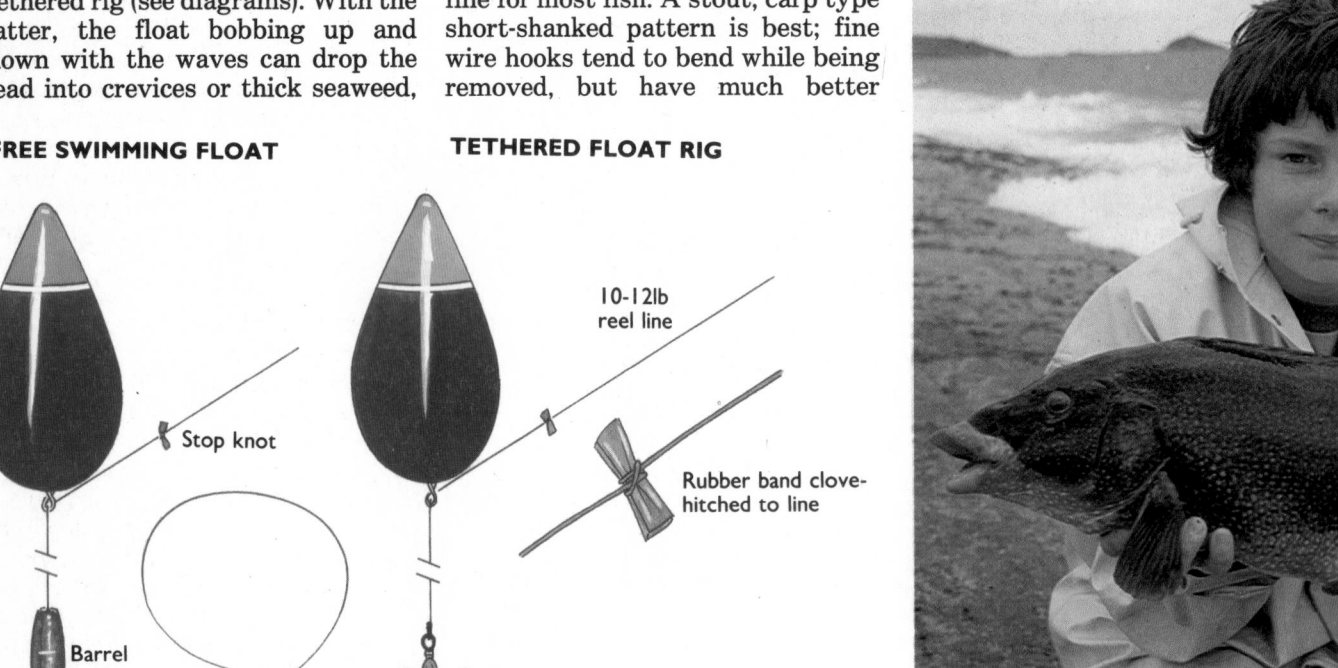

1

Friction   Strike

2

Strike

Friction

3

Stri

Frictio

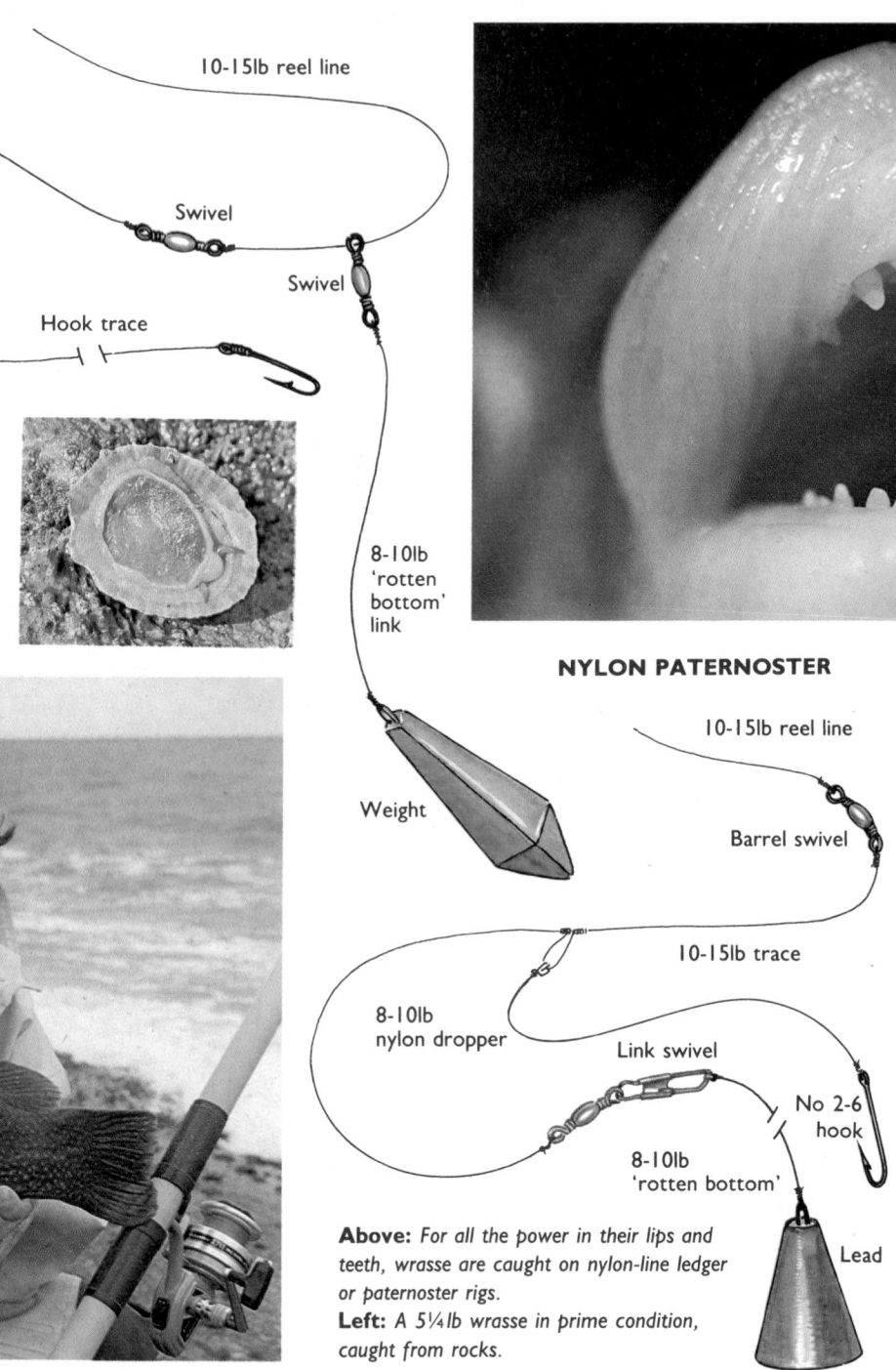

10-15lb reel line

Swivel

Swivel

Hook trace

8-10lb 'rotten bottom' link

Weight

NYLON PATERNOSTER

10-15lb reel line

Barrel swivel

10-15lb trace

8-10lb nylon dropper

Link swivel

8-10lb 'rotten bottom'

No 2-6 hook

Lead

Above: *The mouths are capable of tearing mussel barnacles off the rocks.*

Above: *For all the power in their lips and teeth, wrasse are caught on nylon-line ledger or paternoster rigs.*
Left: *A 5¼lb wrasse in prime condition, caught from rocks.*

Left: *Where there is a known hotspot, the float can be anchored with an old lead, using rotten-bottom. There are advantages of reduced friction in using the inverted float.*

TWO BASIC SEA FLOW ATTACHMENTS

1. On striking, friction centres on top of float stem.
2. As float pulls over, friction transfers to foot.
3. Friction is much reduced by line running through ring.

penetration, which is desirable against the fish's tough mouth. In the West of England the Aberdeen is much favoured in sizes 2/0 to 4/0.

A rocky shore means that landing a wrasse produces further problems. Very few people want to eat wrasse, so a gaff has no place in this fishing. A landing net is the safest and best way to bring a fish ashore. Some wrasse, particularly those taken from water over five fathoms or so, will be blown when landed, as the

species is affected severely by pressure change. But, with light tackle, where fish are played carefully and are not dragged up through the water, the species both gives a powerful fight and is returned to the water with a good chance of surviving the trauma.

Wide range of baits

Baits for wrasse are legion, but there can be no doubt that peeler and soft crab are the best. King ragworm, harbour and tidal river ragworm, and to a lesser extent, lugworm, attract them, followed by mussels, cockles, scallop and limpet. Hermit crabs also make excellent bait. Most anglers know the wrasse's reputation for tearing limpets off rocks, but these do not figure highly in the fish's diet. The author has caught many wrasse on them, but more often resorts to adding a lugworm or a small fragment of ragworm to form a cocktail. The smell of the worm is an added attraction to hunting fish.

Smell is perhaps the key to successful wrasse fishing for, despite the wrasse's good eyesight, holes and kelp beds are areas of deep gloom. Even rubby dubby can help. Alternatively, a small bag of offal, especially oily scraps, is a sure way of encouraging wrasse to feed.

317

Skate

Skate are widely distributed around our coasts, and to catch them you need patience and muscle. They offer the angler a wonderful opportunity to tackle monster fish

Sea fishermen perhaps hunt skate because they offer the chance of a monster fish from waters in which a catch of more than 100lb is rare. Skate is not a great sporting species, and it may be that they are fished, as mountains are climbed, because they are there.

Skate fishing varies little from Scottish and English waters to the marks of Eire. Almost all of it is from an anchored boat under the command of a professional skipper whose job it is to put you over suitable ground. Years ago, a boat-man worth hiring could almost guarantee a fish or two, but today the skate marks have been so ravaged by both commercial and sporting fishermen that success is a reflection of excellent luck, rather than skill or know-how. Established fishing grounds are around Scotland— Ullapool, Scapa Flow and the Western Isles—and over the Irish Sea in Kinsale, Westport and Valencia but it is a rare stretch of coast that has never produced at least one specimen. Skate travel with the tide and are much more active in warmer months than in autumn and winter.

Without good bait, the odds against hooking a skate are long indeed. The species preys upon all kinds of fish, crustaceans and worms, and successful fishing baits are those which exude a powerful scent and are big enough to withstand the predations of smaller fish and marine creatures which attack before a skate locates the tackle.

A waiting game

Among skate fishermen it is generally agreed that fresh mackerel and herrings are best. Both are extremely juicy baits which result in showers of blood, fatty droplets and fragments of meat, spreading a scent lane. This is very important

where the skate are scattered over a large area. Skate fishing is a waiting game: half a mackerel or even a whole fish is certainly not too big to ensure that when the fish eventually comes along, enough bait is left on the hook to spark its interest. The effectiveness of the bait depends on its freshness. Stale bait might well be a complete failure except where the skate are accustomed to fish offal, as they are in the vicinity of commercial fishing ports.

Feeding habits

Skate feed relatively slowly. It is debatable whether this behaviour reflects natural caution or is due to clumsiness in shuffling the enor-mous flat body over the prey. Whatever the reason, a bait that is correctly mounted helps the angler. While it is seldom necessary to hide hook shank and trace wire inside the bait, neat packaging at least ensures that the hook point ends up in the skate's jaw, and is not buried in a mass of squashy bait.

The skate has formidable jaws that literally grind hooks to powder and great care is needed in the selection and construction of the terminal tackle. The hook must be strong, forged, and with a brazed eye. The preferred size is between No 6/0-12/0, but there is much in favour of the smaller hooks because they are far sharper. A needle-sharp point and neat barb are essential to drive the hook into the muscles.

The trace, incorporating a simple running ledger, needs to be short —2ft of cable-laid wire of 150-250lb b.s. are knotted and sleeved to the hook and to a big-game swivel. Attached to the other side of the swivel

A delighted angler showing off a 141lb common skate caught off Stornoway in the Outer Hebrides—a noted area for large fish.

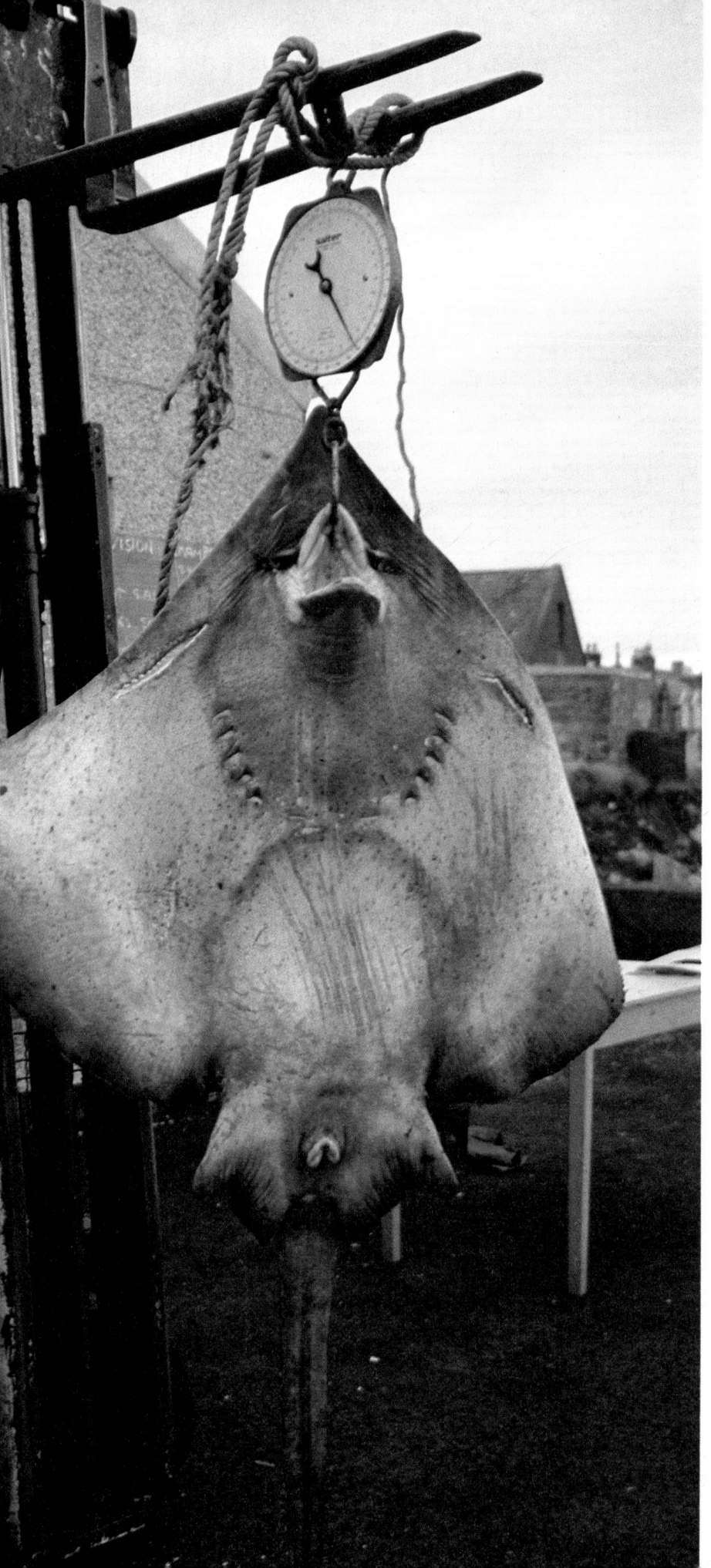

ASK THE EXPERT

How can I fish deep, fast water without using massive leads?
Change from nylon (or Dacron) line to wire. Wire lines are much thinner so water resistance is reduced. Wire under stress needs careful handling, though. Use roller rings or aluminium oxide liners and a deep, narrow reel like the Penn Mariner—and never grab the line when landing a fish.

Under pressure my reel slips around my rod. How can I remedy this?
Use the finest quality winch fitting. Secure the reel with the seat clamp provided by the manufacturer. Best of all, use a reel with harness lugs. Properly rigged to the harness shoulder straps, the reel takes most of the strain and stabilizes the rod.

How long should I delay striking?
In most cases longer than you might think. More fish are lost through premature striking than any other cause. It's almost impossible to wait too long.

My reel broke two days after I boated a big skate. Was it just bad luck or could I have damaged it?
Line wound on to a spool under the pressure of a sea fight imposes a massive crushing force. The spool may weaken and burst within days. Change to a one-piece, aluminium or bronze spool: never use plastic and avoid two or three-section brass spools as they may open under pressure. After landing a big fish, run off the line then rewind it.

Are skate thorns poisonous?
Not poisonous as such, but they can cut badly and their dirt may give rise to secondary infection.

319

is 2-6ft of 80-100lb b.s. nylon monofilament to provide a buffer against abrasion and some insurance against sudden jerks, which nylon, being more elastic than Dacron, is better able to absorb. A Clements boom and sinker are threaded onto the nylon and held at the correct distance with a stop-knot, then a second swivel is tied on. The main line, 50-80lb b.s. Dacron, is secured by the usual combination of doubled leader and Policansky knot.

Good skate rods are inevitably powerful with the emphasis on lifting ability rather than fishing sensitivity. Hauling a big skate off the sea bed is tough work even without burdening yourself with a rod that makes life more difficult due to adverse leverage ratio. Choose the shortest rod you can find. A 6ft rod is more efficient than a 7ft, and

Below: *A 136½lb skate caught on whole mackerel.* **Far right:** *Another view of the fish on page 329; note the muscular mouth.*

longer rods are out of the question for most anglers. As long as the rod reaches far enough over the gunwales for reasonable fishing control, the shorter it is the better.

High grade 50 and 80lb boat blanks cope well with skate. Use glassfibre because there is absolutely no detectable advantage in carbonfibre. Insist on the best fittings and rings: metal winch fitting with locking ferrule for the butt; roller or aluminium oxide lined side rings; always specify a double roller tip; and choose the comfort and control of a soft, fairly wide diameter foregrip. Double-whipped rings are tougher than a single plain wrap.

Recommended reels
The reel has to be very strong rather than large. Skate may run, but seldom as far as sharks. Line pressure is immense, however, and the spool must be able to withstand it without collapsing. Big game multipliers and heavy duty cen-

SKATE RIGS

Below: Mount a sizeable strip of herring on to a Mustad Sea Master and crimp the hook to cable-laid wire. Attach a second trace of nylon monofil of 80-100lb b.s. holding a Clements boom. Link this trace by a heavy-duty swivel to 50-100lb b.s. reel line.

Bottom: Hook a Sea Master crimped on to cable-laid wire of 150-250lb b.s. into the back of a mackerel and bind the bait to the hook and the wire with Alasticum. Crimp the wire to a barrel swivel and attach a long trace holding a Clements boom to it.

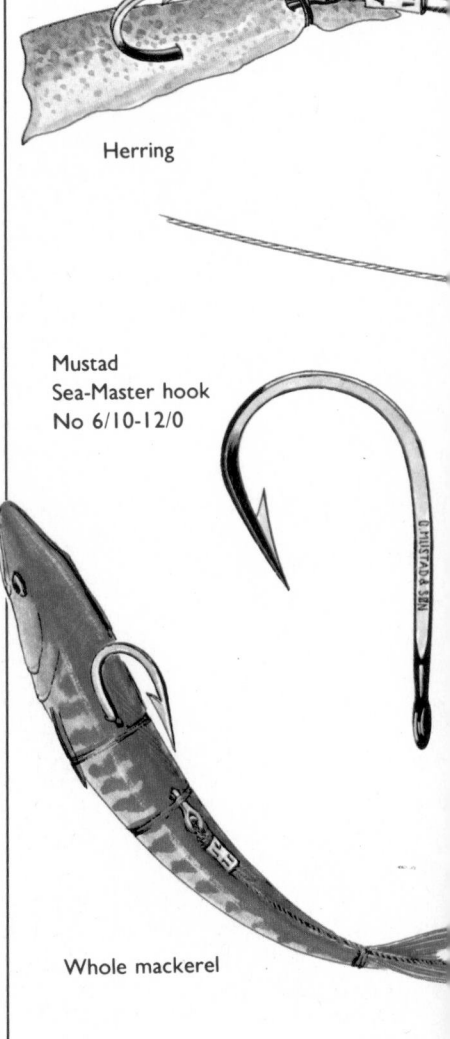

Herring

Mustad
Sea-Master hook
No 6/10-12/0

Whole mackerel

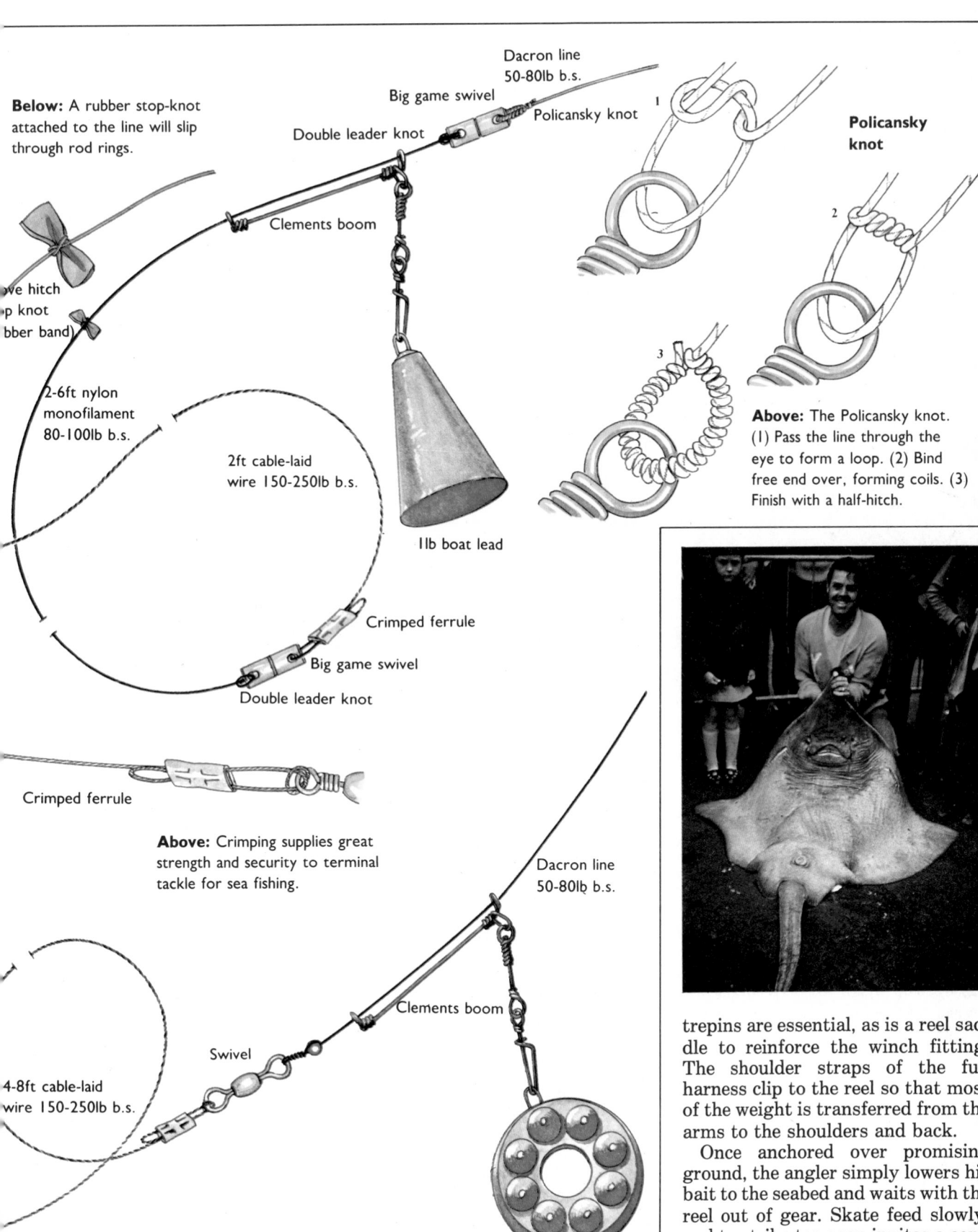

Below: A rubber stop-knot attached to the line will slip through rod rings.

Dacron line 50-80lb b.s.

Big game swivel

Policansky knot

Double leader knot

Clements boom

ve hitch
p knot
bber band)

2-6ft nylon monofilament 80-100lb b.s.

2ft cable-laid wire 150-250lb b.s.

1lb boat lead

Policansky knot

1

2

3

Above: The Policansky knot. (1) Pass the line through the eye to form a loop. (2) Bind free end over, forming coils. (3) Finish with a half-hitch.

Crimped ferrule

Big game swivel

Double leader knot

Crimped ferrule

Above: Crimping supplies great strength and security to terminal tackle for sea fishing.

Swivel

4-8ft cable-laid wire 150-250lb b.s.

Clements boom

Dacron line 50-80lb b.s.

1lb grip lead

trepins are essential, as is a reel saddle to reinforce the winch fitting. The shoulder straps of the full harness clip to the reel so that most of the weight is transferred from the arms to the shoulders and back.

Once anchored over promising ground, the angler simply lowers his bait to the seabed and waits with the reel out of gear. Skate feed slowly, and to strike too soon invites a complete miss or hooking the fish in the wing. Give it time to get the hook well down, then strike hard. Keep up

the pressure because the skate will hunch down on the bottom using its body as a sucker. You have to pull harder than the fish can, and that is backbreaking work. Playing a skate is a tug-of-war.

Many anglers say that one good skate is enough to last a lifetime. For the most part skate fishing is brutal fishing that requires only patience and a strong back. But as long as big skate haunt our coastal waters anglers will fish for them because to land a big one is still an achievement few can boast of.

Skate are rare in many of their former strongholds. Rod and line fishing endangers stocks—in fact it may be more of a hazard than commercial fishing. So, bearing in mind that skate are poor eating anyway, put them back alive. It is best not to boat them in the first place: none of the cartilaginous species withstand manhandling and are best cut free while alongside the boat. The wingspan can be approximately measured and is closely related to the weight of the fish.

Above: *Another big skate landed—finally. A comfortable rod butt rest, like the one around the angler's waist, is a great help.*

Below: *The rod curves low and the shoulders, arms and back begin to ache as a large Irish skate is battled to the boat.*

322

Tope

With a skin as tough as glasspaper and teeth that can slice through nylon line, the tope is a tough fighting fish that needs strong tackle but a gentle touch to be landed unharmed

The tope is a strong, slim-bodied member of the shark family and is found all around our coasts. More numerous in some areas than in others, the Wash, the Thames Estuary, the Solent, Cardigan Bay, the Wexford Coast and Tralee Bay are noted tope fishing venues. The species is found in depths ranging from a few feet along the shore to depths in excess of 50 fathoms, but on the whole it is a fish found in moderate depths and is most plentiful in depths of 5-20 fathoms. The fact that it frequents shallow water facilitates the use of light tackle and permits the tope to show its superb fighting qualities.

While the tope is found over all types of bottoms it has a preference for clean ground and although it inhabits all levels of water it feeds mainly on demersal, bottom-living, species, particularly those found over clean ground. It is almost entirely a fish eater and the most popular baits used for catching tope are mackerel, herring, squid, whiting, pouting and small flatfish.

Tope are large fish running up to 80lb or more, but a more usual size is between 20 and 35lb. For that reason, sizeable baits such as a long lask of mackerel or indeed the whole mackerel can be used.

Tope are taken regularly from the shore in places. Steep-to beaches with a fair depth of water close-in offer the best opportunity, but in calm conditions the tope may be met on very shallow beaches. They run a long way up only those estuaries

Tope fishing provides some of the best big-game fishing to be found around the British Isles, though over-fishing in recent years has made the tope an endangered species.

and tidal channels that are completely saline as they have no great
tolerance to freshwater. The time
and place to fish is directly in the
channel at low water and on the
early flood tide. Tope will be found
quartering little coves and bays
along a rocky coast, usually at the
same stage of the tide, but only persistent fishing of a particular spot
will yield this information.

Shore fishing for tope
For shore fishing a beachcasting rod
capable of casting 6oz is suitable.
Lighter rods will handle the fish but
may be over-loaded by the combined
weight of bait and sinker if a heavy
fish bait is used. Nylon monofilament of 18-20lb b.s. is adequate provided there is enough of it on the
reel—300 yards is not too much as
shore-caught tope can run a very
long way when hooked. Multiplier
reels are most commonly used but in
some cramped rock fishing situations a large fixed-spool reel has
definite advantages.

Right and below: *A shocker knot or
crimping will join a leader to the main reel line.*
Above right: *The lift aboard calls for
confident, correct handling—and preferably
gloves.*
Far right: *Cutting a wire trace with tinsnips:
the fish will be returned unharmed.*

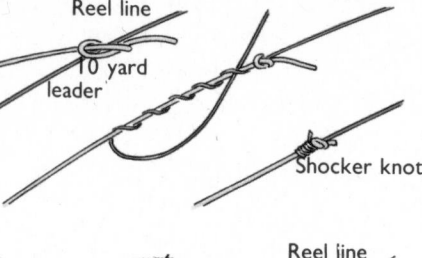

Reel line

10 yard
leader

Shocker knot

Reel line

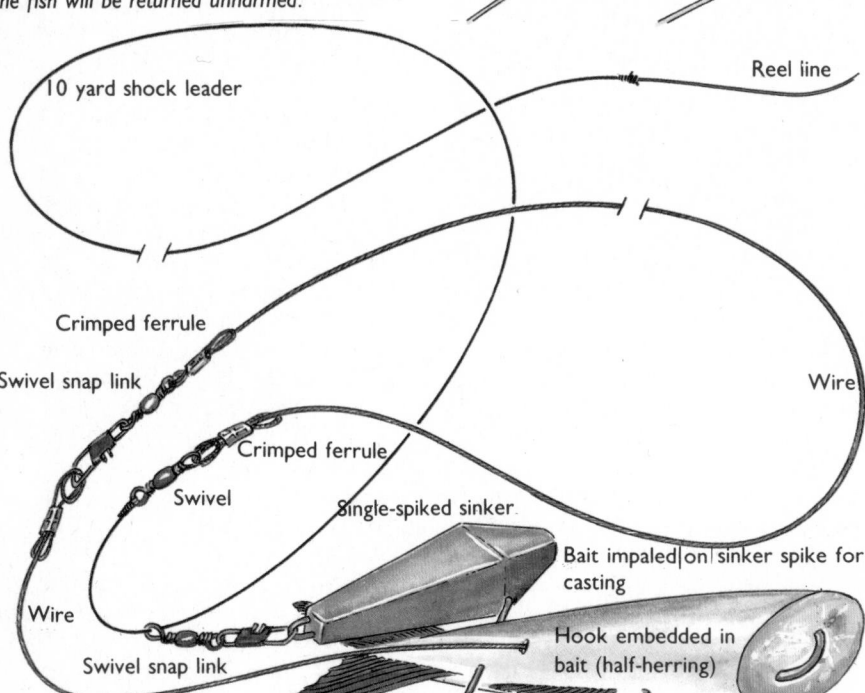

10 yard shock leader

Crimped ferrule

Swivel snap link

Crimped ferrule

Swivel

Wire

Single-spiked sinker

Bait impaled on sinker spike for
casting

Wire

Swivel snap link

Hook embedded in
bait (half-herring)

How to hook tope
Tope pick up a bait and run a short
distance before pausing to turn and
swallow it. A ledger rig, therefore, is
the most suitable terminal tackle as
it allows the fish to seize the bait
and move off with it without feeling
drag or pressure. The fish should not
be struck until it commences its
second run, unless a very small bait
is being used.
   One method is to use an all-wire
trace of 40lb b.s. Its overall length is
4ft as anything longer causes

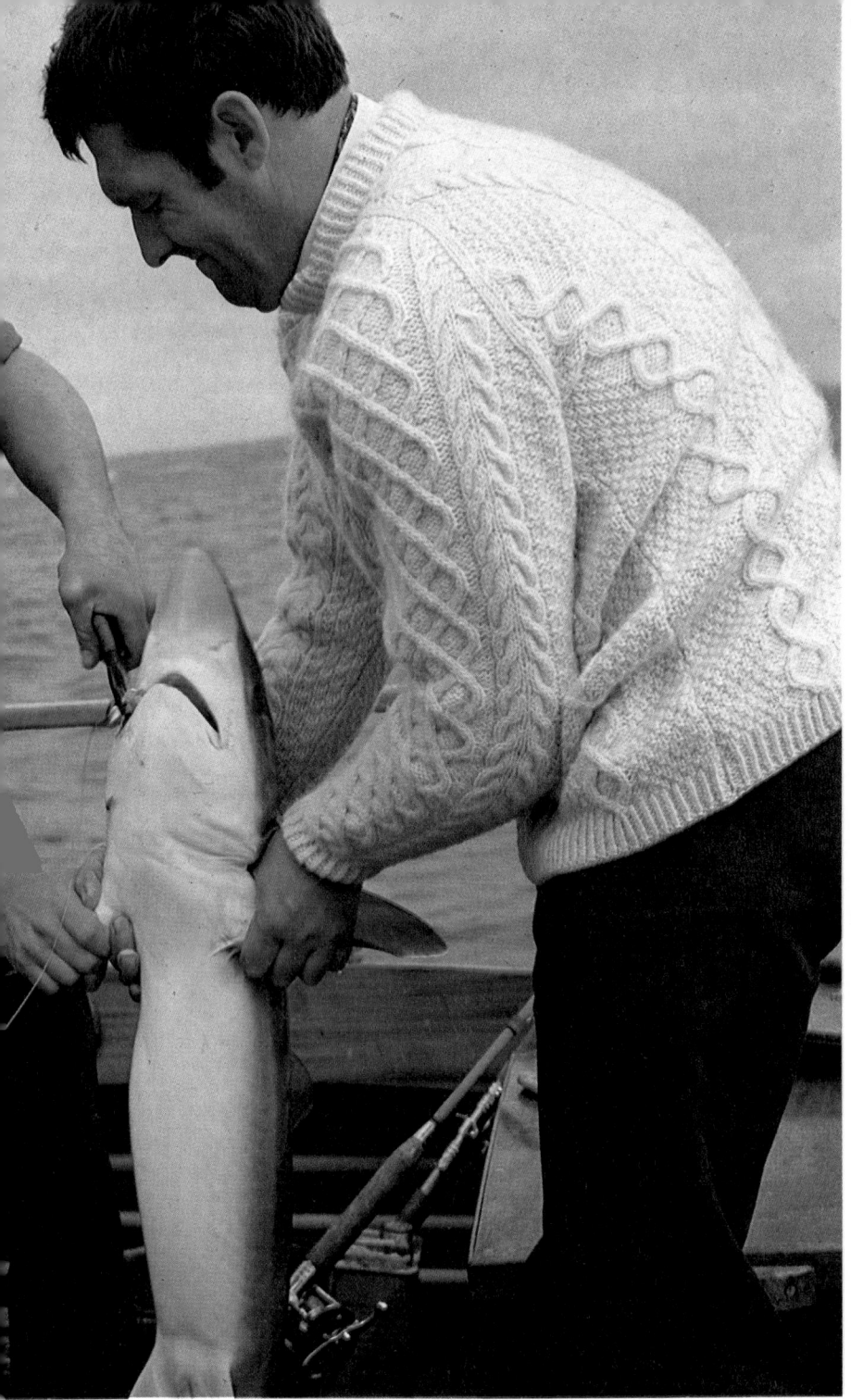

What time of year is best for tope fishing from the shore?
On the North Devon coast, where many 40lb specimens are captured, September and October are best. This will not vary much elsewhere.

What is the growth rate of the tope?
The fish is long-lived but slow growing. Females do not reach maturity until they are at least eight years old. Such a fish weighs about 20lb.

What is the right way to bring a tope aboard a boat?
The wanton use of gaffs has led directly to the decline of the species—even to its disappearance in many areas. A tope should be lifted aboard in gloved hands, the main grip being round the narrow body just in front of the tail. A quick, positive swing is all that is needed. Conservation by this means is vital to the survival of the species.

Is it worthwhile to groundbait from the shore?
Like all members of the shark family, the tope has amazing powers of smell and will quickly 'home in' on a source of food. A bag of fish guts, weighted with stones, should be thrown out as far as possible from the fishing position. A large, weighted tin stuffed with rags soaked in pilchard oil will serve equally well but the tin should be well pierced to let the oil flow out.

What weight of monofilament line should be used for tope traces?
Only 80lb commercial monofilament is thick enough to resist the fish's strong jaws and abrasive skin. It can be purchased by the metre, so need not work out to be too expensive.

serious problems in casting. It is joined to a shock leader of 30lb test and then to the main line. The sinker is attached to a free running swivel on the shock leader, which permits the fish to take line freely. A similar trace is also used except that the short wire hook-link is followed by heavy monofilament of at least 40lb test. Tope have sharp teeth so a short-wire link to the hook is essential. Their skin is as rough as glass paper when rubbed against the grain, and as they have a tendency to roll up on the trace, light nylon will part like thread. All-wire is therefore safer, but heavy nylon is preferred since it is more flexible and fishes better. It should, however, be changed after each fish as it becomes unreliable due to abrasion and chafing. Hook sizes will depend on the size of the bait used, but are normally 6/0 to 9/0. They should be razor sharp.

When casting a long trace, an old spiked sinker is used on which all but one spike is removed. The bait is

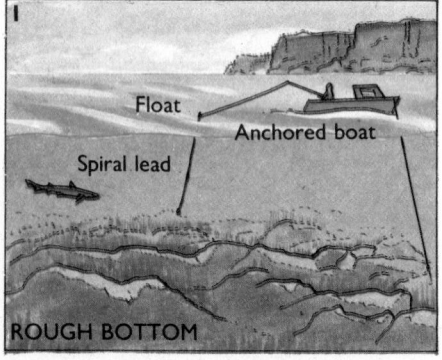

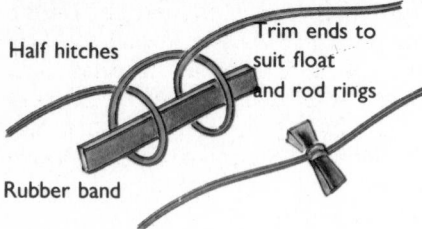

impaled on the single spike, effectively halving the length of the trace and permitting easier casting. When the bait hits the water it parts company with the sinker. A few feet of line should be wound back on the reel when the sinker is on the bottom to ensure that the trace has straightened out along the sea-bed.

Traces for boat fishing are very similar, except that heavier nylon monofilament can be used for the short-wire link—50lb to 70lb test will suit admirably. When fishing from an anchored boat in strong tides or currents a long trace may be preferred and its length can be adjusted by putting a stop (a rubber band or match stick secured by two half hitches) on the line below the free running ledger. When fishing on the drift—that is, from a drifting boat—a shorter trace is desirable. The ledger runs on the monofilament portion of the trace, making a partial ledger and when fishing over rough ground the sinker should be attached by a length of light line or 'rotten bottom'. If the trace fouls, the bottom link to the sinker should break and only the lead will be lost.

To get the best out of tope one must not fish heavy. This is unnecessary as the tope likes to run hard and fast, particularly in shallow water and can be played on light gear. A test line of 25lb to 30lb is adequate and can be matched with rods comparable to those complying to the IGFA specifications for the 20lb and 30lb tackle classes. Multiplier-type reels with a capacity of 300 yards of line are best and they should have an efficient brake or slipping clutch.

While the angler normally fishes on or near the bottom for tope, when drift fishing in depths of up to 10 fathoms or over rocky reefs he can driftline or float fish for them. These methods can at times be most effective. When floatfishing, the depth at which the bait is fishing can be adjusted to keep it clear of the reefs and avoid catching in the bottom. When driftlining in relatively shallow water the aim should be to fish in mid-water. When fishing from an anchored boat or on the drift in shallow water, fish your bait well away from the boat.

Top: *Returning a tope to the sea.* **Above:** *Tope fishing from boats. When at anchor over rough ground (1) adjust the length of trace with the rubber band stopper, shown left. On the drift over a sandy bottom, a shorter trace is best (2) with no float, to avoid snagging.* **Below:** *A slider float rig with rubber band stopper for tope fishing.*

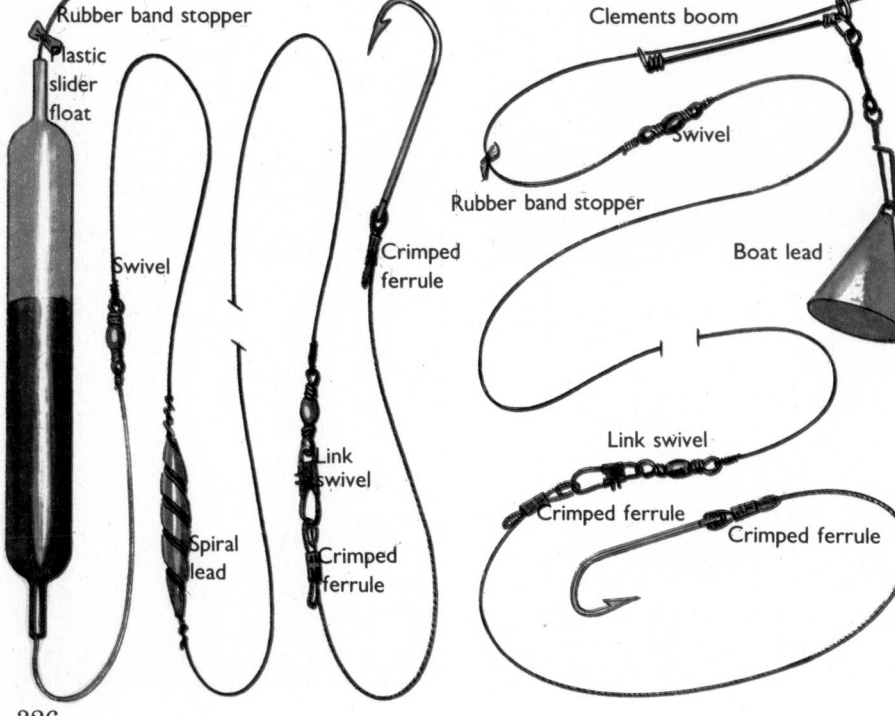

Ling

A novice fisherman's first deep sea boat trip to a chartered wreck or reef is an almost guaranteed pleasure thanks to the shoals of suicidal ling which infest these deepwater marks

Most newcomers to deep water wreck and reef fishing, probably began by catching ling. It is a prolific species with a wide distribution, but the greatest numbers are found at deep-water marks at the western end of the English Channel and Southern Ireland. A very powerful fish, the ling reaches a maximum length of 6½ft, and weight in excess of 100lb. Anglers seldom come into contact with ling of more than 45lb, and so far only five have broken the 50lb barrier. The British Record stands at 57lb 8oz—a fish caught three miles off Stonehaven, Scotland, by I Duncan on 16 May 1982.

The numbers of ling that inhabit wrecks is phenomenal; but some idea can be gained from the catch of 6,200lb made by eight anglers in a two-tide session about 24 miles south west of the Channel Islands. Fishing over a virgin wreck follows a very definite pattern. The first assault will remove several thousand pounds of fish in the 15-25lb class. Successive visits result in fewer fish, but the average weight will be much greater. Until the ling have been drastically thinned out, conger and other species that live on wrecks hardly show among the catches. The hulk may be alive with eels

Left: *A magnificent 34lb wreck ling.*
Below: *Gaffing and boating a ling—a job for two, however small the fish.*

but only the odd one will be caught the first four times the wreck is fished. They are outnumbered.

The ling *(Molva molva)* is a member of the cod family, although at first sight one might think it more closely resembles the conger. It has a long, slimy, eel-like body but the head and back are broad and its coloration, spineless fins, barbules and very small scales are telling indications that it is a member of the great family of the Gadidae.

Habitat and size
It is essentially a deepwater species, and while small fish may be found close to the shore, adult ling are rarely found in depths of less than 15 fathoms and are taken commercially in depths up to 200 fathoms. They are most plentiful in depths of 20-60 fathoms. The ling has a great liking for rough and rocky ground, particularly deep-fissured reefs rising steeply from deepwater. A demersal or bottom-dwelling species feeding almost entirely on other fishes, the ling spawns offshore in deepwater from April to June. It was once considered a mid-summer and autumn fish but with the development of wreck fishing, the angling season is now all year round.

Tackle and bait
When fishing over rough ground from a drifting boat, an ordinary paternoster trace will suffice. The lead or sinker should be attached by some 'rotten bottom' in case it cat-

Does a ling make powerful runs?
Not in the accepted sense, but it puts up a fair amount of pressure, constantly trying to bore downwards as it is pumped up. Ling in the 40lb class can offer you quite a struggle.

What type of reel is best for pirk fishing in deep water?
You need a narrow spool, fast-retrieve multplier with a 5:1 gear ratio. The Penn Senator Special exactly fits these specifications.

How big can ling grow?
The 124lb fish caught near Wolf Rock lighthouse off the tip of Cornwall in 1853 must come close to the maximum possible weight. The catch is well documented in Couch's *History of Fishes of the British Isles*.

What is the shore record for ling?
It now stands at 19lb 4oz, to the credit of D J Rogan of St Hellier, Jersey. He caught it in the winter of 1981 (confirming the fact that large ling move close to the coast during the cold months) from the south west coast of the island.

Should I try whole fish baits?
Unlike its wreck neighbour the conger, which swallows a whole fish more or less intact, the ling rips and tears at a bait with its long needle-like teeth. The secret of catching large numbers is to offer strips of mackerel or squid, and to strike as soon as a bite registers.

When are the biggest wreck catches made?
During December, January and February, when ling congregate in large numbers prior to spawning. The breeding process is usually completed by mid-March.

ches in the bottom. Only the sinker will be lost if it is necessary to break out, and this can be quickly replaced. Hook sizes should be 6/0 or larger, depending on the size of the bait. If fishing specifically for ling, large baits are advisable because pollack and small conger living on the same type of ground will go for the smaller baits. For ling, a whole small herring or the whole side of a mackerel is very attractive bait.

The take is usually deliberate, so wait until you feel the weight of the fish before striking. Should you miss, drop the bait back down quickly to the fish. Ling are fierce predators that will snatch again at a bait that has been whipped from

Top left: *These three specimen ling are of uniform size and probably came from exactly the same part of the wreck they inhabited.*
Above: *Catch from waters off Hoy Island in the Orkneys. Note the butt pad—an item of tackle vital to comfortable 'pumping'.*
Left: *The Eddystone Reef is famous for its specimen fish—including ling.*

their jaws, if given the chance. They do not run when hooked but fight strongly and stubbornly. Like many species with swimbladders, when brought up quickly from deepwater on heavy tackle they come up more easily after the first few fathoms.

However, heavy tackle is not necessary and when taken on light tackle they fight vigorously all the

Successful Red Gill

The Red Gill PVC sandeels are very successful lures for fishing wrecks. These can be fished as a single lure on a following trace, in tandem, or in threes in paternoster fashion. If a feather jig is used it is advisable not

Left: *Snapping and thrashing on the hook, a ling of any size needs careful handling.*

to have more than three feathers either baited or unbaited. When fishing with multiple lures one can hook two or three heavy fish at the same time, but unless very strong traces are used, one lure is almost inevitably broken. Single lure fishing enables the angler to use lighter gear and so derive far more enjoyment from his sport.

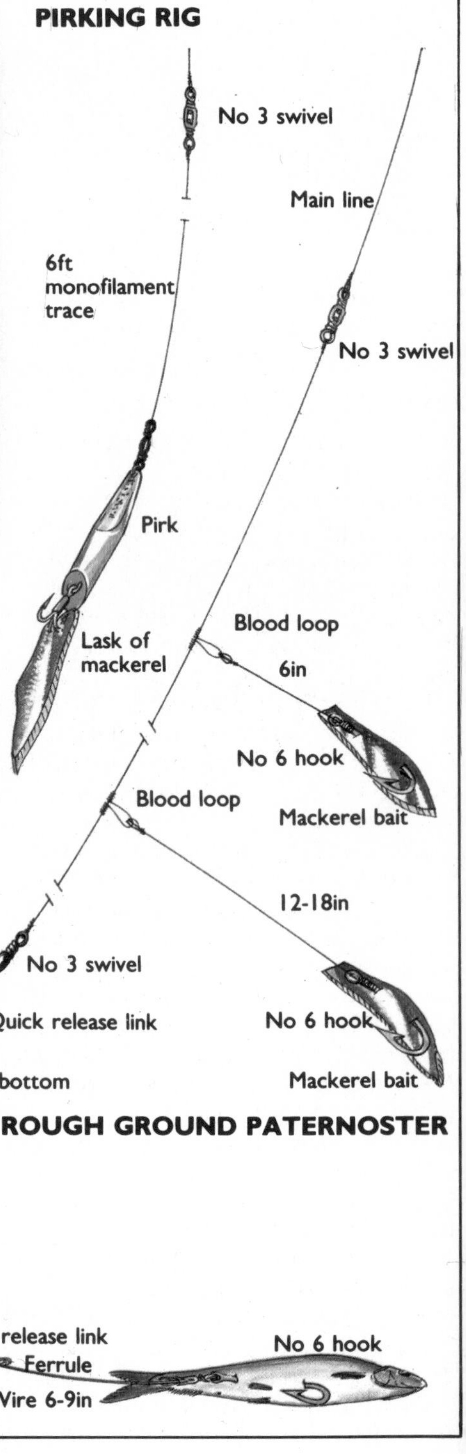

way to the boat. They have a very impressive mouthful of teeth which will make short work of light nylon traces, so heavy gauges are advised for terminal rigs. Extreme care should be taken when you are unhooking the fish as the sharp teeth can inflict nasty wounds.

Seeking ling

When fishing from an anchored position for ling, a simple ledger rig is very effective. As conger are found on the same ground it is advisable to use a short 6-9in wire link to the hook, for conger are likely to sever an all-monofilament trace. When fishing on the drift there is a risk of conger taking the bait. Wire is also recommended when wreck fishing as ling will be found on the bottom together with conger. If you are seeking ling, another hazard when fishing wrecks are the banks of very large pollack. The difficulty here is trying to get a large bait down without it being taken.

A big fish bait is more easily got down when fishing from an anchored boat. Anchored uptide of the wreck, the bait can be worked downtide without encountering the pollack and coalfish. When fishing on the drift, however, artificials such as 20oz pirk will get down through the depths very quickly—usually too quickly for the marauding fish in midwater. Pirks are very good for taking ling and the addition of a lask of mackerel to the treble hook of the pirk can prove very productive.

Background: *Terminal tackle must be sturdy. The Capta lead on the whole-bait rig helps hold bottom. Over rough ground, the rotten bottom stops loss of expensive tackle.* **Inset:** *Mackerel baits can often be bought fresh on the quayside and used whole or cut diagonally into lasks.*

LING FISHING RIGS

Main line

No 3 swivel

6ft monofilament

No 3 swivel

Quick release link

Rotten bottom

Bomb lead

Clements boom

No 3 swivel

Capta lead

Quick release link

Ferrule

Wire 6-9in

No 6 hook

LEDGER RIG

PIRKING RIG

No 3 swivel

Main line

6ft monofilament trace

No 3 swivel

Pirk

Lask of mackerel

Blood loop

6in

No 6 hook

Mackerel bait

Blood loop

12-18in

No 3 swivel

No 6 hook

Mackerel bait

ROUGH GROUND PATERNOSTER

Pollack

Reefs and wrecks are the obvious places to go in search of monster pollack and rod records, but shore fishermen and open-water anglers differ on what counts as a 'specimen' fish

For the pursuit of specimen pollack, the angler must be aware that pollack fishing is divided into three seasons: spring/early summer, summer/autumn and winter. There is a definite migration of fish according to season. Few fish frequent shallow water or the great reefs during the coldest months of the year. Instead they migrate to deep water in the Atlantic. In late April the first few return, and numbers build up rapidly, reaching a peak on the reefs in late August.

During high summer, pollack provide good sport for boat fishermen, but until mid-October those fish coming close to land are rather small. Fish that live in deepwater wrecks are present throughout the year, but the population dramatically increases from the beginning of November, when the residents are joined by migratory shoals.

Many wrecks beyond the 40-fathom line, about 20 miles offshore, hold thousands of large fish during the winter, and provide spectacular sport. Between December and March the females grow heavy with roe. A pollack weighing 18lb in December may, by the end of February, be close to the British boat-caught record weight of 26lb 7oz. There are three kinds of boat fishing: inshore, offshore, and reef and wreck. Each demands a completely different approach and to find specimens in numbers requires quite a lot of dedication.

Light-tackle pollack fishing in shallow water is exciting during the autumn and early winter. In the western English Channel from Torbay to Land's End, pollack up to 14lb are caught within a few hundred yards of land—sometimes in less than four fathoms. While specimen fish can come from any patch of rocky ground, fishing off prominent headlands, where the tide runs strongly, is the best bet for consistent sport.

Among prime marks are Berry Head, Start Point, Bolt Tail, Rame Head and Queener Point, Chapel Point (Mevagissey) and the Gwineas and Manacle Rocks. From late October very large pollack hang around harbour estuaries and it is not unusual to contact them at night on the flood tide in tidal rivers. Good examples of these rivers are the Tamar, Fowey and Helford.

For inshore fishing, most experts favour a 10ft fast taper, hollow glass spinning rod, matched with a small multiplier loaded with 10-12lb b.s. monofilament. It is essential to choose a soft line with a small diameter. End tackle for anchored or drift fishing is a 12ft trace worked from a single wire boom—commonly known as the 'flying collar' rig.

Moody pollack hook themselves
Most inshore pollack are contacted close to the bottom during daylight, and the popular method of fishing is to allow the baited hook to reach the fish and immediately begin a steady retrieve. Very few pollack, big or small, take a stationary bait, so it is vital to keep it moving at all times to give a lifelike appearance.

Shallow-water pollack are moody fish. At times they strike savagely, taking the bait well down without hesitation. More often, the first indication of the pollack's presence is a gentle pressure on the rod, followed by a more pronounced pull, before the tremendous power-dive so characteristic of the species. Striking is unnecessary, as the sheer speed of the dive against the multiplier's drag is sufficient to drive the hook home.

The combination of shallow water and light tackle makes even an eight-pounder seem a giant. In shallow water, pollack do not suffer distortion to the swimbladder through change of water-pressure, so they are able to make a series of line-stripping runs, but it is their

downfall when hooked in deep water.

Unless the drag is set accurately to match the line's breaking strain, the fish will certainly succeed in breaking free—this is always a big hazard when fishing close to shore, and it has been responsible for the loss of many fine specimens.

Keeping a thin profile

It is important to maintain close contact—at no time should the line be allowed to slacken. If it does, the fish will dive deep into thick kelp and you may lose it when the terminal tackle snags. Some idea of a specimen pollack's fighting capabilities in the shallows can be gained

from my own best fish of 12lb 10½oz. It took 25 minutes to beat on spinning tackle.

Sliding-float fishing from an anchored dinghy is also effective, particularly in a strong tide-run. The float—a thin-profile pattern 8in long—is quickly whisked away by the run of water, so a large amount of ground can be worked. The usual practice is to let the float run at least 200 yards before starting a slow retrieve. Unfortunately, pollack weighing more than 6lb are seldom caught on float gear, but it is a method that guarantees a fair bag.

Trolling for pollack close to shore is a method which is effective in the

early morning and late evening.

Live sandeels are by far the most successful bait for inshore pollack. Used with a long trace and worked from a drifting or anchored boat, they take a heavy toll of big fish. A live prawn, hooked through a tail segment and allowed to swim around on a light trace, is most effective.

Pollack are also partial to worms, particularly large king ragworm.

Below: *The rock ledges at the tip of Portland Bill make a productive fishing mark for the pollack specimen hunter.*
Inset: *Pollack fishing off the steep-to cliffs of Stornoway, Lewis.*

How should artificial eels be presented to winter wreck pollack?

A single 177mm eel on a long trace is the most sporting way. Two or three mounted on short snoods to a tough paternoster are more deadly still. This rig is dropped at speed, which often attracts a take. If the lures reach bottom without being attacked, wind up 10ft and jig them.

How effective is trolling?

Unfortunately, the falling pollack population attributable to commercial gill netting has been the ruination of the trolling method. It still pays dividends sometimes, particularly where spring tides rush through shallow-water bays, and near headlands. The lure or live sandeel must work well clear of engine noise—100 yards is not too far.

Can you suggest a good shore rig?

Large pollack move inshore in early winter. Where water is deep close in, mount live sandeel on a sliding float. Rig it so that the eel works just above any kelp. On a steep-to beach, offer a simple ledger rig.

What's so good about a lever-drag multiplier reel for pollacking?

It gives precise control over line drag and is much simpler to use than a star drag multiplier. One movement of the lever engages or disengages the spool. Expensive, but worthwhile.

Is wire line right for deep water?

Its small diameter permits the use of much lighter leads, and you can keep in touch with the fish. But a short length of monofilament is needed as a cushion between wire line and a flying collar boom; the same applies if you are using a paternoster or pirk.

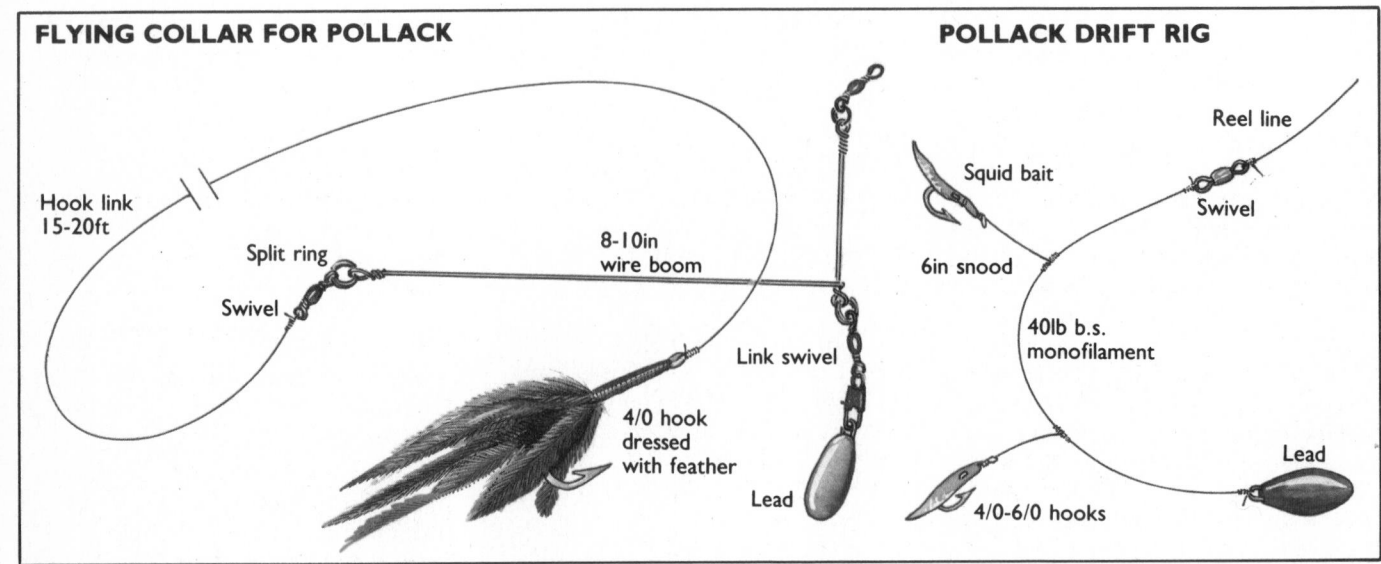

FLYING COLLAR FOR POLLACK

Hook link 15-20ft

Split ring

Swivel

8-10in wire boom

Link swivel

4/0 hook dressed with feather

Lead

POLLACK DRIFT RIG

Reel line

Squid bait

Swivel

6in snood

40lb b.s. monofilament

Lead

4/0-6/0 hooks

Alternatively, small ragworm bunched together are taken greedily. Many of the largest specimens have fallen to these baits. Fish-strip gets little response inshore and should be used only as a last resort.

The cream of pollack sport is found on the concentrations of rock that make up the deep water reefs off Devon and Cornwall. Any conversation concerning fishing for pollack will inevitably touch on Eddystone, Hands Deep, Hatt Rock and Wolf Rock.

Each reef is a maze of gloomy canyons and soaring walls of rock clawing towards the surface. Life of all kinds abounds, providing an endless supply of food for big predators. Here the specimen pollack is king, and, on a rich diet, males and females reach over 20lb.

The Eddystone Reef
Fourteen miles south of Plymouth and nine from Cornwall's Rame Head are the rocks of Eddystone.

The Eddystone light stands on the highest rock, but the reef extends above and below the water for nearly two miles in every direction. The rocks are red gneiss, a very hard rock found at only two places in England—at the Stone itself and two miles away at Prawle Point on the Devon coast.

The best fishing is on a dull day as red gneiss has an unusual mirror-like quality which reflects sunlight underwater. This seems to deter the fish from feeding.

Big pollack are a feature of the Eddystone Reef. Specimens of 14lb and more are commonplace in autumn and winter, and during the summer months large shoals of 6-8lb pollack roam the reef.

At the north east of the reef is a group of rocks at a depth of 20 fathoms, rising to within 10 fathoms of the surface. Here, many specimen pollack weighing over 12lb, and occasionally even more, are taken.

Another good spot is located a mile from the lighthouse on the south side, where a massive pinnacle of rock rises 68ft from the bottom, although there is still 60ft of water above it at low tide. King rag works particularly well, but big mackerel frequently fall to the feathers and baits intended for pollack.

Despite their size, fishing for large reef pollack with heavy tackle is completely wrong. Pollacking requires no more than medium-weight gear, which can consist of a two-handed spinning rod or a 20lb IGFA-class boat rod—although the latter is a bit heavy for the discerning angler. Many enthusiasts use an 11ft hand-made, one-piece, hollow glass rod with an all-through action. Used in conjunction with a multiplier and 15-18lb b.s. monofilament, it has maximum sensitivity in detecting light bites and is perfect for playing large fish.

As in shallow water, experts fishing rough ground use the 'flying collar'. It allows very long traces and baited hooks to be dropped at a

Above left: *Reef tackle. The wire boom is for rigidity: the hook link is monofilament and need not be any thicker than 15 or 18lb b.s. to withstand a pollack's bite.*
Above: *The drift rig is for wrecks where line must withstand snagging and a possible encounter with a conger eel. Some sources recommend lines as heavy as 60lb.*

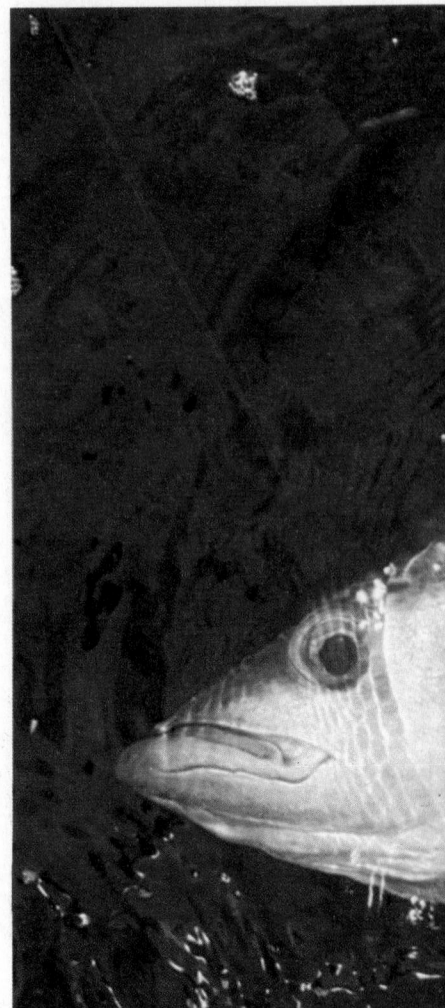

fast pace through any depth of water without their tangling with the reel line. The boom can be purchased, or made from an ordinary wire coat-hanger.

Once the eyes have been twisted at all three points of the boom, split rings are added. These connect swivels to the reel line, the long trace is particularly important, as big pollack revolve on their way to the surface. Without the swivel the trace becomes hopelessly twisted, and needs replacing after each single pollack capture.

Allow the boom to run to the bottom and then retrieve steadily for 60 turns of the reel. This procedure is repeated until the bait is taken. Once the pollack has taken the baited hook, it will bend the rod with its desperately determined dive.

A plastic version of the wire boom is now on the market. The reel line runs through two guiders on the top edge to a swivel, which joins the long trace. With this boom, rigging-up takes seconds. It performs well

enough, but should really be bigger.

The single hook and long trace of the flying collar rig increases the quality of sport, as the fish can quickly work up top speed. When there is a good flow of water, such as during a spring tide, you can use a 20ft trace. In a moderate run, however, you can reduce the length by as much as 50 per cent.

An appetite for currents

Long study of the pollack's eating habits shows that a fast run of water encourages it to feed freely. In slow-moving water and in the slack top and bottom of a tide, few bites will materialize, but, as the tide strengthens, the pollack will begin to hunt around for food.

Medium-weight tackle allows the use of a small lead even in deep, fast-moving water. With 18lb b.s. monofilament it is possible to get away with a 6oz lead, which makes for comfortable fishing and does not hamper the fish's movement.

I mentioned earlier the desirabili-

Below: *Eddystone can be reached with ease from either Looe or Plymouth. The reef itself is of interest, but so too are the sunken hulks of the ships it wrecked. This coast also offers the shore angler some good marks.*
Bottom: *Brought to the boat's side, a specimen pollack awaits the landing net. It's a pity to damage these handsome fish with a gaff, especially if you are intending to eat the meat.*

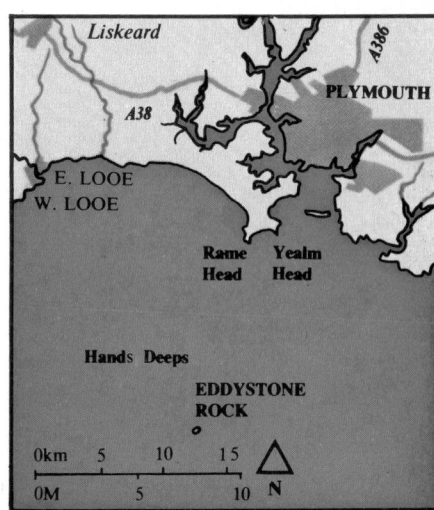

Above left: *A giant fish taken from deep water during the winter.*
Left: *Twin specimens from over a wreck in Lyme Bay, Dorset.*
Above: *The largest of these wreck pollack weighed 22lb. The proud anglers made their bumper catch using artificial eels in a wreck habitat where shoaling sandeel present the easiest prey to hunting pollack.*
Above right: *Not a shore catch, but Michael Bowden was fishing close inshore when he caught this 14lb pollack at Mevagissey.*
Right: *Brian Taylor—well pleased with this pair of specimen pollack taken over a Devon wreck.*
Far right: *Rita Burret, the IGFA world record holder for pollack, holds up another record contender—a 15lb 3oz coalfish. Confusion arises from the failure of the IGFA to distinguish between the coalfish and the pollack.*

ty of retrieving line through 60 turns of the reel before letting the bait sink back to the bottom. Most pollack on a reef will be somewhere within that range. By counting each revolution of the reel-handle and noting the number when a fish is hooked, the exact feeding-level can be determined. Valuable fishing time can be saved in this way, by working only the productive zone. Naturally, it will alter as the hours pass, but it is a simple matter to maintain contact.

A pollack hooked on a long trace usually surfaces close to the boat. As the boom cannot pass through

the rod-rings, the fish must be gently drawn to the net by hand. The majority brought from deep water are incapable of further fight at this stage, so there is little chance of their escaping.

Whether or not you intend to eat it, a pollack should always be lifted from the water with a wide-mouthed net. Gaffing is uncertain and damages the fish.

While any part of a large reef is likely to hold several fish, there are always hotspots. Many charter skippers have precise knowledge of these, and find it comparatively easy to anchor in a position that will

place baited hooks exactly where they are most needed.

If the reef is unfamiliar, move around until a high pinnacle is pinpointed with the echo-sounder. The anchor is then dropped well uptide, as the boat will move back a long way before its anchor takes effect. Baits then run over the top of the pinnacle and end up on the sheltered side of the rock, where many fish will be found—especially in fast tide conditions. Pollack tend to stay out of fierce water.

Although king ragworms are not found in deep water, they make deadly bait for reef pollack, and take

most fish between May and mid-July. Detailed records compiled over a 10-year period show that, except for live sandeel, worm surpasses other baits by a large margin. Consequently, pollack purists spend hours digging for worms. The popularity of the bait for reef fishing has led to overdigging and shortages at many places, and giant worms of 12-18in are now extremely difficult to find.

King rag are offered on a 4/0 hook to which a few red and white feathers have been whipped. Half a dozen white or red beads are threaded on to the trace to rest against the hook's eye. These embellishments

337

induce a take when other baits and unadorned hooks are left untouched.

By the end of July pollack take mackerel, squid-strip and all manner of livebaits. Anglers seeking specimen fish should livebait with small mackerel, hooked through the body behind the vital organs or in front of the dorsal fin. Pouting also make livebaits but, being susceptible to water-pressure, they are usually in a poor state and incapable of displaying much activity when returned to the bottom.

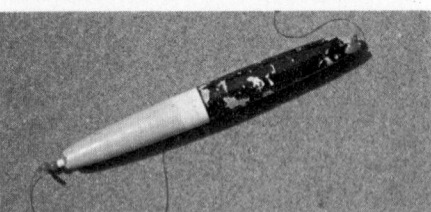

Artificial eels
If large livebaits are used, allow time for the pollack to get a firm hold of the bait fish before striking. It is also important to raise the hook size to 6/0 and employ a 20lb-class rod to cope with both bait and catch.

In recent years artificial eels of various kinds have become popular baits. They are undoubtedly useful, but their full effectiveness is restricted to periods of big tides.

Successful reef pollacking requires a sensitive touch as, quite often, the fish only mouth a bait without making a determined attack.

Wreck fishing for pollack is spectacular, but its sporting level depends on the method used. Pollack run much larger on wrecks than on reefs, and the concentration of fish is considerably greater. Even a small wreck, standing just a few fathoms high, provides shelter for vast numbers of fish.

During the summer the flying-collar technique is widely used from a drifting boat, as few skippers bother to anchor if they are after pollack. Tackle is a 20lb-class 6½-7ft hollow glass boat rod matched with a medium-sized multiplier and monofilament line. Braided lines have no stretch, but their resistance to water demands the use of much larger weights, and spoils the sport.

Working from an anchored boat means slower sport, but is more enjoyable. You can settle down to uninterrupted fishing and, by increasing or decreasing the amount of weight, establish a spot where the big fish are feeding.

Unfortunately, fishing at anchor with medium-weight tackle is possible only during neap tides and on the

first days of the build-up to spring tides. The most productive wrecks lie in deep, exposed water, which can roar along in big tides. To combat a five-knot tide, increase gear to the 50lb-class and use 2lb of lead.

At the other extreme, light-tackle wrecking for pollack is becoming popular on wrecks during the smallest tides. Several British anglers have set IGFA world records for pollack *(Pollachius pollachius)*, with a line standard of 6lb for men and 12lb for women.

A strange discrepancy
Across the Atlantic, where the IGFA is based, *P. virens*—the coalfish of British waters—is referred to as pollack. Ludicrously, British records for *P. pollachius* appear in American lists for *P. virens*. Such a situation must be cleared up without delay, and separate lists established.

Catching specimen pollack of over 18lb on 6lb line requires a high level of skill as well as the right rig. In experienced hands, the one-piece 11ft rod comes into its own, its length and sensitivity allow very large fish to be played out. This type of pollacking can be done only with a few people fishing at the same time—a luxury when charter boats cost over £120 a day.

Good bait presentation is vital when fishing ultra-light over wrecks. Mackerel or squid-strip should be cut into strips 8in long and 1in wide, tapering to a point. The hook is positioned at the thin end. But live sandeel is still the best bait of all.

Wreck fishing during the winter with heavy-duty paternoster rigs and pirks often results in catches up to the record weight of 26lb 7oz.

Plaice

To commercial fishermen, the plaice is the most important flatfish species. Abundant, readily tempted with the right bait, and delicious to eat, it's just as popular with anglers

A handsome adult plaice. Few grow larger than this, though very occasionally they grow to a massive yard in length.

Of all the fishes caught around the British Isles, few are better known than the plaice *(Pleuronectes platessa)*. It has long been a favourite with the housewife as it looks very attractive when displayed on fishmongers' slabs with its eye-catching orange/red spots. The plaice belongs to the order of fish known as *Heterosomata*, which means 'twisted-bodied'. These are the flatfishes which swim on one or other side of their body just above the sea bottom.

The plaice lies and swims left side down. The colouring of its right or upper side varies from a light sandy brown right through to a dark brown according to the locality and the type of seabed on which it lives. The distinctive spots, too, range in colour from pale orange to bright scarlet. Furthermore, if the seabed is chalky, then it is not uncommon to catch plaice with white spots as well as red. The underside, however, is always a translucent bluish white with thin blue streaks.

The skin of the plaice feels completely smooth when rubbed with the finger, although there are several bony knobs on the ridge of the head which distinguish it from other flatfish. The lateral line is very slightly curved in the vicinity of the pectoral fin, and the jaws are lined with very strong teeth. There are also muscles resembling a second set of jaws at the entrance to the gullet, which are used to crush small varieties of shellfish.

Plaice distribution

Plaice are found all round the British Isles, extending northwards as far as Iceland and as far south as the Mediterranean. Spawning takes place very early in the year—usually in January or February—in depths of 15-30 fathoms. The eggs float in the sea and measure approximately $\frac{1}{10}$ inch in diameter. A good-sized female, a fish of, say, 3lb, produces as many as 250,000 eggs in one spawning. Depending on the water temperature, the eggs take anything from 8-28 days to hatch. The newly hatched larvae measure about $\frac{1}{3}$in, and at this stage are not flat but rounded like other fish.

The larva feeds on its yolk sac for about the first week of its existence and normally not until it has exhausted this food supply does it change from its original round shape to the flat shape it will have for the rest of its life. At the same time, the young plaice begins to take in food, which at first, of course, is of microscopic dimensions.

The fish's change in shape begins with a change in the position of the eyes. The left eye moves upwards and forwards and after about ten days arrives on the upper margin of the head just in front of the right eye. A little over four weeks later it

reaches its final position above and in front of the right eye. While the eyes are going through this rotating movement, the young fish begins to take up a new position when swimming. As it has been growing, the whole anatomy of the body has gradually undergone a distinct twisting process, and the fully developed fish finally swims and rests, camouflaged, on its left side with both eyes pointing upwards.

Growth rate

The growth rate of a plaice, though relatively fast for a flatfish, is slow when compared with that of cod, for instance. A four-year-old fish will measure only 12-13in, although this may vary slightly from area to area.

Females mature some time between their third and seventh years, when they are about 9-11in long. Males mature a year earlier, between their second and sixth years.

The early life of a plaice is spent in sandy shallows feeding on very small crustaceans called copepods and large quantities of mollusc larvae. After about six months of this diet the fish attain a length of some 2in, and at about this size they gradually move farther out from the shore, although they still favour areas where the depth is less than five fathoms. Tagging experiments have shown that plaice do not as a rule travel a very great distance, usually staying close to their spawning area throughout their adult life.

Mussel bed

Razorfish

There is one fish on record that was tagged in the North Sea in 1904. It was recaptured in 1920 only a few miles from where it had originally been tagged.

After spawning

Adult plaice return to shallower waters near the shore in March and April to recover from the rigours of spawning. At this time they are thin, but after a few weeks of feeding in the rich shallows they quickly regain weight. The adult fish feed mainly on bivalve shellfish of all kinds, small cockles and mussels being firm favourites. The mussels are swallowed whole and are crushed by the jaw-like muscles in the throat; the fish then digests the contents and excretes the pulverized shell.

If there is ample food, plaice will frequent almost any type of seabed. Some of the best catches are taken in very rocky areas where they are usually feeding on mussels growing on the sides of the rocks. On sandy seabeds they search out razorfish and they will even travel up estuaries in search of cockles and other bivalves. They will eat marine

Far left: A plaice's chosen habitat is usually well seeded with shellfish, which form the major part of its diet. The natural harbour of Lulworth Cove illustrated is one of many such grounds on the Dorset coast.

Below: The product of a day's boat fishing—20 deepwater plaice.

ASK THE EXPERT

What time of year is best for shore fishing?
May and October are good months. Fish weighing 5lb and more are caught then on the South/East Devon coast.

Do plaice travel far up tidal rivers?
They are not found in any great number more than five miles from an estuary and then only if the river is fairly wide. But good plaice rivers include the Dart, the Fowey, and the Firth of Clyde which produced the boat record of 10lb 3½oz.

What bait should I use in winter?
In the depths of winter, good plaice are taken on peeler crab preserved or frozen since the summer glut.

Does the state of tide have any bearing on the success of a boat fishing trip?
Definitely. Plaice lie dormant, just under the sand or shingle during slack water. They only begin to feed when the tide starts to run. Spring tides often bring the best catches.

What kind of rod is best on shore?
An 11-12ft light beachcaster capable of casting a 4oz weight suits most estuarial and river fishing. Choose a medium action, otherwise soft baits will tear loose on the cast.

Does a fast tide merit using wire line to boat fish for plaice?
It is essential to keep the bait very close to the bottom. Wire line cuts through fast water and keeps terminal tackle down with the minimum of lead. But use 4ft of light nylon between weight and hook as a rotten bottom. Let out line slowly, stopping the moment you contact the seabed.

worms, such as lugworms and ragworms, although these do not seem to figure very prominently in the plaice's natural diet. Therefore, it is not surprising that, although trawlers catch great quantities of plaice, rod and line anglers fishing the same area with marine worms usually fail to make big catches.

The most likely area to take plaice on rod and line is on mussel beds—but the mussels should be smallish, no bigger than an inch in length. Mussel beds appear in different areas from year to year, and they are usually located by accident, but once found it is reasonably safe to assume there are plaice to be caught there in good numbers.

The ideal time to try for these 'flatties' is during prolonged settled weather in the summer. Clear water and bright sun make for better fishing. As the fish feed largely on bivalves, one would assume that these would be the best bait, but for some reason they seem reluctant to take them when they have been removed from their shells; and of course it is totally impractical to try

Below: *Cutting thin strips of squid as hookbait for plaice: a surprising choice considering the natural diet.*

to hook the mussel while still inside its shell. Thus the angler is reduced to using less favoured, but nevertheless successful, marine worms as bait. Lugworm usually proves the best, with ragworm running a close second, although this order may be reversed in some areas. Peeler crab, too, is often used.

Size potential
Plaice do not grow to great size and the rod-caught record is a fish of 10lb 3½oz, boated by H Gardiner fishing in Longa Sound, Scotland in 1974. Professional trawlers frequently take bigger fish than this, often well into double figures, but the rod and line angler can usually count himself lucky if he takes fish in the 3-4lb range. For this reason a light hollow glass rod in the 20lb class is to be recommended, providing leads of over 12oz are not going to be used.

For terminal tackle a trace should be used when the tide is running, but paternoster gear is favoured on sluggish tides or slack water. If using a trace, it should be about 8ft in length, either fished through a Clement's boom or a Kilmore boom. If baiting with lugworm, a long-shanked hook, No 2 or 1, is quite large enough. Use three hooks together, as more than one fish is taken at a time quite regularly. This is often because, even if you are holding the rod when the plaice swallows the worm, no bite is detected due to them swallowing the baited hook and remaining still. It is only when you lift the rod tip that you realize that a fish has in fact taken the bait.

Fish caught like this are usually deeply hooked. If, however, a bite is felt it is usually only a light tap, tap, and should be left for the fish to gorge the bait. To avoid the temptation of striking too soon, it is best not even to hold the rod.

To attract the fish, white spoons may be added to the trace, but they must be celluloid and not metal. Celluloid spoons are lighter and even a slight tide will give them movement in the water, and it is this movement that entices flatfish to attack the baited hooks.

Slack-water fishing

A different method of fishing should be used when using paternoster gear on slack water. In these conditions, the rod tip should be continually raised and lowered. This has two effects: first, it gives the bait movement; second, every time the lead strikes the seabed it sends up a cloud of 'dust' which, because plaice are very curious creatures, brings them close to the baited hooks to investigate. Fishing this way, the bite is very positive, being more in the nature of a sudden snatch rather than the gentle tap experienced with a trace. Unlike a bite on a trace, the sudden snatch should be struck immediately. Once hooked, the fish dives for the seabed and on light gear can put up quite a lively fight, diving for the bottom all the way to the boat. A landing net should be used in preference to a gaff for the bigger specimens.

Although plaice generally favour deeper water than other flatfish such as dabs and flounders, good fish can also be taken by shore-based anglers. However, whereas boat anglers will often go out and fish specifically for plaice, plaice taken by shore anglers are more often caught by accident. The most likely areas for shore plaice are river mouths, particularly those of Devon and Cornwall. Notable fish can be caught from the shore, too. A former record fish weighing 7lb 15oz was landed by a youngster fishing at Salcombe, Devon.

Estuaries and bays

When fishing for plaice in estuaries, the baited spoon method is the best. By slowly recovering line the bait is kept on the move, so preventing attack by the crabs which abound in this kind of area. In addition, the spoon, as it revolves, flashes and disturbs the seabed, attracting fish to the area. As well as estuaries, other likely shore-based spots are sheltered sandy bays with a fair depth of water, and rocky shores with sandy gullies. For the latter, a paternoster rig is recommended, the terrain being too rock-covered and snaggy to use a spoon.

Plaice make excellent eating. A fish of over $2\frac{1}{2}$lb can be 'quarter filleted'. To do this, cut through to the bone from head to tail along the lateral line with a sharp knife and then carefully remove the flesh from the bone by cutting outwards towards the fins. Do this on both the top and the underside, thus making four good fillets. A fish in good condition will produce half its total weight in fillets.

Above: *Playing a plaice on light tackle. It can lend a renewed sense of achievement after a day of simply stocking up for the freezer.*
Inset: *A spring balance measures an angler's personal best for the day.*

FISHING FOR PLAICE

Methods	Rod/Reel	Line	Terminal rig	Bait	Season	Habitat	Distribution
Beachcasting	2-4oz Beachcaster with fixed-spool or multiplier reel	10-15lb b.s. with shock leader	3 hook Paternoster 1-4/0 long-shank hooks. Aberdeen pattern for worm baits	Lug or ragworm, cockles, mussels, scallops, and razor-fish	Inshore-April-May Offshore-all year	Sandy, open ground. Mussel and other shell-fish beds	All around British Isles
Boatfishing	Light tackle rod (12lb Class) is ideal for inshore work. Multiplier or centrepin reel	12lb b.s.	Single or twin 1/0 long shank hook. Running or fixed ledger				

Rays

Your choice of coast may determine which species of ray you hunt down, but knowing the right sea marks, owning the right tackle and using the right bait will mark you out as a specialist

Left: *The fine mottle of a thornback ray. Gaffing—even through the relatively sturdy wing—rules out the return of the ray: it would almost certainly succumb to infection.*

Two species of ray indigenous to the waters around the British Isles play a major role in angling. The thornback is the more common, but fishing for the painted or small-eyed ray, *Raja microocellata*, is rapidly growing in popularity. In the western half of the country, more of the latter species are taken, principally after dark. Although they have distinctly different characteristics, they are often mis-identified, and on occasion are also confused with the blonde ray. This situation has led to many sea angling clubs laying down a rule that every ray being entered for award purposes has to be positively identified by a qualified member on the staff of a Marine Biological Laboratory, or similar institution.

All the species mentioned inhabit the same type of ground, and can on occasion look very alike. Similarly, all rays share the same feeding habits and therefore the techniques of fishing for thornback applies equally well to the other species mentioned, to which can be added the spotted, cuckoo, and undulate varieties. None demands specialized tackle: the rays are in the main slow moving fish, but they tend to cling tenaciously to the seabed and have to be prised up. Then in midwater they act like kites, using their wings with the current to generate power out of proportion to their size.

Wide choice of rods

Boat tackle in the 20-30lb class and shorecasters that throw 4-6oz sinkers up to 120 yards are suitable for most beach and inshore boat fishing for thornbacks. Provided it has the necesary backbone, a rod of almost any design will perform adequately. The choice of reels is also straightforward: multipliers for boat work, and either a fixed-spool or casting multiplier for fishing offshore for thornback.

One exception is when boatfishing over shallow ground at long range—a form of angling developed on the Essex coast—in which case it has been found more successful to cast the baits well uptide and perhaps 75 yards out. Short beachcasting rods are used in preference to conventional boat rods, and because of the casting involved, many anglers prefer the trouble-free fixed-spool reel. In this particular situation it is ideal, but for most boat fishing, especially over deep water, the reel is a very bad choice because it lacks sufficient winching power.

Although medium weight gear is quite sufficient for boat fishing where one is, so to speak, 'on top of the fish', it is a very different situation when shore fishing over extremely rough ground. This is particularly the case on Cornwall's rugged north coast where extremely fine thornback and small-eyed ray fishing is enjoyed by those with the will and ability to fish remote patches of sea bottom from precipitous rock ledges. This demands tough tackle: usually a 12ft beach caster,

Right: *Nick Cranfield sets the hook in a ray.*
Below: *A deep sea fishing boat sets out from Ullapool in west Scotland in conditions of dead calm, to hunt skate and ray.*

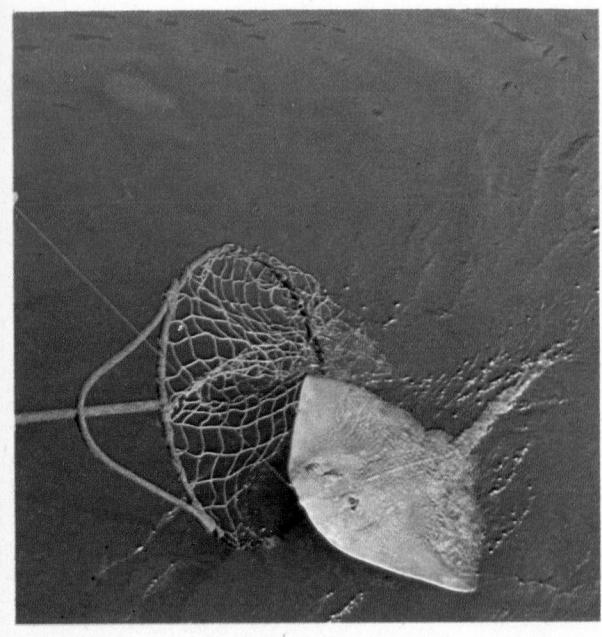

Left: *A well used, heavy duty sea net is held ready to receive a good thornback, patiently drawn close in under the rod tip. Snatching at the fish or thrusting the net at it can easily lose you the ray at this stage.*

Right: *As the skate pans through the water, spreading its wings for maximum resistance, the pull must be strong, steady and confident. A butt pad makes a long skate fight a lot more comfortable.*

Inset: *An undulate ray tagged by marine biologists who still have much research to do into the various ray species.*

matched to a good sized multiplier loaded with 30lb monofilament line and married to a 40lb shock leader. It is often impossible to reach a hooked fish and a direct lift in excess of 30ft is often needed to successfully land a quarry. The fact that the best sport is always during rough weather when incredible seas smash into the rocks naturally adds to the not inconsiderable problems.

Keep your bait near the bottom
Generally, terminal tackle arrangements must take into account the ray's feeding habits and the nature of its skin and teeth. The fish's construction implies that it is a seabed hunter, and baits, therefore, should be presented close to the bottom.

At times, some species of rays feed in midwater—I have landed them on floatfished baits when the sea was alive with sandeels and brit—but, as a rule, the tackle should be down on the sand and mud where the thornback prefers to feed.

The trace may be either a simple paternoster or a running ledger. Contrary to popular belief, a paternoster does not hold the bait up from the seabed, because water and tide pressure push the last few yards of line flat against the bottom, even if it is lowered straight down.

In slow or stillwater, the running ledger has the advantage of allowing a fish to move off with the bait

without feeling any line resistance. In fast water, there is no practical difference between the ledger and paternoster, as water pressing against the reel line will prevent the ledger from running.

Trace length is probably a more significant factor. Two or three feet between hook and sinker seems to induce more bites than does a very short link, and this is because the longer trace allows better bait movement and reduces line resistance when the ray investigates the tackle.

The trace must also be strong enough to withstand the ray's skin and teeth. Many thornbacks are lost because the line catches around the tail and is cut through by the rough skin or one of the many thorns. Strong nylon of at least 35lb b.s. between the hook and the main line acts as a buffer. Wire may be used to the same effect, but it has the disadvantage of kinking and difficult knotting if not used correctly.

The hook
The weakest link in ray tackle is the hook. This must be very strong or the ray will grind it to powder. Thick wire, stainless steel hooks of the kind considered too rank for general fishing, are ideal, as long as they are sharpened. Large hooks are seldom required because rays have relatively small jaws, and therefore swallow moderate baits more quickly than they could a bigger helping that

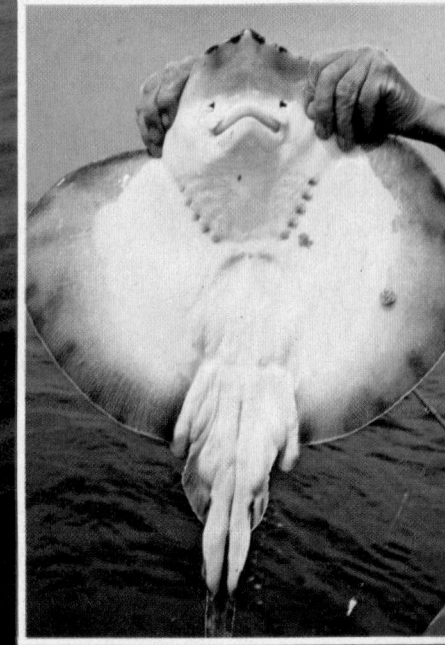

ASK THE EXPERT

Does the thornback venture far up tidal rivers?
Rays weighing upwards of 12lb—which is a good weight for the species—are commonly caught miles from the open coast. Devon's River Dart and Cornwall's River Helford are good examples: waters with soft bottoms, which is liked by the species, and usually a large population of crabs.

Are steeply-shelving beaches worthwhile places to fish for thornback?
Rays like the security of a reasonable depth of water. This sort of beach often means good catches. Outstanding beaches which spring readily to mind for ray fishing are the Chesil Bank off Dorset and Slapton in South Devon.

Does good thornback fishing from the shore depend on specific weather and tidal conditions?
Fishing just after a stiff blow can be excellent, particularly when working from a beach. A flood tide is often the best time to offer a bait.

Is it true that the thornback is being overfished?
Two decades ago the fish was extremely numerous inshore between mid-April and September, and it was possible to take a dozen good fish during the run of a tide. Due to indiscriminate inshore trawling, much of it illegal, the numbers are now just a shadow of what they were, and constantly declining. All female thornbacks should be returned to the water.

SHORE CASTING TACKLE

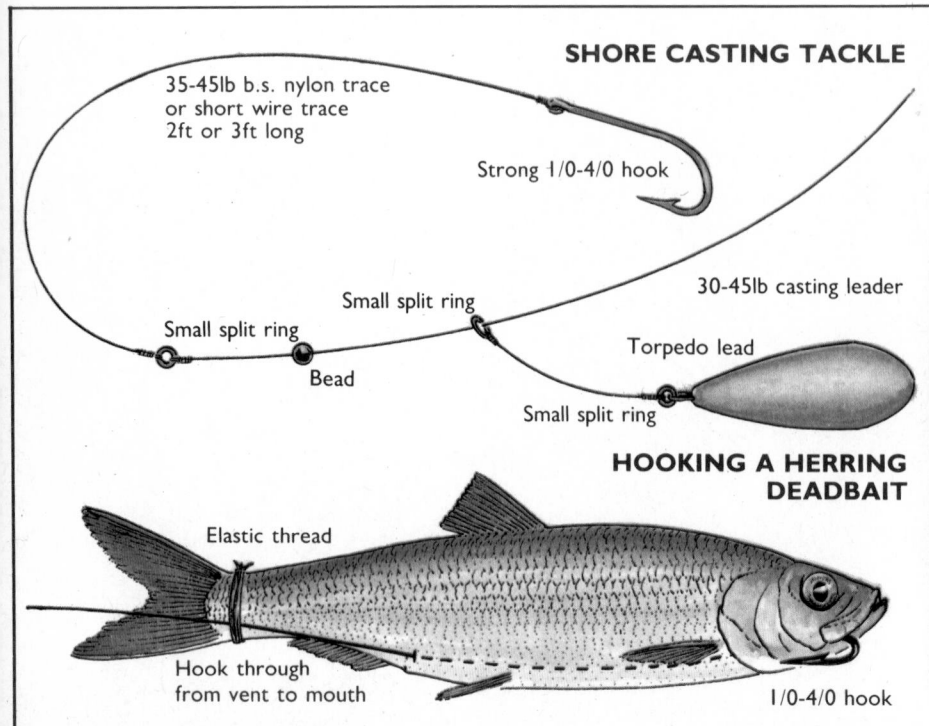

35-45lb b.s. nylon trace
or short wire trace
2ft or 3ft long

Strong 1/0-4/0 hook

30-45lb casting leader

Small split ring

Small split ring

Bead

Torpedo lead

Small split ring

HOOKING A HERRING DEADBAIT

Elastic thread

Hook through
from vent to mouth

1/0-4/0 hook

Above right: *Large thornbacks can be caught close inshore. This specimen was taken in the mouth of the Tamar river.*
Above: *A simple ledger rig for thornbacks and one way to mount a whole herring.*
Below: *Deep water ray taken within half an hour of mooring over the right mark.*

needs to be crunched down to size. The smaller the hook, the sharper it is, and the easier to drive home. Hook sizes recommended for all the British rays are 1/0-4/0.

Bait needs careful attention, for it is the key to success. Rays feed on herrings and mackerel, crabs, sandeels, worms and small fishes like blennies and tiny dabs. The common denominator is absolute freshness. It cannot be over-emphasized that the bait must be freshly killed or deep-frozen. All rays are extremely sensitive to smell and taste, and ignore any bait that is less than perfect. It pays to collect your own baits or to obtain supplies directly from commercial fishermen.

Good bait and reasonable tackle are the foundation of ray fishing, the only other practical requirement being patience, for rays feed very slowly and you must guard against striking too soon. Wait until they run off with your bait.

Unfortunately, really good bait is only half the battle. First of all you must know where to find the rays. The British coastline is tremendously long and varied, making it impossible to stereotype fishing grounds. Rays are widespread, and the thornback is likely to turn up almost anywhere. Noted thornback

marks include the Essex Blackwater, Morecambe Bay, Herne Bay and the Norfolk coast—but those are just a few examples of the vast areas where the species is hooked.

Marks for ray fishing

It is perhaps significant that many good ray marks are over rough ground with moderate depth. More than that cannot be said, because even within a general area known to hold stocks of rays, only a few shore and boat marks produce the majority of catches. The solution is to seek local advice by talking to other anglers, to read the angling press or, best of all, to go to sea with an experienced charter-boat skipper who can pinpoint the most likely spots. If there is a rule of thumb for ray location, it is to look for rough ground and, if shore fishing, for reasonably deep water close inshore.

Ray seasons are neatly summed up in the East Anglian adage which says that the thornbacks arrive when the hawthorn blossoms. Most years, the fish move in from May onwards, first being caught by the boats, then, as the inshore water warms up, by the beach angler. Sport continues until autumn, after which it dies away as the rays move out to deeper water.

Sharks

For the angler in search of big game, sharking represents the most rewarding sea fishing available in British waters. Here we describe what equipment to buy and the best tactics to use

Since sharks grow to a size much bigger than normally caught, most anglers assume that their equipment must be scaled up and that it should be heavy and strong. Consequently, many anglers buy rods and reels suited to fight and land fish many times greater than any ever caught in this country. This imbalance in tackle is further endorsed

A rod-bending experience, with Trevor Housby playing a porbeagle shark off the South West coast. **Inset:** A rare sight on the Cornish coast today, a 95lb blue shark.

by charter boat skippers who tend to provide over-heavy tackle for the angler without his own sharking equipment.

Heavy tackle is not needed

Heavy boats rods and extremely large reels loaded with 130lb b.s. line are well beyond the requirements of any of our sharks since none make the fantastic 400-to-600-yard-runs of marlins and tuna for which such equipment was developed. Only very long runs require such heavy lines: this is because the pressure of the water on the line during a long curving run (or its resistance as such

a length is being moved through the water) would break a lighter line. Since the average angler can only produce a pull of 25lb with, say, a 7A, no angler would ever need a line much heavier than 30lb b.s. Moreover, the weight in water of any of our sharks cannot break the line, for the weight of the fish in water is only a fraction of its weight in air.

Considering the fighting qualities of the various species liable to be taken, and the weight to which they go, the following types of tackle are recommended so that each would allow the fish to give the best sport: blue shark—30lb-class tackle;

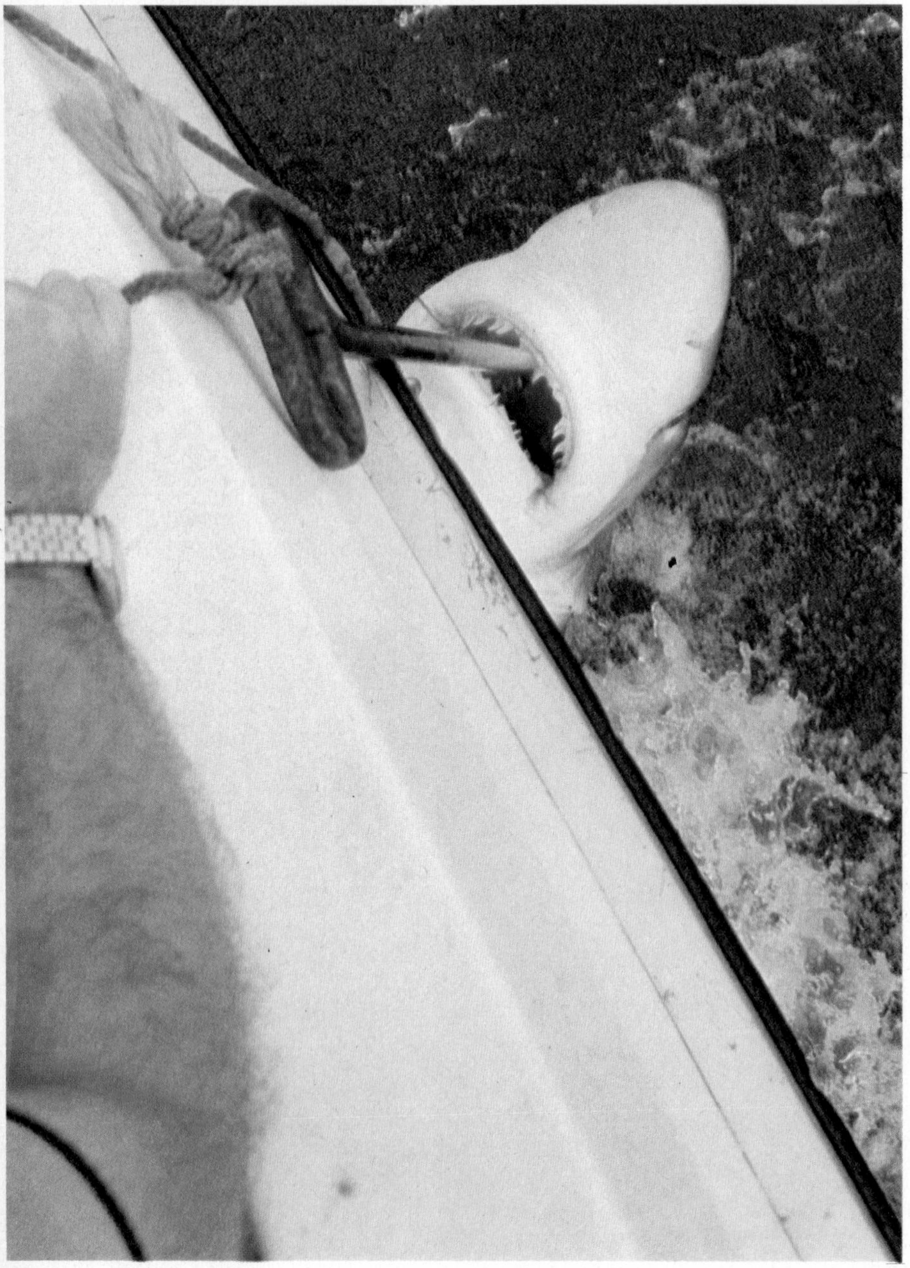

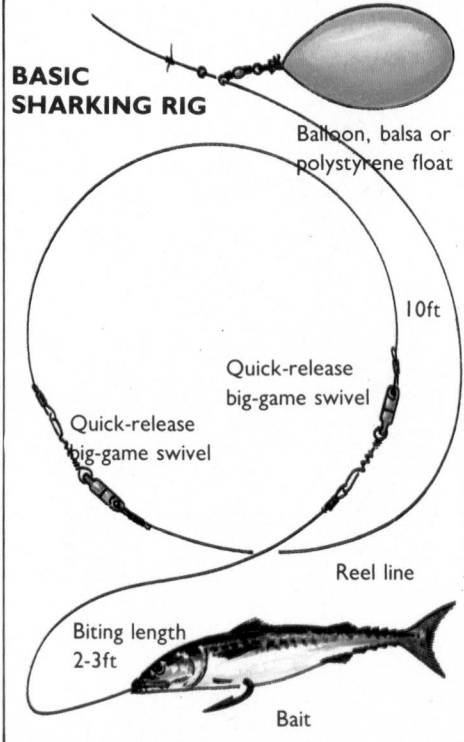

BASIC SHARKING RIG

Balloon, balsa or polystyrene float

10ft

Quick-release big-game swivel

Quick-release big-game swivel

Reel line

Biting length 2-3ft

Bait

porbeagle—50lb-class tackle; mako, thresher and large porbeagle—80lb-class rod and reel. Each one of these tackle classes can be reduced to a lower one with increasing experience in catching shark.

The terminal tackle, because of the size of baits used and the size of sharks' mouths, should consist of large 6/0 to 10/0 good-quality hooks, attached to a biting length of 2 to 2.5mm diameter braided wire, because a shark's teeth are liable to cut through anything else. The biting length, 2 to 3ft long, should be attached to a further 10ft of

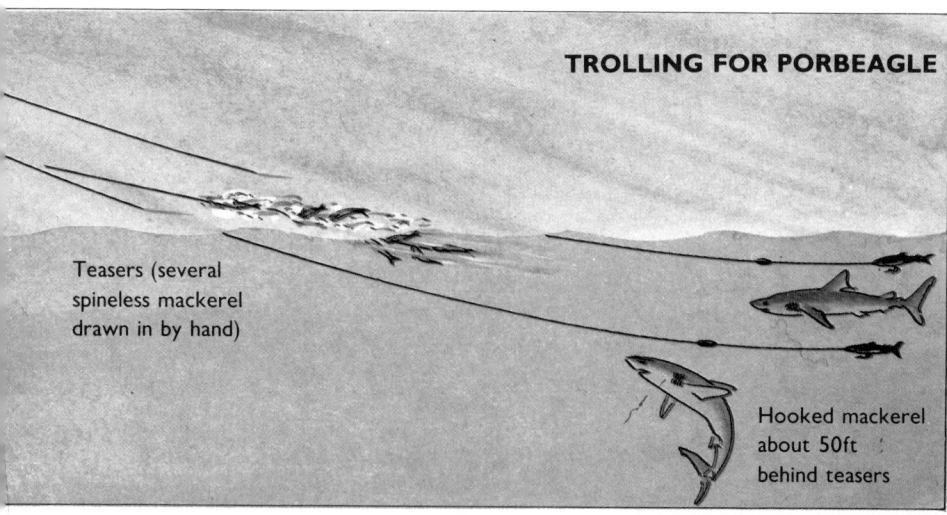

TROLLING FOR PORBEAGLE

Teasers (several spineless mackerel drawn in by hand)

Hooked mackerel about 50ft behind teasers

What are the chances of catching a porbeagle from the shore?
Excellent if you pick the right area. Jack Shine pioneered this exciting branch of sea fishing from the steep cliffs of Lahinch in Ireland. His heaviest catch was a superb 145lb porgie taken off Green Island. The coast of North Cornwall around Hartland Point and Crackington Haven, could provide similar sport.

When do blues appear in our waters?
The first fish of the season are taken in May—but 50 miles offshore. By the middle of June they are 15 miles from the coast. In hot weather, with little wind, they can be found even closer than 10 miles out by the end of July. Most begin to leave for the Atlantic deeps in October.

Where is the headquarters of the Shark Angling Club of Great Britain?
At Looe in Cornwall. Membership details can be obtained from the Secretary, Brian Tudor, The Quay, East Looe (Tel Looe 2642). The club is also a member of the International Game Fish Association.

Do mako sharks hunt close to the shore?
Like its near relative the porbeagle, this species preys within a few hundred yards of the shore, particularly where vaulting cliffs rise out of deep water. The West coast of Ireland and Cornwall's north coast are prime spots.

What is the best shark bait?
Fresh herring is probably the best bait of all. A bunch of three, hooked through the eyes, is a deadly offering.

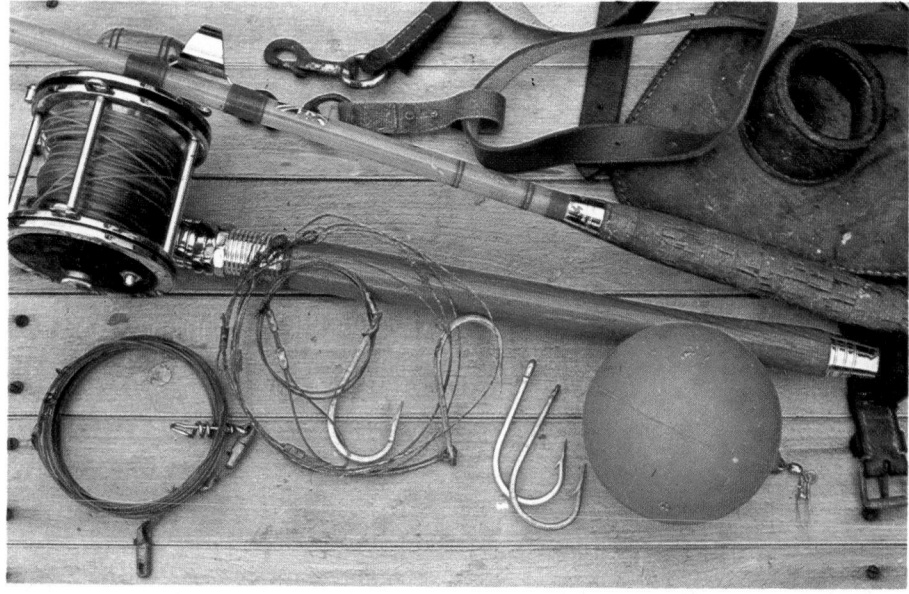

Far left: *Gaffing a blue shark. A flying gaff—in which the head is attached to a rope—is essential since most gaffed sharks thrash about wildly.* **Left:** *A standard, all-purpose shark-angling rig.*

Top: *Trolling for porbeagle using a group of teasers—usually mackerel with their backbones removed.*
Above: *Typical shark tackle—Penn 6/0 reel, wire traces, big hooks and a float.*

slightly thinner, similar wire or long-liner's monofilament nylon to withstand the abrasive action of the shark's skin.

Bait
Bait in shark fishing consists of whole fish used either singly if the fish is large, or in number if they are small. The favourite bait is mackerel which as a shoal fish probably represents the commonest natural food of sharks. However, any other species may be used and many sharks have been taken on pouting or pollack. Various methods of mounting the bait are used with the head or tail pointing up the trace. Each method should ensure that the bait does not come off when first taken, for sharks rarely swallow the bait at once. Natural presentation is not essential, for the movement of the bait should give off the erratic vibrations of an injured or sick fish.

The off-the-bottom rule
Since sharks are usually mid-water or surface fish, the bait should be fished off the bottom. This is achieved by attaching a float, either a balloon or square of polystyrene, to

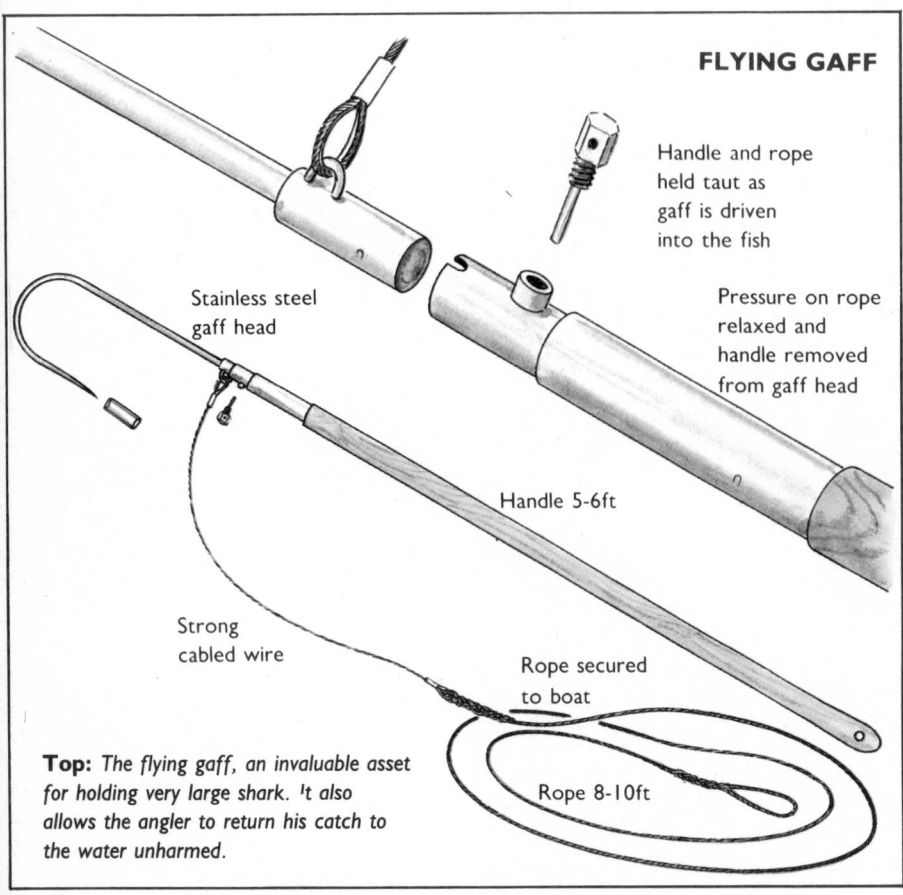

FLYING GAFF

Handle and rope held taut as gaff is driven into the fish

Pressure on rope relaxed and handle removed from gaff head

Stainless steel gaff head

Handle 5-6ft

Strong cabled wire

Rope secured to boat

Rope 8-10ft

Top: *The flying gaff, an invaluable asset for holding very large shark. It also allows the angler to return his catch to the water unharmed.*

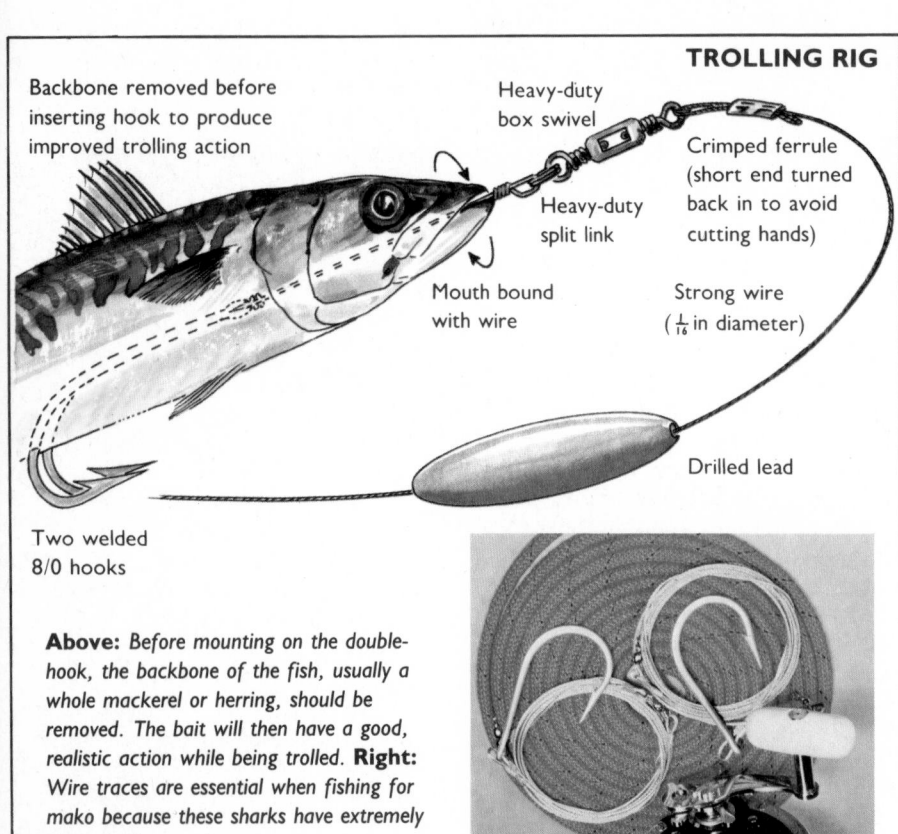

TROLLING RIG

Backbone removed before inserting hook to produce improved trolling action

Heavy-duty box swivel

Crimped ferrule (short end turned back in to avoid cutting hands)

Heavy-duty split link

Strong wire ($\frac{1}{16}$ in diameter)

Mouth bound with wire

Drilled lead

Two welded 8/0 hooks

Above: *Before mounting on the double-hook, the backbone of the fish, usually a whole mackerel or herring, should be removed. The bait will then have a good, realistic action while being trolled.* **Right:** *Wire traces are essential when fishing for mako because these sharks have extremely sharp teeth.*

the line once the depth set for the bait has been reached. The float should always be as small as possible so as not to produce resistance once the bait is taken. This off-the-bottom rule on bait presentation is not absolute, for many sharks are taken with the bait on the bottom fished as a flowing trace.

The method of fishing depends very much on the area, the wind and tides, and both drifting and fishing at anchor are successful. In each case, the use of rubby-dubby is almost essential, especially if blue shark are sought. Any shark swimming through its trail of fine particles will follow them to source and find the bait. The presence of the fine, oily particles of food prompts the shark into feeding.

have often been found to be dead. Once a fish is really tired, then, and only then, should it be brought inboard for a lively shark can do great damage to an angler or a boat. Always fight a shark in the water—not in the boat. Small sharks can easily be lifted into the boat by hand if the freeboard of the boat is not too high.

The flying gaff

The use of flying gaffs, which have detachable handles and where the head itself is attached to or carries a rope, is essential, since most gaffed shark thrash about wildly. It is easier to control them at the end of a rope and there is less chance of injury from the handle which otherwise may break or be moved around erratically by the thrashing fish. A noose passed over the tail of the fish lying at the side of the boat can also be used to tether the fish. This is probably the best method as it always allows the fish to be returned to the water uninjured—an absolute necessity if anglers are to continue to enjoy their sport.

Left: *For the shark fisherman, the mako is perhaps the most respected adversary. The current British record stands at 500lb.*
Below: *Don Melon with a specimen porbeagle.*

Trolling for porbeagle

Recently, trolling a mounted whole fish bait for porbeagle has been successfully tried off Ireland. This is a standard method for mako in many parts of the world and would probably bring good results in British waters. But its one drawback is that only some four baits can be fished by this method. Its obvious advantage is that a much greater area can be covered. Line must be paid out as soon as the bait is taken so that the fish has a chance of swallowing the bait before the hook is set. No rules can be made about striking. While some sharks will take the bait with a rush, others will play with it before taking it properly, or perhaps leave it alone. In every case, should a strike be missed it is advisable to

retrieve the bait slowly with frequent stops. This may induce the shark to have a second go, providing always that the hook is not bare.

Similarly, no rules are possible about the type of fight to be expected. In many cases it will not start until the fish has been brought to the side of the boat for the first time. After this anything may happen: long runs away and towards the boat, periods of inactivity or deep soundings. Two species, the mako and the thresher, will make long runs and will often clear the water completely in repeated, spectacular leaps. But the fish will tire slowly and come to the side of the boat. At this stage it may suddenly sound, or stop fighting altogether. On being brought to the surface such fish

Whiting

The whiting, a member of the cod family, is an extremely common fish which is of great commercial importance. It also provides good sport for the boat or shore angler

This 6lb 1oz whiting, just 11oz below the rod-caught record, was caught over the Skerries Bank off the coast of Devon.

The whiting, *Merlangius merlangus,* is probably the commonest sea fish around the British Isles, with a distribution from Iceland to the Mediterranean, and the fact that it comes into shallow water makes it a favourite with the beach angler.

The species is much smaller than its close relatives, cod, haddock, and pollack, boat-caught specimens being usually of 1-2lb, while from the beaches the average is slightly smaller. For its size, the whiting is a vicious predator. The body is slender and streamlined for speed, and the jaws are lined with needle-sharp teeth. Impaled on these, the unlucky prey stands little chance of escape.

The whiting's coloration

Coloration varies slightly, depending on environment, but generally the back is a pinkish brown and the flanks are silver, blending into a white belly. Whiting in some areas have small black dots along the back, but this is more common in smaller fish.

Like all members of the Gadidae or cod family, the whiting has three dorsal fins, but the caudal or tail fin differs in being quite square. The vent is set very far forward, and the first anal fin is very long, while the second anal fin is much smaller and set close to the tail. The lateral line curves, as in the pollack. but the whiting is easily distinguished by its slightly protruding upper jaw, the pollack having instead a protruding lower jaw.

Spawning times vary considerably with the locality, and it can take place any time from February to June. Whiting spawn in most depths, but water of 15-20 fathoms is generally preferred. A large fish will lay up to 300,000 eggs, each approximately 1.2mm in diameter. The eggs are pelagic and the newly hatched larval whiting is carried by the tides for a considerable period before it becomes demersal when it reaches inshore waters.

Henceforth, growth can be very rapid, depending on the availability of food. At one year, the fish can be 6-7in long, and by the end of the second it may have attained 12in. The growth rate tends to slow down a little in the third year, and at four years old the whiting reaches about 18in. Both sexes mature at about 9-10in, which means that a two-year-old fish is capable of reproducing.

Whiting are predominantly shoal fishes, except immediately after spawning, when they tend to hunt individually to regain their weight and strength after the rigours of reproducing. Anything in the sea that is smaller represents food, provided they can catch it, and, more to the point, swallow it. Small fish make up a major proportion of the diet, the undiscriminating fish finding small whiting very acceptable. Were it not for these strong cannibalistic instincts, shoals of mature fish would be even more abundant.

Merciless pursuit of food

Apart from smaller whiting, other diminutive fish, such as gobies, whitebait, sandeels, sprats, young herring and pouting, and baby flatfish are pursued mercilessly. Pink and brown shrimps, small crabs and all forms of marine worms are also found in their stomachs. Although mainly a bottom-feeding species, larger whiting will come very close to the surface in pursuit of sprat and herring shoals, often ending up in the drifter's nets in consequence. Whiting are found over all types of seabed, but sand, mud and gravel are usually preferred.

Undoubtedly, the best whiting fishing is during the autumn. During the summer the shoals of large fish tend to stay well offshore, but towards the end of August they start to move in to the shallow coastal waters and will travel well up into wider rivers such as the Thames and the Firth of Clyde.

Sole

Over a hundred years ago, stagecoaches rushed fish from the Kent coast to the tables of London's rich. With numbers now declining, the sole has once again become a rare delicacy

The sole, *Solea solea*, perhaps so called because of its footprint-like outline, is one of the most highly esteemed food fishes to be found in British waters. Belonging to the *Heterosomata* (flatfish) group, the sole, like most other members of the flatfish family, swims on its left side and has both its eyes on the right or upper side of its body.

Coloration
The colouring of the right side varies according to the type of seabed on which it lives. It may be almost all black or a light, sandy brown, with darker patches and speckling—although there is always a very dark

spot on the tip of the right pectoral fin. The left or underside is usually pure white. The eyes, which are smaller than in most fishes, are set very close together. The mouth is small and curves downwards, and the snout, which is also rounded, projects beyond the mouth, giving the fish a rather disgruntled expression. Except for the underside of the head, the whole body is covered with small overlapping spiny scales. This makes the fish very rough to the touch, particularly when rubbed from tail to head.

The sole is often called the 'Dover' sole, a name which stems from the time when the gentry of London

paid great prices for it. A regular and fast stagecoach service from Dover carried, among other things, locally caught fish to the capital.

Other names have also been given to the sole. Small soles, under 1ft long, are often referred to as 'tongues' as they resemble an animal's tongue. Fish of between 6oz and 8oz are called 'slips'. Try holding a live one of this size and the reason for the name quickly becomes apparent. Large specimens of over 3lb are nicknamed 'doormats'.

Distribution
Favouring warmer water, the sole is to be found throughout the English Channel, the Irish Sea, the West Coast of Ireland and the southern half of the North Sea as far north as the Firth of Forth, becoming scarce farther north. Spawning takes place in most areas from the end of March until early May. Many fish move

A close-up of the Dover sole's head showing the rounded snout, glove-puppet mouth and fringe of spiny scales covering the underside.

inshore to spawn, particularly into estuaries. A female fish of 1lb will lay over 120,000 eggs, but at least 95 per cent of these eggs are eaten by other creatures before they have had time to hatch. The eggs, which are pelagic, have a diameter of 1-1.5mm and take between six and ten days to hatch, depending on water temperature. The larvae develop into the adult fish shape at about ½in long and adopt the customary demersal life-style.

Sheltered early life

During its first summer, the sole spends its life in sheltered estuaries, often ascending major rivers, such as the Thames and Humber, for considerable distances. In fact, soles are quite commonly caught as far up the Thames as Gravesend. By October in their first year, the young fish have grown to about 2in, but their growth rate slows down during the winter. Rapid growth does not begin again until the following March, but by August the fish are over 4½in long. Male fish mature when about 8in long, on the East Coast, and 9in long on the South Coast, while females mature at 10in and 11in.

Soles live offshore in deep water during the winter, but move inshore, particularly into river estuaries, during early spring. There they inhabit sand or mud-and-sand bottoms, often in very shallow water. During daylight hours they partially bury themselves in the sand, feeding mainly at night on the many marine worms found on this type of seabed.

As summer turns to autumn, the sea temperature falls, so the sole migrates back to deeper water, some fish travelling great distances. In Ministry of Agriculture, Fisheries and Food tagging experiments in the River Blackwater in Essex, fish tagged in May were recaptured from the Dogger North ground, off Flamborough Head in Yorkshire, in the November of the same year. The following May most of the recaptured fish returned to the Blackwater, suggesting that many of the fish return to the same area year after year.

In very cold waters the fish congregate in the deepest parts of the North Sea, and it is then that com-

HOOKING A WORM

mercial trawlers make their heaviest catches. The colder the winter, the bigger the catches, for when the water temperature is very low, the sole becomes lethargic and does not bother to bury itself in the seabed. Consequently it is easy prey for the standard otter trawl. Otherwise, commercial fishermen, especially the Continentals, employ beam-type trawls that literally dig the fish out.

Accidental catches

While the sole is much sought after by commercial netsmen, very few anglers fish for it specifically. Indeed, many rod-and-line-caught specimens are taken by accident rather than design. Some anglers claim that the sole is a very difficult fish to catch on a hook, but this is a fallacy. Despite its peculiar-shaped mouth, it can take a baited hook quite readily, provided a very small hook and small bait are used.

As the sole is nocturnal, the angler should begin fishing at sunset, when the fish are just beginning to feed.

Above left: *The lemon sole,* Microstomus kitt, *is related to the halibut.*

Above: *After death, the eyed side of the Dover sole quickly turns a dark sepia.*

Left: *Small pieces of ragworm are all that's needed as a sole bait: larger pieces would be too big for the fish's relatively small mouth. A broken worm also oozes milky body fluids into the water which adds to the bait's attraction. Alternatively, you might try mussel or shrimp—both are reputed to work well.*

Below: *Sole tagged and released in the Essex Blackwater were found at Flamborough Head, Yorkshire the same year—proof of a remarkable pattern of inshore, north/south migration.*

The areas from which the shore-based angler is most likely to make good catches are shallow sandy bays (particularly near river mouths), shingle beaches which run off into sand or mud towards the low water mark, and river estuaries.

One particularly famous area is the stretch of beach between Dengemarsh and Dungeness in Kent. On beaches such as this, the most productive period is usually one hour either side of low water—when distance-casting is totally unnecessary and is, in fact, very often a disadvantage as most of the fish are lying within 30 yards of the shingle. It is only when the angler is forced back up the beach by the incoming tide that more distance should be given to the cast so that the bait reaches the sand at the base of the shingle. Similarly, when fishing river estuaries, if the edge of the main channel can be reached with, say, a 40-yard cast, it is pointless to cast farther as most of the fish will be found along the shelving bank.

Sole records

Although the rod-caught record sole was a fish of 6lb 1oz 14dr caught by J Bartram from an Alderney, Channel Isles, beach in 1984, most fish encountered when rod and line fishing

What species other than Dovers are found in British waters?
Lemon sole (or Lemon dab) is an even more highly prized relative. The Eyed sole, the Thick-back and the Solenette are also British residents.

What are the record weights for sole?
The boat record goes to a fish of 3lb 12oz 4dr caught off the Isle of Wight in 1980. The shore record is a magnificent 6lb 1oz 14dr fish taken at Alderney in the Channel Islands.

Is it possible to catch sole during daylight hours?
After a fierce storm has coloured the sea to what is termed 'thick water' conditions, catches can be made from muddy esturial beaches.

Do shellfish make good bait?
Many large sole have fallen to mussel. Hermit crabs, which you can often buy on a quayside, also make choice baits.

Do sole really spend the winter inside tidal rivers?
During a flounder-tagging programme carried out by the Marine Biological Association at the end of 1981, at least 600 sole were trawled up in the River Tamar. Strangely, very few are hooked by anglers in the same area.

What is a French sole?
The French (or Sand) sole, *Pegusa lascaris,* is at the northernmost limit of its distribution if it enters British waters at all, though it turns up in the Irish Sea now and then. It is a speckled grey—or yellow brown—with a distinctive 'rosette' nostril on its blind side. As with most things we designate 'french', the French have another name for it: in this case *Sole pole.*

are under 2½lb, with the majority between 8oz and 1¾lb, so heavy gear is completely unnecessary. As most sole fishing is done on quiet summer nights, the lightest possible beachcasters can be used with a line of under 15lb b.s. If the venue demands long casting, then the nylon-type paternoster rig should be used to achieve a good distance, but in other areas a stainless steel paternoster gives the best results. Soles, like all other members of the flatfish family, are attracted by glitter.

Hooks should be long-shanked to make unhooking easier, as the fish usually gorges the hook. The hook should be no larger than a size 6. The best bait depends on the worm commonest in the area. For instance, if there are extensive lugworm beds in or near the fishing area, lugworm is the obvious bait; if the main worm in the area is ragworm, then this should be used.

Best baits
Because of the small size of the hook, small pieces of worm should be used. Too much bait on the hook will cover the point and result in missed fish.

A medium-sized blow lugworm will bait three hooks, and a large king ragworm is sufficient for perhaps a dozen. In estuaries where maddies (small ragworm) are the favoured bait, then one, or perhaps two, fills the hook nicely; but always make sure the point is left exposed for quick penetration. The lead should be as light as possible to hold bottom, and if there is a strong cross-tide then a spiked lead should be used, preferably of the breakaway type with swivelling gripwires.

There is no need to hold the rod, as time should be allowed for the fish to gorge the bait before you strike.

The initial bite
Usually, the initial bite is quite powerful, tempting many anglers to strike immediately, but this results in many missed fish. It is much better to wait for the second bite, which is not usually so vigorous, but which is far more likely to hook the fish. As sole move around in small groups, it often happens that two are caught together, one fish feeding on the bait

358

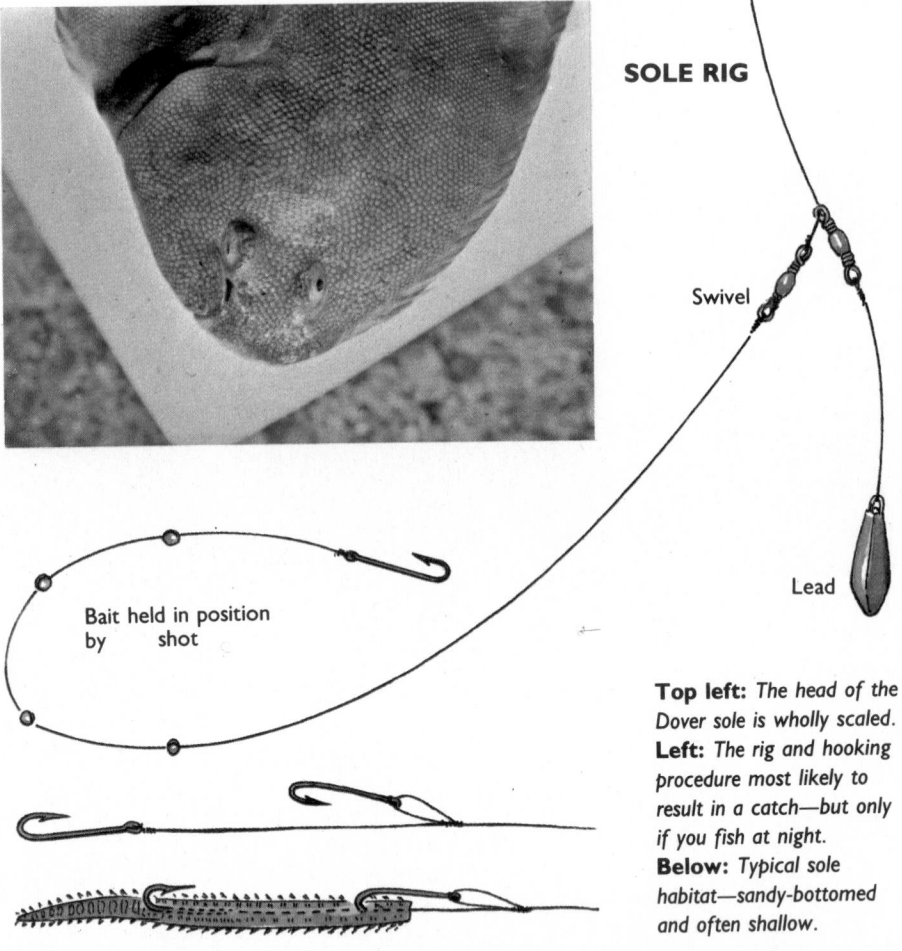

SOLE RIG

Swivel

Lead

Bait held in position by   shot

Top left: *The head of the Dover sole is wholly scaled.* **Left:** *The rig and hooking procedure most likely to result in a catch—but only if you fish at night.* **Below:** *Typical sole habitat—sandy-bottomed and often shallow.*

Worms

Sand and mud bottom

Molluscs

tending to attract a second.

Whereas some beach anglers fish specifically for soles, for some unknown reason very few boat anglers do. Even when they set out to catch one, they often make the mistake of going too far offshore. The best places to moor a boat are just below low-water mark, close to lugworm or ragworm beds. And,

again, the most productive time is from sunset to sunrise, the only exceptions being after heavy seas when the water is very muddy, or while the sole are migrating to or from the estuaries. For a few days in the spring and again in the autumn migration, the fish are just as active by day as by night and, unusually, can be fished for at all times.

Turbot

The turbot is a highly prized flatfish and, as the current rod-caught boat record was set relatively recently, it would appear that there are still plenty of big fish in the sea

Members of the Bothidae, one of the three groups of flatfishes, the turbot (*Scophthalmus maximus*), the brill (*S. rhombus*) and the megrim (*Lepidorhombus whiffiagonis*) are common round the southern coast of the British Isles. The others in this group are comparatively rare; the topknot (*Zeugopterus punctatus*). Eckström's or Bloch's topknot

Sid Jones, looking understandably pleased with this 20lb turbot. Fishing is year-round, generally at its best in the summer.

359

(*Phrynorhombus regius*), Norwegian topknot (*P. norvegicus*) and scaldfish (*Arnoglossus laterna*).

The turbot can be distinguished from the brill by its diamond-shaped body, an absence of scales, and the bony tubercles on the upper surface.

On both sides of the mouth, situated at the end of the snout, are equal bands of numerous, slender and closely set teeth lacking canines. When fully extended, the mouth is usually large—with a sizeable specimen it is possible, though not really advisable, to insert the hand.

The eyes of the turbot are on the left side. A dorsal fin extends to the head, ending in front of the eyes, while the anal fin, although reaching almost around the body, is somewhat shorter, having about 47 rays as opposed to the brill's 60-odd. In both, the lateral line curves strongly over the pectoral fin.

The colouring of the turbot depends to an extent on its environment and the depth of water, being from mid-brown to a light sand. Many specimens are variegated and speckled with light and dark marbling, very often with greys also present. The blind side of the turbot is an opaque white.

Spawning takes place in offshore waters from April to July, or later, a female turbot of, say, 23lb, shedding an estimated 14 million-plus eggs. The young turbot has a long pelagic life, drifting gradually into shallower waters and developing a swimbladder. At 2in it has lost the swimbladder and become entirely demersal. Small turbot, at this stage, are often caught in the shrimper's push-net in less than 2ft of water, but they gradually move into deeper water.

The turbot is a shallow-water fish, rarely taken in depths of over 40 fathoms. My own records, compiled over the last 20 years, show that all catches were made on or close to sandbanks, in water of between 4 and 12 fathoms. The favourite environment of the turbot is around sandbanks situated in deep water, where sandeels, sprats and other immature fish abound.

Muddy or gravelly bottoms in the estuaries of large rivers, where young fish are usually present, also hold an attraction for these large flatfish. Big specimens are taken off the many wrecks off Devon and Cornwall and littering the sandy bays around the south west and west coasts of Ireland. Many small turbot up to 4lb are taken by the surf caster baiting with mackerel strips.

The species is almost entirely fish-

ouring of the two species is similar, the brill often has a greenish tone with shades of brown.

This species is almost exclusively fish-eating, exhibiting a preference for sandeels and sprats. It attains less than half the weight of the turbot, and while the boat record is a 16lb fish from the waters off the Isle of Man in 1950, a fish of 10lb is considered well above average. The spawning period is similar to that of the turbot, although it starts a little earlier, in March, and continues until late July.

The return of the turbot and brill from deep water to the sandbanks in earlier spring excites the imagination, for of all the species none requires greater understanding if the angler is to be successful. The author's findings on the subject are based on his personal experiences over a number of years and embrace a study of the turbot's habits and an analysis of recorded catches.

Both turbot and brill are limited in distribution and are not scattered haphazardly over the seabed. On occasions they can be taken on the most unlikely fishing grounds. However, to be certain of locating these fish in quantity, the angler is advised to study the Admiralty charts of deep-water sandbanks, for here is where they feed on sandeels.

Among the better-known banks are the Varne out from Folkestone harbour, and the Colbert Ridge close by, the Shambles bank close to Portland Bill, the famous Skerries bank at Dartmouth, and the sandbanks extending from Start Point to Salcombe in Devon. They are headlands interrupting a natural tidal flow. The composition of banks can vary considerably—the Varne Ridge, for example, consists entirely of hard, clean sand, while the Shambles is of sand, shingle and broken shell, the latter coming from the vast shell beds beyond the bank itself. Although most sandbanks remain constant, contours are continually changing as heavy seas and fast tides rip gullies out and build up ridges.

Above: *The 32lb 3oz former record turbot hooked by Derrick Dyer, and a 31lb 4oz fish taken a while before by Ben Taylor from a mark 21 miles SE of Plymouth.*
Far left: *A net's far better than the gaff, which can cause severe damage.*
Left: *Turbot fishing on the Skerries Bank.*

eating, obvious from its large mouth and sharp teeth. Considering its bulk, the turbot is a surprisingly strong and rapid swimmer. Sandeels and sprats are the chief food, and in addition small flatfish, whiting and pouting—in fact, any small fry—are readily taken. The author has never found worms or crustaceans in the stomach contents.

The record turbot (boat) is 33lb 12oz, taken in Lannacombe Bay, near Salcombe in South Devon, by Roger Simcox in 1980. The current shore fishing record is a magnificent fish of 28lb 8oz, caught by JD Dorling at Dunwich Beach, Suffolk.

Characteristics of the brill
The brill lacks the angular diamond form of the turbot, being more oval in shape. There are no tubercles on the uppermost side, but cycloid scales are present on both. The brill, with the same geographical range as the turbot, and frequently found at a similar depth, is invariably caught on the same ground. While the col-

Feeding
The feeding habitats of turbot and brill are distinctive, for they do not

361

feed at regular intervals, but according to the state of the tide. During slack water they become listless, lying partly submerged on the seabed, blending with the sand, shingle and shells of the sandbank.

Turbot are stimulated into activity at both the ebb and the flow of the tide. Lying in ambush, they rise suddenly from the seabed to pick off small fish being taken along in the strong tidal flow. They are not affected by sudden bait movements, although this is natural enough when one considers their need to chase small, active food fish. This knowledge is a great help to the angler, for if he misses contact with his first strike, and returns his bait to the bottom, the turbot will come back again until it is either captured or has taken the bait off the hook.

Leads

Some anglers consider slack neap tides more profitable than the stronger springs, but so far as turbot and brill are concerned, the author does not agree. When bait and lead are bouncing on the seabed directly under the boat, the fish are at rest, but when the tide strengthens and the bait streams away, they become active.

There are anglers who maintain that during strong tides it becomes difficult to hold bottom, regardless of the weight of lead used. This could well be true in deep waters, where the water pressure on the total surface area of line is responsible. On sandbanks, however, where the depth is often between four and ten fathoms, water pressure is much less. Here, it is rarely necessary to exceed 14oz of lead, even during the spring tides, and if tides are especially strong, wire lines are recommended, needing very little lead.

Baits for turbot

Bait is important. Without doubt, sandeels are the favourite diet of the turbot and brill. These species are not alone in their weakness for sandeels, for mackerel also chase them until whole areas of the sea boil in the efforts of the prey to escape. To represent the sandeel, filleted flanks from a freshly caught mackerel make excellent turbot and

brill baits. Strips an inch wide are cut the full length and the hook turned twice through one end only, so that the free section moves realistically in the tide.

If neither mackerel nor sandeel is available, small, immature fish of most species can be used successfully. I often bait with small whiting or pouting, and using a fine baiting needle to mount one on the hook, I lash the tail along the nylon snood with cotton elastic. The hook must be located in the mouth of the bait, for turbot, and most other fish, will avoid the sharp spines of the dorsal fin by swallowing the bait head first.

The behaviour of the hooked turbot should be discussed before the tackle is described. In slack water it can dive repeatedly, but it would be wrong to praise the turbot's fighting qualities. Yet many are caught in strong tides, and these fish should not be regarded lightly. They are wily enough not to expend their strength unnecessarily in violent movement, but use their extensive

body area in concert with the tide to impose a great deal of pressure on both angler and tackle. In this way, the weight of a turbot is magnified several times, so that the strength of tackle must be chosen accordingly.

A rod in the 30lb-class is suitable. The reel, preferably a multiplier, should have handles that disengage when line is conceded, otherwise the angler can have his knuckles badly

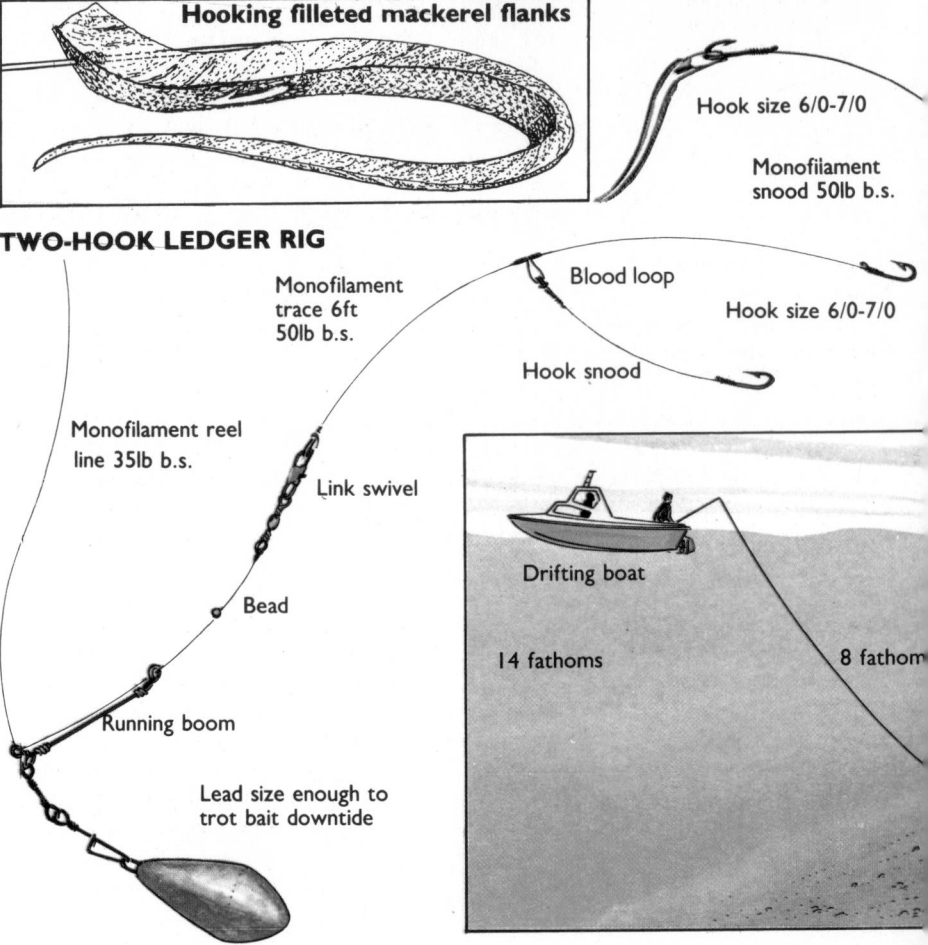

Hooking filleted mackerel flanks

Hook size 6/0-7/0

Monofilament snood 50lb b.s.

TWO-HOOK LEDGER RIG

Monofilament trace 6ft 50lb b.s.

Blood loop

Hook size 6/0-7/0

Hook snood

Monofilament reel line 35lb b.s.

Link swivel

Bead

Drifting boat

Running boom

14 fathoms

8 fathoms

Lead size enough to trot bait downtide

rapped. Avoid plastic or metal fabricated spools as these can burst or distort under extreme loads, especially if loaded with monofilament, the elasticity of which creates high pressure on the spool's flanges. One-piece machined spools are designed to overcome this problem, and are available in sizes small enough.

A main line of 35lb b.s. is advised,

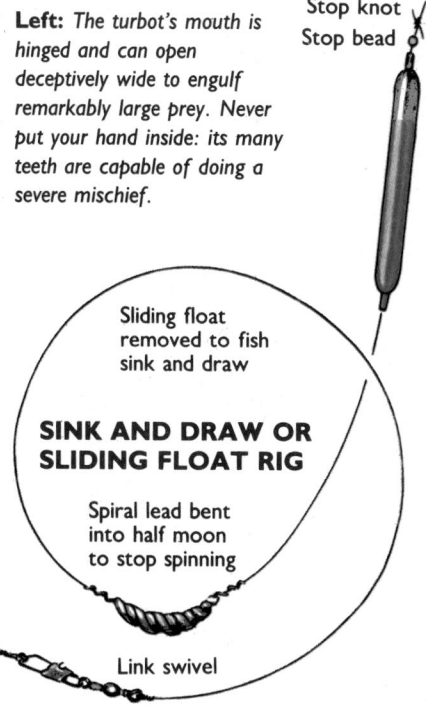

Left: *The turbot's mouth is hinged and can open deceptively wide to engulf remarkably large prey. Never put your hand inside: its many teeth are capable of doing a severe mischief.*

Sliding float removed to fish sink and draw

SINK AND DRAW OR SLIDING FLOAT RIG

Spiral lead bent into half moon to stop spinning

Link swivel

Stop knot
Stop bead

Far left: *Cut thinly enough, a lask of mackerel resembles the sandeel which is a staple part of the turbot's diet. It is 'animated' by being fished sink-and-draw on the sliding float rig illustrated above.*

while traces and hook snood should be 50lb b.s., for turbot laying back against the tide can quickly bite through lighter line with their sharp teeth. Braided lines with less stretch can be used, for bites are more pronounced and the hook can be set in a positive manner. But I prefer monofilament, because its elasticity, plus the cushioning effect of a flexing rod tip, imposes far less strain on the hook when playing a fish. The turbot's mouth is large, so there is no point in using small hooks, and 6/0 or 7/0 are the most useful. Three distinct types of terminal tackle are recommended, all based on the conviction that turbot and brill respond to a moving bait.

The first is a two-hook, long flowing trace, the main line passing through a running boom with lead attached. The fish can pick up and swim away with the bait without feeling the resistance of the weight. The trace, roughly 6ft long, can be clipped to a link swivel which has been attached to the end of the main line. If the fish is deeply hooked the trace can be removed and replaced by another without loss of fishing time. Weights should be as light as possible, depending on tide strength, to allow the bait to be trotted down-tide, so that fish are not disturbed by seeing the boat's hull.

In strong tide I often use the sink-and-draw technique, substituting a single hook mounted to a 6ft nylon snood, again attached to the main line by a link swivel. The weight can be either of the spiral or barrel type and should be attached to the main

VARNE BANK

Backwave shows edge of bank

Tide

Anchored boat

Bait flowing out in tide just above the sandbank

3 fathoms

Bait moving with boat down the sandbank

Left: *The Varne Bank, eight miles out of Folkestone, Kent. It is discernible by the water surging over its shallowest parts in smooth, fast-moving glides. Leslie Moncrieff's two recommended methods are illustrated: the boat either drags the bait off the summit to the lower, brill/turbot territory or anchors and lets baits stream on to the bank's steep-to sides. Only drifting allows the whole bank to be worked, but it does involve frequent repositioning of the boat.*

line above the link. This tackle is very useful with the lead bent into a half-moon shape to prevent spinning, for by lifting and lowering the rod tip, the bait can be kept moving.

If the tide is very light, and to get the bait covering as great an area as possible, I sometimes use the same rig, but attach a float above the lead, controlling it by a stop. This method allows the bait to drag along the seabed, tempting the turbot to bite. Remember that a moving bait is natural to turbot and brill; they expect prey to move off quickly.

Many turbot hooked in a strong tide will adopt the same attitude as the skate, curling up against the flow. With fish of 18lb or over, it is sometimes difficult to break this hold, and line simply cannot be recovered. When this happens, let out a short amount of line. This controlled release frequently disturbs the turbot's posture and if line is recovered immediately the fish will not be able to regain its hold.

If the turbot surfaces well down-tide of the boat's stern, the person netting the fish may attempt to han-

FISHING FOR TURBOT

Methods	Rod	Reel	Reel Line	Terminal tackle	Hooks	Leads/ weights	Bait	Groundbait/ attractor	Season	Habitat	Distribution
Boat Bottom fishing. Ledger (sand, shale) drift or anchored up. Ledger with wire trace (wrecks) from anchored boat	Hollow glass 20-30 6½-7½ft	4/0 or 6/0 multiplier	25-30 mono 30-50 mono	Trace 15ft long to end hook and another on a short snood placed 3ft up the trace. A small barrel lead can be positioned 4ft from hook to keep the baits down as it passes over the sandbanks	4/0, 5/0, 6/0	Barrel lead 8-12oz on reel line stopped off with bead. Alternatively a circular grip tied to a swivel with nylon	Sandeel strip, live sandeel, mackerel or squid strip 8" long 2" wide tapering to point	A bag of fish offal can be tied to another rope a few feet from the hook anchored up fishing only	From April on sandy ground. Fishing slows from October. All year on wrecks	Sandbanks in fairly deep water —Skerries, Varne, etc. Large specimens bury in the sand close to wrecks. All Britain's record breakers for last 10 years have come from wreck marks off Devon coast	English Channel, North coast (Atlantic) of Cornwall
Also caught from the shore in a few places, short trace to 2/0 hook ledger		Small to medium multiplier									

Above left: *John Selmes with a 21lb turbot caught off Brighton.*
Above: *A gaff can tear out of the wing of a flatfish, so the wound must be to the head.*

dle the angler's line. This must be avoided, for the natural stretching of the line, coupled with the cushioning effect of a flexing rod tip, minimizes hook strain. The angler should move towards the bows and bring the fish near enough to be netted by the skipper at the stern.

Gaff these fish in the open mouth, or just below the head. To safeguard the flesh from blood contamination, make an incision about 3in long in the top, close to its tail, and allow the blood to drain away.

The turbot angler must master the art of fishing sandbanks. This includes an understanding of tackle and methods, and a knowledge of the turbot's moves.

The Varne

The Varne is a typical sandbank. Lying eight miles out from Folkestone, in 14 fathoms, the steep-sided bank is roughly seven miles long and a

few hundred yards wide. In parts the top is less than four fathoms under the surface—and in low-water spring tides one can often see the bait lying on the hard, clean sand below. The bottleneck here, between the French and English coastlines, creates extremely fast currents. Although the length of the bank runs roughly in the direction of the flow, the tide is bent as it meets the bank, sweeping diagonally across. On meeting the obstruction of the bank, the deep, fast water is compressed and deflected upwards. As it races across the top of the bank its speed is greatly increased, smoothing the surface of the water and causing giant eddies and swirling currents to form. Then it meets the deeper waters on the farther side, and the sudden check creates a back wave clearly outlining the bank's contours.

This is where the angler must position his boat, presenting the baits so they lie halfway down the slope in about eight fathoms of water, the area found to be most productive. Turbot and brill lie in ambush for

sandeels below the edge of the bank.

When first fishing the Varne, I concentrated on the shallow waters on the top. Here I took plenty of plaice, dabs, whiting, dogfish and cod, but only the occasional turbot or brill. Then I noticed that French longliners always set their hooks along the down-tide edge during slack water, waiting for several hours until the baits were swept down the incline towards the waiting fish. When the lines were recovered, I was surprised at the quantity of turbot and brill that were taken aboard.

Bait presentation

From these observations I started to fish the downtide side of the bank and had immediate success. As the tide changes from ebb to flood, one must move to the opposite edge. Due to water disturbance, the edge of the bank can be easily located during strong tides, but this effect is not so apparent during weaker tides. Here it is essential to use an echosounder to find the correct position.

Two methods can be employed to present the baits at the correct position on the sloping bank. The boat should be anchored on the top of the bank and the cable then played out, allowing the boat to drift back until the bait is positioned correctly.

The second method, and perhaps the more effective, is to fish on the drift. It does mean, however, that the boat must be repositioned every few minutes, otherwise the baits will reach deeper water away from the fish. Drifting ensures that the whole length of the bank can be covered.

On the Varne, my best catches have been from October until Christmas; on the Shambles, April, May and June fish well, and reports of plaice and turbot from the Skerries bank appear throughout spring, summer and autumn.

Last, a serious note of warning. Fishing sandbanks should only be attempted from a sound boat in settled conditions. In troubled weather, with wind against a strong tide, shallow waters, obstructed in their movement, toss in fury. If experienced boatmen consider weather conditions are wrong, take their advice seriously. In doubtful weather, leave judgments to the experienced.

Off-shore fishing

Fishing off-shore will add a new dimension to your sport, and the range of tackle and techniques that you will need is quite different to that used for freshwater fishing in rivers or lakes

The off-shore fishing grounds round the British Isles have something for everyone. There are large skate, halibut, shark and conger, as well as cod, tope, ling, and a wide variety of lesser fish, all of which provide good sport on rod and line.

The secret of off-shore fishing is to know and understand the various species and their favourite habitats. For example, it will be a waste of time fishing over rocky pinnacles for tope. This small shark lives mainly by hunting flatfish and pouting, and usually confines its activities to flat, sandy or shingly ground. But pinnacle rocks are a good place to bottom-fish for conger, ling and cod. In mid-water around the pinnacles you will find the free-swimming fish such as pollack and coalfish.

Vital decision

Deciding where fish should be found is vital. Like people, fish will be found where the most food is available. Around wrecks or weed-covered reefs, for example, there will be a thriving population of small fish, crabs, prawns and immature lobsters. These creatures form the food of bigger fish, such as cod, ling, conger and pollack.

All fish have good times and lean times. During the summer, shoals of mackerel and sand-eels provide a superabundance of food for larger species, and during the winter months, along the south and east coasts, huge shoals of sprat and immature herring drift inshore followed by packs of hungry cod, pollack and spurdog. This is good for the fish, but at times they can become so glutted that they ignore the bait.

Seasons for sea fish

Anglers find that fish come and go through the seasons. In West Country and Scottish waters, huge influxes of coalfish and cod appear to mix with the ever-present pollack and ling. This leads to bumper catches. On the South and East Coasts, fish stocks have declined and anglers now rely on migratory species such as bream to provide good fishing. Off the Sussex coast, it is the April influx of good-sized black bream that everyone looks forward to, while a little later in the year, and farther along, off Hampshire and the Isle of Wight, anglers can find bass and tope, and perhaps even heavy-weight cod during the winter. The same pattern applies right around the country with various species predominating according to latitude.

As basic equipment, the off-shore angler will need a 6ft boat-rod. Longer rods are used, but as the hook is dropped straight down over the side and there is virtually no casting to be done, length is not necessary to provide leverage for distance casting. Most boat anglers use the very effective multiplier reel which has a fast rate of line retrieve (useful when winding in from deep water), good braking and a ratchet which enables the angler to prop his rod securely and adjust the brake to a correct tension so that a bite will be registered by the 'clack' of the ratchet. For off-shore fishing, line breaking strain (b.s.) should be about 30lb, although a stronger line should

Boating a 35lb tope in Cardigan Bay, off Aberystwyth — the finest tope ground in the whole of Europe.

ASK THE EXPERT

In a boat that's not fitted with an echo sounder, is fishing a matter of luck?
You may go out with a skipper who can place you over a known wreck, reef or area of pinnacles. But over an uncertain bottom, there are 'surface indications' which can help even the inexperienced. Even at 15-20 fathoms, rocks on the seabed create a surface disturbance: moor uptide of the swirl. Gulls following a shoal of mackerel for the pickings move with the current, whereas stationary bass lurking behind a sandbank attract hovering gulls.

What boat gear is essential to offshore fishing?
A good compass is vital: take a fix on a promontory or prominent building ashore as soon as you settle to fish — in case visibility suddenly worsens. Don't skimp on anchor rope or you may be dragged out to a depth where you can't hit bottom. In a small boat, ensure that your outboard motor is well maintained and secured with a safety line. Carry a baler and, lastly, flares for use in an emergency.

In fairly shallow water, is it worth trolling from a moving boat?
Wherever sandeel, sprat and mackerel are about, there's a good excuse to troll an artificial rubber eel or limber up a dead one, mount a squid, try a dead herring or a metal lure. Bright, flashing lures, are best for shallow mackerel, pollack and bass fishing. Trolls for reef bass run 100 yards behind the boat from long rods in special mountings. The springy rod and forward movement of the boat really sink the hook on a take.
Don't ever try to steer and fish at the same time in a motor-driven boat.

be used if you are fishing specifically for conger. In shallow water, when fishing for flatties, or out deeper for black bream, a lighter line will be adequate, but the 30lb b.s. line will stand a great deal of punishment if a sizeable conger is hooked.

Terminal tackle
One of the most effective terminal tackles is the running ledger, with the sliding boom holding a lead of sufficient weight to hold the bottom. This will depend on the strength of the tide. Leads come in all the standard shapes — grip, torpedo, and bomb — and all do their job well when used at the right time and place. The running-ledger rig with boom, swivels, a two yard leader and end hook, will work well on practically all types of seabed, except rocks. Here, some form of paternoster is necessary. With this rig, the angler will feel the weight hit bottom but know his hooks are placed above this. If care is taken to keep the sensitivity to a fine degree, with the lead just in touch with the bottom, the hooks will not snag.

Tackling-up is the first job, while the boat is heading out to the mark.

First make sure that any items of gear not needed immediately — extra clothing in case of a squall, spare rods, food and drink — are all stowed away in the cabin, or somewhere out of sight. When fish are coming aboard there must be no unwanted gear to get in the way, especially if a conger is thrashing about in the boat.

Boat owners do not look kindly on anglers using seatboards or the gunnel for cutting up bait strips from mackerel or squid. Always use a baitboard and a sharp knife.

Mackerel taken on feathers specifically for baits should be left in a bucket of seawater or in a keepnet over the side in order to be kept fresh. This lively fish is by far the best bait for almost every type of sea fishing, and in the spring and summer a bout of feathering as soon as the boat is at anchor is advised. Sometimes a boat can halt on the way out and be allowed to drift over a likely area for as long as it takes to get sufficient mackerel for the day's fishing. But don't assume that mackerel will

OFF-SHORE FISHING METHODS

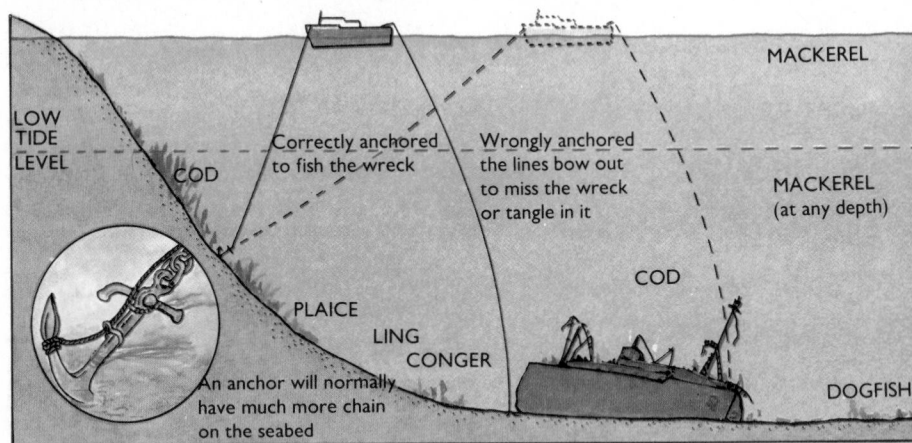

LEDGERED BAIT

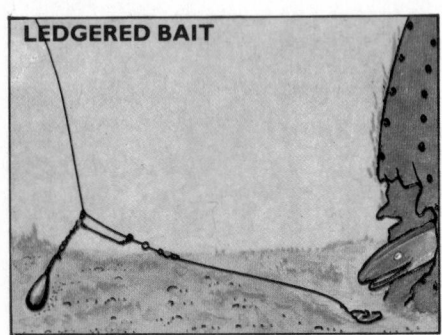

The ledgered bait (above) will sit close enough to lure fish from a wreck. The pirk (below) is a lure that works well drifting over rocky pinnacles.

PIRK

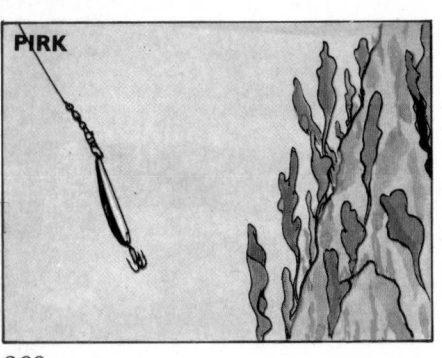

PATERNOSTER RIG

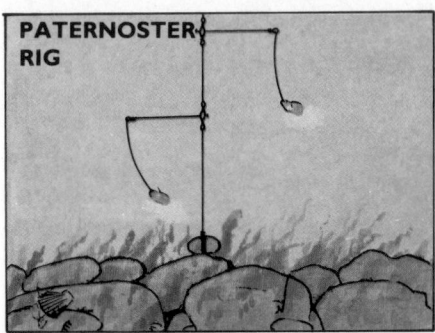

When fishing over a rocky sea-bed a paternoster rig (above) will avoid snagging the bottom. Over sandbanks (below) use a Wessex ledger.

WESSEX LEDGER

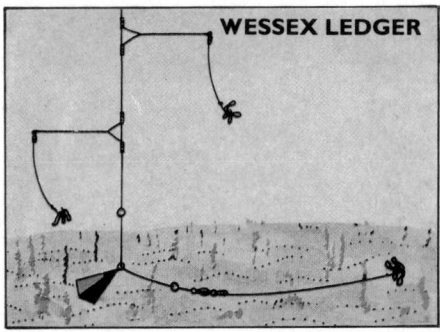

always be around. A standby bait
— herring, squid, lugworm or ragworm — should be acquired before
setting out. Most sea angling centres
have tackle shops nearby which open
early all through the week so that
anglers can buy frozen baits and odd
items of tackle.

Wait before dropping down
When the boat anchors, wait until the
craft is steady before dropping down
the lines. It may take a few minutes
for the boat to sit right in the tide.

Sometimes a small sail may have to
be hoisted to hold the craft steady in
the tide if the wind is coming from the
side. The stern corners are the ideal
places from which to fish. From these
places the lead can be of just enough
weight to get the bait down, and then
allowed to work out with the tide, but
always being kept in contact with the
seabed. The anglers behind them
must have heavier weights to avoid
tangling. The successful off-shore
angler will adjust his tackle so that he
is in constant touch with the bottom.

He will not allow his lead to bounce
up and down in the sand or mud
because this will set up vibrations
and echoes in the water that may well
keep fish away. The ideal method is to
be able to 'feel' the seabed all the
time, and be able to differentiate
between the small tugs and pulls of
the tide and anchor rope, and similar
sensations from fish.

Don't snatch!
Different species of fish have different 'bites'. But as with other forms
of fishing, it is not necessarily the
biggest fish which give the strongest
bites. Some large cod will give tentative pulls at first, but this fish has a
very large mouth, so a hurried snatch
by the angler may well pull the bait
out of its mouth. Wait. Let the take
develop, and strike when the cod has
taken the bait, turned, and is swimming away. The hook will then be set
properly and the fish can be played to
the boat.

Before setting out, whether in your
own boat or not, be sure to have
enough food and drink for the trip, a
thick pullover and some weather-
proof clothing. The day may be fine
and the forecast good, but things can
change in the long periods that sea
anglers stay out — especially if the
day's fishing is good.

Remember not to anchor in a busy
sea lane; watch for the onset of a sea-
mist; keep an eye on the sky. Squalls
can blow up in minutes and the time
taken to up-anchor may be just
enough for real trouble to develop as
the wind rises and turns a calm sea
into a heaving and dangerous place
for a small boat.

Seaway Code
Once you have fallen to the lure of sea
fishing you may want to own a boat.
But the sea does not allow many
mistakes and before setting out in a
boat of your own be careful to make
sure you have a lifejacket. The
Seaway Code is a useful little booklet
giving helpful advice on safety for sea
anglers, and can be obtained free
from the Department of Trade, Room
505, Gaywood House, Great Peter
Street, London SW1P 3LW.

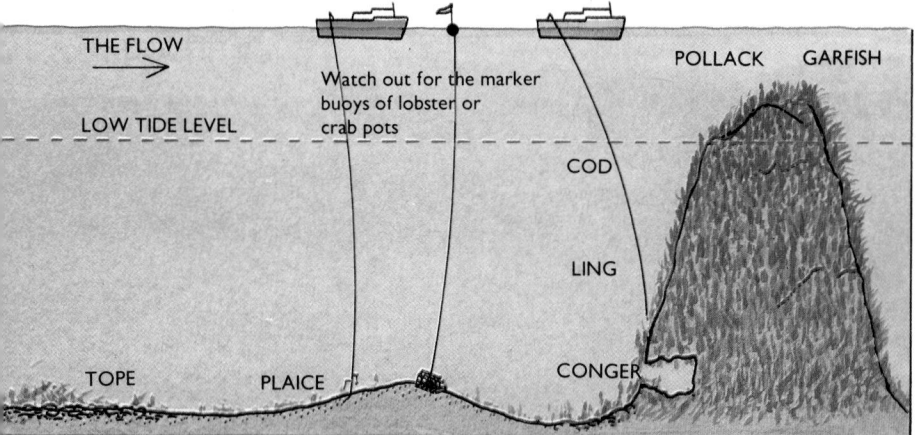

*Many fine pollack like this can be caught in the
waters off the rocky Cornish coast.*

Wreck fishing

To sea fishermen, a wreck represents a guarantee of large numbers of big fish every time baits are lowered in among the tangle of metal, drifts of sand, and jungle of weed

Wreck fishing is the most spectacular branch of sea fishing and it provides anglers with the opportunity to consistently catch specimen fish. Reasonable catches are occasionally made from wrecks lying close to shore, but their accessibility can lead to over-fishing and the numbers of fish living in them is drastically reduced. The best action is now found on sunken hulks lying more than 30 miles out, a distance which can only be reached in good weather conditions by skippers operating large, fully equipped, licensed charter-boats.

Some wrecks lying within ten miles of the shore are pin-pointed by using shore markers, but this is a chancy business. One skipper who made a success of this type of operation was Colin 'Fishy' Williams of Mevagissey, the 'man with the magic eyes', who had the incredible ability to take shore marks and anchor right over hulks when the land was nothing but a mere haze.

The alternative is an electronic Decca Navigator, which receives a continuous stream of signals from shore stations. These are displayed as numbers on green, red and purple dials, which give an accurate cross-bearing of the boat's position in relation to 'lanes' on a special Decca chart listing hundreds of wrecks plotted by hydrographic surveys. Each hulk has a set of coordinates and when these are known it is possible to position the boat right over it.

Secret wreck marks

All charter skippers keep a record of the numbers and jealously guard them. Every year new wrecks are discovered by accident and as each is likely to be sheltering hundreds of fish, it is understandable that skippers prefer to keep such information to themselves. Some skippers go to great lengths to preserve the secrets of such a mark, only visiting the place when no other vessel is in sight. They then keep a vigilant look-out during the time the boat is anchored over it, and should another charter boat be spotted they leave the area quickly.

Finding the wreck is one thing, anchoring accurately is something else. Many West Country skippers

Below: *These six ling—all weighing over 30lb—were landed during the course of a single tide.*

have brought this to a fine science and before letting the anchor go are able to take into account direction of tide, wind strength, and how the hulk is lying on the bottom.

Sometimes the anchor is dropped 600 yards uptide of the mark but, by the time the warp has taken up, the craft is close enough for baits to drop right back into the wreck where the fish are likely to congregate.

Dominant wreck species

While many different species are found on wrecks, the sport is dominated by conger, ling, pollack, coalfish and bream, all of which fall into three distinct categories. Conger and ling are taken on heavy-duty tackle and big baits ledgered on the bottom. The pollack and coalfish fall to medium-weight gear, artificial and natural baits, between the wreckage and the surface, although the bottom 10 fathoms is usually the productive zone. Black and red bream are caught by using more sensitive tackle on baits dropped right into the wreckage.

The techniques for catching each group will be discussed in turn.

Conger and ling reach enormous weights and over the past ten years records have gradually crept upwards. The record conger is now a giant 109lb 6oz, to the credit of Bristol angler Robin Potter, who was fishing 22 miles south of Plymouth. Britain's biggest rod-caught ling fell to Ian Duncan of Scotland fishing 3 miles off Stonehaven on 16 May 1982 and weighed 57lb 8oz. Very stout angling tackle must be used to deal with such fish successfully. The right combination for this heavyweight section of wrecking is a 50lb-test rod with a 6/0 multiplier and monofilament line. Braided lines are unsuitable for deep-water fishing as their drag demands the use of heavy leads.

There are many good British-made hollow glass rods available, but when it comes to reels only the American Penn Senator and British Tatler models stand up well to the terrific punishment that wrecking imposes on fishing tackle.

Terminal tackle for these rough and tough fish is a ledger rig of good quality wire 12 to 18in long, ending

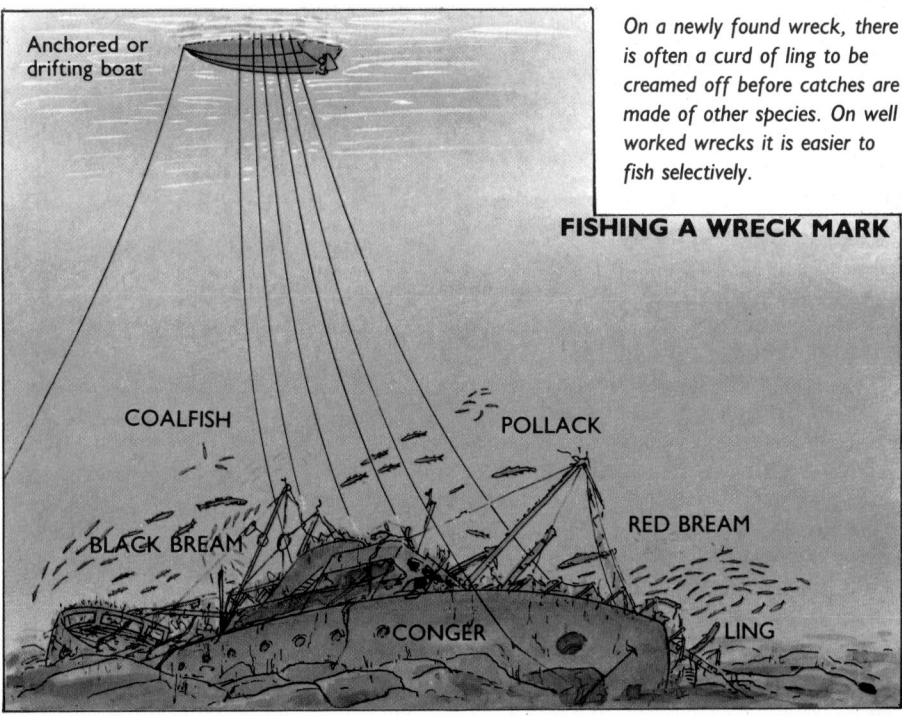

On a newly found wreck, there is often a curd of ling to be creamed off before catches are made of other species. On well worked wrecks it is easier to fish selectively.

FISHING A WRECK MARK

Anchored or drifting boat

COALFISH

POLLACK

BLACK BREAM

RED BREAM

CONGER

LING

in a 10/0 hook, preferably of the off-set forged-eye type. A stout 5/0 swivel connects this to the reel line, and also stops the sliding lead from running down to the hook. It is good practice to use a rotten-bottom to hold the lead. This also obviates the need for a costly running boom.

Old or fresh bait?

Both conger and ling are catholic feeders, and will accept almost any fish bait, although the majority are caught on mackerel or squid. It is a half-truth that conger only take fresh baits, as many 50-pounders are taken on mackerel three days old. But fresh bait increases one's chance of success.

The take from an outsize conger can be quite gentle in spite of its bulk and strength. It often mouths the bait for some time before actually taking it, and only experience will tell you when to strike. But never be in a hurry, for many conger hooked in the lips break free. When the rod tip tells you of the eel's presence the slack line should be wound in slowly until contact with the fish is made.

Get the conger into clear water

Once the hook has been struck home you must pump the conger into clear water above the wreckage. At this

point, never give line—the risk of being broken up must be taken. Later, line can be given under pressure through the slipping clutch. Conger weighing more than 50lb make continuous power-dives in an attempt to regain the wreck, while fish to 80lb have been known to dive back from the surface through 40 fathoms, despite a tight clutch and thumbs on the spool.

Ideally, conger should be brought to the gaff in an exhausted condition. Failure to observe this important rule puts the catch at risk, and can be very dangerous for the chap wielding the gaff.

The big fish charter boat skippers have a fixed procedure for gaffing a specimen conger. Once the fish has been pumped to the surface the angler steps well back from the gunwale to give the gaffer plenty of room to swing. The multiplier is put out of gear and the spool is held in check by a thumb. This ensures that, should the fish make a last second dive for the bottom (which it commonly does), there is no danger of the line snapping. The freeline technique also ensures the man using the gaff will not be hampered as he brings 8ft of writhing eel aboard.

The angler must resist at all costs the temptation to see what is going on in the water. Many big fish have been lost at the gaff simply because of crowding at the gunwale and the excitement shared by all aboard. A conger in the 80-100lb class needs two gaffers, and team work is vital. John Trust and Ernie Passmore of Brixham, in a 15 year career as co-skippers of *Our Unity,* brought thousands of specimens safely aboard from the many wrecks that litter Devon's Start Bay, and the vast expanse of Lyme Bay off the coast of Dorset. These include three British Record conger. Both areas are havens for the wreck angler, and among the hulks that are regularly fished are a 30,000 ton liner and a battleship sunk in wartime.

Ling feed quite differently and wolf big baits without any regard to caution. As soon as a bite is felt, the hook can be driven home, and the fish dragged away from the bottom. Fish weighing 30lb and more give a good account of themselves, but providing the hook has a firm hold, the issue should never be in doubt. After a few wreck trips the difference between conger and ling bites can be easily detected.

Pollack and coalfish

Wrecking for pollack and coalfish is tremendous fun. Both species are grand fighters and the line-stripping plunge of even a 15lb pollack is one of the most thrilling experiences in sea fishing. During the summer, most are caught on medium-weight tackle from anchored boats. The usual rig is a single 4/0 hook to a 20ft trace, worked from an 8in wire boom, or the recently introduced plastic variety. The boom effectively keeps the trace from tangling with the reel line during its long journey to the bottom. It is then steadily retrieved until the bait or artificial eel is taken. At this point the fish will make its characteristic plunge, and line must be given out again or it will certainly break.

The coalfish is a better fighter than pollack because it is less affected by changes in water pressure. On average it will make at least half a dozen tremendous runs before reaching the surface, and the fight is never won until the fish is safely in a net. Pollack, on the other hand, are
372

HEAVY DUTY LEDGERING
Offset forged-eye hook
Heavy duty swivel 5/0
Wire trace 12-18in
Bead
Sliding lead
Fished on the bottom with mackerel or squid bait
Rotten bottom
Reel line
'Red Gill' eel
Hook 4/0
Lead
Wire trace 20ft
Swivel
Bead

MEDIUM WEIGHT PATERNOSTER RIG
Monofilament reel line 15-20lb b.s.
1/0 Aberdeen hook
Swivel
Bead
TWO-HOOK PATERNOSTER
Fished between the wreck and surface using artificial or natural bait
6in snoods
Plastic boom
Link swivel to carry lead
Rotten bottom
Fished in and over the wreck with fish strip or worm bait
Lead
Plastic bag filled with sand replaces expensive leads
Lask of squid

much affected by pressure changes and when pumped up too quickly arrive lifeless at the surface.

Between November and March, females are heavy with roe, and so many fish congregate on deep-water wrecks that echo sounders and fish-finders (sophisticated enough to normally pick out a single specimen) record what appears to be a solid mass. Most of the winter wreck fishing is done on the drift, after dan buoys have been dropped to accurately mark the wreck's position in relation to the tidal run.

Spring tide=frenzied feeding

For several reasons, the best catches are made during spring tide periods, when the fast run of water stirs the fish into frenzied feeding activity. In this mood they strike fiercely at natural baits and various kinds of lures without hesitation. Big tides also ensure fast drifts across the wreckage, which makes it possible

to get in as many as 30 productive drifts during a single tide.

Drift fishing is most successful when not more than six anglers work at a time. A charter boat moves sideways down the length or across the hulk, and the lines stream out naturally from one side only. Working from the wrong side, the lines go under the keel. Apart from the obvious danger of cutting off, it is extremely difficult to have direct contact and bring up the fish. Lines also tangle with those streaming away correctly, and much valuable fishing time is lost. It is a fact that too many leads plummeting down at the same time frighten fish, and the catch is often smaller when a wreck party of 10 fishermen are all active at once.

Most winter fishing is done with heavyweight nylon paternosters rigged with artificial eels on short snoods. For a two-hook rig the nylon must not be less than 60lb b.s., and if three artificials are being used, which is typical rod-and-line 'commercial' practice, the strength is stepped up to 80lb. Even this can be snapped like cotton if two fish run in opposite directions after taking the lures simultaneously as they commonly seem to do.

Crude but effective

While the method of fishing is perhaps a trifle crude, it takes considerable skill to get the best out of it. The lures, weighted with at least a pound of lead, are allowed to plummet at high speed to the bottom. Quite often they are grabbed by fish swimming as much as eight fathoms above the wreckage. When this happens, the multiplier is thrown into gear, and the full weight of possibly three specimen-sized fish comes on to the rod. The sudden, violent jerk is usually enough to drive the hooks home, but it is as well to strike a few times yourself to make absolutely sure. At this stage, the slipping clutch is set to give line under pressure as the fish will immediately

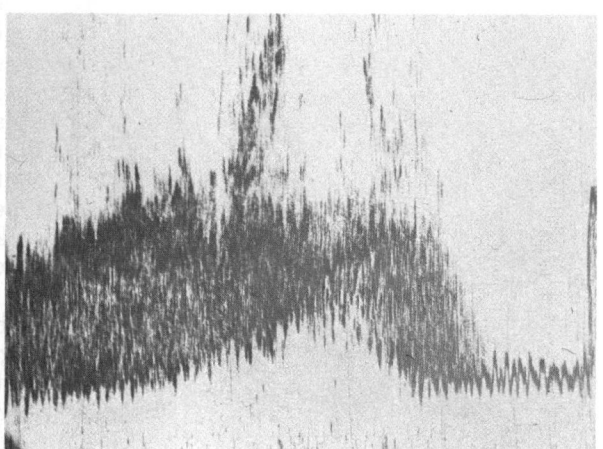

start to plunge downwards.

Successful winter wrecking on the drift depends greatly on the skill of the skipper. He must set each drift up to take advantage of the wreck's position and know exactly where the high parts are. As he watches the sounder, a constant stream of instructions is shouted back from the wheelhouse, and the anglers must be ready to respond instantly to such orders as 'Up 50ft!' 'OK We're over, drop back 50!'

Strong arm tactics

Failure to heed the warnings will almost certainly result in the loss of tackle worth over £3.00. Repeated a few times during the day, winter wrecking becomes a very expensive business. Large pirks, or jiggers as they are also termed, fitted with large forged-eye treble hooks are used effectively for wreck fishing throughout the year, but a great deal of stamina is required to work a 26oz lure correctly for long periods. Charter boat skippers, seldom short on physique, have developed this type of fishing to a fine art. Their method is to stand high on the bows, well out of the anglers' way, and cast the lure as far as possible, letting it run unchecked to the bottom. If it fails to attract a fish on its way down it is retrieved at an ultra-fast pace with a high-geared multiplier until it finds a taker. The largest pollack are taken on pirks, the author's best specimen weighing 23lb 12oz, which is not far short of the national record. Unfortunately, such a fish hooked on a weighty pirk is quite incapable of achieving its fighting potential.

Above left: *A stomach pad is essential if you are going to be fighting big ling or conger. The pad pivots the rod and takes much of the strain off the angler's back and arms.*

Left: *The print-out of an echo sounder monitoring a wreck: the rising streaks show a massive build-up of fish hovering over the hulk. The most modern 'colour' sounders can even differentiate between species.*

What is the most productive fishing period on a wreck?
From the middle of the first hour to the end of the third during a flood tide is generally best. Some wrecks fish well on the ebb, but this depends on how the hulk is lying. If it is whole, and on its side, with the superstructure facing down-channel, the biggest catches will be made during the up-channel run. Wrecks that sit upright or are well broken fish equally well on the flood or ebb.

Are tide times the same far out to sea as they are inshore?
If you are more than 12 miles out from the coast, low or high water will be roughly three hours later than is published in tide tables for the area.

How does pay-by-distance chartering work?
A group of, say, ten anglers pay a minimum fee of about £150 for a trip to marks lying 20 miles out. Beyond that about £10 is added to the overall fee for each additional 10 miles out the boat sails.

Do big conger hunt at night?
The most recent night catch was a 103lb specimen taken from beside a wreck by the Plymouth boat *Zummerzet Maid*. Eels weighing more than 120lb have been taken in nets worked down the side of wrecks at night, when the chances of boating such fish are much improved.

What is a colour sounder?
Very new technology is finding its way into charter boat fishing. Instead of depicting a black image, a colour sounder draws in seven colours. Experienced operators are then able to distinguish between the various species of the shoal fish they see.

Sea leads

When you consider the variety of ground that makes up our ragged coastline, you quickly appreciate why so many different sea leads exist

Leads for sea angling range from split-shot to bombs weighing as much as 4lb which keep a bait on the bottom in deep water during fierce spring tides. There are many different types and each performs a specific task. With a few exceptions, it is of paramount importance to use the right shape and size of weight for the type of fishing being undertaken.

When you have counted all the commercially manufactured leads your tackle dealer stocks, there are still the home-made and improvized varieties to consider.

Wye lead   **Jardine spiral**

Shore fishing

Split-shot, the indispensible lead used in freshwater fishing, also plays a vital role in saltwater, where it is used in float fishing and driftlining for such species as pollack, mackerel, garfish and the wily mullet. Shot is available in a variety of sizes, and should be gently crimped on to the line with pliers.

Ball leads (also known as pierced bullets) and barrel leads, which are designed to run freely on a line, range from $\frac{1}{4}$oz to 3oz. These leads are correct for making up the sliding float rig used to suspend a bait close to the bottom in almost any depth of water. The 'slider' is popular with anglers seeking wrasse, pollack and bass over rough ground. Barrel leads weighing up to 6oz are sold in many tackle shops for bottom ledgering, but they roll around on firm sandy ground, and tend to twist the line. These larger sizes, therefore, make a poor type of lead and are best avoided.

Leads for muddy ground

For ledgering on muddy ground in tidal rivers and estuaries where the water is shallow, flat leads are by far the best. Although they make for poor long-distance casting, those with a thin profile sink to the bottom more slowly than bombs and

consequently do not penetrate more than a few inches into the ooze. Extensions of the smooth, flat weight are the Circular Grip, Capta and the Six Pointed Star. These are useless as casting leads, but they hold well on firm mud, shale and sand—even when the tide pours out of rivers during spring tides.

The long-casting beach angler needs a variety of weights ranging in size from 2oz to 10oz, which offer minimum wind-resistance. Across the years numerous patterns have evolved, and present day beach fishing experts think little of putting an intact bait 160 yards out into the surf where the big fish roam. A small band of men who specialize in this fascinating branch of sea sport, using carbonfibre rods, are already casting way beyond 225 yards and, as this material becomes even more sophisticated, 300 yards may well fall within the range of normal beachcasting as opposed to tournament casting.

Barrel leads

Pierced bullets

Coffin leads   **Arlesey bombs**

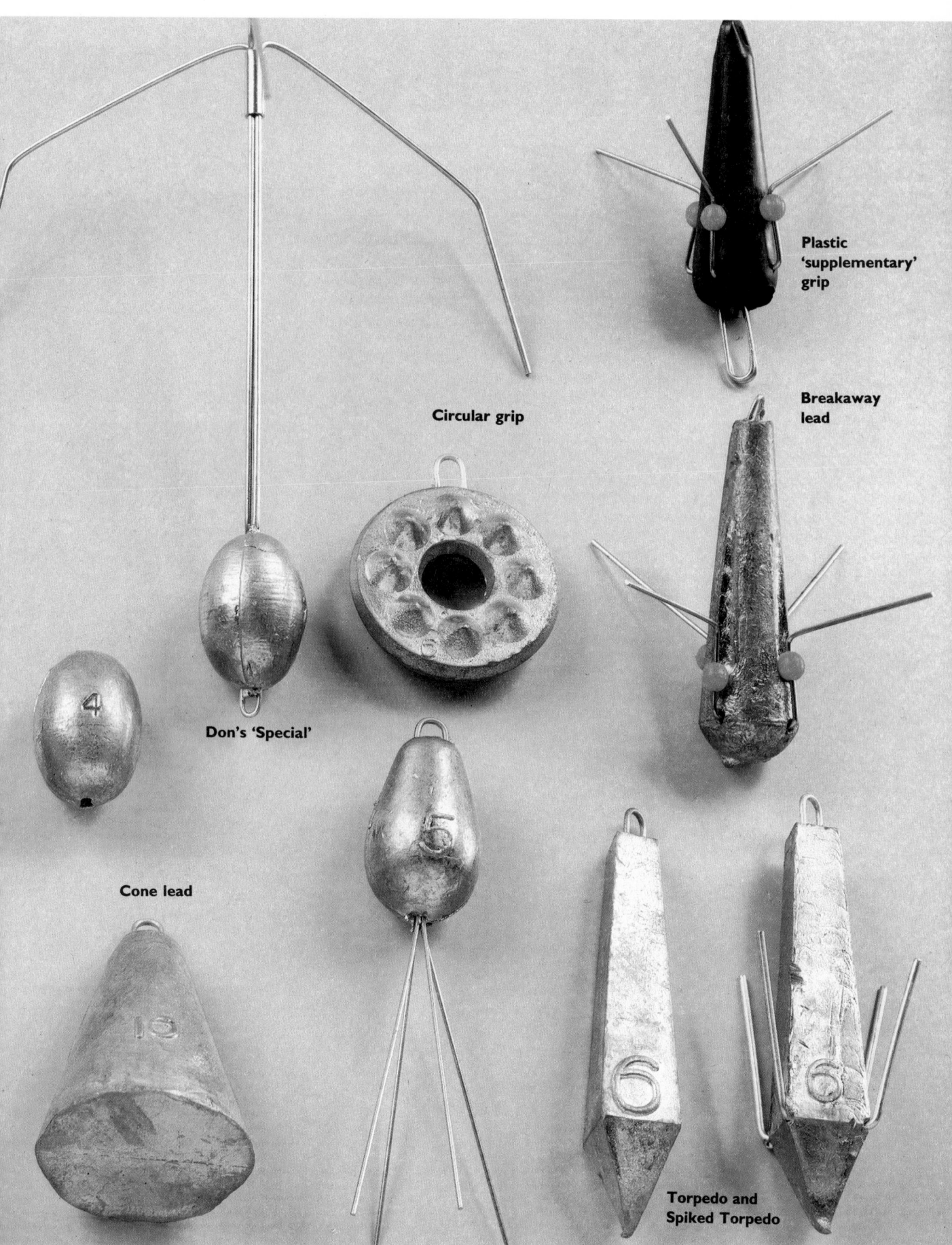

Circular grip

Plastic 'supplementary' grip

Breakaway lead

Don's 'Special'

Cone lead

Torpedo and Spiked Torpedo

375

Rubby dubby

Though evil smelling and not for those with a delicate stomach, a rich concoction of old mackerel mashed up and mixed with fish offal, blood and bran, makes a killing groundbait for sharks

Rubby dubby, a word coined in Cornwall in the 1950s when shark fishing began as a sport, was borrowed from American big game anglers. In America, 'chumming'—throwing chopped up pieces of fish into the water—had long been used to attract tuna and other species of giant game fish.

The best dubby is made from oily pilchards, herring and mackerel, pounded to a pulp with a blunt instrument. Fish offal and unwanted fish are constantly added and some skippers introduce bran to thicken it up. Blood collected from slaughterhouses is also a popular ingredient but contrary to belief it does not stay in a liquid state, due to it being a coagulant. It then resembles jelly, and is a useful additive to existing rubby dubby. Occasionally it is kept separate and after a good stir ladled directly into the sea with an old saucepan. Under the rules of the International Game Fish Association and the Shark Angling Club of Great Britain, the use of blood, flesh, and the guts of mammals for 'chumming' or 'rubby dubby' will disqualify a catch, so if you have a world or British Record shark in mind, make sure none of these are used on the boat.

Conventional dubby is placed in stout meshed bags or in small sacks and suspended over the side of the boat at bow and stern, a length of rope holding it just beneath the surface, where constant wave action keeps the oil and particles of fish flowing. Every so often the bags are bashed heartily against the side of the boat to help thing along.

'Rubby dubby trail'
Once in the water the 'rubby dubby trail' gradually builds up. Pieces of flesh sink quickly or slowly, depending on their oil content, while the

oil droplets stay on the surface. On rough days it is quite remarkable how this trail smooths out the sea. If the trail is 'fed' regularly with fresh bags of dubby it becomes deeper and wider, forming almost a solid lane of attraction, leading a shark straight to the baited hooks.

Quite a few rubby dubby barrels are started at the beginning of the season. The mess is topped up each day; after a couple of weeks it is said to be of superior quality, guaranteed to attract sharks.

Groundbaiting
While the Cornish version is used mainly in British waters for sharking, many skippers operating bottom fishing trips attach a bag of fish guts and mashed flesh a few feet from the boat's anchor rope. When the hook bites into the bottom, the tide flow carries particles of flesh back under the craft, thus attracting fish into the vicinity of the baited hooks. This variation really comes into the category of groundbaiting, and of course by comparison with a sharker's dubby is not at all unpleasant. Dubbying as used in shark fishing is a certain way of attracting mackerel. Drop a set of feathers into a slick that has been working for as little as ten minutes and the chances are that each hook will hold a shining mackerel.

It should be remembered that land predators always hunt upwind. Fish react the same way, and search for food uptide. It usually takes about an hour for the rubby dubby to do its silent but deadly work.

Shark boats leave harbour around 9.00am allowing two and a half hours to reach the ground, set up the drift and get the dubby in the water. It takes a further hour for a useful slick to build up, and half an hour for the shark to swim up it. Quite often

a reel will 'sing' punctually at one o'clock.

Each boat has its own characteristics: those with large wheel-houses and high prows catch the wind rather more than craft with a lower profile. In certain wind-on-tide conditions some boats overrun the slick, and others side-slip, creating an undesirable bend in the trail. When this happens a fish can easily swim past the baits and continue hunting away from the boat.

Once the dubby is working, it is of course bad policy to break trail by moving to another area. When the drift is set, the pattern must be maintained until it is time to draw lines. This rule does not apply in

Top left: *A bucketful of ancient mackerel—the perfect base for all 'good' dubby.*
Left: *Maurice Cleghorn happily mincing old mackerel as a last-minute addition.*
Above: *Rubby dubby seeps out of the sack to trail attractively in the tide.*
Right: *Old deadbait, cut up and placed in a bag will also attract fish if thrown over the side.*

How can rubby dubby be made when there is a shortage of fish to pulp?
Pilchard oil is a good substitute and can be bought in small or large quantities. Stuff old rags into a pierced tin or sack and soak them in the oil. The oil will seep out slowly.

Can any sort of fish be used in a mixture of rubby dubby?
Yes—but those with a high oil content are best. Pilchard rates number one in shark fishing circles. The flesh, as well as oozing grease, sinks more slowly than any other kind of fish.

How often should the dubby bag be changed?
Maximum attraction will be kept up if a fresh bag is put over the side every hour. When the sea is rough, the life of the dubby is shortened considerably.

Is there a danger of sharks actually attacking the bags?
It does happen quite often—mostly on very hot days when the water is very calm. Large sharks have been known to station themselves under a boat and take a baited hook thrown by hand. You should not be fishing for shark from any boat small enough to be upset by your quarry, though in British waters shark fishermen aren't in danger of being eaten!

What size mesh should the net bag have?
In conditions of moderate drift, a small mesh bag will not release too much dubby in too short a time. When the drift is very fast, however, the amount entering the water needs to be stepped up and a wide meshed bag should be used to achieve this.

porbeagle shark fishing, which is confined to quite small areas of rocky ground lying well inshore. Crackington Haven in Cornwall and Hartland Point in Devon are only a matter of 400 yards from the land. In this situation, the boat's drift pattern is short and repetitive; consequently a 'box' of attraction, rather than a lane is created. Unlike blue shark, which keeps to deep water, porbeagles will hunt in less than 30ft, so pure chumming with small pieces of fish is practised, in addition to having the conventional net bags at bow and stern. On several occasions, very large surface-swimming porbeagles have been coaxed to within a few feet of

the boat with tasty morsels.

An alternative method when fishing at anchor over a small patch of rock is to drop a large weighted can filled with crushed fish mixed with pilchard oil. Holes should be punched in the side to allow the juices to flow out.

A word of warning to those who have never smelt rubby dubby—the effect is devastating to most newcomers to the sport of sharking and many old hands alike!

If you have a sensitive stomach, stand as far away from the bin as possible while the skipper is filling the bags. Many an angler's day has been turned into a nightmare of seasickness.

Eire: the coast

Little by little, Eire's working harbours and inshore waters were discovered by foreign anglers. Sporting potential was developed with care and enthusiasm; now it is world-renowned

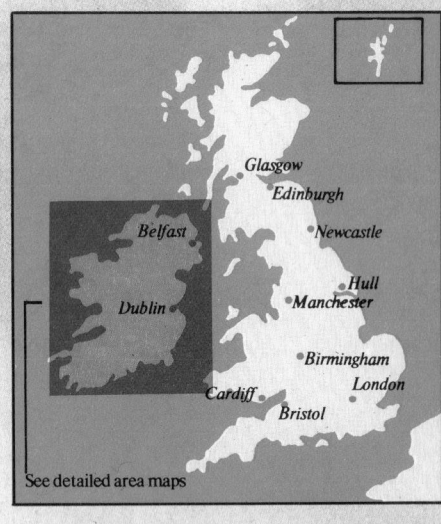

See detailed area maps

Irish sea angling is bountiful—both in terms of statistics and of variety. The Irish coastline covers 3,000 miles, not all of which is fishable, but which offers a mixture of vast beaches, offshore waters and bays, and rugged stretches leading to wrecks such as the *Lusitania* (sunk in 1915) 10-12 miles off the Cork coast, and others off Donegal and Mayo. Standing in warm tributaries of the main Gulf Stream, its southern waters attract warm water species such as mullet and bass. There is no shortage, however, of the cold water species—coalfish, cod and herring. Prevailing westerly and south-westerly winds, however, can suddenly enliven an angler's boating with the wildest of storms.

Statistics demonstrate Ireland's

undisputed angling wealth at sea. In Leinster, for example, there are 60 clubs. And in 1982, 239 sea fishing festivals and competitions are planned. The Irish Marine Record fish include a halibut of 156lb, a cod of 42lb, a 37lb thornback and a 66½lb tope. In 1980 new records were set for black sole (4½lb), monkfish (73lb), turbot (32½lb) twaite shade (2lb 1½oz) and painted ray (14lb 7oz).

Greystones
Greystones, 20 miles south of Dublin, is the prime eastern venue, with three or four clubs and a membership of 500 or more. There is an abundance of fishing from steep shelving beaches north and south of the town—approximately eight miles in all—and pier fishing for codling, bass, pouting, dogfish and some gurnard. Rock fishing at the Flat Rock and Carrigedery accounts for codling, pollack and a few bass. All along this section the tide rip near the shore is strong at peak tides. Ballygannon Strand, two miles south of Greystones along the railway line, is a favourite location.

There are many boats available at Greystones, and the boat fishing is located half a mile to a mile out, parallel to the coast, towards the Moulditch Buoy and the Ridge. The area is full of local marks. In winter, big cod are caught in north-flowing water, and all year round the area is noted for codling (especially in autumn), and for pouting, plaice, thornback, conger, pollack and some skate, tope and wrasse.

Surf sweeps into Co Kerry's north-facing Brandon Bay and gives fine beach fishing.

Visitors to the area can obtain help and information from a number of contacts and clubs. In the Dundalk to Kilmore stretch, one should make a point of contacting the Greystones Ridge Club in Ranelagh, Co Dublin, the Knights of the Silver Hook in Sutton, Co Dublin, the Bray Sea Angling Club, or the East Coast Ladies in Dublin.

Isolated locations
The inquisitive shore angler who has a car will find many isolated locations between Greystones and Wexford, notably at Kilcoole 'Breaches', Kilmichael and Courtown, where mullet in the tiny harbour are excep-

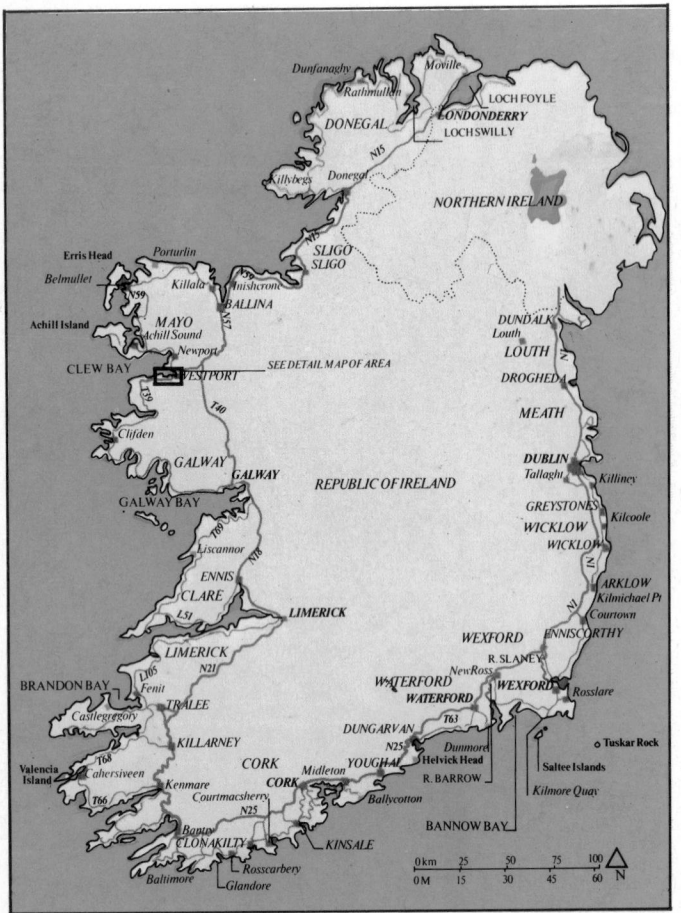

tionally catchable. The tidal stretches of the River Slaney at Wexford also offer good opportunities. Bass fishing at night can be good on both bridges of the town at Wexford, while numerous quay stands are excellent and there is a variety of beach fishing within three miles of the town. Two deep-sea clubs are active there and at adjacent Rosslare, leading to Tuskar Rock five miles out. Splaugh Rock, a vast undersea platform, was once fine for bass, but was overfished, though it still remains some fine cod, pollack, and conger.

Saltee Islands

Off Kilmore Quay there is plentiful angling all around the Saltee Islands, four miles out. The warmer water becomes evident here, and fishing for tope and pollack is excellent, especially when drifting along the Burrow beach near Kilmore Harbour. There is beach fishing everywhere here.

For more information about this area you should contact the Saltee

Sea Angling Club or one of the numerous sea angling clubs in Kilmore Quay, Co Wexford.

The mobile angler will find unlimited shore fishing at Dunmore East, a considerable fishing port, and along Bannow Bay, west of Kilmore, while all shore anglers would do well to explore the swift deep channel on the western side of Bannow Island for bass and flounder. Further information can be obtained from the Dunmore East Sea Angling Club in Waterford City.

Dungarvan

Dungarvan has had ups and downs in deep sea angling lately, mostly because of boat troubles, but has no shortage of good water. There is the four-mile estuary, fished from Cunnigar on shore, with a four-mile strand at Clonea and then a vast crescent-shaped bay leading beyond the Helvic Head. In Dungarvan Town, above and below the railway bridge and along the quay, there is spinning, driftlining and bottom fishing for bass. Mullet fishermen

should float fish the outlet pipe between early ebb tide and low water. Reports tell of estuary pollution or disturbance, but Dungarvan's offshore waters are a fine venue for tope and blue shark in summer.

Youghal has good general angling in reputable blue shark waters. But the shark have been so heavily sought that future stocks are at risk. The codling are about in autumn. Shore fishing includes some surf fishing at such places as Goat Island, Mangan's Cove, Caliso Bay and Youghal Strand. Conger can be caught at night from the pier head. Ballycotton nearby was once a popular Irish angling haven. Fifty years ago, pioneers of sea angling in England went there, trained their boatmen, and set up a sort of angling dynasty. Later, when there were troubles in Ireland, the pioneers left and Ballycotton went off the angling map, but there is some excellent deep sea angling for cod, ling, pollack, skate and blue shark, with boats available. And there's a run of sea trout past the reef at Ballymona

380

Above: *Ling fishing close in to the sheer, dark cliffs of Clare Island.*

Inset: *Co Clare presents 60 miles of rock to a sea harbouring wrasse like this.*

Strand together with bass.

After Ballycotton, enterprising promoters found Kinsale, west of Cork Harbour, with greater shelter and amenities. It is a highly organized, sophisticated angling boat station today, though expensive. For those who like modest outgoings on holiday, however, some of the finest garfish and bass angling from small boats is to be found in the estuary of the River Bandon, running through Kinsale. The Kinsale Sea Angling Club in Kinsale, Co Cork, will help with information about the area.

Centres such as Courtmacsherry, Clonakilty, Rosscarbery, Glandore, and Baltimore in West Cork are noted for their shore fishing, but are rather expensive. Great sea loughs cut into the Cork and Kerry coasts, with angling spots such as Bantry Bay, Kenmare River and Valentia Island. Boat fishing is not readily

available, though the angler has never far to look for action on shore. Cahersiveen on the Kerry has boats suitable for truly big skate, but these, unfortunately, are becoming scarce in Ireland.

In fact, the Irish Federation of Sea Anglers has become extremely conservation-conscious of late. Bass of less than 43cm, for example, should be returned according to its book of *Sea Angler's Rules*. Projects to chart the migratory and reproductive habitats of shark, skate, ray, tope and monkfish have resulted in a great deal of tagging work. It stands to reason that tagged fish should be returned—and since it is not easy to spot a tag during the fight to boat or beach fish, the use of the gaff is strongly discouraged.

Warm west coast

Next, working up the west coast, the Dingle peninsula, jutting into the warm Atlantic, has wonderful shore fishing with long strands noted for bass. Brandon Bay has a 14-mile strand perfect for bass fishing and it is only one beach out of dozens in the peninsula. Castlegregory also has plenty of good shore fishing for bass and flatfish.

At Fenit, in Tralee Bay, there is exciting fishing from the long pier with skate and ray coming regularly, while out in the bay specimen undulate ray are found in great numbers in June and July. Further information about fishing in the area can be obtained at the Old Bridge House in Fenit, Co Kerry.

The first porbeagle shark caught from the rocky shore at Liscannor, Co Clare weighed 145lb and was taken by Jack Shine—but his is certainly not a game for timid anglers. There are, however, 60 miles of rocky eminences from which to practise, all the way up to Galway Bay, which is well served by angling boats. They go along the Clare coast, into the path of north-going porbeagles and blues, and out to the Aran Islands. There is much bottom fishing. Bass fishing in the tidal lagoon west of Galway is available and at the mouths of the Knock and Spiddal rivers. There is also mullet fishing in the harbour.

Clifden in Connemara is popular

How can I join the Irish Shark Club?
A 100lb qualifying catch entitles you to membership. Eddie Cullen of 1, Glenview, South Douglas Rd, Cork, can send details in return for a s.a.e.

Which lures are best in Irish waters?
For bass and pollack in fast seas, use a $\frac{1}{4}$oz or a $\frac{3}{4}$oz German Sprat (smaller Sprats take mackerel). Rubber eels of 7in take early pollack. Silver Devons or Vibro spoons ($1\frac{1}{4}$-$1\frac{1}{2}$in) take sea trout, mackerel and shoal bass, and $3\frac{1}{2}$in white plastic spoons can be baited to catch flatfish.

When can I catch Irish halibut?
The halibut shoals are only within reach of rod and line in June and July. All but bass show best between May and November; even Ireland's superb sea fishing can't be recommended in February and March.

Which baits can I get hold of cheaply, on the spot?
Lugworm abound on flat beaches; mussels, cockles and razorfish are almost as easily come by. Sandeels are abundant only in parts. Big prawns can be hand netted at low tide wherever there is plenty of weed among rocks or growing on harbour walls. And have a word with the inshore trawlermen, who bring up large numbers of unwanted hermit crab: they may lay some aside for you.

Why are there no skate mentioned on recent Irish record and specimen lists?
In the interests of this hard-hammered species, the Irish Specimen Fish Committee want to deter anyone from killing the few remaining giants for the glory of it.

for blue shark fishing and has been discovered by Dutch anglers who have made it their holiday home. While there is little shore fishing, most fishing is done from serviceable catamarans in the three rugged bays—Streamstown, Clifden and Mannin—for pollack, conger, wrasse, mackerel, ray and flatfish. Streamstown is only worth fishing in slack water conditions for conger. Nearby Killary Harbour is so deep and sheer-sided that pollack, mackerel, ray and whiting can be caught close inshore.

Moving into Co Mayo, Westport was a pioneer in sea angling, and is still a fine centre. It has the advantage of lying in the vast, sheltered, island strewn Clew Bay and its fishing suffers few interruptions from the storms outside. It is a maze of eyots and peninsulas offering shore and some rock fishing and is well established as a resort, with its clubhouse on the quayside, boats on call, frequent competitions and a comradely atmosphere. For years monkfish kept Westport in the news: they were being caught even from the end of the pier. But there

Below: *Ron Edwards engages in a fight with a ray from the shallow, sheltered waters of Westport Bay. The islanded bay below the town is inaccessible to all but angling boats.*

are fewer to be had now, and the inroads made by fishing on other species has resulted in club members being urged to return all of their catches alive.

Achill Island has yet to be explored by shore fishermen. Bullsmouth, however, has shown promise with ground fishing in the fierce tidal sweep. The Irish tub gurnard record still stands with a 12lb 3½oz Achill fish. Purteen has boats for pollack fishing under the giant cliffs.

Belmullet, on the north Mayo coast, has splendid venues—Porturlin, Portacloy and Ballyglass. It is a wild area, though, and it takes organized parties to procure boats in advance. There is spectacular fishing for cod, bream, conger and skate off Erris Head, and the finest turbot are found in the water off Ballyglass. Belmullet gave a record turbot of 32½lb in 1980.

Killala Bay, served by Killala and Inishcrone, has plenty of boats and an abundance of fish. Recent specimens caught at Killala include a red gurnard of 2lb 9¾oz, a tub gurnard of 8lb 5oz, a blonde ray of 26lb, and a pollack of 12lb 8oz.

Although the rock fishing at St John's Point is good, Killybegs, in Donegal, has apparently fallen back in organized boat angling, principally because of commercial sea fishing. Along the high Donegal coast, however, places such as Dunfanaghy, Downings and Rathmullan, all with boats, have much mixed bottom fishing, and Lough Swilly was always famous for hordes of tope, although they are now much thinned. Moville, in neighbouring lough Foyle, is noted for large numbers of gurnard as well as cod, dogfish, pollack, coalies, ray, ling, tope and haddock, and holds a week-long fishing festival, usually in August.

Sea fishing in Ireland is organized by the Irish Federation of Sea Anglers. Member clubs pay a Federation charge, but individuals may join for a £5 fee which entitles them to a copy of the Federation periodical, *Gaff,* and the *Sea Angler's Rule Book.* A free copy of *Gaff* can be obtained by writing to Mr Hugh O'Rorke, Secretary of the IFSA, 67 Windsor Drive, Monkstown, Co Dublin.

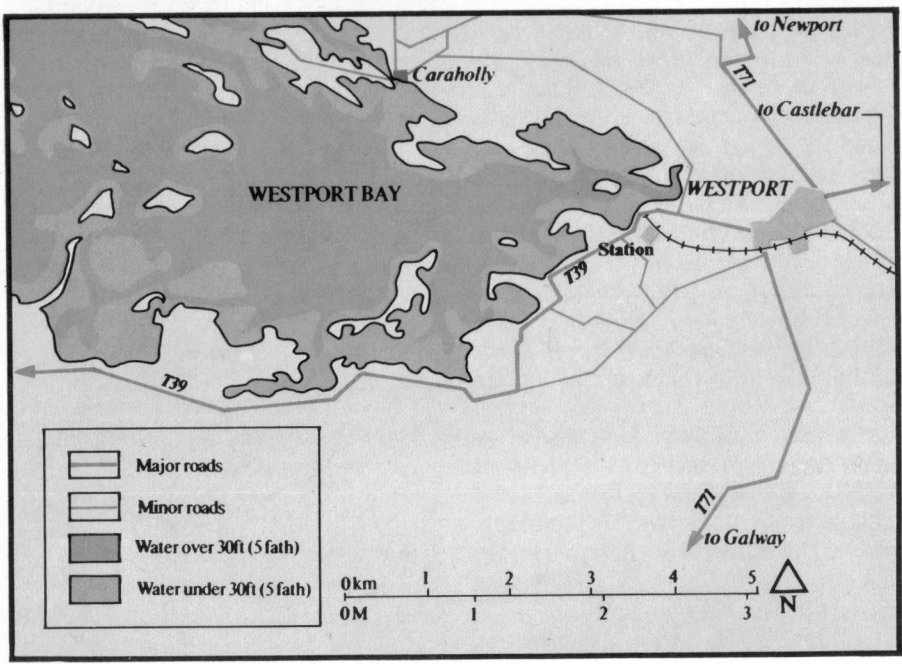

to Newport

Caraholly

to Castlebar

WESTPORT BAY

WESTPORT

T39

Station

T39

T39

to Galway

Major roads

Minor roads

Water over 30ft (5 fath)

Water under 30ft (5 fath)

0 km 1 2 3 4 5

0 M 1 2 3

N

West Country

For the sea angler, the varied, rugged coastline and waters off Dorset, Devon and Cornwall offers some of the most magnificent sea fishing to be found anywhere in the British Isles

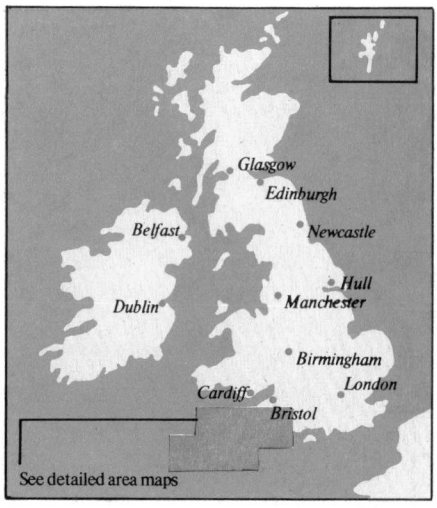

West Bay, not far from Bridport, Dorset, gives the sea angler a choice of shore or boat fishing for a wide variety of species.

The British Record (Rod-caught) list for sea fish shows just how productive the waters off Dorset, Devon and Cornwall are. Currently, 58 records have their origins in the area, the breakdown showing 40 by boat anglers, nine from the shore and nine for boat or shore caught species with a weight up to 1lb. Some records have been broken many times, those for pollack, ling, conger and coalfish, for example, and there is little doubt all of them will change hands again and again as wreck boats in particular push further out into the wastes of the English Channel.

The 'coast of wrecks' would not be an inaccurate description for the lower end of the Channel. From Portland Bill to Land's End the bottom of the sea is littered with the rusting remains of the vessels ranging from coasters, submarines, ocean liners and even a giant battleship. Most were sunk during two world wars and at the height of the German U-boat campaign of World War II it was not unusual for a group of ships to be sunk within a matter of hours in one small area. Such a situation occurred off Falmouth, when five merchantmen went down. The ships lie within a 10 mile box and provide shelter for vast numbers of fish across a wide range of species and superb fishing for the wreck angler.

Lyme Bay

Weymouth and other ports in Dorset have boats that frequently make the run to marks in Lyme Bay. The liner *Empress of India*, among others, is inhabited by fine conger, while off the Devon coast, Lyme Bay and Start Bay are the hunting grounds of Brixham charter skippers. Brixham's skippers started fishing wrecks in the 1960s and the famous boat, *Our Unity,* is seldom out of the angling news. Their biggest haul was 5,000lb of ling, conger and pollack, made by eight anglers in about six hours fishing.

Tides run swiftly in both bays, and good wrecking is restricted to neap tide periods. If you are thinking of tangling with an 80lb conger make sure that you bear the tides in mind when making a booking. Anglers who forget this are naturally disappointed when their big day turns out to be fished on less productive ground, in more sheltered waters, because of tide changes.

Dartmouth

Several top flight boats work out of Dartmouth, with Lloyd Saunders and *Saltwind II* frequently making angling news. In 1980 Saunders smashed the British Record for coalfish with a monstrous fish of 33lb 7oz, at Start Point, S Devon, while six miles to the west in Lannacombe Bay a mark known as the Ridd gave local angler Roger Simcox the British Record turbot of 33lb 12oz.

Thirty miles down the coast is the great seaport of Plymouth, now regarded as Britain's number one

sea angling centre. Over 30 fully equipped and licensed boats are available for reef and wreck charter. Records set by anglers embarking from the port include conger 109lb 6oz, pollack 25lb, mackerel 5lb 6½oz, and bass 18lb 6oz. Wreck fishing is a speciality, but the great reefs of Eddystone, West Rutts and Hands Deeps are also popular. These lie in deep water, but can be reached in a couple of hours.

Inshore boat fishing is also productive. The whiting grounds four miles south of Rame Head are famous for big fish, and specimens of 3-5lb are no surprise. The area's shore fishing can also be recommended, and you can take your pick of rock, storm beach and quiet sandy estuaries. The main species are the colourful ballan wrasse *(Labrus bergylta)*, which reach a weight of seven pounds in the deep kelp-strewn gullies, pollack and bass.

Looe

Looe is perhaps the shark fishing capital of the world. Each day throughout summer, 25 boats go beyond the Eddystone, where 'blues' provide plenty of excitement. They mostly weigh around 50lb and at the end of each week there are at least six fish in the 80-110lb class. Unfortunately, too many small sharks are unnecessarily killed by holiday anglers eager to show off their catch at the end of the day. To qualify for membership of the Shark Angling Club of Great Britain the minimum weight caught is 75lb, and it would probably be advisable for sharks below this weight to be returned unharmed to the sea. Other shark species found off Looe are the mako and porbeagle. The former is a true man-eater and reaches an enormous weight. The current British record fish of 500lb was captured off the Eddystone in 1971 after a battle lasting several hours.

Far left: *There are many spots on the Cornish coasts where rock fishing can be productive for mackerel, bass and pollack.*
Top: *Big pollack roam close to Start Point, S Devon, and go for float-fished sandeel.*
Centre: *Kynance Cove, close to the Lizard, has abundant shore fishing.*
Left: *Boat fishing in the Salcombe Estuary.*

ASK THE EXPERT

What's the average cost of a day's wreck fishing?
About £20 for a single place. Trips last roughly 12 hours, but it's wise to check with the skipper before you leave harbour.

What is meant by a 'two-fish rule'?
Most charter skippers working wrecks impose a fish limit. No matter how many you catch, you can only take two away. But bear in mind that a brace of ling can weigh over 60lb!

Is there good haddock fishing in the West Country?
Yes, but it's very localized. Falmouth Bay is the prime site with at least seven British Record fish taken there. Large specimens are also caught off Rame Head from time to time.

What is the best mark for plaice?
The Skerries Banks which lie a few miles south west of Dartmouth. In April and May large numbers of 4-7lb fish are caught, mostly on peeler crab and sandeel strip.

Where can I hire a self-drive boat for inshore fishing?
Salcombe is easily the best place. Contact any of the following: Edgar Cove, Salcombe 2542; Ian Brodie, 3197; Ken Allen Boats, 2840. A useful publication, *Spotlight Guide to Angling in the South West* contains many boat fishing contacts.

Can tope be caught from the shore?
Yes, two places spring to mind: Chesil Bank which runs for 18 miles between Portland Bill and West Bay; also Trevose Head on Cornwall's North Coast, though this second mark should never be fished alone.

squid and mackerel, and stories of gigantic conger breaking up tackle and gaffs do have some truth in them. A little farther upstream is Old Sawmills Reach where fine flounder and bass are caught on the making tide. Spoons tipped with worms are much favoured locally and account for big flatties.

Shore fishing at Fowey is especially good during the autumn.

Looe craft make regular trips to the Philips Rocks, Hatt Rock and Brentons—marks that quite rightly have an honoured place in British angling history. In these places the pollack is king. It is a hefty green and gold fish whose power-dive for the bottom after it has taken a bait, is something one never forgets. Pollack of 10lb are common, and tackle-busting fish up to 20lb are never far away.

Fowey

These reefs are also fished by skippers from Fowey, but their main quarry is bass on the inshore grounds. Most of them make for the Cannis Rock, due south of Gribben Head, where fish averaging 6lb are taken on live sandeel. Many species find their way into Fowey Harbour, and near the Bodinnick Ferry, where the water is very deep, conger fishing is particularly good at night. Eels up to 75lb have been taken on

From the harbour mouth to the tidal limits there are dozens of spots where you can catch big wrasse, bass, pollack and flounder. Golant, renowned for its flounder, produced the record fish of 5lb 11oz. The fish tend to lie behind sandbanks running across the river, and a moderate cast from the railway siding will put crab or worm bait in the right place.

Outside the harbour to the east, between Pencarrow Head and Lansallos, the water is reached by a very steep path. The effort can be worthwhile, as monster wrasse shelter under rocky overhangs and provide plenty of rod-bending sport. One recent catch gave 27 fish over 4lb, and three over 6lb, which is specimen weight for the species.

Pollack fishing can also be rewarding along this wild stretch of coast.

rocks at night is no game for the lone angler. Always have a friend along, and be fully equipped with lights, 20ft of stout rope and a first-aid kit in case of emergencies.

Mevagissey
The small port of Mevagissey is another sea angling centre. Each day charter boats bring shark, ling, conger, coalfish and pollack ashore, while wreck fishing is a speciality for skipper Bernard Hunkin who has found the British record ling and angler fish. Inshore wrecks off the Dodman Point have also produced record fish—a red bream weighing an incredible 9½lb and an electric ray only fractionally short of 100lb.

The shoreline within 30 miles of Mevagissey is perfect for shore fishing. There are dozens of spots providing all the popular species, while Falmouth, with its huge harbour and miles of tidal rivers cutting deep inland, is a paradise for shore and dinghy anglers. Most species are present throughout the year, but autumn is the best period. Soft back and peeler crab offered on bottom or float gear will be quickly snapped up by flounder, plaice, dabs, wrasse, pollack or bass. Spinning from rocks with artificial or natural baits—from Zone Point, Trefusis Point, or Pendennis Point, produces mackerel, garfish, bass and pollack.

Manacles Reef
A few miles away is the notorious Manacles Reef, a superb spot for bass, pollack and conger fishing. The reef lies directly across the southern approach to Falmouth, and its outer edge is marked by a large red buoy, chained to the sea-bed 200ft below. Many ships have gone to the bottom in the past, and modern wrecks like the *Finisterre* soon become inhabited by large numbers of specimen-sized species.

Over the reef itself is good bass country. Fish of 7-10lb are common, with a percentage weighing 13lb. These are caught by drift-line methods or by trolling with artificial eels. Pollack fall to the same methods, but during daylight the fish lie deep so it is essential to work the bait close to the bottom.

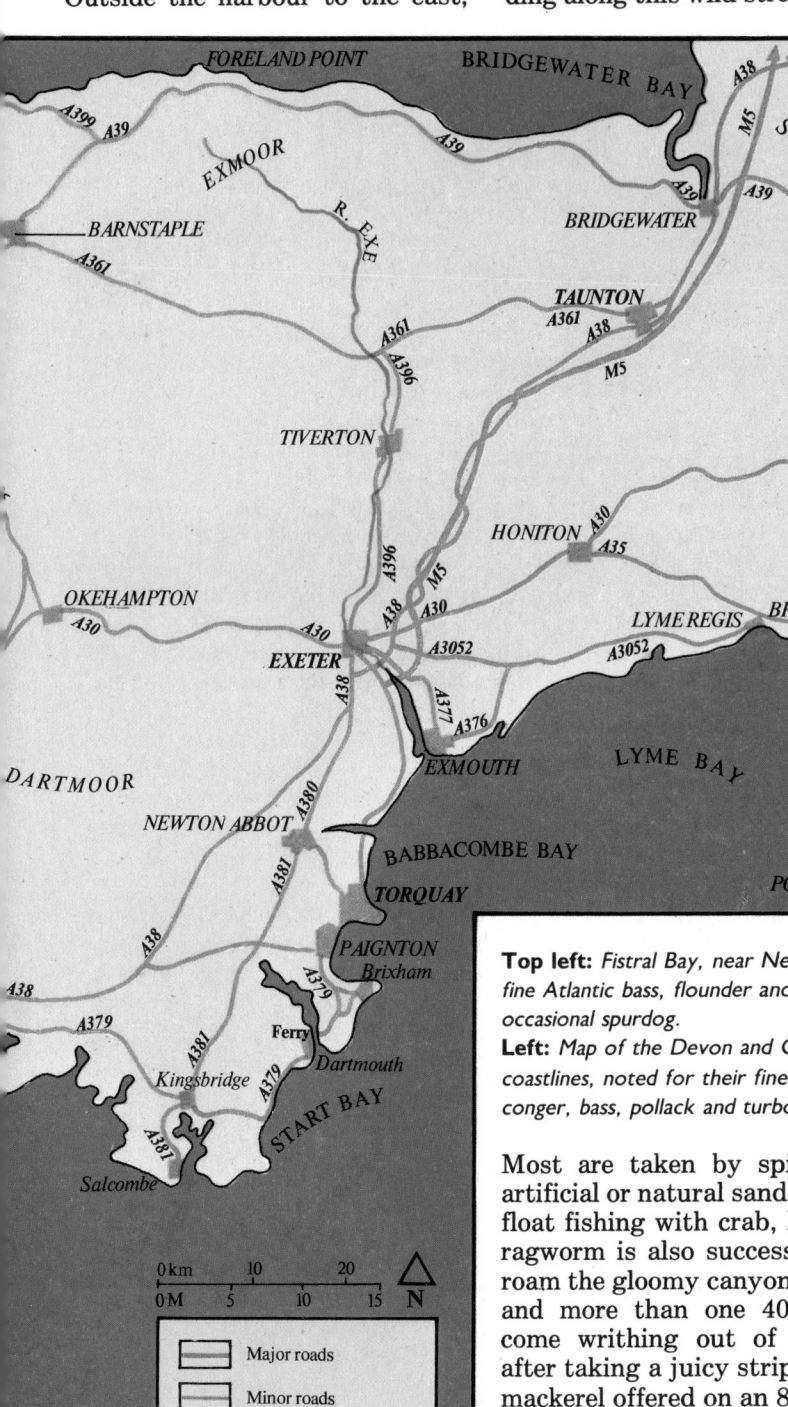

Top left: *Fistral Bay, near Newquay, has fine Atlantic bass, flounder and the occasional spurdog.*
Left: *Map of the Devon and Cornish coastlines, noted for their fine shark, conger, bass, pollack and turbot.*

Most are taken by spinning with artificial or natural sandeels. Sliding float fishing with crab, king rag, or ragworm is also successful. Conger roam the gloomy canyons after dark and more than one 40lb fish has come writhing out of the depths after taking a juicy strip of squid or mackerel offered on an 8/0 hook to a wire trace. Take a word of warning however; congering from desolate

GAME FISHING

THERE WAS A TIME, long ago, when only English gentlemen (and poachers) fished for trout, the 'ordinary' man spending his angling time catching roach, chub, bream and so on and since much of the catch was taken back home as food any pike or perch was considered a welcome bonus because there is not a great deal of nourishment in the carp-like fishes. But the great levelling up of the social orders, the general increase in wealth and leisure time has led to the fact that any angler has access to trout fishing of some kind.

The strictures of space decreed that this section of the book is all that can be alloted to game fishing; it can be no more than an introduction to what is probably the oldest kind of fishing that has been practised. Of all the skills an angler can acquire in order to become successful and accomplished in his chosen sport that of fly fishing is without doubt the most graceful and satisfying of all. The bare bones of casting a fly line are covered lucidly here but a book twice the size of this volume could not adequately describe the beauty of a brook rod and trout line in action in the hands of an expert. It is not that fly casting is difficult, the elements can be picked up in an afternoon, but in the right hands the line with its attached artificial fly moves in perfect arcs to and fro a little to one side and above the angler's head, finally to unfurl and reach out to its farthest extent and deposit that whisp of feather and silk on a hook as lightly upon the water's surface film as a speck of thistledown. From where it touches, concentric rings spread out, mirroring those other rings created by falling mayflies and other insects, spent after their brief nuptial flights.

At these times, when spent flies are fluttering down to the water, the trout feed voraciously, gulping and snapping the tiny morsels up one after the other. If the angler has cast well and accurately one of those flies taken so eagerly will conceal a long-shanked hook and the trout will be on. Now comes the moment for the angler to put into practice another of his skills: and it is not a violent strike, of the kind made in some instances of coarse fishing. All the angler must do – and it takes great presence of mind – is to tighten the line *and keep it tight all the while* until the trout is safely in the net.

Among trout fishermen there is an old and very comfortably familiar little saying: 'Match the hatch'. This rhyming phrase refers to the concept of watching to see which fly is hatching while you are fishing and then tying as near an imitation as possible. The theory is that if the artificial is cast among the natural insects as they flutter back to the surface the chances of a fish are very much enhanced. This is epitomised by the great Frederick Halford's definition:'Dry fly fishing is presenting to the rising fish the best possible imitation of the insect on which he (sic) is feeding in its natural position, or floating on the water with its wings up . . .'. When that was written some 85 years ago the fashion was to create very close copies of the natural insect because writers such as Halford insisted that this was the only way to attract trout. This all refers of course to the dry fly. In today's dry flies things have not changed a great deal, although in the wet fly category some flies bear little resemblance to any living or dead creatures. And there is no doubt that they attract fish consistently.

But fly fishing for wild brown trout is not only concerned with the ultra-delicate approach of the Test angler, waters such as this are very exclusive. Those in the fisheries business have in recent years created many accessible, new reservoirs where trout fishing may be obtained comparatively cheaply and easily. They come in widely differing sizes from those of about an acre to the huge man-made lakes such as Chew Valley with its miles of banks. All these waters are well attended throughout the trout season, with very heavy attendances during the first week or so when introduced trout, fat and lazy after being reared on protein-rich pellets in stewponds, can be quickly tempted. These fish have not developed the shyness and timidity that wild fish have when anglers are about. Reared trout know man as the provider of food and not their executioner.

Reservoir trouting is now big business and allows many more anglers to become adept at fly casting than would otherwise be the case if such fishing were not available. The rule is always 'Fly only' and woe betide the angler seen applying a maggot or worm to the barb on his fly; instant ejection and a ban on his presence in future is the penalty.

One of the greatest and most gratifying experiences that a fly fisherman can enjoy is to hook and land a trout, or any other fish, on a fly that he has tied himself. Some of the great classics in the literature of the sport are those written by the master fly-tiers. Authors such as Halford are sought after in secondhand book shops and the lucky man who finds one of the better editions complete with examples tied by the author's own hand will have an eminently sellable volume on his bookshelf.

So far as fly rods are concerned, there are diehards who insist that their old Hardy built-cane rod is the equal of any new-fangled carbon wand and of course a well-tried and old faithful friend of a rod in its loving owner's hands will continue to catch fish until the owner or the rod comes to the end of its day. When man-made materials came into being, the new rods were made of solid fibreglass; those models soon become known as nothing more than long, green liquorice sticks, with about the same action. Then hollowglass came along and the improvement was immediate. These news rods had some semblance of 'action' and 'feel'. But weight was still something of a problem, especially for fly fishermen who would be fishing actively all day with none of the long periods with the rod in rests that the coarse angler has. Then carbon appeared and rods had suddenly lost 90 per cent of their weight, even having more of the action of the old split-cane and built-cane rods that were the apples of our fathers' eyes.

Now there is boron and with these advances, as might be expected, prices kept in line and climbed steadily at each new introduction, each new gadget that no self-respecting angler would be seen without. Like everything else, the costs of pleasure go up and up.

Of course fly fishing for trout, brown or rainbow, is not all there is to game fishing. There is much more, for fly casting has been whimsically described as an excuse for making trout fishing difficult and the business of the angler is to catch fish and not to create so many hazards, complexities and technical problems that solving them becomes more important than the reason for the angler being at the waterside – to catch fish.

Trout, like pike, perch and chub, can be caught by spinning because they are all predators and when they are feeding they will fall to any lure being worked in such a way as to create the flash and vibrations produced by immature or ailing fish swimming erratically. In Scotland and parts of Wales spinning for trout is an accepted method, but most English waters do not allow it. I have caught trout from that delightful little river the Chess by using a spinning rod and small Mepps, but I was a guest of the United States Air Force, which leases a stretch on the outskirts of London, and the American anglers who fished it were not adept at the fly caster's art, preferring the spinner.

In Ireland, trolling for the large wild brown trout in the huge loughs is probably the only worth-while method that gives the angler much of a chance to cover the acres of water stretching before him. Towed behind the boat the lure has to be worked fairly deep, down to where the big ones lie. At the same time, there is another style with much more refinement and delicacy and one which can be highly successful in the right weather conditions. This is dapping, an old, old technique which uses the breeze to waft a light line and winged artificial out so that it bobbles and bounces along on the surface film, exactly like the dancing of a dragon-fly or another of the water-loving winged insects. As the dimples and rings made by the dapped fly come into the trout circle of vision the fish is drawn to the surface and, hopefully, induced to take. Many fine Irish trout have fallen to this elegant and classic style of fly fishing.

The enclosed waters of the South West, unlike the grey monotony of some of the concrete reservoirs elsewhere, are really delightful places, with the most beautiful scenery to offset what can sometimes be a fruitless day so far as fishing is concerned. Even though the haversack may not carry the limit bag of trout at the end of the day the very atmosphere of a place such as Blagdon means that pleasing memories are nearly as acceptable. Blagdon, near Cheddar, Somerset, is a special place for me. At the beginning of the trout season its bays and inlets are lined with the most gorgeous spring flowers and the wildlife too has a fascination of its own. I have stood, casting hopefully towards the place where I spotted a feeding trout, then looked down to see an adder swimming slowly past my waders.

There is also a very different kind of trout fishing. In the South and West of England most fly fishermen think – and dream – of the giants waiting to be hooked in the glamorous rivers and reservoirs, but travel a mile or so across the border into Scotland or Wales and the trout fishing becomes a very different matter. In mountainous country there are no grand, exclusive waters, except of course those great salmon rivers such as the Tay, Spey, Dee, Wye and a few others.

The mountain trout streams are usually small, rushing burns and brooks and the angler who fishes them has to be content with the trout they support. I have memories of fishing some beautiful burns, nowhere more than a yard or two across, among the lava-moulded hills of Skye and being delighted with a few fat 8oz trout full of shrimp and whose taste was incomparably sweeter than any pellet-fed two-pounder from the South.

Then there is the sea trout, a migratory version of the brown trout. Those who seek this powerful and doughty fighter in the estuaries while the fish are running upstream from the sea, operate mostly during the darkest of nights. These anglers insist that the sea trout is worthy of their entire fishing time and that no other species compares.

Even today, the average angler does not experience salmon fishing unless he lives in the vicinity of a river which has a run of the species, or unless he can afford the very considerable expense of this branch of the sport. It still costs a good deal of money for a rod on one of the noted salmon rivers, and many stretches of those are highly exclusive. The money involved includes expensive fishing gear such as double-handled salmon spinning rods, a costly rod licence, the 'right' clothing, fees for good, reliable ghillies, and – again – expensive hotel accommodation. One could spend huge sums and never see let alone hook a salmon. Not that this will deter the determined angler intent on having the chance to hook and play to the waiting ghillie one of the world's great sporting fishes.

Wet fly lines

A few decades ago wet flies were a quirk of regional game fishing: now a whole range of purpose-made lines has festooned the market and the wet fly fisher must buy intelligently

In the days when the only fly lines available to the game fisherman were of dressed silk, considerable time and trouble had to be expended to maintain or renew the oils and soft substances used in the dressing to ensure that the line remained waterproof and would continue to float on every outing.

This was particularly important for the correct presentation of the floating fly—the order of the day on very many fisheries, particularly the Southern chalk streams. In other parts of the country, fishing a sunken fly was perfectly acceptable, and many anglers discovered that they could work their sunken flies more effectively if the line dressing wore off, resulting in a waterlogging of the line and so, slow sinking.

Plastic-coated fly lines
In recent years the development of plastic-coated fly lines has proceeded apace, offering the angler a very wide choice of line profiles at varying densities. These have enabled him to fish efficiently in any water, no matter at what depth the trout (or salmon) might be feeding.

ICI Fluon coated lines have very little friction, and as a result they shoot through the rod rings positively, enabling long, effortless casts to be made. Such a line handles extremely well, and its flexibility is unaffected by cold conditions—a most important plus during winter fishing. Coated lines are available in a variety of colours. A light coloured one, particularly white when viewed from below, is less visible to the fish as it blends well against the light of the sky. From the fisherman's point of view a light floater makes it easier to see all takes, which is essential for consistent success.

Fly lines are given an AFTM (Association of Fishing Tackle Manufacturers) number. This makes it possible to match a line perfectly with a fly rod carrying a similar number itself. The AFTM number is based on the weight in grains of the first 30 feet of line.

Lines are also coded: F—floating; S—sinking; I—intermediate; WF —weight forward; DT—double taper; SH—shooting head; L—level. The selection of the correct line profile is dictated by necessity. Where casting range is short, and delicacy and accuracy essential, the correct choice will be the double taper profile or the single taper lines offered by some manufacturers. After all, if one is talking about casting a maximum distance of some 15 yards, there seems little point in loading with a line twice that length.

The use of half a double taper line, attached to a backing of nylon monofilament or braided Terylene, reduces the size of reel needed, which, in turn, reduces the weight at the butt end of the rod, leading to more efficient and comfortable casting. It should not be overlooked that half a fly line costs proportionately less than a full one, whether one purchases from a cooperative dealer, or simply buys a full line and shares it with a friend.

Forward taper line
Where longer casting is required, or the water is very deep or fast moving, the forward taper line is preferable. This has the casting weight at the forward end—hence the name—while the rest of the length is made up of fine 'running line'. Forward taper lines vary in length, ranging from the 30 yard standard up to 40 yards or more.

The shooting head is simply a variation upon the forward taper theme, whereby the actual fly line is restricted in length to that needed to give the rod the correct action —usually between 7-12 yards. This short section is spliced to the backing line, generally of nylon monofilament, which can have a circular or oval cross-section. The latter section is far more resistant to tangling, which is possibly the only disadvantage of monofilament as a backing material. This particular set-up of shooting head and monofilament backing is ideally suited to such long-distance casting techniques as the 'double haul', enabling experienced practitioners to cast 50 yards or more with accuracy and comparative ease.

A further benefit is conferred upon the angler hooking a fish at long range, or in very deep water, namely that the fly line is, by its very nature, relatively thick, offering considerable resistance to the water. Thus, there is a risk when using a full line and playing a fish at long range that the pressure exerted by the water against the line can pull the hook clean out or even cause the leader to break. This risk is greatly minimized by the use of a short line and fine backing.

'Torpedo' and 'long belly'
Just as the shooting head is merely a variation upon the forward taper profile, so are there other variations, such as the 'torpedo' taper and the 'long belly', although the principle remains virtually the same in every case. That section of the line which carries the weight necessary to action the rod correctly and enable efficient casting is found towards one end of the line, so that the line is no longer reversible, which is the case with the double taper.

Manufacturers have developed their own specific descriptions for the line densities now produced, and in order not to confuse the issue for newcomers to fly fishing, it is probably as well to discuss individually the densities in common use, offering brief comments on the function of each in turn.

Floating lines
Floating lines are ideal for the presentation of sunken flies which require little 'working' through the water, or require to be worked very

close to the surface, either in stillwater or gently flowing rivers. The depth at which a sunken fly can be fished in stillwater is restricted by the length of the leader—on average some 3-4 yards. It takes quite a long time for an unweighted nymph to sink to that depth, and when trout are feeding close to the bed of a lake, it is common practice to use a dressing containing lead to speed the sink.

On the other hand, where the fish are feeding off the bottom, application of floatant to the leader will ensure that the nymph does not sink too deep. Sometimes, when the fish are feeding and sporting at the surface—and this is particularly common in reservoirs—a lure is fished on a floating line, stripped back so quickly that it skips across the surface, creating a definite wake.

Neutral density lines
Neutral density lines are the modern equivalent of the old silk line, requiring the application of a floatant if they are to be used as a floating line,

A selection of wet fly lines currently on sale in any large tackle shop.

or used untreated as a slow sinking line. The main advantage of this line was that a suitable length of the tip could be left ungreased, allowing it to sink, and enabling a sunk fly to be fished at greater depth than would be possible with a standard floater. This has now been superseded by the sink tip line.

This is carefully manufactured so that the tip, which sinks at medium rate, is adequately supported by the floating body of the line. When fishing a nymph in deepish water, the 'take' is readily signalled by a movement of the floating section. It is equally efficient at indicating a take 'on the drop' (as the fly sinks), and with its use a faster retrieve of the nymph, fly or lure is possible than with the full floating line, because the pattern in use will not rise to the surface as readily as with the floater. This type of line can be very effective in deeper, or medium-flowing rivers, where it is important that depth is achieved quickly and maintained, or in stillwaters where the margins are full of snags which would tend to foul a full sinker. Some anglers claim to find difficulty in casting a sink tip line because of the imbalance between the dense tip and the less dense body, but this can usually be overcome by practice.

Slow sinking lines

With slow sinking lines, the term 'slow' can vary in meaning from manufacturer to manufacturer, because there has never been standardization of terms in this context, but matters seem to be improving, with many firms now offering a full range of densities, so that if a slow sinker is purchased from a range which includes medium and fast sinkers the angler is on safe ground.

The use of a slow sinker does not greatly differ from that of a sink tip, in that it can be used to take fish 'on the drop', or at slow to medium speed retrieve in stillwaters, and in the medium-running or deeper rivers. Nymphs can be fished on slow sinkers, but more commonly the larger wet flies and lures are used. The take of a fish is signalled, as with all sinking lines, by that familiar tug transmitted to the retrieving hand.

392

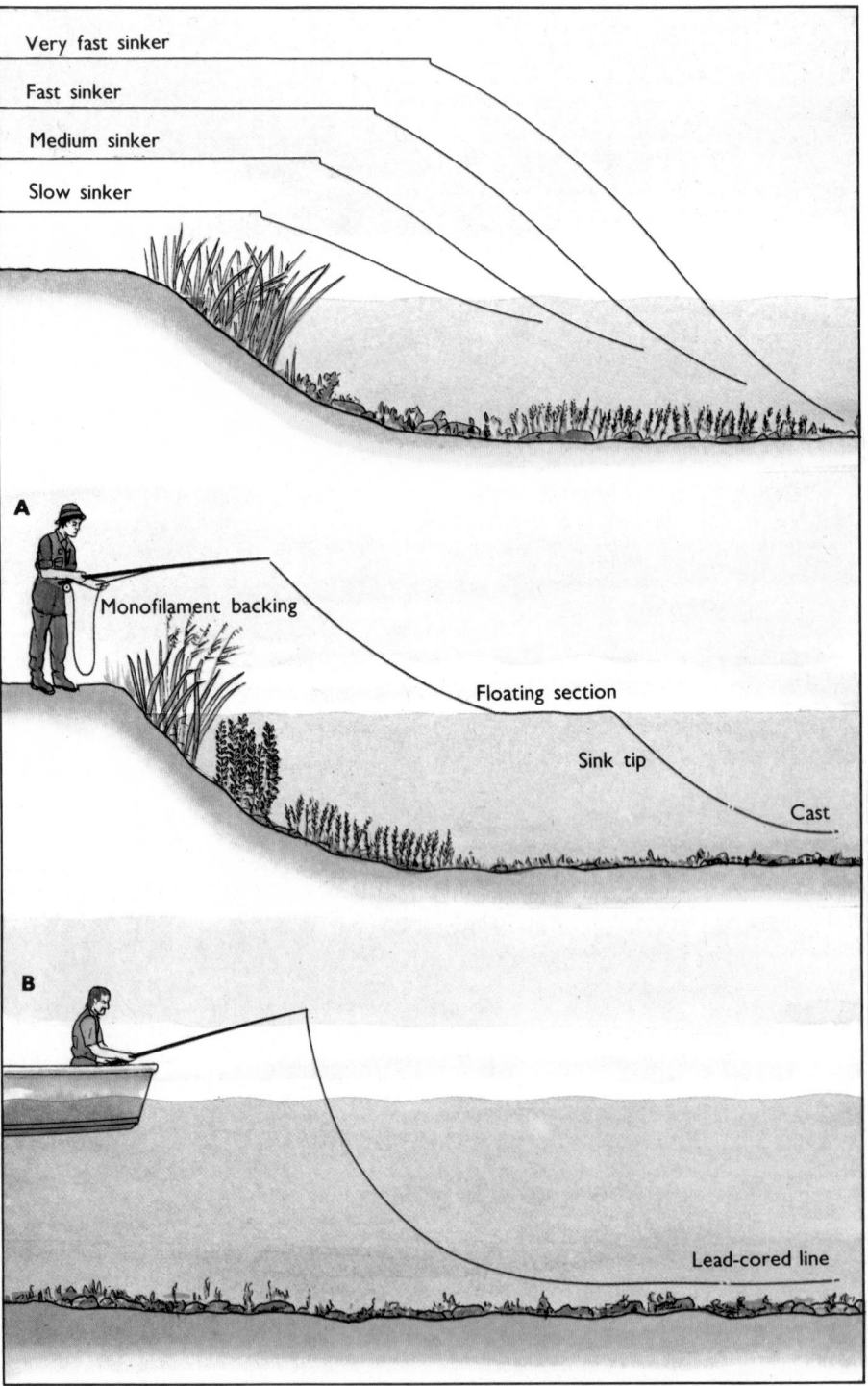

Medium sinking lines
Medium sinkers, as may be expected, sink faster than the slow sinkers, and are therefore more suited to deeper or faster-flowing water, and to faster than medium speed retrieves. However, with maximum speed lure stripping, the lure itself will rise very close to the surface, which can be an advantage especially when the fish are working in the upper levels but demand a fast moving lure which does not break the surface.

Fast sinking lines
Fast sinkers enable fast working of a fly in deep water and ensure that no matter how fast the retrieve, the lure will be unlikely to rise above midwater. Obviously they are well suited to the fast-flowing rivers

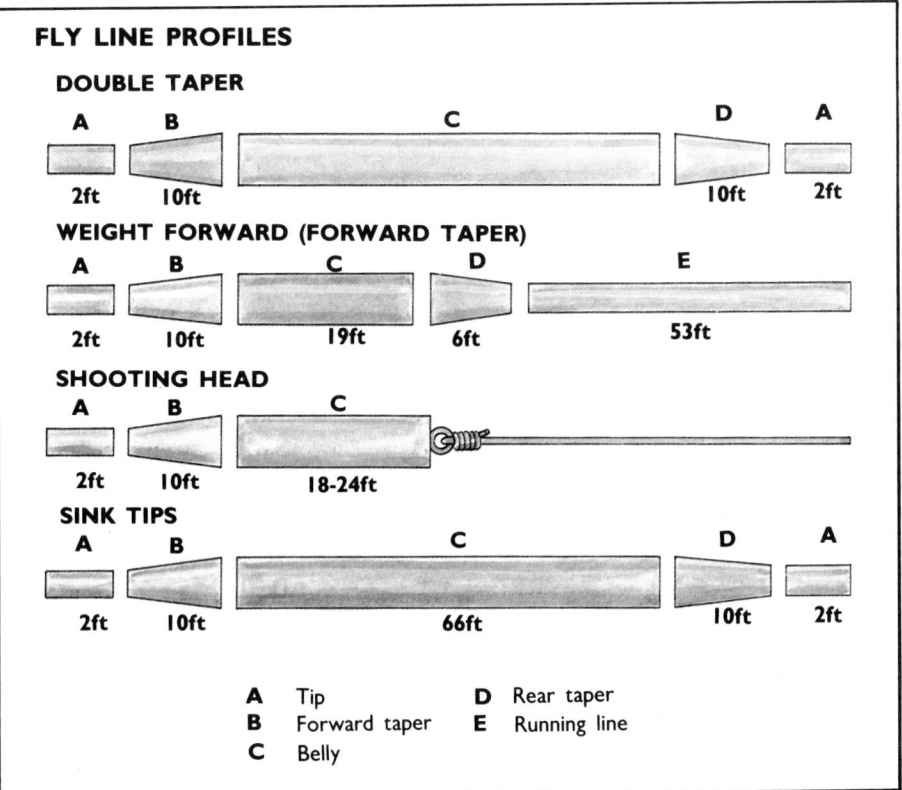

FLY LINE PROFILES

DOUBLE TAPER

A — 2ft
B — 10ft
C
D — 10ft
A — 2ft

WEIGHT FORWARD (FORWARD TAPER)

A — 2ft
B — 10ft
C — 19ft
D — 6ft
E — 53ft

SHOOTING HEAD

A — 2ft
B — 10ft
C — 18-24ft

SINK TIPS

A — 2ft
B — 10ft
C — 66ft
D — 10ft
A — 2ft

A Tip
B Forward taper
C Belly
D Rear taper
E Running line

Left: *Most fly fishermen, unable to afford the full range of lines available, either opt for a medium sinker in the hope of it serving most purposes, or choose one to suit the particular conditions on the water they most often fish—a fast-sinker, for example, for a large, snaggy gravel pit.*

where the trout or salmon are taking fairly deep.

Very fast sinking lines

Very fast sinkers are fairly specialized lines, often carrying lead in the core. By their nature they are ideal for the very deepest reservoirs, lakes and lochs where the quarry is feeding deep, and where it is important that a lure stripped quickly does not rise much above the bottom. Similarly, they are ideal for the biggest, fastest-flowing rivers, enabling the angler to remain in close touch with his fly throughout every cast. In a big stillwater where the bed snags the fly regularly on slower retrieves, it is a useful dodge to shorten the leader, and attach a dressing incorporating buoyancy material, such as Ethafoam, so that the fly floats up off the bottom clear of the snags, allowing retrieval to be slowed right down.

Lead-cored lines

There is one other type of line coming into use for fishing the deepest reservoirs and lakes—the level lead-cored line, without doubt the fastest sinker of all. This is not used for normal sunken fly fishing, but for trolling behind a boat which may be drifting, or propelled by oars or even a motor, depending upon local rules and regulations.

The purpose of the exercise is to drag the largest size of lure at a steady speed across the bottom, in the hope of attracting those very large trout which have adopted a bottom-feeding existence. It could be argued that this is not true fly fishing, being merely a minor variation on spinning tactics, but the fact is that a form of fly is being used, and so it really is a branch of fly fishing, although unorthodox.

Lead core line is offered by several leading manufacturers in 100 yard or metre spools. The American-made Trolling Line is used principally for saltwater trolling for game fish. The average cost of such a spool is between £8 and £10, which makes it an extremely cheap way of obtaining what is almost equivalent to three full fly lines.

Are the diameters of floating and sinking lines the same?
No. The sinker has a much thinner profile which enables it to go below the surface of the water quickly.

Which wet fly line weights are most commonly used?
Most of the fishing you are likely to do on English reservoirs and rivers will be served by line weights of between 5 and 10.

What kind of knot is used most to join line and cast?
The needle knot. A small hole is made in the end of the fly line into which the end of a monofil cast is forced, until it emerges through the wall of the fly line. A whipping is then made to fasten the two together. It produces a very neat knot, which will pass through the small rings of a fly rod quite easily.

What are the advantages of a fly reel with a perforated drum?
It keeps the fly line and backing well aired: consequently it will not become mouldy. However, if the tackle is to be laid up for any length of time it is nevertheless good policy to remove the line and thoroughly wipe it dry.

Will I need a special rod to fish a wet fly line?
Generally speaking the same rod will do for either wet or dry fly fishing. If you can afford another rod exclusively for wet fly fishing, however, be sure to choose one that is strong enough to cope with yards of sunken line.

Fly lines

Good fly lines are expensive, but won't catch good fish unless you're prepared to expend more care in teaming them with backing, leader and point, and more time on maintaining them

The Hardy Flyweight reel takes DT-4-F—double-taper floating line No 4—with no backing.

In the early days of fly fishing, lines were made of plaited horsehair. This was later replaced by a lighter mixture of horsehair and silk, then by pure silk, plaited, tapered and dressed (impregnated and coated) with linseed oil.

The oil-dressed silk line was in universal use for three-quarters of a century, until it was replaced by the modern plastic-coated fly lines which consist of a plaited Dacron core with a coating of polyvinyl chloride (PVC). For sinking fly lines, the PVC is impregnated with powdered metal, the quantity used determining the rate at which the line sinks through the water.

Plasticizer

PVC is a hard material unless it contains a suitable 'plasticizer', which is introduced during manufacture.

The commonest cause of trouble with modern fly lines is loss of plasticizer from the PVC coating. This loss goes on all the time, but certain factors can accelerate it greatly. The use of grease, other than one of the special kinds that themselves contain plasticizer, will

394

draw plasticizer out of the PVC very quickly, as will the various liquids intended to make dry-flies waterproof, should they get on the fly line.

Some of these waterproofing liquids are sold in aerosol cans, and special care should be taken when using them, to ensure that the line is not sprayed.

Another cause of plasticizer loss is leaving reel and line in hot places, such as a car parcel shelf exposed to bright sunshine, in glove pockets adjacent to car heaters, in cupboards near radiators or fires, and so on. There is little risk of ill effects from simply fishing on hot days, since the line is constantly being cooled by the water, but many a line has been ruined by being left in a closed car standing in the sun.

Fortunately it can be restored by the use of special replasticizing grease such as 'Permaplas'. But, if too much plasticizer has already been lost, the line coating becomes hard and cracks. Once that has hap-

pened there is nothing that can be done to repair the damage.

A wide variety of line is now available, identified by a code know as the AFTM (Association of Fishing Tackle Manufacturers) system. This code tells you the kind of taper the line has, the weight of the first 30ft of the line, and whether the line is a floating or a sinking one.

So-called 'level lines' are of the same thickness all along their length; they are little used and their only merit is that they are cheap. They are designated by the letter L.

Double taper lines

'Double taper lines', designated DT, have both their ends tapered for more than 10ft, giving a fine end which falls more lightly on the water. The idea of a double taper is that when one end is worn, you can reverse the line on your reel and use the other. These lines usually come in lengths of 90ft.

'Forward taper lines', otherwise known as 'weight-forward' (WF) resemble the first 30ft or so of a double taper with 40ft of very fine fly line attached. (In fact there is no actual attachment, both core and coating are continuous.) This allows more line to be 'shot' through the rings when casting. Recently, lines have been introduced with the first, heavier part longer than 30ft. These are called 'long belly lines'.

'Shooting heads' are similar in principle to 'forward taper lines', but instead of the fine shooting line being a continuation of the PVC—coated fly line, it consists of nylon monofilament attached to the fly line by a special knot. This allows even more line to be 'shot' in casting, and as the fly line is usually cut from a double taper, shooting heads are much cheaper than either double or forward taper lines.

Shooting heads

Good tackle shops will usually sell halves or 'double tapers' for making shooting heads, which will need a further reduction in length, usually to 30-36ft.

All these lines can be of different floating or sinking qualities. There are floaters, slow sinkers, medium sinkers and fast sinkers, as well as floating lines with sinking tips. They are all available in a range of weights, numbered 3 to '12. The more powerful your rod, the heavier the line it will need.

Let us look at some examples of coding. A line coded DT-7-F is a double-tapered floating line, weight No 7. A WF-9-S is a forward taper sinking line, weight No 9 and so on.

The reason why the weight number refers to the first 30ft or so of the line, is that 30ft is about as much as an average fly caster can control when he whips the line back and forth in false-casting. Good casters can handle more, but in practical fishing there is no advantage in having more than about 45ft, which only very good casters can handle.

When you buy a rod you will find that its maker has specified what size line it will carry. Remember that this refers to 30ft of line in the air. If your rod has a recommendation of No 7 line, that means it will work nicely when you are switching 30ft of line in the air.

Short casting
If the kind of fishing you do involves mainly short casting, and you seldom have more than 24ft in the air, you will do better with the heavier No 8 line. If, on the other hand, you often put 35ft or more into the air, then you should use a lighter line.

For dry fly and nymph fishing, floating lines are used: the sinking lines are mainly for lake and reservoir fishing when wet flies and lures of various kinds are needed. Slow sinkers sink at a rate of about 1ft in 7 seconds: medium sinkers 1ft in 5 seconds: fast sinkers, or as they are sometimes called, 'Hi-D' lines sink about 1ft in 3 seconds. By counting the seconds after casting, you can decide how deep you allow your line to sink before starting the retrieve. This useful ploy is also used when the angler is spinning, but of course the rate of sinking is considerably faster due to the weight of the lure.

Backing line
For most kinds of fly fishing, your fly line needs backing: that is, some monofilament or braided, uncoated line is wound on to the reel first, and then the coated fly line is attached to it. Flattened monofilament of about 25lb b.s., or special monofilament sold for backing purposes, is cheaper than braided backing line, and easier to connect to fly lines.

Monofilament backing line is attached to the fly line with a needle-knot. The same knot can be used to tie a short piece of ordinary round-section monofilament to the other end of the fly line, to which in turn the tapered leader (cast) is knotted with a three-turn blood knot or a Double Grinner knot. All these knots are very secure, and have the advantage of being able to pass easily through the rod rings.

The pale coloured lines are easier

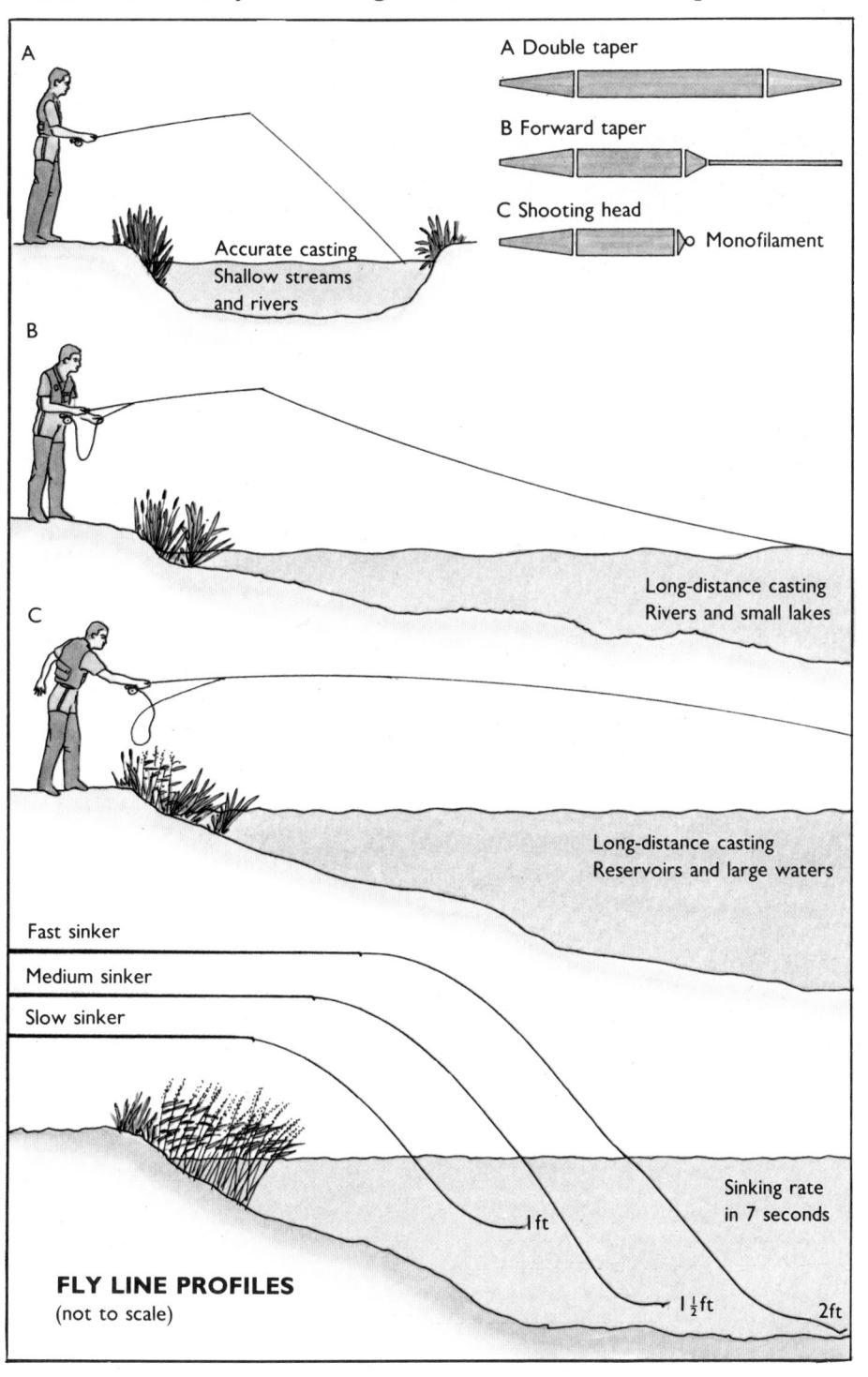

A Double taper

B Forward taper

C Shooting head — Monofilament

A — Accurate casting — Shallow streams and rivers

B — Long-distance casting — Rivers and small lakes

C — Long-distance casting — Reservoirs and large waters

Fast sinker

Medium sinker

Slow sinker

1 ft

1½ ft

2ft

Sinking rate in 7 seconds

FLY LINE PROFILES
(not to scale)

Left: When to use the three different line profiles, and relative rates of sinking lines.

395

ASK THE EXPERT

Can you use both ends of a double taper and thereby save money?

Yes and no. Few anglers reverse a DT line because they find that after a season's fishing or two it has become kinky—usually the result of having been wrongly stored on the reel. The beginner, however, may ruin a line in just one season. If this happens then it is perfectly possibly to use it again by reversing it.

What weight should I use when practising casting?

Absolute beginners will find it quicker to learn using a heavy line, such as an AFTM9. But having learnt the basics, you should try very hard to reduce the number. So don't buy 9—you should only need it for a few hours. Try and borrow one.

Does it matter whether backing line is oval or round in section?

Oval backing is far more resistant to tangling—the main disadvantage of monofilament as a backing material.

What colour should sinking lines be?

They should be—and usually are—either brown or green. The reason why fluorescent orange floaters are becoming more and more popular and accepted is because it is designed to 'invade' the fishes' territory.

I have bought a fly line in a sale. Is it likely to be defective?

If it has been lying around exposed to sunlight for some time it may have lost its plasticity. This, however, can be remedied by simply coating it generously with a plasticising agent. Wipe off the surplus after a couple of hours and the line will be fine.

Above: *Lines and line preparations.*
Left: *At end of season, store lines in loose coils and never leave them on the reel: permanent twists will otherwise develop.*

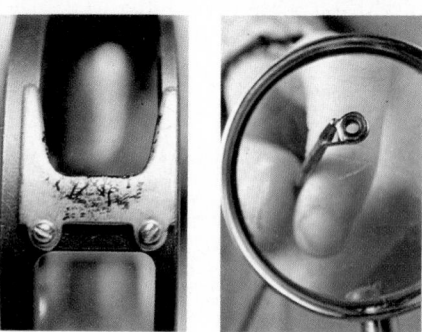

Above left: *Beware of damaged line guards. A layer of ink will highlight any cracks.*
Above right: *Use a magnifying glass to check rod rings or run a pin round inside.*

to see against dark reflections, but harder to see against a ripple or a bright reflection. In certain conditions, such as in bright sunshine or against a dark background of rocks or trees, pale lines being false-cast in the air can scare fish. When lying on the water's surface all lines viewed from below look dark, regardless of their actual colour.

Damaged rod rings, grooved by abrasive matter or with cracked centres, can destroy lines, and these rings should be checked regularly and replaced if defective. Avoid dropping loose line on to sand or gravel, or anywhere involving the risk of its being trodden on with nailed boots or waders.

Good fly lines are expensive; they deserve care.

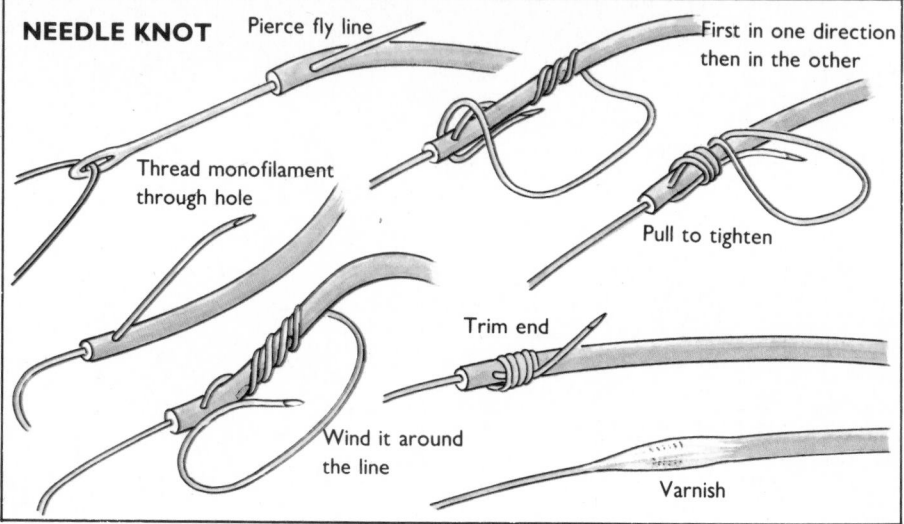

NEEDLE KNOT
Pierce fly line
First in one direction then in the other
Thread monofilament through hole
Pull to tighten
Trim end
Wind it around the line
Varnish

Fly casting

To many coarse anglers, the sight of a fly fisherman casting is tinged with awe. Yet if you follow a few simple rules and take expert advice, casting a fly need not be difficult

The technique of fly casting was described by Izaak Walton like this: 'In casting your line, do it always before you, so that your fly may, first, fall upon the water and as little of your line with it, as is possible'. This advice, in *The Compleat Angler,* is as true today as it was in 1653. The aim is to present the artificial fly to the fish in as natural a way as possible. This means that it must alight on the water in imitation of the natural insect, creating that small spreading ripple which induces the fish to take. But fly casting is a practical skill, very difficult to illustrate as a single, flowing motion. It is not a difficult skill to learn once the basic requirements are understood.

The basic problem

It is important to understand that there is only one basic problem and therefore only one real mistake to be made in fly casting. The problem is that you must make the fly rod do the work, and not your arm. The rod must be made to act as a spring in order to propel a virtually weightless object, the fly, through the air. The function of the spring is

Above: *A fly casting demonstration.*
Below: *With the line going out, the caster is making the final throw with the rod held in the nine o'clock position. The secret of good casting is not to move the rod back beyond the one o'clock position or forward beyond the eleven o'clock position before making your final cast.*

Back Cast
Lift the rod to A, bringing line off the water. In one movement, bring the rod back to the one o'clock position at B. The rod is now fully flexed, ready for the forward cast.

Forward Cast
Bring the rod smartly forward, stopping it at the 11 o'clock position C. The line will straighten ready for the final throw.

Back Cast
Viewed from above, the arm can be seen to move to the right, giving a slightly convex curve to the back cast.

Forward Cast
For the forward cast, the arm must be kept close to the body keeping the rod straight.

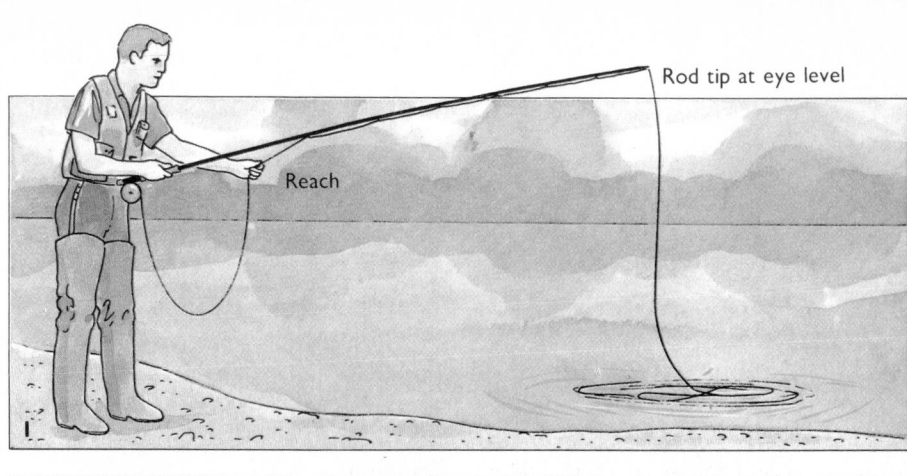

Rod tip at eye level

Reach

Pull

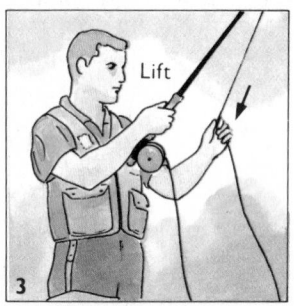

Lift

Stop

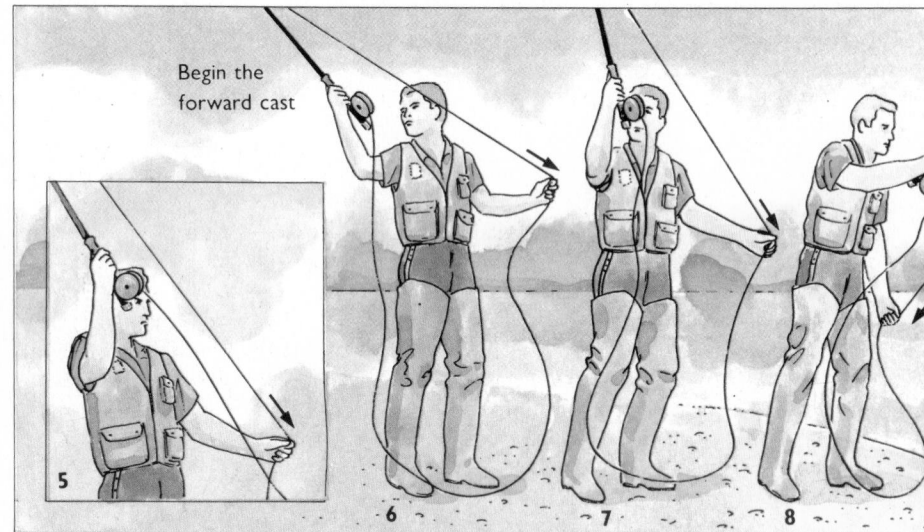

Begin the forward cast

to store up energy, and then release it when required. This can be understood in terms of two simple arm movements, which are equivalent to the loading and unloading of the spring.

The back cast
The action of fly casting, simply described, is that the line is lifted from the water by the rod and briskly thrown back behind the caster. This is called the 'back cast'. There

is a pause while the line streams out and straightens behind the caster, who prevents the rod from straying back beyond the vertical by thumb pressure on the top of the handle. In that essential pause, the line, while streaming out behind the caster, is also pulling back the rod tip, making the whole rod flex. The rod and line are then driven forward again on the 'forward cast'. This flexing of the rod is the equivalent of a spring being wound up.

The base of the spring, in this case, is the butt of the rod. As with all springs, the base has to be locked firmly, or its energy will leak away. The locking action is achieved by the 'stopping' of the wrist at the point when the rod butt is roughly level with the ear during the back cast. The wrist is locked and as it is dragged back by the power applied to the

back cast and the weight of the pulling line, the rod is forced to flex.

Wrist movement
The role of the wrist is actually far more complex than this necessarily simplified description of a cast. Experienced fly casters use wrist movement and virtually nothing else to control the rod and line, both in basic overhead casting and in other kinds of cast. Beginners should concentrate on stopping the wrist from following the rod backwards, as it would naturally do. If this is allowed to happen energy will not be stored in the base of the rod. This means that the angler will have to compensate for the lack of energy in the rod by applying extra muscular power to the forward cast. This in turn will lead to a weak or lazy back cast, simply because it becomes unnecessary to have a strong one.

Correctly done, fly casting will seem to require little effort or have little power behind it but will have maximum results, that is, the angler will be able to cast a long way without feeling tired. It is correct to say that if the casting arm is tired after half an hour, then there is something wrong with the angler's casting technique.

Use the spring—not force
Really good fly line casters are extremely rare, and the gap between the standard of their performance and that of the average fly fisherman is enormous. Many fly fishermen with years of experience do not use their fly rod as a spring. They use force instead, but nevertheless believe that they are casting correctly because they can send the line some distance. In Britain there seems to be very little interest in casting as a separate, important part of fly fishing. There are fly-tying clubs but casting clubs usually fail for lack of support. Most anglers seem reluctant to learn from an expert and seem quite happy to go on casting in a haphazard fashion.

It is important to have several lessons with a professional instructor as this allows the student to gain a natural technique based on direct observation.

The technique of fly casting has

Bring rod down to 11 o'clock position

Basic fly casting for reservoir trouting
1 *Strip about six yards of line from the reel and work it through the rod rings.* 2 *Begin the back cast with the rod tip held roughly at eye level.* 3 *Lift the rod sharply upwards, making sure that line is not pulled through the rings by the surface tension of the water.* 4 *Continue the back cast to* 5, *pulling line with the left hand.* 6 *With the rod stopped at the one o'clock position, the spring of the rod stores energy.* 7 *Begin the forward cast. Pull line while driving rod forward to increase speed.* 8 *Energy stored in the rod is released.* 9 *When the pull through the rod is felt, release line to shoot through and unfurl.* 10 *Lower rod to nine o'clock position.* 11 *The fly gently glides on to the surface of the water.*

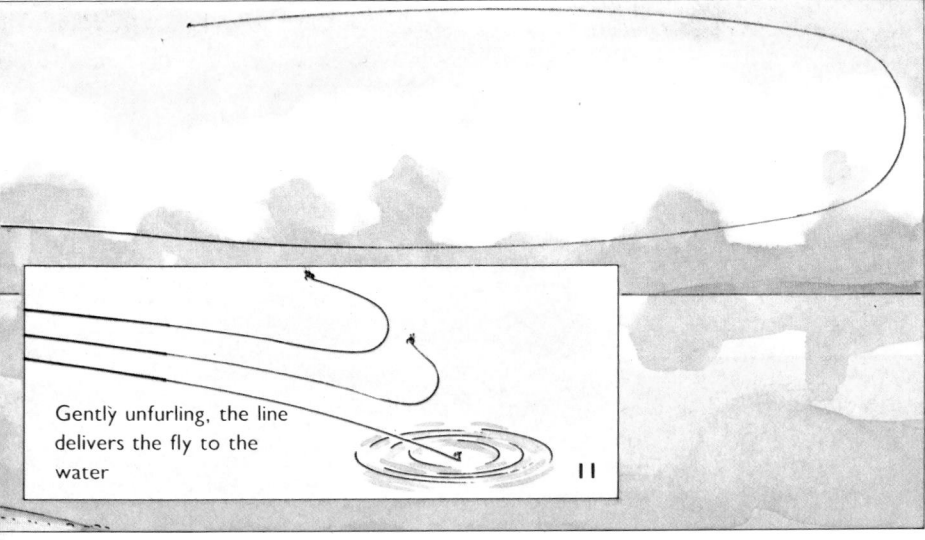

Gently unfurling, the line delivers the fly to the water

ASK THE EXPERT

What basic tackle do I need before I can begin to fish reservoirs for trout?
An inexpensive $8\frac{1}{2}$-$9\frac{1}{2}$ft glassfibre rod—light but with a whippy action—is fine for the novice. The fly reel need not be expensive either, but must give you rim control with the hand holding the rod. To begin with, content yourself with a forward-taper floating line—ask the dealer which weight will match the rod he had sold you. Mount this on 100 yards of 20lb backing line (nylon). Attach a 2ft monofil leader then a cast of tapering strengths: 9lb, 7lb and finally 5lb b.s. Then all you have to do is choose a fly!

Can I learn the rudiments of fly casting without paying too much?
Many local authority adult education centres run evening classes in casting as well as fly tying and rod building. Ask at your library for a prospectus.

My fly line falls repeatedly and infuriatingly in a heap at my feet when I try to cast. What an I doing wrong?
The fault lies—as most casting faults do—in hurrying the final movement. You are starting the forward cast before the back cast has had time to straighten out. The other symptom of the same mistake is a mid-air whipcrack which sends your fly spinning into the bushes.

Can I practise away from the water?
Yes. A lawn or any close-cropped field will do. Place markers on the ground to help you judge accuracy and distance of your casting. Fit the fly line with a length of monofilament to prevent the tip from fraying, and cut off the point and barb of an old fly hook.

Wherever possible it is better to cast from the bank, as this angler is doing, rather than wade into the water and risk scaring away the fish in the swim.

been shown many times as a series of frozen poses, each one illustrating where the angler's arm, wrist, or the line, should be at a given moment. But it must be stressed that the action of the fly rod and line is a fluid motion which should comprise one graceful arm movement. Any errors picked up and not corrected immediately by a teacher could easily become a habit. If you practise the wrong technique several times and become used to it, it will be very hard to correct later. Rather than focusing on the errors and trying to correct them one at a time, you would probably have to start from the beginning again, because the process must be learnt as a whole rather than broken up into stages. It is a mistaken approach to teach or

learn such a technique on the basis of correcting errors, since concentrating on only one small part of the casting routine will cause it to lose its fluidity and be broken up.

In spite of its importance as a technique to be mastered, casting is a means to catch fish, and not an end in itself. Where the fly lands on the water is an essential part of the skill: for example, successful reservoir fishing often depends on the ability to throw a very long line. But wherever you fish, accuracy of casting is vital. Right from the beginning of your tuition in fly casting, aim to reach the fish. Accuracy will enable you to do that.

In recent years fly fishing has lost much of the mystique with which it was once surrounded and is now enjoyed by many reservoir anglers. Though deplored by many purists, this trend does offer the newcomer an opportunity of developing his skills and also of landing a big fish.

Wet fly fishing

Bloody Butchers and Cardinals, Alexandras and Zulus—all wet flies, designed to be fished below the surface of the water. Here we describe the basic techniques of wet fly fishing

Wet fly fishing is, quite simply, the art of fishing an artificial fly beneath the surface of the water, either in imitation of a natural food item, or as an 'attractor'—a pattern which seems to bear no resemblance to any living creature but which induces a fish to strike at it in curiosity, anger or defence. Patterns referred to as 'nymphs' and 'bugs' usually attempt to imitate specific life forms, although there are more than a few patterns which bear a general resemblance to a number of different creatures and therefore are imitative of a range of natural forms, rather than one specific form.

Traditional wet flies
Traditional wet flies very often tend to fall into the 'attractor' category, bearing no close resemblance to anything in nature. Nevertheless, there are others that imitate, either in colour or shape, living creatures such as small fry or the pupal or larval forms of insects. Of the vast range of lures now available, some are designed to resemble small fry of all manner of species, while others merely suggest small fish by their outline and the way that they move in the water when retrieved correctly. It is probable, however, that the majority are neither shaped nor coloured like small fish or fry, and succeed in catching trout by the attractor principle.

'Point' and 'dropper' flies
The traditional version of wet fly fishing involves the use of a team of three flies, although in times past there are records of anglers using a dozen or more patterns at the same time. A modern wet fly leader has one fly attached to the end of the leader: this is the 'point' fly, and more often than not is a dressing tied to simulate a nymph or bug. Perhaps a yard above the point fly there is a 'dropper', a loose length of nylon projecting from the leader to which the second fly, also called a dropper, is attached. This often tends to be an attractor pattern, like a Bloody Butcher, which some anglers believe to be recognized by the trout as a tiny minnow or stickleback. A yard or so above the dropper is another dropper, to which the 'bob' fly is tied. This usually tends to be a biggish, bushy dressing, such as a Zulu or a Palmer, which bounces across the surface of the water when retrieved.

Standard tactics when river fishing are to commence at the upstream end of the beat, casting upstream at an angle of 45°, allowing the line to sweep around with the current, and lifting off again when the line forms an angle of 45° downstream. After each retrieve, the angler moves a yard or so downstream and repeats the process. This is virtually the opposite of the dry fly fisherman's tactics, since he will normally prefer to work upstream, so it is easy to understand why there is conflict between the two schools of thought.

Modern practice
Of course, there is no reason why the wet fly exponent cannot adopt the tactic of working upstream, and modern practice is very often to use just one fly on the leader—the point fly, in fact—and follow exactly the same tactics as the dry fly purist —working upstream and casting

Wet fly fishing in a New Forest stream. Normal tactics are to start at the upstream end and work methodically downstream.

only to an observed fish. In such cases, the selected fly will almost always be a sound copy of a natural life form, preferably one which exists in good numbers in the particular fishery. Specific nymph copies can be excellent, as can shrimp patterns. In stillwater fishing, with no current to work the flies, the angler has to learn to manipulate the flies manually. When fishing from the bank, the choice of a floating line, or one or other of the sinking lines is the same as it is on the river. Whereas line selection on the river, however, may be dictated more by current speed than any

other factor, on stillwaters the final selection may well be dictated by the depth of water in front of the angler, the depth at which the trout are feeding, and the speed of the retrieve required to induce a take.

What line to use?

If the trout are taking food close to the surface on slow moving food items, then a floating line and slow retrieve—or no retrieve at all—is indicated, and the take of an interested trout is signalled by a movement of the end of the line. Where the trout are deeper, and only willing to accept a fast-moving ob-

ject, it will be necessary to use a sinking line. The rate of sink depends on the circumstances.

On the larger waters, lure fishing has come into prominence in recent years. Normal practice, almost invariably, is to attach one lure at the point of the leader and cast this out as far as possible by means of the double haul cast. Distances of 50 yards can be achieved with practice using this technique. A sinking line is usually employed, and retrieval tends to be very fast indeed, so fast that it is known as 'stripping'. Occasionally trout are willing to accept a lure stripped across the surface

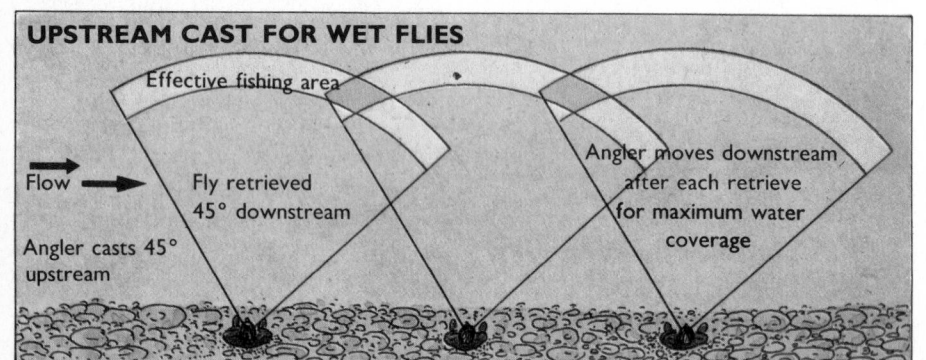

UPSTREAM CAST FOR WET FLIES

Effective fishing area

Flow

Angler casts 45° upstream

Fly retrieved 45° downstream

Angler moves downstream after each retrieve for maximum water coverage

Left: The upstream cast. Below left: A classic composition: the fish is a 5lb 3oz rainbow trout and in the wallet are lures, on the left, and nymphs on the right.
Below: This fine rainbow was caught on a pheasant tail nymph, which you can see in the corner of its mouth. Right: When the trout are not feeding on surface insects the nymph can be fished sink-and-draw. Trout feeding on hatching flies might be tempted by using the style shown in the lower picture. Below right: Making your own 'team of three'.

HOW TO MAKE YOUR OWN 'TEAM OF THREE' LEADER

Fly line

Needle knot   Knotless taper 48in
0.020in to 0.012in approx

using a floating line, which creates a pronounced wake behind the lure.

It seems to be less well known that a lure on a sinking line, fished so slowly that it bounces along the bottom, can be very productive, and often leads to the capture of larger trout. Where it is permitted, the static sunken fly can also prove very killing. This involves casting out a fairly heavily dressed lure on a medium sinking line, letting it sink on the bottom, and just waiting for a trout to snap it up. Sometimes the lure will be taken as it sinks, or is picked up off the bottom shortly after it has settled, but on other occasions one has to resort to an occasional short retrieve before allowing it to settle again. The bed of the lake has to be clear of weed and obstructions for this to be successful, and the water should preferably be at least 6ft deep.

Fishing the traditional 'team of three' from a boat can be very exciting. The method is to let the boat drift, casting before you, and retrieving line just fast enough that you keep in touch with your flies as the boat drifts towards them. Often it pays to retrieve faster, so that the bob fly dibbles along the tops of the waves. Sometimes a trout will take

STILLWATER NYMPH FISHING

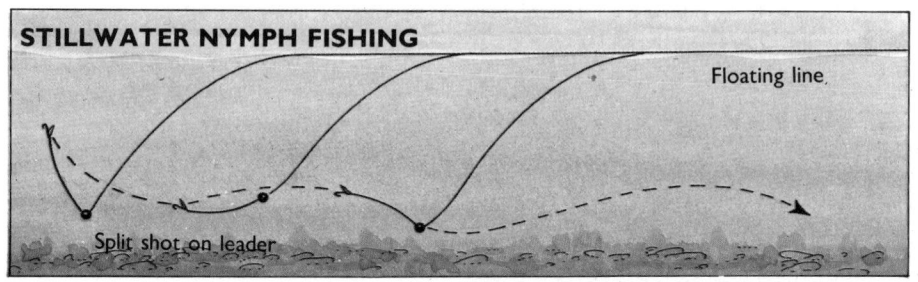

Floating line

Split shot on leader

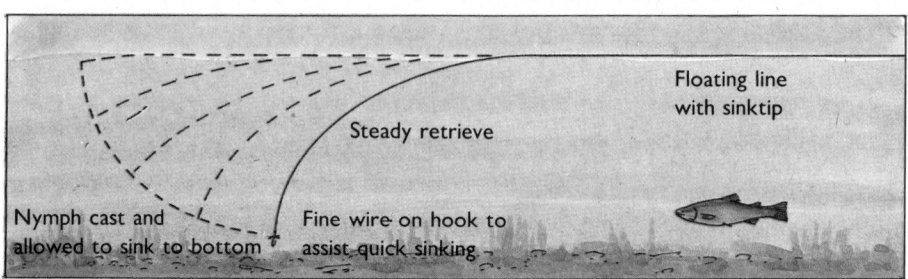

Floating line with sinktip

Steady retrieve

Nymph cast and allowed to sink to bottom

Fine wire on hook to assist quick sinking

THE WATER KNOT

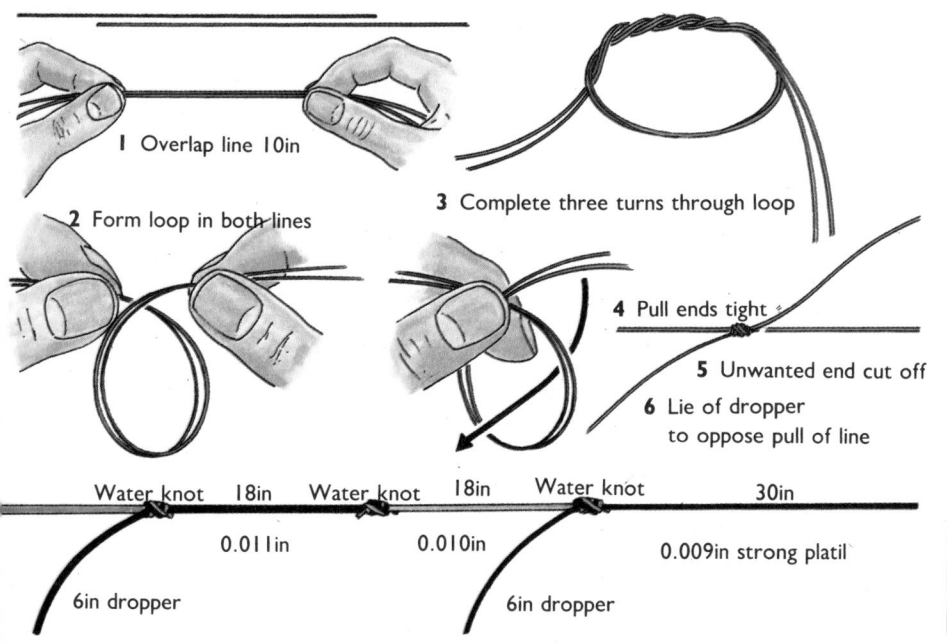

1 Overlap line 10in

2 Form loop in both lines

3 Complete three turns through loop

4 Pull ends tight

5 Unwanted end cut off

6 Lie of dropper to oppose pull of line

Water knot   18in   Water knot   18in   Water knot   30in

0.011in   0.010in   0.009in strong platil

6in dropper   6in dropper

What is a 'dropper'?
The dropper is the length of nylon sticking out at right angles after joining two lengths of line. Alternatively, a fly tied at the end of this length of nylon is also called the dropper. When boat fishing it is quite common to use a cast of three or four flies: the end fly is the 'point' fly, then come the droppers, and the top fly is known as the 'bob' fly.

What is the best time of day to fish for a sea trout?
The best time to fish for them is at night. The rivers sea trout inhabit are usually clear, rocky spate rivers and the water is much too clear for you to compete with the fish's eyesight. Good patterns to use are Peter Ross, Butcher and the Hugh Falkus range of lures.

What is 'false casting'?
That's the name given to lengthening your line while casting without letting the line touch the water.

If I see two rises in the same spot, can I hold one fish responsible for both?
Trout select a place at which they station themselves to wait for the current to bring food within reach. They rise again and again in the same spot and this plays into the hands of the observant angler.

What are 'redds'?
These are holes scooped out of a gravel river bed by a salmon or trout into which it lays its eggs before lightly covering them with a little more gravel.

A good rainbow is netted in the evening glow. Fishing in the evening can be productive, especially after a hot day, during which the fish may have gone down.

his trout, and guess what the trout is feeding on—or likely to feed on. Once the trout has been seen, and the decision made which fly to tie on, the angler casts his nymph or bug to that trout, just as the dry fly anglers does with surface feeding trout.

This type of wet fly fishing is, however, a little more difficult than dry fly fishing because the trout might be feeding 6ft down from the surface and the angler has to be very accurate with his cast, not only to get the distance right, but also to know that his fly will sink fast enough to reach a trout before it moves on to feed elsewhere. If the water is very deep, it may be necessary to use a sink tip line, but usually it is sufficient to use a floating line with a long leader, and perhaps some lead wire added to the artificial fly when it is being dressed.

Salmon and the wet fly

Wet fly fishing for salmon can be grand sport, although usually very expensive. The usual practice is to make long casts across the river, let your fly drift downstream over likely holding areas, and then retrieve slowly. The flies are often very large—larger even than reservoir lures—and mostly look like nothing on earth. Full dressed traditional salmon flies include Dusty Miller, Jock Scott, Durham Ranger and Thunder-and-Lightning. When the water is low much smaller flies are used, with fairly sparse dressing, and indeed, it is probable that some of the more effective reservoir lures have been developed from low water salmon flies.

Low water patterns that have found favour with salmon enthusiasts are Blue Charm and Logie. Such a selection to hand will cover most salmon fishing situations. Although there are always local preferences most of the flies mentioned are also traditional patterns in remote foreign lands. In British Columbia, for example, every tackle shop carries a range similar to that found in England and Scotland. Or fish Nova Scotia's salmon rivers and you will find virtually no difference in the local pattern, size of fly, or techniques employed, from those used in home waters.

the bob fly so close to the boat that the hapless angler is taken completely by surprise.

Drift problems

Lures can be fished very efficiently from a boat, and so can a single fly or nymph, usually on a sinking line. If the boat drifts too quickly this can create difficulties, so the normal practice is to slow down the rate of drift by using a drogue or 'sea anchor'—a cone of heavy canvas attached securely to a spreader ring, and allowed to trail over the side—acting as a brake. Alternatively, anchor the boat in a chosen position and fish exactly as one would from the bank.

Catching the biggest trout from reservoirs and very large lakes can be difficult because of the vast expanse of water that has to be covered. Fortunately, a great many small stillwater fisheries have opened up across the country, and many

of these have the twin attributes of possessing clear water and quite large trout. Usually it is more expensive to buy a day ticket on these small fisheries than it is on the reservoirs, but value for money is obtained because the average size of the fish is larger and the density of stock very much higher. The average angler catches one reservoir trout of about a pound in weight on each visit. On small fisheries the average is usually three trout which weigh more.

Many of the small fisheries have rules banning lure fishing, or the use of more than one fly on the leader. This makes sense because long casting on a small water is hardly ever necessary, and would interfere with the enjoyment of other anglers. Also, it is easier to persuade a good-sized trout to take an imitation of a natural insect than it is to get it to take a gaudy lure. The most successful anglers study the water very carefully, first of all to locate a trout, and secondly to try to see what it is likely to be eating. The more visits an angler makes to a particular water, the easier he finds it to locate

River trout

If you learned your fishing on a reservoir, the sight of river trout can be a disappointment. But once you have hooked a specimen, no stocked water will ever hold the same appeal

AT-A-GLANCE

Specimen sizes
Water and parentage are all-important in determining specimen sizes for brown trout: hatchery-bred fish should weigh 10lb, natural fish betwen 1lb on upland becks and 4lb on rich rivers

Tackle, Bait, Techniques
Rod
Mark IV Avon, reservoir trout fly

Reel
Fixed-spool/fly reel

Line b.s.
6-8lb

Hooks
6-14 spade-end (worms), 10-12 (livebaits)

Baits
Dry fly, wet fly, nymph, Mepps spinner, Devon minnow, fly spoon, marsh worms, lobworm head/tail

Techniques
Dapped or floated dry fly, wet fly, nymph, paternoster spinning, roller ledgering

Arthur Oglesby writes:
First of all, we must ask ourselves what a specimen river trout is.

It might be a fish of double figures bred in a hatchery and released into one of the lush, hallowed sanctuaries of Hampshire's chalk country. But, just as easily, it could be a darkly spotted fish barely touching the pound mark, or a fish born and bred in an upland beck or burn that literally has had to fight for every morsel of food coming its way. In fact, the 1lb beck trout could represent more of a prize than the double-figure leviathan which has been fed and nurtured in a stewpond for most of its feather-bedded life.

Water chemistry
A trout can only become as big as its environment will allow. Alkaline waters, such as the chalkstreams of Hampshire, are much more capable of producing the weed and aquatic insect life on which trout feed, than the acid, upland streams. Water chemistry and temperature have great bearing on the amount of food which will be available to the fish. Those which are to grow to specimen size must also have adequate places of sanctuary.

One great factor to be borne in mind is that, wherever the water, the big fish have not become specimens by being easy to deceive.

Such fish might well have felt the temper of the angler's hook more than once; may even have had a brief excursion into a landing net when they were of inconsequential size. The only reason that they normally acquire specimen notoriety is that they have learned to take great care of themselves. We have to differentiate between recently released hat-

Trevor Housby with a 7½lb brown trout taken from the River Test—perhaps the most famous of trout rivers. The fly is still in its mouth.

chery fish and those which have been in the water since birth or since they were small yearlings.

Although there is much controversy about what constitutes a specimen fish, let us assume, in dealing with river trout, that we are seeking the natural-bred leviathan.

In order to catch a specimen of any species, it is important to know where and when the fish is likely to be found and what, in fact, constitutes a specimen for the particular water concerned.

One eminent game fishing writer once wrote of a well-known trout river that any trout in it of over 2lb was worthless to the fishery. What he meant was that when a fish has acquired such a weight in this particular water it had ceased to rise to the small hatching flies and the facsimiles of them which were being offered by the angler. The principal diet of this fish had become other, smaller, trout. In this way, by taking young fish and depleting the

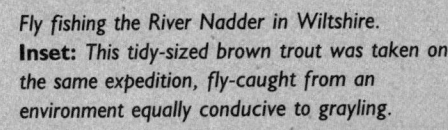

Fly fishing the River Nadder in Wiltshire.
Inset: *This tidy-sized brown trout was taken on the same expedition, fly-caught from an environment equally conducive to grayling.*

larder of other food which potentially sporting fish might take, it worked to the detriment of the fishery rather than being an asset.

Any angler seeking to capture a species of river trout should first ask the question: what does it feed on? Armed with the answer, the angler should then use the food, or an artificial version of it, upon which the fish regularly feeds.

We must decide which methods of capture appeal to us most. It might well be that by limiting ourselves to a fly-only rule we inhibit our chances of catching the real monsters. Certainly, some of the largest trout have been taken on worms, minnows

Why are there so few specimen river trout?
Quite simply, too many are killed before they reach specimen proportions. The growing popularity of the sport leads to more and more pressure on the waters. You can help by returning small fish carefully and paying strict heed to Water Authority size limits.

Where in a river should I look for a big trout?
River trout are territorial. A trout grows to specimen size only when it has chosen for its territory one which provides a good supply of food and affords it security: an undercut bank off a main stream, a channel between weedbeds, the water round a fallen tree—wherever the current concentrates food on the surface or keeps it in suspension. It is true that as soon as a good trout is taken from one of these 'specimen' lairs, another moves in to take its place.

Have you any tip which might help me trick an 'educated' trout into biting?
By the time a trout has grown big, it has met most baits and ruses. The best idea is probably to try something different but something natural to the trout's environment and diet. The minnow, for example, is a much neglected bait and may well be living in the water you choose to fish. Be systematic and patient at all times.

If big trout are cannibals, what is the point of fly fishing for them?
It is fairer to say that *most* big trout are *mainly* cannibalistic. A good evening hatch will bring many really big trout to the surface and give the fisherman using an artificial fly an excellent chance of a specimen catch.

and salmon spinning tackle. But there are times when any fool can catch trout—even specimens—on worms, and this is why many trout fisheries operate a fly-only rule.

We must also decide which species of trout interests us most—rainbow or brown? The diehards among us might decide that the brown trout is the chosen species and that they will limit their activity to the fly. Let us also confine ourselves to this method. Traditionally, this gives us three basic options: the use of the dry fly, the wet fly and the nymph.

The dry fly—dapped or floated —and the nymph offer a slight advantage in that the angler generally sees his fish before he casts to it. This way, we have advance knowledge of the dimensions of our fish and know whether or not it qualifies as a specimen. I recall one devout dry fly angler who devoted an entire season to the capture of one big fish. The fish was generally

408

in the same lie or area of water. Scorning other rising trout, the angler would merely observe his fish until it started feeding, then he would try to catch it. When, in an unguarded moment, the fish finally took his fly, it weighed in at 4lb and was as good a trout as the water had been known to produce.

Following that, he was a slightly disappointed angler, but it was not long before he had located another good fish worthy of attention.

It was the great American angler E R Hewitt, who listed the three stages of the fisherman's development as: when he wants to catch the most fish, when he wants to catch the biggest and when he wants to catch the most challenging fish the water can produce, regardless of its size.

When you have located your fish, observe it carefully, with the rapt attention of a champion boxer watching his opponent in training or

fighting another contender. In particular, study its feeding habits, the kind of flies it takes and the time of day when most of its serious feeding takes place.

Know your fish

Get to know your fish, its weaknesses and foibles. Watch its reaction to other trout which stray into its territory. Does it compete with them for food? Greed has seen the downfall of many a good fish. And always bear in mind that you are taking on a special kind of quarry—one that has seen all the mismanaged attempts to extract it from the water and that will scornfully retreat the moment you have the slightest laspe of concentration or expertise.

In dry fly fishing, the biggest cause of failure with sophisticated trout is undetected drag. It is, of course, helpful to have some idea of the fly on which the fish is feeding

Far left: *Playing a big rainbow trout. Stocked rainbows have a tendency to drop gradually downriver until they are lost in the sea.*
Left: *The River Anton in Wiltshire is an idyllic setting in which to fish for the water's specimen browns and rainbows.*
Above: *As yet, fishing has barely made inroads on Ireland's trout river stocks despite the popularity of the sport with holiday anglers.*

and to be able to choose a reasonable facsimile to put on the leader. But the paramount factor is a presentation that makes the fly look like a natural insect alighting on the water's surface film.

Drag—the ultimate deterrent

Some years ago I was casting over one or two very good rising trout. The casting was careful and dextrous, but, although none of the fish was alarmed and they continued feeding on the naturals, there was not one which would condescend to take the artificial. I could have concluded that I was presenting the wrong fly, but when I carefully withdrew to a small bridge just upstream, the fish were still rising boldly to naturals I had imitated.

It was then that I snipped the artificial off my leader and dropped it on to the water so that it would float down over the fish. A good trout promptly came and took it as

though it had been looking for that fly all day. That it would subsequently spit it out seconds later was of no account. What is more, other trout in the vicinity rose to and took three more artificials chosen at random and dropped on to the water. Pattern had nothing to do with the problem. It was all allied to the fact that, when presented from the bridge, the flies were untethered to a leader, line or, ultimately, to me. Drag was the enemy!

A specimen trout knows all about drag and may well locate itself in a lie where drag can be easily detected, but not easily overcome, by the angler. One trick which may be tried is to cast so accurately that the fly is dropped on to the nose of the rising fish. This calls for great skill and is often best attempted as the rings recede from an earlier use.

Usually one of two things happens. Either the fish takes the fly with a greedy grab, or it bolts for

cover as though the devil himself had been after it. Properly attempted, though, it enables the angler to cover the fish before drag occurs. Additionally, it does not give the fish much time to scrutinize the fly and decide that it is not the real thing. The technique has caught some good trout, but it has frightened many more.

Many trout are caught just before or after a very prolific hatch of naturals. At the peak of the hatch, there are often too many naturals for fish to bother with the artificial.

Sometimes, the best way of securing a specimen is by the use of the nymph. This may be tantalizingly passed in front of a feeding fish before the main hatch of naturals occurs. But always bear in mind that the specimen trout is most likely to take your fly when you least expect it to do so.

All the good wild trout that I have caught have demanded the utmost skill. We need all the skills of the hunter if we are to get on to terms with such fish. Practice casting until you can drop an artificial fly into a soup plate at 20ft and so that it alights like thistledown. Learn to move with the stealth of a cat and always aim to spot your specimen before it sees you. Bear in mind that it only takes one cast to catch a fish.

Barry Potterton writes:

River trout sport in the South can be divided into fishing chalkstreams, the rivers and streams of Wales, Devon and Cornwall, and the few other southern rivers which have not fallen foul of pollution or water abstraction. Chalkstream fishing has been discussed on pp. 337-339.

The rivers and streams in Wales, Devon and Cornwall are mainly fast-flowing spate rivers which hold a natural stock of wild brown trout. They may well hold the odd rainbow trout if the river has been stocked and they may also have a seasonal run of salmon and/or sea trout.

These rivers can be fished with fly, but I will concentrate on spinning and worming in the three different water conditions that one is likely to meet: clear water at normal level (which is most common), low-water, and a coloured spate.

Spinners and spoons

Clear water at near normal level is the most appropriate condition for light spinning. Rather than a spinning rod, I like to use a Mark IV Avon or reservoir trout fly rod, both of which have extra length and play fish better in fast water. I use a Mitchell fixed-spool reel loaded with 100 yards of 6 or 8lb b.s. nylon. My favourite baits are a small Mepps spinner, a fly spoon or a very small Devon minnow.

The height that the bait fishes in the water is most important, and this is determined by the overall weight of the end-tackle. Too little weight and the bait will skate across the surface of a fast stream. Too much weight will cause continual snagging on the bottom.

Weight can be added to end tackle by putting split shot or swan shot 18in above the bait. In the case of a snaggy bottom, shot should be added until the bait fishes at a good depth, perhaps even touching the bottom once or twice as it is fished across the stream.

If the bottom is relatively snag-free, use a simple paternoster set-up, incorporating a three-way swivel, which allows the bait to ride just above the bottom. The short perpendicular length of line should be about 8in long and of less breaking

strength than the main line—so that you do not lose the lot if your weights become snagged. Use swan shot or smaller split shot because these are easily changed and can slide off the short length if they become snagged.

Right: *Fishing an awkwardly situated pool. A preliminary cast ensures that weights touch bottom lightly, then subsequent casts lengthen until the bait swings into the pool.*
Below: *A brown and a rainbow caught from the same river on very light fly tackle.*
Below right: *Keir Muter fishes the North Tyne River. His rod is carbonfibre, 8½ft long, and fishes tirelessly for hour upon hour.*

Reaching deeper pools

Fish down and across the river with just enough overall weight to feel the bottom once or twice as the bait swings round. Good-sized trout are most likely to be found in these deep pools, so look for a position where the main pool and flow of water is towards my bank. Start fishing the very top of the pool with short casts down and across at an angle of about 45 degrees. This ensures that you are fishing with the correct weight, bearing in mind that a cast at an angle farther upstream allows the bait to search deeper water and *vice versa.*

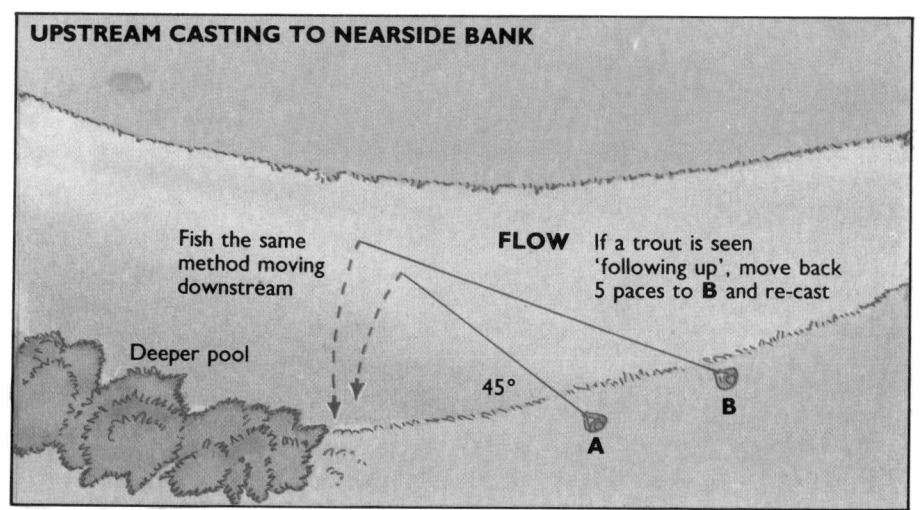

UPSTREAM CASTING TO NEARSIDE BANK

Fish the same method moving downstream

Deeper pool

FLOW

If a trout is seen 'following up', move back 5 paces to **B** and re-cast

45°

A

B

When I am satisfied with the overall weight I am fishing, I gradually increase the length of each cast. It is most important to let the bait hang momentarily after it has swung across the river and then to retrieve it quite slowly. It is quite common to get a take during the retrieve, or to catch sight of a fish 'following up'. In the latter case, I take five paces back upstream and start all over again. Where there is little current the same method can be used, fishing up and across, and winding in slowly enough to keep the bait from bobbing up.

Tasteless worms

Worming for wild trout is every bit as skilful as fly fishing for 'stockies'. In a river with varying currents and depths, straightforward trotting of a float and worm is not practicable. I prefer to fish an adaptation of a rolling ledger down and across the current. This gives the worm a natural movement with the current, taking it into the pool itself.

My rod, reel and line are the same as for light spinning, but I whip a good quality spade-end hook (size 6-14) straight on to the main line, and use a small ring and a stop-shot to produce my version of a paternoster/sliding ledger rig.

I like to use marsh worms or small red worms for clear water. I avoid brandling if possible, particularly if they have not been scoured properly in moss. Trout tend to spit them out as soon as they have sunk their teeth in and tasted the yellow slime which comes out of a brandling that has not been properly cleaned.

After the worm has swung across the current, I let it rest at the bottom of the pool for a few minutes. The amount of weight for fishing a worm is less critical than with light spinning, and in a steady current I try to fish the worm quite slowly —down and across—by adding extra weight 18in above it.

Spinning in coloured water can be surprisingly effective but, generally, worms are the food that the trout will be after. Coloured water usually means a stronger current than normal, so trout tend to lie in the less turbulent pools and eddies to avoid the mainstream current.

411

This is the time when I hope to have a few lobworms with me, as well as smaller worms. The tail or head of a lobworm is a superb bait in these conditions. I use my normal tackle with an 8lb line straight to a No 6 spade-end hook. Do not be put off by the water colour until you have covered all the likely spots thoroughly but without success.

Warm-weather wading

The greatest challenge to the trout fisherman comes when the river is at low summer level, with the main pools connected by a mere trickle. These conditions are often brought about by hot, sunny weather. A mid-day stroll down the river bank can virtually convince you that the river is completely devoid of fish. But, in fact, trout and salmon abhor strong sunlight and seek shelter from it in places unlikely to be spotted.

The trout do continue to feed, and do so in the early morning and late evening, which are the times to go after them. In these conditions, the banks are bone-hard. Vibrations from the angler's footsteps scare fish as surely as the sight of him on the skyline. For these reasons, I often wade upstream, fishing up and across each pool I come to.

My tackle is a light fly rod for easy casting, a fixed-spool reel, and 100 yards of 6lb b.s. nylon carrying my paternoster/sliding ledger device. The shotting required is often very light and I have caught trout with this method using no weight at all apart from the stop-shot.

Early morning and late evening sessions tend to pass very quickly, so it helps to walk the beat during the day to pick out the most likely spots, such as the odd pool where the water is too deep or obscured for you to see the bottom.

I start with short casts to the bottom of the pool and gradually lengthen my cast until I have covered the whole pool. Some snagging is inevitable with this style of fishing, so I carry plenty of spare hooks and shot in my pockets to avoid splashing out of the water every time I lose a piece of tackle.

I only use a float on large pools of even depth, weirpools and pools beneath rapids or waterfalls. Such spots tend to have more than their fair share of snags and obstructions, but these in turn provide excellent cover for trout. I like to use a large float, which will support two or three swan shot, to ensure that the worm gets down through the tangled maze of cross-currents which are common in such pools.

These are ideal places to try livebaiting with minnows, if you can lay your hands on some, fished on the float tackle described above. The minnow should be lip-hooked on a size 10 or 12 hook and allowed to drift around the pool. It is a first-class bait for sea trout, 'brownies' and rainbows.

Pollution

Many rivers in the South have suffered from pollution and/or water abstraction on a small scale which have been sufficient to wipe out the stock of wild brownies without affecting the coarse fish.

These rivers tend to be sluggish and of even depth, so trotting a float-fished worm will provide sport with coarse fish—and the chance of a trout. With rivers becoming cleaner in the area, it is to be hoped that riparian owners and the relevant Water Authorities will take the first opportunity to re-introduce trout to these waters.

The most encouraging example of cleaner rivers is the Thames. Thames trouting in the large weirs used to be a very fine and rewarding art. I hope that the Thames Water Authority, in addition to their

Below: *On the River Frome, the East Stoke weirpool (shown in diagram) responds to several different techniques.* **Bottom left:** *Fly-caught browns from a stream.*

salmon stocking policy, considers restocking brown trout.

Barry Potterton's Spotlight

I have chosen a pool on a private stretch of water—the weirpool on the River Frome at East Stoke near Wareham, Dorset—because it exhibits all the features of the deep, turbulent pools where one is most likely to come across large trout.

Within less than 50 yards of the bank, the angler has the choice of spinning, ledgering, fly fishing or float-fishing a worm or minnow.

At first glance, the pool appears to be simply a fast race with an eddy either side, but the surface currents have little bearing on what happens below. For this reason, the position I take on the bank to fish one part of the pool is vital to the correct presentation of the bait.

The diagram shows how I fish from six different positions, A-F, to give myself the best possible coverage of the pool.

Positions A and F, on either side of the main race, are the best places to fish the lower half of the race. Both spinner and ledger are cast down and right across the current. From here, a float baited with worm or minnow can be trotted down the edge of the main race. Trotting a float presents a problem of line drag in the confused currents, so I make a point of greasing my line and regularly lifting the line from the surface as I trot, to ensure direct contact with the float.

The pool gradually shallows away from the weir, and a float-fished worm will eventually lay on the bottom. Laying-on with the occasional movement of the bait is a very effective method in such a pool. By altering the depth of the float-tackle I can lay-on over different parts of the pool. From these positions (A and F) I can also drop a light ledger into the tail of each eddy so that it works its way under the main race to the calmer water below.

Positions B and E give me access to the end of the eddies, where the current quickens and flows at right-angles directly under the main race. The eddy by position E is stronger and deeper than the other one, and the bankside bushes provide additional cover for fish. Both swims can be spun, ledgered or float-fished.

Position C at the top of the island gives me access to the streamy water at the bottom of the race. The water is too shallow here for float-fishing, but is ideal for a wet fly, spinner or a ledger rig.

Position D is the place where I fish a dry fly upstream to cover fish at the bottom of the race. As with many pools, the current runs off through a deep channel under the bank below this position. This swim, too, can be fished with wet fly, spinner or ledger.

Such a pool makes an ideal resting place for salmon and sea trout during their upstream migration. If the river has a run of these, I make sure I have 8lb b.s. line to give myself the best chance of landing one.

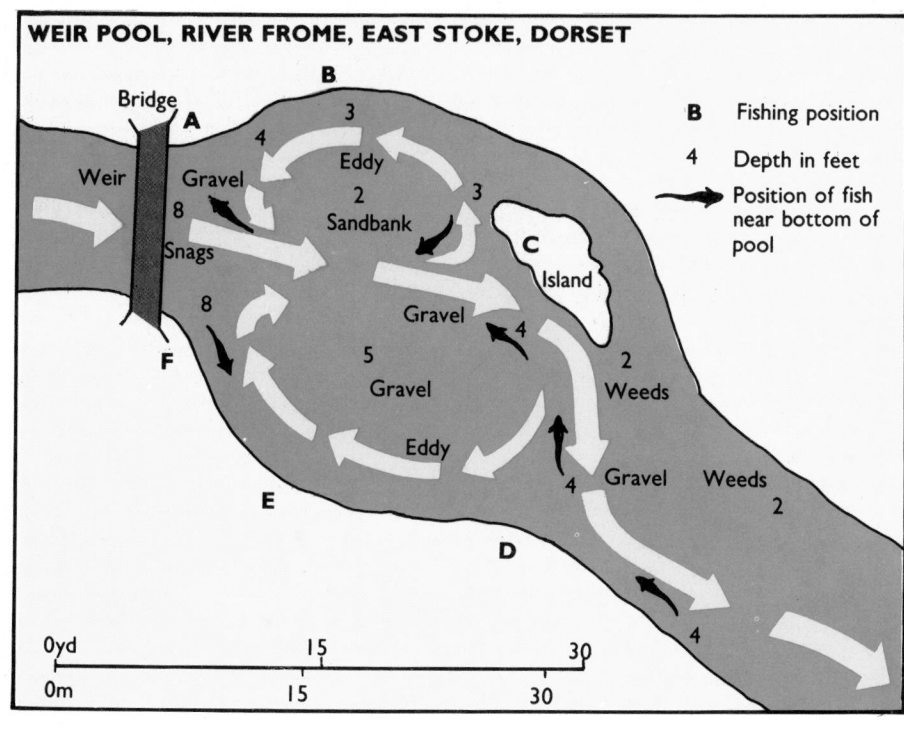

WEIR POOL, RIVER FROME, EAST STOKE, DORSET

Bridge

B

A

3

Weir

4

Eddy

Gravel

2

B — Fishing position

4 — Depth in feet

→ — Position of fish near bottom of pool

8

Sandbank

3

Snags

C

Island

8

Gravel

4

F

5

Gravel

2

Weeds

Gravel

Weeds

Eddy

4

2

E

4

D

0yd   15   30

0m   15   30

INDEX

Page numbers in *italics* refer to illustrations only

PICTURE CREDITS

ARTWORK CREDITS